# HISTORICAL GRAMMAR OF APABHRAṀŚA

# *Historical* GRAMMAR OF APABHRAṀŚA

GANESH VASUDEV TAGARE

MOTILAL BANARSIDASS
*Delhi Varanasi Patna Madras*

*First Edition*: *Poona, 1948*
*Reprinted in Delhi, 1987*

MOTILAL BANARSIDASS
Bungalow Road, Jawahar Nagar, Delhi 110 007
*Branches*
Chowk, Varanasi 221 001
Ashok Rajpath, Patna 800 004
120, Royapettah High Road, Mylapore, Madras 600 004



ISBN: 81-208-0290-x

PRINTED IN INDIA
BY JAINENDRA PRAKASH JAIN AT SHRI JAINENDRA PRESS, A-45 NARAINA INDUSTRIAL AREA, PHASE I, NEW DELHI 110 028 AND PUBLISHED BY NARENDRA PRAKASH JAIN FOR MOTILAL BANARSIDASS, DELHI 110 007.

*most respectfully dedicated to*

H. H. RAJA SHRIMANT SIR

RAGUNATHRAO SHANKARRAO

*alias*

BABASAHEB PANDIT PANT SACHIV, K.C.I.E.

*for his generous patronage to learning*

*and*

Dr. SUMITRA M. KATRE

# CONTENTS


| | Page |
|---|---|
| FRONTISPIECE | |
| DEDICATION .. .. .. .. .. .. .. | v |
| PREFACE .. .. .. .. .. .. .. .. | ix |
| ABBREVIATIONS .. .. .. .. .. .. .. | xiii |
| INTRODUCTION .. .. .. .. .. .. .. | 1 |
| CHAPTER I. APABHRAṀŚA PHONOLOGY .. .. .. | 39 |
| CHAPTER II. DECLENSION IN APABHRAṀŚA .. .. .. | 104 |
| CHAPTER III. CONJUGATION IN APABHRAṀŚA .. .. .. | 282 |
| CHAPTER IV. NOMINAL STEM-FORMATION IN APABHRAṀŚA | 335 |
| INDEX VERBORUM .. .. .. .. .. .. .. | 343 |

# PREFACE

The present dissertation on Apabhraṁśa was accepted by the University of Bombay for the degree of Ph.D. in September, 1946. It required six long years to complete this work as I was then working as a secondary teacher at Bhor where there are no library facilities for such type of research work. If I could complete this work in spite of indifferent health and under very trying circumstances, it is due to the encouragement of His Highness the Rajasaheb of Bhor and the infinite patience with which my esteemed *Guru*, Dr. S. M. Katre, went through all my material and made valued suggestions from time to time, giving me loan facilities of important books on the subject whenever required.

"A Historical Grammar of Apabhraṁśa" is such a vast subject as would require the study of a lifetime. The application of the chrono-regional method of study to Apabhraṁśa literature, published so far, has its own obvious limitations and the time-space context of some Apabhraṁśa texts being still unsettled, one has to accept the earlier and later dates of the texts as the upper and lower *terminii* of the linguistic phenomena represented therein. As this is the first historical grammar of Apabhraṁśa, the chrono-regional method of study had to be emphasised. Though I had to criticise occasionally some of the theories of the great *savants* like Pischel, Grierson, Bloch and others, I express my indebtedness to all of them as early pioneers in the field but for whose labours the present work would have been impossible.

It was intended to add some more sections and chapters on Reductions and Extensions in Apabhraṁśa, NIA and Apabhraṁśa, Apabhraṁśa and Extra-Indian Prakrits and other topics in Apabhraṁśa linguistics in general; but they are published separately in Oriental Journals as they could not be included under Historical Grammar.

His Highness, Raja Shrimant Sir Raghunathrao Shankarrao *alias* Babasaheb Pandit Panta Sachiv, K.C.I.E., the Rajasaheb of Bhor, to whom the present work is most respectfully dedicated, is already known as a progressive ruler. His patronage to learning and munificent donations to educational, social, humanitarian and other cultural activities (even outside the State) have given him a highly respected position in the hearts of his subjects as well as in those of others in the Indian Dominion.

Born in 1878 in the historical family of Panta Sachivs who saved the Maratha Kingdom in the most critical period of the early 18th century, His Highness inherited a noble tradition of self-sacrifice. After receiving his higher education in the Deccan College, Poona, the Rajasaheb carefully equipped himself with the necessary accomplishments and varied practical administrative experience both at Poona and in the State. Even as a prince, he was noted for his love of learning, progressive democratic views, sociable nature and nobility of character. Small wonder it is that his accession to the *gadi* on 18th July, 1922 inaugurated a new era in the history of the State. At the very outset the Rajasaheb removed the longstanding and legitimate grievances of his subjects by giving them freedom of thought, speech and association and by abolishing certain invidious mediaeval types of taxes. Removal of untouchability by law marks the liberal spirit of his administration on the social side. In order to improve the efficiency of the Public services of the State, His Highness had to overhaul and to reform the State departments with their various branches of administration.

The most outstanding feature of his reign is the rapid progress of constitutional reforms. Soon after his accession in 1922 he introduced representative institutions as part of the administrative machinery of the State. The establishment of the Executive Council (1924), the Legislative Council (1928), and Local Self-Government bodies was but a beginning of granting responsible Government in the State. The Government of Bhor State Act (1932), the Diamond Jubilee Celebrations of the Rajasaheb (1938), the Silver Jubilee of his Accession to the *gadi* (1947) were important landmarks in the rapid process of transformation of a mediaeval type of benevolent autocracy into a limited monarchy of the English type. After the Independence Day on 15th August, 1947, His Highness showed a statesmanlike foresight in the interest of his subjects by entering into the proposed Union of the

Deccan States. But his greatest act of self-renunciation—perhaps the noblest one that an Indian Prince can do—is his agreement to integrate his State in the free Dominion of India from 1st March 1948. (The State of Bhor has been merged in the Indian Dominion since 8th March, 1948).

During the quarter of a century since his accession, His Highness made vast improvements in nation-building departments in the interest of Public well-being, convenience and comforts by constructing roads, bridges and buildings, opening of new charitable dispensaries and by providing other amenities of life. It is, however, in the field of education that His Highness took keen interest from the very beginning. Free Primary Education in the State, founding free-studentships and scholarships for deserving students receiving secondary and collegiate education, housing schools and libraries in excellent buildings, special facilities to Harijan pupils in the form of books and scholarships, and donations to educational and cultural institutions both inside and outside the State, founding of a prize of Rs. 500 in the name of the founder of the dynasty for encouraging good works in Marathi Literature are but a few instances of his love of learning. Actuated by this noble sentiment, the Rajasaheb granted study leave and gave a munificent donation of Rs. 3,000 to the Deccan College Research Institute, Poona, for publishing this dissertation. It is, therefore, no mere formality when I respectfully dedicate this work to him.

I owe a great debt of gratitude to my teacher Dr. S. M. Katre. If there is any real contribution to our knowledge of NIA linguistics in this work, the whole credit is due to him ; the shortcomings, however, are due to my limitations. It is again Dr. Katre who arranged for the printing of this dissertation and it is due to his meticulous care that we have such a fine edition of a linguistic work. I am thankful to my referee Professor Dr. Siddheshwar Varma, M.A., D.Litt., of Jammu for his critical appreciation of my work. Professor Dr. A.M. Upadhye, M.A., D.Litt. of Kolhapur, in spite of his onerous undertakings, always found time to respond to my queries promptly and was kind enough to read the type-script of my thesis before it was sent to the press and offer many useful suggestions, a number of which have been incorporated herein. My thanks are due to Professor Dr. P. L. Vaidya, M.A., D.Litt. of Poona and Professor Dr. H. L. Jain, M.A., D.Litt. of Nagpur for their prompt replies to my queries about Apabhraṁśa works and their space-time location ; and lastly to my wife Mrs. Shanta Tagare who goaded me on to complete this work.

The Staff of the Examiner Press in Bombay have shown a rare patience and competence in dealing with the complicated typography of this work, and my thanks are due to the Superintendent for the great care that he has bestowed on the actual printing.

In conclusion, I would very much welcome constructive criticism from my readers to help me further in my studies.

Bhor, February 28th, 1948. G. V. Tagare.

## ABBREVIATIONS

| | | |
|---|---|---|
| Ā | .. | Āvantī. |
| *ABORI* | .. | *Annals of the Bhandarkar Oriental Research Institute, Poona.* |
| *Alt. Gram.* | .. | J. WACKERNAGEL's *Altindische Grammatik.* |
| AMg. | .. | Ardha-Māgadhī (sometimes Amg.) |
| Ap. | .. | Apabhraṁśa. |
| As. | .. | Aśokan Inscriptions (At times referred to as Aśokan). |
| *AUS* | .. | *Allahabad University Studies.* |
| *BBe.* | .. | *Bezzenberger Beitrage.* |
| *BDCRI* | .. | *Bulletin of the Deccan College Research Institute, Poona.* |
| Beng. or Bg. | .. | Bengali. |
| *Bh.* | .. | Bharata's *Nāṭyaśāstra* (Refers to Ap. verses in it also). |
| *BhK.* | .. | *Bhavisatta kahā*—H. JACOBI, München, 1918. (Reference to GUNE's edition is clearly mentioned) |
| Br. | .. | Braj. |
| *BSL* | .. | *Bulletin de la Société de linguistique de Paris.* |
| *BSOS* | .. | *Bulletin of the School of Oriental Studies, London.* |
| *BV* | .. | *Bhāratīya Vidyā.* Bombay. |
| *Cd.* | .. | Caṇḍa's *Prākṛta Lakṣaṇa*—HOERNLE, Calcutta 1880 |
| D. | .. | Dākṣiṇātyā. |
| Ḍh. | .. | Ḍhakkī. |
| *Dkk.* | .. | Kāṇha's *Dohākoṣa*—M. SHAHIDULLA, Paris 1928. |
| *Dkṅ.* | .. | *Ḍākārṇava-tantra*—N. N. CHAUDHARY. |
| *Dks.* | .. | Saraha's *Dohākoṣa*—M. SHAHIDULLA, Paris 1928. |
| *Dn.* | .. | Hemacandra's *Deśīnāma-mālā*—R. PISCHEL. |
| *DS.* | .. | Ap. verses in *Daśarūpa*—SUDARSANASASTRI Gujarati Printing Press, Bombay 1914. |
| EAp. | .. | Eastern Apabhraṁśa. |

*EI* .. *Epigraphia Indica.*

*FLM* .. J. BLOCH'S *La Formation de la Langue marathe.* Sometimes mentioned as *La Langue marathe.*

G. .. Gujarati.

GOS .. Gaekwad Oriental Series.

*Gram.* .. PISCHEL'S *Grammatik der Prakrit Sprachen*, Strassburg, 1900.

H. .. Hindi.

*Hc.* .. Hemacandra's *Siddha-Hema* (Prakrit Grammar).—P. L. VAIDYA, Poona 1928. Generally the 8th Chapter is implied.

*Hv.* .. *Harivaṁśa-purāṇa*—L. ALSDORF, Hamburg, 1936.

IA .. Indo-Aryan.

*IAnt.* .. *Indian Antiquary* (Sometimes shortened as *IA*).

IE .. Indo-European.

*IHQ* .. *Indian Historical Quarterly.*

II .. Indo-Iranian.

*JA* .. *Journal Asiatique.*

*JAOS* .. *Journal of the American Oriental Society.*

*JASB* .. *Journal of the Asiatic Society of Bengal.*

*JBBRAS* .. *Journal of the Bombay Branch of Royal Asiatic Society.*

*JC* .. *Jasahara-cariu* - P. L. VAIDYA, Poona, 1931.

*Jdc.* .. Jinadatta's *Carcarī* (*Ap. Kāvayatrayī*)—L. B. GANDHI GOS No. 37.

*Jdu* .. Jinadatta's *Upadeśa-taraṅgiṇī* (*Ap. Kāvyatrayī*)—L. B. GANDHI. GOS No. 37.

JM .. Jaina Māhārāṣṭrī.

*JRAS* .. *Journal of the Royal Asiatic Society.*

JŚ .. Jaina Śaurasenī.

*JUB* .. *Journal of the University of Bombay.*

*Kc.* .. Hemacandra's *Kumārapāla-carita*—S. P. PANDIT.

*Ki.* .. Kramadīśvara's *Saṁkṣipta-Vyākaraṇa*.

*KKC* .. Kanakāmara's *Karakaṇḍa-carita*- H. L. JAIN, Karanja Jain Series, No. 4, 1934.

*Kp.* .. *Kumārapāla-pratibodha*—Ap. portion as edited by Ludwig ALSDORF, Hamburg, 1929.

*Ld.* .. Lakṣmīdhara's *Ṣaḍbhāṣā-Candrikā*—Ed. TRIVEDI (BSS LXXI, 1916).

*LSI* .. *Linguistic Survey of India*—G. A. GRIERSON.

M .. Marathi (sometimes Mar. is used).

Mah. .. Māhārāṣṭrī.

Marw. .. Mārwārī.

*MASB* .. *Memoirs of the Asiatic Society of Bengal*.

Mg. .. Māgadhī.

MIA .. Middle Indo-Aryan.

*MK* .. Mārkaṇḍeya's *Prākṛta-sarvasva*—Ed. BHATTANATHA-SWAMIN, Vizagapatam, 1912.

*MP* .. Puṣpadanta's *Mahāpurāṇa*—P. L. VAIDYA, Poona.

*MSL* .. *Memoires de la Société de Linguistique de Paris*.

*MSPP* .. *Mahārāṣṭra-Sāhitya Patrikā, Poona*.

*Mt.* .. *Materialien zur Kenntnis des Apabhraṁśa*—R. PISCHEL.

*Nc.* .. Puṣpadanta's *Nāga-kumāra-carita*—Ed. H. L. JAIN, Amraoti, 1936.

Nep. .. Nepali.

NIA .. New Indo-Aryan.

*NIAnt.* .. *New Indian Antiquary*.

NS .. Namisādhu's quotations of sūtras on Ap. in his Commentary on Rudraṭa's *Kāvyālaṅkāra*.

*ODB* .. S. K. CHATTERJI's *Origin and Development of Bengali*, Calcutta, 1926.

OIA .. Old Indo-Aryan.

OWR .. Old Western Rajasthani.

Pa. .. Pali.

*Pai* .. Dhanapāla's *Pāïa-lachhī-nāma-mālā.*

Paiś. .. Paiśācī.

*Pd.* .. Rāmasiṁha's *Pāhuḍa-dohā.* H. L. JAIN, Amraoti, 1933.

P. or Panj. .. Panjabī (Often shortened Panj.).

Pk. or Pkt. .. Prākrit.

*PPr.* .. Joïndu's *Paramātma-prakāśa*—A. N. UPADHYE, Kolhapur, 1937.

*Pu.* .. Puruṣottama's *Prākṛtānuśāsana,* Ed. L. NITTI-DOLCI Paris.

Raj. .. Rajasthānī.

*Rt.* .. Rāmaśarma-tarka-vāgīśa's *Prākṛta-kalpa-taru.* Edited by G. A. GRIERSON, I. *Ant.*, 1922, 23, 27, 28.

Ś. .. Śaurasenī.

SAp. .. Southern Apabhraṁśa.

*Sc.* .. *Sanatkumāracarita*—Ed. H. JACOBI, München, 1921.

*Sdd.* .. Devasena's *Sāvaya-dhamma dohā*—Ed. H. L. JAIN, Amraoti, 1932.

*Sh.* .. Siṁharāja's *Prākṛta-rūpāvatāra*—Ed. HULTZSCH, RAS London, 1909.

Singh. .. Singhalese.

Sk. .. Sanskrit.

*Sn.* .. Lakṣmaṇagaṇi's *Supāsaṇāhacaria,* Edited by Pt. H. T. SETH.

*Tr.* .. Trivikrama's *Prākṛta-vyākaraṇa.*

*Vk.* .. Ap. verses in Kālidāsa's *Vikramorvśīya,* as edited by PISCHEL in *Materialien.*

WAp. .. Western Apabhraṁśa.

*Ys.* .. Joïndu's *Yogasāra*—Edited by A. N. UPADHYE, Kolhapur, 1937.

*ZDMG* .. *Zeitschrift der Deutschen Morgenlandischen Gesellschaft.*

In the body of the work, there are some obvious abbreviations e.g., *Pali Lit. u. Spr.* (GEIGER's *Pali Literatur und Sprache*), *Form. Koṅk.* for S. M. KATRE's *Formation of Koṅkaṇī*, etc. As these longer abbreviations are indicated in their proper places, they are not included here. As usual an asterisk (*) before a form indicates its reconstructed nature. Other marks and abbreviations are common to all linguistic works.

# *INTRODUCTION*

## THE TERM APABHRAṀŚA

§1. The contemptuous term '*Apabhraṁśa*' expresses the prejudice of ancient Indian grammarians and rhetoricians against all deviations from standard Sanskrit which was looked upon as divine speech. For example Patañjali who does not use the word Ap. in its modern linguistic connotation, regards the Prākritic and dialectal forms of Sk. *go* 'a cow' as Ap.[1] Some of these are used in Amg. in the Śvetāmbara Jain canon.[2] Some are regarded as Pkt. or Mah. in *Cd.* 2.16, and *Hc.* 8.2.174. Daṇḍin clearly remarks that in śāstric works deviations from Sk. were called Ap.,[3] a view endorsed by Vāmana.[4]

It is in Bharata's *Nāṭyaśāstra* (circa 300 A.D.) that we come across the first real reference to Ap. It is mentioned as '*vibhraṣṭa*' as distinct from Sk. and Deśī,[5] as a dialect abounding in *-u*,[6] as 'the dialect of the Ābhīras'.[7] It contains some verses[8] in a dialect, the characteristics of which agree with those of the Ap. of Pk. grammarians. Ap. morphemes are found in the proto-canonical Buddhist Pk.[9] Some Ap. forms appear in an early text like Vimalasūri's *Paumacaria* (circa 300 A.D.).[10] Desinences of the type of Ap. are found in Pāli.[11] All this evidence shows the probability of Ap. being a linguistic stage at least as early as 300 A.D.

Bharata assigns to Ap. the position of a barbarous dialect spoken by nomadic people who rear cattle, sheep, horses and camels.[12] The option to use Śābarī in the case of these characters shows Bharata's confusion regarding Ap. though he is careful enough to distinguish it from Drāviḍī.[13]

---

1 *ekaikasya śabdasya bahavo 'pabhraṁśāḥ tadyathā gaurityasya śabdasya gāvī, goṇī, gotā gopotāliketye-vamādayo' pabhraṁśāḥ. Mahābhāṣya* 1.1.1.

2 See L. B. Gandhi, Intro. to *Ap. Kāvyatrayī* p. *GOS* XXXVII.

3 *Kāvyādarśa* 1.36. See also Pischel, *Gram.* § 4.

4 *pūrvanipāte' pabhraṁśo rakṣyaḥ.* 'care should be taken regarding wrong order of words in compounds.' -*Kāvyālaṅkāra-sūtravṛtti*, 5.2.21. As quoted by Bloch in FLM § 22.

5 *Bh.* 17.3.

6 *Bh.* 17.61.

7 *Bh.* 17.49, 54,55. For "Ābhīrī and Apabhraṁśa" see the article of G. V. Tagare in *ABORI* XXIII. 563-7.

8 *Bh.* 17.66, 74, 99, 108, 169.

9 Franklin Edgerton, in *BSOS* VIII. ii-iii pp. 501-17.

10 *e.g.*, *kavaṇa* for *kiṃ*, gerund in *-evi*. See H. Jacobi, Intro. to *BHK.* 59-60. A. N. Upadhye, Intro. to *PPr.* p. 56, Footnote 1 also accepts this.

11 H. Smith, 'Desinences du type apabhraṁśa en pali,' *BSL* XXXIII. 169-72 (1932).

12 *Bh.* 17.47, 48, 55.

13 Bharata is not a grammarian. He might be following some unnamed text in the classification and description of Pk. dialects. The Eastern School of Pk. grammarians follows the same treatment.

Three centuries later, Ap. attained the status of a literary dialect. Thus Bhāmaha regards Ap. as the name of a dialect of poetry and that too of a particular form of literature.[14] Daṇḍin thinks that poetic composition in the dialect of Ābhīras etc., is Ap.[15] but in an earlier verse he refers to a traditional classification of literature (*vāṅmaya* and not *kāvya* as in Bhāmaha) where Ap. literature has got a distinct place and was used on the stage along with Sk.[16] This literary status of Ap. is confirmed by the pride in the ability of composing in Ap. found in the copper-plate of Dharasena II of Valabhī in Kathiawar (600 A.D.). Caṇḍa's recognition of Ap. in his Pk. grammar (*Cd.* III. 37) points to the same conclusion.

Some two centuries later, Uddyotana, the author of *Kuvalayamālā* (778 A.D.) which contains portions written in Apabhraṁśa (*Kiṁci avabbhaṁsa kayā* as the author says in his introductory verses) refers to the mixture of Sanskritic and Prākritic elements in literary Ap. in a highly poetic way: '*tā kiṁ Avahaṁsaṁ hoii? tam Sakkava-paya-ubhaya-suddhā-suddha-paya-sama-taraṁga-raṁganta-vaggiram . . . . . . paṇaya-kuviya-piya-māṇini-samullāva-sarisaṁ maṇoharam.*'[17]

In the 9th cent. A.D., Rudraṭa regards Ap. as a generic term for provincial dialects which were many in number.

*ṣaṣṭho 'tra bhūri-bhedo deśa-viśeṣād Apabhraṁśaḥ.*[18]

It seems that the threefold division of literature as found in Bhāmaha was antiquated by this time and as NITTI DOLCI observes Rudraṭa's sixfold classification of literature was already in vogue by that time.[19]

In the 10th cent. A.D., Rājaśekhara (900-925 A.D.) takes Ap. as a literary dialect distinct from and equal in status to Sk., Pkt. and Paiś.[20] Copious Ap. literature discovered so far, selections of Ap. verses in works like Bhoja's *Sarasvatī-Kaṇṭhābharaṇa* and Dhanañjaya's *Daśarūpa* prove that Rājaśekhara's connotation of Ap. was correct.

---

14 *Kāvyālaṅkāra* 1.16,26.

15 *Kāvyādarśa*, 1.36.

16 *Ibid.*, 1.32.

17 *Kuvalaya-mālā* Palm leaves No. 57-8 as quoted by L. B. GANDHI, Intro. to *Ap. Kāvyatrayī*, pp. 97-8.

18 *Kāvyālaṅkāra* 2.12. Its last mention in this verse does not reflect its degree of importance, as in that case, Sk. will have a secondary place to Pkt.—which a non-Jain rhetorician from Kashmir would never have meant even in those days.

19 L. NITTI DOLCI, *Les Grammairiens prākrits*, p. 158.

20 Vide *Kāvya-mīmāṁsā*: the description of the person of Kāvya-puruṣa Ch. III, p. 6, seating arrangement in the court of the king-poet Ch. X pp. 54-5, capacity of Ap. to express some implication in its own special way ch. IX p. 48, mastery in Ap. composition a condition precedent to the title Kavirāja ch. V p. 19.

In the 11th cent. A.D. Puruṣottama, an 'Eastern' Buddhist Pkt. grammarian, regarded Ap. as the speech of the elites '*śiṣṭas*' of the day, and asks us to refer to the usage of the cultured people for the remaining characteristics of Ap.[21] His sections on Ap. (*Pu.* XVII, XVIII) and Namisādhu's commentary on Rudraṭa's *Kāvyālaṅkāra* 2.12 where he (NS) freely quotes a number of Sūtras from some unnamed work on Pk. grammar (which seems to have been amplified by Hemacandra) show that Ap. was predominently Pkt. *i.e.*, Mah.[22] NS points out that Ap. was then freely mixed with Śaurasenisms, Māgadhisms etc. This mixed state may represent the development of Śaur. Mg or Mah. into Ap. or a free inter-borrowing which was very common in MIA.

Later writers like Mammaṭa, Vāgbhaṭa, the author of *Vāgbhaṭālaṅkāra* (1123-56 A.D.), the author of the *Viṣṇudharmottara*, Rāmacandra and Guṇacandra in *Nāṭyadarpaṇa*, Jinadatta (1200 A.D.) in *Viveka-vilasita* 8.131, Amaracandra in *Kāvya-kalpa-latā-vṛtti* p. 8 and finally Hemacandra, the great Pkt. grammarian, unanimously agree in regarding Ap. as a literary dialect, equal in status to Sk. and Pkt. By the term Ap. these writers seem to understand 'spoken language' or 'provincial language.' Thus Vāgbhaṭa defines it as a pure form of provincial languages.[23] According to *Viṣṇudharmottara* Ap. is infinite as there is no end to provincialisms.[24] Rāmacandra and Guṇacandra endorse the view that Ap. is the provincial speech.[25] Hemacandra, by whose time, Ap. seems to be a dead classical language like Sk. or Pkt., distinguishes it from the spoken language.[26] His grammar too shows a confusion of dialects.[27] Vāgbhaṭa, a later author of *Kāvyānuśāsana*, also distinguishes between Ap. and grāmyabhāṣā.[28]

1200 A.D. is the limit of our studies. It may be noted that grammarians, commentators and rhetoricians after Hemacandra made a confusion in the interpretation of the term and its location. To mention a few: Siṁhadeva in his commentary on Vāgbhaṭa's *Vāgbhaṭālaṅkāra* 2.3, and Mārkaṇḍeya in his Pkt. grammar, are clearly misled in locating some Ap. dialects in Dravidian provinces. *Tr. Ld. Sh.* and *Rt.* had only academic interest in Ap. and their views need not be discussed.

---

21 *śeṣaṃ śiṣṭa-prayogāt*, *Pu.* 17.91 (17.90 according to Sircar's '*A Gram. of the Pkt. Lang.*', p. 115).

22 *tathā prākṛtam evā 'pabhraṁśaḥ* NS. on Rudraṭa's *Kāvyālaṅkāra* 2.12.

23 *Apabhraṁśas tu yacchuddhaṃ tat taddeśeṣu bhāṣitam*—*Vāgbhaṭālaṅkāra* 2.3.

24 *Apabhraṣṭaṃ tṛtīyaṃ ca tad anantam narādhipa deśa-bhāṣā-viśeṣeṇa tasyānto neha vidyate. Viṣṇudhar..* 3.3

25 *deśasya Kuru-Magadhāder uddeśaḥ prākṛtatvam tasmin sati sva-sva-deśe saṁbandhinī bhāṣā nibandhanīyeti iyaṃ ca deśagīś ca prāyo' pabhraṁśe nipatīti -Nāṭyadarpaṇa*, p. 124, as quoted by L. B. Gandhi in Intro. to *Ap. Kāvyatrayī*.

26 *Kāvyānuśāsana* VIII, 330-7, *Abhiddhāna Cintāmaṇi*, II. 199.

27 Compare *Hc.* 8.4.341, 360, 372, 391, 394, 399, 414, 438 with other sūtras on Ap.

28 *Kāvyānuśāsana*, ch. I, p. 15.

To sum up :

(1) The term Ap. originally meant 'a corrupt or deteriorated form' and was applied to usages not sanctioned by the School of Pāṇini.

(2) In the 3rd cent. A.D., the word '*vibhraṣṭa*' was probably used in the sense of Ap. As a dialect it was known as 'the speech of the Ābhīras' and as 'a dialect abounding in *-u*.'

(3) From the 6th cent. A.D., the term Ap. or *Avahaṁsa* or *Avahaṭṭa* designated a literary dialect in the works of grammarians and rhetoricians. Caṇḍa is the first Pk. grammarian to recognise it as such and the copper-plate of Dharasena II of Valabhī is the first inscribed record of this term in this connotation.

(4) Upto 1100 A.D. Ap. connoted the literary form of provincial speeches or the speech of the elite, indicating thereby that the speech of the *śiṣṭas* or the upper classes of the society had many features common with Ap.

(5) Lastly, like other Pk. dialects, this stage became crystallized in literature and grammar. In the 12th cent A.D., and onwards Ap. was a classical language like Sk. and Pk. As Hemacandra notes it, *grāmya-bhāṣā* 'the language of the towns and villages or masses' seems to be distinguished from Ap. by the end of the 12th cent. A.D.

§2. Linguistically Ap. is the name of a stage in the development of the Indo-Aryan branch of the Indo-Iranian group of the Indo-European family of languages. This stage is supposed to have intervened between secondary MIA and NIA (to use the terminology of GRIERSON) and IA speeches are assumed to have gone through this during 500-1200 A.D. The term Ap. is used here as the name of a literary dialect in which poetic works were composed between 500-1200 A.D., and which was regarded as Ap. by the authors themselves and by Pk. grammarians. This tract of literature shares, at least in spirit, the main features of this tertiary stage of MIA and thus forms the basis of the present investigation. The importance of this literature can never be exaggerated, as it is impossible to have a correct picture of the development of IA from its Middle to its Modern phase, unless a scientific study of the historical development of Ap. is undertaken. It must be made quite clear that hereby we do not subscribe to the view of G. A. GRIERSON, who, in the Introductory volume of *LSI* proposed a hypothetical Ap. as preceding each NIA dialect, as that assumption is unsupported by documentary evidence discovered so far.

### APABHRAṀŚA AND DEŚĪ

§3. The use of the term Ap. as 'a provincial language' chiefly from the 9th cent A.D., brings in the problem of the relation between Ap. and Deśī. As PISCHEL points out the terms '*deśī*,' '*deśya*,' '*deśīmata*,' '*deśīprasiddha*' denote a 'heterogeneous element.'[29] It is used for a class of Pk. vocabulary as distinct from *tss.* and *tbhs.* in *Bh.* 17·3 In *Bh.* 17·46-8 the term *deśabhāṣā* included all Pk. dialects including Ap. though the last was assigned a lower status. (See § 1). As Bharata does not give any instance of 'provincial words' (*deśīmata*) we are left in darkness regarding the relation between Ap. and *deśī*. Some two centuries later Pādalipta used the word '*desī-vayaṇa*' for Mah. and not for Ap.[30] In the 6th cent. A.D., Caṇḍa uses the word '*deśī-prasiddha*' for a class of non-Sk., non-Pkt. words and not for a dialect.

The use of the term Ap. for provincial languages has been already noted in § 1. It is chiefly from the 9th cent. A.D., that Ap. authors from this cent. use the term *deśī* for the dialect of their works which we *i.e.*, Pk. grammarians and modern linguisticians, regard as Ap. To quote a few instances:[31]

(1) *Rāma-kahā-ṇaï eha kamāgaya*

.. .. ..

*sakkaya-Pāyaya-puliṇālaṁkiya*
*desī-bhāsa-ubhaya-taḍujjala*
*kavi-dukkara-ghaṇa-sadda-silāyala*
Svayambhu's *Paümacariu* (circa 700-1000 A.D.)

(2) *ṇa viyāṇami desi*
—Puṣpadanta *Mp.* 1·8·10 (965 A.D.)

(3) *vāyaraṇu desi-saddattha-gāḍha*[32]
*chandālaṅkāra-visāla poḍha.*
*jaï evamāï-bahu-lakkhaṇehi*
*iha viraïya kavva viyakkhaṇehi*
*payaḍivvaü kiṁ appaü ṇa tehi*
—Padmadeva's *Pāsa-ṇāha-cariu* (1000 A.D.)

---

29 PISCHEL, *Grammatik*, § 9.

30 *Pālittaeṇa raïyā vittharao taha ya desi-vayaṇaehiṃ nāmeṇa Taraṅgavaī kahā vicittā viulā ya*—Quoted by JACOBI in Intro. to *Sc.* p. XVII

31 Most of the quotations from unpublished Ap. works are taken from H. L. JAIN, Intro. to *Pd.* pp. 33-46.

32. Here the words "*desi-saddatha-gāḍha*" do not imply Ap. but rather the non-derivabl element called *deśī* words. The word "*deśī*" has been used with different shade of meaning in different contexts.

(4) *ṇa samāṇami chandu ṇa bandha-bheu.*

.. .. ..

*ṇa sakkaya pāyaü desa-bhāsa*
*ṇau saddu vaṇṇu jāṇami samāsa.*
—Lakṣmaṇadeva's *Nemi-ṇāha-cariu*

The use of the term *deśī* or *deśi-bhāṣā* for one's spoken language persisted down to NIA. Thus Jñāneśvara, a 13th cent. author of Mahārāṣṭra, uses it for Marathi. *e.g.*,

*yā-lāgī amhā̃ prākṛtā deśi-kārē bandhe Gītā*
*mhaṇaṇē hē anucitā kāraṇa nohe*
—*Jñāneśvarī*. XVIII. 1721.

Sanskrit rhetoricians and Pk. grammarians are consistent in implying 'non-derivable words in Pkts.' by the term '*deśī* words.' *Bh.* and *Cd.* are quoted above. Rudraṭa in 900 A.D., clearly states:

*prakṛti-pratyaya-mūlā vyutpattir nāsti yasya deśyasya*
*tan maḍahadi kathaṁcana rūḍhiriti na Saṁskṛte racayet.*[33]

Hemacandra understands non-Sanskrit, underivable provincial words by the term '*deśī*.' He says:

*je lakkhaṇe ṇa siddhā ṇa pasiddhā sakkayāhihāṇesu*
*ṇa ya gaüṇa-lakkhaṇā-satti-saṁbhavā te iha ṇibaddhā*
*desa-visesa-pasiddhīi bhaṇṇamāṇā aṇantayā huṁti*
*tamhā aṇāi-pāïya-payaṭṭa-bhāsā-visesao desī.*[34]

Hemacandra attests to the existence of such provincial words in *Hc.* 8·2·178 but excludes those from his lexicon which he included in his Pk. grammar.[35] His list of *deśī* words is different from that in Dhanapāla's *Pāi.* and from those in other Pk. grammars. Pischel rightly remarks: 'They (*i.e.*, Pk. grammarians) consider as such (*deśī*) every word of which the form or meaning cannot be derived from Sk. In proportion to their erudition in Sk. and their skill with etymology, they declare a particular word to be *deśya* which is considered by others to be *tbh.* or *ts.* Thus there are found among the *deśī* words which although clearly traceable to Sk. root, have yet no exact form in Sk.'[36]

P. L. Vaidya showed that a majority of these words are traceable to Sk.[37] while A. N. Upadhye traced some of these to Kanarese[38] which shows the Dravidian element in these words.

33 *Kāvyālaṅkāra,* 6.27.

34 Intro. to *Dn.* (Cal. University, 1931) p. 34 as quoted by H. L. Jain in Intro. to *Pd.* p. 40 footnote.

35 See the Com. on the word *lakṣaṇa* in the above quoted verses.

36 Pischel, *Grammatik* § 9.

37 'Observations on Hemacandra's Deśīnāma-māla,' *ABORI*, 8, pp. 63-71.

38 'Kanarese words in Deśi Lexicons,' *ABORI*, 12, pp. 274-84. Some Kannaḍa words in Upadhye's list e.g., *tuppa* 'ghee,' *vāhalī* 'a stream' are, however, IA loans to Kannaḍa.

Thus the term '*deśī*,' as applied to words is different in implication than when applied to a dialect. '*deśī bhāṣā*' is generally the spoken language of a particular province whether it be Mah. Pkt. or Ap. or one of the NIA languages. *Deśī* as applied to word implies a word non-derivable from Sk., expressing thereby the limits of the philological studies of the author who classes it thus. These words are found in Pkt., Ap. and NIA. The identification of *deśī* with non-Aryan element in IA is a hasty conclusion of CALDWELL and his followers, as the problem is yet to be adequately studied by scholars with sound grounding in IA, Dravidian and Austro-Asiatic Philology.

## REFERENCES TO AP. LITERATURE

§4. There are many references to Ap. literature in Pk. grammars and Sk. rhetorical literature, where many Ap. verses are quoted as illustrations of the theories propounded in them. In §§1 and 3 we have referred to the different Alaṅkāra works where the term Ap. and its usage are given. Here the references are arranged in a chronological order, the dates of the authors being those given by M. M. P. V. KANE in his 'History of Alaṅkāra Literature' in the Introduction to Viśvanātha's *Sāhitya-darpaṇa* 2 (1923).

(1) Bharata (circa 300 A.D.), *Nāṭyaśāstra* (Kāvyamālā No. 42) Ap. is an uncultured dialect (*vibhāṣā*) spoken by herdsmen e.g. cowherds. shepherds, tenders of herds of horses, camels, etc., (17·48, 55). As noted in §1 above Ap. was then called Ābhīrī and a dialect abounding in *-u*. It had a lower status on the stage, lower than that of Pk. Its use for the ravings of mad Purūravas in the *Vikramorvaśīya* IV shows that Kālidāsa regarded Pk. as too dignified a medium to be used for this purpose, even in the case of an *uttamapātra* like the king.[40] (See §8 later.)

(2) Bhāmaha (circa 600 A. D., but before Bāṇa). In *Kāvyālaṅkāra* 1st Chapter[41] he divides *kāvya* dialectically in Sk., Pkt. and Ap. (1·16). In distinguishing between *Kathā* and *Ākhyāyikā*, he remarks :

*na vaktrāparavaktrābhyāṁ yuktā nocchvāsavatyapi*
*Saṁskṛtam saṁskṛtā ceṣṭā kathāpabhraṁśabhāk tathā* (1·28)

(3) Daṇḍin (6th cent. A.D. ) in his *Kāvyādarśa*[42] 1·23-8 differs, and he does not recognize the distinction between *kathā* and *ākhyāyikā*.

40 The genuineness of these Ap. verses is still a moot point. A strong case in favour of their genuineness can be made. See A. N. UPADHYE, Intro. to *PPr.* p. 56 Footnote 1 and G. V. TAGARE, 'Madhyayugīna Mālavasāhtya,' *Puruṣārtha*, June 1942.

41 Printed as an Appendix to the *Pratāparudrayaśobhūṣaṇa* (*BSS* LXV, 1909).

42 Edited by BELVALKAR and RADDI, *BSS* LXXIV, 1919.

He classifies literature (*vāṅmaya*) in four categories according as it is in Sk. Pkt. Ap. and a mixture of these. The word '*āpta*' in this shows that this fourfold classification is older than Daṇḍin.[43] Ap. connotes the speech of Ābhīras and others as it is recorded in poetic works. In śāstric works[44] non-Sanskrit expression is regarded as Ap. (1·36). Ap. is characterised by the use of metres like '*osara*' (1·37).

Taking a synthetic view of these works we find that in the 6th cent. A.D. the *-u* abounding dialect in Bharata's *Nāṭyaśāstra* came to be known as Ap. *Kathās* and poems were written in it and it rose to such a literary eminence as to claim a place in works on Poetics, along with Sk. and Pk. Ap. developed a number of metres peculiar to it. The then Ap. literature assumed such an importance and wide influence as to attract the attention of representative rhetoricians from Kashmir to South India. It was still looked upon with contempt as a speech of low castes or nomadic tribes.

(4, 5) Rudraṭa (800-850 A.D.) in his *Kāvyālaṅkāra*[45] divides '*vākya*' in six kinds according to dialects.

*bhāṣā-bheda-nimittaḥ ṣoḍhā bhedo'sya sambhavati* (2·11)

Namisādhu (1069 A.D.), the commentator, remarks that the division of literature in three languages *viz.*, Sk., Pk. and Ap. (as found in Bhāmaha), is set aside by the word '*ṣoḍhā*,'[46] This six-fold division of literary dialects includes Ap. along with its many sub-dialects.[47] Perhaps as Nitti Dolci says this six-fold classification is older still.[48]

The examples of *bhāṣāśleṣas* are given in 4·15, 16,21. He states that a mixture of dialects would give us 30 kinds of *bhāṣāśleṣas* (4·22) It is important to note that Rudraṭa quotes Ap. verses while his predecessors Bhāmaha and Daṇḍin do not do so. It shows that Ap. grew in literary eminence by the 9th cent. A.D. as a non-Jain rhetorician in far off Kashmir is quoting these verses—a fact borne out by the history of Ap. literature. Ānandavardhana quotes an Ap. *dohā* in the *Dhvanyāloka*.[49]

(6) In the 10th cent. A.D. Rājaśekhara, the author of *Kāvyamīmāṁsā* (900-925 A.D.) tells us a great deal about the importance of

---

43 *tadetad vāṅmayaṃ bhūyaḥ Saṃskṛtam Prākṛtam tathā Apabhraṃśaś ca miśraṃ cetyāhu āptāś caturvidhaṃ* (1.32).

44 *śāstra=śabdaśāstra* in the Com. in Belvalkar's Ed. but 'Vedic works' in the Com. of Jīvānanda Vidyāsāgara Calcutta Ed.

45 Kāvyamālā 2, Ed. Pt. Durgaprasad and Panashikar, 1909.

46 '*Prākṛtaṃ Saṃskṛtaṃ caitadapabhraṁśa iti tridhā*' *ityetan nirastaṃ bhavati*. This reference is most probably to Bhāmaha's *Kāvyālaṅkāra* 1.16.

47 '*bhūribhedo*' in Daṇḍin's *Kāvyālaṅkāra* 2.12.

48 *Les Grammairiens prakrits*, p. 158.

49 See Pischel, *Materialien*, p. 45.

Ap. According to him, Ap. is a 'very elegant dialect,'[50] capable of expressing some implication in a special way, just as Sk., Pk. and Paiś. have a speciality of their own in doing so[51]. A special place of honour is given to Ap. in the court of the king Poet[52]. The description of the body of the mythological Kāvyapuruṣa shows the same[53].

(7, 8) *Daśarūpa* of Dhanañjaya (974-94 A.D.) with the Com. of Dhanika and Bhoja's *Sarasvatīkaṇṭhābharaṇa* (1030-50 A.D.) have been utilised in the body of the present dissertation. They show the flourishing state of Ap.

(9) Namisādhu's commentary on Rudraṭa's *Kāvyālaṅkāra* 2·11, 12 is mentioned above (§4·4). He states that Ap. was predominently Pk. i.e., Mah. and was freely mixed with Śaurasenisms, Māgadhisms etc.[54] The mixed state may represent the development of Śaur. Mg. etc., into their pre-NIA stage or free interborrowing as stated in §1.

(10-15) The views of Vāgbhaṭa (1123-56 A.D.) the author of the *Vāgbhaṭālaṅkāra*, the author of *Viṣṇudharmottara*, of Guṇacandra and Rāmacandra (in their Commentary on *Nāṭyadarpaṇa*), of Jinadatta in *Vivekavilasita* 8·131, of Amaracandra in *Kāvyakalpalatā-vṛtti* and of Hemacandra are already mentioned in §1.

The different references to Ap. literature show that Ap. was rising slowly from the low status as an Ābhīra dialect to that of literary importance during 300-600 A.D. Its importance went on increasing as centuries rolled on and it finally became equal in status to Sk. and Pk. by the 10th cent. A.D. It retained this to the end of our period. The *Alaṅkāra* works bear testimony to this historical development of Ap.

§5. Though there is a vast field for research in Ap., very little of it was known to PISCHEL when he wrote his monumental grammar of Pkt. languages. Many Pkt. grammars were available only in Mss. when he studied them. The Pkt. grammars of Puruṣottama and Rāmaśarma Tarkavāgīśa were not known then. The knowledge of Ap. literature was limited to the disputed verses in Kālidāsa's *Vikramorvaśīya* Act IV, anthology of Ap. verses in Bhoja's *Sarasvatīkaṇṭhābharaṇa*, and in Hemacandra's Pkt. grammar, and a few more strophes

---

50 *subhavyo' pabhraṃśaḥ—Bālarāmāyaṇa* 1.10.

51 *eko 'rthaḥ Saṃskṛtoktyā sa sukavi-racanaḥ prākṛtenāparo' smin anyo' pabhraṃśa-gīrbhiḥ kimaparamaparo bhūta-bhāṣā-krameṇa.* —*Kāvyamīmāṃsā* Ch. IX. p. 48.

52 *Kāvya-mīmāṃsā* Ch. X. pp. 54-5.

53 *Kāvya-mīmāṃsā*, Ch. III, p. 6.

54 *tathā prākṛtam evāpabhraṁśaḥ* Namisādhu is not a grammarian and the fact that the ūtras quoted by him regarding the characteristics of Pk.dialects, are copied *verbatim* by *Hc.*, shows that he used some treatise on Pk. grammar before him.

quoted in some Sk. rhetorical works. He edited these critically in his *Materialien zur Kenntnis des Apabhraṁśa*. But his critical apparatus was limited. When one reads Ludwig ALSDORF's *Apabhraṁśa Studien*, one realizes what PISCHEL would have done, had he a few more and better Mss. for collation. Moreover PISCHEL's *Grammatik* is neither a historical nor a comparative grammar of Prakrits. As collection of material it is quite good, but it is unsatisfactory from the point of Ap. linguistics.

Critically edited works form the very basis of linguistic studies, as it is impossible to prepare a descriptive, comparative or a historical grammar without them. It is this paucity of the elementary apparatus of linguistic studies which formed the limitations of PISCHEL's *Grammatik*. It is in 1918 that we get a critical edition of the first independent literary work in Ap.—the *Bhavisattakaha* edited by Hermann JACOBI. Since then a number of Ap. works (some uncritically edited) appeared. The following is the list of these works in an alphabetic order (in the abbreviations.)

(1) *Bhavisattakaha* : Edited by Hermann JACOBI with a German Introduction and the text in Roman Script. The text is more accurate than the Devanāgarī text in P. D. GUNE's edition. It is hence used for form-collection. The introductory essays in both of these editions are interesting from the point of Ap. language and literature.

(2, 3) *Dohākoṣas of Kāṇha and Saraha* : Edited in French by M. SHAHIDULLA. The introduction gives a good analysis of the dialect in addition to other information regarding the authors, their dates etc. M. SHAHIDULLA's date of Kāṇha (700 A.D.) and S. K. CHATTERJI's opinion about the same (1200 A.D.) are taken as the two extremes; and 700-1200 A.D. is taken to be the period of this dialect.

(4) Ap. verses in the ***Daśarūpa***: ***DS*** as edited by Pt. SUDARŚANA-ŚĀSTRI, printed in Gujarati Printing Press, Bombay, 1914. The text of the Ap. verses is not critical.

(5) *Harivaṁśa Purāṇa*: edited by Ludwig ALSDORF of Hamburg University, in German with the text in Roman Script. He based his text on Mss. A, B, C (designated as B, P, S by P. L. VAIDYA in his edition of MP Vol. III). ALSDORF's edition is informative, and contains dialect-analysis and a very good glossary.

(6) *Jasahara Cariu*: edited by P. L. VAIDYA, Poona, 1931. It is chiefly based on Mss. S and T of Senagaṇa and supplemented by P, A and B of Balātkāragaṇa. As noted by the editor, S was copied

at Surat and then the copies travelled to Karanja in Berar. The editor does not give the analysis of the dialect.

(7, 8) *Jinadatta's Carcarī and Upadeśarasāyana*: Edited by L. B. Gandhi in G.O.S. The introduction is learned, but the text is not so much critical. The forms from these are used only as supplementary examples.

(9) Hemacandra's *Kumārapāla Carita* Ch. VIII. : It was first edited by S. P. Pandit and the edition was revised by P. L. Vaidya (BSPS No. 60). This work is composed mainly to illustrate the rules of Hemacandra's grammar and naturally its style is artificial.

(10) Kanakāmara's *Karakaṇḍa Carita* : Edited by H. L. Jain of King Edward College, Amraoti. The text is critically edited although the introduction does not deal with the characteristics of Kanakāmara's dialect.

(11) *Kumārapāla-pratibodha* of Somprabha : It is edited in GOS. The Ap. portion is re-edited by Ludwig Alsdorf in German, with the text in Roman Script. It is a critical text with a good analysis of the dialect and glossary. Here all references are to Alsdorf's text.

(12) Puṣpadanta's *Mahāpurāṇa* Vol. I, II, III : The monumental text is critically edited by P. L. Vaidya. It is unfortunate that the paper situation during this world-war should deprive us of the promised introduction by this eminent scholar.

(13) *Materialien zur Kenntnis des Apabhraṁśa.* : R. Pischel's edition of the then available Ap. material is already criticised above. This contains Ap. verses in Kālidāsa's *Vikramorvaśīya* Act IV, Bhoja's *Sarasvatīkaṇṭhābharaṇa*. For the anthology of Ap. verses in Hemacandra's Pkt. grammar, P. L. Vaidya's edition (Poona, 1928) is used.

(14) *Nāgakumāra Carita* by Puṣpadanta. This is a critical edition by H. L. Jain. It contains a brief analysis of Puṣpadanta's dialect, in addition to the general introduction and a good glossary.

(15) Rāmasimha's *Pāhuḍadohā*: Critically edited by H. L. Jain in Hindi with the usual introduction, brief but important dialect analysis, translation and glossary. We have followed H. L. Jain regarding the date and province of Rāmasiṁha.

(16-17) Joïndu's *Paramātmaprakāśa* and *Yogasāra*, an excellent edition by A. N. Upadhye of Kolhapur in 1937. The text is critically edited and the linguistic portion of the Introduction is brief yet lucid.

UPADHYE places Joindu *c.* 600 A.D., while H. L. JAIN assigns him to 1000 A.D. Hence 600-1000 A.D. is regarded as the period of his dialect.

(18) *Sanatkumāra Carita*: Edited by H. JACOBI in German, with Introduction, text in Roman Script, translation and glossary. Though this is one of the earliest Ap. publications, the text is critically accurate, Introductory essay (especially regarding Ap. literature) instructive, dialect analysis reliable, with a useful translation and glossary. It is an indispensable work to a student of Ap.

(19) Devasena's *Sāvayadhamma-dohā*: Edited in Hindi by H. L. JAIN. As usual with such editions, a critical text, a short dialect analysis, an instructive Introduction and glossary are the main features of this work. We follow H. L. JAIN regarding the authorship of the text.

(20) Hemacandra's *Siddha-Hema* : Here P. L. VAIDYA's edition (Poona 1928) is used.

(21) Ap. verses in *Supāsanāha Carita* : edited by Pt. H. T. SHETH. The text is not so much critical. Ap. forms are used only as supplementary examples.

Though we have consulted Maheśvara's *Saṁjama-Mañjarī*, N. N. CHOUDHARI's edition of the *Dākārṇava Tantra* and such other works, the forms are not used in this dissertation as they are composed after 1200 A.D.

§6. Since the close of the last great War in 1918, some grammatical studies of Ap. have been published. The first and foremost mention must be made of the two Introductions in H. JACOBI's editions of *BhK*. and *Sc.* The Introductions to *BhK*. (in JACOBI's and GUNE's editions) are now known to all. The term Ap., opinions of Pk. grammarians on Ap., Ap. as the Ābhīrī dialect, the then extant Ap. literature etc., are discussed by both these scholars. Moreover they provide us with sound grammatical analysis of the dialect. Although JACOBI is misled in designating the dialect of *BhK*. as Vrācaṭa,[55] his masterly study of the dialect of Ap. is perfectly reliable.[56]

The introduction to *Sc.* notes a few more Ap. works. Herein JACOBI gives his regional division of Ap. literature into Eastern, Western, Southern, and Northern groups. He seems to believe that Eastern Ap. works follow the rules of Eastern Pk. grammarians. A

55 See Intro. to *BhK*. pp. 71, 72, 77, 81.
56 Intro. to *BhK*. pp. 24-43.

comparison between the dialects of *DKK.* and *DKs.* and the Ap. of *Pu, Rt.* and *Mk.* disproves the theory. The only work in the 'Northern' Ap. is a 15th cent. poetic composition by a Bania.[57] As will be seen later on in §8, the regional classification of Ap. literature followed in this work is different and more natural.

As we have seen in §5 above, some editors of Ap. works e.g., ALSDORF, SHAHIDULLA, JAIN and UPADHYE, have devoted a few pages of their introductions to the dialect study of the texts edited by them. Out of these editors JACOBI, ALSDORF, SHAHIDULLA and UPADHYE, give us a detailed analysis of the texts they have edited, while others are very brief.

Out of the linguistic studies in Ap. we must mention Jules BLOCH's *L'indo-aryen*, Louis GRAY's papers on MIA morphology and IE. element in Pkt.[58] and lastly *Apabhraṁśa Studien* by Ludwig ALSDORF. BLOCH in his *L'indo-aryen* evaluates the Ap. tendencies and notes its contribution to NIA linguistics. The work being a rapid survey of the evolution of IA during the last 2000 years, is very unsatisfactory from the point of view of Ap. linguistics. Louis H. GRAY's "Observations on MIA Morphology" (*BSOS* VIII ii-iii, pp. 563-9) are interesting from a comparative point of view. His paper on 'Fifteen Prakrit Indo-European Etymologies' (*JAOS* 60·360-9) is not directly connected with Ap. In both of these he tries to attract the attention of the students to the II and IE elements in MIA, though we must be very cautious in accepting his theories and etymologies which are sometimes far-fetched. ALSDORF, in his *Ap. Studien* critically re-edits PISCHEL's *Materialien* and gives some linguistic notes on the *-ha* element in Ap. morphology, Greek counterpart of Ap. *appaṇa*, a few Ap. post-positions etc. The notes are unconnected and few in number—a fact minimising its importance either as a comparative or as a historical grammar of Ap. The learned author does not claim it and he designates it modestly as '*Studien*' and not '*Grammatik.*'

Lastly we may mention S.M. KATRE's *Wilson Philological Lectures*, 1941, in which the author takes a succinct survey of IA developments wherein Ap. is cursorily surveyed in passing.

§7. It will be clear from the above discussion that none of the scholars tried to study Ap. in its chrono-regional perspective, though Historical Linguistics has advanced to some extent since the publication of E. BENVENISTE's *Origines de la formation des noms en indo-européen* I

57 Intro. to *Sc.* p. XXIII.
58 In *BSOS* VIII ii-iii and *JAOS* 60, pp. 360-9.

(Paris 1935) and J. KURYLOWICZ's *Études indo-européennes* I (Krakow 1935). Historical Linguistics as applied to Ap. being still an unexplored region, it is pertinent to explain this new point of view here.

As pointed out by S. M. KATRE in his *Wilson Philological Lectures* (1941), Historical Linguistics is 'the science of comparative grammar applied to a given family of languages, consciously attempting to place before oneself the space-time context of each linguistic fact so far as that was determinable, and thus build up a linguistic approach at once chronological and regional.'[59] It is in this manner that we are to fill in the large gaps in our understanding of IA developments, wherein constant interborrowing between the cognate dialects has taken place on such a large scale, as to render the method of isoglosses unintelligible. This method is a distinct advance over the old method of comparing vocables from different cognate languages belonging to unrelated periods of history. This new method has shown that it alone can solve the linguistic problems raised by the discovery of Hittite and Tocharian, as mere comparative linguistics applied to non-synchronic elements belonging to distinct but cognate groups, fails to solve etymological problems.

Time and Space are thus the two important co-ordinates for defining the linguistic history and development of this important stage of IA. It is this special significance of the Space-Time Context which necessitates a chrono-regional study of Ap. literature. And it is here that difficulties begin to crop up, as in the history of old Indian literature, we have no definite means of ascertaining exact chronology. For example, *DKK* is located by M. SHAHIDULLA in 700 A.D., by Bagchi in 1100 A.D., and by S. K. CHATTERJI in 1200 A.D. H. L. JAIN regards *PPr.* as a work of the 10th cent. A.D. while A. N. UPADHYE claims it for the 6th cent. A.D. The date of *BhK.* is also uncertain though he is assigned to the 10th cent. A.D. by P. D. GUNE, the editor of the Devanāgarī text. Thus although our knowledge of Ap. extends over 900 years, we have to take recourse to relative chronology as a means of fixing the literary strata.

During these eventful nine centuries (300-1200 A.D.) some considerable changes must have taken place in IA. As is well known, the real development of language takes place upon the lips and in the minds of men and not in written documents. But as matters stand now, we must rely on documents, as the representatives of the psycho-physical factor in the change of language, though a script is but a poor record of human sounds, and factors *e.g.*, Mss. traditions, competence of scribes, redactors and

59 *BV*, 2 pp. 220-2.

editors, provincialism etc. affect adversely the objective representation of the author's original composition. Moreover, if we depend entirely on documentary evidence, Ap., being a literary language, may not represent the then prevalent popular idiom. As Jules BLOCH puts it:

"Our knowledge of its (India's) languages, at least in their most ancient stages, is based only, or nearly so, on literary languages of which we know neither the local basis, nor the degree of connection with the vernaculars. They do not give expression to the thoughts and feelings of the people, at the most, they give an ideal picture of the culture of a small community. They may differ in character, some highly religious and aristocratic, some popular, but religious, too; the majority are mainly adapted for purely literary usages. The linguist has to be careful in giving their evidence its proper value, before trying to construct the details of the history of Indo-Aryan."[60]

This passage is quoted here, *in extenso*, to state succinctly the difficulties that face a student of Ap.

In §§1 and 3 we have seen that Ap. was a living idiom upto 1100 A.D., and that it was in the 12th cent. A.D., that the divorce between Ap. as a literary dialect and the *grāmya bhāṣā i.e.*, vernacular became apparent. It is the Ap. literature upto 1200 A.D., that forms the basis of this study. Ap. literature during this period is expected to be much more akin to the popular speech, as this literature was chiefly composed for the masses, and the general paucity of Pkt. Inscriptions after 400 A.D. most probably indicates that Prakrits ceased to be understood by the common people after that period. As Pk. became stylised and artificial as Sanskrit itself during our period (500-1200 A.D.) and NIA languages were yet to appear in the development of IA, Ap. alone affords us valuable material for evaluating this post-Prakrit and pre-NIA period linguistically.

§8. Ap. literature is regionally classified in three main divisions according to the place of composition of the particular work. They are roughly as follows :

(1) Western Apabhraṁśa (Abbr. WAp.) : This roughly corresponds to the Śaur. region in GRIERSON's *LSI* Vo. I. 1. It comprises of the provinces where Gujarati, Rajasthani and Hindi are the spoken medii to-day.

(2) Southern Apabhraṁśa (Abbr. SAp): It mainly corresponds to the Māhārāṣṭrī region in *LSI* Vol. I. 1 and includes Mahārāṣṭra, Berar

60 Jules BLOCH, Furlong Lectures for 1929. 'Some Problems of Indo-Aryan Philology,' *BSOS* V. 4 (1930).

and the Marathi speaking districts in C.P. and H. E. H. the Nizam's dominions and the country adjoining them.

(3) Eastern Apabhraṁśa (Abbr. EAp.): This is corresponding to the land of Magadhan speeches *viz.*, Bengal, Bihar and Orissa where the modern descendants of Mg. hold the sway.

This classification is somewhat different from that of JACOBI who classified Ap. literature according to cardinal points. The so-called "Northern Ap." is not represented by a single work during our period. The work mentioned by JACOBI in Intro. to *Sc.*, p. XXIII is a very late composition when all the Modern Indo-Aryan languages were fully developed all over India. We do not subscribe to GRIERSON's theory of postulating one Ap. per every NIA language. This hypothesis is unsupported by the evidence discovered so far. It is expected that this classification will throw more light on the linguistic developments in the pre-and proto-NIA periods, as it reflects the popular usages in those regions where the great NIA languages of today have been crystalized.

The following is the division of Ap. works according to their Space-Time Context :

(i) WESTERN APABHRAṀŚA.

| *Name of the author and the work* | *Date (A.D.)* | *Province* |
|---|---|---|
| 1) Kālidāsa—Ap. verses in *Vk.* IV if genuine. | 5th cent. | Malwa. |
| 2)3) Joindu—*PPr.*, *Ys.* | 6th-10th cent. | .. |
| 4) Devasena (?)—*Sdd.* | 933 | Dhārā (Malwa) |
| 5) Rāmasiṁha—*Pd.* | 10th cent. | Rajputānā. |
| 6) Dhanañjaya—*Ds.* | ,, | Malwā. |
| 7) Dhanapāla—*BhK* | ,,(?) | Gujarat. |
| 8) Bhoja—Ap. verses in *Sarasvatī-kaṇṭhābharaṇa.* | 1000-1050 | Malwa |
| 9, 10) Jinadatta-*Jdc.*, *Jdu.* | 1113-1155 | Gujarat. |
| 11) Lakṣmaṇagaṇi—*Ap.* verses in *SN.* | 1142 | ,, |
| 12) Haribhadra—*Sc.* | 1159 | ,, |
| 13, 14) Hemacandra —*Hc.*, *Kc.* | 1088-1172 | ,, |
| 15) Somaprabha—*Kp.* | 1195 | ,, |

The Time-Space location of a few of these works needs some explanation.

(1) *The genuineness of Ap. verses in Kālidāsa's Vk.*:

The following are the main objections against Kālidāsa's authorship of these verses: (*i*) The king being an *uttama-pātra* cannot utter verses in Pkt. (*ii*) The Commentator Kāṭayavēma knows nothing about them. (*iii*) South Indian Mss. do not include them. (*iv*) Most of these verses are tautological, some vague in allusions and references, several of them interrupting the sentiment expressed by Sk. verses. (*v*) Other dramas of Kālidāsa do not contain Ap. passages.[61]

The objections may be refuted as follows.[62]

(*i*) *Nāṭya śāstra* allows change of dialects (*bhāṣāvyatikrama*) for *uttama pātras* on certain occasions. Here in *Vk.* IV the king is insane. Moreover as PANDIT himself suggests someone else sings these songs for the king, giving (as Prin. R. D. KARMARKAR notes it in his Intro. to *Vk.*) occasional rest to the actor representing the king.

(*ii*) Ignorance of Kāṭayavema is no argument. If Kāṭayameva ignores them Raṅganātha comments on them.

(*iii*) Northern Mss. include these verses and Kālidāsa himself belonged to Northern India. Moreover, the Dravidian audience in the South might have no interest in Ap., as it was not connected with their speech. Hence their exclusion in the Southern Mss. and inclusion in the Northern ones. Really speaking an argument based on the Southern recension of *Vk.* is inconclusive.

(*iv*) These are purely subjective considerations. A lunatic is expected to be vague and tautological in his ravings. The imagery in the songs is of no mean order. To quote A. N. UPADHYE : 'Even in present day dramas meaningless songs are introduced; they do not advance the plot in any way but they are sung merely to amuse the audience. Anyone acquainted with the phonology of Ap. will readily accept that it is perhaps the best medium for songs.'[63]

(*v*) A negative argument requiring no refutation.

Though these are strong grounds in favour of the genuineness of these verses, we regard it an open question.

---

61 S. P. PANDIT, Intro. to the *Vikramorvaśīya*.

62 For details : G. V. TAGARE's article in *Puruṣārtha*, June, 1942. Prof. Dr. A. N. UPADHYE holds a similar view, Intro. to *PPr.* (1937) p. 56, note 1.

63 Intro. to *PPr.* p. 56, footnote 1.

(2) *The date of Joindu*:

The date of Joindu is still a disputed point. A.N. UPADHYE, the editor, places him in the 6th cent. A.D. [64] But as some assign him to the 10th cent. A.D. 6-10th cent. has been regarded as the period of his dialect. We referred to Prof. Dr. UPADHYE, the editor of *PPr.* regarding the province of these works. As he supposes that the works were composed somewhere in Rajputana or Northern Gujarat (his letter dated 2-1-1942), Joindu's works are placed in this group.

(3) *The authorship of Sāvayadhaṁmadohā*:

H. L. JAIN, the editor, claims *Sdd.* to Devasena and says that it was composed in 933 A.D., at Dhara, while A.N. UPADHYE regards it as Lakṣmīcandra's composition (earlier than 1528 A.D.).[65] We have tentatively accepted JAIN's date, province, and authorship of *Sdd.*

As UPADHYE now gives up the theory of Joindu's authorship of *Pd.*,[66] we may regard Rāmasiṁha as the author of *Pd.* We may also accept P. D. GUNE's date of *BhK* as no contrary evidence has yet appeared.

The dates and authorships of the remaining texts are already settled. As noted above the critical nature of *DS.*, *Jdc.*, *Jdu.* and *Sn.* is doubtful. The examples from these are of a supplementary nature.

(ii) SOUTHERN APABHRAṀŚA.

The second important yet allied group is that of Ap. works belonging to the Deccan. As these Mss. travelled to Gujarat where they were copied and some of these copies were taken from that province and deposited at Karanja in Berar, some westernisation of these texts is not improbable.

The following are the dates and places of composition of these works.

| *Name of the author and the work* | *Date* | *Place* |
|---|---|---|
| 1) Puṣpadanta—*Mp.* | 965 A.D. | Mānyakheṭa |
| 2, 3) ,, *Nc.*, *Jc.* | 965-72 | ,, |
| 4) Kanakāmara—*KKc.* | 975-1025 | Assaye (Nizam's Dominion). |

64 Intro. to *PPr.* pp. 63-7.
65 *Ibid.*, pp. 59-61.
66 *Ibid.*, p. 62.

P. L. VAIDYA has now definitely settled the place and time of Puṣpadanta.[68] Mānyakheṭa is modern Malkhed (17° 10″ N. and 77° 13″ E) in H. E. H. the Nizam's dominions.

We differ from the learned editor of *KKc.* regarding the province of the author and claim him to Assaye in the Nizam's dominions, where a battle was fought between the Marathas and the English in 1803 A.D. The following are the grounds for this theory.[69]

Kanakāmara states that he composed *KKc.* at Āsāiya. This Āsāiya should be identified with modern Assaye in the Nizam State and not somewhere in Bundelkhand on account of the following reasons :

(*i*) The details of the description of the Terāpura caves (so minutely described by Kanakāmara in *sandhis* IV and V of his work) are corroborated by BURGESS in his account of the Dhārāśiva caves in his *Archaeological Survey of Western India*, Vol. III. Assaye, Terāpura (modern Ter), Dhārāśiva (Mod. Osmanabad) formed a part of the Rāṣṭrakūṭa kingdom. These very places have been taken as a background for a greater part of *KKc.*

(*ii*) Rāṣṭrakūṭa king Kṛṣṇa III (mentioned as 'Kaṇha' by Puṣpadanta and 'Kaṇṇa' by Kanakāmara)[70] conquered the kings of the South *e.g.*, Cera, Cola, Pāṇḍya, Siṁhala etc. Kanakāmara shows his hero to have done the same.

(*iii*) The princes, their feudatories associated with Āsāiya in *KKc.* are not properly identified elsewhere outside the Deccan.

(*iv*) H. L. JAIN, the editor of *KKc.*, does not satisfactorily identify Āsāiya with any place in that part of the country (*i.e.*, Bundelkhand). On the contrary he suggests Assaye as an alternate place for identification.[71]

---

68 Intro. to *Jc.* pp. 19-24 and Intro. to *MP.* Vol. III, pp. XVIII-XXIII.

69 For details see G. V. TAGARE's article in *MSPP.*, March 1942. pp. 23-33. In his letter dated 3-12-42, Prof. JAIN appreciated the force of the following reasoning, but Prof. UPADHYE differs. Owing to pressure of our work in different fields, we could not continue the discussion.

70 We have epigraphic evidence of the hyper-Sanskritisation of this '*Kaṇṇa*' into '*Karṇa*' with reference to this very king Kṛṣṇa III.

*āśritya karṇa-rājākhya-Vallabham Bāḍapādhipaḥ*
*vinirgamayya taṃ deśād Amma-rājākhyam ūrjitam.*

—Aruṁbaka Plate (*EI* XIX, p. 137 Vallabha is a designation of the Rāṣṭrakūṭas while Ammarāja mentioned here is Ammarāja II of Eastern Cālukyas. For historical details about these See A. S. ALTEKAR *Rāṣṭrakūṭas and their Times* (Poona, 1934), pp. 121-2.

Kṛṣṇa > Kaṇha > Kaṇṇa > Karṇa (Hyper-Sanskritisation) is quite clear.

71 Intro. to *KKc.* pp. 40-1.

### (iii) Eastern Apabhraṁśa

The third and the last important group of Ap. works is of 'Eastern Ap.' It consists of the *Dohākoṣas* of Kāṇha and Saraha. Though we consulted the *Ḍākārṇava-mahā-yoginī-tantra-rājya*, briefly mentioned as *DKn.* and Vidyāpati's *Kīrtilatā*, they are excluded from this study, as they were composed after 1200 A.D. These works are composed in Eastern India by persons who were the natives of that part of the country, and as such present a homogeneous dialect, no matter whether it is called 'Buddhist Ap.' according to Tibetan tradition, or 'Östlicher Ap.' after Jacobi.[72] We do not designate these as 'Eastern Ap.' because they follow the rules of 'Eastern Pk. grammarians.' As we shall find it in the body of this work, the Ap. described by these 'Eastern' Pk. grammarians is different from EAp. Nor do these grammarians describe the Magadhan Ap., the parent of Beng. Maith. and Oriya. Nor is the dialect of the *Dohākoṣas*, Western Ap. though as Ap. it shares some characteristics with WAp.

The following works have been mainly used as the basic texts of EAp.

| *Name of the author and the work.* | *Date* | *Province* |
|---|---|---|
| 1 Kāṇha—*DKK.* .. | 700-1200 A.D. | Bengal. |
| 2. Saraha—*DKs.* .. | 1000 A.D. | ,, |

The first work of this group is a small collection of 32 dohās expressing the mystical experience of Kāṇha or Kṛṣṇācārya who is popularly known as Kāniph Nāth or Kānupā. From the data presented by M. Shahidulla,[73] it appears that Kāṇha was a native of Samataṭa or Eastern Bengal. His preceptor Jālandhari or Jālandhar Nāth was a contemporary of Matsyendra Nāth who was in Nepal in 657 A.D. in the reign of Narendra Deva. Gopīcandra, another contemporary of these was a near relative of Bhartṛhari, the King of Malwa, who died according to Itsing in 651 A.D. The evidence presented by M. Shahidulla shows that Kāṇha should be located in 700 A.D. rather than in 1200 A.D., as was supposed by S. K. Chatterji. We have allotted 700-1200 A.D., as the period of this dialect. This includes 1100 A.D., the date proposed by Bagchi.

Saraha, the author of *DKs.*, composed his work in a dialect which is a continuation of the dialect in *DKK.* The comparative table of morphological frequencies (with reference to Nom. sg.) as given in this work will show that Saraha is most probably later than Kāṇha.

72 Intro. to *Sc.* pp. XXV, XXVII.
73 Intro. to *Les Chants Mystiques*, pp. 25-9.

§9. *Method of Approach*

The chrono-regional classification of Ap. literature brings us to the problem of linguistic approach. Broadly speaking, there is practically absence of clear-cut characteristics of Ap. vocabulary, phonologically separating it from other MIA dialects. As a matter of fact, phonology is the weakest part in MIA dialectology. For example, what are the phonological *differentiae* between the great Pk. dialects Mah. and Śaur? It is the voicing of OIA, *t* and *th* and the change *ry*>*yy*. (See *Hc*. 8.4.286-98). Paiś devoices *d* to *t*, dentalizes *ṇ*>*n* and cerebralizes *l*>*ḷ* (See *Hc*. 8.4.303-24). Mg. is characterized by the changes *r*>*l*, *s*, *ṣ*>*ś*, *j*>*y* and retention of *y*, *ññ* pronunciation of the nasal conjuncts, *ny*, *ṇy*, *jñ*, *ñj*, the peculiar *jihvāmūlīya* (ᳵ*k*) pronunciation of *kṣ and śc* of *cch*. (*Hc*. 8.4.288-98).

Though Pk. grammarians note the retention of *ṛ* and -*r* conjuncts, voicing of intervocalic voiceless consonants (viz., *k*, *kh*, *t*, *th*, *p*, *ph*.>*g*, *gh*, *d*, *dh*, *b*, *bh* respectively) and the change *m*>*ṽ*- as the peculiarities of Ap. phonology, the analysis of actual Ap. literature convinces one that the above-mentioned generalisation holds good. As matters stand now, morphology is a more reliable criterion in dialect classification in MIA in general. In the case of Ap. in particular, it is Ap. Morphology which distinguishes it from other MIA dialects.

The above discussion will bring home the necessity of collecting data from morphological examples bearing Ap. characteristics as defined by Pk. grammarians and linguisticians. It is hence that the part on Ap. Phonology is based on deductions from the declined or conjugated forms which may be claimed as true Ap. forms. As far as possible, forms common to Mah. Śaur. or other MIA dialects are scrupulously set aside as there is no propriety in discussing the development of literary Pkts. or secondary MIA in a work dealing with Ap. or tertiary MIA linguistics. Our aim is to determine exactly the genuine Ap. developments in their chrono-regional context. This being the case, all the data, whether phonological or morphological, is clearly analysed and tabulated in their Space-Time context as far as it is determinable.

The peculiarities common to all regions will be naturally evident. The source of forms quoted will be indicated in the Index Verborum at the end of this work.

§10. *The Method of Presentation*:

In describing every phenomenon, the statements of Pk. grammarians and their illustrations are (wherever possible) given first by way of juxta-position and a comparison is made with the findings from actual Ap. literature. As stated above only factual illustrations of the particular characteristics are selected. The illustrations are arranged in their chronological order and they are classified according to the general conditions surrounding them. When the particular dates of certain forms are not known with certainty as in the case of works *e.g.*, *PPr.*, *DKK.* the upper and lower limit is clearly indicated while citing the form. The history of a particular Ap. feature is traced throughout the entire period (500-1200 A.D.), as far as it is possible. The regional distribution is also attempted wherever possible.

The present state of published Ap. literature is not satisfactory as some works are uncritically edited. No conclusions are based on the illustrations from uncritical editions, but they are used as supplementary examples. Critical editions alone form the basis of this work.

The terminology OIA, secondary MIA and tertiary MIA is the same as in GRIERSON'S *LSI* and S. K. CHATTERJI'S *ODB.* Thus Pre-Ap. MIA means Aśokan, or Primary Pk. and secondary or literary Pkts. Pre-Ap. IA includes OIA and pre-Ap. MIA.

As in the case with every research work, the present state of knowledge of IA linguistics forms the limitation of the truth or otherwise of the theories proposed herein.

## SUMMARY OF THE IMPORTANT FINDINGS

§11. The following is the summary of the important findings regarding Ap. dialectology. Ap. literature shows the following characteristics of regional and temporal evolution in Ap. during 500-1200 A.D.

### I. PHONOLOGY

As stated above (§9), there are practically very few clear-cut characteristics of Ap. vocabulary, phonologically separating it from other MIA dialects. Pkt. grammarians enumerate the *differentiae* of Ap. phonology as follows :

(1) Irregularity in vowel changes.
(2) Retention of *ṛ*.
(3) Voicing of intervocalic voiceless consonants.
(4) The change of intervocalic *-m-* to *-v-*.
(5) Retention of *-r* conjuncts (*i.e.* conjunct consonants with *-r* as the 2nd member).
(6) Insertion of *r* where historically there was none in OIA.

(1) A reference to §§16-32 will show that vowel-changes are not so 'irregular' as *prima facie* they appear to be in the superficial interpretation of *Pu.* 17. 17, *Hc.* 8.4.329, *Tr.* 3.3.1 and *MK.* 17.9. They generally follow the main outlines of vowel changes in literary Prakrits. They, however, show the beginnings of NIA vowel-changes as follows :

(*i*) General reduction and loss of final vowels inherited from OIA and earlier Pkts. (see §§17-19).

(*ii*) Preservation of the quantity of vowels in penultimate position. (§20). The quantitative changes (if any) are generally due to the following consonant cluster. It is chiefly in EAp. that due to loss of the intervocalic consonant in the final syllable, penultimate and final vowels come together and coalesce (§21). It is in EAp. again that changes like *ubeśa*<*upadeśa* indicate that non-initial vowels in prepenultimate position are glided over. Some qualitative changes in penultimate vowels in EAp. as well as in other regions are due to the weakness in accent or the principle of assimilation and dissimilation (§ 22).

(*iii*) Preservation of the quality of the initial syllable inherited from OIA and earlier MIA. This is due to the accent on the initial syllable although a few instances of accentless initial syllable resulting in aphaeresis, qualitative change etc., are met with occasionally (§§ 23-29).

(*iv*) Reduction of the double consonants (resulting from OIA consonant clusters) to single consonant with compensatory lengthening of the vowel in the initial syllable (§ 36).

(*v*) Contraction of vowels in contact supply the basis for corresponding NIA vowel-changes though some of these are common to literary Pkts. as well (§§ 31, 32).

It will be found that under the outward irregularity of Ap. vocalism, Ap. has a system of its own and it supplies in general a sound basis for the vowel-system in the NIA of that region.

(2) ***Retention of ṛ***

In spite of the prescriptions of the Pk. grammarians, *ṛ* is not conserved in Ap. literature, except as a characteristic of certain families of Mss. SAp. (especially in *Hv.*) is the only region where it is retained in some *tss.* and sometimes *ṛ* is represented by *ri-* testifying to its then pronunciation in SAp. Although changes of *ṛ* were useful as a distinguishing feature in early isoglosses, Ap. literature from the 10th cent. A.D. shows a mixed state due to interborrowing on a large scale. In the earlier Ap. works, initial *ṛ*->*i*- was the characteristic of EAp. and it went on increasing in WAp. Initial *ṛ*->*a*- was less in vogue in EAp. than it was in WAp., although it was decreasing in both. Medial -*ṛ*->-*i*- was the general rule in WEAp. From the 10th cent. A.D. *ṛ*>*a* went on increasing and in WAp. of 1200 A.D. its frequency is similar to that of SAp. We find it in a great number of cases in Gujarati also (§16).

(3) *Voicing of intervocalic voiceless consonants* :

The treatment of intervocalic surds and aspirated surds is the same as in Pkts. The voicing is not the *differentia* of Ap. despite Pkt. grammarians (See §§55-57).

(4) *Intervocalic -m-* :

The treatment of intervocalic -*m*- is less important as a characteristic of Ap. than as a regional *differentiae*. The change -*m*>-*ṽ*- although looked upon as the speciality of Ap. by Pkt. grammarians like *Hc.* (8.4.397), is found in earlier Pkts. *e.g.*, Amg., Mah. and JM. (PISCHEL, *Gram.* §251), and as such it cannot be regarded as a distinguishing feature of Ap. In Ap. literature intervocalic -*m*- is generally retained rather than changed to -*ṽ*-. This conservatism persisted down to 1200 A.D. As expected -*m*->-*ṽ*- or -*v*- (which is a later stage) appears from the beginning of our period (500 A.D.) in WAp., and -*ṁ*->-*b*- in EAp. This is in consonance with the early isoglosses where we find -*m*->-*ṽ*- in the Central and Eastern regions (and in the Southwest), where this literature came to be written. The same is the case with SAp. in 1000 A.D. *KKc*. (1100 A.D.) is more conservative for -*m*->-*ṽ*- or -*v*- is practically absent, although we have it in the works of Puṣpadanta and in Old Marathi.

The change of -*m*- to a simple vowel with the loss of -*v*- and the introduction of vocal glide (-*y*-) is found in SWAp. from the 10th cent. A.D. but not in EAp. In general, it appears that in 1000 A.D. SAp. was more conservative than EAp. We need not attach much importance to the general preference to -*ṽ*- in SAp. and -*v*- in WAp. (§58).

(5) *Retention of -r conjuncts* :

Although this is unanimously sanctioned by Pkt. grammarians and was probably a faithful representation of spoken Ap., such forms with *-r* as the second member of the consonant cluster are rare in Ap. literature due to stylisation. The normal treatment of *-r* conjuncts is not much different from that in Pkts. (see §64).

(6) *Insertion of r*:

Insertion of *r* in vocables where there were none in OIA, is unanimously regarded as a characteristic of Ap. phonology by Pkt. grammarians. It is quite probable that Ap. speakers attempted to add a *r* for giving it the grandeur of Sanskrit. We possess some examples in the treatises on Pk. grammar. But there are very few such cases in Ap. Literature and most of these are in a work like *Kc.* which was specially written to illustrate the rules of *Hc.* (§68).

Ap. literature is regionally divided into three groups—WAp., EAp., and SAp. When we compare these groups with the classification of early MIA dialects in TURNER's *Position of Romani* §27, WAp. corresponds to the Central and to some extent to the South-Western region, chiefly in the later Ap. works written in Gujarat. EAp. corresponds to the Eastern group and SAp. to the South-Western and Southern ones. In modern times WAp. has developed into Hindi and Gujarati. Bengali and other Magadhan languages are spoken in the EAp. region, and Marathi in the SAp. region. There is so much interborrowing in olden times that the criteria of early isoglosses cannot be applied to Ap. literature for regional differentiation. It is, however, important to review the treatment of OIA, *ṛ, kṣ, sm, tv, dv, y-* and *-m-* in Ap.

(1) The treatment of *ṛ* is noted above. In general it corresponds to early isoglosses in earlier Ap. works.

(2) In EAp., OIA *kṣ-*>*kh-* and *-kṣ-*>*-kkh-* are the only treatments without exception. WAp. was originally a *kṣ*>*kh* dialect. From 600 A.D. *kṣ*>*ch* forms began to appear in WAp. But these are most probably loan-words which slowly increase upto 1000 A.D. After 1000 A.D. (and most of these works upto 1200 A.D. are written in Gujarat) we find a greater number of *kṣ*>*ch-*, *-cch-* forms in WAp. There is a mixture of *kh-* and *ch-* (*-kkh-* and *-cch-*) though SAp. appears to be more inclined to *-ch-*. *KKc.*, however, has more *kh-* forms than *ch-* ones (§61).

(3) In EAp.. OIA *tv*>*tu-*, *-tt-* is the only treatment while in *Vk.* (WAp. 500 A.D.) *tv-*>*p-* and *-tv-*>*-p-*>*-v-* is the rule. From 600 A.D. there is a mixture of *-tt-* and *-pp-* treatments in WAp. as well as in SAp. (§62). The isoglossal import-

ance of OIA *dv* is lost in Ap., as *d-*, *-dd-* and *b-*, *-bb-* treatments are freely mixed from the beginning of our period (§63). The same is the case with OIA *sm* which is changed to *s-* initially and *-mh-* or *-mbh-* non-initially (§65).

(4) Initial *y-* was consistently changed to *j-* in all regions (§52) The treatment of *-m-* is given above.

In addition to these points of differentiation given by TURNER (*Position of Romani* §27) we have a few more which serve as regional *differentiae.*

(1) OIA *v*>*b* without exception in EAp. It may be due to orthography but the same is not found in WSAp. although some forms in WAp. indicate the change *v*>*b* in that region (§53).

(2) Retention of *ś* and the use of *ś* for *ṣ* and *s* are the characteristics of EAp. only. In WSAp. all sibilants are reduced to dental *s*. (§§54 and 59).

(3) The consonant group *-ṣṇ-* is changed to *-ṭṭh-* in SAp in some forms (chiefly in *nomina propria*). We do not find this in WEAp. *Biṭṭhu* (*Viṣṇu*) is the only exception in EAp. (§65).

(4) There is generally the insertion of a plosive *-b-* in *-mh-* <*-hm-* in WSAp. but it is retained as *-mh-* in EAp. (§67).

(5) There is no case of initial aspiration in EAp.

In other respects Ap. has the same phonetic characteristics as those in Pkts. The processes of vowel-colouration and dis-colouration (§37), Anaptyxis (§38), Prothesis (§39), Epenthesis (§40), Umlaut (§41), Aspiration (§43), Deaspiration both initial and non-initial (§44) etc., have been considered in their proper places but they do not serve as regional *differentiae*.

## II. MORPHOLOGY

§12. Ap. is distingished from other literary Pkts. by its Morphology. The continuous process of reduction and regularisation in the general development of IA Morphology has reduced the stems in Ap. to *-a*, *-i*, *-u* ones (although theoretically-*ā*, *ī*, *-ū* endings in Fem. gender are found) but the declension of *-a* stems predominates (§§75, 76).

According to Pk. grammarians Ap. gender system is irregular (*atantraṁ*). As a matter of fact OIA gender system is continuously crumbling down in Aśokan Inscriptions, Pali and Pkts. Although gender in WSAp. is a continuation of the same system in Pkts. the confusion is on a larger scale. EAp. represents still greater disintegration than in WSAp.

The main reason of this confusion is the tendency to normalisation in Ap. declension, where it is rather the end-vowel than its gender in OIA, which determines its gender in Ap. The neut. gender tends to disappear morphologically. The common terms of Masc. and Fem. *-a*, *-i*, *-u* stems show the strong influence of Masc. *-a* stems on Ap. declension resulting in the confusion in the gender, which embarrassed the Pk. grammarians. (§§76 also 87, 94, 97 and the discussion of term.s in §§87-99).

As in Pkts. there is no dual number in Ap. (§77) The number of cases has been reduced in this stage and we have the Direct, the Instr. Loc. and the Dat. Gen. Abl. as the only three cases in Ap. Some common term.s between the Ins. Loc. and Dat. Gen. Ablative go to show the formation of the Oblique in Ap. (§78).

The declension of Masc. and Neut. *-a* stems is important as it was the norm after which the declension of other stems and Pronouns was modelled. In the direct sing. of *-a*, stems, Ap. literature shows a number of term.s not noted by Pk. grammarians. *e.g.*, SWEAp. *-ā̃*, WAp.- *ḍā̃*, WSAp. *-ũ*, *-aũ*, and EAp. *-e*, *-ha*, *-ho*, *-hŏ*. On the other hand, *i-* though sanctioned by Mk. 17·42, is not found in literature unless we interpret it as another form of *-ĕ* in EAp.

Out of the various desinences of the direct sing. WSEAp. *-u* is a stable term which is the characteristic of our period, and it is extended to indeclinables also. *-o* or *-ao* is a Prakritism, though its use for Neut. in EAp. shows a confusion of gender. Zero is a doubtful term. as the speech habit of that period was to use the stem itself for the direct case. This habit which is represented in Buddhist Sanskrit, is amply illustrated in Buddhist Ap. *i.e.*, EAp., although WAp. presents some instances of this throughout our period (500-1200 A.D.). SAp. however rarely uses such desinence-less stems. *-e*, *-ae* and *-aye* which is a distinguishing feature of EAp, is the development of the termination-less *-aka* extension of the base, and *-e* Nom. sg. in Mg. in that region afforded favourable ground for such development. This desinence-less *-aka* was changed to *-ā̃* in WAp. and sometimes in EAp. (and very rarely in SAp.) and its use for the Neut. in EAp. shows a confusion of gender. -*ḍā* (<OIA *ṭaka*) is another form of -*ā* in WAp. WSAp. -*aū* and -*ū* is probably a contamination of Nom. sg. -*u* +Acc. sg. -*m*. EAp. -*ha*, -*ho ho* are the cases of -*ha śruti* according to SHAHIDULLA.[74] The comparative percentage of the frequency of term.s shows that Kāṇha was probably a predecessor of Saraha (§ 80).

There is a strong evidence in Ap. literature of the fusion of Loc. and Instr. cases, and a confusion of numbers, neither of which has been recorded by Pk. grammarians. Granting that -*iṁ*, -*ī* (sometimes -*i*) <-*eṁ*, < and -*iṇa*<-*eṇa* of the Instr. sg. have been sanctioned by Pk. grammarians under -*eṁ* and -*eṇa* (-*eṇaṁ* of grammarians is not found in Ap. literature), we have -*e* (not in every case a scribal error for -*eṁ*), -*ạhi*, -*ehi*, -*ehĩ* as the additional term.s in literary Ap. The last two are traceable to Ved. Instr. Plur. -*ebhiḥ* in which cases we have a confusion of numbers. These are common to Instr. and Loc. plurals as well. In EAp. -*e*, -*ẽ*, -*ehĩ*, -*ehi*, -*ahi*, are common to Instr. and Loc. sgs., but -*eṇa* is rare there, though it is very popular to the end of the 12th cent. in WAp. It is a Prakritism which is not much in vogue in SAp., and in some of the earlier WAp. works. -*ẽ* is the stable desinence in WSEAp. though it appears less popular in Kp. and some WAp. works of the same century. The relationship -*ẽ*<-*eṇa*<-*ena* is an open question.

GRIERSON's suggestion of OIA -*a-smin*<-*a-hiṁ*, -*a-hĩ* developing into -*ẽ* is worth consideration. This Loc. sg. -*a-smin* has given us Ap. Loc. and Instr. sgs. -*a-hi*, (-*ahĩ*, -*a-hiṁ* in Loc. sg.) Ap. shows that the fusion of Ins. and Loc. which began in JM. was completed during our period. (§ 81). In the Loc. sg., EAp., -*ẽ*, WSAp. -*iṁ* (although not noted byPk. grammarians) prove the same point. EAp. is characterised by the additional -*ahĩ*, -*ahi*, -*ehi* and -*ita* (in DKK. 2), out of which-*ita* is probably a borrowal from Bengal. -*ahĩ* is rare, and has probably developed into -*ẽ*. Both -*ahĩ* and -*ahi* are clearly traceable to -*a-smin*. -*i* which is a weakened form of OIA -*e* is a stable desinence in SWAp. though it is not found in EAp. A few termination-less Loc. forms in EAp. are noted by SHAHIDULLA (§ 83). Out of these term.s Fem. -*ā* stems use -*ẽ* (WEAp. 1000 A.D.), -*iṁ or* -*ī* (WAp. 1000 and 1200, SAp. 1100 A.D.) SAp. -*i* (?) see §§ 88, 90).

In Ap. there is a gradual absorption of the Abl. into the Dat. Gen. case, and that compound case forms the main basis of NIA oblique. Out of the 11 term.s of the Ap. Dat. Gen. in Pk. grammars, 3 viz. -*he*, -*hu*,-*ho* are common to Gen. and Abl. Gen. -*e* and -*hassu* are unrepresent-

---

74. *Les Chants Mystiques*, p. 38.

ed in literature. Abl. -*adu* is a Prakritism (JŚ and Ś. Mg. as well). The fusion of Abl. and Dat. Gen. is achieved in EAp. from the very beginning of Ap. period, and in WSAp. after the 10th cent. A.D. Regionally speaking WAp. possesses a rich variety of term.s which can be classified into three types *viz.*, -(*a*)*hā̃*, -(*a*)*ho* and (-*a*)*hi*. SAp. has only -(*a*)*ho* type which is exceptional in EAp. -*ha* is generally found therein. WAp. -*hi* is an extension of Fem. Gen. sg. -*he* to Masc. stems. All these -*h* term.s show a tendency to pronounce OIA *s* as *h* in MIA speech. Out of these -(*a*)*hā̃* is traceable to OIA Pronominal plur. -(*ā*)*sām* which has been reduced to -*ha* in the 12th cent. A.D. in WAp. -(*a*)-*ho* is, as BLOCH points out in *L'indo-aryen*, p. 143, on the pronominal model, -(*a*)*ha* +-(*a*)*hu* and -*hu* is its weakening. Zero is exceptional while -(*a*)*su*, (-*a*)*ssu* are Pkt. desinences with the characteristic -*u* ending in Ap. (§ 83).

The term.s of the direct Plur. exhibit two chief tendencies: (*i*) the use of the sing. for the plur., and (*ii*) the use of Masc. term.s with Neut., and vice versa. The first is not much popular although it is attested to in earlier WAp. texts (*PPr.* Ys.) and in EAp. The illustrations show that this is due to the constant association of the enumerated things in one group. The second tendency is traced in EAp. (700-1200 A.D.) and later in WAp. (1000 A.D.) and SAp. (1100 A.D.) Its converse *viz.*, the use of the desinences of the Neut. for Masc. stems is traced in WSAp. from 1000 A.D. but it is absent in EAp. This is probably due to the confusion of genders which is found even in earlier Pkts.

Out of the Ap. term.s in Pk. grammars, -*he*-, -*ho* and -*du* are unrepresented in literature. -*ḍā̃* though sanctioned by the Eastern Pk. grammarian Pu., is not traced in EAp. but in WAp. of the 10th cent. (chiefly in *Pd. Sdd.* ). The use of stem without any term. for the direct plur. is the common characteristic of SWEAp. throughout this period. -*ā̃* (<*āḥ* or- *akāḥ*) is chiefly found in EAp. In Voc. plur. -*ho* and -*hu* were separate particles originally. Termination-less Vocatives derived from OIA -*āḥ* are numerous in Ap. (§ 84).

As in Instr. and Loc. sings. (§§81, 82), the plural forms of these cases prove the fusion of the two cases in Ap., although they are separate in Pkts. The term.s of this joint case can be classified in two groups —(*i*) -*ehiṁ* (<Ved. -*ebhiḥ*) group and -*a-hiṁ* (<OIA -*a-smin*) group. The first illustrates the fusion of the Instr. and Loc., and is a common characteristic of WSEAp. throughout our period. The second signifies both a confusion of number and a fusion of case, and is illustrated in all these regions from 600 A.D. SEAp. -*ahi* and EAp. -*ehi* (and the few -*ahi*, -*ehi* forms in WAp. of 12th cent. A.D.) are denasalisations of Ap.-*ahĩ* and-*ehĩ*. The extension of -*āhaṁ* of the Dat. Gen. to these cases shows the

process of the formation of the Oblique in Ap., though such examples are rare and appear in WAp. from the 10th cent. and onwards. *-ihĩ* group is a weakened form of *-ehĩ* (§ 85).

According to Pk. grammarians *-huṁ* and *-haṁ* were the chief term.s of Abl. and Gen. plurs. respectively, although Eastern Pk. grammarians sanction these for the Gen. *and* Abl. plurs. as well. Ap. writers, however, made little distinction between these two cases. They also neglected *-huṁ* which is absent in EAp., and a rarity in WSAp. *-(a)haṁ* or *-(a)hā̃* is a stable desinence in WSAp., and is traceable to Pk. and OIA **-āsaṁ* rather than to *-(a)ha* + *-ã*<MIA *-āṇaṁ* as *-ṇam*>*-ã* is rare in IA. EAp. *-(a)ha* is the extension of the sing. to the plur. Abl. plur. *-hũ* in SAp. and in Pkt. grammars is an analogical formation after the Gen. sg. *(a)-ha*: Gen. plur. *(a)-hã*. *-(a)hiṁ* though a rarity, is the extension of the Instr. Loc. to this compound case forming a prelude to the Oblique in NIA (§86).

These are the main characteristics of the declension of Masc, and Neut. *-a* stems which was regarded as the standard for other declensions to follow.

Fem. stems in *-ā* serve as a model to the declension of Fem. *-ī* and *-ū* stems. (§ 97). They (*i.e.*, Fem. *-ā* stems) follow the declension of Masc. and Neut. *-a* stems as they share 11 common term.s in sing. *viz.*, Direct: Zero, Ins. *-ẽ*, *-iṁ* (*-ĩ*), *-i* (?), Dat. Gen. *-ha*, *-haṁ*, (*hã*), *-hu* *-hũ*, Loc. *-i*, *-iṁ* (*ĩ*), *-hiṁ* (*-hĩ*), and 5 in plur. *viz.*, Direct -Zero, *-aĩ* (BhK.), Dat. Gen. Abl. *-haṁ* (*-hã*), *-hu*, Loc. *-hĩ* (§88).

Fem. *-ī* and *-ū* stems have adopted 10 (7 from sg. + 3 from plur.) desinences from Masc. and Neut. *-a* stems (§ 97).

That there should be 11 (sing. 7 + plur. 4) terms common to Masc. *-i*, *u-* and Fem. *-a* stems and 7 (sing. 5 + plur. 2) terms common to Masc. and Fem. *-i*, *-u* stems (§ 94), shows that the confusion of gender was on a very large scale in Ap. (see § 76).

In the declension of these stems, the direct case was formed before 600 A.D. Ins. and Loc. remained distinct upto the end of the 11th cent. (and probably to the end of our period). In contrast to Pk., Gen. and Loc. are distinct and the former absorbed the Abl. upto 1000 A.D. Some common term.s in Dat. Gen. Abl. and Instr. Loc. show the preparation of the ground for NIA Oblique (§§ 87, 88, 89). In Instr. sg- *-āe* is common to Ap. and Pkt. and this was probably reduced to *-aĩ* in SAp. (1000 A.D.), the remaining are Masc. and were applied first in EAp. (700 A.D.), then in WAp. (1000 A.D.), and lastly in SAp.

(1100 A.D.). Dat. Gen. Abl. -*a-hi*<-*a-hĕ* or -*ahe*<-*a-syāḥ* is quite common in SAp. (965 A.D.), though it occasionally occurs in contemporary WAp. where it got established upto 1200 A.D. Loc. -*a-hi* is probably derived from Masc. -*a-smin* or *adhi*. There is a greater use of Masc. terms in WAp. than in SAp. Loc. -*ahi* is first found in EAp. in which it does not alternate with -*ahĩ*. It may be traceable to the OIA postposition *adhi*, but in WAp. it appears first in *BhK*. (1000 A.D.) and in contemporary SAp. But WAp. has -*a-hiṁ* and SAp. shows -*aĩ*, -*aiṁ* as the alternative term.s. (§§ 90, 91, 92).

In plural number there are few purely Ap. Fem. term.s as most of them are either common to Ap. Masc. Neut. -*a* stem.s or to Pkts. The direct plur. -*aũ*<Pkt. -*āo* and -*aĩ* (Neut. direct plur.) are obvious. The Loc. Instr. -*ahiṁ* (which is common to Pkts. and Ap. Masc. -*a* stems) is seen in WSEAp. from the 10th cent. A.D. -*a-ĩ* is the extension of Masc. Loc. sg. to Loc. plur., while -*a-hã* (in Sc.) shows the confusion of this case with Dat. Gen. Abl. in 1200 A.D. in WAp. Zero indicates the tendency to apply the term. to the last word when a number of related words in the same case come together consecutively. Dat. Gen. Abl. -*ahu*, -*ahaṁ* are common to Masc. -*ahu* is popular in WAp. upto the end of Ap. period. -*a-hã* was first used in SAp. (1000 A.D.) and then in WAp. (1100 A.D. and onwards) and it underlies the half-nasalised forms of NIA oblique (§ 93).

The declension of Masc. -*i* and -*u* stems is more influenced by the declensions of Fem. -*i*, -*u* stems than by the one of Masc. -*a* stems. It appears that it was the ending (rather than its OIA Gender) which influenced the declension of the stems (See § 77 and § 95 ). Thus terminationless direct sing. and plur., Dat. Gen. Abl. sing. -*hi*, -*he* (cf. Fem. -*a* stems § 92), Loc. sg. -*hi* smack of the influence of Fem. declension (for details see § 94).

There are 8 (sing. 6+plur. 2) term.s common to Masc. and Fem. -*i*, -*u* stems and 11 (sing. 7 + plur. 4) desinences common to Fem. -*a* and Masc. -*i*, -*u* stems. There are very few term.s, which are special to this declension and their history has been treated in different contexts (§§ 95, 96).

The number of Fem. -*ī̆*, -*ū̆* stems is limited as many of them take pleonastic -*ka*. The declension of Fem. -*ī*, -*ū* stems is closely allied with similar Masc. endings, although Fem. and Masc. -*a* stems have contributed some desinences to this. The common term.s of Loc. and Dat. Gen. Abl. sg. (and these are distinct from those of Pkt.) show the process of the formation of the oblique of NIA type. We find the same in the plural Number. Dat. Gen. Abl. sing. term.s have regional differences *e.g.* EAp. *-ha*, WSAp. *-he* (1000 A.D.) WAp. *-hu* (1200 A.D.) (see §§ 97, 98, 99).

A synthetic view of the declension of all the stems in Ap. shows the following facts :

(1) The Direct case was formed in the Ap. period.

(2) The Indirect cases had two groups *viz.*, the Instr. Loc. and the Dat. Gen. Abl., and there was a tendency towards the fusion of these groups resulting later on in the Oblique in NIA.

(3) The strong tendency to normalisation led to the confusion of gender, and in EAp. the Neut. was morphologically getting obsolete.

(4) The confusion of genders and numbers gave an appearance of uniformity to Ap. declension but it had some regional and temporal differences.

(5) The tendency to use the term. with the last word (generally substantive), although the previous ones also stand in the same case.

Due to the confusion of cases mentioned above, there arose a greater necessity to use post-positions to denote particular cases in Ap. period and later. In Ap. *honta, hontaü, honti* is used for Abl. *ṭhiu* coupled with Loc. gives the Abl. sense. *keraa, kera* denotes the Gen., and *taṇa* is construed with Instrumental. A careful investigation into the history of these shows that originally these were used in a different sense. Thus *honta* or *hontaü* was a Pres. Part. which was used in the Abl. sense in SAp. of the 11th cent. A.D. first, and in WAp. at about 1150 A.D. (though some WAp. works of the same century do not attest to it). Its Abl. use in NIA shows that it must have become more popular in the proto-NIA period. *ṭhia* or √ *ṭhā* when coupled with Loc. does not give the Abl. sense in WEAp. upto the end of 11th cent., and the instance quoted from Hc. is doubtful. *kera* is used in WAp. (600-1200 A.D.), SEAp. (1000 A.D.) with the Gen., and is found as a post-position and suffix in NIA of WAp region, as a suffix in Eastern NIA, though it is lost in NIA of SAp. region. *taṇa* is more used as a Gen. post-position than as an Instr. one. As an Instr. post-position its earliest use is in *PPr.* (WAp. 600 A.D.) but it is more in vogue in SAp. of 1000 A.D. (but not in contemporary WAp.) and finally in WAp. of the 12th cent. A.D. (§§ 100-104).

## NUMERALS

Numerals in Ap. present a stage which though closely allied to Pkts., is the immediate predecessor of numerals in NIA. *ekka* 'one' is the only cardinal to possess different forms for Masc. and Fem. genders. These cardinals follow declension of *-a* stems. Most of the formations follow the older Pkts. and show a state of confusion and mixure (§§ 105-115). Ap. follows Pkts. in fractionals as well (§ 116). The ordinals also corroborate the same finding. In SAp. ordinals from 5th onwards (except the 6th ) take *-va* optionally for *-ma* (cf. *-va* in M.). These, being adjectives, are declined like nouns (§ 117).

## PRONOUNS

Personal pronouns of the 1st and the 2nd person form one group which presents a rich variety of forms. 1st p. pron. has *aha-*, *ma-* in sing., and *amha-* in plur., while 2nd p. pron. has *tu-*, *ta-*, *pa-* in sing. and *tumha-* in plur. as the bases. Both of these accept mostly desinences of Masc. and Neut. *-a* stems with a few relics of old Pkt. and OIA forms. It was the declension of the 1st person which influenced the paradigm of the 2nd one. Ap. literature does not represent some forms of these declensions, although they are sanctioned by Pk. grammarians. There is much stability in the declensions of these throughout our period. These declensions supply us with the history of the NIA forms of these pronouns, and are useful as a connecting link between MIA and NIA (for details see §§ 119-120).

The next important group is that of Adjectival pronouns which is thus designated from a functional point of view. It consists of the 3rd person, Remote Demonstrative and Correlative *ta-* (<*tad*), the Proximate Demonstratives *ea-*, *eya* (*etad*) and *āya-*, *āa-* (=*idam* which has **a-* base from Instr.), the Relative *ja-* (*yad*), the Interrogative *ka-*, *kavaṇa* (*kiṁ*) and the Reflexive *appa-* (*ātman*). *adas-* is only exceptionally used in Hc. 8.4.364. These pronouns generally accept the term.s of the noun qualified by them, and as such the process of simplification of themes and paradigms, tendencies to normalisation, confusion of genders and number, and the fusion of cases, as in Noun declension are found here. Out of the above mentioned pronouns *yad*, *tad*, *kim* are declined exactly alike. The forms of *etad* and *idam* are freely mixed together. *ātman* is declined in Masc. gender and sing. number. The remaining pronouns are unimportant, and have no declensional peculiarities as distinct from Noun Declension (§§ 122-130).

Personal, demonstrative, relative, interrogative and other pronouns contributed different types of adjs. Though the formative suffixes are noted in Ch. IV, only 12 are considered here. Out of these, formatives from *kārya* (*e.g.*, *-āra*, *-āraa*, Fem. *-erī*) make possessive adjectives, and are applied to personal pronouns in WSEAp. during our period (500-1200) and down to NIA, except in SAp. region. Out of the suffixes from OIA *-dṛśa* (*e.g.*, *isa*, *-risa*, *-eha*), *-isa* has remained popular in NIA e.g., Hindi, Marathi and their cognate dialects. Adjectives showing extent are of two type : (*i*) *kiyat* types e.g., *-(e-,i-)ttiya*, *-(e-i-)ttula* etc., and (*ii*) -*vṛddha type e.g., *-vaḍḍha*, *-vaḍu*. Both of these types are conserved in NIA. Of the second *-vaḍḍha* is popular in Marathi, and *-vaḍu* in NIA of WAp. region e.g., Gujarati.

## CONJUGATION

§ 13. Conjugation in Ap. forms the intermediate stage between Pkts. and old NIA, and represents a stage in the continuous process of simplification and modification in the verbal system in IA. Like Pkts. and NIA, substitution of the nominal phrase for verb system is the normal rule in Ap. Thus this system appears to be based on (*i*) the verbal group depending on OIA Present Ind. and (*ii*) a group of nominal forms based on the above mentioned verbal system (§§ 132). Herein Ap. is a precursor of NIA.

Verbal themes in Ap. rest on the Present system and P.P. Participles in OIA. As usual Ap. roots are transitive and intransitive, primitive or causative in form. Ap. derives its verbal bases from OIA bases which are either normal (levalised to *-a* ending irrespective of their original class), phonologically modified, or linguistically reconstructed. The OIA verbal bases are (1) Present Active, (2) Present Passive, (3) P.P. Participles, and (4) Onomatopoeia. These bases are enlarged by pleonastic suffixes *e.g.*, *-ra*, *-ḍa* etc., (§ 133).

Causative formations take the suffix *-ăva* in WSAp., and *-aba* in EAp., sometimes there is a *vṛddhi* of the radical vowel *-a-* of the primitive root (and *guṇa* of radical *-i-*, *-u*), while some primitive and causal forms are identical. Gunating of the radical vowel and the application of *-ā* (*va*) e.g., H. *paknā*: *pakānā*, and the addition of pleonastic *-āṛ*, *-āḍ*, *-āl* are found in NIA (§ 135).

The desinences of the Pres. Ind. show an unbroken continuation from OIA, and a strong influence of Sk. and Pkt. on Ap. To note purely Ap. desinences: 1 p. sing *-aũ* is due to the influence of 1 p. Nom. sg. pronominal ending *-aũ* < OIA *-akaṁ*. It is absent in 500 A.D. in WAp. but is the most frequent term in *Kp*. (1200 A.D. WAp.), *-ami* is the characteristic term in SAp. In 2 p. sing. *-ahi*<OIA Imp. 2 p. sg. *-dhi* was popular in early WAp. texts and in speech throughout the Ap. period, as it is the source of 2 p. sg. forms in NIA of the WAp. region. Though *-ahi* is extremely popular in SAp., it seems to have lost its influence in the proto-Marathi period. *-asi* is consistently found in MAp. and the modern Magadhan languages. 3 p. sg. *-aï* is obviously from OIA<*-ati*, and is the source of 3 p. sg. in NIA. EAp. *-a*<*-aï* is probably *metri causa* and is found rarely. Pres. Ind. is under the influence of Imp. This is seen from the common and contaminated term.s. Out of the three term.s of 2 p. pl. *-ahu* and *-aha* are used in Imp. 2 p. pl. The terms. of 2 p. pl. are traced to OIA **-thas*, analogically with 1 p. pl. *-mas*. It is the source of the desinences of 2 p. pl. in NIA, and its influence probably explains *-h-* in Ap. 1 and 3 p. plurals, *-ahũ* and *-ahĩ* (though OIA pron. *asmaka* must have some share in the formation of the former). Thus we have 1 p. *-aũ*: *-ahũ*:: 3 p. *-ai*: *-ahĩ*. 3 p. pl. *-ahĩ* appeared in *PPr.* (600 A.D.) first, and remained popular in WAp region throughout the Ap. period, and supplies the 3 p. pl. desinences. to the NIA, while *-anti* is chiefly found in SAp. and EAp., and is the source of term.s of 3 p. plur. in Modern IA languages of these regions (§ 136).

Imperative in Ap. literature has a richer variety of terms than that noted by Pk. grammarians. Although there are few (practically none) for 1 p., 2 p. sg. and pl. present the greatest number of desinences. The 2 p. sg. has 11 term.s in SAp., 9 in WAp., 7 but a different set in EAp. Only 6 are common to WSEAp. There appears a gradual growth in the number of desinences in WAp. *-ahi*<OIA *-dhi*, originally found in *VK*. (WAp.), spread all over Aryan India in 1000 A.D., and became the most popular one in SAp. (though not much so in EAp. The influence of *-u*<OIA *-tu* of 3 p. sg. is found in many term.s of 2 p. e.g., *-hu*<OIA -**thu*, *-asu*, *-esu*<OIA *-sva* and *-u* (the last not much popular even in WAp.) The popularity of *-u* endings in Ap. (used with indeclinables also) afforded full scope for such development. The Pres. Ind. and Imp. have many common term.s. (Imp. is of the Present tense even from the OIA period). Thus Imp. 2 p. pl. *-ha* (*-aha*, *-eha* is of the Pres. Ind. WAp. of 1200 A.D. appears under the strong influence of Pkt. In 2 p. sing., speaking regionally, we find *-ahi*, *-i*, and *-u* popular in SAp. (1000 A.D.), and *-aha*, *-ahu*, *-u* in EAp. In WAp. *-ahi* is very popular in 500 A.D., *-ahu*, *-ahi*, *-i* in 1000 A.D., and *-asu*, *-esu* in 1200 A.D. In 2 p. plu., WAP. has *-ahu*, *-ahũ*, *-aha* (in 1100-1200 A.D.), SAp.*-ahaṁ* *-aha*, *-ahu* (rarely), and EAp. *-aha*, also *ijja-ha* and *-ahu* (only in *DKs.*)

Out of these *-ahu* is traceable to OIA *-*thu*. *ahũ* has a nasal due to its pl. number, and the influence of 3 p. pl. (cf. the term. of Pres. 3 p. pl.); *-aha*<OIA *-tha* becomes *-ahã* by the same analogy. The influence of the Pres. Ind. on Imp. is immense. 3 p. sg. *u* <OIA *-tu* is clear. 3 p. pl. *-ahũ* is on the analogy of Pres. Ind. -i : *ahĩ*:: *-u*: *-ahũ*. NIA is deeply indebted to Ap. for its variety of term.s.

As in Pkts. Future in Ap. is of 2 types *-sa* and *-ha-*, both of which are traceable to OIA *-sya-* and the term.s of Pres. Ind. are added to them. *-sa* Future is very popular in SAp. (and Marathi), while there is a mixed state in WAp. to which we can trace the different developments of the Future in NIA of that region (§ 139).

The Past was a participial tense in Ap., and was expressed by using the pp. of the verb with "to be" (√*as* or √*bhū*) expressed or implied. *-la* forms existed in spoken Ap., and became very popular in post-Ap. period (§ 140).

The Optative in Ap. is used in the place of OIA Potentional Mood, and sometimes for the Imperative. Its augment is *-ijja*<Primary Pkts. *-eyya* and is confused with the *-ijja* Passive. Sometimes it takes *-iavva* (<*tavya*) of the Pot. Part. In later WAp. desinence-less *-ijja*. was used for all persons. SAp. takes the term.s of the Pres. after *-ijja* (§ 141).

The denominatives(§ 142), duplication of verbs to express intensity, frequency etc., (§ 143), the Ap. defective verb √*as* (§ 144) and the use of different forms of OIA *nāsti* (and sometimes of *mā*) as negatives (§ 145) show the continuity of IA and Ap. as the mediate stage between MIA and NIA.

The Present, Past Passive and Future Participles, Infinitives, and Absolutives are the important nominal forms of verbs Ap. Out of these, the first three are adjectival and the last two indeclinable. In Ap. *-anta* and *-māṇa* (*i.e.*, the phonological modifications of these suff.s). are applied to roots irrespective of their *pada* in OIA. Both these are found in WSAp. (and in the NIA of these regions) though *-anta* is more popular. EAp. uses only *-anta*. The details of the use of the Pres. Part. show the importance of Ap. as a formative stage of the NIA tenses and syntax. (§ § 146-47).

As in pre-Ap. MIA, Ap. uses the phonological modifications of OIA *-i-ta* to form pp. This *-ita*, with or without stem-widening *-ka*, is applied to the Prakritic form of OIA roots or to *deśī* ones. We find (though to a lesser extent) *aniṭ* type of formations with OIA roots direct, or reconstructed, and with *deśī* roots. We find both these types of pp. in NIA. EAp. has some pp. forms in *-a*, and these are different from those ending in *-(i)a* <*ita*. *-uya* ending of *deśī* roots is on the analogy of *-iya* or *-ia*. No *-la* forms in literary Ap. are traced (§ 148).

The Future and Obligatory Parts. in Ap. are chiefly derived from OIA *-tavya* and Ved. Pali *-eyya*. SAp. has *-evva* (*va*), *-evaya* and *-eva* which developed in M. *-vā̆*, *-vī*, *-vĕ*. WAp. favours *-avvu* chiefly in the latter half of the 12th cent. A.D., (cf. Guj. *-vū* infinitives and root-endings) EAp. has *-iba*. cf. Beng. *-ibā̆* infinitives. Prakritisms and ending with *-ssa*+*māṇa*, or *anta* need not be noticed. (§ 150).

Infinitives in Ap. retain many of the Ved. suffixes, and has a mixture of the Absolutive ones. In WAp. *-aṇa* suffixes (*i.e.*, *-aṇa*, *-aṇu*, *-aṇahiṁ*, *-anahaṁ*) are the most popular, and form the source of *-na* Infinitives in NIA of that region. Out of these *-aṇahaṁ* is preserved in SAp., but *-aṇa* is absent in *DKK.*, and a rarity in *Dsk.* (both EAp. works). EAp. does not represent such a mixture of Inf. and Abs. suffixes, although it is sanctioned by Pk. grammarians. In WAp. this appears in the 1000 A.D., and is widely popular in 1200 A.D. *-huṁ* is the most influential suff. in SAp., and is probably the source of M. *-ū̃* Infinitives. In 1100 A.D. SAp. uses the obligatory suffixes *-evvaiṁ*, *-evaeṁ* <OIA *-*tavyakaṁ* for Inf. Though such a usage is a rarity in WAp., it seemed to have spread in WEAp. regions in proto-NIA, as is evident from the Inf. forms in the Modern IA languages of these provinces. In M. *-vā̆*, *ïvī*, *-vĕ* are still used in the obligatory sense. EAp. extends the Absolutive suff. *-aï* to Inf., and this is a special term in EAp. No such mixture appears in SAp. (§ 150).

Absolutives in Ap. literature EAp. is characterised by *-ī* and *-iā̆* <OIA *-ya* (*lyab*) which developed as *-ia*, *-iya*, *-iu* in Wap. from 1000 A.D. *-i* is absent in Hv., and rare in other SAp. works. Suffixes from Ved. *-tvī*, *-tvīnam*, went on increasing in WAp., and we get *-eppi*, *eppiṇu*, *-epi*, *-epiṇu*, *-evi*, *eviṇu*, *-ivi*, *-avi*, *-ppi*, *-pi*, *-vi* and *-piṇu* in Ap. *-tti*< *-tvī* is not much productive in WSAp. In Ap. literature there are two currents of Absolutive term.s, one traceable to OIA *-tvā* and the other to *-ya*. In EAp. *-tvā* term.s are not found, while *-ya* forms begin to appear in WSAp. from 1000 A.D. EAp. is free from Prakritisms. Due to the absence of *-tūṇa* or *-(i)uṇa* forms in Ap., M. Abs. Suff. *-ūn* cannot be traced to them, but to the contamination of OIA *-tvāna* +*tvīna* which satisfactorily explains the various types of *-ūn* endings in Old and Modern Marathi and Koṅk. Modern absolutive suffixes of WSEAp. region are derived from OIA *-ya* > WEAp. *-ī̆*, *-ĭ* (§ 151).

Adverbs (§ 152), Conjunctions (§ 154) and Interjections (§ 155) have much in common with other literary Pkts., and possess little that is chrono-regionally important (except in EAp.). NIA is greatly indebted to Ap. in many respects with regard to these indeclinables, as the variety of forms in NIA is traceable to these.

§14. Ap. has the following suffixes which may be classified according to their powers as follows :

(1) Suffixes added to Substantives to form Substantives : *-tta*, *-ttaṇa*, *-ppa*, *-ppaṇa*, *-maī*, *-riṇa* (?), *-vaṇḍa*.

(2) Suffixes applied to Adjs. for forming Abstract Substantives: *-ima*, *-tta*, *-ttaṇa*, *-ppaṇa*.

(3) Suffixes added to Substantives for forming Adjs.: *-ara*, *-āla*, *-ālu(ya)*, *-i(ya)*, *-itta*, *-illa*, *-ira*, *-va*, *-vanta*, *-vi(ya)*.

(4) Suffixes added to Adjs. to form Adjs. : *-iya*, *-ra*, *-era*.

(5) Suffixes for forming Adjs. from Verbs : *-ira*, *-evva*.

(6) Suffixes added to Adverbs to form Adjs.: (*-(a)ḍa*, *-(a)ḍḍa*, *-ttia(ya)*, *-ttula*, *-risa*, *-ha(u)*.

(7) Pleonastic suffixes : *-a*, *-ya*, *-aya*, *-iya*, *-uya*, *-kka* (rarely as in *gurukkī*<*guru-*), *-ḍā*, *-ḍī* and not *-du* though it is sanctioned by Eastern Pk. grammarians. *-la*, *-kī*, *-āla*, *-ālu*, *-illa*, *-ulla-* and different combinations of the chief Pleonastic suffixes *-ka*, *-ḍa*, *-la*. In Ap. *-ra* is rare.

(8) Feminine suffixes : *-ā*, *-ī*, *-ṇī*.

Primary suffixes showing Agent or doer, action are also noted in Ch. IV. (For details see §§ 156-158).

# *CHAPTER I*

## APABHRAṀŚA PHONOLOGY.

§ 15. Sounds in Ap.

The following are the sounds in Ap. literature :

Vowels : *a, ā, i, ī, u, ū, ṛ* (generally in *tss.*), *ē̆, ō̆*. With the exception of *ṛ* these could be nasalised.

Consonants : *k, kh, g, gh, c, ch, j, jh* (both palatals and palato-alveolars), *ñ* (very rarely), *ṭ, ṭh, ḍ, ḍh, ṇ t, th, d, dh, n* (in Jacobi's editions and in some uncritically edited works), *p, ph, b, bh, m, r, l, v, ś* (in EAp.), *s, h, ḷ* (in Southern Mss. and in spoken Ap.).

Devanāgarī script has no separate signs to indicate the two values of *e*, and *o*. The Northern scribes have a tendency to represent short *ĕ* and *ŏ* as *i* and *u*—the latter at times being a mistake of the copyist for *o* in Jain Mss. in which it is represented with a vertical stroke on the head of *u*. We have also no separate symbols to show the open (*vivṛta*) and closed (*saṁvṛta*) sounds of *a*, although these values have been recognized by old Sanskrit grammarians like Pāṇini[1] and Patañjali.[2] The different values of *a* in Koṅkaṇi, Bengali and Awadhi along with the close neutral *a* normally found in the whole group of IA, lead one to posit a similar state in Ap., but there is little Ms. evidence to support the theory.

The OIA diphthongs were already lost in the early stages of MIA, and have come down as *ē* and *ō*, or as *ĕ* and *ŏ*, or even as *i* and *u*. As this is not a speciality of Ap., we may pass on to the treatment of OIA *ṛ* in Ap.

§ 16. Treatment of OIA *ṛ*.

Retenion of *ṛ* is a *bona fide* characteristic of Ap. phonology according to all schools of Pkt. grammarins. (See *Pu.* 17.15, 18.3 for Vrācaṭa Ap.,grammar quoted by Namisādhu on Rudraṭa's *Kāvyālaṅkāra* 2·12, ex.s on *Hc.* 8-4-329 *Mk.* 17·4 for Vrācaṭa Ap.), In practice

---

1 *Aṣṭādhyāyī* 8.4.68.

2 *Mahābhāṣya*—discussion on *Savarṇagrahaṇa*. Also at the beginning of his Com. on *Śiva-Sūtras*.

however, it is limited to certain families of Mss.[3] We may safely ignore these *tss* e.g., *mṛga*, *vṛnda*, *nṛ* and others, as the speciality of certain Ms. traditions, although we know that the total absence of *tss* is due to the stylisation in MIA, and that OIA *tss.* were present in the contemporary Dravidian literature, and in the oldest stage of NIA.

The prākritic tendencies in the treatment of *ṛ* in Vedic literature,[4] the changes of *ṛ* in Aśokan Inscriptions,[5] and its changes in Prākrits,[6] are enough to show the artificiality of this injunction of Pkt. grammarians. A reference to the comparative tables (§ 17A) shows that the geographical distribution of the changes of OIA, *ṛ* (*viz.* initial >*ṛ*>*a* in the South-West, *ṛ*>*i* in the North and in the East) found in Aśokan Edicts, is lost in our period. In the post-Aśokan Pkt. Inscriptions one finds that OIA, *ṛ* initially tends to be *a*- in all regions, and that in the non-initial syllables, it nerally becomes -*a*- in all regions and at all times. The change of the vowel *ṛ* to *u* is found mostly in nouns of relationships in all regions, but in the east and the centre it also tends to be *i*.[7]

As in Pali[8] and in Pkts.,[9] OIA *ṛ* is changed to *a*, *i* and *u* in Ap. The following table of statistics will, however, show how the treatment of OIA *ṛ* differed during 500 (?)—1000 A.D.

| (1) Initial *ṛ* | WAP | | EAP | |
|---|---|---|---|---|
| | *VK* 500 A.D. | *PPr* 600 A.D. | *DKK* 700 A.D. | *DKS* / *DKS* 1000 A.D. |
| > *a* | 2) | 2) | ) | 1) |
| | )28·5% | )13·3% | )16·6% | ) 10% |
| > | ) | ) | 1) | ) |
| > *i* | 3) | 9) | 3) | 7) |
| | )43% | )66·6% | )50% | )80% |
| > *ī* | ) | 1) | ) | 1) |
| > *u* | 2) | 2) | 1) | 1) |
| | )28·5% | )20% | )33·3% | )10% |
| > *ū* | ) | 1) | 1) | ) |
| > *e* | | | | |
| Total | ..7 | 15 | 6 | 10 |

3 A. N. UPADHYE, Introduction to *PPr.* p. 56, Footnote 2.

4 For example *avaṭa*, *kaṭuka*, *vikaṭa*. For more vide WACKERNAGEL, *Alt. Gram.* I. §§ 9, 146, 172.

5 M. A. MEHENDALE, "A Comparative Grammar of Aśokan Inscriptions," *BDCRI* 3.3.227-31 (March 1942).

6 PISCHEL, *Grammatik.* §§ 47-58.

7 M. A. MEHENDALE, "Historical Grammar of Inscriptional Prākrits" *BDCRI* 6-1-2.67.

8. S. M. KATRE, "Treatment of Ṛ in Pali", *ABORI* 16.189-201.

9 PISCHEL, op. cit. §§ 47-58. The *ra*, *ri*, *ru* treatments noted by PISCHEL and KATRE are really (*r*)*a*, (*r*)*i*, (*r*)*u* ones.

| | | | | | |
|---|---|---|---|---|---|
| 2 2) Medial ṛ | | | | | |
| > *a* | | | | | 1(?) |
| > *ā* | | | | | |
| > *i* | 1 | 50% | 1 | 1 | 3 |
| > *ī* | | | | | |
| > *u* | 1 | 50% | 1 (√*suṇa*) | | |
| > *ū* | | | | | |
| > *e* | | | | | |
| Total | ..2 | | 2(?) | 1 | 4(?) |
| (3) Final ṛ | | | | | |
| > *a* | | | | | |
| > *ā* | | | | | |
| > *i* | | | | | 1 |
| > *ī* | | | | | |
| > *u* | | | | | |
| > *ū* | | | | | |
| > *e* | | | | | |

In calculating the ṛ forms in these works, words traceable to IE e.g., **g^w^horo-*>*ghara, ghariṇi, gharavai* etc, to OIA non-ṛ variants e.g., *ṇisuṇa-*<√*śru-* (and not √*śṛ-*), √*gaha, gahia*<√ *grabh-* or √*grah-* (and not to √*gṛh-*) are omitted as they are not the treatments of OIA ṛ although they are commonly supposed to be such. Repetition of the same form either in compounds (e.g., *mṛga-* in *miaṅka, mia-locaṇa*) or otherwise e.g. *diṭṭha, diṭṭhaa, diṭṭhi* (all from √*dṛś-*) or *tisia, tisittaṇa*<*tṛṣā*, are regarded as one form. Forms which were already changed in OIA e.g., *bi-sara-*<*vi-smar-*√*smṛ-*, *kārima*<*kār-ima* (though usually quoted with *kṛtrima*) are excluded from the above calculation in the table of statistics.

The comparative table given above shows the following facts :

(1) Initial ṛ> *a-* was less in vogue in EAp. than in WAp., although it was disappearing fast in both the regions.

(2) Initial ṛ->*i-* which was the main characteristic of EAp. in early Pkts., predominantly remained unchanged in our period. In WAp. it went on increasing from 43% to 66·6%

(3) Initial ṛ->*u-* is chiefly due to the labial element.

(4) It is generally in metrically heavy syllables that OIA *ṛ* was changed into a long vowel *e.g.*, *kāṇha* <*Kṛṣṇa* in EAp. This was found in other regions at a later period *e.g.*,*būḍhau* <*vṛddhaḥ*.

(5) Medial -*ṛ*->-*i*- was the general rule in WEAp. upto 1000 A.D.

There is only one example of final -*ṛ*, and that is a meagre evidence to base any conclusion regarding the treatment of final *ṛ* in Ap. upto 1000 A.D.

From the 10th cent. A.D., and onwards, Ap. literature testifies to a large-scaled interborrowing. We find that the geographical distribution of the treatment of OIA *ṛ* as found in Aśokan Inscriptions or given by TURNER in *Position of Romani in Indo-Aryan* § 27, is only a thing of the past, and we meet with a number of cases with *ṛ*> *i* both initially and medially in SAp. *e.g.*, *tiṭṭhā*<**tṛṣṭā*=*tṛṣṇā*, though the usual *taṇhā* is frequent. So is the case with *hṛdaya*> *hiyaa*, *hiyavaya* (cf. Paiś. *hitapaka*), the latter of which appears at least 10 times in *Hv*. (See *Hv*. *Glossar* p.489). We have many instances of medial -*ṛ*->-*i*- in this region *e.g.*, *nipphia*< *nispṛha*, *amhārisa*<*asmādṛśa*, *eyārisa*<*etādṛśa* and others.

On the other hand, instances of *ṛ*>*a* go on increasing in WAp. till at last in *Kp*. the proportion of *ṛ*>*a* is similar to that in *Hv*. e.g. *vasahi* <**vṛsabhī* "a bull,"[10] *parimalaï*<*pari-*mṛdati*, *viyambhaï*<*vi-jṛmbhate*. Probably this explains the predominance of the -*a*- treatment of this vowel in Guj.

There is one characteristic which distinguishes SAp. from WAp. It is the value of Sk. *ṛ* as pronounced in loan-words. In SAp. one finds OIA *ṛ*>*ri* and conversely *ri*>*ṛ*. The converse change clearly proves the phonetic habit of pronouncing *ṛ* as *ri*, although it is a scribal device. Kannaḍa Inscriptions from 800-1000 A. D. attest to this phonetic habit as we find *ṛ* written as *ri* in them. e.g. *risiyaru*<*ṛṣi*- "sages," *Nripatunga* <*Nṛpatunga*[11]. It is in SAp. alone that one finds exs. e.g., *sṛya*< *śrī-ka*, *tṛya*<*strī-ka* (though the normal forms *siri* and *tiya*, are not absent). SAp. (and chiefly *Hv*.) shows numerous cases of *ṛ*>*ri*. e.g. *riya*<*ṛc*, *rijjha-u*<*ṛdhya-tu*, *riddhilla*<*ṛddhi-mat*, *rikkha*<*ṛkṣa*, *riddhi-he*<*ṛddheḥ*. A few exs. of this are found in WAp. as well e.g. *risi*<*ṛṣi*, *Risaha*< *Ṛṣabha*,*rīṇa*< √*ṝ-na*, *riṇiya*<*ṛṇika*.

---

10 ALSDORF in *Kp*. J. 71-4 *Glossar* regards this as a contamination of *vṛṣabha* + *vahati*. The use of *vahati* "an ox" is found only in lexicons of a later date.

11 G. S. GAI "Historical Grammar of Old Kannaḍa," *BDCRI* 6.56. In footnote No. 8, he quotes from Keśirājas *Sabdamaṇidarpaṇa* 268 from which it appears that the phonetic habit of the Kannada speaking people of that period was the pronunciation of OIA *ṛ* as *ri*.

Corresponding to the change *ṛ*>*i*, we have some instances of *ṛ*>*e* chiefly in WAp. *e.g.*, *geṇha*<**gṛhṇa*, *gheppaï*<**ghṛpyate*=*gṛbhyate* or *gṛhyate* (also in SAp.), √*dekkha-* as well as √*dikkha-*<√**dṛkṣ-*, *dekhanta* <√*dekha-*<**dṛkṣ-*.

Under the superficial uniformity of this literary *lingua franca*, one finds some chrono-regional variations in the vocalisation of *ṛ* during our period.[12]

§16A. TREATMENT OF OIA *ṛ*

| Cent. A.D. | Region | Examples |
|---|---|---|
| 500 ? | WAp. | (a) *Initially* |
| | | 1. *-ṛ>-a-* : *Kasaṇa* (*Kṛṣṇa*), √*ṇacca-* (**nṛtya-*) |
| | | 2. *-ṛ->-i-* : *hiaa* (*hṛdaya*), *diṭṭhī* (*dṛṣṭā*), *miaṁka* (*mṛgāṅka*), *mia-locaṇa* (*mṛga-locana*). |
| | | 3. *-ṛ->-u-* : *pucchimi* (*pṛcchāmi*), *puhavi* (*pṛthavī*). |
| | | (b) *Medially* |
| | | 1. *-ṛ->-a-* : nil. |
| | | 2. *-ṛ->-i-* : *sarisa* (*sadṛśa*) |
| | | 3. *-ṛ->-u-* : *parahua* (*parabhṛta*). |
| | | (c) Finally: nil. |
| 600-1000 | WAp. | (a) *Initially* : |
| | | 1. *-ṛ->-a-* : *maya* (*mṛgāḥ*), *vi-yambhiya* (*vi-jṛṁbhita*) only two cases. |
| | | 2. *-ṛ->i-* : *tiṭṭhā* (**tṛṣṭā*), *ghiṇā* (*ghṛṇā*,) *diṭṭha* (*dṛṣṭa*)—9 cases. |
| | | 2A *-ṛ->-ī-*: in metrically heavy syllables : *dīsaï* (*dṛśyate*)—5 times. |
| | | 3. *-ṛ->-u-*: *pucchiu* (**pṛcchita*), *puhavi-* (*pṛthavī*) only two cases. |
| | | 3A. *-ṛ->-ū-* : Metrical long syllable *būḍhaü* (*vṛddhaka*)—1 form. |
| | | (b) *Medially* |
| | | 1. *-ṛ->-a-*: nil. |
| | | 2. *-ṛ->-i-*: *ṇivitti* (*nivṛtti*). |
| | | 3. *-ṛ->-u-* : nil. *nisuṇaï* (*ni-śṛ-ṇū*)—3 times. |
| | | (c) *Finally* : nil. |

12 For the treatment of *ṛ* in IA and in Marāṭhī see Jules BLOCH, *L'indo-aryen* pp. 34-6 and *FLM* §§ 30, 31.

700-1200 EAp. (a) *Initially*

1. -*ṛ*->-*a*-: nil in *DKK*. *maṭṭī* (*mṛttikā*), *gahia* (*gṛhītvā*).

1A. -*ṛ*->-*ā*-: *Kāṇha* (*Kṛṣṇa*) *ā*- in heavy syllables.

2. *ṛ*->*i*- : *diḍha* (*dṛḍha*), *diṭṭha* (*dṛṣṭa*), *kiaü* (*kṛta*), *śiāla* (*śṛgāla*).

2A. -*ṛ*->-*ī*- : *dīsaï* (*dṛśyate*). *ī*- due to metrically long syllable.

3. -*ṛ*- >-*u*-: *pucchaï* (*pṛcchati*), *muṇāla* (*mṛṇāla*),

3A. -*ṛ*->-*ū*- : *pūhabi* (*pṛthavī*).

4. -*ṛ*->-*e*- : *dekkhaï* (**dṛkṣ*-), *cellu* (**cṛt*-) both in *DKs*.

(b) *Medially*:

1. -*ṛ*->-*a*- : Only 1 in *DKs*. 78. *akkaṭa* (*akṛta*) ("wonder").

2. -*r*->-*i*-: *aïsa* (**adṛśa*), *sarisa* (*sadṛśa*), *amiya* (*amṛta*).

(c) *Finally* :

1. -*r*->-*i*-: *māi* (*mātṛ*), Only 1 in *DKs*. 86.

1000 WAp. (a) *Initially*

1. *ṛ*->*a*- : *taṇa* (*tṛṇa*), *ṇaccaï* (*nṛtyati*), *ghaya* (*ghṛta*), *kaya* (*kṛta*).

2. *ṛ*->*i*-: *hiyaya*, *hiaḍaa*(*hṛ aya*), *kiya* (*kṛta*), *vicca* (**vṛtya-vartman*), *kiviṇa* (*kṛpaṇa*) *ghiya* (*ghṛta*), *dikkha* (**dṛkṣ*-=*dṛś*-), sometimes *ṛ*->*e*- e.g., √*dekkha*- (**dṛkṣ-dekkhanta*.

3. *ṛ*->*u*-: *pucchaï* (*pṛcchati*), *puṭṭha* (*pṛṣṭha*).

3A. *ṛ*-▷*ū*-: before a heavy syllable : *būḍhaü* (*vṛddha-ka*).

4. *r*->*ri*-: *rikkha* (*ṛkṣa*), *rīṇa* (√*ṛ-na*)

(b) *Medially*

1. -*ṛ*->-*a*-: *sukaya* (*sukṛta*), *amaya* (*amṛta*), *Jiṇa-hara*[13] (°*gṛha*).

2. -*ṛ*->-*i*-: *amia* (*amṛta*), *nigghiṇa* (*nirghṛṇa*). *ṇivitti* (*nivṛtti*), *sukiya* (*sukṛta*) also *dukiya*, *erisa* (*īdṛśa*).

(c) *Finally*

1. -*ṛ*->-*a*: *piya* (*pitṛ*), *bhāya* (*bhrātṛ*), *māya* (*mātṛ*).

---

13 Really <**ghara*-PIE < ***gʷhoro*-

2. -ṛ>-: *māī* (*mātṛ*), *bhāi* (*bhātṛ*).

1000 SAp. (a) *Initially*

1. *ṛ->a-*: *paṭṭhi* (*pṛṣṭhe*), *saṃkhala* (*śṛṅkhalā*) *taṇha tṛṣṇā*).
2. *ṛ->i-*: *tiṭṭhā* (**tṛṣṭā*), *hiyavaya* (*hṛdaya*).
3. *ṛ->u-*: *uḍu* (*ṛtu*).
4. *ṛ->ri-*: *riya* (*ṛc*), *rijjhau* (*ṛdhyatu*), *riddhilla* (*ṛddhi-mat*), *rikkha* (*ṛkṣa*).

(b) *Medially*

1. *-ṛ->-a-*s *amaṇṭha* (*amṛṣṭa*)
2. *-r-▷-a-*: *amhārisa* (*asmādṛśa*), *nipphia* (*niḥspṛha*)
3. *-ṛ->-ū-*: *āucchaṇa* (*āpṛcchana*), *pautta* (*pravṛtta*), *māuya* (*mātṛka*).

(*c*) *Finally*

1. *-ṛ>-a* : *varaitta* (**varayitra*=*varayitṛ*).

1100 WAp. (a) *Initially*

1. *ṛ->a-* : *maacchi* (*mṛgākṣī*).
2. *ṛ->i-* : *diṭṭha-* (*dṛṣṭa-*), *bhiuḍiā* (*bhṛkuṭikā*), *hiaa* (*hṛdaya*).
3. *ṛ->e-* :√*geṇha-*√**gṛṇh-*), *gheppaï* (**ghṛpyate*= *gṛbhyate* or *gṛhṇāti*).

(*b*) *Medially*

1. *-ṛ->-a-*: *visaṭṭho* (*visṛṣṭa*).
2. *-ṛ->-i-* : *sariṇāu* (*sadṛśa-nāmā*), *saricchu* (*sadṛkṣaḥ*.)

1100 SAp. (a) *Initially*

1. *ṛ->a-* *taṇha* (*tṛṣṇā* ), *taṇuvaṇa* (*tṛṇa-vana*), *vaḍḍha* (*vṛddha*).
2. *ṛ->i-* : *titti* (*tṛpti*), *dhiṭṭha* (*dhṛṣṭa*), *hiyaya* (*hṛdaya*).
3. *ṛ->u-* : *puhaï* (*pṛthavī*), *būḍhaü* (*vṛddha-ka*), *muiya* (*mṛtā*), *muṇāla* (*mṛṇāla*).
4. *ṛ->ri-* : *riddhi* (*ṛddhi*), *riṇa* (*ṛṇa*,) *risinda* (*ṛṣīndra*).

(b) *Medially*

1. *-ṛ->-a-*: *daramalīya* (=*durmṛdita*), *saṁghaṁia* (*saṅgṛhīta*).
2. *-ṛ->-i-* : *amiya* (*amṛta*), *ṇigghiṇa* (*nir-ghṛṇa*) *bhāiya* (*bhrātṛka*).

3. -ṛ->-u- : nil.

(c) *Finally*

1. -ṛ>-a : *dhīya* (**dhitṛ=duhitṛ*) cf. Pa. *dhītā ; bhāya* (*bhrātṛ*), *māya* (*mātṛ*) also *māa*.
2. -ṛ->-i : nil.
3. -ṛ->-u : *piu* (*pitṛ*).

1200 WAp. (*a*) *Initially*

1. ṛ->a-: *vasahi* (**vṛṣabhi*), *malaï* (**mṛdati*), *taṇha* (*tṛṣṇā*).
2. ṛ->i- : *hiya* (*hṛda-ya*), *hiyaya*, *hiyaḍaya* (*hṛdoya*) *tiṇasama* (*tṛṇa-*), *vintāgi* (*vṛntāka*).
3. ṛ->u-: *vuṭṭhi* (*vṛṣṭi*), *puṭṭhi* (*pṛṣṭha*), *pucchai* (*pṛcchati*), *suṇai*, *-suṇahi* (√*śṛ-ṇa-*).
4. ṛ->ri-: *riu* (*ṛtu*), *riṇiya* (*ṛṇika*), *riddhi* (*ṛddhi*).

(b) *Medially*

1. -ṛ->-a- : *amaya* (*amṛta*), *pagaï* (*prakṛti*), *pahaṭṭhaï* (*prahṛṣṭa-*), *viyambhaï* (*vi-jṛmbhate*).
2. -ṛ->-i- : *tārisa* (*tādṛśa*), *visarisa* (*visadṛśa*), *samiddha* (*samṛddha*).
3. -ṛ->-u- : *parahuya* (*parabhṛta*), *pāusa* (*prāvṛśa*).

(c) *Finally* :

1. -ṛ>-a - : *māya* (*mātṛ*).
2. -ṛ>-u : *piu* (*pitṛ*).

§16B. TREATMENT OF OIA ṛ

| Cent. A.D. | WAp. | SAp. | EAp. |
|---|---|---|---|
| 500 ? | (a) Initially: ṛ->a- >i- >u- | | |
| | (b) Medially : -ṛ->-i- > u- | | |
| | (c) Finally : nil. | | |
| 600-1000 | (a) Initially : ṛ->a- | | |

| | |
|---|---|
| | >i- : ī (In metrically heavy syllables)<br>>u- ū- (Metrically long syllable). |
| (b) Medially: | -ṛ>-i-<br>>-u- |
| (c) Finally | nil. |

| Cent. A.D. | WAp. | SAp. | EAp. |
|---|---|---|---|
| 700-1200 | | | (a) Initially:<br>ṛ->a- in heavy syllables<br>>i-<br>>ī- (In metrically long syllables)<br>>-u-, ū- -do.- |

| Cent. A.D. | WAp. | SAp. | EAp. |
|---|---|---|---|
| | | | (a) Initially:<br>ṛ->e-<br>(b) Medially:<br>-ṛ->-a-<br>>-i-<br>(c) Finally<br>-ṛ>-i |

| Cent. A.D. | WAp. | SAp. | EAp |
|---|---|---|---|
| 1000 | (a) Initially :<br>ṛ- >a-<br>>-i- sometimes<br>ĕ-<br>>u-<br>>ū- before a heavy syllable.<br>>ri-<br>(b) Medially :<br>-ṛ->-a<br>>-i- | (a) Initially:<br>ṛ- >a-<br>>-i-<br>>u-<br>>ri-<br>(b) Medially:<br>-ṛ->-a-<br>>-i-<br>>-u- | |

| Cent. A.D. | WAp. | SAp. | EAp. |
|---|---|---|---|
| | (c) Finally<br>-ṛ>-a<br>>-i . | (c) Finally ;<br>-ṛ>-a | |
| 1100 | (a) Initially:<br>ṛ->a-<br>>i-<br>>e- | (a) Initially: :<br>ṛ->a-<br>>i-<br>>-u- (Labial influence)<br>>ri- | |

| Cent. A.D. | WAp. | SAp. | EAp |
|---|---|---|---|
| 1100 | (b) Medially :<br>-ṛ->-a-<br>>-i-<br>(c) Finally : | (b) Medially :<br>-ṛ->-a-<br>>-i-<br>(c) Finally :<br>-ṛ>-a<br>>-u | |
| 1200 | (a) Initially:<br>ṛ->a-<br>>i-<br>>u-<br>>ri-<br>(b) Medially·<br>ṛ->-a-<br>>i-<br>>-ū-<br>(c) Finally<br>-ṛ>-e<br>>-u | | |

§17. Although Pk. grammarians are almost unanimous in asserting the irregularities of vowel changes in Ap., [14] we find that they generally follow the main outline of changes in literary Pkts. It is, however, interesting to observe the beginning of NIA tendencies during our period.

14 For example *Pu.* 17.17 *ajjhalau ca bahulam* "There is no hard and fast rule regarding the changes of vowels and consonants in Ap." Vide also *Pu.* 17.9. It is only *Pu.* which mentions the irregularities of consonant changes. Others refer to vowel changes only. Thus we find in *Hc.* 8.4.329 *svarāṇāṁ svarāḥ prāyo'pabhraṁśe* cf. *Tr.* 3.3.1 followed by *Sh.* and *Ld.* See *Mk.* 17.9 as well.

The following are generally regarded as the characteristics of NIA vowel-changes :

(1) General reduction and loss of final vowels inherited from MIA, except in very few cases, where traces of the final vowels are seen.

(2) The preservation of the penultimate vowel in quantity.

(3) Loss of pre-penultimate vowels except in the initial syllables, first through reduction of all vowels to the neutral vowel *-a-* which is later glided over in current pronunciation.

(4) Preservation in general of the quality of the initial syllables inherited from MIA.

(5) Reduction (except in Panjabi) of the double consonants inherited from MIA to single consonants with compensatory lengthening of the vowel in the initial syllable (except in Sindhi where the original OIA quantity of the vowel is preserved.[15]

The treatment of OIA vowels in different positions during the Ap. period will show that Ap. is the real background of most NIA as NIA, languages, although some tendencies in Ap. are as old as OIA, Pāli, or literary Pkts.

## FINAL VOWELS

§18. There seems to be a tendency in OIA to pronounce the final syllable weakly, as it was probably unaccented. Thus Vedic *yatrā* and *tatrā* became *yatra* and *tatra* in classical Sk. The consonant endings were lost in MIA.[16] In Aśokan edicts of the East, *-ā* ending words were written as *-a* ending ones. In spite of the conservatism of spelling which Bloch attributes to the longer pronunciation of these shortened vowels as compared with the originally OIA short vowels, we see some forms in literary Pkts. which must be traced to this tendency. e.g., *kadua gadua* in Śaur., shortening of nasalized long vowels in the final position the change of *e* and *o* to *i* and *u* in Dutreuil de Rhins fragments.[17]

That this tendency persisted down to the NIA period is clear from almost all NIA languages except in Bihari, Kāshmīrī Sindhi and the

15 S. M. Katre, *Prākrit Languages and their Contribution to Indian Culture*, Bharatiya, Vidya Studies, No. 3, 1945, p. 75.
16 Pischel, op. cit., § 339.
17 Bloch, *FLM* §37. He refers to the relevant sections from Pischel's *Grammatik* therein.

Southern dialects of Koṅkaṇī.[18] We may safely assume the existence of this tendency in the Ap. period.

The following are the instances of this tendency in our period.

(1) *-a*, *-aaṁ* dropped out or shortened. The total loss of final syllables is included under this. (See 2b below).

WAp. *khettī*<*kṣetrita*, *ujjhā*<*upādhyāya*, *sayaḍi*, *sagaḍiya* <*śakaṭikā* 'a fire-pan,' *eu* or *iu*<*evam*, *paccala*<**pratyalam* though ALSDORF following Dn. 6·69 takes it as *samartha* (See *Glossar* to *Kp.*)

SAp. *dhruu*<*dhruvam*, *saṁca*<*saṁcaya*.

EAp. *indi*, *īdi*<*indriya*, *e*<Pk. *eaṁ*=*etad*, (in WAp. VK. 22- also), *aṇabara*, *aṇabaraa*<*anavarata*, *cellū*<**celluka* or *cella*<√**cṛt*- cf. Low Sk. *ceṭaka*, *kaha*<*katham*.

Ins. sg. *-eṁ*<*-ena* may be regarded as an instance of phonetic weakness of the termination, if the connexion between *-eṁ*<*-ena* is correct as BLOCH[19] and TURNER[20] suppose it. This desinence is common to WSEAp.

(2) Shortening of OIA *-ā*, *-āṁ*, *-āḥ*, *-āni* to *-a* or its loss.

(a) Examples of *-ā* of Fem. nouns reduced to *-a*;
WAp. *pia*<*priyā*, *parāiya*<*parakīyā*, *saṁjha*<*sandhyā*
SAp. *bhukkha*<*bubhukṣā*, *pāvajja*<*pravrajyā*, *Aṇaṁga--leha* <°*-lekhā*.

EAp. *abejja*<*avidyā*, <*dakkhiṇa*<*dakṣiṇā*. We have a greater number of *tss.* and *semi-tss.* in EAp. than in WSAp.

(b) Loss of final syllable containing *-ā*. (See §19·1 above e.g. WAp. *āṇī*<*āṇīā*<*ānītā*, *ceya*<*ceyaṇā*<*cetanā*, also *ceṇa* in *Bhk.* 330·4.

EAp. nil in *DKK*. There are only two such examples in *DKs.* viz., *maṭṭī*<*maṭṭiā*<*mṛttikā*, *picchī*<*picchiā*<*picchikā*
For the rest see Ap. Morphology.

(3) OIA *-ĭ*, *-in*, *-iṇī*>Ap. *-i* or *-a* :

---

18 S. M. KATRE, *Form Koṅk.* §§ 17 ff. BLOCH, *FLM* § 37 last para.
19 BLOCH *FLM* § 193 (1).
20 TURNER, "Phonetic Weakness of Terminational Elements in Indo-Aryan" (*JRAS* 1927, pp. 227-39).

Out of these -*in*>-*i* and -*ĭ*>-*i* need not be illustrated as they are normal Prākritisms. In Ap. morphology we do not have Acc. sg. -*im*>Ap. -*i*, but the use of the stem itself for the direct case without any termination. Instances like *ekkai*<*ekākīnī*, *pahua*, <*prabhṛti* are very rare. The last is an example of vowel-discolouration.

(4) OIA, -*ŭ*, -*ŭṁ*>Ap. -*u*, -*a*, :

As noted above reduction of *ŭ*>-*u* and -*ŭṁ*>-*u*, in Ap. needs no illustrations. Forms e.g., *dhaṇa*<*dhanus*, *Vijja* (-*ppaha*) <*Vidyut-prabha* are rare. They are probably due to the discolouration of weakly pronounced -*u*. The discolouration of vowels comes more in vogue in NIA.

(5) OIA -*e*>Ap. -*i* :

*amhi*<**asme*, *tumhi*<**tuṣme* and the reduction of OIA inflectional -*e* to -*i* are found all in Ap. works. So also Interjections e.g., *ari*<*are*, *arari* <*arere*, *hali*<*hale*. In *āha ra*<*ehi re*, *jāha ra*<*yāhi re* (*Kc*. 69), there is a further reduction of -*i*>-*a* as noted above.

§19. TREATMENT OF FINAL -*a*.

Following are the different treatments of OIA -*a* in Ap. in this position :

(1) OIA -*a*>Ap. -*i*:

WAp. *parim* (*v. l. pari*) <*param*, *kiri*<*kira* or *kila*; such instances are, however, rare.

SAp. *saïṁ*<*svayam*, *avasiṁ*<*avaśyam*. Here -*a*>-*i* is due to the semi-vowel -*y*-. Similarly in EAp. (*DKS*.) *māi*< MIA *māyā*<*mātā*, *māi*<OIA *māyā*.

(2) OIA -*a*>Ap. -*u*:

It is the characteristic of this period that -*u* of Nom. sg. is applied to indeclinables also, in all the regional Aps.

e.g., WSAp. *sahu*<*saha*, *sahũ in Jdc*. 32·1, *Kp. S*. 53·4 cf. *He* 8·4·419 (all in WAp.), *etthu*< *ittha*=*atra*, *ketthu*=*kutra* *ajju*<*adya*, *ciru*<*ciram*.

(3) OIA -*a*>Ap. -*e*:

All from SAp. (See §19·1 above).

*sae*<*svayam*, *avaseṁ*<*avaśyam* etc. In this the original forms seem to have a pleonastic -*ka*. Thus *avaśyakam*>*avassayam*>**avasayam* >*avaseṁ* is the probable history of this form.

## PENULTIMATE VOWELS

§20. Generally vowels are preserved in the penultimate position, though there may be some change of quantity.

(1) Ap. *-a-* <OIA *-a-*:
*goro-aṇa* <*goro-cana*, *khavaṇau* <*kṣapaṇakaḥ*, *payaḍaṇa* <*prakaṭana*, *kaccāsaṇa* <(*kacca* = *apakva*) *-aśana*, *avarupparu* <*parasparam*, *goraḍī* <**gauraṭī* = *gaurī*, *andhaāra* <*andhakāra*. SAp.: *korava* <*kaurava*, *Johayau* <*Yaudheyakaḥ*, *matthaya* <*mastaka*, *ṇiyaṁsaṇa* <*nivasana*,[21] *bhuvaṁgama* <*bhujaṁgama*. EAp.: *huabaha* <*hutavaha*, *pokkhara* <*puṣkara*, *bisama* <*viṣama*, *hiyaya* <*hṛdaya*.

Quantitative changes are either due to the following consonant cluster or sporadic. e.g., :

WAp: *miaṅka* <*mṛgāṅka*, *rahaṁga* <*rathāṅga*, *pāhaṇa* <*pāṣāṇa*.
SAp.: *bambha-cāra* <*brahmacarya*, *sokkha-khāṇi* <*saukhya-khani*.

(*ii*) Ap. *-i-* <OIA *-i-* :
WAp.: *laliya* <*lalita*, *vivajjiu* <*vivarjitaḥ*, *orāliya* <*avaraṭita*, *puṇḍariya* <*puṇḍarīka*, *vāmiya* > **vāmita* = *vāmīkṛta*, *ummattia* <*unmattikā*, *kavvāḍiya* <**kapāṭika* 'a porter.' SAp. *ṇatthiya* <*nastita*, *PWB* as quoted in *Glossar* to *Hv.* '*caught by the nose,' gloss—*nāthita*, *pahila* <**prathila*, *bahiṇie* <*bhaginyā*.

EAp. *guhira* <*gabhīra*, *joiṇi* <*yoginī*, *thabira* <*sthavira*.

(*iii*) Ap. *-u-* <OIA *-u*:
WAp: *samudda* <*samudra*, *lhasuṇa* <*lasuṇī*, *sarūva* <*svarūpa*, *bhiuḍi* <*bhṛkuṭi*, cf. *bhiuḍiā* <*bhṛkuṭikā* (*Mt.* 20), *samuha* <*samukha*, *ūsuya* <*utsuka*, *kappūra* <*karpūra*.

SAp. *pharusa* <*paruṣa*, cf. *Hc.* 8.1.232, *kappūra* <*karpūra*, *sammuham* <*sam-mukham*, *maṇua* > *manuja*

EAp.: *kalūsa* <*kaluṣa*, *niuṇa* <*nipuṇa*, *jamuṇā* <*yamunā*.

§21. Occasionally with the loss of occlusion of the intervocalic consonant in the final syllable, the penultimate and final vowels come together and coalesce. This is chiefly found in EAp. e.g.,

EAp. *tāla* <*tālaa* <*tālaka*, *maṭṭī* <**maṭṭiā* <*mṛttikā*, *muṇḍī* <*muṇḍia* <*muṇḍita*, *pāṇī* <*pāṇia* <*pānīya* (contrast *pāṇia*, *pāṇiya* in *Sdd* 89 and 18), *indi*, *īdi* <*indiya* <*indriya*.

21 Or more probably < **ni-taṁsanana-*

Absolutive term. *-i*<*-ia*. In *DKS*. 93 *mara*<*maraī*< **marati*.

This was less in vogue in SWAp. It is totally absent in *Vk*. and *Mt*. A few examples from the 10th cent. A.D. are found here and there. Thus we find :

WAp. *khettī*<*khettiā*<*kṣetritā* 'agriculture.'

*gandhoa*<*gandhodaka*, *parāī*<*parakīyā*, *poṭṭali*<*poṭṭalika* (but *poṭṭaliya* elsewhere). These are the only 4 forms in the 224 *dohas* of *Sdd*. in the 222 *dohas* of *Pd*. there are only 2 or 3 such examples viz. *caurāsī* <*caturaśīti*, *puttha* and *potthā*<*pustaka*. It is noteworthy that *DKS*., *Sdd*., *Pd*. belong to the same century wherein we find this regional difference.

Though all the occurrences of such forms in SAp. were not calculated due to the vast extent of the works of Puṣpadanta, such examples in SAp. of the 10th cent. A.D. are not frequent although examples like *bhaḍḍārī*<*bhaṭṭārikā* show that this was not totally absent in SAp.

This seems to be a well established tendency in NIA.[22] Although Ap. literature attests to its existence from the 10th cent. A.D., its beginning may be still earlier.[23]

§22. There are some cases where the penultimate vowels undergo qualitative change, perhaps due to the absence of accent or to the principle of assimilation and dissimilation, e.g.

WAp. *khayara*<*khadira*, *ukkhiṇa*<*ut-*√*khan*<according to, JACOBI,[24] but traced to *-kṣiṇati* by KATRE in his *Wilson Philological Lectures*. *sāhika*<*sādhaka* as equated by H.L. JAIN in the translation (*Pd*. p. 37) and glossary to *Pd*. p. 99. The alternative equation *sahāyaka* or rather **sāhyaka* is better. The line in question runs as follows: *visayā sevahi jīva tuhuṁ dukkhahaṁ sāhika* (v. 1. *sāheka*) *ena* "Oh Jīva, you enjoy objects of sensual pleasure, but this leads to misery."

SAp. *majjhiva*<*madhyama*, cf. *majjhima* also, *geruya*<*gairika*, *puṇḍucchu*<*puṇḍra-ikṣu*. As a matter of fact it is an instance of initial *i-*>*u-*, a change found in literary Pkts. also.[25]

---

22 BLOCH, *La Langue Marathe* § 41 ; KATRE, op. cit., § 23.
23 For similar examples in other MIA dialects see PISCHEL *Grammatik* § 150.
24 Glossar to *BHK*. p. 132.
25 PISCHEL, *Grammatik* § 117.

EAp. *uttima*<*uttama* cf. *Hc.* 8·1·46 and PISCHEL, *Gram.* §101; *kuccha* in *DKK* 10, though equated with *kiñcit* by M. SHAHIDULLA (*Les Chants Mystiques Vocabulaire*, p. 100), should better be traced to *kaścit.*

In EAp. the following changes are worth noting: *ubeśa*<*upadeśa.* The intermediate stages—*ubaesa*, *uaesa*—as well as *uesa*<*upadeśa* are also found therein. *ekkāra*<**ekkāāra*<*ekākāra*, *andhāra*<*andha-āra*< *andhakāra*; *datta*<**daitta*<*daitya* is semi-*ts*, but the *tbh.* as *daïcca* is in WSAp.*pariṭṭhabo*<*pari-ṭṭhāvio*<*pāristhāpitaḥ.*

These examples are enough to show that the penultimate syllable was definitely unaccented in EAp. As this tendency is seen in *DKK*, it may be assumed that 700 A.D., is the earliest record of this so far as Ap. literature is concerned. It may be earlier still as we find similar instances in literary Pkts.[26]

## PRE-PENULTIMATE VOWELS

### §23. VOWELS IN INITIAL SYLLABLES

Normally Ap. preserves vowels in the initial syllable irrespective of its nature, probably due to accent, though instances of accentless vowels resulting in (*i*) aphaeresis, (*ii*) change of quantity and sometimes (*iii*) change in quality are not wanting. Quantitative change further shows (*a*) lengthening of short vowels in closed syllables and (*b*) *vice versa* sporadically.

From the treatment of vowels in initial syllables in NIA,[27] it appears that most of the phonetic tendencies in NIA go back to Ap. period and generally to their respective parent-regional group.

As these changes are found all over Aryan India from very old times, they are arranged alphabetically rather than chrono-regionally.

§24. Ap. *a*-<OIA *a*- :

WAp. *avicallu*<*avicālyaḥ*, *kavaḍḍiya*<*kapardikā*, *khapparau*< **skarparakaḥ*, *gahira*<*gabhīra*, *ghaḍa*<*ghaṭā*, *candaṇaim* <*candanena*, *chaḍa*<*chaṭā*, *jahaṇa*<*jaghana*, *jhaya*<*dhvaja*, *ṭhaviya*<**sthapita*, *ḍara*<*dara*, *ḍhakka*<*ḍhakkā*, *ṇaha*< *nabhas*, *talāu*<*taḍāgaḥ*, *thaṇa*<*stana*, *dasa*<*daśan*, *dhavalaṇaham*<*dhavalayitum*, *naḍa*<*naṭa*, *pavāṇa*<*pramāṇa*,

26 *Ibid.*, §§ 148-50.

27 For Bengali, See S. K. CHATERJI, *ODB* §§ 155-166 ( § 143 as well); for Marathi *vide* BLOCH, *FLM* §§ 43-49 where North-Indian languages are also noted; for Koṅkaṇī, KATRE *Form. Koṅk.* §§ 25-29; for a synthetic review of the whole field, see BLOCH, *L'indo-aryen*, pp. 43-5.

phaṇivaï<phaṇipati, bahutta<bahutva, bhaḍa<bhaṭa, mahisa<mahiṣa, rayahaṁ<rajasām, lahu<laghu, vayaṇu <vacanam, sau<samam, hattha<hasta.

SAp. Asoya<Aśoka, karoḍi<Pk. karoḍiya cf. M. karaṭī or karoṭī, khala (ts), khagga<khaḍga, √gavesa<√gaveṣaya, ghaḍa<ghaṭa, caukka<catuṣka, chaḍayaṇa<ṣaḍayana, jaḍia<jaṭita, jhasa-cindha<jhaṣa-cihna, ḍasiya<*daśita=daṣṭa, ḍhakkā (ts)., navaï<namati, tarucchu<tarakṣu, thaṁbhaṇī<stambhanī, Dasāraha<Daśārha, dhavala 'a bull,' natthiya<nastita, pahilau<*prathila-kaḥ phaḍa<phaṭā,=phaṇā, balāla<bala-vat, Bharahesara<*Bharatheśvara, maṇuva<manuja, Rahu<Raghu, lahuyāraya<*laghukatara-ka=laghutara, vaṭṭa<vartman, samaïriya<samīrita, Haṇuva<Hanumat.

EAp. abikkala<avikala, kalūsa<kaluṣa, kharaḍa<√khara-ṭa, gabba<garva, cauṭṭthaa<catuṣṭaya, tabbẽ<*tad-vakam=tadā, but tavve in Vk. 22, dahābia- causal PP. of √dah, naggala<nagna-ṭa, pabīna<pravīnaḥ, pharanta<spharant, bhaabā<Pk. bhaavam<bhagavan, majjhye<madhe, rahia <rakṣita, sahāba<svabhāva, hattha<hasta.

§25. Ap. ā-<OIA ā- :

WAp. āhāsanta<ābhāṣamāṇa, kāṇaṇa<kānana, khāya<*khāta =khādita, gāma<grāma, ghāya<ghāta, cāyaga<cātaka, chāya<chāyā, jaya<jāta, jhāṇa<dhyāna, ṭālai<ṭālayati, ṭhāṇa<sthāna, ḍāha<dāha, ḍhālaï—caus. of √ḍhala, ṇāsia<nāśita, tālanti<tāḍayanti, dāliddau<dāridryakam, dhāvira<√dhāv-, ṇāḍaya<nāṭaka, pāuriya<prāvṛta, phāḍiya<sphāṭita, bālī<bālā, bhāvami<bhrāmayāmi, mārisa< mādṛśa, rāya-ha<rājñaḥ, lālasa (ts.), vāvāra<vyāpāra, sāmala<śyāmala, hāriya< ta.

SAp. āluṁkhiya<ārukṣita, kāsāya-paḍa<kāṣāya-paṭa, √khā <√khād-, gāma<grāma, ghāṇa<ghrāṇa, cāriu<cārita, chāhi<chāyā, jāvāya<jāmāta, jhāṇa<dhyāna, ṭhāu=< *sthāpa?=sthāna, ḍāiṇiu<ḍākinyaḥ, nāmāla√nāmavat, tāva<tāpa, thāla<sthālī, dālidda<dāridrya, dhāha<dhāhā 'expression of sorrow,' onomatopoetic, Dhāidīva<Dhātakīdvīpa, pāḍihera<prātihārya, phāra<sphāra, bāyara<bādara, bhāviṇi<bhāminī, māṇikka<māṇikya, rāṇaa<rājan, lāyaṇṇa<lāvaṇya, vāvaṇa<vāmana, sāmiṇi<svāminī, hāliṇi< hālinī.

EAp. *ābaï*<**āpaï*<**āpati* though usually equated with *āyāti*[28], *ṭhāba*<*sthāman*, *tālā*<*tālaka*, *nāhi*<*nāsti*, *bhābiaï* <*bhāvyate* and *bhābaï*<*bhāvayati*, *māï*<*mātar*, *rāba*<*rāva*, *sāmaggi*<*sāmagrī*

§26. Initial *a*- is lengthened to *ā*- generally in heavy syllables, and sporadically in open syllables Conversely we find *ā*- shortened to *a*- (sometimes with the doubling of the next consonant, even though it be simple in OIA.) Such examples are sometimes found in other MIA dialects.

(A) Ap. *ā*-<OIA *a*- :

(*i*) *In heavy syllables* :

WAp. *tāsu*<*tassu*<*tasya*, *kāsu*<*kassu*<*kasya* and similar gen. sg., *kāyavva*<*kartavya*, *ṇāsaï*<*naśyati*, also *ṇāsira*<*naśya-ira*, *dāhiṇiya*<*dakṣiṇīya*, also *dāhiṇa*<*dakṣiṇa*, *dāḍhā*< *daṁṣṭrā*, *khāla*<*khalla*.

SAp. *Āsōya*<*Aśvayuja* (?) 'pertaining to the month of Āśvina,' *gāva*<*garva*, *tāyatiṁsa*<*trayastriṁśa*, but most probably from **trā-triṁśa* on the analogy of *dvātriṁśa* "thirty two," *dāhiṇa*<*dakṣiṇa*, *phāsa*<*sparśa*.

EAp. *ābhāsa*<*abhyāsa*, *bājīra*<*vajrin*, *lābhaï*<*labhyate*, *kāsu* <*kasya*, *sāndhi*<*sandhi*.

(*ii*) *In open syllables* :

WAp. *gāla*<*gala*, *pāroha*<*praroha*, *pāyaḍa*<*prakaṭa*, *bāhira* <*bahiḥ*, also *bāhirau*, *bāhiri*, *bāhiṁ*, cf. *bāhera* in *DKK*. 2 (EAp.).

SAp. *kāliṅga*<*kaliṅga*, *cāuṭṭha*<*caturtha*, *pāyaḍa*<*prakaṭa* cf. *Hc*. 8·1·44, *sāyatta*<*sapatnī* *pāikka*<*padātika* or *pādika* as equated by P. L. Vaidya in glossary to *JC* p. 142? Some trace it to Old Persian.

EAp. *ṇāhī* or *nāhui*<*nahi*, *ālē*<*alam*.

(B) Ap. *a*-<OIA *ā*:

(*i*) With the doubling of the next consonant even though simple : WAp. *khaddhaï*<*khādati* in SAp. (*Nc*. 7.13.5) used figuratively for *hata*. cf. *Dn*. 2·67,

---

28 Turner *Nepali Dictionary*, p. 30. See under *āunu* where he compares the semantic cognate Eng. get=arrive. See also Pischel, op. cit., § 254 for *āvaï*=*āvāti*.

EAp. *natha*<*nātha.*

(*ii*) When the following syllable is simple.

WAp. *ahāṇa*<*ābhāṇaka*, *paliu*<*pālitaḥ.*

SAp. *chaïya*<*chādita*,

EAp. *aïriya*<*ācārya*, *amaṇā*<*āgamana*,*pharāa*<*sphārita*, *Baṇārasi* <*Vārāṇasī.* This is more frequent in EAp.

(*iii*) When the following syllable is a consonant cluster:

WAp. *aṁva*<*āmra*, *gatta*<*gātra*, *pabbhāra*<*prāgbhāra*,[29] *vajjiya*<**vādyita*=*vādita.*

SAp. *atthāṇa*<*āsthāna*, *kaṁci*<*kāñcī*, *gatta*<*gātra*, *Jambāvaī* <*Jāmbavatī*, *ṇāṭṭa*<*nāṭya* or **nṛtta* ?, *Tamalitti*<*Tāmralipti*, *thatti*<**sthā-p-ti* in the sense of *sthiti*[30] *patthiya*<*prārthita*, *bhajja*<*bhāryā*, *maṁjara*<*mārjāra*, *rakkhasa*<*rākṣasa*, *laṁgūla* <*lāṅgūla*, *vaggha*<*vyāghra*, *sakkhiyara*<*sākṣicara.*

EAp. *adda*<*ārdra*, *appā*, *appāṇa*<*ātman* (in WSAp. as well), *kajja*<*kārya*, *natthi*<*nāsti*, *bakkhāṇa*<*vyākhyāna* (both a subtantive and a verb), *bamhaṇa*<*brāhmaṇa*, *bhanti*<*bhrānti*, *magga* <*mārga*, *sattha*<*śāstra.*

As will be seen from above Ap. *a*- < OIA *ā*- is mainly found when *ā*- in OIA is followed by a conjunct consonant.

§27. Generally *i*- and -*u*- (both in light and heavy syllables) are preserved in their initial position. Their elongation is due to the following consonant cluster.

(A) Initial *i*- :

(*i*) Ap. *ī*<OIA *i*- :

WAp. *pia*<*priyā*, *tihuyaṇa*<*tribhuvana*, *Jiṇa-vara*<*Jina-vara*, *piyaulliya*<*priyā-ullī-ka* (both pleonastic) *ciṭṭhaï*<*tiṣṭhati*, *kīlā*<*krīḍā*, *kittiyu*<*kiyat.*

SAp. *vijigicchā*<*vicikitsā*, *ṇihasaṇa*<*nigharṣaṇa*=*nikaṣaṇa*,[31] √*thippa*<√*stip-ya*-, *Viṭṭhu*<*Viṣṭu* cf. *Biṭṭhu in DKS.* 52, contrast *Hc.* 1·85.

---

29 In *Kp.* J. 102.5 this word means "a collection" as the context "*bhūsaṇāṇa pabbhāru bhāru va*" shows. In *Dn*, 4.66 it is a synonym for a collection "*saṅghāta.*"

30 P. L. Vaidya takes it as *deśī* for *sthiti*, see Glossary to *JC.* p. 132. It is, however, possible to explain it as a noun ending in -*ti* from the causal base of √*sthā.*

31 Cf. Pischel, *Grammatik* § 206.

EAp. *biḍambiya<viḍambita, biphāria<visphāritam, dība<dīpa dīha<dīrgha.*

(*ii*) Ap. *ī-* <OIA *i-*+ conjunct consonant :

WAp. *jīhaḍī, jīhaḍiya, jīha<jihvā-, ṇīrukkha<nir-*rukṣa (=vṛkṣa), vīsanta<viśrānta, Sīhapura<Siṁhapura.*

SAp. *Sīhaura<Siṁha-pura, vīsā-suhiuyā=viśvāsaṁ sukhaṁ karotī'ti* 'N. of a *vidyā*' (*Nc.* 6·6·23), *jīha-i<jihvayā, vīsamiya <vi-śramita.*

EAp. *dīsaï<dṛśyate.* Only one form repeated thrice.

(*iii*) Sporadic changes of OIA *ī-*>Ap. *i-* (a) with or (b) without the gemination of the following consonant, though it be a simple one in OIA.

(*a*) With the doubling of the next simple consonant :
WAp. *ṇiccu<nīca, ṭikkaïm<ṭīkayā, khilla-hī<krīḍanti.*
SAp. *ṇitta<nīta, ṇicca<nīca, ṇitti, <nīti.*
EAp. *tiṇṇa<trīṇi.* Only one form.

(*b*) WAp. *jiya<jīva, ciṇṇa<cīrṇa*
SAp. *tittha<tīrtha,*
EAp. nil.

(B) (i) Ap. *ū-*<OIA *ū-* :
WAp. *sulalia<sulalita, uppari<upari, uttiḍaa=uttarīya* (*Sdd* 151) *ullāva<ullāpa, luddha<lubdha, nūṇa<nūnam, pūyaṇa<pūjana.*
SAp. *duva<druma, duhikka<durbhikṣa, jujha<*Pk. *jujjha <yuddha, kumbhi-he<kumbhinaḥ.*

EAp. *ubaesa, uaesa, uesa<upadeśa, ūha<ūrdhva, uttima<uttama.*

(*ii*) Ap. *ū-*<OIA *u-*+consonant cluster :
WAp. *ūsāra<*utsāra, ūsava<utsava.,*

SAp. *Dūsāsaṇa<Duḥśāsana, ūvaḍiya<utpatita, ūsasei<ut-śvas.*
EAp. *ūala<utpala* contrast *Hc.* 8·2·77.

(*iii*) Ap. *u-*<OIA *ū-* :
WSAp. *puvva<pūrva, ubhham, uddha<ūrdhva, ubbhubbha <ūrdhva-ūrdhva, kuppara<kūrpara, suṇṇa<sūnya,* also in EAp.
EAp. *juttha<yūtha* but *jūha* in Mah., Amg. JM. (PISCHEL-*Gram.* §§ 188, 221).

§28. In Ap. initial *e-* and *o-* in dissyllabic words are long: e.g., *ēka* (*ts*), *mēha<megha, ōha<ogha, jōa<yoga.*

Initial *e-* and *o-* are generally short before consonant clusters, and are weakly pronounced as terminal sounds giving *-i* and *-u* as Loc. and Nom. sgs. Ap. *e-* and *o-* sometimes result from stressed *i-* and *u-* in OIA.

(*i*) Ap. *ĕ-*, *i-*<OIA *e-* :

WAp. √*pĕkkha* or *pikkha*<√*prekṣ*, *ciṭṭha*<*ceṣṭā*, *tilla*<*taila*, *līha*<*lekhā*,

SAp. *cillaṇa-devi*<*Celanā-devī*, *chitta*<*kṣetra*, *tilloya*<**trailoka*.
EAp. *khetta*<*kṣetra*.

(*ii*) Ap. *e-*<OIA *i-* :
WAp. *kheḍḍa*<*krīdā*, cf. *Hc.* 8·4·168. *ētthu*<*itthā* cf. PISCHEL *Gram.* §107, *erisa*<*īdṛśa*. SAp. *celī*<*cīrī*, *pehuṇaya*<**picchanaka*, *bekkhura*<*dvi-khura*.
EAp. *ettha*, *etthu*<*itthā*.

(*iii*) Ap. *o-*<OIA *u-* :
WAp. *potthaya*<*pustaka*, also *potthā*, *mokaliya*<**mukna-*, *koḍi* <MIA *kuḍḍa* (*deśī*), *thora*<*sthavira* but JACOBI equates it with *sthūla* (*Glossar* to *Sc.* p. 124). In *Sc.* we have no cases of Ap. *o-*<OIA *u-*. The few stray forms e.g., *hōya* <*bhūta* (Sc. 784·6) are really √*ho*<*bhō*<*bhū*+pp. term. *-ya*<*-ta*.

SAp. *toṇḍa*<*tuṇḍa* cf. *Hc.* 8·1·116, *tōṇīra*<*tūṇīra*, *gomccha*, *guṁccha*<*guccha*, *konti*<*kuntī*, *tolā*<*tulā*. The number of such cases is next to that of the retention of *u-*.
EAp. *sojjha*<*śuddhi*, also *sojjhuka*, √*sojjha*.

Examples of reduction of OIA *ō-* to Ap. *u-*, before conjunct consonants (e.g., *mukkha*<*mokṣa*, *cukkha*<*cokṣa*) are found in common with other MIA dialects.[32]

§29. The initial vowel and syllable were sometimes lost in OIA,[33] Pali,[34] and Prakrits,[35] as they were not stressed. Their number is on the increase as we proceed from OIA to Pkts. Cases of such aphaeresis and syncope are found in Ap. of all regions, testifying thereby to the absence of stress on the initial syllables in these cases.

WAp. *vahelia*<*avahēḍita*, *bhintara*<*abhyantara*.
WSAp. *raṇṇa*<*araṇya*, *pi*, *vi*<*api* cf. *bi* in EAp. *va*<*iva*, *pakkhara*

32 PISCHEL op. cit., § 84.
33 J. WACKERNAGEL, *Alt. Gram.* I. § 53.
34 Cf. W. GEIGER, *Pali Lit. u. Spr.* § 20.
35 PISCHEL, op. cit., §§ 141-45.

*<upaskara*, *bhukkiya<bubhukṣita*, *ḍhillaa<śithilaka*,
WSEAp. *haũ<ahakam*,
SEAp. *baïṭṭha<upaviṣṭa*,
SAp. *mayāsi<amṛtāśī*, *rahaṭṭa<araghaṭṭa*, *valagga<avalagna*, *viṭṭāla<apavitra-la*, *ṇesara<dinēśvara*.

As the treatment of vowels in non-initial position is much the same as in other Pkts., we may pass on to the treatment of vowels in contact.

### VOWELS IN CONTACT

§30. Due to slackness in articulating OIA intervocalic stops, the unaspirated stops, *k*, *g*, *c*, *j*, *t*, *d*, *p*, became spirantised, and finally lost their occlusion in MIA. The *udvṛtta*-vowels came in contact and resulted into :

(1) Retention of the hiatus.

(2) Preservation of the individuality of the vowels by insertion of *-y-*, *-v-*, *-b-*, *-h-* and sometimes *-r-* as '*hiatus-tilgers*.'[36]

(3) Contraction into a single vowels.

Ap. shares (1) and (2) in common with other MIA dialects. Literary Ap. does not attest to diphthongisation of *udvṛtta* vowels, although(3) tends to show the possibility of its existence in spoken Ap. As the contraction of such vowels into a single one is interesting from the point of NIA, it is briefly noted here. As these are general developments in Ap., the venue is sometimes not indicated before some WSAp or WSEAp. forms.

### CONTRACTION OF VOWELS

§31. The following are the results of vowel-contraction when the first vowels is *ă* :

(1) *ạ+i>e* :

36 Insertion of such vocalic glides is an old phenomenon. For such glides in Pali see GEIGER, *Pali Lit. u. Spr.* § 36, in Amg. PISCHEL, op. cit., § 187 ; for a historical discussion see S. K. CHATTERJI, *ODB* § 170.

Out of the above-mentioned *Śrutis*, *-ba-śruti* is the same as *-va- -śruti*, and is found in EAp. only e.g., *ubesa* (*uddeśa*), *ubāharaṇa* (*udāharaṇa*). *-ha- śruti* is rare *e.g.*, *cihura* < *cikura*, *chāhi* < *chāyā*, and perhaps *sihiṇa* (*stana*) and EAp. *gāhia* < **gāyita=gīta*. *-ra-* glide is rarer still e.g., *paritthiya* < *prati-sṭhita*, *maraṭṭa* < *mada-iva* < **mṛd*?

*eha*<*aïsa*<**ā-dṛśa*, similarly *jeha*<*jaïsa*<*yādṛśa*, *teha*<*taïsa* <*tādṛśa* and other pronominal adjectives. *suhellī*<*sukha-kelī* in *NC* 1·15·2. Is *-ellī* pleonastic, as the word means '*sukha*' only, in *Dn.* 8·36?

The problematic forms in NIA e.g., M. *ãśī*, Guj. *aisi* 'eighty,' M. *basṇē* 'to sit' do not appear in this stage. We have for them *asī* <*asii*<*aśīti*, *baïṭṭha*<*upaviṣṭa*.

(2) *a*+*u*>*o*, sometimes reduced to *u* :

WSAp. *mora*, *moraa*, *morullaa*<*mayūra*, *cotthī*<*caturthī*, *coddaha* <*caturdaśa*, *bholau*<*bahulaka*, *poma*<**paduma*=*padma*, *Pomāvaï* <**Padumāvatī*.

SAp. *āhuṭṭha*<*ardha*- **tūrtha*.

(3) *ă*+*ă* :

(*i*) *ā*+*a*>*ā* :

OIA *-āga* : *āya*<*āgata*, EAp. *āmaṇa*<*āgamana*

*-āja*: *rāula*<*rāja-kula*, *bhāṇa*<*bhājana*, but WAp. *reï* <*rājate* has *-e-* due to *-ya-*<*-ja*.

OIA *-āda*: *khāi*<*khādati*, *khāṇa*<*khādana*.

WAp. *chāṇa*<*chādana*, √*chāya*<√*chāday*

OIA *-āya*: *palāṇa*<*palāyana*, SAp. *pacchittu*<*prāyaścitta*; *ā* is contracted to *a* due to the next heavy syllable.

EAp. shows the contraction of OIA *-āya* to *a*, e.g., *rasaṇa*<*rasāyana* *atthamaṇa*<*asta-mayana* (?) It is traceable to simple *astamāna*.

WSAp. *kera*<*kārya*, *pāḍi-hera*<*prāti-hārya* show an *-e-* development.

OIA-*āva*>*ā* or *o* due to the labial element *-v-* : *talāra*<*talavāra*[37] *saloṇa*<*salāvaṇya*, *ōli*<*āvali*.

(*ii*) *-a*+*-ā*>*ā* :

OIA *-akā* : SAp. *soṇṇāra*<*suvarṇakāra*.

WAp. *piyāri*<*priyakāri*.

WSEAp. *andhāra*<*andhakāra*, *sāhāraa*<*sahakāraka*

---

37 Pischel, op. cit., § 167; P. L. Vaidya equates it with *talavara* (Glossary to *JC.* p. 130) in which case it will be an unusual development for OIA *-ava-* >Ap. *-o-* is the general rule. See §31 (iv) b. below.

EAp. *ūāra*<*upakāra* .if the lengthening of *u-* be not due to *ua-*<*upa-*.

OIA *-avā* : *akkhāḍaya*<*akṣavāṭaka.*

(*iii*) *-ā*+*-ā*>*ā* :

OIA *-ākā* : EAp. *āra*<*ākāra.*

(*iv*) *-a*+*-a* when separated by *-y-* or *-v-* :

(a) OIA *-aya:-*>*-e-* : *Ujjēṇi*<*Ujjayanī, Ujjenta*<*ūrjayanta, Ujjanta* in *Hv.* 89·17·3 is traceable to **ūrjanta. te-*<*traya-* as in *teraha* <**traya-daśa, tettiya,*<*trayastriṁśat.*

(b) OIA *-ava-*>*-o-* : SEAP. *loṇa*<*lavaṇa.*

WSAp. *ohulliya*<*ava-phullita, thora*<*sthavira, dora* <*davaraka.*

WAp. *ovagga*<*apa-valg-, orālia*<*ava-raṭita,*√*olagga* <*ava-lagna.*

(c) Others :

OIA *-aka -* : When no *ya-śruti* develops : e.g., *campā-*(*vaṇṇī*)<*campaka-*(*varṇā*),

EAp. *tālā*<*tālaka, dohā*<*doddhaka.*

*-aga-* : SAp. *Tera*<**Tayara*<*Tagara, -ē-* due to *-ya-śruti.*

*-aja* :

*-ata* : PP. Participles e.g., *gaa* (*gata*), *maa* (*mṛta*) etc., seem to have been reduced to **ga-*, **ma-* in spoken, Ap., as the NIA forms with the *-la* terms of the past (although originally pleonastic) go to prove e.g., M. *gelā*, Konk. *gello* (MIA *gaa-*).

OIA *-ada* : *kelī*<**kayalī*<*kadalī. -ē-* due to *-ya-śruti.*

It is the *-ya-śruti* which solves satisfactorily why *-a*+*-a* is contracted into *-e-* in Marathi.[38]

OIA *-apa-*<*-ava-*<*o* :√*osara*<*apasara,*
SAp. *karoḍi*<*karapatrikā*
WSAp. *soaï*<**svapa-ti,*
WAp. *voiya* (PP. of√*vyap-*).

---

38 Bloch, *La Langue Marathe* § 62.

§32. When the first vowel is *-i-* (or *-ĕ-*), it results into *-ī-*, *-ū* when combined with *-i-* or *-u-*. But when the first vowel is *-u-* or *-o-*, it remains predominant.

e.g. OIA *-ī-*+*-ī-*>*-ī-* : *bīa*<*dvitīya*, *tīa*<*tṛtīya*.
*-i-*+*-u-*>*-ū* : *dūṇa*<*dvi-guṇa*.
*-u*+*-a-*>*-o* : *ōlakkhaï*<*upalakṣayati*, *soṇṇāra*<*suvarṇakāra*, *popphala*<*pūga* (or *pūgī*)-*phala*.
*-u-*+*-u-*>*-u-* WAp. *umbara*<*udumbara*,
SAp. *ukhala*<*udūkhala*.

As there are very few instances of the contraction of more than two vowels (e.g. *ujjhā*<*upādhyāya*, *dora*<*davaraka*, *vivarēra*<*viparīta*+*ira*) we may ignore these here.

## NASALISATION OF VOWELS

§33. Nasalisation of vowels is a late MIA characteristic which has come down to the NIA languages.[39] Spontaneous and compensatory nasalisation are noted below (§ 34.)

In a vocable with a final nasal, when the last two vowels contract, there is nasalisation *e.g.*

WSEAp. *haũ*<*ahakam*,
WSAp. *saĩ*<*svayaṁ*, *avasaĩ*, *avasẽ*, *avasĩ*<*avaśyam*.
EAp. *ālẽ*<*alakaṁ*=*alam*.

The Neut. direct Pl. in *-āĩ*<*-āni*, Ins. sg. *-ẽ*<*-ena* (if these be the correct derivation) are the instances of this. It is, however, the class-nasal *-m-* which has brought about nasalisation of the preceding vowel e.g. the nasalisation in the desinence of Pres. 1 sg. *-ũ* or *-aũ*. There is no orthographic evidence of the nasalisation of other class-nasals although we find a few forms e.g. *pãka*<*paṅka*, *-payãgama*<*pataṅgama* in EAp. This, coupled with the nasalisation in old NIA, leads one to believe in its existence in spoken Ap.

Words e.g. WSAp. *peranta*<*paryanta*, *cunca*<*cañcū* and *vaṁjha* <*vandhyā*, *saṁjha*<*sandhyā*, *toṇḍa*, *tuṇḍa*<*tuṇḍa*, *aṁjaṇa* (*ts*)., go to show that in Ap., in the group short vowel+nasal+consonant (both voiced and unvoiced) there is no lengthening and nasalisation of the short vowel as we find it in some NIA languages.

---

39 For nasalisation in Bengali see S.K. CHATTERJI, *ODB* §§ 175-77, and that in Marathi *vide* BLOCH, *FLM* § 66 ff.

## SPONTANEOUS NASALISATION

§34. Spontaneous nasalisation i.e. the tendency to insert nasals though none existed in the corresponding OIA form, belongs to earlier MIA, as we find it in Pali,[40] and in Prakrits.[41] Grierson showed that most NIA words with nasalised vowels can be referred to MIA forms actual or hypothetical.[42]

In Ap. spontaneous nasalisation comes as a compensation for the loss of a consonant or sporadically, e.g. SWAp. *payampa*<*pra-√ jalp*, *piṁcha*<*pṛcch*, *iṁcha*<√*icch*, *phaṁsa*<*sparśa*, *vaṁka*<*vakra*, SAp. *goṁcha*, *guṁcha*<*guccha*<*gutsa*, *kaṁcāiṇi*<*kātyāinī*, WSAp. *daṁsana*<*darśana*, *baṁhiṇa*<*barhin*, *maṇṭha*<*mṛṣṭa*. WAp. *pankhi*<*pakṣin*, *āluṁkhiya* <*ārukṣita*, SAp. *vindhaï*<*vidhyati*, WAp. *īsim*<*īṣat*, *ṇiyaṁsaṇa*<*nivasana*, *maṁjara*<*mārjāra*, *vimbhala*, *vembhala*<*vihvala*, *thimbha*<√*step-* EAp. *jimghaï*<*jighrati*.

## DENASALISATION

§35. As opposed to spontaneous nasalisation, we have some cases of the loss of OIA nasals inAp. e.g.SWAp.*sīha*<*siṁha*, *vīsa*<*viṁsati*, *tīsa*<*triṁśat*, *dāḍhā*<*daṁṣṭrā*, SAp. *agāa*<*agamya* (?), *pacchāuhuṁ*< *paścāt-mukhaṁ*.

The treatment of post-consonantal nasal i.e. that of stop+nasal, of nasal+nasal, and of sibilant+nasal is the same as in literary Pkts..[43]

§36. In Ap., as in NIA, the OIA group of vowel+conjunct or double consonant, reduces itself to

(*i*) long vowel+single consonant after assimilation and reduction with compensatory lengthening of the vowel, if short, or

(*ii*) short vowel+double consonant after assimilation and retention of the group with reduction of the vowel, if long.

(*i*) Long vowel+single consonant :
WSAp. *sahāsa*<*sahasra*,
WAp. *jayāsi*,<*jayaśrī*.
WESp. *dīha*<*dīrgha*.
SAp. *Sarāsaï*<*Sarasvatī*, *vaṇāsaï*<*vanaspati*, *baṁbhaṇa-cāra* <*brahma-carya*, *sīsakka*<* *śīrṣaska*.

---

40 Geiger, *Pali Lit. u. Spr.* § 6.3.
41 Pischel, op. cit., §§ 74, 86.
42 Grierson, "Spontaneous Nasalisation in the Indo-Aryan Languages," *JRAS* (1922) pp. 381 ff.
43 See for example Pischel, op. cit., §§ 269, 348, 349. For sibilant+nasal §§ 312-14.

EAp. *ūha<ūrdhva*, *ūala<utpala*.

(*ii*) Short vowel+double consonant :
WAp. *kaḍaccha<kaṭākṣa*, *dukkhannu<duḥkhārṇava*.
SAp. *Paṇḍava<Pāṇḍava*, *Kammuya<kārmuka*. We may include examples, e.g., *ṇikka<nīka*, *ṇiccu<nīca*, *kacca<kāca*, *pujja<pūjā* etc.

For further examples see §§26 (B)(*i*), 27 (A) iii (*a*), and (B) iii.

### VOWEL-COLOURATION

§37. In Ap. we find labial and palatal colouration of *a* more conspicuous than that of *i* and *u*. The presence of a labial vowel or *v* is generally responsible for labialisation while that of *y* for the palatalisation of *a*.[44]

(A) *Labialisation of a* :
WSAp. √*jūra<*√*jvar*, √*muṇā* : *maṇṇa<*√*man* cf. OIA *muni*, *jhuṇi<dhvani*.

SAp. *paülaṇa*: *jalaṇa<pra-jvalana*, *viusa<vidvas*, *guhila<gahvara +gabhīra*?, *khuruppa<kṣurapra*, *puḍhama* : *paḍhuma*, *puḍhuma* : *paḍhama<prathama*.

EAp. *biṇua<vijña* or **vijñuka* or the analogy of *savvaṇṇu<sarvajña*.

(B) *Palatalisation of a* :
SAp. √*picca*, WAp. *pikka*: *pakka<pakva*, WAp. *avasi* : SAp. *avasu<avaśyam*, *ṇiḍala*: *ṇaḍāla<lalāṭa*,

WSAp. √*abbhiḍa<*abhyaṭ* (*abhi-*√*aṭ*), SAp. *akkhiya<ākhyāta*, *aṇṇetta-he<anyatra*, (*aho-*) *gaiṇam*: °*gagaṇam<*(*adho-*) *-gaganam*
WAp. *tiriccha<tiryakṣa*.

For a few more see § 22.

There are very few examples of vowel-discolouration in Ap. e.g. *halola<hilola*, *ucchu<ikṣu*, *kāiṁ<kim* (?). It is more prominent in NIA,

### ANAPTYXIS

§38. As in other literary Pkts., we meet with a number of cases of Anaptyxis in Ap. They are found in learned borrowals from OIA.

---

44 Although this phenomenon is more prominent in NIA (for which see, for example, Bloch, *FLM* §§ 75, 76), examples *e.g.*, *pūñjila*: *piñjūla* in OIA (for more Wackernagel, *Alt. Gram.* § 277) shows its antiquity.

as we have distinct *tbhs.* used in the same works. They are greater in number in *-r-* and *-l-* conjuncts, although Pk. grammarians allow the use of *-r-* conjunct in Ap.

WSAp. *paṇayaṁgaṇa*: *pan'aṁgaṇa* (*paṇyāṅganā*).
WAp. *murukkha*: *mukkha* (*mūrkha*).
WAp. *kārima*: *kamma* (*karman*).
WSAp. √*varisa* <√*varṣ*, *kilesa* <*kleśa*, *arahanta*, *arihanta*, <(*arhat*),

WAp. *aruha* <*arhat*, *arisaya* <*arśa*,√*garaha* <√*garh*, *kilīṇa* <*klinna*, *kasaṇa*<*kṛṣṇa*, but EAp. *kānha*.

SAp. *vaïrāyas*<*vairāgya*, *bhaviya*<*bhavya*, *vāhiyāli*<*vāhyāli*, *barihaṇa*<*barhin*, *sukkila*<*śukla*, *gilāṇa*<*glāna*,√*salahijja*<√*ślāgh-*

PROTHESIS

§39. Prothesis is rare in Ap. The groups of *sk*, *st*, *sp*, *sm* were either assimilated or changed to *kh*, *th* (*ṭh*), *ph* and *mh*. A few forms e.g., WAp. *ittiya* <*strī-ka*, *hedisa*<*īdṛś*, *yevva*<*eva* show the existence of this tendency in Ap. No instance of prothetic *v* was traced in Ap.

EPENTHESIS

§40. As in other literary Pkts., there are some cases of the epenthesis of *-i-* and *-u-*, in Ap. *e.g.*

WSAp. *kera*<*kārya*, *peranta*<*paryanta*.

SAp. *mera*<*maryāda*, *acchera*<*āscarya*.

WAp. *accheraya*<*āścarya*.

WSAp. *baṁbhacera*<*brahma-carya*,
SAp. *sundera*<*saundarya*, *pāḍihera*<*prātihārya*.

WSAp. *poma*<*padma*, *Pomāvai*<*Padmāvatī*.

UMLAUT

§41. Instances of the qualitative change in a vowel through the influence of another vowel or semi-vowel of a different quality, are found in Ap. Sections on vowel-contraction (§§ 31, 32), vowel-colouration and discolouration (§37) and Epenthesis (§ 40) contain sufficient examples some of which are found in other literary Pkts. as well.

CONSONANTS IN APABHRAMSA

§42. The history of IA consonantism is well-nigh clear from the works of J. WACKERNAGEL[45], W. GEIGER[46], R. PISCHEL[47], J. BLOCH[48], R. L. TURNER[49], S. K. CHATTERJI[50], S. M. KATRE[51] and others. Its history in our period is briefly as follows:

(*a*) Final consonants of OIA > lost in early Pkts. > lost in Ap.

(*b*) Initial consonants of OIA > preserved in Prākrits > preserved in Ap.

(*c*) Intervocalic stops of OIA :

(1) Surd in OIA > sonant in Prākrits > possibly spirant in Ap. leading to zero in NIA.

(2) Surd aspirate in OIA > sonant aspirate or -*h*- in Pkts. dialectically > sonant aspirate or -*h*- in Ap. leading to loss of occlusion in NIA.

(*d*) Consonant clusters of OIA > double consonants in Pkts. through assimilation

(1) Single consonants with compensatory lengthening in Ap., or

(2) Double consonants in Ap.

The following table of Ap. occlusives will show the general nature of Ap. consonantism :

| | Initial or resulting from consonant groups or double consonants. | | | | OIA intervocalic consonants. | | |
|---|---|---|---|---|---|---|---|
| | Unaspirated | | Aspirated | | Unaspirated | Aspirated | |
| Velars .. | *k* | *g* | *kh* | *gh* | *g*, *y*, zero | *gh* | *h* |

45 J. WACKERNAGEL, *Alt. Gram.* I §§ 96-239.
46 W. GEIGER, *Pali Lit. u. Spr.* §§ 35-64.
47 R. PISCHEL, *Grammatik der Prakrit Sprachen*, pp. 135-239.
48 BLOCH, *La Langue Marathe*, §§ 14-15 for Marathi consonantism §§ 81-175. The general development of consonants in YA is treated in *L'indo-aryen*, pp. 50-95.
49 R. L. TURNER, "Gujrati Phonology," *JRAS* (1921), 505-508.
50 S. K. CHATTERJI, *Origin and Development of Bengali*, pp. 36-63, 82-98, 239-61. For Bengali consonantism, see pp. 433 ff. For the general development in IA, see *Indo-Aryan and Hindi* Lectures II and III (pp. 28-95).
51 *Form. Koṅk.* § 76. Koṅk. Consonantism §§ 77-174.

| | | | | | | |
|---|---|---|---|---|---|---|
| Palatals | *c* | *j* | *ch* | *jh* | *j*(rarely) | |
| (Palato-alveolars & dento-palatals) | | | *s* | | *y*, zero | |
| Cerebrals | *ṭ* | *ḍ* | *ṭh* | *ḍh* | *ḍ* (*ḷ*) | *ḍh* |
| Dentals | *t* | *d* | *ṭh* | *dh* | *d*, *y*, zero | *dh*, *h* |
| Labials | *p* | *b* | *ph* | *bh* | *b*, *v*, zero | *h bh* (rarely). |

Changes in Ap. dialects *e.g.*, Vrācaḍa(ṭa), Upanāgara are not noted here. Although initial single consonants have come down unchanged, *y*->*j*- is the general rule in Pkts. (except Mg.) Editors differ regarding the preservation of initial *n*-. Eminent text-critics *e.g.*, Pischel, Vaidya, Jain, Upadhye and others have, however, built up a tradition of initial *ṇ*-.

The treatment of intervocalic surds is practically the same as in Pkts. in spite of the rules of Pkt. grammarians for voicing them (§§ 55-57).

### ASPIRATION

§43. The following are the examples of initial and non-initial aspiration of occlusives in Ap. Many of these are found in literary Pkts. also[52].

(a) *Initial*

WSAp. *khilliyaiṁ*<*kīlakāḥ*, *khiliya*<*kīlita*, √*jhala*<*jval*- and its related forms √*jhala-phala*, √*jhalajhala*, √*jhalakka*, *bhisa*<*bisa*, also *bhisiṇī*<*bisinī*, *bholaa*<*bahulaka*, hence √*bholava*-.

In the following the presence of *ṛ*, *r*, and a sibilant is responsible for aspiration :

*khapparaü*<*karparaka* (but rather **skarparaka*), √*kheḍḍa*, *khella*, √*khilla*-<√*krīḍ*-, and its derivatives, *gheppa*-, √*ghippa*-<√*gṛbh*-.

52 Such aspiration is really an old phenomenon in IA. For aspiration in OIA see Wackernagel, *Alt. Gram.* I. § 203, § 109, etc., for Pali vide Geiger, *Pali Lit. u. Spr.* § 40 (pp. 57-8), § 62 (p. 70), for Pkts. see Pischel, *Grammatik* §§ 205-10, for aspiration in NIA see Chatterji, *ODB.*, §§ 236-40; Turner, "Gujarati Phonology," § 40, Bloch, *FLM* §§ 84-6, *L'indo-aryen*, pp. 59-60. S. M. Katre, *Form. Koṅk* § 78.

WAp. *bharasu*<*paraśu*; *if dhamdha*<*dvandva* as understood by Brahmadeva in his Kannaḍa gloss on *PPr.* 2·21 be corrrect, its meaning 'business,' 'transaction' or 'shame' as in *Pd* 122 (see *Pd* 7, 91 also for 'business') seems semantically connected with Sk. *dvandva* although the phonological equation may be doubtful. *lhasuṇa*<*lasunī*.

SAp. *khujjava*<*kubjaka*, *ghoṇasa*<*gonasa*, *jhuṭṭha*<*juṣṭa* (?) at least semantically, *pharusa*<*paruṣa*, also *bharusattaṇa*=°*tva*, *bhisiya*<*bṛsikā*. Is *b*>*bh* due to *r*?

EAp. Nil

Forms in which the aspiration is due to the presence of *ṛ*, *r*, a sibilant, or metathesis of *h* are not, strictly speaking, cases of real aspiration. Hence forms e.g., *ghara*, *ghariṇi* etc.<IE**g*$^w$*horo*, or the changes of *sk*>*kh*; *st*>*th*, *ap*>*ph*, *sn*>*ṇh* and *sm*>*mh* are excluded from this section.

(2) *Non-Initial*:

Non-initial aspiration is very rare in Ap. The following instances are, however, exceptional:

WAp. *vaḍha*<*baṭu* (?) also in *DKS*. *dhandha*,

EAp. *dhandhā*, *dhandhī*<*dvandva* (?).

SAp. *sa-jhuṭṭha*<*sajuṣṭa* (?); *-h-* in *Bharaha*, *Bhārahī*, *Bharahe-sara* implies *-*th*-for regular *-ta-*. Thus the original forms are **Bharatha* **Bhārathī*, **Bharatheśvara*, rather than the usual *Bharata*, *Bhāratī* etc. Can we include instances of *-h- śruti* e.g., *sihiṇa*<*staṇa*, *bhaūha*<*bhrū-*, *chāha*, *chāhi*<*chāyā*, etc., under this?

## DEASPIRATION

§44. The process of de-aspiration is found in OIA,[53] Pali,[54] and Pkts.[55] in pre-Ap. IA, as well as in post- Ap. period, as in Marāthī[56] Bengai,[57] Koṅkaṇi,[58] and Sindhi. In Ap. de-aspiration is comparatively rare when compared with NIA.[59]

53 Wackernagel, *Alt. Gram.* I §§ 104,109.
54 Geiger, *Pali Lit. u. Spr.* § 40.
55 Pischel, *Grammatik*, §§ 213-4.
56 Bloch, *FLM* §§ 87-9.
57 Chatterji, *ODB* §§ 241-3.
58 Katre, *Form. Koṅk.* § 80 *ABORI* 18.4 (1937).
59 Bloch, *L'indo-aryen*, pp. 60-62.

The natural position of de-aspiration is the final one, especially the terminational endings, but as the use of the stem itself for the direct case has been proved to be the characteristic of MIA Sk. (e.g., Buddhist Sk.) we need not assume that forms e.g., *sappa*<*sarpāḥ*, *ghaṇṭa* <*ghaṇṭāḥ*, are due to this process.

In other cases, it is sometimes due to dissimilation and metathesis of *h*. To take a few examples :

> *kuhia*<**khuhia*<*kṣubhita*, *sandhukki*<*sandkukṣita*, *saṁkala*< *śṛṅkhalā*, *cuppaï*<*Pk.*√*chupa-*, *dihi*<*dhṛti*, *bahiṇi-hi*<*bhaginī*, the intermediate link *bhaiṇi* is also traced, *bīha*<*bhī*, *jagaḍanta* <*jhakaṭa* (a Sk. vocable according to *Hc.* 442·2), EAp. *jatta* : *jattha*<*yatra*, *tatta*: *tattha*<*tatra*, *ṇ*(*n*)*iccala*<*niścala*.

It seems that the process of de-aspiration was accelerated in the post-Ap. period, as there are fewer cases of de-aspiration in Ap. than in NIA. Some de-aspirated forms in NIA, e.g., M. *bhūk*<Ap. *bhukkha* (*bhubhukṣā*), *māj*<Ap. *majjha* (*madhya*), appear to be aspirates in Ap. The NIA languages however show no uniformity in de-aspiration. Thus along with Ap. *cumbhala*, *combhala*>M. *cumbaḷ*, Ap. *dhandha* >M. H. *dhandā*, Ap. *ghuraghura*>M. *gurgurṇē* we find Ap.√*sikkha*-< *śikṣ*- leading to *śikṇe* in M. and *sikhnā* in H.

## CEREBRALISATION

§45. The problem of cerebrals and cerebralisation in the different stages of IA is sufficiently discussed by different scholars.[60] As in OIA and Pkts. Ap. has the following retroflex sounds—*ṭ*, *ṭh*, *ḍ*, *ḍh*, *ṇ*, *ḷ*. OIA dentals undergo cerebralisation in Ap. under the following circumstances.

(1) Preceded immediately by *ṛ*.
(2) Preceded at a distance by *r*.
(3) Preceded immediately by *r*.
(4) Followed immediately by *r*.
(5.a) Single and intervocalic dentals.
(5.b) Double and Intervocalic dentals.
(5.c) Initials dentals.
(6) Initial *n*- and *l*- and intervocalic -*n*- and -*l*- :

---

60 For OIA see WACKERNAGEL, *Alt. gram.* I. §§ 143-51; for Pali *vide* GEIGER, *Pali Lit. u. Spr.* § 42 and § 64; for Prakrits, PISCHEL, *Grammatik* §§ 289-94, 308, 309, 333; for Marathi, BLOCH, *FLM* §§ 108-119, for Bengali, S. K. CHATTERJI *ODB* §§ 266-72, for Koṅk., S. M. KATRE, *Form. Koṅk.* §§ 84-90, *ABORI* 18.4, for Sindhi, TURNER, "Cerebralisation in Sindhi," *JRAS* (1924) pp. 558 ff., for that in IA, BLOCH, *L'indo-aryen*, pp. 53-9.

As TURNER points out in his critical review of *L'indo-aryen*, the 2nd case is an ablaut of *ṛ*. [61] Thus Ap. *√paḍha*<*√paṭh*<*√*pṛth-*, *paḍhama* <*prathama*<**pṛthama*, show that cases 1 and 2 are identical. Each of the above cases has exceptions where dentals are not cerebralised. These testify to the survival of old dentals in two currents: dentals and cerebrals.

§46. The following are the examples of cerebralisation in Ap. The retention of dentals under the same circumstances is also noted side by side.

(1) *Preceded immediately by ṛ* :

(*a*) Cerebralised : WAp. *kaḍa*<*kṛta*, *otthāḍiya*<*ava-√stṛ-maṭṭī* <*mṛttikā*. Sap. *uḍu*<*ṛtu*, *vāuḍa*<*vyāpṛtsa*, *vaḍḍa*<*vṛddha*

(*b*) Dental remains : WSAp. *samiddha*<*samṛddha*, WEAp. *kia*, WSAp. *kaya*<*kṛta*, WAp. *aṇuvitti*<*anuvṛtti*.

(2) *Preceded at a distance by r*:

As noted above, TURNER regards this as an ablaut of *ṛ* in OIA[62].

(*a*) Cerebralised: WSAp. *caṭṭa*, EAp. *cellu*<**√cṛt-*,also *ciḍaulla* 'a sparrow,' a cognate of Sk. *caṭaka*. WSEAp. *paḍhama*< *prathama*, SWAp. *ḍhilla*<*srithira*, *paḍicchavi*<**pratīcchatvī*= *pratīṣya*, WAp. *gaḍḍāyarau*<**gartākaraka*=*gartaka*. *pāḍihera* <*prātihārya*, SEAp. *paḍhai*<*prathati*<**pṛthati*, EAp. *paḍi*< *prati*, *paḍibakkha*<*pratipaṣa*, *paḍijjaï*<*pratīyate*.

(*b*) Dental remains : WSAp. *bhāya*, *bhāyara*<*bhrātar*. SAp. *paija*, WAp, *paijja*<*pratijñā*, SAp. *paisāra*<*pratisāra*.

§47. (3) *Preceded immediately by r* :

(*i*) *rt* (*a*) cerebralised : WAp. *vaṭṭaḍiyā*, SAp. *vaṭṭa*<*vartman*, WAp. *vaṭṭaï*<*vartate* cf. SAp. *vaḍḍa-ü*, SAp. *vaṭṭula* <*vartula*, SAp. *bhaḍāra*, °*rī* WAp. *bhaḍāraya*, *bhaḍāriya* <*bhartāra-ka*, °*ri-kā*.

(*b*) Dental remains : WAp. *atta*<*ārta* but *aṭṭa* in SAp. *vatta* <*vārtā*, *kattī* <*kartari*, SAp. *kattiya*<*kārtika*.

(ii) *rth* : (*a*) Cerebralised : *āhuṭṭha*<*ardha-*turtha*, *gamanaṭṭhiya* <*gamanārthita*.

---

61 *BSOS* VIII. i. p. 205.
62 *BSOS*. 8.1.205.

(*b*) Dental remains : SWAP. *attha*<*artha*, WAp. *aṇattha* <*anartha*, SAp. *samattha*<*samartha*. EAp. *paramattha* <*paramārtha*.

(*iii*) *rd* : (*a*) Cerebralised : WSEAp.√*chaḍḍa*, √*chaṇḍa*<*chard-*, WAp. *kavaḍḍiya*<*kapardikā*, SAp. *niḍḍāriya*<*nir-*√*dṛ* usually explained as '*niskāsita*.'

(*b*) Dental remains : WAp. *addiya*<*ārdrita*, *gaddaha*<*gardabha*, *niddaya*<*nirdaya*, *maddala*<*mardala*, SAp. *kitti*<*kīrti*.

(*iv*) *rdh* :

(*a*) Cerebralised : WAp. *uḍḍha*<*ūrdhva*, SAp. *saḍḍha sārdha*, *pavaḍḍhaī*<*pravardhate*.

(*b*) Dental remains : WAp. *vaddhavaṇa*<*vardhāpana*, *uddhīkaya* <*ūrdhvī-kṛta*, SAp. *uddha-hatta*<*ūrdhva-hasta*, *addhaddha* <*ardārdha*.

EAp. shows a further development *viz*., reduction to *h*. e.g., *ūha*<*ūrdhva*, and not *ubbha* and *uddha* as elsewhere.

In general it appears that WAp. retains the dental to a greater extent than SAp.

(4) *Followed immediately by r* :

(*i*) *tr* : (*a*) Cerebralised : SAp. *viṭṭala*<*apavitra-la* by haplology.

(*b*) Dental remains: WAp. *khettī*<*kṣetrita*, SAp. *chetta*<*kṣetra*, WAp. *tigu*<*trika*, WSAp. *kattha*<*kutra*, SAp. *pattala*< *patra-la*.

(*ii*) *ntr* : WSAp. *anta*<*antra*, WSEAp. *manta*<*mantra*. EAp. *tanta*<*tantra*. No cerebralisation.

(*iii*) *dr* : WSAp. *nidda*<*nidrā*, WAp. *suhadda*<*subhadra*. Cerebralised : WSAp. *tevaḍḍa*<**tayavadra* and similar other forms from pronouns, according to Pischel, but actually <**vṛddha*- ?

(*iv*) *ndr* : (*a*) Dentral remains : WSAp. *canda*<*candra*-and proper names derived from it. Exception *Caṇḍa-utta* <*Candra-gupta*.

(*v*) *dhr* :

(*vi*) *ndhr* : SAp. *purandhi*<*purandhrī*, *randha*<*randhra*, SAP. *Andha* <*Āndhra*.

It will be observed that generally dentals are preserved in such cases although cerebralised forms are not wanting.

§48. (5a) *Single intervocalic dentals* :

Out of these some are elided, some take vocal glides (*śrutis*), some become voiced, some are retained while some are cerebralised. Cases under the last category are noted here:

-*t*- : WSEAp. √*paḍa*<*pat*-, *nivaḍa*<*nipat*, WSAp. *saḍiya*< *śātita*, *sāḍa*√*śātay*, *Dhāḍaï-saṇḍa*<*Dhātakī ṣaṇḍa*.

-*d*- : √*vaḍa*<*vad*- and its frequentative *vaḍavaḍa*, *khuḍia* <**kṣudita*, SAp.√*ḍara*-<√*dar*, *nisāḍa*<*niṣāda*=*miśā*-

-*th*- : *cara*. SAp.√*kaḍha*√*kvath*- also√*kaḍhakaḍha*

-*dh*- :

(5.b) *Double and intervocalic dentals* :

These are generally preserved either as double consonants or single ones with compensatory lengthening of the preceding vowel (cf. §27A [iii.a], B. iii, 36, 72) a tendency so common in NIA. Cerebralisation due to the influence of immediately preceding *r* is noted in §47. The remaining cases are given below :

-*t*- : EAp. *cauṭṭhaa*<*catuṣṭaya* but *cauṭṭha* is due to -*r*- in *caturtha*.

-*th*- : WSEAp. *uṭṭhiya*<*utsthita*, *kaviṭṭha*<*kapittha*, *aṭṭhi* <*asthi*, *paṭṭhava*<*prasthāpay*.

-*d*- :

-*dh*- : SAp. *thaḍḍhattaṇa*<*stabdhatva*.

In many of these, sibilant+dental has resulted into cerebralisation due to the influence of the sibilant.

(5.c) *Initial dentals* :

As in §48 (5.b) above, the cluster of a sibilant+dental leads to cerebralisation of the dental, although there are some cases of 'spontaneous' cerebralisation.

-*t*- : *ṭhaḍḍha*<*stabdha*- For aspiration of *t*- see §44 a.

-*th*- : SEAp.√*ṭhā*<OIA *sthā*. Hence the following forvms WAp. *ṭhāharaï*, *ṭhāvaï*, *ṭhāya*. SAp. *ṭhāu*, *ṭhaaala* 'a stake at dice.' EAp. *ṭhāi*, *ṭhia*, *thāṇa*, *thāb*<: *sthāman*.

*-ḍ-* : WSAp. √*ḍaha* < √*dah*, √*ḍasa* < *daśa*,
SAp. *ḍahu* < *dahara*(?) 'a child.'
EAp. *ḍahābia* < **dahāvita* = *dāhita*.

*-ḍh-* : SAp. *ḍhaṁkha* < **dhvaṅkṣa* 'dry, withered.'

§49. (6) *Initial and Intervocalic* n *and* l : (a) *Initial n-* and *l -*:

There is so much irregularity regarding the use of *n* and *ṇ* in Mss. that eminent text-critics like PISCHEL, VAIDYA, JAIN and UPADHYE have set an editorial tradition of levelling all *n* to *ṇ*. JACOBI and SHAHIDULLA differ and retain *n* initially (JACOBI preserves *-nn-*).

Initial *l-* is not cerebralised e.g., WSAp. *laṁgūla* < *lāṅgūla*, *lāyaṇṇa* < *lāvaṇya*, *loṇa* < *lavaṇa*, EAp. *loyaï* < *lokayati*, *loaṇa* < *locana*.

There is no documentary evidence (except in Southern Mss) of the change of intervocalic *-l-* to *-ḷ-*. In Ap. intervocalic *-d-* and *-ḍ-* were changed to *-l-*, but the Northern Mss. do not give a *-ḷ-* although we find this phonetic habit in Vedic and in Pali, and the change of intervocalic *-l-* to *-ḷ-* is common in NIA. e.g., Marathi[63]

(b) Intervocalic and double *n* and *l* :

Intervocalic double *-nn-* and *-ll-* remain dental. The editorial convention of cerebralising all *n* is noted above (§ 49.a) Thus in JACOBI's editions e.g. that of *Sc.* we have *kaṇṇa* < *kanyā*, *maṇṇaū* < *manye* etc., and SHAHIDULLA has *sunna* < *śūnya*, *anna* < *anya* etc., in EAp.

*-ll-* : WAp. *sallai* < *sallakī* SAp. *vallaha* < *vallabha*, *pallala* < *palvala*, WSAp. *salla*, *sella* < *Śalya*.

It will be found that in many of these cases of cerebralisation, Ap. follows the main out-lines of literary Pkts.[64]

## CONSONANTS IN INITIAL POSITION

§50. Final consonants being already lost very early in MIA, we have to consider consonants only in their initial and intervocalic positions. Although Ap. does not differ much from Pkts. in its treatment of initial consonants, it is worthwhile to consider some of them, due to their regional and other importance.

## NASALS

§51. Normally the class-nasals *ṅ*, *ñ* and *ṇ* (?) are not found in literary Ap. According to S. K. CHATTERJI there is some epigraphic

63 BLOCH, *FLM.*, §§ 144-7, S. M. KATRE, *Form. Koṅk.*, § 89 (b).
64 See PISCHEL, *Gram.* §§ 289-94, 308, 309, 333.

evidence of ṅ pronunciation in the Tipperah Inscription of Lokanatha (700 A.D.).[65] But its contemporary work, *DKK*, does not show it, probably due to stylisation, as the persistence of this pronunciation in Bengali suggests its existence at least in spoken Ap.

*ñ* is found only in the *dhātvādeśa* for √*vraj*, viz., *vañña* (*Pu.* 17·81) or *vuña* (*Hc.* 8·4·392). Whether this is a relic of Magadhism or a special development of OIA **vrajñāti* as suggested by PISCHEL,[66] does not concern us as this form or *ñ* never recurs in Ap. literature except in the illustrative work *Kc.*, and there, too, rarely.

*n* was definitely used in EAp. region as we find it initially and intervocalically in the *Dohākoṣas* and the *Dākārṇava*. Examples like *gaana* : *gaaṇa*<*gagana*, *pabana* : *pabaṇa*<*pavana* in the *Dohākoṣas*, show the irregularity in the use of intervocalic *-n-*. Regarding this SHAHIDULLA remarks, "To sum up, the use of *ṇ* is more frequent than that of *n* with Saraha and less frequent with Kānha.[67]"

Initially *n-* is retained by JACOBI in *BhK.* and *Sc.*, and even by P. L. VAIDYA in his edition of *Hc.*, (Poona, 1928). The hesitation between initial *n-* and *ṇ-* in Mss. of the IA region, the consistent use of *ṇ-* by Southern scribes, and the new editorial tradition of the use of *ṇ-* consistently both in initial and intervocalic positions are already noted above (§ 49). NIA preserves initial dental *n-*. The same might have been the case of Ap. in WAp. region.[68] We hear an initial *ṇ-* occasionally in the speech of peasant (Jains, Marathas etc.) of the Southern Maratha country. Is it a relic of the Ap. period (especially of SAp.) as *ṇ-* is absent in standard Marathi? *n-* is absent in SAp. texts.

A few instances of initial *n-* are noted below from WEAp. texts :

EAp. *naggala*<*nagnaṭa*, WAp. *nāha*, EAp. *nattha*<*nātha*, WEAp. *niccala*<*niścala*, WAp. *niāsvannu*<*niḥ-sāmānya*, *nūṇa*<*nūnam*, but the *ts.* form used in *DKS* 42, *nevattha*<*nepathya*. EAp. *neha*<*sneha*.

Initial *ṇ-* being so much common in modern editions of Ap. works, needs no illustration.

Initial *m-* : WSEAp. *maṇa*<*manas*, *māi*, *māyī*, *māya*<*mātar*. SEAp. *miccha*<*mithyā*, *mukka*<**mukhna*=*mukta*, WAp. *metta*<*metta*<*mātra*+*mitra* or IE **metrom* giving *metta* in WAp. and *matta* in EAp ; WSEAp. *mokkha*, <*mokṣa*.

---

65 *ODB* p. 518.
66 *Grammatik*, § 237.
67 *Les Chants Mystiques*, p. 36.
68 TURNER "Guj. Phonology," § 48, *JRAS* 1921.

SEMI-VOWELS (*y* and *v*)

§52. With the exception of words e.g. *ycalaï* (*calati,*) *yjalaï* (*jvalati*) in *Mk.* 17·2 which is an attempt of the grammarian to represent one type of palatal pronunciation, initial *y*- always becomes *j*- in Ap. In EAp. *yena* (*Dkk* 19), *yojjaï* (*DKS.* 10), *yojaï* (*DKS.* 82) are *v. ll* for *jena, pabbajjaï* and *polaï* respectively. As the editor does not accept them, and the speech habit of Bengal does not support it, we may ignore them. It is non-existent in SAp. and Marathi.[69]

The following are some examples of initial *y*- in OIA.

> EAp. *Jamuṇā*, WAp. *jaṃ̃ṇā* <*Yamunā*, WSAp. *jāma*, WAp. *jāva*, EAp. *jāba*<*yāvat*, WSAp. *juāṇao*<**yuvānakaḥ*, WSEAp. *jeṇa*<*yena*, *joi*<*yogin*.

Thus *y* has no phonemic value in Ap. except a a *hiatus-tilger* and as a palatizing factor when it followed the dental or *r*- in consonant clusters. Its revival in NIA is due to the influence of Sanskrit and the factors noted by BLOCH[1].

§53. Ap. *v* stands for OIA *v, p, b,* intervocalic *-m-* and MIA *-vv-*. The conjunct of a dental with *-v-* has two treatments—dental and labial. The labial treatment seems to be favoured in spoken WEAp. regions where it is found even today. The consistent use of *b* for *v* in EAp as opposed to its preservation (except in clear borrowals) lends support to the theory that the labial treatment of dento-labial. consonant conjuncts is a loan from the East and the Midland in NIA. Sometimes *v* and *b* are interchanged in SWAp. due to the resemblance in the characters in the Devanāgarī and cognate scripts.

(1) *Initial v- retained* :

> SAp. *vaddala*<*vardala*, WAp. *vāli*<**vālya*, Absolutive of √*val*-, SAp. *vihatthi*<*vitasti* with *ha-śruti*,
>
> WAp. *vīsaï* (*viṁśati*), WSAp. *vuḍḍha*<*vṛddha*, *vihavia*< *vaïbhāvita*.

(2) *Initial v-*<OIA *b*- :

> WSAp. *vāha*<*bāṣpa*, WAp. *vībhaccha*<*bībhatsa*.

(3) *Initial b-* <OIA *v*- :

An EAp. characteristic e.g. *bajja*<*varjya*, *bajjaï*<*varjyate*, *bāsa* <*āvāsa*, *bāsia*<**vāsita*=*uṣita*, *biappa*<*vikalpa*, *bīra*<*vīra*, *Bea*<*Veda*.

---

69 BLOCH, *FLM*, § 151.

This is still the trait of the EAp. region. In WAp. we occasionally meet with *b-*<*v-* e.g. *baṁsa*<*vaṁśa*. There too we find this tendency even today.

## SIBILANTS

§54. Out of the three sibilants in OIA, Ap. conserves only *s* in all regions except the East and *ś* in EAp. *ṣ* is exceptional in the *Dohākoṣas* though it became more popular later on in the *Ḍakārṇava tantra*. Ap. *s*<OIA *ch* was probably a dento-palatal, in other cases it was a dental fricative.

Initial *ś-*, *ṣ-* became *s-*, while *s-* was retained in WSAp. Its treatment in EAp. is irregular although *ś-* was preserved only in that region.

(1) *ś-*>*s-* : WSAp. *saṁkha*<*śankha*, WAp. *sakhaṇḍa*<*śākharaṇḍa* (*Sdd*. 61), WSEAp. *siri*<*śrī*, SAp. *sukkila*<*śukla*, EAp. *suṇā*. SEAp. *suṇṇa*<*śūnya*, SAp. *seṇī*<*śreṇi*. WSEAp. *sosa*< *śoṣa*.

(2) *ś* conserved in EAp.

e.g. *śattha*<*śāstra*, *śihara*<*śikhara*, *śuna*<**śuna*=*śvan* (*DKS*. 7). Only 8 cases of initial *ś-* (5 in *DKK* and 3 in *DKS*).

(3) *ṣ-*>*ch-* or *s-* :

*chaṭṭhama*<*ṣaṣṭha-* **ma* analogical, *solasa*<*ṣoḍaṣa*.

(4) *s-* >*s-*:

SWAp. *savva*, WAp. *savu*<*sarva*, WSAp. *sāyara*<*sāgara* WEAp. √*sijjha-*<*sidh-ya*, EAp. *suratta*, SAp. *suraya*<*surat-va*, WSAp. *sevijjanta*=*sevyamāna*, WSEAp. *sokkha*<*saukhya*

(5) For the treatments of sibilant+nasal see § 65.

(6) For *kṣ-* see § 61.

(7) Lastly there is one important treatment of *s* viz. its change into *h* in terminations, numerals and other words. e.g. Abl. and Gen. sg. *-ha*< *-ssa*<*-sya* ? (§83), Loc. sg. *-hĩ*, *-hi*<*-smin* (§82), the augment of Future *-ha*<*-ssa*<*-sya*. Numerals e.g. *daha*<*daśan*, *eyā*(*gā*)*raha*<*ekdāśan*, *bāraha*<*dvādaśa*, *hulaī*<*śūlayati*.

## INTERVOCALIC CONSONANTS

§55. According to Pk. grammarians intervocalic stops are voiced. Thus *-k-*, *-t-*, *-p-* become *-g-*, *-d-*, *-b-* (see *Pu.* 17·6, 13; *Hc.* 8·4·396, *Tr.* 3·3·2 followed by *Sh.* 22·2 and the com. on it, also *Ld.'s* comm. on *Tr.* 3·3·2; *Ki* 5·1 *Mk.* 17·2)[70]. Intervocalic *-kh-*, *-th-*, *-ph-* were changed into *-gh-* *-dh-*, *-bh-*. (*Pu.* 17·7, 13. *Hc.* 8·4·396, *Tr.* 3·3·2 followed by *Sh.* and *Ld.*, *Mk.* 17·2.).[71]

In literary Ap. intervocalic *-k-*, *-g-*, *-c-*, *-j-*, *-t-*, *-d-*, (and *-p-* also) lose their occlusion and disappear. It is only at times that *-k-*, *-c-*, *-t-* become voiced. *-p-*, is sometimes changed to *-v-*. Ap. writers are more inclined to drop these intervocalic stops or use vocal glides (*śrutis*) in stead, rather than change them to *-g-*, *-j-*, *-d-* according to the prescription of Pk. grammarians. (see §56 below).

Similarly intervocalic aspirated stops- *-kh-*, *-gh-*, *-th-*, *-dh-*, *-ph-*, *-bh-* generally become *-h-*. It is only occasionally that *-kh-*, *-th-*, *-ph-* were changed to *-gh-*, *-dh-*, *-bh-* respectively. But that might be a relic of the older stage as in Ap. literature such forms are few although Pk. grammarians have sanctioned them specially for Ap. (For the treatment of aspirated stops in Ap. see §57 below.)

Literary Ap. follows literary Pkts. to a greater extent than the rules of Pk. grammarians.

§56. The following is the treatment of intervocalic stops (*k*, *g*, *c*, *j*, *t*, *d*, *p*) in Ap.[72]

(1) (*i*) *-k-* > *-g-* : WSAp. *maragaü*, *maragaya* < *marakata*,
WAp. *ahigāra* < *adhikāra*, *pagāma* < *prakāmam*.
EAp. *jegaḍa-ha* < *jhakaṭa-* also in WAp. (*Bkh.* 3·8).

(*ii*) *-k-* simply dropped :

WAp. *paräiya* < *parakīyā*,
SAp. *soṇṇāra* < *suvarṇākāra*.
EAp. *āra* < *ākāra*, *maṭṭī* < *mṛttikā*.

---

70 *Pu.* 17.5 notes the loss of occlusion of *k*, *g* and others but gives no indication about their intervocalic nature. *Ki.* 5.1 combines *Pu.* 17.13, 6, 7 into one, and amounts to the same as *Hc.* 8.4.396 or *Tr.* 3.3.2, while in *Ki.* 5,3 we find the loss of single, intervocalic *-k-* in some words (cf. *Pu.* 17.5). *Rt.* 3.2.2 does the same and follows *Pu.* 17.13 (viz., voicing of intervocalic *-k-*, *-kh-*, *-t-*, *-th-*). *Mk.* gives no rule like *Pu.* 17.5 for his Nāgara Ap. but prescribes optional voicing of *-k-*, *-c-*, *-t-* etc. *Hc.*, *Tr.*, *Sh.* and *Ld.* however, are unanimous regarding the voicing of intervocalic *k.*, *c.*, *t.*, *kh*, *th*, *ph*.

71 *Pu.* 17.8 states that *kh*, *gh*, *th*, *bh* become *h*. Thus *Pu.* 17.8 is not in accord with *Pu.* 17.7 or 17.13. The *adhikāra* "*bahulam*" is not given probably due to the corrupt nature of the text. Ap. literature including the illustrative *dohās* in *Hc.*, however, reduces these aspirated surds to *-h-* rather than voice them according to grammarians' injunctions.

72 Cf. Pischel, *Gram.* §§ 186, 187, 192, 202.

(*iii*) -*k*- with vocal-glides :

WAp. *loyāloya*<*lokāloka*, *ghūyaḍa*<*ghūka*,
SAp. *Alaya*<*Alakā*, *sayajja*<*sva-kārya*.
WSAp. *thovaḍa*<*stoka*, *thova* also in WAp.

(*iv*) -*k*- retained :

WAp. *ika*,
SEAp. *eka*,
EAp. *ekku*<*eka*,
WAp. *aṇukiya*<*anukṛta*,
SAp. *jīva-kae*<*jīva-kṛte*.

The first may be due to MIA *ekka*-, and the last two need not be considered as instances of intervocalic -*k*-, since *kiya*-<*kṛta*- has independant existence.

2. (*i*) -*g*- dropped :

SWAEp. *jōī*<*yogin*,
SAp. *Raīveya*<*Rativegā*,
EAp. *bhaa-bã*<*bhagavān*.

(*ii*) -*g*- with vocal glides :

SAp. *Ṇāyadatta*<*Nāgadatta*, *avayaṇṇiu*-*PP*. of *ava*√*gaṇ*.
WAp. *juyala*<*yugala*, *uvveva*<*udvega*.

(*iii*) -*g*- remains in *tss*. and *tbhs*. e.g. *pari-gaṇa*, *sugaya*<*sugata*.

3. (*i*) -*c*->-*j*- : SAp. *vijigicchā*<*vicikitsā*.

(*ii*) -*c*- dropped :

WAp. *goroaṇa*<*gorocana*.
EAp. *aīriya*<*ācārya*.

(*iii*) -*c*->*hiatus-tilgers* :

WAp. *āyamvilaya*<*ācāmla*, *āyariya*<*acārya*.
SAp. *riāyā*<**ṛcā*=*ṛc*. *ullova*<*ulloca*. *paḍi-vayaṇu*<*prati-vacana*

(*iv*) -*c*- is retained in *tss*. and *tbhs*. *e.g*. *acala*, *aceyaṇa*<*acetana*.

4. (*i*) -*j*- dropped :

WSAp. *rāa*<*rājan*, SAp. *rāī*<*rāji*,
WSEAp. *tea*<*tejas*.

(*ii*) -*j*->-*y*-, -*v*- *śrutis* :

WAp. *ayāṇuya*<**a-jānaka*=*ajña*, *Gayaura*<*gajapura*,
SAp. *jhasoddhaya*<*Jhaṣadhvaja*, *maṇuva*<*manuja*, *bhuvaṁgama*.
<*bhujaṅgama*.

(*iii*) *-j-* conserved in *tss.* and *tbhs.* e.g. *aja*, *ajarāmara*, *Ajiya*<*Ajita*.

5. (*i*) *-t-*<*-d-* :

WAp. *āgado*<*āgataḥ*.
SAp. *samidi*<*samiti*, *samii* also.

(*ii*) *-t-* dropped :

WSAp. *caüttha*<*caturtha*, EAp. *caüṭṭha*<*catuṣṭaya*.
WAp. *caüraṁsa*<*caturasra*.
SAp. *Vaivasa*<*Vaivasvata*, EAp. *kiau*<*kṛta*.

(*iii*) *-t-*>*-y-*, *-v-* glides :

WAp. *saṁkeya*<*saṅketa*, *dāyāra*<*dātā-*
SAp. *Amayamaī*<*Amṛta-matī*.
WSAp. *bhūva*<*bhūta*, *suva-paṁcamī*<*śruta-*°
SAp. *huvāsaṇa*<*hutāśana*, *accabbhuva*<*atyadbhuta*.

(*iv*) *-t-* preserved :

EAp. *eta*<*etāvat* but *etta*, *ettiya* etc., in SWAp.
Normally *-t-* is not preserved in Ap.

6. (*i*) *-d-* dropped :

WSEAp. *pāa*<*pāda*, SAp. *pāikka*<*pādika*.
WSAp. *eyāraha*<*ekādaśa*, (*-ra śruti*,)
WSEAp. *jaï*<*yadi*.
WSAp. *paüma*, *poma*<**paduma*=*padma*.
EAp. *uesa*<**udesa*<*uddeśa*.

(*ii*) *-d-*>*-y-*, *-v-*, *-b-* *śrutis* :

SAp. *Vioyara*<*Vṛkodara*.
WAp. *kheviya*<*khedita*, *uvahi*<*udadhi*.
SAp. *mahovahi*<*mahodadhi*, *Jasova*<*Yaśodā*.
EAp. *ubāharaṇa*<*udāharaṇa*, *ubesa*<**udeśa*<*uddeśa*.

(*iii*) *-d-*>*-l-* :

WSAp. *galatthiya*<*kadarthita*.
WAp. *palitta*<*pradīpta*, *Kālaṁbiṇī*<*kādambinī*.

(*iv*) *-d-* retained in *tss.*

WAp. *udaya-sela*<*udaya-śaila*.

7. (*i*) *-p->-b- -v-* :

WSAp. *ṇaravaï<narapati*, WAp. *khavaṇau*.
EAp. *khabaṇa<kṣapaṇaka*. SAp. √*khavaya<kṣapay-*.
EAp. *dība<dīpa*, *ubesa<upadeśa*.
SAp. *vāvāra<vyāpāra*.

(*ii*) *-p-* dropped :

WSAp. *pāa<pāpa*.
EAp. *uarē<upareṇa*, *ūāra<upakāra*, *uala<*ūpala*, *uppala<utpala*.

(*iii*) *-p->-y-* glide :

SAp. *sāyatta<sāpatna*.

8. (*i*) *-b-* retained : In *tss.* e.g. EAp. *Śabara* (*ts*).

(*ii*) *-b->-m-* or *-v-* : Out of this *-v-* is a scribal confusion for *-b-* and SAp. *Kuvera<Kubera*, *siviya<śibikā* may be due to that confusion.

WSAp. *samara<śabara*. SAp. *savara* also,
SAp. *simira<śibira*, *samari<śabari*, are due to the development and confusion of *-m-* (>*-ṽ-*>*-v-*)>*-b*.

§57. The following are the treatments of intervocalic aspirated surds in Ap.[73]

1. (*i*) *-kh->-gh-* : Probably a relic of older stage before its reduction to *-h-*, e.g. WAp. *sughĩ<sukhena*. But rare in Ap. literature.

(*ii*) *-kh->-h-* :

WSEAp. *sahi<sakhi*.
WSEAp. *līha*, *leha<lēkhā*.
EAp. *suha-base<sukha-vāsaḥ*.
SAp. *suhelli<sukha-+elli* pleonastic.

2. (*i*) *-gh->-h-* :

WAp. *vihāya<vighāta*. The context (*BhK*. 18.4.2 in Gune's edition suggests '*vidhāta*,' as the original form as the line in question is : *paramesara taho kaiṁ vihāyau*
SAp. √*salahijja-* pass. of √*ślāgh-*,
EAp. *dīha<*dīgha<diggha<dīrgha*.

73 Cf. Pischel, *Gram.* §§ 188, 192, 202.

3. (*i*) *-th-*>*-dh-* : A Śaurasenism. Although attested to in *Hc.* 8.4.397.3 as *sabadhu*<*śapaham*, *kadhidu*<*kathitam*, it is rare in WAp. itself, and practically absent in SAp. and EAp.

(*ii*) *-th-*>*-h-* : WSAp. *ahava*, EAp. *ahabā*<*athavā*.

WSEAp. √*kaha*<√*kath-*, SAp. *mehuṇaya*<*maithunaka*.
EAp. *pūhabi*<*pṛthavī*.

(*iii*) *-th-*>*-ḍh-* : Cerebralisation. See §48 (5.b).

4. *-dh-*>*-h-* :
WAp. *ahuṭṭha-ham*<*adhastāt*, *sahiṭṭha*<*sadhṛṣṭa*, *Sohamma* <*Saudharma*.
SEAp. *bohi*<*bodhi*.
EAp. *sāhia*<*sādhita*, *nibboha*<*nirbodha*.

5. (*i*) *-ph-*>*-bh-* :
Although *Hc.* (and other grammarians also) regard this as a characteristic of Ap., it is as old as Mah. e.g. *Sebhālia* <*śephālika*, *Sibhā*<*śiphā* etc. See *Hc.* 8.1.236. Instances like *Sabhalaüṁ*<*Saphalakam* (*Hc.* 8.4.396.3) are rare in Ap. literature.

(*ii*) *-ph-*>*-h-* : As in Mahārāṣṭrī. See *Hc.* 8.11.236. *bimbī-hala*<°*phala*, *muttāhala*<*muktāphala* etc. (See also PISCHEL, *Gram.* §200.)

(*iii*) *-ph-* is retained when it forms the initial syllable of the 2nd member of a compound. e.g. EAp. *siri-phala*<*śrīphala*.

5. *-bh-*>*-h-* :
WSAp. *sahāu*, EAp. *sahāba*<*svabhāva*.
WSAp. *soha*<*śobhā*. EAp. √*nihāla*<*nibhālay-*, *guhira*.
SAp. *gahiraü*, WAp. *gahira*<*gabhīra*.

It will be observed that literary Ap. follows Pkt. rather than the rules of Pkt. grammarians regarding the voicing of intervocalic aspirated stops.

§ 58. There is little to add to the treatment of *-n-* as all *-n-* has been normalised to cerebral *-ṇ-* by most of the modern editors. The treatment of *-m-* is important since it is looked upon as a phonological characteristic of Ap. by Pk. grammarians (e.g. *Hc.* 8.4.397), and secondly it served as a distinguishing point in the early isoglosses.[74]

---

74 TURNER, *Position of Romani in Indo-Aryan* § 27

## TREATMENT OF -m-

A glance at the comparative Table § 58A will show that the treatment of -m- depended upon its position in the vocable. It is generally retained, and especially so when followed by a conjunct consonant, and in *tss.*, although the examples selected in the Table § 58A show that -m- was conserved in positions where it is (or ought to be according to Pk. grammarians) changed to -ṽ- in other works. The conservative tendency of retaining -m- persisted throughout the Ap. period in all regions. Thus we have such pairs e.g., *gāma : gāṽa, sāmala : sāṽala, pamāṇa : pavāna* and others.

The second stage in the history of -m- viz. its change to a nasalised and unnasalised -v- is also attested to from very early times e.g., WAp. *bhāvamı (bhrāmyāmı)* in Vk. 39, *javalā (yamalaka)* in PPr. EAp. *ṭhāba (sthāman), -b-* for -v- is always found in EAp., SAp. *pacchıṽa (paścıma) duṽa (ćruma), Govaī (Gomatī), Jauṇā (Yamunā).* A reference to Pk. grammarians (see PISCHEL's *Gram.* § 251) will show that this change is not limited to Ap., but is found in Pkts. like Mah. JM. and Amg. as well. The Ap. period marks only a greater vogue of this tendency. Thus -m- > -ṽ- cannot be regarded as the *differentia* between Pkts. and Ap.

Though it is understandable that ṽ preceded v in the chronology of the changes of -m-, Comp. Table § 58A does not support the theory as the only form in Vk. is an unnasalised -v- viz., *bhāvamı (\*bhrāmamı = bhrāmyāmi)*, while in 1200 A.D., we find a number of nasalised forms e.g., *kaṽalu (kamalam), bhaṽaru (bhramaraḥ), jaṽāiya (jāmātṛka).*

KKc. the last SAp. work of 1100 A.D., presents an interesting problem as we do not meet with forms with -m- > -ṽ- or -v-. The only case of -m- > -v- is the doubtful form *ravaṇṇa (ramaṇya* according to PISCHEL[75] but cf. Sk. *lāvaṇya* along with it). The other two forms are *Jauṇā < Jauṇā < Yamunā* and *cauryya < \*camarīka = camarī.* The main problem is why -m- > -ṽ- should be found in the works of Puṣpadanta and in Marathi under the Yādava dynasty (e.g., *bhaṽāra < bhramara, kuvaṛī < Pk.. kumari, cavarē < cāmara)* and why it should be absent in *KKc.*

The further stage in the development of -n- < -ṽ- or -v- viz. the loss of -v- leaving a hiatus or the use of a hiatus-tilger instead, are also noticed in Ap. from 1000 A.D., in WSAp. It is not found in EAp.

---

[75] *Grammatik* § 251.

We have more examples of unnasalized vowels *e.g.*, *dhūa* (*dhūma*), *indiya-gāa* (*indriya-grāma*) in WAp. than in SAp. where we have SEAp. *dhūma* (*ts.*) and *-gāma* and the vowels are nasalized *e.g.*, *saũhũ* (*sammukham*) : *samuhũ*, *kheuṁ* (*kṣema*): *kheva*. SAp. *kũyari*<*kūmārī* (as well as *kumari*) has a nasalized vocal glide for *-m-*.

Regionally the following treatments of *-m-* are seen.

| Cent. A.D. | WAp. | SAp. | EAp. |
|---|---|---|---|
| 10th | (1) *-v-*, at times *-ṽ-*. | *-ṽ-* sometimes *-v-*. | *-b-* |
| | (2) un-nasalized vowel. | Nasalized vowel, sometimes unnasalised one. | |
| 11th. | (1) un-nasalized vowel. | unnasalised vowel. | |

Paucity of WAp. literature in 1100 A.D., makes it unsafe to generalize but in spite of the mixed state of isoglosses in our period, 10th cent. A.D. provides us with some regional differences in the treatment of *-m-*.

§ 58A. *Treatment of Intervocalic -m-*

| Cent. A.D. | Region | Examples. |
|---|---|---|
| 500 | WAp. | 1) *-m-* retained : *sāmalo* (*śyāmalaḥ*), *bhamanteṁ* (√ *bhram*), *kuṁkuma* (*ts*), *pia-ama* (*priya-tamā*). |
| | | 2) *-m->-v-* : *bhāvami* (*bhrāmyāmi*). Only one instance *Mt.* 34. |
| 600-1000 | WAp. | 1) *-m-* retained : *gāmu* (*grāmaḥ*), *pamāṇu* (*pramāṇam*) *sāmalau* (*śyāmalaḥ*), Majority of cases. |
| | | 2) *-m->-v-*: *javalā* (*yamalaka*). |
| 700-1200 | EAp. | (1) *-m-* retained : *bhumayanti* (√ *bhram-*), *bhama-hu* (√ *bhram*), *gāma* (*grāma*), *-m-* generally conserved. |
| | | 2) *-m->-b-* : *ṭhāba* (*sthāman*), *nibesi* (*nimiṣya*). |
| 1000 | WAp. | 1) *-m-* conserved : *kunkuma* : (*ts.*), *pagāma* (*prakāmam*) *sumaṇasa* (*sumanas, sumaṇa*). |

| | | |
|---|---|---|
| | | 2) -*m*->-*ṽ*-, -*v*-: *pavāṇa* (*pramāṇa*), *dāvaṇu* (*dāman*), *ujjavaṇa* (*udyamana*,) *suvaṇa* (*sumara*, *sumanas*), *kunkuva* (phonetically °*vã-kunkuma*), *kuṽara* (*kumāra*).<br>3) -*m*->un-nasalised vowel : *dhūa* (*dhūma*), *indiyagāa* (*indriyagrāma*). |
| 1000 | SAp. | 1) -*m*- retained : *sāmisāla* (*svāmi-sāra* ?), *Sīrimai* (*Śrīmatī*), *Amayamai* (*Amṛtamatī*).<br>2) -*m*->-*ṽ*-, -*v*- : *pacchiṽa* (*paścima*), *duṽa* (*druma*), *jāmvāya* (*jāmāta*); *ārāva* (*arāma*), *bhāviṇī* (*bhāminī*) *Govaï* (*Gomatī*), *vāvaṇa* (*vāmana*).<br>3) -*m*->nasalised or unnasalised vowels : *saũhũ* (*sammukham*) also *samuhū*, *kheuṃ* (*kṣema*). *kheva* also, *Jauṇā* (*Yamunā*). |
| 1100 | WAp. | 1) -*m*- retained : *ṇāma-hu* (*nāman*-), *sāmala* (*śyāmala*) *bhamaï* (*bhramati*), *samuha* (*samukha*).<br>2) -*m*->-a vowel : *ṇāu* (*nāma*), Only 1 form in *Mt*. |
| | SAp. | 1) -*m*- retained : *Veyamaï* (*Vegamatī*), *Amiyavega* (*Amitavega*) *sāmi-sāla* (*svāmi-sāra*), *samāhi*-(*samādhi*).,<br>2) -*m*-> -*v*->unnasalised vowel : Rare. *Jauṇā* (*Yamunā*), *caüriya* (*camarī*) and the doubtful form *ravaṇṇa* (**ramaṇya*=*ramaṇīya*) but cf. Sk. *lāvaṇya*. Only 3 forms, out of which the first two are -*m*->-a vowel-. |
| 1200 | WAp. | 1) -*m*- retained: *sāmala* (*śyāmala*), *kamala* (*ts*), *pamāṇa* (*pramāṇa*), *kumārī* (*ts*,), *bhamaru* (*bhramaraḥ*), *Rāma-ha* (*Rāma*-); *majjhima* (*madhyama*), *sāmi-sala* (*svāmin*.).<br>2) -*m*->-*ṽ*-, -*v*- : *asavaṇṇa* (*asāmānya*), *navakāra* (*namaskāra*), *kaṽalu* (*kamalam*), *bhaṽaru* (*bhramaraḥ*, *jaṽāiya* (*jāmātṛka*), *dāvaṇa* (*dāman*-). |

### §58 B. Treatment of Intervocalic -*m*-

| A.D. | WAp. | SAp. | EAp. |
|---|---|---|---|
| 500 ? | 1) -*m*- retained<br>2) -*m*->-*v*- | | |

| | | | |
|---|---|---|---|
| 600-1000 | 1) *-m-* retained<br>*-m-*>*-v-* (rare) | .. | .. |
| 700-1200 | .. | .. | 1)*-m-* generally conserved.<br>2) *-m-*>*-b-* |
| 1000 | 1) *-m-* conserved<br>2) *-m-*>*-ṽ-*, *-v-*<br>3) *-m-*>-vowel (unnasalised) | 1) *-m-* retained.<br>2) *-m-*>*-ṽ-*, *-v-*.<br>3) *-m-*>nasalised or unnasalised vowel. | |
| 1100 | 1) *-m-* retained<br>2) *-m-*>a vowel | 1) *-m-* conserved.<br>2) *-m-*>*-v-* rare.<br>3) *-m-*>a vowel. Not frequently. | |
| 1200 | 1) *-m-* retained<br>2) *-m*>*-ṽ-*, *-v-* | | |

§59. The treatment of other intervocalic consonants in Ap. is practically the same as in other Pkts. In the treatment of sibilants, we find *-ś-* and *-s-* for OIA *-ś-*, *-ṣ-*, *-s-*, in EAp. There the *-s-* influence is probably external, and is more predominant in later works e.g., *DKs.* and the *Ḍākārṇavatantra.*

*-ś-* remains : EAp. *pabeśa*<*praveśa*, *deśa*(*ts*), *ubeśa*<*upadeśa.*
*-ṣ-*>*-ś-*: EAp. *beśa* (*veṣa*), *biśaya* (*viṣaya*).

In WSAp. we have uniformly *-s-* for *-ś-*, *-ṣ-*, and *-s-*. Even in EAp. we find *-s-*<*-ś-*, *-ṣ-*.

*-ś-*>*-s-* : EAp. *āsa*<*āśā.*
*-ṣ-*>*-s-* : EAp. *sosa*<*śoṣa*, *bisaya*<*viṣaya.*

Sibilants>*-ha* :

WSEAp. *eha*<*eṣaḥ* WSAp. *daha*<*daśan.*
WAp. *pāhaṇa*<*pāṣāṇa.*

## CONSONANTS IN CONTACT

§60. The changes of OIA consonant clusters to MIA have been ably discussed by BLOCH[76] and CHATTERJI[77] in general and by GEIGER and PISCHEL with reference to Pali and Prakrits. Ap. does

76 *L'indo-aryen*, pp. 79-90.
77 *Indo-Aryan and Hindi*, pp. 79-83.

not differ much from Pkts. in its treatment of conjunct consonants. The treatments of the following consonant clusters, however, deserve attention:

OIA *kṣ*, *tv*, *dv*, *ṣṇ*, *sm*, consonant+*r*.

The importance of these clusters lies in the fact that these were the crucial points in the isoglossal distinctions in olden times and their development in our period is linguistically interesting.

### TREATMENT OF OIA *kṣ*.

§61. A chrono-regional study of the treatment of OIA *kṣ* (see Comp. Table § 61A leads us to the following conclusions :

(1) In EAp. OIA *kṣ* whether initial or non-initial, was uniformly changed into -*kh*- and -*kkh*-. There is not a single exception to this rule.

(2) WAp. was originally *kṣ*>*kh* dialect. In *Vk*. *kṣ* is always changed to *kh*- or -*kkh*- according to its initial or non-initial position. In 600 A.D. *kṣ*>*ch* forms began to appear in *PPr*. Thus initially *kṣ*->*ch* is found in *chāra*>*kṣāra* in *PPr*. 2.90, but that is exceptional, the normal treatment being *kṣ*->*kh*- as we find it in *khattiu*<*kṣatriya*, *khavaṇau* <*kṣapaṇakaḥ* and many other forms. Similarly intervocalic -*kṣ*->-*kh*- is the general development. -*kṣ*->-*ch*- as in *acchi* (*akṣi*), *vaccha* (*vṛkṣa*) and a few more forms mark the beginning of a new tendency if they be not loan-words from SAp.

This tendency was very slowly gaining popularity in WAp. Thus, excluding the repetitions, we find only two forms with initial *kṣ*->*ch*- in *Sdd*. viz., *chaṇasasi*<*kṣaṇa-śasi* (*Sdd*. 177), and *chijjau*<*kṣīyatām* (*Sdd*135), but here too the form is traceable to√*chid*- as well, as the line in question is

*mohu ṇu chijjau dubbalau hoi iyaru parivāru* *Sdd*. 135

There is no *kṣ*->*ch*- in *Pd*. In the big WAp. work of the 10th cent. A.D., *BhK*., there are only two *ks*->*ch*- forms viz., *chaṇa*<*kṣaṇa*- and *chitta* <*kṣetra*, √*chuha*=√*kṣip* is a *dhātvādeśa* in *Hc*. 8.4.143, and is not its linguistic equation as is clearly indicated by JACOBI (*Glossar* to *BhK*. p. 150). So initially *kṣ*->*kh*- is the normal rule.

In its non-initial position *kṣ*->-*ch*- is more in use, although it was a slow process in the 10th cent. In *Pd*., in 933 A.D., *picchaï* (*prekṣ*-) and *acchaïta* (*ā-kṣi*) are the only two examples of this. In *Sdd*. we have only three forms of this. It is only in *BhK*. that we get some more instances of *-kṣ->-ch-*. It is thus clear that *-kṣ->-ch-* forms whether borrowals or genuine were slowly on the increase in 1000 A.D.

In 1100 A.D., in the anthology of Ap. verses in the *Sarasvatī-kaṇṭhābharaṇa*, *khittaa* (*kṣiptaka*) appears twice and it is the only vocable with *kṣ->kh-*, and we have no example of *kṣ->ch-*. Intervocalically *-kṣ->-cch-* is found in the majority of cases, *pekkhami* (**prekṣyāmi*) is the only instance of *-kṣ->-kkh-*. The treatment of *kṣ* in these verses illustrates how *-kṣ>-cch-* went on increasing in WAp. in 1100 A.D. As we do not know the sources of these verses, we cannot infer anything regarding the venue of these from this small selection of *dohās*.

In 1200 A.D., we find *kṣ>kh* initially and intervocalically as usual. There are a few cases of initial *kṣ->ch-*. We have only two in *Sc.*, viz., *churiya* (°*kṣurikā*) and *chuha* (*kṣudhā*). Though there are a few more examples of *-kṣ->-cch-*, WAp. prefers *-kṣ->-kkh-* treatment rather than the *-cch-* one.

It may now be safely asserted that in spite of mutual borrowings, standardisation as a literary dialect, and other levelling factors, the treatment of OIA *kṣ* is more inclined to *kh-* or *-kkh-* rather than to *ch-* or *-cch-* in WAp. This fact is in consonance with TURNER's findings regarding old isoglosses noted in *Position of Romani in Indo-Aryan*, §27.

When we come to SAp., we have a mixed state of affairs in the changes of *-kṣ-* in the non-initial position, even from the 10th cent. A.D. The same confusion is found in *KKc.* But initially *kṣ->ch-* is quite frequent in the works of Puṣpadanta, but in *KKc.* the proportion between *kh->ch-* treatments is 8:3. In the early MIA isoglosses *kṣ>ch* was the peculiarity of the south-west. The discussion of the *kṣ>kh, ch* problem in Pkts. as found in PISCHEL's *Grammatik* §§318-21 does not clarify the position. That WAp. and SAp. show a mixture of *kh-*, *ch* forms is certain. But just as WAp. is mainly based on a *kṣ>kh* dialect, SAp. may be said to be a *kṣ>ch* dialect to a less extent. We find a similar state in Marathi,[78] and in spite of the mixture of *kh* forms in Puṣpadanta and Kanakāmara, SAp. is more or less a literary form of *ch-* dialect. *kṣ->jh-*. as in SAp. *jhīṇa* (*kṣīṇa*) has correspondence in Pkts. For example see PISCHEL, *Gram.* §326 also √*jhara*<√*kṣar* quoted therein. In NIA Ap. *jh-* has been conserved as *jh-* e.g., M. *jharaṇẽ*<√*jhara* in Ap. *jhijṇẽ*< Ap. *jhijja-*. For more BLOCH, *FLM* §107.

78 BLOCH, *FLM.* § 104.

## §61A. Treatment of OIA *kṣ*

| Cent. | Region | Examples |
|---|---|---|
| 500 ? | WAp. | a) Initially : *khuhia* (*kṣubhita*). |
| | | b) Non-Initially : *pekkhu* (**pṛekṣa*), *sikkhia* (*śikṣita*), *lakkhijjai* (*lakṣyate*), *ā-akkhiu* (**ā-cakṣitam*). |
| 600-1000 | WAp. | a) 1. *khirai* (*kṣarati*), *khattiu* (*kṣatriyaḥ*), *khavaṇau* (*kṣapaṇakaḥ*). |
| | | 2. *chāra* (*kṣāra*). *kṣ->kh-* the normal treatment. |
| | | b) 1. *rukkha* (**rukṣa*), *pekkha*, *pikkha* (*prekṣ-*), *viyakkaṇu* (*vicakṣaṇaḥ*), *lakkhana-* (*lakṣaṇa*) |
| | | 2. *acchi* (*akṣi*), *vaccha* (*vṛkṣa*), √*accha* √(**ā-kṣi-*). *-kṣ->* *-kkh-* the normal treatment. |
| 700-1200 | EAp. | a) *khaṇa* (*kṣaṇa*), *khiti* (*kṣiti*), *khabaṇa* (*kṣapaṇaka*), *khetta* (*kṣetra*). |
| | | b) *takkhaṇe* (*tatkṣaṇe*), *akkhara* (*akṣara*), *akkhoha* (*akṣobha*), *lakkhai* (*lakṣate*) also *lakkha* (*lakṣya*). |
| 1000 | WAp. | a) 1. *kṣ->kh-*: *khoja* (*kṣoda*), *khāra* (*kṣāra*), *khettī* (*kṣetritā*), *khoï* (*kṣapayitvā*), *khayara* (*khadira*), *khuhiya* (*kṣubhita*), *ghitta*<**khitta*<*kṣipta* (?). |
| | | 2. *kṣ->ch-*: *chaṇa-* (*kṣaṇa-* ?), *chijjaü* (*kṣīyatām*), nil in *Pd.* *chitta* (*kṣetra*). Only 2 in *Bh.K.* repetitions excluded. |
| | | b) 1. *-kṣ->-kkh-*: *mokkha* (*mokṣa*), *rukkhaḍa* (**rukṣa-*), *rakkha-hu* (*rakṣ-*), *-kkh->-kh->-h-* in *rahanti* (*rakṣ-*) *Sdd.* 138.; *mokkha- ha* (*mokṣa-*), *akkharaḍa* (*akṣara-*) *aṇu--pehā* (*anuprekṣā*). *-kṣ->-h-* as above. *abhakkha* (*abhakṣya*), *akkhara-* (*akṣara*). |
| | | 2. *-kṣ->cch-*: Only 3 in *Sdd.* *picchai* (*prekṣate*), *-acchau* (*ā-kṣi*), *Lacchi* (*Lakṣmī*). 2 in *Pd.* *picchaï* (*prekṣ-*), *acchanta* (*ā-kṣi*). Many more in *BhK.* e.g., *-acchi* (*-akṣi*), *Lacchi* (*Lakṣmī*), *vacchayala* (**vakṣa-tala=vakṣassthala*), *saccha* (*sākṣāt*), *ucchu* (*ikṣu*). |

1000 SAp. a) 1. *kṣ-> kh-*: *khīriṁ* (*kṣīreṇa*), *khundivi* (*kṣud-*)

2. *kṣ-> ch-*: *chaṇa-* (*kṣaṇa-*), *chohiya* (*kṣobhita*) *choha* (*kṣobha*), *-choṇi* (*-kṣoṇi*) more frequent than *kṣ-> kh-*.

3. *kṣ->jh-*: *jhīṇa* (*kṣīna*), *jhjjanta* (*kṣi-*), √*jhara* (*kṣar*).

b) *-kṣ-> -kkh-* more popular than *-kṣ- >-cch-*. *akkhāḍaya* (*akṣavāṭa*), *lekkhahi* (*lakṣ-*), *nirikkha* (**nirīkṣa=cora*), *duhikkha* (*durbhikṣa*), *dakkhavahi* (**dṛkṣ-*), *Lakkhaṇa* (*Lakṣmaṇa*), *saṁkhohaṇikā* (*saṁkṣobhaṇikā*); *-kṣ- -cch-*: *kaccha* (*kakṣā*), *Lacchi* (*Lakṣmī*), *ucchu* (*ikṣu*), *manchuḍu* (*maṅkṣu*), *ucchala*—(*ut-*kṣal-*).

1100 WAp. a) *kṣ->kh-*: *khittaa* (*kṣiptaka*), *khaṇa* (*kṣaṇa-*)

b) 1. *-kṣ- >-cch*: *-accha* (*-akṣa*) as in *-kaḍaccha-* (*-kaṭākṣā*), *maachi* (*mṛgākṣī*), *tirriccha* (*tiryakṣa*). *saricchu* (*sadṛkṣa*), *Mahālacchihī* (*Mahālakṣmī*),- *vicchuhiai* (*vi-kṣubh-*).

2. *-kṣ- >-kkh-* : Only 1 form viz., *pekkhami* (**prekṣyāmi*).

1100 SAp. a) *kṣ-> kh-*: 8 forms excluding repetition. e.g., *khaṇaddha* (*kṣaṇārdha*), *khīṇa* (*kṣīṇa*), *khetta* (*kṣetra*).

2. Only 3 forms : *chaṇa-* (*kṣaṇa-*), *churia* (*kṣurikā*), *chuha-taṇha* (*kṣudhā-tṛṣṇā*).

b) 1. *-kṣ->-kkh-*: *rakkhavāla* (*rakṣāpāla*), *lakkhārasa* (*lākṣā-*), *akkhara* (*akṣara*), *bhukkhā* (*bhukṣā*).

2. *-kṣ->-cch-* : *kucchi* (*kukṣi*), *Lacchi* (*Lakṣmī*), *vicchoya* (*vikṣobbha*).

1200 WAp. a) 1. *kṣ->kh-*: *khitta* (*kṣetra*), *khivai* (*kṣipati*) *khaṇeṇa* (*kṣaṇa-*), *khaya-* (*kṣaya-*), *khavaga* (*kṣapaka*).

2. *kṣ-> ch-* : Only 2 forms in *Sc.* viz., *churiya* (*kṣurikā*), *chuha* (*kṣudhā*); *chāra* (*kṣāra*) Very few forms.

b) *-kṣ->-kkh-* : *rakkha* (*rakṣā*), *Lakkhaṇa* (*lakṣaṇa*), *ahikaṅkhira* (*abhikāṅkṣin*), *rakkhejjahu* (*rakṣ-*), *lakkhehiṁ* (*lakṣa-*) *mokkha*, *mukkha* (*mokṣa*), *cukkha* (**cokṣa*), *akkha-* (*akṣa-*).

*-kṣ->-cch-* : *acchi* (*akṣi*), *icchu* (*ikṣu*), *Lacchi* (*Lakṣmī*), *acchōḍiya* (*ākṣoḍita*).

## § 61.B. Treatment of OIA *kṣ*.

| A.D. | WAp. | SAp. | EAp. |
|---|---|---|---|
| 500 ? | a) Initially : *kh-*<br>b) Non-initially : *-kkh-* | | |
| 600-1000 | a) Initially :<br>(1) *kh-* (normally)<br>(2) *ch-* (rare).<br>b) Non-initially :<br>(1) *-kkh-* (Normally)<br>(2) *-cch-* not frequently. | | |
| 700-1200 | .... | a) Initially : *kh-*<br>b) non-initially : *-kkh-* | |
| 1000 | a) Initially : (1) *kh-*<br>(2) *ch-* still rarely.<br>b) Non-initially :<br>(1) *-kkh-*<br>(2) sometimes *-kkh*>*kh-* >*-h-*<br>(3) *-cch-* | a) Initially : (1) *kh-*<br>(2) *ch-* more frequent than *kh-*.<br>(3) *jh-*<br>b) Non-initially:<br>(1) *-kkh-* more popular than *-cch-*.<br>(2) *-cch-* | |
| 1100 | a) Initially : *kh-*<br>b) Non-initially :<br>(1) *-cch-* normally<br>(2) *-kkh-* only 1 form | a) Initially : (1) *kh*<br>(2) *ch-* only 3 forms.<br>b) Non-initially :<br>(1) *-kkh-*<br>(2) *-cch-* | |

| | | |
|---|---|---|
| 1200 | | a) Initially : (1) *kh-* (2) *ch-* few forms. b) Non-initially (1) *-kkh-* (2) *-cch-* |

### Groups of Dental+*v*

#### Treatment of *tv*

§ 62. In the early isoglosses OIA *tv* was changed to *tt* in the Southwest, *pp* in the centre, *pp* (?) in the East and *tt* (?) in the South. This leads us to expect *tv*>*pp* in WAp., *tv*<*tt* in SEAp. The facts, however, are as follows :

(1) EAp. changes OIA *tv* to *tu-* initially and *-tt-* intervocalically.

(2) In WAp. in 500 A.D. *tv-*>*p-* is the only change in the initial position, and *-v-* i.e.,*-eviṇu*<*-tvīnam* indicates the same treatment (*-tv-*>*-pp-*>*-p-*>*-v-*). It is from 600 A.D. that the *tv-*>*-t-* and *-tv-*>*-tt-*>*-cc-* changes begin to take place initially and intervocalically, and from the 10th cent. A.D., there is a free admixture of *-tt-* and *-pp-* as well as *t-* and *p-* treatments in WAp. The same is found in the subsequent centuries, both in initial and non-initial *tv*.

(3) In SAp. from the very beginning, we find that OIA *-tv-*> *tu-*, *p-*, and *-tv-*>*-tt-*, *-pp-* are freely mixed together. The same is the case in *KKc* in 1100 A.D.

It is probable that most of the forms with initial *tv-* being 2nd person pronouns, and *-tv-* forms being Absolutives and abstract nouns already in vogue in the WSAp. tract (as Ap. was a literary *lingua franca* in this contiguous region) such mixture was inevitable, although the original tendency was evident in early WAp. works. EAp. however, preserves its special characteristic.

### § 62A. Treatment of OIA *tv*.

| Cent A.D. | Region | Examples |
|---|---|---|
| 500 ? | WAp. | a) Initially : *tv-*>*p-*: for examples e.g., *paĩ* (**tvayam*= *tvam*) see 2nd p. Pronoun §120. |

b) Non-initially : *-tvīnam*>(*e*)*viṇu*. For exs. e.g., *rundheviṇu* (*rundh-tvīnam*) see Absolutives § 152.

600-100 WAp. a) *tv-*>*tu-*: For exs. s.e.g., *tuhum*(*tvam*) see 2nd p. Pron. § 120.

b) 1. *-tv-*>*-v-* : As in *-evi*, *-eviṇu* from Vedic *-tvī*, *-tvīnam*. For ex. see Absoluties § 152.

2. *-tv-*>*-tt-* *-cc-* e.g., *taccu* (*tatvam*).

700-1200 EAp. a) *tv-*>*tu-*: e.g., *tuhu* (*tvam*) for more see 2nd p. Pron. § 120.

b) *-tv-*>*-tt-* e.g., *-tta*<*-tva*, *-ttaṇa*<*-tvana* of Abstract nouns see Ch. IV. *tatta* (*tatva*).

1000 WAp. a) 1. *tv-*>*tu-*: See 2nd p. Pron. § 120. for ex. see √*tura* (*tvar-*)

2. *-tv-*<*p-* : Forms e.g., *paī* (*tva-yā* etc.) see 2nd p. p. Pron. § 120.

b) *-tv-*>*-tt-* e.g., *-tta* (*-tva*), *-ttaṇa* (*-tvana*) of Abstract nouns. See Ch. IV. *mitthettiya* (*mithyātva*).

2. *-tv-*>*-pp-* or *-p-* e.g., *-eppi*, *-ppi* (*-tvī*), *eppiṇu* *-ppiṇu* (*-tvīnam*). For exs. see Absolutives § 152.
3. *-tv-*>*-tt*>*-cc* : *taccu* (*tatvam*).

1000 SAp. a) 1. *tv-*>*tu-*: For exs. see 2nd p. Pronoun § 120.
2. *tv-*>*p-*: for exs. see 2nd p. Pron. § 120.

b) 1. *tv-*>*tt-* e.g. Suffixes of Abstract nouns *-tta* (*-tva*), *-ttaṇa* (*-tvana*).

2. *-tv*>*-pp-*: Suffixes of Abstract nouns e.g., *-ppa* <*-tva*, *-ppaṇa*<*-ytvana*.

1100 WAp. a) *tv-*>*p-*: e.g. *paī* (*tvayā*) see 2nd p. Pron. § 120.

b) 1. *-tv-*>*-tt-* : e.g., *visittī* (*viśitvī*) see Absolutives § 152.

2. *-tv-*>*-p-*>*-v-* : e.g. *suṇivi* (**śruṇitvī*) see §152.

SAp. a) *tv-*>*tu-*: e.g. *tuhuṁ* (*tvam*). see 2nd p. Pron. § 120, *turia*, *turanta* (*tvar-*).

*tv-*>*p-* : See 2nd p. Pron. § 120.

b) 1. *-tv->-tt-* : *caccara-vanta* (*catvara-*), <*-tt-* of Abstract Noun see Ch. IV.

2. *-tv->-v-* : *-ivi, -evi, -eviṇu* <*-tvī, -tvīnam* of Absolutives §152.

1200 WAp. a) 1. *tv->tu-* : see 2nd p. Pron. §120. *turiu* (*tvaritam*), *turanta* (*tvar-*).

2 *tv->ta-, pa-* : see 2nd p. sg. §120.

b) 1. *-tv->-pp-* : *-ppi, -ppiṇu -eppi, -eppiṇu*<*-tvī, -tvīnam* of the Absolutive. *-ppaṇa* <*-tvana* of Abstract Nouns.

2. *-tv->-pp-, -p-*<*-v-*: *-ivi, -evi, -eviṇu*<*-tvī -tvīnam*. See Absolutives §152.

3. *-tv->-tt-*: *-ttaṇa,*<*tvana, -tta-*<*-tva* of Abstract nouns. *tatta* (*tatva*).

## §62B. Treatment of OIA *tv*.

| A.D. | WAp. | SAp. | EAp. |
|---|---|---|---|
| 500 ? | a) Initially : *p-*<br>b) Non-initially : *-v-* | .... | .. |
| 600-1000 | a) Initially: *tu-*<br>b) Non-initially<br>(1) *-v-*<br>(2) *-tt->-cc-*. | .... | .. |
| 700-1200 | .... | | a) Initially : *tu-*<br>b) Non-initially : *-tt-* |
| 1000 | a) Initially : (1) *tu-*<br>(2) *p-*<br>b) Non-initially :<br>(1) *-tt-*<br>(2) *-pp-, -p-*<br>(2) *-tt->-cc-*, | a) Initially : (1) *tu-*<br>(2) *p-*<br>b) Non-initially :<br>(1) *-tt-*<br>(2) *-pp-* | |
| 1100 | a) Initially : *p-* | a) Initially : (1) *tu-*<br>(2) *p-* | |

| | | |
|---|---|---|
| | b) Non-initially : | b) Non-initially : |
| | (1) *-tt-* | (1) *-tt-* sometimes *-tt->-cc-* |
| | (2) *-p->-v-* | (2) *-v-* |
| 1200 | a) Initially : (1) *tu-*, (2, 3) *ta-*, *pa-* | |
| | b) Non-initially : (1) *-pp-*, (2) *-p->-v-* (3) *-tt-* | |

§63. The treatment of OIA *dv* shows a mixture of *dv* and *bb* forms from the very beginning of our period both initially and intervocalically. *Vk* is the only Ap. work showing purely *-vv-* (*-bb-*) treatment. The reason of this admixture from 600 A.D. is most probably due to the fact that the majority of *dv-* forms being numerals have spread beyond their provinces, or have been freely borrowed in the interprovincial communication from very old times. This was the state before Ap. period, and it is due to the paucity of Ap. material in 500 A.D. that adherence to the older phonological tendency is seen.

The old isoglossal line of demarcation appears to have been lost in Ap. from 600 A.D. onwards and WSEAp. between 600 A.D. to 1200 A.D. shows a free inter-borrowing among the provinces regarding the changes of *dd* and *bb*.

## §63A. Treatment of OIA *dv*.

| Cent A.D. | Region | Examples |
|---|---|---|
| 500 ? | WAp. | a) Initial : nil. |
| | | b) Non-initial : *-dv->-vv-* : *uvvellia* (*udvelita*), *uvvellira* (*ud-vel—*) |
| 600-1000 | WAp. | a) 1. *dv->d-* : *dēsu* (*dveṣa*), *do-hĩ* (*dva--yoḥ*). |
| | | 2. *dv->b-* : *bĩhi* (*dvayoḥ*), *be* (*dvau*). |
| | | b) *uvvasu* (*udvasaḥ*) *PPr.* 1.44. |
| 700- | EAp. | a) 1. *dv->du-*: *duāra* (*dvāra*) only 1 form in *DKK*. 22. Nil in *DKS*. |

2. *dv->b-: beṇṇi, benna (dvi-), biṇṇa (dve), beṇima dvidhā.*

b) *-dv->-d-* : *adaa* (*advaya*) only 1 form in *DKS*. 100

1000 WAp. a) 1. *dv->d-: do, dui, duṇṇi* (*dvi*), *duviha* (*dvividha*).

2. *dv->b-* : *bāraha* (*dvādaśa*), *biyaya, bidia* (*dvitīya*), *bihim* (*dvābhyām*).

3. *dv->v-* : *ve-* (*dvi-*), *vāra* (*vāra*), *vijjaya* (*dvitīyaka*).

b) *-dv->-vv-*: *uvveva* (*udvega*), *uvvali* (**udvali=udvartana*)

1000 SAp. a) 1. *dv->-d-* : *Dīvāyaṇa* (*Dvīpāyana*), *Dujaḍa* (*Dvijaṭa*), *deha* (*dvaidha*), *dohāviya*(*=dvidhākṛta*), *dohāīhuya* (*dvibhāgī bhāūta*).

2. *dv->b-* : *Bārāvaipura* (*Dvārāvatī-pura*), *bāvīsa* (*dvāviṁśat*) and numerals with *dvi-* as the first part of compounds.

b) 1. *dv->-dd-* : *addaiyavāya* (*advaitavāda*). *caüddāra* (*catur-dvāra*).

2. *-dv->-vv-* : *uvvāra* (*udvāra-ṇa*), *uvvevira* (*ud-vep-*).

3. *-dv->-u-* -: *viusa* (*vidvas-* but rather<**viduṣa*).

1100 WAp. a) *dv->d-* : *doṇha* (*dvayoḥ*) only 1 viz. *Mt*. 16.

b) *-dv->-vv-* : *viuvviṭṭhi* (*vyudviṣṭa*)- *Mt*. 19 only one form.

1100 SAp. a) *dv->d-* : *doṇṇi* (*dvau*), *dovālasa* (*dvādaśa*). *dv->b-* : *bāraha* (*dvādaśa*) -*KKc* 5.10.1 only one form.

b) *-dv->-d-* : *Jambu-dīva* (*Jambu-dvīpa*) but this is really initial *dv-*.

1200 WAp. a) *dv->d-* : *dāra* (*dvāra*), *duha* (*dvidhā*), *do* (*dvi*) *duguṇa* (*dvi-guṇa*).

2. *dv->v-* : *vāra* (*dvāra*).

3. *dv->b-* : *be, behiṁ* (*dvi-*).

b) 1. *uvvasiya* (*udvasita*), *uvvigga* (*udvigna*), *uvveya* (*udvega*).

2. *viusa* (*vidvas*).

### §63B. Treatment of OIA *dv*.

| A.D. | WAp. | SAp. | EAp. |
|---|---|---|---|
| 500 ? | a) Initially : nil<br>b) Non-initially : *-vv-* | ....<br>.... | ..<br>.. |
| 600-1000 | a) Initially : (1) *d-*<br>(2) *b-*<br>b) Non-initially : *-vv-* | .... | .. |
| 700-1200 | .... | .... | (*a*) Initially :<br>1) *du-* only one form in *DKK*.<br>2) *b-*<br>(b) Non-initially.<br>1) *-d-* only one form in *DKs*. (1). |
| 1000 | 1) Initially : (1) *d-*<br>(2) *b-*<br>(3) *v-*<br>b) Non-initially : *-vv-* | (2) Initially : (1) *d-*<br>(2) *b-*<br>(b) Non-initially : (1) *-dd-*<br>(2) *-vv-*<br>(3) *-u-* (?) | |
| 1100 | a) Initially : *d-*<br>b) Non-initially : *-vv-*<br>Both (a) (b) rare. | (a) Initially : (1) *d-*<br>(2) *b-* only 1 form<br>(b) Non-initially : *-d-* | |
| 1200 | a) Initially : (1) *d-*<br>(2) *v-*<br>(3) *b-*<br>b) Non-initially : (1) *-vv-*<br>(2) *-u-* | | |

### Groups with *r*

§64. According to Pk. Grammarians *r* as a second member of consonant clusters is optionally retained. (*Cd.* 3.37, *NS.* on Rudraṭa's *Kāvyālaṅkāra* 2.12, *Pu.* 17.15 and 18.3 for Vrācada Ap., *Hc.* 8.4.398 and examples on *Hc.* 8.4.329, *Tr.* 3.3.5 followed by *Sh.* and *Ld.*, *Ki* 5.2.5, 16, *Mk.* 17.4 and 18.4 for Vrācaḍa Ap.). The illustrations probably express the real state of affairs in spoken Ap. as *tss.* with *r* as the second member are used even in the oldest stage of NIA and Dravidian literature contemporaneous with the Ap. works. Thus *grāmo* (*grāma*), *vaghro* (*vyāghra*) in *Cd.*, *bhrāyara* (*bhrātar*), *vaghreṇa* (*vyāghreṇa*) in *NS.*, *priyeṇa* (*priya-*) in *Hc.* etc., show how *tss.* were used in spoken Ap. with an admixture of Pk. influence on the vocable.

In Ap. literature we do possess such clusters e.g., tss. like *prāṇa*, *priya*, pro-*ts.* forms e.g., *praṁgaṇa*<*prāṅgaṇa*, *praāvadi*<*prajāpati*, *prāu*, *prāiva*<*prāyaḥ*, *dhruvu*<*dhruvaṁ* and -*r* conjuncts like *dhrum*, *tram*, *jrum*, etc. These forms are enough to show that -*r* conjuncts were in existence in our period, although the general tendency is towards assimilation due to the stylisation in literature. Exceptional as these forms are in the mass of Ap. literature, they show that it was nearer to the spoken idiom than we are usually apt to regard it.

The following examples show that the treatment of conjuncts with -*r* as the second member of the group in Ap., is practically the same as in literary Pkts.[78]

*kr-*>*k-*, *kh-* : WSAp. √*kanda*<*kranda-*, √*kheḍḍa*, √*khella*, *khilla* <√*krīḍ-*.

*-kr-*>*-kk-* : WSAp. *cakka* (*cakra*).

WAp. *ahakkamiṇa* (*yathā krameṇa*)

*-kr-*>*ṁk-* : WSAp. *vaṁka*<*vakra*.

*gr-*>*g-* : WSAp. *gāma*<*grāma*, *gimbha*<*grīṣma*

*-gr-*>*-gg-*, *-g-* : WSAp. *agga*<*agra*, EAp. *sāmaggi*<*sāmagrī*

WAp. *asagāha*<*asad-grāha*.

*ghr-*>*gh-* : SAp. *ghāṇa*<*ghrāṇa*.

*-ghr-*>*-ggh-* : WAp. *agghāiya*<*āghrāta*.

*-ṁgh-* : EAp. *jiṁghaï* (*jighrati*)

*ḍr-*>*-ḍ-* : SAp. *puṁḍucchu*<*puṇḍra*+*ikṣu*.

For the treatment of *tr*, *dr*, *dhr* see § 47(4).

*pr-*>*p-*: WAp. *pāvami*<**prāpami*, *pesu*<*praveśa*.

SAp. *païṭṭha*<*praviṣṭa*, EAp. *pabiṇa*<*pravīṇa*.

*-pr-*>*-pp-* : WAp. *vippa*<*vipra*, SAp. *sippā*<*śi* (*kṣi*)*prā*.

*br-*>*b-* : SWAp. *Bambhu* (*Brahman*), E. *Bamha*, *Bamhaṇa* (*Brāhmaṇa*).

---

78 For the treatment of -*r* clusters in Pkts. see Pischel *Grammatik*, §§ 287-95.

*bhr->bh-*: WSAp. *bhamei, bhamijjaï*<√*bhram-*,
EAp. √*bhumaya-*<√*bhram.*
*-bhr->-bbh-*: WAp. *abbha*<*abhra.*
*-mr->-mb-*, *-mv-* See §67 (1).
*vr->v-*: WAp. *vajjaï*<*vrajati*, SAp. *vaya*<*vrata.*
*śr->s-* : WSAp.√*suṇu*<√*śru-ṇu, SAp. soṇiyāhiṁ* (*śroṇyoḥ*)
*-śr->ṁs*: WSAp. *aṁsuya*, °*va*<*aśru.*
*-sr->-ṁs-*: WAp. *cauraṁsa*<*caturasra.*

These changes, being common to Pkts. and Ap., need not be discussed.

## GROUPS WITH SIBILANT + NASAL

§65. Out of the OIA clusters of sibilant + nasal only *-ṣṇ* and *sm* deserve attention. As in Pkts., in Ap. also, such groups result in *h*+ nasal, and consequent Metathesis reducing them to nasal+*h*. But the regional differences in the treatment of *-ṣṇ-* are too obvious to be ignored (especially in Proper names). Thus *-ṣṇ-* is changed to *-ṭṭh-* in SAP. e.g., *Viṭṭhu* (*Viṣṇu*), *-Viṭṭhi* (*-Vṛṣṇi*). *Biṭṭhu* (*Viṣṇu*) is the only form (*DKS.* 52) in EAp., and may be a loan-word there. The normal treatment of *-ṣṇ-* is *-ṇh-* in WEAp. *tiṭṭha*<*tṛṣṇā* in *PPr.* 2.132 is properly **tṛṣṭā* the corresponding form in SAp. being *tiṭṭhi*<**tṛṣṭi* in 1000 A.D. In SAp. also, the majority of forms (even *nomina propria*) shows *-ṣṇ-* >*-ṇh-* treatment. e.g., WSAp. *Kaṇha*<*Kṛṣṇa*, EAp. *Kāṇha*, WSAp. *taṇhā* (*tṛṣṇā*) etc.

### (ii) *sm* :

a) Initial *sm->s-*: WSAp.√*sara*<*smar* as in *sarevvaü*<*smartavyaḥ sarivi* (*smṛtvā*), *sara-*<*smara* ; *visārijjaï*<*vismāryate*, EAp. *bi-sariaa*<*vi-smṛtaka.*

In the last two examples, *sm* is initial in the second member of the compound.

b) Non-initial *-sm-*: Plur. form of 1st person pron. e.g., *amha, amhaĩ, amhāṇaṁ*<OIA **asma-*. For this see 1st P. Pron. §119 A.

c) *-sm->-h-*

Loc. sg. *-hiṁ*<*-smin*, also found as *-hĩ*, *-hi* as in *jahĩ* (*yasmin*), *kahĩ* (*kasmin*) etc., through normal MIA *-mhi-*.

d) Insertion of the plosive *-b-* between *-m* and *h-* resulting from *-sm-*. See §67.

In *Jc.* 1.13.8 *bhappa-ra*<*bhasman-* is an exceptional form showing *-sm->-pp-*.

### Anaptyxis (Svarabhakti)

§66. Like other Pkt. dialects, Ap. sometimes inserts a light vowel to break a consonant cluster. The instances are noted in §38.

### Insertion of Plosives

§67. In a group of nasal+liquid in Ap., as in literary Pkts., a voiced plosive of the same class as the nasal is at times used between the nasal and the liquid. Thus we have:

(1) OIA *-mr-*>-**mbr-*>Ap. *-mb-* at times written as *-mv-*. e.g., WSAp. *tamba*<*tāmra*, *tamba-cūla*<*tāmra-cūḍa* in SAp., *āmba*, WAp. *amva*<*āmra*, SAp. *āyamba*<*ātāmra*.

(2) OIA *-ml-*>**-mbl-*>Ap. *-mb-* or *-mv-* with anaptyxis. e.g., WAp. *amvila*<*amla*, *āyamvila*<*ācāmla*. SAp. *semva(ba)li*< *śālmalī*, after Metathesis; but initially *ml-*>*m-* is seen. e.g., *meccha*<*mleccha*.

(3) A similar insertion of plosives is found in the OIA cluster of *-h-*+nasal which results into nasal+*-h-* by Metathesis in Ap. *-hn-*>**-nh-*>*-ndh-* e.g., *cindha*<*cihna*.
*-hm-*>*-mh-*>*-mbh-* e.g., *ba(va)mbhaṇa*<*Brāhmaṇa*, but EAp. has *Bamha*<*Brahmā*, *bamhaṇa*<*brāhmaṇa*.

(4) When the OIA cluster of sibilant+nasal results into *-mh-* (<*-ṣm-*, *-sm-*), we sometimes find *-b-* inserted between *-m-* and *-h-*. e.g.
WSAp. *sambhariya*<**saṁsmarita*=*samsmṛta*, *vimbhaya*<*vismaya*.
SAp. *sembha*<*śleṣma*, *gimbha*<*grīṣma*, *vimbhaiẽ*<*vismitena*.

### Insertion of *r*.

§68. According to Pk. grammarians, the insertion of *-r-* as a second member of a consonant group where no such historical relation is traceable to OIA, is one of the distinguishing characteristics of Ap. (See *Pu.* 17.14, *Hc.* 8.4.399, *Ki*, 5.2,5,16; *Tr.* 3.3.6, *RT.* 3.3.2, *Mk.* 17.3). The retention of *-r-* in *r-* clusters is a different phenomenon for which see §64. We find the following examples in treatises on Pk. grammars: *vracala*, *uvraca*, *vracau*, *krāka*, *krukhi* in the Com. of *Ns.* on Rudraṭa's *Kāvyālaṁkāra* 2.12, *jram* (*Pu.* 17.55), *jrum* (*Ki* 5.49), *dhrum*=*yad* (*Hc.* 8.4.360, 438, 1; *Sh.* 40), *tram*=*tyad* or *tad* (*Hc.* 8.4.360), *drum*=*tad* (*Ki.* 5.49), but *yad* in *Tr.* 3.4.31 and *Ld.* on the same *sūtra*. *prassadi*<*paśyati* (*Hc.* 8.4.393), *bhrantri*<*bhrānti* (*Hc.* 8.4.360), *bhrāsa*<*bhāṣya* (*Ki.* 5.5),

*Vrāsa*<*Vyāsa* (*Hc.* 8.4.369, *Ki.* 5.5, *Ld.* 3.3.6). In *etrula, jet-rula, ketrula, tetrula* for *iyat, kiyat, yāvat, tāvat* (*Hc.* 8.4.435) the *-r-* is probably due to the influence of Sk. *atra, kutra, yatra, tatra. Mk.* 17.3. gives *vrākrosu* (*vyākrośa*), *vrāḍi* (*vyāḍi*), *vrāgaraṇu* (*vyākatraṇa*).

It is important to note that this is not the characteristic of literary Ap. Exceptional forms like *Vrāsu, prassadi* are found very rarely, and in a work like *Kc.* which is specially written to illustrate his own Pk. grammar by Hemacandra.

### Prothesis

§69. See §39.

### Interchange of Consonants

§70. The following consonants are interchanged in Ap. Many of these are found in literary Pkts. as well :

(1) *-ḍ-* and *-l-*, (*-ḷ-*) interchanged. e.g.
WAp. *ōrālia*<*avaraṭita, duddhaḷā*<**duddha-ḍaa dugdha-ṭa-ka.*
SAp. √*pīla*<√*pīḍ*
EAp. *naggala*<**nagga-ḍa*<*nagna-ṭa, cellu*<*ceṭaka* or its cognate like *ceḍa-*<√**cṛt.*[79]
SAp. *ciḍaülla.*

(2) *-d-* and *-l-* interchanged :
WSAp. *galatthiya*<*kadarthita,*
WAp. *palitta*<*pradīpta,* cf. *Hc.* 8.1.221,
SAp. *Kālambiṇī*<*Kādambinī.*

(3) *-n-* and *-l-* interchanged.[80]
WSAp. *loṇa, loṇiu, lavaṇīya*<*navanīta, nāhala*<*lāhala, ulūkhaṇa* <*ulūkhala, ṇaḍāla nalāḍa,*<*lalāṭa* or from *niṭala* ?

(4) *-m-* and *-b-* interchanged :
WSAp. *samara*<*śabara,* SAp. *simira*<*śibira.*

(5) *-m-* and *-v-* interchanged :
WSAp. *jāma,* WAp. *jāmu*<*yāvat,* also, *tāma, tāmu*<*tāvat,*
SAp. *Dumaya*<*Duvaya*<*Drupada.*

---

79 S. M. Katre, 'Pk. ucciḍima' in *Mm. P.V. Kane Festsehrift,* pp. 258-9.
80 For corresponding changes in OIA e.g. *naktaka* : *laktaka,* see Wackernagel, *Alt. Gram.* I. § 175.

(6) *-v-* and *-b-* interchanged :

The use of *b* for *v* is an EAp. characteristic e.g., *baaṇa*<*vacana*, *bāca*<*vācā*, *biḍambia*<*viḍambita*, *butta*<**vukta*=*ukta*, *bohittha* <**vohitra*=*vahitra*. Rarely in WAp. *baṁsa*<*vaṁśa*. Sometimes we find *v*<*b* e.g., WSAp. *vāha*<*bāṣpa*, WAp. *vībhaccha*<*bībhatsa*. The phonetic habit of pronouncing *b* for *v* and, the corresponding scribal practice may be the reason of this.

(7) *-r-* and *-l-* interchanged :[81]

(a) Ap. *-l-*<OIA *-r-* : WSAp. *dālidda*<*dāridrya*, *somāla* <*sukumāra*, (*saumya*+*āla?*) *āluṁkhiya*<*āruksita*.

Ap. *-r-* <OIA *-l-* : *sāmari*<*śālmali*,

EAp. *ebaṁkāla*<*evaṁkāra*.

### Metathesis

§71. As in OIA,[82] Pāli[83] and Pkts.[84] we have some cases of metathesis in Ap. e.g., *Vāṇārasī*, EAp. *Baṇārasi* <*Vārāṇasī*, *dīhara*<*dīrgha*, *pahirāviya*<*paridhāpita*, *halua*<*laghu-ka*, *draha*< *hrada*. MIA has, by nature, a repulsion for a consonant cluster beginning with *h-*, and hence transposed it by Metathesis. *śn*, *śm ṣm*, *sn*, *sm*, *hn*, *hm* became *ṇh* and *mh* in Ap., but as it shares these in common with Pkts., they need not be illustrated.[85]

### Consonantal Gemination

§72. Sometimes non-initial single consonants are doubled simply, or to compensate the shortening of a long vowel. We find this in Ap. of all regions.[86]

WAp. *kacca*<*kāca*, *kōuhalla*<*kautūhala*, *ṭikka*<*ṭīkā*, *ṇāikka*<*nāyaka*, *ṇihitta*<*nihita*, *tella*<*taila*, *duritta*<*durita*, *pemma*<*preman*.

SAp. *ujjuya*<*ṛjuka*, *uppari*<*upari*, *ekka*, *ikka*<*eka*, *callia*<*calita*, *ṇiccapphala*<*niscāpala*, *pāikka*<*pādika*.

EAp. *abikkala*<*avikala*, *ekka*<*eka*, *juttha*<*yūtha*, *ṇakkha*<*nakha*, *nattha*<*nātha*, *paṁḍitta*<*paṇḍita*.
See §27 (A) iii (a) , (B) iii.

---

81 Pischel, *Grammatik*, § 257, § 259.
82 Wackernagel, *Alt. Gram.* I. § 354.
83 Geiger, *Pali Lit. u. Spr.* § 47.
84 Pischel, *Grammatik*, § 354
85 Pischel, Ibid., §§ 312-4
86 For similar examples in literary Pkts. and their explanation see Pischel, *Grammatik*, § 90, § 194.

## Compensatory Nasalisation

§73. Sometimes a consonant cluster becomes a nasalized simple consonant, the nasalisation being a compensation for the loss of one member of the conjunct. e.g.

WSAp. *daṁsaṇa*<*darśana*,√*jampa*<√*jalp-*, *vaṁka*, *vaṁkī*<*vakrā*,

WAp. √*piṁcha*<√*pṛcch-*, *paṁkhi*< *pakṣin*, *āluṁkhiya*<*ārukṣita*, *baṁhina*<*barhin*, *maṁṭha*<*mṛṣṭa*,

SAp. *goṁcha*, *guṁcha*<*guccha* or *gutsa*, *Kaṁcāiṇi*, <*Kātyāyanī*, *vayaṁsi* <*vayasyā*.

EAp. *jiṁghaï*<*jighrati*.
See § 34 also.

# *CHAPTER II*

## DECLENSION IN APABHRAṀŚA

### §74. Ap. Morphology—in a synthetico-analytic stage

Ap. Morphology represents the essential *differentia* between literary Pkts. and Ap., and as such its importance cannot be exaggerated. A synthetic review of the general development of IA Morphology shows a continuous process of reduction and regularisation.[1] Ap. morphology represents a phase later than that of Pkts.[2]

In Ap. we find that the number of stems is practically reduced to one type—the *-a* ending one. The number of cases is reduced to three as the Nom. and Acc. are identified, the Instr. merges into Loc., and the Abl. and the Dat.-Gen. become one. As a matter of fact, we have three and sometimes (in Fem. stems) practically two cases here—the Direct and the Oblique. The analytic tendency is set in. Ap. Morphology is in a synthetico-analytic stage. Its comparison with the old flexional system in NIA, shows that Ap. is only a precursor of the old NIA.

### §75. Declension in Ap.

Ap. preserves the declensional system of Pkts. in a reduced degree but to a greater extent than the old stage of NIA. It has regional variations, but all of them show that the ground is being prepared for NIA. The direct case was already formed in Ap., and the remaining two supplied the oblique bases to NIA.[3]

As in other MIA dialects, all themes or stems in Ap. end in vowels. Normally they end in *-a*, *-ā*, *-i*, *-ī*, *-u*, *-ū*. Stems in *-e* and *-o* (their number is negligible), are reduced to *-i* and *-u* ones respectively. Thus we have :

*-a* : *ṇāha*, *ṇattha* (*nātha*), *rāya* (*rājan*), *kamma* (*karman*), *vijja* (*vidyā*).

Masc. Fem. and Neut. genders.

*-ā* : *kīlā* (*krīḍā*), *cīriyā* (*cīrikā*), *riyā* (*ṛc*). All Fem.
*-i* : *laṭṭhi* (*yaṣṭi*), *māi* (*mātṛ*), *suhi* (*suhṛd*), *risi* (*ṛṣi*), *dahi* (*dadhi*).

---

1 Bloch, *L'indo-aryen* pp. 99-300.
2 Although Pischel mixes up these stages, his description of the Morphology of Pkts. (*Gram.* pp. 241-407) is still worth reading.
3 Bloch *L'indo-aryen*, pp. 172-78.

Masc., Fem., Neut. genders.

-*ī* : *rāṇī* (*rājñī*), *Lacchī*(*Lakṣmī*), *Amarāurī* (*Amarapurī*). All Fem.
-*u* : *mahu* (*madhu*), *Vi*(*Bi*)*ṭṭhu* (*Viṣṇu*), *vahu* (*vadhū*), *vijju* (*vidyut*).

All genders.

-*ū*: *bhū* (*bhrū*). Fem.

In actual declension all the long end-vowels merge into short ending ones, and we have practically stems ending in short -*a*, -*i*- -*u* out of which the declension of -*a* ending stems remains predominant.

§76. Gender in Ap.

It was long before the beginning of our period that disruptive influences had set in, in the OIA gender system. Aśokan Inscriptions,[4] Pali,[5] and Pkts.[6] show that there was already a confusion of genders in pre-Ap. period.

Ap. represents a state in which the old gender-system was crumbling down rapidly. It baffled the Pkt. grammarians so much that they declared the impossibility of laying down definite rules for the gender system in Ap. (See *Pu.* 17.21, *Hc.* S.4.445, *Tr.* 3.4.67, *Mk.* 17.9). Pischel correctly remarks that gender in Ap. is more fluctuating than that in all other dialects, although it is not completely irregular as Hemacandra implies it in *Hc.* 4.445.[7]

A passing reference to the comparative Tables of Declension in the following sections will show that though gender in WSAp. is a continuation of the same system in Pkts., the confusion is on a larger scale. There is a greater disintegration in the gender-system in EAp. than in that of WSAp.

It appears that normalisation in declension was an important factor which affected Gender in Ap., as many times, it was the ending rather than its gender in OIA, which seems to have influenced the declension of a word. The neut. gender tends to disappear morphologically in Ap. Masc. and Fem. -*ī* and -*ū* stems have many desinences in common, and the reduction of Fem. -*ā* stems to -*a* ending ones has resulted in the borrowal of Masc. term.s on a large scale.[8] (see §89, 95, 98).

4 Bloch, *FLM.* § 180 where he quotes Senart, *Inscriptions de Piyadasi* II, p. 339.
5 Geiger, *Pali Lit. u. Spr.* § 76, p. 78
6 Pischel, *Grammatik*, § 356-59.
7 Ibid., § 359.
8 For details see Comparative Tables.

In Ap. there is very little difficulty regarding the gender of stems ending in *-ā*, *-ī* and *-ū*. They were always Fem. irrespective of their gender in OIA. *e.g.*, *vaṭṭā* (*vartman-* Neut. in OIA), *antraḍī* (*antra-*Neut. in OIA) ; *Tss.* and *tbhs.* ending in *-ā*, *-ī*, *-ū* were naturally Fem. *e.g.*, *Rāhā* (*Rādhā*), *Ramā* (*ts.*), *Lacchī* (*Lakṣmī*), *vahū* (*vadhū*). The real difficulty arises about the gender of themes ending in *-a*, *-i*, and *-u*, as these endings are common to all genders. Thus in *-a* stems we get *kumbhaiṁ* for Masc. *kumbhān* (the use of Neut. for Masc.), *rehaïṁ* for *rekhāḥ* (Neut. for Fem.) *amhaiṁ*<**asme* (Neut. for common gender). Pkt. grammarians quote many examples of this confusion (literally "a change") of genders, *liṅga-viparyaya*, which is only a preparatory stage to the state of affairs in NIA.[9]

§77. Number in Ap.

Although OIA had three numbers as in IE. and II, the dual was lost very early in MIA. In Aśokan Edicts the word *dvi* was used with a noun ending in the Plur. in order to express duality e.g., *duve morā* (Girnar 14). The same is the case in Pali[10] and in Pkts.[11] Ap. also expresses duality by the use of the numeral "two", the following noun being Plur. in Number e.g.,

*thiyaī ve vi ganjolliya-gattaī* *BhK.* 85.4.
*avarāha doṇṇi ajja vi khamīsu* *KKC.* 2.18.3.

We find the same in NIA. The use of the honorific plural is not a speciality of Ap. as it is found even in OIA.

§78. The tendency to normalisation and reduction of cases in IA has resulted in the formation of two cases in NIA—the direct and the oblique. It is in Ap. that Nom. Acc. and Voc. merged together and formed the Direct case, although Prakritisms sometimes obscure this achievement during our period. The fusion of the Dat. and the Gen. took place in pre-Ap. MIA,[12] (and sometimes in OIA also).[13] In Ap. the Abl. was gradually absorbed in the Dat.—Gen. case, so that after 1000 A.D. we have one comprehensive Dat.-Gen.-Abl. case supplying the basis for the oblique in NIA.

Comparative Tables of the Ap. Morphology and the free use of Instr. and Loc. absolutive constructions in the same sense in Ap. (which is also evidenced in JM.) show that the merging of the Loc. and Instr.

---

9 Bloch, *L'indo-aryen*, pp. 152-3. For the treatment of gender in NIA see *FLM* § 180 and *L'indo-aryen*, pp. §§ 150-53.
10 Muller, *Pali Gram.* §§ 61-2 as quoted by Bloch *FLM* § 177.
11 Pischel, *Gram.* § 360.
12 Ibid., § 361, in spite of *Hc.* 8.3.132.
13 Speyer, *Ved.u.Sansk. Syntax* §§ 43, 71-2, as quoted by Bloch, *FLM* § 183.

was complete in Ap. Although some desinences of the Loc. Instr. and the Dat.-Gen.-Abl. are common especially in the declension of Fem. stems, the Loc-Instr. seems to have retained its distinct existence to the end of our period, and supplied some bases for the oblique in NIA.[14]

§79. We shall now discuss the declension of Nouns ending in different vowels and trace the chrono-regional developments in declension in our period on their pre-Ap. MIA (literary Pkts.) back-ground, and their contribution to the formation of NIA in different regions. The Ap. desinences, as given by Pkt. grammarians, are juxtaposed with those which are traced in actual Ap. literature. It will be observed that the rich variety of terminations as found in Ap. literature is not seen in the sections on Ap. in Pkt. grammars.

## DECLENSION OF NOUNS

### Stems ending in -*a* (Masc. and Neut.)

#### *Singular*

§80. The Nom., Acc. (and Voc.) sgs.

The following are the term.s of Nom. sg. of -*a* ending stems (Masc. and Neut.) according to Pkt. grammarians.

(1) -*u* (*Pu.* 17.42, *Ns.* on Rudraṭa's *Kāvyālaṅkāra* 2.12,

*Hc.* 8.4.331, *Ki.* 5.22, 23, *Tr.* 3.4.2, *Sh.* 22.27.

*Ld.* 4.2, *Rt.* 8,16, *Mk.* 17.10. In *Cd.* 27 (Appendix) if the quotation 25 *kālu laheviṇu*. . . . from *PPr.* 1.85 be a part of *Cd.'s* genuine work -*um* (Neut. with -*ka* suffix *Hc.* 8.4.354).

(2) -*o* (*Cd.* 3.37, *Pu.* 17.42, *Hc.* 8.4.332, *Ki.* 5.23, *Tr.* 3.4.3, *Sh.* 22.6, *Ld.*, 4.3, *Mk.* 17.13).

(3) Zero (*Cd* 3.37, *Pu.* 17.42, *Hc.* 8.4.344, *Ld.* 4.17. Examples in the grammars of *Hc.*, *Sh.*, *Ld.* and *Pu.* suggest the optional lengthening of the final vowel).

(4) -*i* (*Mk.* 17.12).

The following are the desinences of Acc. sg. :

(1) -*u* (The same as the above for Nom. sg.)

14 For the general development of the case in IA, see BLOCH, *L'indo-aryen*, pp. 156-61, also *FLM* § 183.

(2) -*o* (In the works of Southern Pkt. grammarians e.g., *Tr.* 3.4.3, *Sh.* 22.8.

(3) -*i* (*Mk.* 17.12).

The following are the term.s of this case in Pkts.[15]

Nom. : -*o* ; Mg. Amg. -*e*.

Acc. : -*m*.

The Comp. Table (§ 80A) of chrono-regional classification of desinences shows that -*u* is the only common and stable term. throughout the Ap. period in all regions. This is generally regarded as weakened form of the nom. sg. -*o* in Pkts. as the phonetic weakness in the terminational endings in IA is a well established fact.[16] This desinence is older than 500 A.D. as it is found in the Ap. illustrations in *Bh.* 17. e.g., *moru* (*mayūraḥ*), and probably in the protocanonical Buddhist Texts under-lying the extant texts of Sanskrit Buddhism e.g., *Saddharma-puṇḍarika*.[17]

The term. -*o*, though sanctioned by Pk. grammarians and used freely in WAp., is less frequent in EAp. and SAp. In EAp. it is used for Neut. direct sg., showing thereby a confusion of gender in that region. -*o*, being common to Pkts. is a classicism in Ap., but it may be traced to -*ao* and *aü* (?) also.

The frequent use of zero as a term. of the direct case in EAp. deserves attention. The tendency to use the stem itself for the direct case is found in Buddhist Sanskrit, and EAp. writers, being Buddhists, assimilated this speech-habit. But the use of this from the beginning of our period in WAp. shows that this tendency was not limited to the East alone, although the term. zero never enjoyed the popularity in WAp. as it did in EAp. There are a few cases of vowel discolouration (e.g. §37) but they are too few to base the theory of the discolouration of -*u* to -*a*, as early as 500 A.D. in WAp. This desinence is not found in SAp.

-*e* is the characteristic term. of EAp. The influence of Mg. -*e* on EAp. is understandable. But the direct sg. -*e* of EAp. is *not* the same as Mg. -*e*. It is just probable that this is the result of the -*aka* (>-*aya*->-*e*) of the extended stem which was used by itself for the direct case. Thus

15 PISCHEL, *Grammatik*, §§ 363-4.

16 Although TURNER's theory regarding the Phonetic weakness of Terminational Elements in IA (*JRAS* 1927, pp. 227-39) is a sufficient explanation of this change—Pk. -*o* > Ap.-*u* Louis H. GRAY regards this -*u* as a "dulling" of *[ɔ : ] < *a < *az of which *z* is not a Sk. phoneme. GRAY supposes that *az was pronounced in spoken Sk. and Sk.-*ō* (before sonants) for -*as*, -*ah* is a mere *façon d'ecrire* for this *az (*BSOS* VIII.ii-iii p. 564).

17 F. EDGERTON, *BSOS* VIII.ii. iii.

*maarandae*<*makarandaka* in Kāṇha and *home*<*homaka*, *abbhāse*<*abhyāsaka* in Saraha, can be explained. We cannot rule out the possibility that Mg. *-e* was reduced to *-*i* and gave rise to *-e* after its combination with the *-a* of the (extended or unextended) stem.[18] The use of *-e* for the nom. sg. in Mg. in that region afforded a favourable ground for such development, but that Mg. *-e* could not have remained intact when the general tendency was towards weakening such flexional end.s in IA.

This *-e* appears as *-ae* or *-aye* (in EAp.) when it is applied to the stem extended with pleonastic *-ka*. e.g., *arabiṇḍae* (*aravindaka*), *maarandae* (*makarandaka*), *paramatthaye* (*paramārthaka*), *surattaye* (*surata-ka*). (For the consonantal gemination in the last see §72). There are four such forms in *DKK*. 6 and 8, and one in *DKS*. 63—all of which take *-ae*. The remaining three are in *DKS*. 63, and they take *-aye*.

*-ẽ*<*-akam* is found only in three forms in *DKS*. Thus we find *tullẽ*<*tulyakam*, *bhullẽ*<*bhraṣṭam* in *DKS*. 3. It is absent in *DKK*.

The next important term. is *-ā*. Though it is sanctioned by a standard western grammarian like Hemacandra (*Hc*. 8.4.330), it was never popular with WAp. writers. The two forms with *-ā* in *VK*. viz., *cakkā* (*cakravāka*)., *morā* (*mayūraka*) are due to syncope. This desinence is rare in *PPr*. and *Pd*. Even the 12th cent. WAp. works *e.g.*, *Sc*. and *Kp*. do not use it, although they were contemporaries of Hem. The examples in *Hc*. are due to the compilatory nature of the work. This desinence is practically absent in SAp.

*-ā* is not used as a Voc. term. upto 1000 A.D. in WAp. It is less frequent even after that. *-a* ending vocatives are popular throughout the Ap. period (500-1200 A.D.) in WSAp.

It is EAp. which uses *-ā* for the direct Sg. It is largely used in the neut. gender also in EAp. where it is the normal desinence. From 1000 A.D. some *-ā* forms of the neut. gender appear in WAp. e.g., *thakkā* (**stha-kka* or *-kna*), *bhaggā*<*bhagna-ka*. in *Pd*. They persist down to the end of 1200 A.D. e.g., *bhallā*<*bhad-ra-ka*, *hiyaḍā*<*hṛdayaka* etc. Only SAp. resisted this innovation. The use of *-ā* both for Masc. and Neut., indicates the confusion of gender in those regions at that time (see §76).

As *-ā* appears earliest in EAp. where it is used as a general rule, we may regard it as the contribution of EAp. We have a number of such forms which substantiate this claim. e.g., *tālā* (*tālakam*), *biphāriā*

---

18 Cf. S.K. CHATTERJI's explanation of Beng. Nom. sg. *-e* in *ODB* § 497. L.H. GRAY regards the Mg. *-e* in *putte* as the "dulling" of *putta* (*BSOS* VIII.ii-iii, 564).

(*visphāritakam*), *dhaṇṇā* (*dhanya-kaḥ*), *paḍi-bakkhā* (*prati-pakṣa-kaḥ*). The OIA genders are given to show how this was a common term. both to Masc. and Neut. in *DKK* and *DKS*. This *-ā* is probably nothing but the use of an extended stem without any term. in the direct case in which the final *-aka* developed into *-*aa*>*-ā*.[19] The usual explanation of the use of Nom. plur. *-ā* (<OIA *-āḥ*) of Pkts. for Nom. sg. need not be repeated.

Closely connected with this is *-ḍā* which is nothing but pleonastic *-ṭaka*>Ap. *-ḍaa*>*-ḍā*. This *-ḍā* of nom. sg. is a special characteristic of WAp. It was a fashion in Ap. period to extend the stem by adding pleonastic *-ka*>*-a* resulting into *-aü*, *-aũ* and *-ao* in the direct case. Neither Pk. grammarians nor PISCHEL have noted *-ũ* and *-aũ* as the morphemes of the direct sg. In EAp. we have very few forms like *jāṇaũ*<*jñātam*,[20] *bhaabā̃*<Pk. *bhaavam* (*bhagavān*) which end in *-ũ* or *ã*. WSAp. contains many examples of this term. ALSDORF's remark that forms with *-ũ* are from stems ending in *-ma*,[21] is doubtful, e.g., WAp. *kaya-uṇṇũ* (*kṛta-puṇyaḥ*), *antarāũ* (*antarāya*), *jampaṇayũ* (*jalpanaka*), *loaṇavantaũ* (*locanavat*) etc., do not end in *-ma*. Similarly SAp. *hittaũ* (*hṛta*), *bhallaũ* (**bhad-la-ka*), *jhullantaũ* (Pres. part of √*jhulla*) cannot be explained that way. This *-ũ* is due to the contamination of nom. sg. *-u*+acc. sg. *-m*, as the direct case is a fusion of Nom. and Acc.

In EAp. we have *-ha*, *-ho*, *-hŏ* as the special term.s of this (direct) case. M. SHAHIDULLA explains them as the cases of *-haśruti*.[22] The explanation appears satisfactory as we cannot regard this as the extension of the gen. to the direct case as *-ha* (and not *-ho*, *-hŏ*) is the normal desinence of gen. in EAp.

Though the date of Kāṇha be disputed, he does not seem to be a contemporary of Saraha. The following comparative table of frequency of terms. in the direct case, is based on SHAHIDULLA's calculation of the desinences.[23] This table will clearly indicate that they are separated by some 2 or 3 centuries, and that Kāṇha is probably the older of the two. The *DKn.* is such a corrupt text, and so late in date, that it is difficult to give a consistent evolution of Ap. flexion in EAp.

---

19 For PISCHEL's explanation see *Grammatik*, p. 249.

20 SHAHIDULLA takes this as Pres. 1 P. sing. in *Les Chants Mystiques*. The words *maĩ jāṇaũ* are taken here as *mayā jñātam* as *jānāmi* is a regular verb in the next line (*DKS* 92)

21 Introduction to *Hv.* § 41 remarks.

22 SHAHIDULLA, *Les Chants Mystiques*, p. 38.

23 Ibid.

## A Comparative Table of Relative Frequency of Terminations of the Direct Case in EAp.

(The percentage is based on Shahidulla's calculations of the frequency of terms.)

| S. No. | Termination | % in *DKK* (700 A.D.) | % in *DKS* (1000 A.D. | Remarks. |
|---|---|---|---|---|
| 1 | *-a* i.e., Zero | | | General in both, hence not calculated. |
| 2 | *-u* | 28·57 | 41·04 | |
| 3 | *-aü* | 10·71 | 13·43 | Generally used with pp. though Saraha used it with 3 nouns. |
| 4 | *-o* | 17·86 | 17·16 | In *DKK*. for adjs. and verse-ends. In *DKs*. with 5 nouns and 15 verse-ends. |
| 5 | *-ao* | 7·14 | 2·98 | In *DKK* with adjs. at the end of the Soraṭṭha metre. In *DKs*. with 1 noun and 3 verse ends. |
| 6 | *-ĕ* | 7·14 | 5·22 | |
| 7 | *-ẽ* | nil | 2·24 | |
| 8 | *-ae, -aye* | 14·28 | 2·98 | |
| 9 | *ā* | nil | 12·68 | In 5 final verses in *DKS*. |
| 10 | *-ha* | 3·57 | 1·49 | |
| 11 | *-ho* | 10·71 | 0·74 | |
| | Total | 99·98 | 99·96 | |

§80A. Stems ending in *-a* (Masc. and Neut.)

DIRECT SINGULAR

| Cent A.D. | WAp. | SAp. | EAp. |
|---|---|---|---|
| 500? | 1) *varu, kolu, ṇisiaru* | .. | .. |
| | 2) *juāṇao, ṇāhao, santāvio* | .. | .. |
| | 3) *parahua, haṁsa,* | .. | .. |
| | 4) *morā, cakkā* (syncope) | .. | .. |
| | Voc. *morā, baṁhiṇa* | .. | .. |
| 600-1000 | *Masc.* | | |
| | 1) *mohu, kālu, būḍhau, khovaṇu, khavaṇcu, khaḍillau.* | | |
| | 2) *roya, sayala, mokkha.* | .. | .. |
| | 3) *sāsaḍā, jiyā.* | .. | .. |
| | Voc. *jiya, joïya.* | .. | .. |
| | *Neut.* | | |
| | 1) *jagu, daṁsaṇu, suhu* | .. | .. |
| | 2) *dhuttima, siddhi-suha* | .. | .. |

| | WAp. | SAp. | EAp. |
|---|---|---|---|
| 700-1200 | .. | .. | *Masc.* |
| | | | 1) *ṇāhu, tasu, paramesaru, bhamarū* (*DKs.* 73) |
| | | | 2) *haṁkāro, sariso* (fcw). |
| | | | 3) *kāṇha, siddha, Saraha, bohi-cia.* |
| | | | 4) *biralā, paḍibakkhā,* (5) *sunnae, paripuṇṇae.* |
| | .. | .. | 5) *uese, bhaṁge, sahābe,* |
| | .. | .. | 5A) *paramatthaye, rahiye.* |
| | | | 6) *loa-ha.* |
| | | | 7) *dība-ho, pabanaho.* |
| | | | Acc. : |
| | | | 1) *ujjoa, bhanba, māṇa, gabba.* |
| | | | 2) *bhaṭṭāra-ha* (*DKs.* 82). |

3) *karahā* (*DKs*. 45).
Voc. *baḍha, baḍhie* (*DKK*. 8).

*Neut.*
1) *jagu, jalu, jāṇaũ* (*DKs*. 92).
2) *nibbāṇo, biruddho.*
3) *mahāsuha, nīra, jaga.*
4) *ṭhāṇā, biphāriā, tuḍiā, diṇṇā, tālā.*
5) *cange, arabindae maarandae*

5A) *tullẽ* (*DKs*.3) , *bhullẽ* (*DKs*. 3).
6) *kahiye, surattaye.*

| Cent. A.D. | WAp. | SAp. | EAp. |
|---|---|---|---|
| 1000 | *Masc.* Nom. | *Masc. Direct* (Nom. Acc.) | |
| | 1) *pesu, uvvevu, Rāmaṇu vilalullu, sukhiyaü vappuḍaü,* Acc. *samsāṛu, bheu, pettu.* | 1) *kāu, Sudattu, aruhu, vesu, sāhāraü varaittu, bholaü, viṭṭalaü, a-cokkhaü, rāṇaü.* | |
| | 2) *kaya-uṇṇũ aṇuharamāṇaũ antarāũ.* | 2) *samprāiyaũ, jhullantaũ, ḍhaliyaũ.* | |
| 1000 | 3) *ḍhuraḍhullio, upiyo, suo.* (Acc.) *savatti-vehaọ* (*Bhk*) | *Neut.* | |
| | | 1) *pacchittu, kheu, juṇṇaü, āiddhaü maṇiṁgiyaü.* | |
| | 4) *hariya valaa, bhāya.* Acc. *Sumiṭṭhāhāra.* | 2) *bhallaũ, cilisāvaṇaum̐, hittaũ.* | |
| | 5) *dusahā.* | | |
| | Voc. : 1) *jiya, joïya, vaḍha, bhaviya.*<br>2) *mūḍha* (*Pd.* 13). | 3) *caraṇa-juyala viusattaṇa* (rare) | |
| | *Neut.*<br>1) *sāsu, loṇiu, pāü , khemu, kheu, thoḍaü, thovaḍaü, ḍhillaü, gharu, suhu, jampaṇayũ.*<br>2) *pāṇiya, siva, suha.*<br>3) *thakkā, bhaggā* (Pd.) | | |

1100 *Masc.*

1) *sariṇāu, moru, sarosiru khittaü, khapparaü, Jaṇaddaṇaü,*

(Acc. ) *kantu, kālu.*

2) *aüho, bhullallio*

*Neut.*

1) *loaṇavantau, gaaṇu.*

2) *duddhalā*

*Masc.*

1) *siu, vaccharāü, vinjjhu,*
2) *pukkāra, sāmisāla*
Acc. *rukkha.*

*Neut.*

1) *gamu, caraṇu, maṇu.*

Acc. *kittaṇu, vayaṇu, ṇararūu*

1200 A.D. *Masc. Nom.*

1) *viṇṭalu, kumaru, mukkhu, kāu, huaü, asāraü, pāraü, ghaḍiaü.*

2) *khagga, vaḍavānala, sārasa.*

3) *beṭṭā, ḍhollā, ghoḍā, nehaḍā.*

*Acc.*

1) *kantu, ghāu, vāyasu, māṇu.*

2) *aggalaüṁ, vīsāṁvū.*

3) *vamkima, kara, kāvāliya.*

*Neut.*

1) *ṭhāṇu, kamalu, taṇu, uṇhau.*

2) *vallahaüṁ, hiaḍaüṁ, hiaüṁ, vaḍḍattaṇaüṁ.*

3) *daḍḍhā, bhallā, hiaḍā, visamā.*

4) *kavala, kuḍḍa.*

*Voc.* (both Masc. and Neut.)

1) *ḍhollā, bappīhā, puttā, hiā, hiaḍā.*

2) *pia, kuṁjara, priya, vaḍha.*

3) *bhamaru.*

## §80B. Stems ending in -a (Masc. and Neut).

Direct Sing.

| A.D. | WAp. | SAp. | EAp. |
|---|---|---|---|
| 500 ? | Nom. Acc. : -*u*<br>-*o*, -*ao*, (Pkt.)<br>zero<br>-*ā* (syncope ?)<br>Voc. : -*ā*<br>-zero. | | |
| 600-1000 | *Masc.* Nom. Acc. :<br>-*aü*, -*u*<br>zero<br>-*ḍā*<br>Voc. : zero.<br>*Neut.* Nom. Acc. :<br>-*u*,<br>zero. | | |
| 700-1200 | .. | *Masc.* Nom. - *u*-<br>-*o* (few)<br>zero<br>-*ā*<br>-*e*, -*ye*<br>-*ha* (few)<br>-*ho*, -*ho̐*.<br>Acc. : zero (majority)<br>-*ha* (*DKs*. 82)<br>-*ā* (*DKS*. 45)<br>Voc. : zero, -*ie*<br>(*DKK*. 8)<br>*Neut.* : -*u*, -*ũ*<br>(*DKs*. 92)<br>-*o*,<br>zero.<br>-*ā*,<br>-*e*, -*ē*,<br>-*ye*. | |

| | | |
|---|---|---|
| 1000 | *Masc.* Nom. : -*u*, -*aü*<br>-*ũ*, -*aũ*,<br>-*o* (Pkt. ism.)<br>zero.<br>-*ā* (*Pd.* 102)<br>Acc : -*u*<br>-zero<br>*o*- (*BhK.* 27702)<br>Voc. : zero (majority.)<br>-*ā*<br>*Neut.* : -*u*, -*aü*<br>-*ũ*<br>zero<br>-*ā* | *Masc.* Nom. Acc. :<br>-*u*, -*aü*,<br>-*aũ*<br>Voc. : zero<br>-*u*<br>*Neut.* : -*u*, -*au*.<br>-*ũ* (not many)<br>zero. |
| 1100 | *Masc.* Nom. : (1) -*u*, -*aü*<br>(2) -*o* (Pktsm.)<br>Acc. : -*u* | *Masc.* Nom. Acc. : -*u*<br>-zero<br>Voc : zero |
| 1100 | *Neut.* Nom. Acc. :<br>-*u*<br>-*aũ* (rare)<br>-*ā* ,, | *Neut.* Nom. Acc. :<br>-*u* |
| 1200 | *Masc.* Nom. - -*o* (Pktism.) Hence not noted in §80A.<br>-*ũ*, -*aü*<br>zero.<br>-*ā*<br>Acc. : -*u*<br>-*um*, -*ũ*.<br>zero.<br>*Neut.* : Nom. Acc. : -*u*, -*aü*<br>-*uṁ*<br>-*ā*<br>zero (not many).<br>Voc. : -*ā* (numerous)<br>-zero (a great many)<br>-*u* | |

## §81. The Instrumental-Locative Case.

Pkt. grammarians prescribe the following desinences for Instr. sg.:

(1) -*eṁ* (*Hc.* 8.4.333, 342; *Sh.* 12, *Ki.* 24, *Mk.* 17. The references are to the relevant sections or chapters on Ap. in these works.)

(2) -*eṇa* (*Pu.* 17.46, *Hc.* 8.4.333, 342, *Sh.* 12, *Ld.* 4.5, *Ki.* 24, *Mk.* 29.)

(3) -*eṇaṁ* (*Mk.* 17.29)

(4) -*e* (*Ld.* 4.5, *Rt.* 15 also 12).

The following terms. in literary Pkts. serve as a background for Ap. developments.[24]

(1) -*eṇa* (Mah. Amg. JM. JS. Śaur. Mg. Pais. CP.)

(2) -*eṇam* (Mah. Amg. JM.)

A reference to Comparative Table §81A will show that

-*ēṁ* (sometimes represented as -*ẽ* or -*e* ̐ ),

-*iṁ* or -*ĩ* (at times written as -*i*), -*e*, -*ahi*, -*ehi*, *ehĩ*, -*eṇa* and -*iṇa* are the chief term.s of Ins. sg. in literary Ap. In the South and the West -*e* is probably a scribal error as such forms are comparatively rare in SWAp. literature. The Easterner, *Rt.*, was correct in giving this desinence, as -*e* Ins. sgs. are quite common in EAp. (see §81 A), but we cannot give the same credit to *Ld.* who does not show his knowledge of such a tract of literature like EAp., and was probably misguided by the omission of the scribes to give a nasal on *e* (-*eṁ*) in the Mas. before him.

Out of the above-mentioned term.s -*eṇa* and -*iṇa* need not detain us as they are obvious Prakritisms, -*iṇa* being another way of writing -*eṇa* <OIA -*ena*. -*eṇaṁ* (which is again a Pkt. desinence as seen above) is rare although it is sanctioned by *MK*. This does not mean that the number of -*eṇa* and *iṇa* Ins. sgs. was negligible. It is so only in EAp. where it occurs only in two forms viz., *saddena* < *śabdeṇa* (*DKs.* 94), and *bhananteṇa* < *bhaṇatā* (*DKK* 17) one ending with the dental -*n*. The predominance of -*eṇa* forms is due to the spell of Pkt. literature which Ap. never escaped throughout its career. The critical apparatus of PISCHEL's *Materialien* discloses the existence of -*eṇa* forms both in the Mss. of *VK.* and in the *Sarasvatīkaṇṭhābharaṇa* though the editor uniformly represents -*ẽ* as the term. of Ins. sg. In *Hv.* the proportion of -*eṁ* forms to -*eṇa* ones is 580: 355 (the latter includes -*ĕṇa* 336 + -*eṇa* 19). Out of the last, -*eṇa* is found only in the *ghattā* strophes. (*careṇa* in *Hv.* 87.5.8 is the only exception). In *Kp.* -*eṇa* forms (*i.e.*, Ins. sgs. in -*ēṇa*, -*eṇa*, and -*iṇa*) are the rule, and -*eṁ* ones (*i.e.*, forms ending in -*iṁ*, -*ĩ*, for there are no -*ēṁ* ones in

24 PISCHEL, *Grammatik*, §§ 363-4.

ALSDORF's edition of *Kp.*) are the exception. Their proportion is 95: 5. The *-i* forms in *Kp.*, as we shall see later on, have no relation with *-eṁ*.

In WAp. there appear to have been two waves of *-eṇa* forms, one wave appeared in 1000 A.D., and the other in 1200 A.D. Perhaps this may be due to the paucity of published Ap. literature of the 11th cent. A.D. The published Ap. works show that *-eṇa* was not much popular in WAp. upto the 10th cent., and that after a temporary subsidence in the 11th cent., finally superseded *-eṁ* (*-ẽ*, *-iṁ*, *-ĩ*) upto 1200 A.D.

On the contrary, *-eṇa* was less popular in SAp. The above-mentioned proportion of *eṁ* : *eṇa* (580 ; 355) is found in *Hv.* i.e., *Mp.* in which Puṣpadanta deliberately tried to imitate the high-flown, ornate style of Sk. and Pk. classics. One has simply to turn to *Jc.* (which is a work of a more popular nature), and one finds the popularity of *-iṁ* <*-eṁ* term. These *-iṁ* Ins. sgs. remained the characteristic of *KKc.*

*-eṇa* is practically absent in EAp. of our period, and even a later work like the *Ḍākārṇava* shares this speciality of EAp. to a great extent.

. *-eṁ* (*-ẽ*, *-e* ů, sometimes *-e*, *-iṁ* *-eṁ*, *-ĩ*, occasionally *-i* also) is a *bona fide* Ap. desinence. It is the only stable term. found in SWEAp. from 500—1200 A.D. It survived in NIA as *-ẽ* and *-e* in Marathi,[25] and *-ẽ*, *-ẽ* in Bengali,[26] to mention a few prominent languages. Its derivation has long been a bone of contention. Jules BLOCH traces it to Sk. *-ena*,[27] while GRIERSON connects it with MIA Loc. sg. *-ahĩ*,[28] TURNER traces Ins. sg. *-e* in Guj. to Sk. *-akena*>Ap. *-aeṁ*>OWR *-aĩ*, with the remark that in forms with *-eṇa* (Ap. *-eṁ*) and *-āṇam*, *-ṇ-* probably represented *anusvāra*, but the spelling lagged behind the pronunciation.[29] This probably explains the predominance of *-ṇ-* element in the flexion of a late WAp. work like *Kp.*, and the number of *-eṇa* Ins. sgs. in *Mp.* Even the oldest stages of Marathi and Gujarati presuppose Ap. *-eṁ* rather than *-eṇa* in forms of this case.

In his later paper on 'The Phonetic Weakness of Terminational Elements in Indo-Aryan"[30] TURNER again reiterates the connection between Sk. *-ena* and Ap. *-eṁ*. On the analogy of Sk. *phalāni*<Pk., Ap. *phalāiṁ*, BLOCH also repeats his old view regarding the connection

25 BLOCH, *La langue marathe* § 193.
26 S.K. CHATTERJI,, *ODB* § 498.
27 BLOCH, *FLM* p. § 193.
28 GRIERSON, Critical review of M. Jules BLOCH's *La langue marathe*, *JRAS*, 1921, p. 260.
29 *JRAS*, 1921, pp. 525-6 § 66(2).
30 Ibid., 1927 pp. 227-39 (1927).

between Ap. *-eṁ* and Sk. *-ena*,[31] in spite of GRIERSON's criticism of the same quoted above.[28]

The crux of the problem is whether phonetic weakness affected the *-n-* element in the term. *-ena* at all (if we except Neut. Nom. Acc. Plur. *-āni*>Pk. *-āiṁ*, Ap. *-āĩ*)[32] and whether there is any other instance of such weakness of *-n-* in the whole field of IA. We have not come across such weakening of *-n-* in other cases. It appears that the Ins. and Loc. merged into one case, and the desinences of the Loc. came to be substituted for the Ins., as we find it in some forms in JM. In Ap., as in JM., we have a number of Instr. Absolute constructions for the Loc. Absolute ones.

We may explain these desinences as follows: Instr. sg. *-eṁ* (*-ẽ*, *-eũ*, at times *-e*, *-iṁ*, *-ĩ*, sometimes *-i*) may be connected with Loc. sg. *-ahiṁ* or *-ahĩ* as pointed out by GRIERSON.[33] In Kp. *-i*, the Loc. sg. term. which is clearly traceable to OIA *-e*, is repeated 15 times for Ins. sg., and we cannot treat all these as *schreibfehlers* for *-ĩ*. The editor (Ludwig ALSDORF) also regards *-i* as the term. of Ins. sg.[34] In early WAp. works we have a few *-i* Ins. sgs. e.g., *paesi*<*pradeśa* (*Ys*. 47), but their number being negligible, we may regard them as scribal errors. In the 10th cent., however, we have a number of Ins. sgs. in *-i*. For example in *BhK*., we have a number of such Ins. sgs. e.g., *sambhandhi*<*sambandha-* (*BhK*. 8.6), *jaṇi*<*-jana-* (*BhK*. 26.1), *paüri*<*paüra* (*BhK*. 34.10), *mahāyaṇi*<*mahājana-* (*BhK*. 34.10) *aikilēsi*<*atikleśa-* (*BhK*. 37.1) etc.[35] These show the continuation of the tradition of JM. in Ap. its immediate successor in Gujarat.

The use of *-i* for Ins. sg. was well-established in SAp. of the 10th cent. A.D., e.g., *kāli*<*kāla-*, *suhi*<*sukha-*, *daṁsaṇi*<*darśana* in *Jc*. It is surprising that ALSDORF's edition of *Hv*. should contain no *-i* forms.

The term. *-e*<*-(a)ĩ*<Loc. sg. *-(a)e* shows the merging of the Instr. and the Loc. The use of common term.s for Instr. and Loc. Plur. point to the same conclusion. Thus in *Bhk*. we have *-hĩ* for both. JACOBI notes one such form in *turaṅgihi—turaṅgeṣu* (*BhK*. 51.10).[36] In *-ihi*<*-ehi*<OIA *-ebhiḥ*, the Loc. and the Instr. cases become identical. Some two centuries later in the same region *i.e.*, Gujarat, we get, in Kp.

---

31 *L'indo-aryen*, pp. 143-4.
32 L.H. GRAY sees the survival of an I-I element in this. See *BSOS* VIII ii-iii, p. 566.
33 *JRAS* 1921, p. 260.
34 Introduction to *Kp*. § 21, p. 57.
35 For more examples see JACOBI's Intro. to *BhK*. p. *34, footnote 1.
36 Intro. to *BhK*. p. *34.

*-ihĩ* (27), *-ehĩ* (25), and *-ahĩ* (3) for Instr. Pl., while Loc. Pl. has *-ihĩ* (9), *-ehĩ* (1), *-ehi* (1) as term.s[37] Both the cases are derived from Ved. Instr. Plur. *-ebhiḥ*>Pk. *-ehiṁ* and the identity is complete. In SAp. of the 10th cent. A.D., *-ahĩ* and *-ehĩ* are common both to the Instr. and the Loc. plurals.

That this was a common feature of Ap. is still more strongly evidenced by EAp. in which *-e*, *-ẽ*, *-ahi*, *-ehĩ* and *-ehi* are common to Ins. and Loc. sgs.

They are also common to the Plur. number. It shows that the distinction between number was getting blurred in EAp. For our purpose it is sufficiently proved that during the Ap. period the Instr. and Loc. cases merged into one. This fact leads us to believe that *-e* is a regular term. of Ins. sg. in Ap., though it was originally of the Loc. sg.

Out of the remaining terms. *-ehĩ*, *-ehi* are directly traceable to Ved. Ins. Pl. *-ebhiḥ*>Pk. *-ehiṁ*. Here we cannot rule out the possibility of *ehẽ*<*-e*+*-smin* both of Loc. sg. On the model of double term.s like Ved. *-āsaḥ*, we have in Pkts. double desinences *-āo*, *-ādo* for Abl. sg. In Ap. also the claims of a double term. of OIA *-e*+*smin*>Ap. *-ehiṁ* are linguistically possible. But the evidence of the confusion of number is so strong that it leans to the probability of *-ehẽ*<Ved. *e-bhiḥ*, than to *-ehĩ*<OIA *-*esmin*.

*-ahiṁ*, *-ahĩ*, *-ahi* should rather be connected with OIA Loc. sg. *-a-smin* as *-ehĩ* and *-ehi* generally weaken into *-ihĩ* and *-ihi* and not into *-ahĩ*, *-ahi*.

Chronologically, merging of Ins. and the Loc. cases appears first in *DKK'* (700 A.D.) in EAp. so far as Ap. literature is concerned. In SAp. it is an established usage in the 10th cent. A.D. Although it appears in JM., its popularity began to increase in WAp. from 1000 A.D.[38]

§81A. Masc. Neut. -*a* stems

Instrumental Singular

| Cent. | WAp. | SAp. | EAp. |
|---|---|---|---|
| 500 ? A.D. | 1) *aṅgeṁ*, *joeṁ*, *pahāreṁ*. | .. | .. |
| | 2) *ciṇhẽ*, *paāṛẽ*, *raṇṇẽ* | .. | .. |

37 The term. *-esu* (9) of Loc. Plur. is not discussed here as it is due to classicism. The calculation of the term. is based on Alsdorf's edition.

38 The old stage of NIA inherits most of the terms. discussed in this section. See Bloch, *FLM* §§ 193, 194, S.K. Chatterji *ODB* §§ 498-9.

| | | | |
|---|---|---|---|
| | 3) *kāraṇe, ṇae, raṇṇe.* | | |
| 600-1000 A.D. | 1) *appẽ ṇiyamẽ, pariṇāmẽ, pasāeö* (*Ys.* 41) *aggiyae* (*PPr.* 101) [39]<br>2) *appiṁ, ṇāṇiṁ, ṇiyamiṁ, appaiö* (*Ys.* 34).<br>3) *kammaĩ, mohaĩ, saṁsaggaĩ.*<br>4) *paesi* (*Ys.* 47 Loc. ?).<br>5, *vavahāreṇa* (*PPr.* 2.28).<br>6) *kāraṇiṇa* (*PPr.* 1.7). | .. | .. |

| Cent. | WAp. | SAp. | EAp. |
|---|---|---|---|
| 700-1200 A.D. | - | - | 1) *sahajẽ, cittẽ, sahābẽ, dhūmẽ, sarahẽ, jhāṇẽ*<br>2) *śabare* (*DKK.* 25), *nehe, dehe* (*DKK*), *kajje, gahaṇe, baṇdhe, nāme* (*DKs.*).<br>3) *pāṇiehi* (*DKK.*31) *khabaṇehi, cittehi,*<br>4) *micchehĩ* (*Dks.*3).<br>5) *appahi, bisahi* (*DKs.*)<br>6) *bahanteṇa* (*DKK.*17) *saddena* (*DKs.* 94). |

| Cent. | WAp. | SAp. | EAp. |
|---|---|---|---|
| 1000 A.D. | 1) *tilleṁ, saṁkheveṁ, pasāeṁ, ajoeṁ, aṇumaggeṁ viaṇakkheṁ.* | 2) *saücceṁ, ḍoreṁ, parihattheṁ, rāeṁ, sae* (?) in *Nc.* 9.21.5. | |

| Cent. A.D. | WAp. | SAp. | EAp. |
|---|---|---|---|
| 1000- | 2) *sappiṁ, paritosiṁ, -ṇāhiṁ, kāyaĩṁ. arahantaĩṁ, kāraṇaĩṁ, candaṇaiṁ.* | 2) *khuruppiṁ, ṇakkiṁ, paṁguttiṁ* *Jc.* abounds in *-iṁ* Ins. Sg.s. *-iṁ* Ins. Sg. s. | |

39 Prof. A.N. UPADHYE kindly informs me that this can be taken as Loc. Sg. also in his letter dated 9-2-47.

| | | |
|---|---|---|
| | 3) *kacceṇa, -kameṇa* (*Sdd.*), *viaggehṇa* (*DS.*), *dhammeṇa* (BhK.). | 3) *kāli, suhi, daṁsaṇi, akkhiya- mettī* (*MP.* 2.6.2) -*ī* metri causa |
| | 4) *tamiṇa, baddhaïṇa* (*Sdd*) *vaḍiṇa, laïyaiṇa* (*Pd.*), *gaṇahariṇa* (*BhK.*) | 4) *cāeṇa, kaṁjieṇa, ammā-hīraeṇa.* |
| 1100 | 1) *mattheṁ, upparẽ* | 1) *rāeṁ, gīyeṁ, jāyaeṁ.* |
| | 2) *saĩ* | 2) *sangaïṁ, ṇicchaïṁ, jharisaïṁ, dāṇaïṁ* (Majority of forms). |
| | 3) *dosiṇa, māṇiṇa, jovaṇiṇa* (*Sn.*) | 3) *Dhāḍīvāhaṇeṇa, rāṇaeṇa.* |

| Cent. A.D. | WAp. | SAp. | EAp. |
|---|---|---|---|
| 1200 | 1) *sugheṁ, pieṁ, daïeṁ.* | | |
| | 2) *akkheviṇa, aïriṇa, ahakkamiṇa, succhandiṇa* (very numerous). | | |
| | 3) *aïreṇa, -saeṇa, pavasanteṇa* (PKt. sm.). | | |
| | 4) *vihavi, rūvi pamāĩ* (*Sn.*), *laüḍaĩ, ṇicchaĩ. adaṁsaṇi* (*JdC.*). | | |

§81B. Instrumental Singular

| A.D. | WAp. | SAp. | EAp. |
|---|---|---|---|
| 500 ? | -*eṁ*<br>-*ẽ*<br>-*e* | | |
| 600-1000 | -*ẽ̄*,<br>-*e*(*PPr.* 1.1. Loc. Sg. ?<br>-*iṁ*<br>-*ĩ*<br>-*i* (*Ys.* 47 Loc. ?)<br>-*eṇa* (Pktsm.)<br>-*iṇa.* | | |

| A.D. | WAp. | SAp. | EAp. |
|---|---|---|---|
| 700-<br>1200 | .... | .... | -*ẽ*<br><br>-*e*<br>-*ehi*<br>-*ehĩ* (*DKS*.3)<br>-*hi* (*DKs.*)<br>-*ena* (*DKs*.94)<br>-*eṇa* (*DKK*.17)<br>rarely. |
| 1000 | -*eṁ*, -*ẽ*<br>-*iṁ*<br>-*eṇa*<br>-*iṇa.* | -*eṁ*<br>-*e* (*Nc*, 9.21.5)<br>-*iṁ*<br>-*i* (Jc.)<br>-*ĩ* (*Mp.* 2.6.2 *Metri causa*)<br><br>-*eṇa.* | |
| 1100 | -*eṁ*<br>-*ẽ*<br>-*ï*<br>-*iṇa* (*Sn.*) | -*eṁ* (few)<br>-*iṁ*<br>-*eṇa* (few) | |
| 1200 | -*ẽ* (rare)<br>-*iṇa* (numerous).<br>-*eṇa*<br>-*ï*, -*aï*, | | |

## 82. The Locative Singular

The discussion of the Instr. leads us directly to that of the Loc. case. The following are the terms. of Loc. sg. according to Pk. grammarians :

(1) -*i* (*Hc*. 8.4.334, *Sh*. 20, *Ld*. 4.6)

(2) -*e* (*Hc*. 8.4.334, *Sh*. 20, *Ld*.4.6, *Ki*. 28, *ERt*. 15, *Mk*. 23,29)

(3) -*hiṁ* (*Ki*. 28, *Rt*. 3.2.12, Examples in *Hc*. 8.4.386, 422.-15).

(4) -*eṁ* (*MK*. 23, *Ki*. 5.132 as quoted by Shahidulla p. 48.

Literary Prakrits take the following desinences.[40]

40 Pischel, *Grammatik*, § 363, § 366 a.

(1) *-ammi* (Mah. JM. JŚ. Amg.)

(2) *-e* (Ma. JM. JŚ. Amg. Ś. Pais. Cp. Mg.)

(3) *-aṁsi* (Amg.)

(4) *-āhiṁ* (Mg.)

In literary Ap. we find the following inflections (see Comparative Tables §82 A).

WAp. : *-e, -i, -iṁ, -ahiṁ, -ahĩ,* (*-mi, -mmi*).

SAp. : *-e, -i, -iṁ, -ahiṁ* (*-mi, -mmi*).

SAp. : *-e, -ẽ, -ahi, -ahĩ, -ita* (in *DKK* 2).

The bracketed terms *-mi* and *-mmi* may be ignored as Prakritisms. It is one more proof of the strong influence of Pkts. on Ap.

Out of the remaining desinences *-e* <OIA *-e* is common to WSEAp. This Sanskritism was on its wane, and WAp. of the 10th and 12th cent. A.D., prefer its weakened form *-i*<*-ĕ*<*-e*, to the pure Sk. *-e* (which is really *-a* ending + the term. *-i*). *-e* in Ap. is due to the existence of the stem-widening pleonastic *-ka,* whenever it is not a Sanskritism. The OIA and Pkt. *-e* soon weakened into *-ĕ*, and was pronounced and written as *-i* which is a stable desinence in WSAp. throughout the Ap. period. It was applied to the stem directly or to the extended stem when it appeared as *-aï*. In SAp. the proportion of *-i* is greater than that of *-aï*. This *-i* is the source of the terms. of Loc. sg. in M., Old Guj., and Sdh.[41]

The next important group of terminations is *-a-hiṁ, -a-hĩ,* and *-a-hi*. These are looked upon as *bona fide* Ap. terms. of Loc. sg. This group reminds us of Mg. *-ā-hiṁ*. These desinences are clearly traceable to OIA *-a-smin,* and it was during the Ap. period that they gave rise to *-ẽ* in the East (EAp.) developing into *-ẽ* and *-e* in Old Maithili,[42] and *-e* in Oriya and Bengali.[43] GRIERSON regards this *-ahĩ* as the source of Ap. Ins. sg. *-ẽ*[44], and we have a proof of the reduction of *-ahĩ* into *-ẽ* in EAp. e.g., *rasẽ* (*rasa-*), *andhārẽ* (*andhakāra-*), *paḍhamẽ* (*prathama-*) etc.

---

41 BLOCH, *FLM* § 194.

42 GRIERSON, *Intro. to the Maithili Dialect* § 78.

43 BEAMES (*Compa. Gram.* II p. 223) and BLOCH (*FLM* § 194) differ. They connect it to the contamination of Loc. sg. *-i* and Pk. *-āhi* of the Abl. sg.

44 GRIERSON, Critical review of M. Jules BLOCH's *La langue marathe*, *JRAS*, 1921, p. 260.

*-iṁ* which appears regularly in WAp. of the 10th cent., and frequently in SAp. of the same period, should be connected with this *-ẽ* of the Loc. sg., as *-iṁ* or *-ĩ* is only a weakened form of the same. The frequency of this term. is too great to be classed as a scribal mistake for *-i*. In *Pd.* 5 there is only one exceptional form *ṇaraya-haṁ* 'in hell,' in which *-haṁ* is inexplicable unless it is the mistake of the copyist for *-iṁ*, both of which appear alike in the Devanāgarī script.

We may now arrange the possible chronology of these term.s as follows :

700 A.D., EAp. *-ẽ* <Ap. *-ahĩ* <OIA *-a-smin.*

1000 A.D. WSAp. *-iṁ*, *-ĩ* < *-ẽ* as above.

*-a-hĩ* is very rare in EAp. but it was either reduced to *-a-hi* or *-a-ĩ* giving rise to *-ẽ* by being combined with the previous *-a*. In *DKK.* 18 *khaṇehi* 'in a moment' is an instance of the fusion of Ins. and Loc., and the merger of sg. and plur., as this *-ehi*<OIA *-ebhiḥ* is a term. of Ins. plur. In *DKK*. 2:

*pakka-siriphale alia jima bāherita bhumayanti*

in *bāherita* 'from outside,' *-ita* for Loc. sg. is (as M. SHAHIDULLA notes)[45] a borrowal from Bengali. The same scholar regards *pāsa*=*pārśve* (*DKK.* 23) and *taḍa*=*taṭe* (*DKS.* 102) as examples of the suppression of desinences of Loc.

§82A. LOCATIVE SINGULAR

| Cent. A.D. | WAp. | SAp. | EAp. |
|---|---|---|---|
| 500 ? | *kāṇaṇe, gahaṇe.* | | |
| 600-1000 | 1) *devali, -citti, pai, dehi, tihuyaṇi, uppahi, titthaï, lippaï*<br>2) *siddhe, citte* (Skt. Sm.) | | |

| Cent. A.D. | WAp. | SAp. | EAp. |
|---|---|---|---|
| 700-1200 | | | 1) *ghare, dūre, dhamme, hiyae, lirāre.*<br>2) *rasẽ, anahārẽ, paḍhamẽ, gharẽ.*<br>3) *dehahi* (*DKK*. 3), *gharahi, desahi, jalahi* |

45 SHAHIDULLA, *Les Chants Mystiques*, p. 42.

4) *jala-hī* (*DKS*. 34).

5) *khaṇehi* (*DKK*. 18).

6) *bāherita* (*DKK*. 2).

| Cent. A.D. | WAp. | SAp. | EAp. |
|---|---|---|---|
| 1000 | 1) *kandaïṁ, atthamiyaïṁ vibhāviyaïṁ, khāraghaḍaïṁ, kuḍilliyaïṁ.* | 1) *-vimāṇe, -kappe, Dhāḍaïsaṇḍe, vitthiṇṇae.* | |
| | 2) *sūri, maṇuyattaṇi, saravari, hiyaï, ummaṇi, devali, hiaḍaï, dhandhaï khavayaï* (quite common). | 2) *jaṇṇi, gosi, vari, vicci, suvihāṇi, pavvi, paṭṭhi, paraï, bhallaï, Puvva- viaehaï, tarumūlaï.* | |
| | 3) *sāāyara-gayahiṁ* (*Sdd*. 3) | 3) *dhūrahiṁ* (*Nc*. 3.3.5). *pāsahiṁ* (*Nc*. 1.10.10). | |
| | 4) *kaccāsaṇahaṁ* (*Sdd*. 13). *ṇarayahaṁ* (*Pd*. 5). | 4) *jammiṁ, gharakammiṁ, kaddamiṁ.* | |
| | 5) *majjhami, pasu-vāhami* (Pkt. sm.) | 5) *jimiyammi, ṇarayammi, ṇahantammi, ṇirasami* (*Jc*. 1.15.16). | |

| Cent. A.D. | WAp. | SAp. | EAp. |
|---|---|---|---|
| 1100 | 1) *jame, ulle, ure, āhasantae.* | 1) *maṇe, sivapahe, dine.* | |
| | 2) *paï, pāantī, panki, hatthi, āuyathambhi, entaï, bolantaï, cauppahaï.* | 2) *maṇi, pāsi, diṇi.* | |
| | 3) *panthahī, māhahī. ṇāhahī.* | 3) *hiyaïṁ,* (*KKc*. 1-14-12). | |
| | 4) *diṭṭhammi vayaṇammi* (Pktsm.) | 4) *pahāṇahiṁ* (*KKc*. 1.3.1). | |
| | | 5) *vaṇṇami, maṇṇami* (*KKc*. 1.14.9) | |

| Cent. A.D. | WAp. | SAp. | EAp. |
| --- | --- | --- | --- |
| 1200 | 1) *oyaṇḍi, cei-hari, desi, tali diṇayari, aggaï, supotthaï, thoḍaï, desaḍai.*<br>2) *cittaha, māsaha* (*Sn.* 18-468).<br>3) *kihĩ, gharahiṁ,* (°*hi,* VAIDYA), *desahiṁ.*<br>4) *kayaïṁ* (*Jde.* 34.1), *diṭṭhaĩ* (*Hc.*) °*i* (VAIDYA's Ed.)<br>5) *tale, dūre* (*Ts.*) *appie.* | | |

§82B. LOCATIVE SINGULAR

| A.D. | WAp. | SAp. | EAp. |
| --- | --- | --- | --- |
| 500 ? | *-e* | .. | .. |
| 600-1000 | *-ï* | .. | .. |
| | *-e* | | |
| 700-1200 | .. | .. | *-e,*<br>*-ẽ*<br>*-hi*<br>*-hĩ* (*DKs.* 34)<br>*-ehi* (*DKK.* 18)<br>*-ita* (*DKK.* 2) |
| 1000 | *-iṁ*<br>*-i*<br>*-hiṁ* (*Sdd.* 3)<br>*-haṁ*<br>*-mi* (*Pd.* 23) | *-e*<br>*-i*<br>*-hiṁ*<br>*-iṁ*<br>*-(a)mmi* | |
| 1100 | *-e,*<br>*-i*<br>*-hĩ*<br>*-mmi* (Pktsm.) | *-e*<br>*-i*<br>*-iṁ*<br>*-hiṁ*<br>*mi-* | |
| 1200 | *-i*<br>*-ha*<br>*-hĩ, -hi*<br>*-hiṁ*<br>*-iṁ, -ĩ, -i* | | |

## §83. The Dative—Genitive—Ablative Case.

This is the most important case in Ap., and may well be designated as the oblique case in Ap., as the oblique cases in many NIA languages are traceable to this, although the Ins-Loc. also supplies some bases in NIA oblique. The fusion of the Dat-.Gen.-Abl. cases is, however, gradual. We find that the use of the Gen. for Dat. is as old as the Brāhmaṇa period[46] and the fusion of these two cases was achieved in literary Pkts.[47]. It was during the Ap. period that the Abl. and the Gen. gradually fell in together, and merged into one compound case.

Pkt. grammarians have noted the following desinences of the Abl. and the Gen. cases :

*Ablative* :

(1) *-he* (*Pu.* 17.44, *Hc.* 8.4.336, *Sh.* 18, *Ld.* 4.7 but optionally, *Ki.* 30, *Rt.* 12, *Mk.* 19).

(2) *-hu* (*Hc.* 8.4.336, *Ld.* 4.7 optionally *Sh.* 18).

(3) *-adu* (*Ki.* 30).

(4) *-e* (*Rt.* 15).

(5) *-ho* (*Pu.* 17.44, *Ki.* 30, *Rt.* 12, 15. *Mk.* 19).

*Genitive* :

(1) *-su* (*Hc.* 8.4.337, *Ld.* 4.9, *Sh.* 15, *Ki.* 31, *Rt.* 14).

(2) *-ho* (The same as above except *Rt.* Here *Rt.* 13).

(3) *-ssu* (*Hc.* 8.4.337, *Ld.* 4.9, *Sh.* 15).

(4) *-ssa* (*Ki.* 31, *Mk.* 29).

(5) *-ha* (*Rt.* 7).

(6) *-he* (*Rt.* 13).

(7) *-hassu* (*Rt.* 14).

(8) *-e* (*Rt.* 12).

(9) Zeιo (*Hc.* 8.4.345, *Sh.* 17, *Ld.* 4.16).

(10) *-haṁ* (*Rt.* 13).

(11) *-huṁ* (*Rt.* 13).

---

46 Bloch, *FLM* § 183 where he quotes Speyer, *Ved. u. Sansk. Syntax* §§ 43, 71, 72.
47 Pischel, *Grammatik*, § 361.

Out of these *-he*, *-hu*, *-ho* are common to Gen. and Abl. *-e* (in *Rt.* 12, 15) is ignored as it is not found in Ap. literature, and like *-hassu* (*Rt.* 14) which is an artificial combination of *-ha* and *-ssu*, it may be a grammarian's invention. *-adu* (<Śaur. Mg. *-ado*) in *Ki.* 30 is a Śaurasenism. The rest are attested to in Ap. Literature.

The following term.s in literary Pkts. show us the background of Ap.[48].

*Ablative* :

Mah. *-āo, -āu, -ā, -āhi, -āhiṁto* (*-tto*)

Amg. JM. *-āo, -āu, -ā*; JŚ. *-ādo, -ādu, -ā*.

Ś. Mg. *-ādo*; Pais. CP. *-āto, -ātu*.

*Genitive*:

Mah. *-ssa*, Mg. *-śśa, -āha*.

A glance at the Comparative Table of Term.s ( §83A) will show that with a few unimportant exceptions in WSAp., Abl. and Gen. sgs. have got common desinences, and that after the 10th cent. A.D., the distinction was practically lost in WSAp. In EAp., both *DKK.* and *DKS.* represent a complete fusion of the two cases from the very beginning (700 A.D.). Its beginning in EAp. may go back earlier still, as there was a greater disintegration of old grammatical order in EAp. than in WSAp. The NIA languages of that region have changed faster than those in the WSAp. region. It is natural that the fusion of the Abl. and Gen. should be achieved first in EAp., although such a tendency is clearly seen in OIA in the declension of Fem. nouns, and Masc. and Neut. stems in *-i, -u, -ṛ*.

Out of the desinences of the Dat.-Gen.-Abl. case, we can easily dispose of *-ssa, -ssu, -(ā)su* as Prakritisms, as the latter two are clearly traceable to Pkt. *-ssa*, the *-u* ending being a fashion of that period in which it is used with some indeclinables also.

It is the *-h-* element in these term.s which requires some explanation. If we set aside the problem of relative frequency, the following desinences are found in Ap. literature.

WAp. *-ha, -haṁ, -ha, -hŏ, -hu, -hi*, zero.

48 PISCHEL, *Grammatik*, § 363.

SAp. *-ho, -hu, -huṁ* (?)

EAp. *-ha, -ho, ho.*

It was already in pre-Ap. MIA that we find OIA *-s-*>*-h-*. e.g., *daha* (*daśan*), *eyāraha* (*ekādaśan*), *bāraha* (*dvā-daśan*), Mg. Gen. sg. *-ha* <-**sa*<Pkt. *-ssa* <OIA *-sya*. In Ap. we find such a change in other term.s, as well. e.g., Loc. sg. *-a-hiṁ*, *-°hĩ*, *-°hi*<OIA *-a-smin*, the *-ha-* Future from OIA *-sya-* Future. This is enough to show that as in the case of Mg., in Ap. too, we have the *-h-* formations of OIA *-sya* for Gen. sg. One may go to the extent of regarding this *-h-* element as the survival or continuation of Magadhi *-ha*.

But these *-h-* desinences are found in WSEAp. This shows that these must have existed in spoken MIA, and that Mg. was the first literary Pkt. to record them. We cannot regard this as a survival of the I-I speech-habit to pronounce OIA *s* as *h*, because I-I and Ap. are not cognate in space or time, and secondly every OIA *s* is not transformed to *h*, in Ap.

Linguistically these term.s may be classified into two groups :

(i) *-haṁ, -ha, -ha,* zero.

(ii) *-hŏ̄, -ho, -hu, -huṁ.*

*-hi* is exceptional and limited to a few forms in *Sdd.* and *Pd.* e.g., *phullatthāṇaya-hi*=*puṣpa-sthānasya* (*Sdd.* 34), *joiyahi*<*yogikasya*=*yoginaḥ* (*Pd.* 192). This *-hi* may be connected with *-he* which was a popular desinence of Fem. *-ă̄* stems in WSAp. of the same (10th ) cent. Such interchange of term.s is (as we shall see later on) not unusual in Ap.

Out of the first group, *-ha* is used both for Gen. and Abl. Sing. and Plur., in *PPr.* OIA *-āsaṁ*>*-(a) haṁ*, *-(a) haũ*, or *(a) hã* is the application of a pronominal term. to nouns. OIA **putrāsam*>Pk. *puttāsam* >Ap. *putta-haṁ* (cf. Mg. *puttă̄haṁ*) is another example of the change of OIA *-s-* to *-h-*.

It is doubtful whether Ap. *-ha* can be regarded as a simple continuation of Mg. *-ha*. It is absent in SAp. EAp. preserves this, though sometimes it uses *-ho* for Gen. sg. In WAp. *-ha* became popular from 1000 A.D., We have only *-haũ* in *PPr.* for Gen. Abl. sgs. In 1200 A.D. in Kp. *-haũ* is totally absent, and *-ha* is the most popular term. Its

49 For the explanation of Gen. terms. in MIA vide Pischel *Gram.* §363, 66. Also S. K. Chatterji, *ODB* §§ 502, 507-8.

proportion to its alternative desinence *-hu* is 55 : 1.[50] This leads us to believe that *-ha* is simply a denasalized form of *-hā̃* which is of a pronominal origin. Bloch regards this on the model of Pkt. *ma-ha, tu-ha* and of pronominal origin in a different sense.[51]

The use of terminationless Gen. is sanctioned by Pk. grammarians like *Hc., Sh., Ld.* But the illustrations of zero term. are doubtful. Thus in *aïmattahaṁ cattaṁkusahaṁ gaya kumbhaï dārantu* *-Hc.* 8.4.345. *gaya-kumbhaï* 'temples of elephants' may be regarded as a *tat-puruṣa* compound as well. The next example of zero term. is in *Hc.* 8.4.384. But there, too, *bali-abbhatthaṇi* is a *tatpuruṣa* compound. In *Mt.* 3, Pischel equates *joiā* as **yaugika* with the Gen. term. dropped. But *PPr.* 1.85 which is the real source of that quotation, it is a Voc. form of *yogin* (see the *chāyā* also).

There are, however, a few forms which appear to be of Gen. sg. with zero term. e.g.

*pia joantihe muha-kamalu* (*Hc.* 8.4.332.2)

*pia=priyasya.* This can be taken as Voc. sg., but that would be rather farfetched. In *Pd* 52 we have another such instance :

*jīvahu janta ṇa kuḍi gaiya*

*janta=yātaḥ* qualifying the noun *jīva* in Gen. sg. However exceptional it might be, the existence of zero term. must be admitted. This might be a later development of Ap. *-ha.*

Out of the second group, *-ho* is the original desinence. *-hō̃* and *-hu* are the cognates of *-ho* as the latter is only a weakened form. This term. is found in WSEAp., although it was never so much popular in EAp. as it was in SWAp. It was used both for Abl. and Gen. sgs. The history of this term. is given by Bloch in *L'indo-aryen,* p. 143. The Abl. desinences in Pkt. (already quoted above), and the use of this for Abl. sing. support Bloch's view. *-hu* its weakening.[52]

---

50 The calculation is based on Alsdorf's edition of *Kp.* In his Intro. to *Kp.* p. 57, he represents these as *-ahā -ahu* etc.

51 Bloch, *L'indo-aryen,* p. 143.

52 Prof. Louis H. Gray advances an alternative theory on purely comparative grounds. He connects Ap. Abl. sg. *puttahe* to **putrasyās, -syās* being the term. of the Gen. Abl. of Fem. pronouns. (cf. Amg. JM. Dat. sg. *puttāe* < **putrāyaï*). Ap. Gen. Abl. sg. *putta-hu* is traceable to **putra-bhas.* In other words he proposes *-hu* < formative *-bh-* + Gen. Abl. sg. *-as,* as the history of *-hu.* In support of this formative *-bh-* he gives non-IA forms e.g. *deābus, luisarifs.* (*BSOS* VIII ii-iii). In the above mentioned paper, Gray juxtaposes so many forms unconnected in space-time context to Ap. that one begins to think that anything is possible in Linguistics. There is no reason why **-bhas* and **-syās* should be assumed for *-hu* and *-he.* If OIA Nom. sg. *saḥ* > *so* : *se* is possible in Pkts. **-bhas* > *-ho* : *-he* is equally possible, and *-hu* is a weakened *-ho.* There is no need to assume a hypothetical from like **putrasyās* in accepting which we have to postulate the application of Fem. term. to Masc. stem even in OIA.

*karaṇḍa-ho* (*DKK.* 21) is the first occurrence of this term. in EAp. (and in Ap. in general). It was never popular in EAp. In 1000 A.D. *-ho* began to appear in *BhK.* It was used more and more in the same region so that in 1200 A.D., *-ho* became the normal desinence in the anthology of Ap. verses in *Hc.* This *-ho* was the most popular term. in *Hv.* (SAp. 1200 A.D.) in which, according to ALSDORF's calculation, the proportion of the Gen. sg. terms. *-(a)ho* : *-(ā)su* is 421.22[53]. The *-āsu* forms are found at the end of verses. In *KKc.* in the 11th cent. A.D., *-ho* is the chief desinence and not *-hu* as in contemporary WAp. *-huṁ* in *haṇaṇahuṁ*<*hananāya* (*KKc.* 2.3.10) is rare. Is it due to the influence of Inf. *-huṁ* which was very popular in SAp., and which conveyed the same sense as the Dative? The line runs as follows :

*asilaya karayali parivi puṇu, so kaheṁ haṇaṇahuṁ uṭṭhiyau.*

We can pass over the nasal in *haṇaṇahuṁ* without affecting the metre. It appears to be a handslip of the scribe to add one *anusvāra* to *-hu* of the Gen. sg.

This case forms an important background for the oblique sing. in NIA.[54]

§83A. GENITIVE (DATIVE-ABLATIVE) SINGULAR

| Cent. A.D. | SAp. | EAp. |
|---|---|---|
| 600-1000 | Abl.—*jīva-ha̐*, *gantha-ha̐*<br>Gen.—*cittaha̐*, *deha-ha* , *-tayaha̐*, *taĭ-loyaha̐*, *jiṇaṇāhaha̐*, *mokkhaha̐*. | |
| 700-1200 | | (1) *karaṇḍahŏ* (*DKK*) *pabaṇaho* (*DKs.*)<br>(2) *saṁsāraha*, *cittaha* (*DKs.*) |

| Cent. A.D. | WAp. | SAp. |
|---|---|---|
| 1000 | (1) *ahuṭṭha-haṁ*, *saṁsārahaṁ* *maraṇahaṁ*, *-kālattayahaṁ*, *muttahaṁ*, *kaḍḍhantahaṁ*, | (1) *kamalaho*, *Coḍaho*, *Kaṁsaho*, *arahanta-ho*, *siviṇaho*, *rāyaho*. |

53 Introduction to *Hv.* § 41.
54 For the oblique sing. in NIA see BLOCH, *L'indo-aryen*, pp. 177-80.

| Cent. A.D. | WAp. | SAp. |
| --- | --- | --- |
| | *tailoyahaṁ.* | 2) *iyarahu, Rāmahu,* |
| | 2) *jīvaha, māṇusaha, kaṇta-ha, kuḍumbaha.* | *vimāṇa-hu.* 3) *riumaddaṇāsu, -mahayarāsu.* |
| | 3) *sangha-hō, -rāyaho, dhammaho* (All from *BhK.*) | 4) *pacchae, bhāiyae* (Abl. Sg.) |
| | 4) *sāyahu vīppahu jūyahu, gottahu, timirahu gīvahu, siddhattaṇahu.* | |
| | 5) *guruvahi, joïyahi, -phullattha-ṇayahi.* | |
| | 6) *mandirāsu* (only 1 in *BHk.* 342.7), *mahāṇarāsu, paramesārasu ṇayaṇā-nandirāsu* | |
| | (7) *janta* (*Pd.* 52) | |
| 1100 | 1) *thirahu, ṇāmahu, pia-hu-, vacchahu.* | 1) *kusuma-uraho ; ṇarindaho, viṇāsaho, tāyaho,* |
| | 2) *bhaṇanta-hŏ* (*Mt.* 2) | *jiṇavaraho.* |
| | 3) *vaïriya-ha* (*Sn.* 34-199), | 2) *ṇaravarāsu.* |
| | 4) *jaṇassu, maṇassu.* | 3) *haṇaṇahuṁ* (?) in *KKc.* 2.3.10. |

| Cent. A.D. | WAp. |
| --- | --- |
| 1200 | 1) *jaṇahŏ dullahahŏ, kantahŏ, sāyaraho* (Quite common in *Hc.*) |
| | 2) *avaruppara-hu, tihuyaṇa-hu jaṇahu* (*Sc.*), *nahayahu* (Abl. *Sc.* 364.8). |
| | 3) *parassu, suaṇassu* (Pkt.) |
| | 4, 5) Abl. Sg. *vaccha-he* (*Hc.* 336) ; *sayaṇijja-ha* (*Sc.* 459.3), *gharavāsaha* (*Sn.* 25.-22). |
| | 6) *gaya* (*Hc.* 345), *Pia* (*Hc.* 332.2). |

## § 83B. Genitive (Dative-Ablative) Singular.

| A.D. | | WAp. | | EAp. | SAp. |
|---|---|---|---|---|---|
| 500 ? | | .. | | .. | .. |
| 600- | Abl. | *-ha* ̐ | | .. | .. |
| 1000 | | | | | |
| | Gen. | *-ha*̐ | | | |
| 700- | | .. | | .. | *-hŏ*, *-ho* |
| 1200 | | | | | |
| | | | | | *-ha*. |
| 1000 | Abl. | *-haṁ* | Abl. | *-ho*. | |
| | | *-hu* (*Sdd.*) | | *-e* (rare) | |
| | Gen. | *-haṁ*. | | *-(ā)u* (*Hv*. Pktsm.) | |
| | | *-ha* | Gen. | *-ho* | |
| | | *-hŏ* (*Bh.K*) | | *-hu* | |
| | | *hu* | | | |
| | | *-hi* | | *-(ā)su* (less numerous) | |
| | | -nil (*Pd.* ) rare | | | |
| | | *-āsu* (3 in *BhK*.) | | | |
| | | Zero | | | |
| 1100 | Abl. | *-hu* | Abl. | *-ho* | |
| | | *-ā* (*Mt*. 3 | Gen. | *-ho* (common) | |
| | | Skt. sm.) | | | |
| | Gen. | *-ho*(*Mt*. 2) rare | | *-(ā)su* (rare) | |
| | | *-hu* (common) | | *-huṁ* (? *KKc*. 212.3-10) | |
| | | *-ha* (*Sn*. 34-199) rare | | | |
| | | *-ssu* | | rare. | |
| 1200 | | *-ha* (common) | | | |
| | | *-ho* (common in *Hc*) | | | |
| | | *-hu* | | | |
| | | *-ssa* (Pkt. sm.) | | | |
| | | *-ssu* (Pkt. but very rare) | | | |
| | | *-su* | | | |
| | | -nil. (*Hc*. 345, 384) | | | |

PLURAL NUMBER

§ 84. THE DIRECT CASE :

The following are the term.s of the Direct Plur. according to **Pkt.** grammarians :

*Masc.*

(1) zero (*Hc.* 8.4.344, *Ki.* 21, *Sh.* 8, *Ld.* 4.17).
(2) *-he* (*Mk.* 14, *Rt.* 10).
(3) *-ho* (*Rt.* 18).
(4) *-ḍā* (*Pu.* 18).
(5) *-du* (*Pu.* 20).

*Neut.*

(1) *-iṁ* (*Hc.* 8.4.333, *Mk.* 16, *Rt.* 11, *Ld.* 4.24)
(2) *-(ā)iṁ* (*Hc.* 8.4.353, *Ld.* 4.24, *Mk.* 16, *Rt.* 11).

We find the following desinences in Pkts.[55]

*Masc.*

Nom. : Mah. *-a*, Amg. *-āo.*
Acc. : Mah. Amg. *-ā*, (Mah.)*-e* .

*Neut.*

Mah. Amg. JM. *-āiṁ*, *-āĩ*, *-aĩ*.

Amg. JM. *-āṇi*, *-ā*, JŚ. *-āṇi*, Ś. Mg.. *-āiṁ*.

In Ap. literature zero is the common term. in all regions throughout our period. It is derived from Pkt. *-ā*,<OIA *-āḥ* reduced to *-ă* before sonants. The desinence *-ā*<OIA *-akāḥ* is rare in WSAp. ALSDORF ignores it altogether in his analysis of the dialect of *Hv.* [56] WAp. texts of the 12th cent. A.D., e.g., *Kc. JDc. Sn. Kp.* do not testify to it. It is only in EAp. and some WAp. texts especially *Pd.* and *Sdd.* (both of 1000 A.D.) that we meet with numerous *-ā* forms. Forms ending in *-ḍā-*<*-ṭa-kāḥ* e.g., *divahaḍā* (*divasa-*), *rukkhaḍā* (**rukṣa=vṛkṣa-*), *kaṭṭhaḍā* (*kaṣṭa-*) are the speciality of WAp. (chiefly of *Sdd. Pd.*) and are still found in NIA of that region e.g., Raj. (For the Neut. *-ā* see below).

The remaining term.s of Masc. Direct Plur. exhibit two tendencies, the space-time location of which is interesting. They are as follows :

(1) The use of sing. for plur.

55 PISCHEL, *Grammatik*, § 363.
56 Intro. to *HV.* § 41.

(2) Extension of the desinences of the Neut. to Masc. and *vice versa.*

(1) The first tendency is not so common. The use of **-u** in WEAp., and *-e*, *-ẽ*, *-u* in EAp. is rare. e.g., *Hari-Hara-Bamhu* (*PPr.* 2.8) *caubbeu*<*catur-Vedāḥ*, (*DKS.*1) *kesẽ*<*keśān* (*DKS.* 6) as in *naggala hoia upāṭṭia kesẽ*, *-baranālẽ* 'the chief stem or stalk' in the *dvandva* compound.

*saṇḍa-puaṇi-dala-kamala-gandha-keśara-baraṇālẽ* . . . . . . *karahu sosa.* 'The group, the lotus plant, the lotus-leaf, the flower, the odour, the stamen, and the chief stem or stalk . . (you) dry up the spirit' (*DKS.* 51).

It is quite probable that the sing. no. in these forms is due to the constant association of the things or deities mentioned therein which led the authors to look upon them as one. Thus the trinity of Gods, Hari, Hara, Brahmā, or the group of four Vedas, or the mass of hair form but one idea, hence the sing. term. But this confusion of number is not limited to this case alone, but to the Instr. Loc., and the Dat-Gen. Abl. cases as well (§ 85, §86).

(2) The second tendency is much more powerful. It is not seen in WAp. in 600 A.D., (in *PPr.* and *Ys.*). Its predominance in *DKK.* and *DKS.* shows the distinction between the Masc. and Neut. genders was (morphologically at least) lost in EAp. Thus *bhūtā* (*bhūtāni*), *bhava-nivvāṇā* (*bhava-nirvāṇāni*), *bea-purāṇa* (*Veda-purāṇāni*), *suṇṇāsuṇṇa* (*śūnyāśūnye*), *amaṇāgamana* (*āgamanāgamane*), *-maṇa* (*manāṁsi*) etc. show that *DKs.* and *DKs.* make little difference between Neut. and Masc., as *-a* stems of Neut. gender take desinences of the Masc., and *-iṁ* or *-ĩ* which are special term.s of the Neut. in WSAp. are absent.

In WSAp. though the distinction between genders is blurred, or is in the process of falling together, Masc. words take the Neut. term.s from about 1000 A.D. It is chiefly in *BhK.* that we get numerous examples of this type e.g., *coraĩ* (*corāḥ*), *gāmaĩ* (*grāmāḥ*), *hāraĩ* (*haārān*), *dosaĩ* (*doṣān*) and others. They are exceptional in *Sdd.* e.g., *dīvaḍaiṁ* (*dīpa-*). Though ALSDORF does not notice such forms, there are some in Puṣpadanta e.g., *kumāraĩ* (*kumārān*), *Veyaĩ* (*Vedāḥ*). It seems to have disappeared in *KKc.* (1100 A.D.) and probably in the contemporary WAp., although verses in *Hc.* contain some such forms. *SN.*, *Sc.*, and *Kp.*, *do not exhibit* this peculiarity of *BhK.*

The counter-part of this linguistic habit *viz.*, the application of Masc. term.s to Neut. nouns as in EAp. e.g., *Bea-purāṇa* (*Veda-purāṇāni*), *bhūtā* (*bhūtāni*)—both appear as early as 700 A.D., in *DKK.* —is seen in WAp. from the 10th cent. A.D. Forms like *uttiyō*, *vihīna* in *PPr.* show that this tendency commenced as early as 600 A.D., in WAp. It is not found in SAp. of the 10th cent. as Neut. direct plurs. end in *-aĩ*. It is in the 11th cent. that we find zero applied in exceptional forms e.g., *kama-kamala* (*krama-kamale*), *uggaya* (*udgatāni*). Zero for the Neut. Direct Plur. are found in many forms in 10th cent. WAp. If we except some purists like Haribhadra (the author of *Sc.*), this characteristic is found in Ap. of the 12th cent. In *Kp.* (1194 A.D.) zero is rather the rule than an exception as according to ALSDORF's calculation we find :

Nom. Acc. Neut. : *-a* (26), *-aĩ* (4), *-āĩ* (4) as the term.s in *Kp.*

We are now in a position to formulate the chrono-regional growth of these tendencies :

(1) *The use of sing. for plur.*
WAp.—*PPr.* (600-1000 A.D.)
EAp.—*DKK. DKS.* (700-1200 A.D.)

(2) *The use of Masc. term.s with Neut. -a stems*
EAp.—700-1200 A.D.
WAp.—1000 A.D. In SAp. also (?)
SAp.—1100 A.D.

(3) *The use of the desinences of Neut. with Masc. -a stems*

WSAp. 1000 A.D.

Lost in SAp. in 1100 A.D. ?

The contributions of LUEDERS, KEITH, BARNETT, and others in *Ind. Ant.* and other journals have made it quite clear that confusion of genders is seen in other MIA dialects, and is in no way the special characteristic of Ap. The synoptic statement of the temporal and regional growth is what appears from Ap. alone.

The Neut. direct Plur. *-ā̆ĩṁ*, *-ā̆ĩ* sometimes represented as *-ĩ*, *-iṁ*, *-ĩ̆* are traced to OIA *-āni*. The difficulty of the change of the intervocalic *-n-*>nasalisation of the surrounding vowel is discussed above in connection with Ins. sg. *-ẽ*<*-ena* ( §82). TURNER believes the possibility of such *-ṇ-*, *-n-*>˘̇[57] though it is limited to Ins. sg. *-ena* and Gen. pl. *-ānām* in addition to this *-āni*. As there is no other instance of such nasalisation in IA., this should be regarded as an open question.[58]

57 TURNER, Gujrati Phonology, *JRAS*, 1921, pp. 525-6 § 66 (2)

58 L. H. GRAY, thinks that the long vowels in *phalāiṁ*, *mahūiṁ* etc., in Pkt. and Ap. are traceable to Ved. *phalā*, *madhū* etc. In Pk. and Ap. *-iṁ*, *-ī* etc., there is the survival of the I-I doublets **-ni*, and **-n*. (For details see *BSOS* VIII ii-iii p. 566)

Neut. Direct Plurs. in *-ā* cannot be traced to Vedic Direct Plur. *-ā* due to the IA tendency of pronouncing the terminational sounds weakly. Ap. *-ā* of the Neut. Direct should rather be regarded as the extension of Masc. *-ā* < OIA *-akāḥ* to the Neut. Reduction of Ved. *yatrā* to *yatra* in classical Sk. is enough to show the improbability of the Ved. Neut. *-ā* surviving intact down to Ap.

Voc. Plur. *-ho, -hu* were independent particles for addressing, which later became case-terminations. The *pluta* vowel of the Voc. resulted in *-ā* which was perhaps reduced to *-a* (or it may be that the old *-āḥ* of OIA Voc. plur. gave rise to these). Hence we have these varieties in Ap. vocatives.

### §84A. Masculine and Neutral stems in *-a*

### Direct Plural

| Cent. A.D. | WAp. | SAp. | EAp. |
|---|---|---|---|
| 600-1000 | *Masc.*<br>1) *pasuya, jiṇavara, roya, rāya, rosa, jīvājīva, mūla-guṇa.*<br>2) *joiyā.* (*Voc.*) *joiya-hu* (*Ys.* 50)<br>3) *Hari-Hara-Bamhu* (*PPr.* 2.8).<br>*Neut.*<br>1) *davvaĩ̐, puṇṇaĩ̐, duhaĩ̐, kiyāĩ̐.*<br>2) *uṭṭiyā* (?) *vihīṇa, padesa.* | | |

| Cent. A.D. | WAp. | SAp. | EAp. |
|---|---|---|---|
| 700-1200 | | | *Masc.*<br>1) *surāsura, ṇirasa, tuḍia, sama* (*DKK.*); *naggala, dhammādhamma, bhābābhāba.*<br>2) *paṁḍittā, bisayā, jaḍā, dībā, kāyā, dosa-guṇā.*<br>3) *japa-homĕ*<br>4) *kesẽ, baraṇālẽ* (*Acc.*)<br>5) *caubbeu* (*Nom.*)<br>6) *paṇḍia-loa-hu* (Voc.) |

| | | |
|---|---|---|
| | | *Neut.*<br>1) *bea-purāṇa, -gaaṇa, suṇṇāsaṇṇa* (*DKK*) *bikhaṇḍia, amaṇāgamaṇa,* °*mana.*<br>2) *bhūtā, paā, bhavanivvāṇā.*<br>3) *-kamme* (*DKK.* 29). |

| Cent. A.D. | WAp. | SAp. |
|---|---|---|
| 1000 | *Masc.*<br>1) *mūlaguṇa, sappa, bahuya, tusa.*<br>2) *divahaḍā, dummehā, rukkhaḍā, kaṭṭhaḍā, bhallā, kālā.*<br>3) *dīvaḍaī, suaṇaī, hāraī, dosaī* (Ac.), *coraī, gāmaī* (Nom.) Mostly in in *BhK.*<br>Voc. *joiyahu.*<br>*Neut.*<br>1) *kamma, vattha, vaya, ghara, saya.*<br>2) *mokaliyaiṁ, sikkha-vayaiṁ, ṇiyalaiṁ*<br>3) *suhā, mokkalē.*<br>4) *upalāṇahiṁ* (*Pd.* 42). | *Masc.*<br>1) *gaya, suravara, amara, raha.*<br>2) *saṇandaṇā, visaṇṇā, bhārayā, Magahā,*<br>3) *kumāraī, veyaī.*<br>4) *hae* (*Nc.* 6.13.11).<br>*Neut.*<br>1) *pillāī, jalāiṁ, bhīsāiṁ*<br>2) *riṇaī, Pupphaim, sīsakkaī.* |

| Cent. A.D. | WAp. | SAp. | EAp. |
|---|---|---|---|
| 1100 | | *Masc.*<br>1) *bhaviysasāra, ṇiva, pāya, bhāya.* | |

| | | |
|---|---|---|
| | | *Neut.* |
| | *pankaā*, (*Mt.* 19) | 1) *hariṇaiṁ*, *laggaiṁ*, *seṇṇaiṁ*,<br>2) *joyaṇāiṁ*.<br>3) *uggaya*, *kama-kamala*. |

| Cent. A.D. | WAp. |
|---|---|
| 1200. | *Masc.*<br>1) *jaṇa*, *sambhariya*, *tarugaṇa*, *visaya*, *dīha*, *navullaḍaa*.<br>2) *khalāiṁ*, *bhaggāīṁ*, *viguttāīṁ*.<br>3) *payaḍā*, *thovā*, *dosaḍā*.<br>Voc. 1) *loaho*, *taruṇaho*, *gaṇahu*, *suyaṇahu*, *bhaviyaṇahu*, *daṇḍadharahu*.<br>*Neut.*<br>1) *avalaī* or *aṁvalaī*, *soiviṇaī cittaiṁ* (*Jdc.* 7.3).<br>2) *kāyavvāī*, *savvāī* (*Sc.* 459.3) *rayaṇāīṁ*.<br>3-5) *pamāṇaī* (*Jdc.* 2.1) *suddhigara* (*Kc.* ), *phala hiaullā*, (*Kc.*) *abbhā* (*KHc.*), *lihiā*, *valayā*. |

84B. MASC. AND NEUT. STEMS IN *-a*

| A.D. | WAp. | | SAp. | EAp. |
|---|---|---|---|---|
| 500 ? | | .. | .. | .. |
| 600-<br>1000 | *Masc.* : | zero<br>*-ā*<br>*-u* | .. | .. |
| | Voc. | *-hu*, *-ā* | | |
| | *Neut.* : | *-ā̆ĩṁ*<br>-zero, *-ā* ? | | |

| | | | |
|---|---|---|---|
| 700-<br>1200 | .. | .. | *Masc.*: zero<br>*-ā*<br>*-e*<br>*-ẽ*<br>*-u*<br>Voc. *-hu*<br>zero<br>*Neut.*: *-ā*<br>*e* (*DKK*.29) |
| 1000 | *Masc.* zero<br>*-ā*<br>*-iṁ*, *-ĩ*<br>Voc. Masc. Neut.<br>*-hu*<br>*Neut.*: zero<br>*-iṁ*, *-ĩ*<br>*-ā*<br>*-hiṁ* (*Pd.* 42). | *Masc.* zero<br>*-ā*<br>*-iṁ* *-ĩ*.<br>*-e* (*Nc.* 6.13.11).<br>*Neut.*: *-āĩ*<br>*-aĩ*, | |

| A.D. | WAp. | SAp. | EAp. |
|---|---|---|---|
| 1100 | *Neut.*: *-ā* | 2) *Neut.*: *ā̆iṁ*<br>zero.<br>1) Masc. zero. | |
| 1200 | *Masc.*: zero<br>*-āiṁ*.<br>*-ā*.<br>Voc.: *-ho*, *-hu*.<br>*Neut.*: *-aĩ*<br>*-āĩ*<br>*-i*<br>zero<br>*-ā* | | |

## §85. The Instr. Loc. Plural.

Pk. grammarians prescribe the following desinences for Ins.-Loc. Plur:

(1-2) *-ahiṁ* (*Pu.* 43, *Hc.* 335, 47, *Ld.* 4.19, 44, 46.
*-ehiṁ* (*Sh.* 13, 14, *Mk.* 18.29, *Rt.* 3.2.12).

(3) *-e* (*Rt.* 3.2.12, *Ld.* 4.4).

(4) *-su* (*Ld.* 4.6 with optional lengthening of the previous *-a*).

The following are the term.s of these cases in Pkts.[59].

*Ins. Pl*:

(1) *-ehi*, *-°him̐*, *-°hĩ* (Mah., Amg. JM. JŚ.)

(2) *-ehim̐* (Ś. Mg.)

*Loc. Plur.* :

(1) *-esu*, *°sum̐*, *°sũ* (Mah. Amg. JM. JŚ.)

(2) *-esum̐*, *°su* (Ś. Mg.)

Literary Ap. shows that the Pkt. term.s of Loc. Plur. were absolutely lost, and those of Ins. Plur. were extended to it, supplying thereby another proof of the merging of Loc. and Instr. discussed above (§ 81). Pk. grammarians admit it frankly.

The desinences in literary Ap. can be divided in two groups :

(1) *-ehim̐*, *°hĩ*, *°hi*, *-i(ẽ) him̐*, *°hĩ*, *°hi*.

(2) *-ahim̐*, *°hĩ*, *°hi*.

We have some forms ending in *-āham̐*, *-ahā̃* e.g., *ṇara ṇarayaham̐ ṇivaḍanti* 'Men fall *into* the infernal regions' (*Pd.* 5), *kum̐jaru annaham̐ taruaraham̐*, *kuḍḍeṇa ghallaï hatthu* 'The elephant passes his trunk *on* other trees out of curiosity.' (*Hc.* 8.4.422.9). Such forms are exceptional and limited to WAp. They show the confusion of the Loc. and the Gen. for which the accommodative nature of Gen. in OIA is responsible.

Out of these groups of term.s the first group is generally traced to Ved. Ins. Plur. *-ebhiḥ*[60] while the second group is related to OIA *-a-smin* of Loc. sg. Thus the first group signifies the merging of the cases and the second group shows the confusion of number in Ap.

The chrono-regional comp. of terms. (§ 85A) shows that SEAp. contains some more forms with unnasalized terms. than WAp. (except in an uncritical text like *Sn.*). *-ahim̐* in SAp. and *-ehim̐* in EAp. seem to have dropped their nasals occasionally. Is this probably due to the pre-

59 Pischel, *Grammatik* § 363.

60 Pischel, *Grammatik*, § 363. It may be urged that linguistically *-e-him̐* <OIA Loc. sg.* *-e-smin* is equally possible. Such double desinences e.g., *-āo*, *-ādo* for Abl. are found in Pkt. Thus *-e-him̐* for Loc. plur. will be an extension of sing. to plur. which is not uncommon in Ap.

ponderence of *-ahĩ* in SAp ? Thus in *Hv.* the proportion of *-ahĩ* : *-ehĩ* is 194 : 113. The denasalised *-ahĩ* i.e., *-ahi* forms are found in *KKc* also. In EAp. the claims of OIA *-adhi*> *-ahi* are doubtful as the exceptional term. *-ahi* may be a scribal error if not a tendency to denasalisation.

The change of *-ehiṁ*, °*hĩ* to *-ihiṁ*, -°*hĩ* etc. is explicable on TURNER's theory of the phonetic weakness of terminational endings in IA.[61] We find these in WAp. Thus in *Kp.* we have :

*-ihĩ* (9) *-ehĩ* (1) *-ehi* (1) as the term.s *-esu* forms being Prakritisms need not be noted.

These *-ehĩ*, *-ahĩ* groups have supplied the following desinences to NIA.[62]

*-ehĩ* >M. -ĩ e.g, *paṇḍaĩ*, 'by learned men,' *cinhĩ* 'by the signs.

>Beng -ẽ e.g., *tiṇiẽ paṭẽ* 'with (or in) three.'

*-ahĩ* >Guj. *-e*, e.g., *hāthe* 'by hands,' *nayane* 'by eyes,' *ṅārie* 'by women.'

>Raj. Guj. *-i* e.g., Raj. *ghoṛai*, Gur. *hāthi*.

§85A. THE INSTRUMENTAL LOCATIVE PLURAL

*-a* Stems (Masc. Neut.)

| Cent. A.D. | | SAp. | EAp. |
|---|---|---|---|
| 500? | *turaehĩ*, *vajjantehĩ*. | | |
| 600- | Ins.: (1) *veyahi* ँ, *paesahi* ँ, | | |
| 1000 | *lakkhaṇahi* ँ. | | |
| | (2) *potthā-picchiyai* ँ. | | |
| | Loc.: (1) *titthahi* ँ, *kasāyahi* ँ, | | |
| | *dehādehahi* ँ. | | |
| | (2) *devālihi* ँ (*Ys.* 43). | | |

61 TURNER, 'Phonetic Weakness of Terminational Elements in Indo-Aryan, *JRAS*, 1927, pp. 227-39.

62 For details see BLOCH, *L'indo-aryen*, pp. 172-3, 174-6.

| Cent. A.D. | WAp. | SAp. | EAp. |
|---|---|---|---|
| 700-1200 | | | Instr.: (1) *akkhohehī, pañcānanehī bamhanehī micchehī, paḍhantehī.* (2) *khaṇehi, -gaṇehi,* (3) *bisahi.* Loc.: (1) *āgama-bea-purāṇe* (*DKK* 2). *bhābābhābe* (*DKS*. 61). |

| Cent. A.D. | WAp. | SAp. |
|---|---|---|
| 1000 A.D. | *Instr.*: | *Instr.* |
| | (1) *akkharaḍehiṁ guṇehī, duvvayāṇehī -attantehī* | (1) *puttehiṁ, īriehiṁ, dahehiṁ, kiṁkarehiṁ.* |
| | (2) *akkharahiṁ, maṇa-vaya-kāya-hiṁ, uvavāsahiṁ, kusumahiṁ, divasahī, kaṇahiṁ.* | (2) *jaya-vanda-hiṁ, lallakkahiṁ, ṇāhalahiṁ.* |
| | | (3) *suṇahahi, viddhani saṇahi.* |
| | *Loc.* | *Loc.* |
| | (1) *guṇehī, thovaehī* | (1) *thāvarahiṁ, rukkhahiṁ, vayaṇahiṁ,* |
| | (2) *rāyahiṁ, rūvahiṁ rasahiṁ, bhavahiṁ, uvavāsahiṁ.* | (2) *kulehiṁ.* |
| | (3) *sukkāhaṁ, saravarahaṁ, visayahaṁ, bhogayahaṁ, calaṇahaṁ.* | |
| 1100 A.D. | *Ins.* | |
| | (1) *vaaṇehī juyalehī.* | (1) *bhalluehiṁ, rayaṇehiṁ, dīvaehiṁ.* |
| | (2) *aṇṇoṇṇahī saahī.* | (2) *loyahiṁ, dantahiṁ,* |
| | | (3) *jāṇahi.* |

| Cent. A.D. | WAp. |
|---|---|
| 1200 | *Ins.* |
| | (1) *visaehiṁ, lakkhehiṁ, loaṇehiṁ, payārehiṃ, sarehiṁ.* |
| | (2) *maṇa-pavaṇihiṁ, -dosihiṁ, -saïhiṁ* (*Sn*) ; *narihĩ, purisihĩ* (*Sc.*) |
| | (3) *ruddhahiṁ, guṇahiṁ, -kerahiṁ, sayatthahĩ* (*Kp.*) |
| | (4) *guṇihi, viṇaihi, susaṇehi* (All from *Sn.*). |
| | *Loc.* |
| | (1) *saehiṁ, maggehiṁ, ḍuṅgarihiṁ* (*Hc.* 4.445). |
| | (2) *kesahiṁ, raṇagayahiṁ, cittahĩ.* |
| | (3) (4) *tihi-pavvahi* (*Jdc.* 33.4) ; *taru-arahaṁ* (*Hc.* 4.422.9). |

§85B. The Instrumental-Locative Plural

| A.D. | | WAp. | | SAp. | | EAp. |
|---|---|---|---|---|---|---|
| 500 ? | | *-ehĩ* | | .. | | .. |
| 600- | Ins.: | *-(a)hi̐* | | .. | | .. |
| 1000 | | | | | | |
| | | *-(a)ĩ̐* | | | | |
| | Loc.: | *-(a)hi̐* | | | | |
| | | *-ihi̐* (*Ys.* 43) | | | | |
| 700- | | .. | | .. | Ins.: | *-ehĩ* |
| 1200 | | | | | | *-ehi* |
| | | | | | | *-(a)hi* |
| | | | | | Loc. : | *-e̐* |
| 1000 | Ins.: | *-ē̐hiṁ, -ēhĩ* | Ins.: | *-ehiṁ* | | |
| | | *-(a)hiṁ, -(a)hĩ* | | *-(a)hiṁ* | | |
| | | | | *-(a)hi.* | | |

| | | | | |
|---|---|---|---|---|
| | Loc.: | *-ehĩ* | Loc.: | *-(a)hiṁ.* |
| | | *-(a)hiṁ* | | *-ehiṁ* |
| | | *-(ā)haṁ.* | | |
| 1100 | | *-ehĩ* | | *-ehiṁ* |
| | | *-(a)hĩ* | | *-(a)hiṁ.* |
| | | | | *-(a)hi.* |
| 1200 | *-ehiṁ* | | | |

Ins.

*-ihiṁ, -ihĩ*

*-(a) hiṁ, -(a)hĩ*

*-(a, i, e)hi* (*Sn.*)

Loc. : *-ehiṁ,*

*-ihiṁ* (*Hc.* 4.445)

*-(a)hiṁ, -(a)hĩ*

*-(a)hi, (a)haṁ* (*Hc.* 4.22.9)

## §86. The Dative-Genitive-Ablative Case

This is perhaps the most important case in Ap., and it is during this period that the fusion of these cases was achieved. Pk. grammarians supply us with following desinences of this case:

*Ablative* :

*-huṁ* (*Hc.* 337, *Ld.* 4.8, *Sh.* 19, *Ki.* 5.29, *Rt.* 13, *Mk.* 20).

*-haṁ* (*Mk.* 20, *Rt.* 13).

*Ld.* prescribes optional lengthening of final *-a* before *-huṁ.*

*Dative-Genitive*

*-haṁ* (*Pu.* 45, *Hc.* 339-40, *Ld.* 4.10, *Sh.* 16, *Ki.* 32, *Rt.* 3.2.14).

*-huṁ* (*Pu.* 45).

Zero (*Ld.* 4.10 with the optional lengthening of previous *-a*).

Though Pk. grammarians were conscious of the process of fusion between the two (Abl. and Dat.-Gen.) cases, *-huṁ,* for Abl. and *-haṁ* for Dat-Gen. were the outstanding term.s according them.

The following were the term.s in Pkts.[63]

*Ablative*:

*-(a-,e-) suṁto, -āhiṁto, -(ā-,e-)hi, -āo*

*-āu, -atto*, (Mah.)

*-ehiṁto, -ehiṁ* (Amg.)

*-ehiṁ* (JM).

*Genitive*:

*-āṇa, -āṇaṃ, -āṇā̃* (Mah. Amg. JM. JŚ.)

*-āṇaṃ* (Ś. Mg.)

*-āhā̃* (Mg.)

It will be found that Ap. Abl. *-huṁ* has no cognate in Pkts., and Abl.-Pkt. desinences are unrepresented or unrelated to Ap.

From the Comp. Morphological Table (§86A) it appears that Ap. writers made little distinction between Gen. and Abl.,and that *-huṁ* which is unanimously sanctioned by Pk. grammarians is not favourite with them, but only a rarity in WSAp. and totally absent in EAp. In *Hv*. the nine cases of *-ahū̃* are doubtful,[64] while it is not seen in WAp. texts upto 1100 A.D., and in the critical editions of *Sc*. and *Kp*. in 1200 A.D. It appears that Ap. writers assumed the fusion of Abl. and Dat. Gen. from the very beginning of our period.

*-āṇa-* being a Prakritism, need not detain us. *-hiṁ* in *bhūvahiṁ*, as in

*jāsu maṇu bhaggā bhūvahiṁ*. *Pd*. 104.

"whose mind is turned away from material object," is (if not a scribal error) an extension of the Ins. Loc. term. to Abl. as we find Amg. and JM. *-ehiṁ* common to Abl. and Instr. Plur. *-a-hū̃* of the Gen. pl. is derived from Gen. sg. *-a-ha*+*-ā*<MIA *-āṇaṁ* of the Plur.[65] and is thus a double Gen. The only difficulty in this is the assumption MIA. *-ṇaṁ* >nasalisation of the surrounding vowel. The only way to avoid this difficulty and the correct derivation seems to be Ap. *-ahā̃*<Pk. OIA **-āsām*. Thus *puttahā̃* Pk. **puttāsam*<OIA **putrāsām* cf. Mg. *puttāhaṁ*.

---

63 Pischel, *Grammatik*, §§ 363, 369-70.

64 Intro. to *Hv*. § 41.

65 Bloch, *L'indo-aryen*, p. 144.

-(*a*)*ha* in EAp. is the extension of the term. of the sg. to the Plur., and has no relation with -*ahā*. Abl. Plur. -*hũ* is connected with OIA Abl. dual -*bhyām* by PISCHEL,[66] but the change -*yām*>-*ũ* is highly improbable. We have in Gen. sg. -*ha* : plur. -*hā̃*, so by analogy we get Abl. sg. -*hu* : Plur. -*hũ*. BLOCH accepts this explanation.[67]

## § 86A. THE DATIVE-GENITIVE-ABLATIVE PLURAL

| Cent. A.D. | WAp. | SAp. | EAp. |
|---|---|---|---|
| 500 ? | | | |
| 600- | *visayahaũ*, *ṇāṇiyahaũ*, | .. | .. |
| 1000 | *dehiyahaũ*, *mukkahaũ*,<br>*mūḍhahaũ*, -*jīvahaũ*. | | |
| 700-<br>1200 | | (1) *jarā-maraṇaha*, *turaṅgaha*,<br>*nitambaha*.<br>(2) *khabaṇāna* (*DKs.* 8).<br>(3) *suṇṇāsuṇṇa* (*DKK.* 13). | |

| Cent. A.D. | WAp. | SAp. |
|---|---|---|
| 1000 | (1) *Abl.* : *dehahaṁ*, *guṇahaṁ*,<br>*paṁcumbarahaṁ*.<br>*Gen.* : *kammahaṁ*, *dosahaṁ*,<br>*baliyahaṁ*, *jīvahaṁ*,<br>*rāyahaṁ*, *guṇahaṁ*,<br>*sāvayahaṁ*, *bhoyahaṁ*.<br>(2) *Abl.* *bhuvahīṁ* (*Pd.* 104).<br>*Gen.* *mukkāhaṁ*, (*Sdd.* 18). | (1) *tūrahaṁ*, *baṁbhaṇahaṁ*,<br>*sarīrahaṁ*, *kaṇāsaṇahaṁ*,<br>(2) *kammayāhaṁ* (*Mp.* 2.9.18),<br>*khalāhaṁ* (*Jc.* 3.37.8).<br>(3) *soṇiyahuṁ* (*Jc.* 3.34.13),<br>(4) *jagaha* (*Jc.* 1.6.1). |

66 *Grammatik*, § 369.
67 BLOCH, *L'indo-aryen*, p. 144.

| 1100 A.D. | WAD | SAD. |
|---|---|---|
| | | (1) *maṇuvahaṁ, bhamantahaṁ, saṁsārahaṁ.* |
| | | (2) *sajjaṇāhaṁ, sāvayāhaṁ, paṁkayaruhāhaṁ.* |
| | | (3) *mantāṇa, pāya-pomāṇa, kammāṇa* (Pktisms) |

| Cent. A.D. | | WAp. |
|---|---|---|
| 1200 | *Abl.* : | (1) *karaṇābhāsahu* |
| | | (2) *girisiṅgahũ, muhahũ* (*Hc.*) |
| | *Gen.* : | (1) *juyarāyahaṁ, visayahaṁ, mattahaṁ, Paṇḍavahā̃, -cittahā̃, bhuṁjantahā̃.* |
| | | (2) *dusaṁga-susaṁga-ha* (*Jdc.* 10-3), *juṭṭa-ha* (*Jdu.* 77.1). |
| | | (3) *chaḍḍaisaṇu* (*Jdc.* 2.1), *visaya* (*Kc.* 22), *gaya* (*Hc.* 4.345), *-āṇa* forms being Pktisms. are not noted. |

## 86B. The Dative-Genitive-Ablative Case

| A.D. | | WAp. | SAp. | EAp. |
|---|---|---|---|---|
| 500 | | .. | .. | .. |
| 600-1000 | | -(*a*)*haṁ* | .. | .. |
| 700-1200 | | .. | .. | -(*a*) *ha*<br>-(*ā*)*ṇa* (*DKs.* 8)<br>zero |
| 1000 | Abl. | -(*a*)*haṁ*<br>-(*a*)*hiṁ* (*Pd.* 104) | | |
| | Gen. | -(*a*)*haṁ*<br>-(*a*)*hā̃*<br>-(*ā*)*haṁ* (*Sdd.* 18) | -(*a*)*haṁ*<br>-(*ā*)*haṁ*<br>-(*a*)*huṁ* (*Jc.* 3.34.13)<br>-(*a*)*ha* (*Jc.* 1.5.1) | |

| | | | |
|---|---|---|---|
| 1100 | .. | -(*a*) *haṁ*<br>-(*ā*)*haṁ*<br>-(*ā*)*ṇa* (Pktisms.) | |
| 1200 | Abl. -(*a*)*hu*<br>-(*a*)*hũ*<br>Gen. -(*a*)*haṁ*<br>-(*a*)*hã*<br>-(*a*)*ha*<br>-zero | .. | .. |

## Feminine Stems Ending in *-a*, *-ā*.

§ 87. The OIA and Pkt. Fem. *-ā* stems are generally reduced to *-a* ending ones in Ap. This does not mean that *-ā* ending stems are totally absent in Ap. but that the *-a* stems predominate. As there is no difference in the declension of *-ā̆* stems , they are classed here under one head. Moreover the number of purely Ap. peculiarities is not so great as to deserve a detailed treatment of every case as we did with regard to Masc. and Neut. *-a* stems. We should leave aside the desinences which are common to other Pkts. and concentrate on purely Ap. development. But at the same time we must recognise the possiblity of Ap. influence on Pk. literature as well.

The importance of the declension of *-ā̆* stems lies in the fact that it served as a model for Fem. *-ī̆* and *-ū̆* stems.

§88. The following are the terms. of these themes in Pkts. [68]

### STEMS IN *-ā*.

*Singular* :

Nom.: zero.

Acc. : *-aṁ*.

Ins. : *-āe*, *-āi*, *-āa* (Mah.). In other dialects *-āe* only.

Dat. : *-āe* in Amg. only.

Abl. : *-āo*, *-aāu* (*-āhiṁto*, *-āi*, *-āa*, *-atto*) in Mah. Amg. JM. *-ādo*, *-āe* (Ś. Mg.)

68 Pischel, *Grammatik* § 374.

Gen. Loc.: -*āe*, -*āi*, -*āa* (Mah.) In others only -*āe* i.e., the term.s are the same as those of the Ins.

Voc. : -*e* (Pktism), zero.

*Plural* :

Nom. Acc. Voc. : -*āo*, -*āu*, zero (Mah. Amg. JM.), -*āo*, zero (Ś. Mg.)

Ins. : -*āhĩ*, -*āhī*, -*āhiṁ* (Mah. Amg. JM. ) -*āhiṁ* (Ś. Mg.)

Abl. : -*āhiṁto* (-*āsuṁto*, -*āo* -*āu*) in Mah. Amg.

Gen. : -*āṇa*, -*āṇã*, -*āṇaṁ* (Mah. Amg. JM. ) -*āṇaṁ* (Ś.Mg.)

Loc. : -*āsu*, -*āsũ*, -*āsuṁ* (Mah. Amg. JM.), -*āsu*, -*āsuṁ* (Ś. Mg.)

A comparison of the term.s of Fem. -*ā* in Ap., (§88A) with those in the chrono-regional tables of the terms. of -*a* stem.s in Ap. (§§80-86) discloses the following facts :

(1) The declension of Fem. -*ă* stems borrowed a number of desinences from the declension of Masc. and Neut. -*a* stems as tabulated below :

*Terms. common to Masc. and Fem. Stems ending in -a.*
*Singular* :

Nom.: zero (sometimes in the case of Acc. also)

Instr.: WEAp. -*ẽ* (1000 A.D.) -*e* (WAp. 1000 and 1200 A.D. and SAp. 1100), -*iṁ*, -*ĩ*, SAp. -*i*.

Gen. : WAp. -*ha*, -*haṁ* (1000 A.D.), -*hu* (1100 A.D.) -*ha* (1200 A.D.), SAp. -*huṁ*.

Loc. : A distinctly different case from Gen. as contrasted with secondary MIA.

WAp. -*i* (600 A.D.), WSAp., -*i*, -*iṁ*, -*hiṁ* (1000 A.D.) -*hĩ* (1100 A.D.).

WAp. -*i*, -*hiṁ*, -*hĩ* (1200 A.D.), -*hĩ* forms less common.

*Plural* :

Direct : zero, in *BhK.* 52.4 -*aĩ*.

Dat. Gen. : Abl. WAp. *-haṁ*, *-hã* (1100-1200 A.D.) Abl. pl. WAp. *-hu* (1200 A.D.)

Loc. : *-hĩ*.

(2) Fem. themes in *-ă* show that the fusion of Nom. and Acc. cases (both sing. and plur.) was complete before 600 A.D. With the exception of the borrwed masc. teıms. of *-a* stems, Ins. and Loc. sings. remained distinct upto the end of 1100 A.D. or even upto 1200 A.D. Ins. sg. conserved the old Pkt. term. (*ā*)*e* throughout the Ap. period —at least apparently. Gen. and Loc. appeared amalgamated in Pkts., but in Ap. they are quite distinct, while the process of the absorption of the Abl. into Gen. is seen upto 1000 A.D. Though we roughly class together Dat. Gen. Abl. sing. and plur. from their use in literature, Abl. is an independent case in Pkts., but not so in Ap. Hence *Hc.* 8.4.350-51.

## §89. The Direct Case

As in NIA, Ap. shows only two important cases—the Direct and the Oblique. The former is already formed while common desinences of Dat. Gen. Abl. and Instr.—Loc. in 1200 A.D. show the formative process of the latter. In the direct case, very few terms. remain to be explained after eliminating those of the masc. *-a* stems. *ă* as in *disā*<*diśam* in *Vk.* (*Mt.* 32) is a mediate stage between Pkt. *-ṁ* and Ap. zero which must be assumed as the stem was used in the direct case from 600 A.D., in WSEAp. The later *-ṁ* forms e.g., *muddaṁ* (*mudrām*) are Prakritisms.

Vocatives in *-e* are Sanskritisms, and these with zero term. are found in Pkts. Voc. sg. in *-i* e.g., *kanti* (*kāntā-*), *vacchi* (*vatsā-*) are weakened forms of *-e* viz., *kānte*, *vatse*.

## §89A. Feminine Stems Ending in *-ā*

*Direct Singular.*

| Cent. A.D. | WAp. | SAp. | EAp. |
|---|---|---|---|
| 500 | *Nom.* : *saria*, | .. | .. |
| | *Acc.* : *disā* (*Mt.* 32) | .. | .. |
| 600- | *Nom.* : *mudda*. *āsā* | .. | .. |

| Cent. | WAp. | SAp. | EAp. |
|---|---|---|---|
| 1000 | *Acc.* : *veyaṇa, bhukkha.* | .. | .. |
| 700-1200 | .. | .. | *Nom.* *dakkhiṇa, bhajja niccala, Jamuṇā, dhāraṇa.*<br>*Acc.* *karuṇā, ghaṇḍā beaṇu* (*DKs.* 77). |

| Cent. | WAp. | SAp. | EAp. |
|---|---|---|---|
| 1000 | *Nom.* *kaṁculiya, līha, gira, vallaha, daya, kiriyā.*<br>*Acc.* *bhikkha, ḍāla, veyaṇa, daya, dikkha, -sāla, -kīla, Pujja, vaṭṭaḍiyā, chāyā.*<br>*Voc.* : *jāe, kanti.* | *Nom.* *rayāṇiyā, aṁciya pasāhiya, kaüsiya, ṇāïṇiya.*<br>*Acc.* : *dhīya, sayala,*<br>*Voc.* *māi, ammi* (?) | |
| 1100 | *Nom.* :<br>*Avc.* : *muddaṁ soha*<br>Voc. : *muddhe* | *Nom.* : *mahila, bāla, vijjāhariya.*<br>*Acc.* : *asilaya, kaṇṇa, līla*<br>*Voc.* : *bhaḍārie.* | |
| 1200 | *Nom.* : *Jīha, dhaṇa, sila, chāyā, phukka.*<br>*Acc.* : *-māla, pūya, hiṁsā, boḍḍia.*<br>*Voc.* : *ammi muddhi, vacchi, ammie.* | | |

§89B. Feminine Stems Ending in -ā.

| Cent. A.D. | WAp. | SAp. | EAp. |
|---|---|---|---|
| | *Direct Singular.* | | |
| 500 | Nom. : zero<br>Acc. : –~ | .. | .. |
| 600-1000 | Nom. : Zero. | .. | .. |

| | | | |
|---|---|---|---|
| | Acc. : zero | | |
| 700-1200 | .. | .. | Nom. : -zero |
| | | | Acc. : -zero<br>-*u*(*DKs.* 77) |
| 1000 | Nom. : -zero | Nom. : -zero. | |
| | Acc. : -zero | Acc. : -zero | |
| | Voc. : -*e*, -*i* | Voc. : -*i* | |
| 1100 | Nom. : | Nom. : -zero | |
| | Acc. : -zero | Acc. : -zero | |
| | *ṁ*- | Voc. : -*e* | |
| | Voc. : -*e* | | |
| 1200 | Nom. : -zero | | |
| | Acc. : -zero | | |
| | Voc. : -*i*, -*ie* | | |

## The Oblique Cases

### §90. The Instumental Case

The predominance of Masc. terms. in this case is so great that although -(*ā̆*)*i* is the term. of Fem. -*ā* stems even in Pkts., one is tempted to regard it as a denasalised form of Masc. -*iṁ* and -*ĩ*, in Ap., instead of taking it to be a weakened form of -(*ā̆*)*e* which appears in Pkts. and Ap. These (*a*)-*i* forms are limited only to SAp. of the 10th cent., and in that too to *Mp.* and *Jc.* for Alsdorf's edition of *Hv.* gives (*a*)*e* for Fem. stems in -*ā̆*, -*ī̆*, -*ū̆*.[69] *KKc.* has -*iṁ*, -*eṁ* and -(*ā*)*e* term.s which evidently shows the tendency to use Masc. term.s to Fem. stems. We find the same in M. for Instr. sg. e.g., *āplyā kṛpẽ karūn* 'by your favour' wherein -*ẽ* is used with the Fem. -*ā* stem viz. *kṛpā*. [70]

The evidence of WSEAp. Ins. sg. of -*ā̆* stems. shows that there was a very strong tendency to apply Masc. term.s to Fem. -*ã* stems, and

69 Alsdorf, Intro. to *Hv.* §§ 43, 45.

70 In Coll. M. The nasal ~ has now disappeared and we generally say *kṛpe-karūn* in our Poona Marathi speech.

its persistence in M. tends to prove Fem. Ins. sg. -*i*<Masc. -*ī*, -*iṁ* rather than -*i*<Fem. -*e*, though linguistically that is equally probable. *Sn.* is an uncritical text, so *līlaha*<*līlayā* (*Sn.* 334-127) may be a scribal error for *līlai*, as *h* and *i* in the Devanāgarī script look alike. Otherwise this exceptional form shows the application of the Gen. term. to the Instr. case.

Chronologically the use of Masc. term.s for Fem. Ins. sgs. is as follows :

700 A.D.—EAp.

1000 A.D.—WAp. (SAp. if the Ins. sg. -*i* discussed above be traceable to -*iṁ*.)

1100 A.D.—SAp

## § 90A. Feminine Stems Ending in -*a*

*Instrumental Singular...*

| Cent. A.D. | SAp. | SAp. | EAp. |
|---|---|---|---|
| 500 | .. | .. | .. |
| 600-1000 | *bhattiya-ĕ, uddehiyaĕ* .. | .. | .. |
| 700-1200 | .. | *bhaba-muddẽ, bācẽ, icchẽ* (*DKs.* 81). | |

| Cent. A.D. | WAp. | SAp. |
|---|---|---|
| 1000 | (1) *tattïṁ, lālaïṁ, ṭikkaïṁ, visakaṇiyaïṁ.* | (1) *Jīvaṁjasaï, mantaṇaï, ṇisāsuṇhaï, hiṁsa-ï, jīhaï, māyaï.* |
| | (2) *nettae*ⁿ, *līlaẽ, kamalaẽ.* | (2) *suttāe, kahāe, vāyae.* |
| | (3) *jarāe, -gattae, kantae.* | |
| 1100 | (1) *ṇiddae, aṇahijja-e* (*Mt.*) | (1) *kusumattaiṁ, karuṇaïṁ, mahilaiṁ, āṇaïṁ, mucchāiṁ.* |
| | | (2) *Pomāvayaeṁ.* |
| | | (3) *uṭṭhiyāe, icchantiyāe, vīhiyāe.* |

| Cent. A.D. | WAp. |
|---|---|
| | (1) *līlae, vayaṇiyae, avāhāe.*<br>*candimae, ṇiddae, uḍḍāvantiae.* |
| | (2) *kavaḍḍiĩ* (*KPs.* 56.4). |
| | (3) *lila-ha* (*Sn.* 334-127). |

§90B. INSTRUMENTAL

| | | | |
|---|---|---|---|
| 500 | .. | .. | .. |
| 600-1000 | *-ĕ* | .. | .. |
| 700-1200 | .. | .. | .. *ĕ* |
| 1000 | *-iṁ* (*Sdd. Pd.*)<br>*-e$^{n}$* (i.e., *-ẽ*) *BhK.*<br>*-e* (*Bh.K*). | *-i*<br>(*ă*)*e*) | .. |
| 1100 | *-e* | *-iṁ*<br>*-eṁ*<br>*-*(*ă*)*e.* | .. |
| 1200 | *-*(*ă*)*e*<br>*-ĩ* (*Kp.* S. 56.4)<br>*-ha* (*Sn.* 334-127). | .. | .. |

§ 91. THE DAT. GEN. ABL. CASE.

Unlike Pkts. Ap. has separate Dat-Gen.-Abl. and Loc. cases. There are some common term.s in these two (Dat-Gen. Abl. and Loc.) cases, but they should not be confused as their linguistic history is different. Thus Dat-Gen-Abl. sg. *-hi* is a weakened form of *-hĕ* or *-he*<OIA *-syāḥ* (according to PISCHEL).[71] The scarcity of this in *Pd.*, *SDD.*, and its appearance in *BhK.*, and the regular occurrence as *-hĕ* in Hv., and *-hi* and *-he* in *Mp. Nc.* and *Jc.* show that it was already a well-established usage in SAp. before 965 A.D., while it was coming in use in contemporary WAp. in which it got recognition as late as 12th cent. A.D. In SAp., however, it continued as *-he* in 1100 A.D.

71 PISCHEL, *Grammatik*, § 375, p. 260.

*-hi* of the Loc. sg. should be connected with OIA *-a-smin*<*-a-hĩ* or with OIA *adhi*. Such similarities in terms. with different histories lead to confusion of cases.

The *-hiṁ* form in *Jc.* 3.11.6.

*ammahiṁ tāma dehi pau leppiṇu.*

'Having cut the leg, give it awhile *to the mother*,' is an exception, and may be a scribal error, as the metre does not require even a half-pronounced nasal *-hĩ*.

The remaining desinences are the same as of Masc. *-a* stems. A greater number of these are found in WAp. rather than in SAp. (For their linguistic history see § 83). Some forms of this case e.g., *ḍāla-haṁ*=*śākhāyām*, appear to have been used in the Loc. sense. The accommodative nature of the Dat.-Gen.Abl. case and the common terms. led to the confusion of cases in that period.

## § 92. THE LOCATIVE CASE

If we exclude Pkt. term.s and those of the Masc. *-a* stems from those of this case, *-(a)hi* is the only desinence worth consideration. ALSDORF identified Gen. and Loc. of Fem. *-ā̆*, *-ī̆*, *-ū̆* stems (as well as those of Masc. *-ī̆* and *ū̆-* stems).[72] In his earlier work (*KP.*), he rightly treated them separately.[73] From ALSDORF's presentation (Intro. to *KP.* § 22) it may appear that Fem. *-ahi* is a denasalisation of Masc. *-ahĩ*. Can we not trace this *-ahĩ* to Fem. *-ā- syām*>**-ā-hẽ*>*-a-hẽ* ? The proportion of desinences as presented by ALSDORF, there, is :

Loc. *-ahĩ* (3), *-ahĩ* (1), [+1 E], [*-āi* 4]

But the real Fem. term. in Ap. is *-ahi* and appears in EAp. for the first time as *PPr.* and *Vs.*, give only *-i* and *-e* endings like the Masc. *-a* stems. There is no other alternative term. like *-hiṁ* or *-hĩ* so this *-hi* (or *-a-hi*) must be connected with OIA *-adhi* as suggested in §91. *-hĩ* appears only in *BhK.* in WAp. (1000 A.D.) for the first time. Other WAp. works of the same cent. e.g., *Pd.*, *Sdd.* use *-hiṁ* forms in stead *-hĩ* alternates with *-hiṁ* or *-hĩ* in 1100-1200 A.D., in WAp. SAp. has *-hi* and *-i* and *-iṁ* as the alternative endings. So *-hi* is the only real Fem. term. of Loc. Sg., and the denasalized endings of WAp. *-hiṁ* and *-hĩ* were mixed up with it.

---

72 Intro. to *Hv.* §§ 43, 45, 44.
73 Intro. to *Kp.* 22, 24, 23.

As Masc. Loc. Sing. term.s of the -*a* stem were freely applied to the Fem. stems from 600 A.D., in WAp., and later in SAp., we need not assume the extension of Fem. Instr. Loc. plur. -*hiṁ* to the sing., though we have some instances of such confusion of numbers in other cases. e.g., Gen. sg. and plur. of Fem. -*ā* stems. Thus Loc. sg. -*hā̃* found generally in *Sc.* (and found as early as 1000 A.D. e.g., *ḍāla-haṁ* in (*Sdd.* 95) is a term. of Gen. plur., and such a Gen.-Loc. case may be an indication of the process of the formation of the Oblique in the last stage of Ap. The Loc. Instr. and Dat.-Gen.-Abl. cases are at the basis of the Oblique in NIA.[74]

### §92A. Feminine Stems Ending in -ā̆

*Locative Singular.*

| A.D. | WAp. | SAp | EAp. |
|---|---|---|---|
| 500 | .. | .. | .. |
| 600-1000 | *sili, kuḍilliyaĩ, silaẽ* (*PPr.* 1.123). | | |
| 700-1200 | .. | .. | *nisa-hi* (*DKs.* 89. |
| 1000 | (1) *avatthahiṁ, dihahiṁ, vesahiṁ.* | (1) *uttarāsāḍhai* (*MP.* 87.13.7). | |
| | (2) *gaṅgaĩ, garuvaĩ piḍi* (*Sdd.* 8), | (2) *volīnahi* (*Mp.* 2.4.6). | |
| | (3) *rāmaiṁ, āyaĩṁ* (*Pd.* 6), *disaĩṁ,* | *saṁjhāi* (*Jc.* 2.9.4. | |
| | (4) *ḍālahaṁ* (*Sdd.* 95). *akhaiṇi* (*Pd.* 42.) *sahāe, kahāe.* | | |
| 1100 | *chāhahi,* (*Mt.* 14), *joṇha-hĩ* (*Mt.* 14). | *Campahiṁ, Gaṁgahiṁ, puvvāhiṁ disihiṁ,* (?) (2) *manjūsaiṁ.* | |
| 1200 | *ṇisi* (*Jc.* 16.3) . Skt. *ṇisihiṁ* (*Jdc.* 18.2). *piyahā̃, niyahā̃* (Intro. to *Sc.* P. 12). | | |

74 Bloch, *L'indo-aryen,* pp. 172-81.

## §92B. Feminine Stems Ending in -*ă*

### *Locative Singular.*

| Cent. A.D. | WAp. | SAp. | EAp. |
|---|---|---|---|
| 500 | .. | .. | .. |
| 600 | -*i* | .. | .. |
| 1000 | -*e* (*PPr.* 1.123) | | |
| 700-1200 | .. | .. | -(*a*)-*hi*. |
| 1000 | -*hiṁ*<br>-*i*<br>-*iṁ*<br>-*haṁ*<br>-zero<br>-*e*. | -*i*<br>-*hi* | .. |
| 1100 | -*hi*<br>-*hĩ* | -*hiṁ*<br>-*iṃ* | .. |
| 1200 | -*hiṁ*, -*hĩ*<br>-*i* (Sktsm.)<br>-*hã*. | | |

PLURAL NUMBER

§93. There are very few purely Ap. desinences of Fem. -*ă̆* stems. Most of them are common to Pkts. and to Masc. -*a* stems in Ap. As most of these are discussed by Pischel, Bloch or in the previous sections of this work, the remaining few are treated here.

THE DIRECT CASE

(1) The stem was directly used for the Direct case in Ap. As similar forms are found in Mah. Ś and Mg., [75] WSEAp. inherited these from the previous speech habits of their respective regions. -*ao* and -*au*, being already used in Mah. Amg. JM. as *āo*-*āu* (-*āo* in Ś. as well), need not detain us. The fusion of Fem. Nom. and Acc. plurs. of -*ā* stems already took place before the Ap. period. In WAp. we find that the term. of the Neut. direct plur. is applied to Fem. -*ā* stems. e.g., *desa-*

75 Pischel, *Grammatik*, § 374, and § 88, of the present work.

*bhāsa-ĩ* (*deśa-bhāṣāḥ*), *sayalaĩ* (*sakalāḥ*). These are the precursors of a similar tendency in Hindi and Punjabi.[76]

THE INDIRECT CASES

(2) *The Instr. Loc. Case*:

The Instr.-Loc. *-hĩ* (or-*hiṁ*) is found in Pkts. as the term. of Instr. plur., whence it was extended to Loc. plur. in Ap. We cannot exactly ascertain the date or the original province of this amalgamation of cases, but in 1000 A.D., it was common to WESAp., and that is the lower limit of this tendency.

Out of the remaining terms., *-i* is a Masc. Loc. sg. term. extended to Fem. Loc. plur. e.g., *saṁjhai* (*sandhyāyāṃ*=°*su* in *Sdd.* 12), *pīḍi* (*pīḍāyām*=°*su Sdd.* 9). Zero, as in *saṁjhā* (*Sdd.* 68) is more interesting. The context shows that in Ap. there was a tendency to apply the desinence to the last word when two or more words (related to each other) are in the same case. Thus here we have *saṁjhā tihiṁ mi* 'In three twilights (?)' (*Sdd.* 68). So in *Pd* 42:

*jasu akhaïṇi rāmaiṁ gayau maṇu*

'One whose mind is fixed on the beautiful lady of a perpetual nature (*viz.* the Final Spiritual Beatitude).' Here Loc. sg. *-iṁ* is dropped in the case of *akhaïṇi* and is applied only to the next word *rāmaiṁ*.

*-hã* which is found chiefly in *Sc.*, is an evidence of the process of the fusion of Gen. and Loc. Plur.

(3) *The Dat. Gen. Abl. Case*

Out of the different terms. of this case, *-hu*, *-haṁ*, and *-hã* are common to Masc. and Fem. stems. They underlie the half-nasalized oblique forms in NIA. These are freely used with Fem. *-a* stems from the 10th cent. A.D. In WAp. *-hu* was popular and was used down to 1200 A.D. *-hã* was used originally in SAp. (1000 A.D.) whence probably it spread to WAp. in the 11th cent. and onwards. By the way, we may note the use of *-hĩ* in *joi -hĩ* =*yogināṃ* (*PPr.* 2.166) which is a puzzle. Are we to assume that the process of the fusion of Loc. and Gen. began as early as 600 A.D. in WAp. even in Masc. gender? Its use in later works e.g., *KKc.* (as in Fem. *soṇiyāhiṁ*= *śroṇikayoḥ* or *śroṇyoḥ*), or the use of the converse tendency *viz.*, the use of *-hã* for Loc. plur. in

76 For a similar tendency in H. and Punj. see BLOCH, *La langue marathe*, § 189.

a still later work like *Sc.*, is understandable as a percursor of NIA oblique. But *-hĩ* does not appear in WAp. in a later period. Is it a scribal error for *-hā̃* ?[77]

### §93A.1. Feminine Stems Ending in -ā. *Direct Plural.*

| Cent. A.D. | WAp. | SAp. | EAp. |
|---|---|---|---|
| 500 | .. | .. | .. |
| 600-1000 | .. | .. | .. |
| 700-1200 | .. | | *lalanā-rasanā* (*DKK*.5). *cintā-cinta* (*DKs.* 59.) |
| 1000 | (1) *ghaṇṭa, paṭṭiya, cinta, aṇupehā.* (2) *desa-bhāsaī* (*Bh.K.* 52.4), *sayalaiṁ* (*Pd.*) | | (1) *ṇikkhantau, Paḍimaü* (2) *riyāü, maïlāü.* |
| 1100 | .. | .. | *vajjaü, ramantiyau, ramaṇiyāu.* |
| 1200 | (1) *kannayau* (*Sc.*), *jajjariāu* (*Hc.*) (2) *dhūya* (*Sc.* 500.9). | | |

### §93A.2. Feminine Stems Ending in -ā *Instrumental & Locative Plural.*

| Cent. A. D. | WAp. | SAp. | EAp. |
|---|---|---|---|
| 500 | | .. | .. |
| 600-1000 | *kuṁḍiyahi̐* (*PPr.* 2.89) | .. | .. |
| 700-1200 | .. | .. | Loc. *daha-diha-hĩ* (*DKs.* 45) |

77 For the development of these oblique cases in NIA see Bloch, *L'indo-aryen*, pp. 172-81.

| | | |
|---|---|---|
| 1000 | *-dīviyahī̃* | *-dhārahiṁ, caüdisahiṁ,* |
| | *Loc. samjhai* (Sdd. 12) | *lanjiya-him, avarāhim,* |
| | *pīḍi. samjhā* (Sdd. 68) | *jamghāhiṁ, māucchiyāhiṁ, bhaühahiṁ.* |
| 1100 | (1) *vahantiahī̃* (*Mt.* 14) *unmmattiahī̃.* | *bālahiṁ, sahiyahiṁ,* |
| | (2) *-gattiahi* (*Mt.* 14). | *samasīlahiṁ* |
| 1200 | *kahahī̃, girahī̃* (2) *tadilayahā̃* (*Sc.* 511.4), *dhūyāhā̃* (*Sc.* 260.9) Loc. *Kahāsu* (Pkt. sm.) | |

§93A.3. Feminine Stems Ending in *-ā*.

*Dative-Genitive-Ablative Plural.*

| Cent. A.D. | WAp. | SAp. | EAp. |
|---|---|---|---|
| 500 | .. | .. | .. |
| 600-1000 | | .. | .. |
| 700-1200 | .. | | .. |
| 1000 | (1) *mahilahā̃, sampayahā̃* (*BhK.*) | .. | .. |
| | (2) *mahilāṇa* (*Pd.* 157) Pktism. | .. | .. |
| 1100 | *mahila-haṁ* (*Sn.* 168-115) | (1) *disāhaṁ* (*KKc.* 7.13.8) | |
| | | (2) *soṇiyāhiṁ* (*KKc.* 1.16.5) | |
| | | (3) *kaṇṇāṇa* (*KKc.* 8.10.1) Pktism. | |
| 1200 | (1) *bhāriya-hā̃, laya-hā̃, devaya-hā̃, kannayāhā̃* (*Sc.* 708.3), *kannahā̃ dhūyahā̃, duhiyahā̃,* | | |
| | (2) *māya-haṁ* (*Hc.* 399). | | |
| | (3) *vayaṁsiahu* (*Hc.* 351). | | |

## §93B (*i*) Feminine Stems Ending in -*ā*

*Direct Plural.*

| Cent. A.D. | WAp. | SAp. | EAp. |
|---|---|---|---|
| 500 ? | .. | .. | .. |
| 600-1000 | .. | .. | .. |
| 700-1200 | .. | .. | zero |
| 1000 | zero<br>-*aĩ*<br>-*ao* | -(*a*)*u*<br>-(*ā*)*u* | .. |
| 1100 | ◡ | -(*a*)*u* | .. |
| 1200 | -(*ā*)*u*<br>zero | .. | .. |

## §93B (*ii*) Instrumental-Locative Plural.

| Cent. A.D. | WAp. | SAp. | EAp. |
|---|---|---|---|
| 500 | .. | .. | .. |
| 600-1000 | -*hi* ँ | .. | .. |
| 700-1200 | .. | .. | Loc. : -*hĩ* |
| 1000 | Instr. : -*hĩ*<br>Loc. : -*i*<br>-zero | -*hiṁ* | .. |
| 1100 | -*hĩ*<br>-*hi* (*Mt.* 14). | -*hiṁ* | .. |
| 1200 | -*hĩ*, -*hã* (Intro. to *Sc*. p. 12).<br>-*su* (Pktam.) | | |

## 93B (*iii*) Dative—Genitive—Ablative Plural

| Cent. A.D. | WAp. | SAp. | EAp. |
|---|---|---|---|
| 500 | .. | .. | .. |
| 600-1000 | .. | .. | .. |
| 700-1200 | .. | .. | .. |

| | | | |
|---|---|---|---|
| 1000 | -*hā̃* (*Bh. K.*) | .. | .. |
| | -*āṇa* (*Pd.* 157) | -*hā̃* (*Vide* Intro. to *Hv.* §43). | |
| 1100 | -*haṁ* (*Sn.* 168-115) | -(*ā*)*haṁ*<br>-(*ā*)*hiṁ*<br>-*āna* (Pkt.) | .. |
| 1200 | -(*ā̆*)*hā̃* (*Sc.*)<br>-*haṁ* (*Hc.*)<br>-*hu* (*Hc.* 351.) | .. | .. |

### MASCULINE STEMS ENDING IN -*i* AND -*u*.

§94. It was already in OIA that Masc. themes in -*i* and -*u* were mostly declined alike. In this stage of MIA, the declension became so identical that there is no need to treat them separately although PISCHEL appears to do so in his treatment of Pkts.[78] In Ap. as in Pkts. some OIA -*ṛ* endings are also included under this.

The following are the term.s of these stems in Pkts.:

*Masc. and Neut. Stems in -i.*

*Singular* :

*Nom.* : -*ī i.e.*, elongation of the final vowel, (-*ṁ*)

Acc. : -*ṁ*.

Instr.: -*ṇā*.

Abl. -(*ī*)*o*, -(*ī*)*u*, -*ṇo*, -(*ī*)*hiṁto*, [-(*ī*)*hi*, -*tto*] in Mah. Amg. JM (*ī*)*do in* JŚ [Ś.Mg.]

Gen. : -*ṇo*, -*ssa*, [-(*ī*)*o*] in Mah. Amg. JM. -*ṇo* (Ś.Mg.)

Loc. : -*mmi* (Mah. Amg. JM.), -*ṁsi* (mostly in Amg.)

Voc. : zero with optional elongation of the final vowel.

*Plural* :

Nom. : -*ṇo*, -(*ī*) zero, -(*ī*)*o*, -*ao*, -*aü*, (Mah. Amg. JM.) -*ṇo*, -(*ī*)*o* in Ś.

Acc. : -*ṇo* -(*ī*) zero, -*ao* (Mah. Amg. JM.)

Instr. : -(*ī*)*hi*, -(*ī*)*hĩ*, -(*i*)*hiṁ* (Mah. Amg. JM.) -(*ī*)*hiṁ* (Ś. Mg.)

Abl. : -(*ī*)*hiṁto*, [-(*ī*)*suṁto*, -*tto*, -(*ī*)*o*] in Mah. Amg. JM.

78 *Grammatik*, §§ 377-88. As a matter of fact he treats them together in §§ 379-82.

Gen. : *-(ī)ṇa*, *-(ī)ṇā*, *-(ī)ṇaṁ* (Mah. Amg. JM.), *-(ī)ṇaṁ* (Ś.Mg.)

Loc. : *-(ī)*, *-(ī)sū*, *-(ī)suṁ* (Mah. Amg. JM.) *-(ī)su*, (*-(ī)suṁ* (Ś. Mg.)

Voc. : *-ṇo*, zero (Mah. Amg. JM.)

With the exception of a few forms *e.g.*, Acc. pl. *vāavo*, and Gen. sg. *-śśa* in Mg. verses, the inflexions of *-u* stems are the same as those of *-i-* ones.

A comparison of the terms. of Masc. *-a* stems and *-i*, *-u* stems shows that the desinences of these declensions are different, and that the common terms. show different frequency. The following terms. are common to *-a* and *-i*, *-u* stems Masc. and Neut.

(*i*) *The Direct Case* : The stem was used for the direct case throughout the Ap. period. Though the same was the case with regard to *-a* stems, *-u* was the chief desinence of the Masc. and Neut. themes in *-a*.

The proper history of the terminationless direct case may also be explained as follows :

OIA *muniḥ*>Pk. *muṇī*>Ap. *muṇi*.

OIA *guruḥ*>Pk. *gurū*>Ap. *guru*.

*-ṁ* of Masc. and Neut. direct sg. is a Prakritism.

(*ii*) *Dat.-Gen.-Abl. sg.* :

*-ha* in *kari-ha*, *guru-ha* (in EAp.) is the same as that of *-a* stems.

*-hu* forms are very few and they are due to the influence of *-hŏ* or *-hu* of Masc. and Neut. *-a* stems. The normal desinence of *-i*, *-u* stems is *-he* or *-hi*. This *-he* or *-hi* is due to the influence of the declension of Fem. stems in *-ĭ*, *-ŭ* and *-ă* (for its history see §91.). *-huṁ* in *Pd.*, is a nasalization of Ap. *-hu* on the model of Pkt. *-ṇa* : *-ṇaṁ*, *-su* : *-suṁ*, etc.

(*iii*) *Loc. Sing.* : *-mmi*, being a Prakritism, may be ignored. As to WSAp. *-hi* and WAp. *-hiṁ*, these are less common in *-a* stems, the normal term. of which is *-i*. These terms. are more used with Fem. *-ă*, *-ĭ*, *-ŭ* stems. As a matter of fact *-hiṁ*<*-smin* is a term. of the Masc., and Masc. *-hi* (a denasalized form of this *-hiṁ*) and Fem. *-hi* (<Ap. *-hĕ*) were confused together in Ap.

(*iv*) *The Direct Plural* : The stem was used in this case as in Masc. *-a* stems and Fem. themes in *-ă*, *-ĭ*, *-ŭ*.

(*v*) *The Dat.-Gen. -Abl. plur.*: As in *-a* stems, *-haṁ* and *-hā̃* were used in WAp. (600-1200 A.D.). These are used with Fem. *-ā* stems in SAp. (1000 A.D.).

A detailed comparison of the terms. of Masc. *-a* and *-i*, *-u* stems, and Fem. *-ă̄*, *-ĭ̄*, *-ŭ̄* stems[79] will show that the declension of Masc. *-i*, *-u* stems is more influenced by that of the Fem. stems than by that of Masc. *-a* stems. It appears that there was only one set of terms. which was used with *-i* and *-u* stems irrespective of their gender in OIA, puzzling thereby the Pk. grammarians who attributed it to the lawlessness of gender.[80]

*Terminations Common to Masc. & Fem, -i, -u stems.*

*Singular* :

Nom. Acc. Voc. : zero.

Instr. : *-e-* cf. Fem. *-a* stems as well.

Dat.Gen. Abl. : *-hi* (WSAp. 1000 A.D.)

*-he* WAp. of 1200 A.D.)

Loc. : *-hi* (WSAp. 1000 A.D., and WAp. of 1200 A.D.)

*-hiṁ*, *-hĩ* (WAp. of 1000 A.D. and of 1200 A.D.)

*Plural* :

Nom. Acc. and Voc. : zero.

Instr. Loc. : *-hiṁ*, *-hĩ* (600-1200 A.D.)

Dat.-Gen.-Abl. : *-hiṁ* (WAp. 1000 A.D.)

*Desinences Common to Masc. themes in -i and -u and Fem. themes in -a.*

*Singular* :

Nom. Acc. : zero.

Instr. : *-e* (WAp. 1000 A.D.)

Dat. Gen. Abl. : *-hu* (WAp. 1000 A.D.), *-hi* (SAp. 1000 A.D.)

*-he* (WAp. 1200 A.D.)

---

79 See § 97 below.
80 cf. *Hc.* 8.4.445.

Loc. : *-him̐*, *-hĩ*, *-hi* (WAp. 1000-1200 A.D.)

*-hi* (SAp. 1000 A.D.)

*Plural* :

Nom. Acc. : zero.

Instr. Loc. : *-hi*, *-him̐*.

Dat. Gen. Abl. : *-ham̐*, (WAp. 1200 A.D.)

Granting that the apparent similarity in terms. with different linguistic history have been classed together in the above tables, it cannot be gainsaid that the Ap. authors themselves forgot the gender system in OIA., and promiscuously applied these terms. irrespective of the original gender of the substantive. This was especially true in the case of writers of 1200 A.D.

As most of these terms. are already discussed in their historical perspective, we may pass a few critical observations on the terms. of each case and discuss the divergences and special points.

### Singular

§ 95. (*i*) The formation of the direct case took place before 600 A.D., as we find the stem itself used for the direct case from *PPr.*, *DKK.* to *Kp.* OIA *agniḥ*>Pk. *aggī*>Ap. *aggi*, and OIA *vāyuḥ*>Pk. *vāū* >Ap. *vāu* are perfectly natural developments in OIA. *-m̐* of the Masc. Acc. sg. and Neut. direct sg. as in *Harim̐*, *mahum̐* (*madhu*) in SAp. (1000 A.D.) is, as noted above, a Prakritism.

(*ii*) Ins. sg. *-ṇā* (SAp. 1000 A.D.) and *-ṇa* as in *aggiṇa* (*agninā*), *gahirajjhuṇiṇa* (*gabhīra-dhvaninā*) are also Prakritisms and semi-Prakritisms. It is SAp. of the 10th cent. which possessed a majority of such Prākritic forms. The porportion of Ins. sg., *-iṇā*: *-im̐* is 37: 6 in *Hv.* (Intro. §44). The *-u* stems in *Hv.* also give 3: 1 as the proportion between (*ū*)*ṇā* (13): -(*u*)*m̐* (4) terms. (Intro. to *Hv.* §44). It was later in the 11th cent. A.D., that we find this Pk. terms. (viz., *-ṇī*) giving place to Ap. *-he*, and *-him̐* in *KKc*.

Though *Hv.* and *KKc.* are not separated by a great period of time, Puṣpadanta seems more of a purist when he writes an epic like *Mp.*

in which he tries to emulate Sk. and Pk. epics. *BhK.*, a contemporary WAp. work, also shows *-ṇa* and *ĩ* or *-ṁ* Instr. sg. s.[81]. But we have *-e* of Fem. Instr. applied to *samāhi* (viz. *samāhie*<*samādhinā*) in the same work (*BhK.* 143.10). Probably the word was looked upon as Fem. in 1000 A.D. In *Sdd.* 193 we have *hoi samāhi-hi ṭhāṇu* 'becomes fixed (stable) in samādhi.' But the use of *-ṁ* for Instr. sg. shows the influence of *-a* stems. Thus the formation of *aggĩ* or *aggiṁ* (*agninā*) is analogous to *sappiṁ*<*sarpeṇa*, *paritosiṁ* <*paritoṣeṇa* (already discussed in §81). That OIA *agni* was treated as **agna* in speech is clear from Pk. Nom. pl. *aggao*, *aggau*. Desinences common to *-a* and *-i*, *-u* stems (the table is given above) show that Masc. *-a* stems wielded some influence on the declension of *-i*, *-u* stems. There are some Fem. *-a* stems with Instr. sg. in *-iṁ*, in 10th cent. WAp. e.g., *tattiṁ*<*tṛptyā*. We are thus justified in regarding Ap. Instr. sg. *aggiṁ* on the analogy of Masc. *-a* stems rather than accepting *agninā*>*aggiṇa*>*aggiṁ*. The evidence of *Kp.* (Intro. §23) and *Sc.* (Intro. p. *13) shows that *-ṇa* was the standard term. of Instr. sg. in WAp. of 1200 A.D., but the use of *-eṁ* in *Hc.* is a pointer to the the influence of the declension of *-a* stems.

(*iii*) Dat. Gen. Abl. terms. of this case were originally different from those of *-a* stems. Out of them *-ha* as in *kari-ha* (*karin-*), *guru-ha* (*guru-*) was the only term. in EAp. and to some extent its speciality upto 1100 A.D. Forms like *paṁgu-ha* (*PPr.* 1.66) show that it was found in earlier WAp. works of the 6th cent. A.D. This *-ha* is the extension of Gen.sg. *-ha* of *-a* stems to this declension. *-hu* which alternates with *ha* and which is limited to WAp., may be looked upon as its special feature (for the history of *-hu* see §83.).

SAp. accepts the Fem. desinence *-hi* found common in WSAp. of that period (1000 A.D.). Thus *sāmi-hi* (*svāmin*), *kukai-hi* (*kukavi-*), *Hari-hi* were the normal Gen. sg. forms. It seems to have spread to WAp. which has *-hu* and *-huṁ* as additional terms. dating from 600 A.D. in WAp. and limited to that region. For the history of *-he* see §91.

(*iv*) Loc. sg. *-hiṁ*, *-hĩ*, *-hi* are common to *a* stems. Masc. and Fem. and Fem. *-i*, *-u* stems in WSEAp. in 1000 A.D. Due to the undetermined age of Ap. works, it is difficult to locate the exact beginning and the venue of this term. But in EAp. *-hi* is used as early as 700 A.D. (in *DKK*), and *-hĩ* and *-hi* in 1000. A.D, (in *DKs.*) in the case of *-a* stems. (*Pd.* a WAp. work of the 10th cent. has *-hiṁ* Loc. sgs.).

---

81 Intro. to *BhK.* p. *36.

## §95A(*i*) Masculine Stems Ending in -*i* and -*u*

*Direct Singular.*

| Cent. A.D. | WAp. | SAp. | EAp. |
|---|---|---|---|
| 500 | *kappa-aru, mahu.* | | |
| 600-1000 | *Nom. muṇi, guru.*<br>(*Neut.*) *āu.*<br>*Acc. susamāhi, sattu, heu.*<br>*Voc. joi* (*joiă joiyā*). | | |

| 700-1200 | WAp. | SAp. | EAp. |
|---|---|---|---|
| | | | *Nom.*: *kālāgni, gaaṇagirī* (*DKs.* 102), *bimala-mai- bhikkhu, cellū* (*DKs.* 10) *Biṭṭhu.*<br>*Neut.*) *batthu.*<br>*Acc.* *aggi.*<br>Voc. *sahi, joi.* |

| A.D. | WAp. | SAp. |
|---|---|---|
| 1000 | *Nom.* (Masc.) *muṇi, jai, suvisuddha--mai,* (*Neut.*) *akhai.*<br>(Masc.) *guru, bhavasindhu*<br>Acc. (Masc.) *jiṇa-muni, bhava-jalahi.*<br>*heu, taru, guru*<br>(Neut.) *mahu, dhaṇu* | Nom. *giri, hari, ṇihi*<br>Acc. *hariṁ, mahuṁ*<br>Voc. *ṇaravari.* |

| A.D. | WAp. | SAp. | EAp. |
|---|---|---|---|
| 1100 | | *ṁanti, kari, divvacakkhu, uṇi* (Acc.) | |
| 1200 | Nom. *parattha-rui, dhamma-maï* (Sc. 4448-3).<br>*kessari.* | | |

Acc. *bali*, *moha-mahoyahi* (*Sn.* 334-127), *heu.*

§95A. (*ii*) Masculine Stems Ending in -*i* and -*u*

*Instrumental Singular.*

| Cent. A.D. | WAp. | SAp. | EAp. |
|---|---|---|---|
| 500 | .. | .. | .. |
| 600-1000 | .. | .. | .. |
| 700-1200 | .. | .. | .. |
| 1000 | *samāhie* | *Haliṇā*, *-paṁjaliṇā*, *phaniṇā*, *vaṇiṇā* (*Nc.* 1.14.10). | |
| 1100 | .. | *kuṁbhi-he* *-mālihiṁ* (*KKc.* 1.14.4). | |
| 1200 | *gahira-jjhuṇiṇa*, *aggiṇa*. *aggieṁ*. *aggiṁ* (*Hc.* 344). | | |

§95A (*iii*). Masculine Stems Ending in -*i* and -*u*.

*Dative-Genitive-Ablative Singular*

| A.D. | WAp. | SAp. | EAp. |
|---|---|---|---|
| 500 | .. | .. | .. |
| 600-1000 | *guru-hu*, *paṁguha* (*PPr.* 1.66). | .. | .. |
| 700-1200 | .. | .. | *kariha* (*DKs.* 8). *guruha.* |
| 1000 | (1) *sūrihi*, *muṇihi* (2) *guruhuṁ* (*Pd.* 81) (3) *Murāriu-hu* (*Bh.K* 451.1) | (1) *sāmihi*, *kukaihi*, *dantihi*, *Harihi*, *samaihi*, *piuhi.* | |

| | | | |
|---|---|---|---|
| | | (2) *sumaï-hu, arihu.* | |
| | | (3) *ṇaravaïṇo* (*Jc.* 1.19.1). (Pktism.). | |
| 1100 | .. | *maṃtihe.* | |
| 1200 | (1) *girihe, taruhe.* | | |
| | (2) *Payaga-taruhi* (*Kc.* 20), *himagirihi* (*Kc.* 20). | | |
| | (3) *girihiṁ* (*Jdu.* 6.1). | | |
| | (4) *suraguruhu* (*Jdc.* 4.4). | | |

§95A (*iv*) MASCULINE STEMS ENDING IN -*i* AND -*u*.

*Locative Singular*

| A.D. | WAp. | SAp. | EAp. |
|---|---|---|---|
| 500 | .. | .. | .. |
| 600-1000 | .. | .. | .. |
| 700-1200 | .. | .. | .. |
| 1000 | (1) *vāhihiṁ, suragirihiṁ, aggihiṁ.* | *viulairihi, sasirihi, harihi, Uttarakuruhi.* | |
| | (2) *samāhi-hi* (*Sdd.* 193). | | |
| 1100 | *Paāvaihiṁ, acchihiṁ, dehi-hĩ.* | (1) *karihiṁ* (2) *tarummi* (Pkt.). | |
| 1200 | (1) *-pantihi, kalihi.* | | |
| | (2) *akkhihiṁ* (*Hc.* 357). | | |
| | (3) *ṇivaimmi.* | | |

§95B(*i*) MASCULINE STEMS ENDING IN -*i* AND -*u*.

*Direct Singular*

| A.D. | WAp. | SAp. | EAp. |
|---|---|---|---|
| 500 | .. zero .. | .. | .. |
| 600-1000 | .. Nom. -zero | .. | .. |

| A.D. | WAp. | SAp. | EAp. |
|---|---|---|---|
| | Acc.: -zero<br>Neut.: -zero | | |
| 700-1200 | .. | .. | *Masc.*: Nom. -zero (occasionally final vowel lengthened).<br>Neut.- zero.<br>Acc. - zero.<br>Voc. -zero. |
| 1000 | *Masc.*: Nom.: zero<br>Acc.: zero<br>Neut. Nom. & Acc.: zero | *Masc.*: Nom: zero.<br>Acc. -*ṁ*.<br>*Neut*. Nom. & Acc. -*ṁ*. | |
| 1100 | .. | zero | .. |
| 1200 | *Masc*. Nom. zero<br>Acc. : zero. | .. | .. |

§95B (*ii*) Instrumental Singular.

| A.D. | WAp. | SAp. | EAp. |
|---|---|---|---|
| 500 | .. | .. | .. |
| 600-1000 | .. | .. | .. |
| 700-1200 | .. | .. | .. |
| 1000 | -*e* | -*ṇā* | .. |
| 1100 | .. | -*he*<br>-*hiṁ* (*RKc*. 1.14.4) | .. |
| 1200 | -*ṇa*<br>-*eṁ*<br>-(*i*)*ṁ* (*Hc*. 344) | .. | .. |

§95B (*iii*) Dative-Genitive-Ablative Singular.

| A.D. | WAp. | SAp. | EAp. |
|---|---|---|---|
| 500 ? | .. | .. | .. |
| 600-1000 | -*hu*<br>-*ha* .. | .. | .. |

| | | | |
|---|---|---|---|
| 700-1200 | .. | .. | -*ha* |
| 1000 | -*hi* (*Pd.*, *BhK.*)<br>-*huṁ* (*Pd.* 81)<br>-*hu* (*Bh.K.* 451.1) | -*hi*<br>-*hu*<br>-*ṇo* (Pktism.) | .. |
| 1100 | .. | -*he* | .. |
| 1200 | -*he*<br>-*hi*<br>-*hiṁ*<br>-*hu.* | .. | .. |

§95B (*iv*) Masculine Stems Ending in -*i* and -*u*
*Locative Singular.*

| A.D. | WAp. | SAp. | EAp. |
|---|---|---|---|
| 500 | .. | .. | .. |
| 600-1000 | .. | .. | .. |
| 700-1200 | .. | .. | .. |
| 1000 | -*hiṁ*<br>-*hi* (*Sdd.* 193) | -*hi* | .. |
| 1100 | -*hiṁ*, -*hĩ* | *hiṁ*<br>-*mmi* (Pkt.) | .. |
| 1200 | -*hi*<br>-*hiṁ* (*Hc.* 357)<br>-*mmi.* | .. | .. |

## Plural

§96, As expected the stem itself was used in the direct case as it is found in Masc. and Fem. -*a* stems and Fem. -*ī*, -*ū* stems as well. The fusion of Nom. and Acc. is found from the 10th cent. A.D. But EAp. of 700 A.D., shows more than one term. for this case. Thus *sāmaggi-e* (*sāmagri-*) in *DKK*. 7 is ont he analogy of *japa--home*<*japa-homāḥ* (*DKK* 29), *maṇḍala-kamme*< °-*karmāṇi* (*DKK*.29). That these are plur. forms is already noted by M. Shahidulla,[82] and is a speciality of *DKK*. But *alia*=*alayaḥ* is rather puzzling unless we trace

82 M. Shahidulla, *Les Chants Mystiques*, Intro. pp. 38 and 41.

it to OIA *ali-ka* (pleonastic) used directly for direct plur. SHAHIDULLA regards these two forms as unique in the dialect of *DKK*.[83]

Ins. and Loc. plur. *-hiṁ* and *-hĩ* are already discussed (see §§85, 93.2). They are common to Masc. and Fem. *-a* stems and Fem. *-ĭ* and *-ŭ* stems.

Dat. Gen. Abl. plur. *-haṁ*, *-haŭ* or *-hã* is common to Masc. *-a* stems, but is limited in this declension to WAp. from 600-1200 A.D. SAp. has *-hiṁ*, *-hi*, *huṁ*, and *-hũ* out of which *-hĩ* is found in *PPr.* (WAp. 600-1000 A.D.). It is really the term. of Loc. sg. and its use here shows that the fusion of Gen. and Loc. began as early as 600 A.D., in WAp. It extended to SAp. later on in 1000 A.D.

It appears that *huṁ* and *-hũ* were common to WSAp. in the 10th cent. A.D. It may, however, be pointed out that in SAp. *-huṁ* or *-hũ* was used with *-u* stems rather than with *-i* stems which generally take *-hi* or *-hiṁ*. e.g., *aṇāi-hi* (*anādi-*), *-kuvāi-hi* (*-kuvādi-*), *sukai-hi* (*sukavi-*). Not that forms e.g., *vaïrihuṁ* (*vairin*) are totally absent, but this is a general observation. *BhK*. shows the use of *-hu* and *-hũ* with Masc. *-i* stems.[84] These terms. persisted down to the 12th cent. A.D., as in *Hc. Kc. Sn.* etc. Though an attempt is made to draw some distinction between the Abl. and Dat.-Gen. cases in the Comparative Table of this declension (§96A) the distinction is either superficial and unreal or it is very difficult to locate the space-time context of this amalgamation. It is, however, certain that it is earlier than the 10th cent. A.D. *-ṇa* terms. being Prakritisms are left out of consideration though they occur to the end of 12th cent. A.D.

## §96A. MASCULINE STEMS ENDING IN *-i* AND *-u*.

*Direct Plural.*

| Cent. A.D. | WAp. | SAp. | EAp. |
|---|---|---|---|
| 500 | .. | .. | .. |
| 600-1000 | *ṇāṇi*, *sāhū*. | .. | .. |
| 700-1200 | .. | .. | *Nom.* : *alia*, *sāmaggie* *rabi-śa sī* (*DKK* 5) *Acc.* (Neut.) *akkhi* (*DKs*. 2, 5). |

83 'Les forms *alia*, *sāmaggie*, sont spéciales pour notre langue'—Intro. to *Less Chants Mystiques*, p. 41.

84 JACOBI, Intro. to *BhK*. p. * 36 § 27.

| | | | |
|---|---|---|---|
| 1000 | | *Nom. kari,* | |
| | *Neut.* | *Neut. -ṇāu* | |
| | *Acc.* : (*dāṇaccaṇa-*) -*vihi.* | (*Mp.* 100.5.3). | |
| | *rajju, pañca-guru.* | | |
| 1100 | .. | .. | .. |
| 1200 | *Nom. sasi-rāhu,* | | |

*Instrumental and Locative*

| Cent. A.D. | WAp. | SAp. | EAp. |
|---|---|---|---|
| 500 | .. | .. | .. |
| 600-1000 | *joihiṁ* (*Ys.* 38, 39). *ṇāṇihi* (*PPr.* 2.16). | .. | .. |
| 700-1200 | .. | .. | .. |
| 1000 | *cakkihiṁ, joihiṁ, ravi-sasi-hiṁ, kusumaṁjalihiṁ.* | *muṇi-hiṁ, manti-hiṁ, sasāsīhiṁ, ṇaggudi-hiṁ; aṇāīhi* ? (*Jc.* 1.2.14), *paṁjalī-hī̃. Loc. Uttara-kuru-hī̃* (*Hv.*) | |
| 1100 | .. | *Gangāṇai-sindhuhu* (*KKc.* 1.3.3)? *mantihiṁ* (*KKc.* 3.101). | |

| Cent. A.D. | WAp. |
|---|---|
| 1200 | -*hatthi-hī̃, ari-hī̃, viḍavi-hī̃ -sāhi-hī̃ karaḍihiṁ* (*Sn.* 76-176). *satthihiṁ hatthihiṁ, sukaihiṁ, vayarihiṁ* (*Sn.* 307-169). *sāhūhī̃ gurūhi* (*Sc.* 127-7-9 and 413.3 respectively).<br>*Loc.* : *vandi-hī̃* (*Sc.* 459.2). Intro. to *Sc.* §17, p.13. |

*Dative-Genitive-Ablative.*

| Cent. A.D. | WAp. | SAp. | EAp. |
|---|---|---|---|
| 500 | .. | .. | .. |
| 600-1000 | *Gen.*<br>*joi-haũ*, *joī-hiũ* (*PPr.* 2.160), *ṇāṇi-hiũ* (*PPr.* 2.30). | .. | .. |
| 700-1200 | .. | .. | .. |
| 1000 | *Gen.*<br>*micchādiṭṭhi-hiṁ* (*Sdd.* 82)<br>*bhāihũ* (*BhK.* 185.7). | *Gen.*<br>*sukkaīhiṁ* (*Mp.* 1.12.8) *aṇāihi*, *-kuvāihi* (*Jc.* 1.126).<br>*riu-huṁ*, *vairihuṁ* (*Nc.* 1.4.4).<br>*sāhu-hũ*, *guru-hũ*, *bandhu-hũ* (*Hv.*) | |
| 1100 | .. | .. | .. |
| 1200 | *Abl.* WAp.<br>Abl. *sāmi-huṁ*, *girihũ* (*Kc.* 19). *taru-huṁ*.<br>Gen. (1) *muṇiham*, *sauṇi-haṁ*, *bandhuhaṁ*.<br>(2) *muṇi-ha* (*Kp. J.* 7.5).<br>(3) *taru-huṁ*, *bandhu-huṁ*, *sāhu-huṁ*.<br>(4) *jiṇa-garu-hu* (*Jdc.* 20.4). | | |

96B. Masculine Stems Ending in *-i* and *-u*

*Direct Plural.*

| Cent. A.D. | WAp. | SAp. | EAp. |
|---|---|---|---|
| 500 | .. | .. | .. |
| 600-1000 | -zero | .. | .. |
| 700-1200 | .. | .. | Nom. *-a* (*DKK*<br>*-e*<br>-zero (final vowel lengthened)<br>Neut. Acc : -zero. |

| | | | |
|---|---|---|---|
| 1000 | -zero | *Masc.* zero<br>*Neut.* Nom. & Acc.<br>-zero. | |
| 1100 | .. | .. | .. |
| 1200 | Masc. Nom: zero | .. | .. |

*Instrumental and Locative Plural*

| | | | |
|---|---|---|---|
| 500? | .. | .. | .. |
| 600- | *-hi* ŏ | .. | .. |
| 1000 | *-hi* | | |
| 700-1200 | .. | .. | .. |
| 1000 | Ins. *-hiṁ* | Ins. *-hiṁ*<br>*-hi* (*Jc.?* 1.2.24)<br>Loc. *-hĩ* | .. |
| 1100 | | Ins: *-hiṁ*<br>*-hu* ? | |
| 1200 | Ins.: *-hĩ*<br>*-hiṁ*<br>Loc.: *-hĩ*. | .. | .. |

96 *B.*(*v*) *Dative-Genitive-Ablative Plural*

| Cent. A.D. | WAp. | SAp. | EAp. |
|---|---|---|---|
| 500? | .. | .. | .. |
| 600- | *-ha* ŏ | .. | .. |
| 1000 | *-hi* ŏ | | |
| 700-1200 | .. | .. | .. |
| 1000 | *-hũ*<br>*-hu*<br>*hiṁ* (*Sdd.* 82) | *-hĩ*, *-hiṁ*.<br>*-hi*<br>*-*(*u*)*huṁ*, *-hũ*. | ..<br>.. |

| | | | |
|---|---|---|---|
| 1100 | .. | .. | .. |
| 1200 | Abl. : *-huṁ*<br>*-hũ*<br><br>Gen. : *-haṁ*<br>*-ha*<br>*-(u)huṁ*<br>*-(u)hu* (*Jdc.* 20.4)<br>*-hĩ* (Intro. to *Sc.* §17. p. 13). | .. | .. |

### FEMININE STEMS ENDING IN -ĭ AND -ŭ

§97. Closely allied with the above declension is that of the Fem. stems ending in *-ī* and *-ū*. Their number is very limited as most of them are reduced to Fem. *-a* stem by the addition of pleonastic *-ya* or *-a*<OIA *-ka*. e.g., *vahu-ya*<*vadhūkā*=*vadhū*, *ṇāhiyā*<*nābhikā*=*nābhi*, *icchantiyā* *<*icchantī-kā* etc. Some of the *-ṛ* stems in OIA are reduced to this e.g., *māi*<*mātṛ*, while some *-ā* stems take this ending in Ap. e.g., *vacchi* <*vatsā*, *viuvviṭṭhi*<*vyudviṣṭā*.

Putting together the information supplied by PISCHEL,[85] we can tabulate the terms. of these endings in Pkts. as follows :

*Singular* :

Nom. and Voc. : zero.

Instr. : *-īa*, *-īe* (M. Amg. Ś. Mg. P.)

Abl. : *-īo*, *-ūo* (M. Amg.), *-ido*, *-udo* (JŚ. Ś. Mg.)

Gen. : *-īa*, *-īe* (M. Amg. Ś. Mg.)

Loc. : *-īe* (M. Amg. JM. Ś. Mg.), *-iṁsi* (Amg.), *-mmi* (Ś).

*Plural* :

Nom. Acc. Voc. : *-īo*, *-īu*, *-ūo*, *-ūu* (M. JM. Ś. Amg.) zero (M.Amg.)

Instr. : *-ihiṁ* (M. Ś. also in JŚ. Amg.)

Gen : *-īṇa* (M.), *-īṇaṁ* (Amg. also M. Ś.)
*-ūṇa*, *-ūṇaṁ* (M.)

---

85 PISCHEL, *Grammatik*, §§ 384-7. The desinences for grammarians' Ap. are quoted from these sections here. In sections quoted from PISCHEL's *Grammatik* M=Mahārāṣṭrī.

Loc. : -*īsu* (M. AMg. JM.), -*isuṁ* (M. Ś.)

The Ap. desinences given by Pk. grammarians are as follows :

*Singular* :

Ins. : -*ie*, (-*ī* in *Pk. Pingala*), Abl. -*he*.

Gen. : -*he*, -*ie*,

Loc. : -*hĩ*, -*ĭ* i.e., zero.

*Plural* :

Direct Case : *iu* , (Vco. -*ho*),

Ins. : -*hĩ*, -*hi*.

Loc. : -*hĩ*.

The desinences common to Masc. and Fem. -*ī* and -*ū* stems are already given in §94. The following terms. are found common in the declensions of Fem. stems ending in -*a*, -*ĭ* and -*ŭ*.

*Singular* :

Nom. and Acc. : zero.

Ins. : WEAp. -*e*, SAp. -*i*.

Dat. Gen. Abl. : WSAp. -*hĕ*, -*hi*, WAp. -*hu* (1000-1100 A.D)

(-*hĕ* in WAp. from 600-1200 A.D.)

Loc. : WAp. -*hiṁ*, -*hĩ*, -*i* ; WSAp. -*hi*.

*Plural* :

Nom. Acc. : zero, WSAp. -*u*.

Ins. Loc. : WSAp. -*hiṁ*, -*hĩ* WAp. -*hi*.

Dat. Gen. Abl. : -*hiṁ*, -*hĩ*.

TERMINATIONS COMMON TO FEM. -*ĭ*, -*ŭ* STEMS AND MASC. -*a* ONES.

*Singular*:

Nom. : Acc. zero (Less common in WSAp. -*a* stems.

Ins. :-*e*, -*ehi* (In EAp. -*a* stems.); -*i* ? (SAp.)

Dat. Gen. Abl. : EAp. -*ha*, WAp. (1200 A.D.) -*hu*

Loc. : -*hiṁ*, -*hĩ* (Less common in WAp. -*a* stems) -*hĩ* (EAp.).

*Plural* :

Nom. Acc. : zero.

Ins. Loc. -*hiṁ*, -*hī*.

Dat. Gen. Abl. : -*hiṁ* (Rarely in WAp.)

*Singular*

§98. The Direct Case.

The fusion of the Nom. and Acc. took place in Pkts., and zero was one of the terms. in that period. In Ap. the stem itself was used in Direct sing. in all regions.

*Indirect Cases* :

Instr. Loc. Case : In Ins. sg., SWAp. -*e* and EAp. -*a* are Prakriisms. EAp. -*ehi* as in *gharaṇi-ehi* (*gṛhinyā*) is a Masc. term. extended to Fem. stems analogically. cf. *khabaṇehi* (*kṣapaṇaka-*), *cittehi* (*citta-*). As we have seen it in §81 it is traceable to Ved. -*ebhiḥ*>Pk. -*ehiṁ* but used as sg. in EAp. In SAp. -*i* as in *Lacchi-i* (*Lakṣmī-*), *Siva-devi-i* (*Śiva-devī-*), is a weakening of (Ins. sg.) -*e* which is by no means rare in that region. The term. zero with the lengthening of the final vowel (e.g., *kittī*<*kīrtyā*, *bhattī* <*bhaktyā*) as found in *Pk. Pingala*[86] is not seen in any region during our period. This elongation is probably a contraction of Pk. Ins. sg. -*īi* or -*īa*. There are some exceptions *e.g.*, *ṇiya-satti*<*nija-śaktyā* (*Sdd.* 121), *caṁcū* <*cañcvā* in *Jc.* 1.12.8. The former being at the end of the metrical line is expected to be long in pronunciation, though the spelling represents it as ending in short -*i*.

-*hiṁ* which appears in WAp. (1200 A.D.) is Loc. sg. extended to Ins. sg.; cf. Loc. sgs. *vāṇārasi-hiṁ* (*Vārāṇasī-*), *Ujjeṇi-hiṁ* (*Ujjayinī-*), *nisi-hī* (**niśī—niśā*), *mahi-hī* (*mehi-*) etc.

-*ṇa* as in *bhatti-ṇa*, is originally Pk. Masc. Ins. sg. of -*i*, -*u* stems conserved in WAp. of the 12th cent. A.D., cf. *aggiṇa* <*agninā*, *gahira-jjhuṇiṇa*<*gabhīra-dhvaṇinā* (see § 95.)

Loc. sg. terms. are quite different from those in Pkts. That they are used with Dat. Gen. Abl. sg., shows a state wherein a real oblique was in the process of formation by the fusion of non-direct cases.

---

86 Pischel, *Grammatik*, § 386, p. 269.

As we have already seen it in §82, Loc. sg.-*hiṁ*, -*hĩ*, *hi* are originally traceable to OIA -*a-smin*. Its use with Masc. and Fem. -*a* stems and Masc. and Fem. -ī̆ and -ū̆ stems, shows its wide popularity during our period. Hence its importance to NIA.[87] *disi*<*diśi*(*Sdd.* 66) is either (bu*i* more probably) a Sanskritism or a formation after Masc. -*a* stems. cf. *sūri* <*sūrye*, *saravari*<**sarovare* in the same text. In SAp. (1000 A.D.) -*he* and -*heṁ* are the desinences of Gen. sg. applied to this case, cf. *Lacchi-he* (*Lakṣmyāḥ*), *dharaṇi-he* (*dharaṇyāḥ*) in the works of Puṣpadanta. There being no -*hĩ* forms, these forms lead one to connect this term. -*he* with OIA Fem. pronominal **-syās* which resulted in Ap. -*he*, -*hi*. -*hẽ* as in -*siri-hẽ*< *śrī*- (*BhK.* 17.2), *bhāyaṇi-hẽ*<*bhājana* (*BhK.* 27.12), *vāvi-heṁ* <*vāpī*- (*Nc.* 2.8.3), is a development of OIA pronominal **-syām*. -*i* in *diṭṭhi-i*<*dṛṣṭyāṁ*, (*Jc*, 3.10.4) is the same as Ins. sg. -*i* in SAp. of the 10th cent. A.D. We need not notice Prakritisms here.

The table of Pk. desinences given above will show that Ap. terms. of the Dat. Gen. Abl. are different from those in Pkts. The Ap. terms. show regional differences *viz.*, -*ha* in EAp., -*hĕ* in WSAp., but -*hu* in WAp. (1200 A.D.) The same was the case with Dat. Gen. Abl. sgs. of Fem. -*a* stems. (See the table of common terms. of Fem. endings in -ā̆, -ī̆, -ū̆ given above). The terminations of this compound case show that the desinences of the Loc. came to be used with this case as early as 600 A.D., as we get forms like *siddhi-hĩ* (*siddheḥ*) in *PPr.* 2.48.69. In OIA Gen. and Loc. dual became one. The complete fusion of these two in sg. number of -*ā* stems in Fem. gender was achieved in Pkts.[88] In Ap. some new factors bifurcated them, but terms. like -*hiṁ* or -*hĩ* of this case, show that MIA hold was strong upto the end of this period. The terms. also show a fusion of the two classes. Thus we find

WAp.<Masc. -*hiṁ*, -*hĩ*, -*hi* -*hu* e.g., *vahu-hu*<*vadhū*- (*Sc*, 44.1)

Fem. -*he*, -*hĕ*, -*hi*.

EAp. Masc. -*ha*.

For some more cases of the confusion of genders see tables of common desinences of Masc. and Fem. endings given above in §94, §97.

Although -*heṁ* -*hẽ* or -*hĕ*ⁿ (as JACOBI represents it in *BhK.*) are common to WSAp. in 1000 A.D., it continued only in SAp. in 1100 A.D., e.g., *disi-heṁ*<**disī*=*diś*—(*KKc.* 2.2.10).

---

87 For its further developments in NIA see BLOCH, *L'indo-aryen*, p. 175.

88 For Fem. -ā̆ -ī̆ -ū̆, stems see PISCHEL, *Grammatik* § 374, §§ 385-7.

It is doubtful whether the zero term. was used with these stems. in Dat. Gen. sg. as we have no clear example where we cannot regard it as a gen. *Tatpuruṣa* compound. Thus in

*rayaṇihi rai saṁgami avagannaĭ.* (*BhK*. 21.4)

We can very well take *rai-saṁgami* (*rati-saṁgame*) as a compound.

It is only in SAp. that pure Fem. terms. were used to denote Dat. Gen. Abl. sing. Prakristisms in *-e* need not be noted.

### §98A. Feminine Stems Ending in -ĭ and -ŭ.

*Direct Singular.*

| Cent. A.D. | WAp. | SAp. | EAp. |
|---|---|---|---|
| 500 ? | *Nom.* *kīlanti, gai, diṭṭhĭ*<br>*Acc.* *gaĭ* (*Mt*. 24). | | |
| 600-1000 | *Nom.* *gurukkī, velladī, raĭ.* *saṁsāriṇī, uḍu-*<br>*Acc.* (1) *paṁcama-gaĭ, taṇu.* (2) *sivamai* ◡ (*PPr*. 2.56). | | |
| 700-1200 | | | *Nom.* : *ghariṇĭ, uatti, mutti, abadhŭi, Bāṇārasi debī.*<br>*Acc.* : *buddhi, keli, dhammagai, bhatti, joinimāi, gharinĭ, maṭṭī.*<br>Voc. *taruṇī.* |
| 1000 | *Nom.*: *pāraddhi, nivitti, savisuddhamaĭ, kuḍi, parivāḍi, sāmiṇi, mukkī dhammadheṇu.*<br>*Acc.*: *aṇumai, panti, gāĭ. bohi, vāhi, puhavi, Sivapuri, raĭ, gurubhatti, keli, tiḍikkī tālū, taṇu.* | *Nom.*: *tiṭṭhi, māibahiṇi, rāṇī.*<br>Acc.: *mahi, Jayasiri, māyari, caṁcū.* | |

| A.D. | WAp. | SAp. | EAp. |
|---|---|---|---|
| 1100 | *Nom.*: *goraḍi, viuvviṭṭhī,*<br>*siddhī.* | *Nom.*: *ṇāri, māṇiṇi,*<br>*Dhaṇamaī, Pomāvaī.*<br>*Acc.*: *Sarāsaī, divvavāṇī, meiṇi.*<br>*Voc.*: *bahiṇie, sundarie.* | |
| 1200 | *Nom.*: *dāli, gori, Uvvasi, Dovaī,*<br>*Acc.*: *sāmaggi, ghariṇi, thui.*<br>*Voc.*: *devi, sahi, ammi,*<br>*ammie* (*Hc.* 396). | | |

*Instrumental Singular*

| A.D. | WAp. | SAp. | EAp. |
|---|---|---|---|
| 500 | .. | .. | .. |
| 600-<br>1000 | *bhattie, bhantie.* | | |
| 700-<br>1200 | .. | .. | *tāsi-e*<br>*bhanti-a*<br>*gharani-ĕhi* |
| 1000 | (1) *satti-e, -suddhi-e,*<br>*kiraṇā-valie,* (*Sdd.*),<br>*jutti-e, jaṇaṇi-e,*<br>*ghittie* (*BhK.*)<br>(2) *Lacchie, rakkhasie* (*BhK.*)<br>*ṇiya-satti* (*Sdd.* 121). | (1) *patti-i, jaṇaṇi-i,*<br>*Siva-devi-i, Lacchi-i,*<br>(2) *buddhī-e, vayaṁsī-e, Kumarīe,*<br>*bhanti-e, salahanti-e* (*Hv.* 92.17.8).<br>(3) *caṃcū* (*Jc.* 1.12.1). | |
| 1100 | .. | *kitti-eṁ, ghariṇi-eṁ, koumaieṁ,*<br>*mahāsaīeṁ, haṁsiṇieṁ.* | |
| 1200 | *riddhī-e,* (*Sc.*), *gaṇanti-e,* | | |

*Radi-e, atiratti-e* (*Hc.*)
*pupphavai-hiṁ* (*Hc.*)
*bhatti-ṇa* (*Sc.*) (*Pktsm.*).

*Dative-Genitive-Ablative Singular.*

| Cent. A.D. | WAp. | SAp. | |
|---|---|---|---|
| 500 | .. | .. | .. |
| 600-1000 | *siddhihi, kittihi,*<br>*siddhi-hi̐* (*PPr.* 2.48.2.69) | .. | .. |
| 700-1200 | .. | .. | *koḍi-ha* |

| A.D. | WAp. | SAp. | EAp. |
|---|---|---|---|
| 1000 | *Abl. mahāevihĕ* (?*BhK.* 296.2)<br>*daṁsaṇa-bhūmihiṁ*<br>(*Sdd.* 57.)<br>*Gen.* (1) *Lacchi-hi,*<br>*suyapaṁcamihi*<br>*bahiṇi-hi* (? *Sdd.* 42)<br>*jaṇ ērihi.*<br>(2) *paṇaīṇihĕ, ghariṇihĕ*<br>*jaṇaṇihĕ, suvapaṁcamihe,*<br>*kamalasirihe.*<br>(3) *paṁkayasiri-he*ⁿ*,*<br>*hāyaṇi-he*ⁿ<br>(4) *raï* (*BhK.* 21.4). | *Gen.* (1) *sai-hi, jara-sarihi, ṇaha-sirihi,*<br>*ṇayarīhi, puṇṇālihi, devihi,*<br>*rayaṇi-vahuhi,*<br>(2) *dharaṇihe, Lacchihe*<br>(3) *Mārīe, devīe,*<br>*mahaevīe,* (*Jc.*) | |

| A.D. | WAp. | SAp. | EAp. |
|---|---|---|---|
| 1100 | .. | (1) *riddhi-he, vegavaihe,*<br>*kuṭṭiṇīhe.*<br>(2) *disiheṁ* (*KKc.* 2.2.10). | |

| A.D. | WAp. | SAp. | EAp. |
|---|---|---|---|
| 1200 | (1) *mahi-hi*, *devi-hi*, *mālai-hi*, *vacchihi*.<br>(2) *gori-he*, *mellanti-he*, *joanti-he*, *tumbiṇihe*, *kaṁguhe* (*Hc*. 367).<br>(3) *siri-hĩ* (Sc. 484.1).<br>(4) *Uvvasĩe* (*Sc*. 491.1).<br>(5) *-vahu-hu* (*Sc*. 444.1) | | |

*Locative Singular*

| A.D. | WAp. | SAp. | EAp. |
|---|---|---|---|
| 500 ? | .. | .. | .. |
| 600-1000 | *puhavihĩ* (*PPr*. 2.131) | .. | .. |
| 700-1200 | .. | | (1) *marutthali-hĩ*<br>(2) *bisayassatti* (*DKs*. 73.) |

| A.D. | WAp. | SAp. |
|---|---|---|
| 1000 | (1) *sippihiṁ*, *kariṇihiṁ*, *dhariṇihiṁ*, *pamuiṇihiṁ*,<br>(2) *rayani-hĩ* (*BhK*. 21.4)<br>(3) *behiṇihi*, *bhittihi* *muṭṭhihi*, *guttihi*, | (1) *Alayāurihi*, *Kosambihi*, *tuṭṭihi*, *puṭṭhi-hi*, *ghariṇihi*, *rayaṇi-hi*, *Sivadevihi*, *bhūmihi*.<br>(2) *sippi-he* (*Nc*. 2.8.10). |

| A.D. | WAp. | SAp. |
|---|---|---|
| | (4) *mahaĕvihu*ⁿ (? *BhK*. 302.9)<br>(5) *disi* (*Sdd*.66) A Sktism.<br>(6) *akhaiṇi* (*Pd*. 42). | (3) *vāvihem̐* (*Nc*. 2.8.3)<br>(4) *joṇohiṁ* *Ujjeṇihiṁ*, *diṭṭhihiṁ*.<br>(5) *diṭṭhi-i* (*Jc*. 3.10.4). |
| 1100 | *Mahālacchi-hĩ*, *-lehi-hĩ*. *-accehihĩ*, *aṇuṇentihĩ*, *-dehi-hĩ*. | *aḍavihiṁ*, *bhūmihiṁ*, *pāraddhihiṁ*, *disihiṁ*. |
| 1200 | (1) *ṇisi-hĩ*, *mahi-hĩ*, *rayaṇi-hĩ*, *dharaṇihĩ*. | |

(2) *sallai-hiṁ*, *Vāṇārasi-hiṁ*.
*Ujjeṇi-hiṁ*.

(3) *mahi-hi*.

(4) *vaṇa-rāi-mmi* (*Sc*. 479.7).

## §98B. Feminine Stems Ending in -ī̆ and -ū̆.

*Direct Singular*

| A.D. | WAp. | SAp. | EAp. |
|---|---|---|---|
| 500 | -zero<br>Acc. -(Mt. 24) | .. | .. |
| 600-1000 | Nom.: -zero<br>Acc.: -zero<br>-̐ (*PPr*. 2.56) | .. | .. |
| 700-1200 | .. | .. | Nom.: -zero<br>Acc.: -zero<br>Voc.: -zero. |
| 1000 | Nom.: -zero<br>Acc. : zero | Nom.: zero<br>Acc. : zero | |
| 1100 | Nom.: zero | Nom.: zero<br>Acc. : zero<br>Voc. : -*e* | |
| 1200 | Nom.: zero<br>Acc. : zero<br>Voc. : zero<br>-*e* | .. | .. |

*Instrumental Singular*

| A.D. | WAp. | SAp. | EAp. |
|---|---|---|---|
| 500 | .. | .. | .. |
| 600-1000 | -*e* | .. | .. |
| 700-1200 | .. | .. | -*e*<br>-*a*<br>-*ehi* (*DKS*.) |

| A.D. | WAp. | SAp. | EAp. |
|---|---|---|---|
| 1000 | *-e* | *-i* | .. |
| | *-i* (*Sdd.* 21) | *-e* | |
| | | -zero | |
| 1100 | .. | *-eṁ* | .. |
| 1200 | *-e* | .. | .. |
| | *-hiṁ* | | |
| | *-ṇa* (Pktsm.) | | |

*Dative-Genitive-Ablative Singular*

| A.D. | | WAp. | SAp. | EAp. |
|---|---|---|---|---|
| 500 | | .. | .. | .. |
| 600-1000 | | *-hi* | .. | .. |
| | | *-hi*ँ (*PPr.* 2.48.69) | | |
| 700-1200 | | .. | .. | *-ha* |
| 1000 | Abl.: | (1) *-hiṁ* (*Sdd.* 57) | | |
| | | (2) *-he* (*BhK.* 296.2) | | |
| | Gen.: | *-hi* (*Sdd.* | *-hi* | |
| | | *-he* (*BhK..* | *-he* | |
| | | *-heⁿ* (i.e., *hẽ*) (*BhK.*) | *-e* | |
| | | zero (*BhK.* 21-.4) | | |
| 1100 | | .. | *-he* | |
| | | | *-heṁ* (*KKc.* 2.2.10) | |
| 1200 | | *-hi* | .. | .. |
| | | *-he* | | |
| | | *-hĩ* (*Sc.* 484.1) | | |
| | | *-e* (*Sc.* 491.1) | | |
| | | (*u*)*-hu* (*Sc.* 444.1) | | |

*Locative Singular*

| A.D. | WAp. | SAp. | EAp. |
|---|---|---|---|
| 500 | .. | .. | .. |
| 600-1000 | -*hĩ* (*PPr*. 2.131) | .. | .. |
| 700-1200 | .. | .. | -*hĩ*<br>zero (*DKs*. 73). |
| 1000 | -*hiṁ*<br>-*hĩ* (*BhK*.21.4)<br>-*hi* (*Sdd*. 42, *BhK*. 293.4)<br>-*hu*$^n$ (? BhK. 302.9)<br>-*i* ? (Sdd. 66) Sktism.<br>-zero. | -*hi*<br>-*he* (*Nc*. 2.8.10)<br>-*heṁ* (*Nc*. 2.8.3)<br>-*hiṁ*<br>-*i* (Jc. 3.10-4) | .. |
| 1100 | -*hĩ* | -*him* | .. |
| 1200 | -*hĩ* (*Sc*.)<br>-*hiṁ* (*Hc*.<br>-*hi* (*Hc*.<br>-*mmi* (*Sc*. 479.3) | .. | .. |

§99. *Plural*

There are not many plural forms of these stems, and they show very few peculiarities as being distinct from Pkts.[89]. Thus -zero and -*u* of the Direct plur. is met with in Pkts., although it is Ap. which generalized the use of terminationless direct plurals to all regions.

The fusion of the Loc. and Instr. cases of these stems took place before 1000 A.D. -*su* endings, being Prakritisms, are ignored here. -*hu*$^n$ as in *mahāevi-hu*$^n$<*mahā-devyoḥ* 'of the two queens' (*BhK*. 302.9) is probably a combination of Gen. -*hu*+Loc. -*iṁ* or -*hiṁ* (both of Masc. gender originally). There are not many pure Ap. forms of the Dat. Gen. Abl. and they show the identification of the Gen. and the Loc. e.g. *Siva Satti-hiṁ*<*Śiva-śaktyoḥ* (*Pd*. 127).

89 Pischel, *Grammatik*, § 387.

## §99A. Feminine Stems Ending in -ī and -ū

*Plural*

*Nom Acc. and Voc.*

| A.D. | WAp. | SAp. | EAp. |
|---|---|---|---|
| 500 | .. | .. | .. |
| 600-1000 | .. | .. | .. |
| 700-1200 | .. | .. | .. |
| 1000 | *Nom.*: *taṇu-maṇa-vaya -sāmaggi.* (2) *angulīu.* | *Nom.*: (1) *livi-u, sāīṇi-u ḍāiṇi-u, bhūmiū.* (2) *rāī* (*Nc.* 6.5.8) *rāyāṇiyā* (? *Jc.* 4.2.7). | |
| 1100 | .. | .. | .. |
| 1200 | *Nom.* (1) *taruṇi-u, saraṇī-u, aṁguliu, Acc. sallai-u, vilāsiṇīu* (*Hc.* 348). (2) *paḍivatti* (*Sc.* 461.1). *Voc. taruṇi-ho* (*Hc.* 346). | | |

*Instrumental-Locative*

| A.D. | WAp. | SAp. | EAp. |
|---|---|---|---|
| 500 | .. | .. | .. |
| 600-1000 | *Loc.* (1) *siddhihi, vitti-ṇivittihi.* (2) *puhavi-hi* ◡ (*PPr.* 2.131.) | | |
| 700-1000 | .. | .. | .. |

| A.D. | WAp. | SAp. |
|---|---|---|
| 1000 | *Ins.* (1) *borihiṁ, Rohiṇihiṁ diṭṭhihim, devihim* (*Pd.* 3), | *Ins.*: *siddhi-hiṁ, riddhi-hiṁ, devihiṁ, kitti-lachhihiṁ,* |
| .. | | .. *ghaggharolihiṁ,* |

(2) *vilāsiṇī-hī*, *-gāhiṇīhī*. — *panti-hiṁ*, *vajjantihiṁ*, *urūhiṁ*.

*Loc.* (1) *ṇaliṇihiṁ*, *vidisihiṁ*, *-aṭṭhamihiṁ* (Sdd.), *-manjari-hiṁ*, *joni-hiṁ*, *sippi-hiṁ* (Sdd.) (2) *mahāevi-hũ* (BhK. 302.9). — *Loc.* *joṇihiṁ* (Mp. 82.10.11) *Mahīsu* (Jc.1.1.7 Pktism.)

1100 *Loc.* (2) *valli-hiṁ*. (1) *Ins. li lāvai-hiṁ* — *Ins.* (1) *sahayarīhiṁ*, *laharihiṁ*, *ṇārihiṁ*. (2) *Ganga-ṇai-sindhu-hu* *Loc.* *dasadisihiṁ*. (KKc. 1-3-3)

1200 *Ins.* *piya-sahi-hī*. *disi-hiṁ*, *asai-hiṁ*, *ramaṇihiṁ* (Sn. 77-176), *pupphavaī-hiṁ* (*Hc.* 438), *sarihiṁ*

*Loc.* *paḍhantihī*, *gāyanti-hī*. *gāyaṇihī*.

*Dative-Genitive-Ablative*

| A.D. | | WAp. | SAp. | EAp. |
|---|---|---|---|---|
| 500 | | .. | .. | .. |
| 600-1000 | | .. | .. | .. |
| 700-1200 | | .. | .. | .. |
| 1000 | *Gen:* | (1) *sivasattihiṁ* (*Pd.* 127). *devi-hiṁ* (*Pd.* 3) *-aṭṭhamihiṁ* (*Sdd.* 13.) (2) *suīṇaṁ* (*Pd.* 98). | | |
| 1100 | | *taralacchi-hũ*. | | |
| 1200 | | *vahuhũ* (*Sc.* 556-8) | | |

## §99B. Feminine Stems Ending in -ī and -ū.

*Direct Plural*

| A.D. | WAp. | Sap. | EAp. |
|---|---|---|---|
| 500 | .. | .. | .. |
| 600-1000 | .. | .. | .. |
| 700-1200 | .. | .. | .. |

| | | | |
|---|---|---|---|
| 1000 | Nom.: -zero<br>-*u* | -*u*<br>-zero | .. |
| 1100 | .. | .. | .. |
| 1200 | Nom.: -*u*<br>zero<br>Voc.: -*ho* | .. | .. |

*Instrumental-Locative Plural*

| | | | |
|---|---|---|---|
| 500 | .. | .. | .. |
| 600-1000 | Ins.: -*hi*<br>Loc.: -*hĩ* ? | .. | .. |
| 700-1200 | .. | .. | .. |
| 1000 | Ins.: -*hiṁ*<br>-*hĩ* (*BhK*)<br>Loc.: -*hiṁ*<br>-*hu*$^{n}$ (*BhK* 302.9) | Ins.: -*hiṁ*<br>Loc.: -*hiṁ* | |
| 1100 | Ins.: -*hiṁ*<br>Loc.: -*hiṁ* | *Ins*.: -*hiṁ*<br>-*hu* (*KKc.* 1.3.3)<br>Loc.: -*hiṁ* | |
| 1200 | Ins.: -*hĩ* (*Sc.*)<br>-*hiṁ* (*Hc.*)<br>Loc.: -*hĩ* | | |

*Dative-Genitive-Ablative Plural*

| A.D. | WAp. | SA.p. | EAp. |
|---|---|---|---|
| 500 | .. | .. | .. |
| 600-1000 | .. | .. | .. |
| 700-1200 | .. | .. | .. |
| 1000 | Gen.: -*hiṁ*<br>-*ṇaṁ* (Pd. 98) | .. | .. |
| 1100 | -*hũ* | .. | .. |
| 1200 | -*hũ* | .. | .. |

POSTPOSITIONS

§100. The use of post-positions is already found in OIA.[90]. In Sk. and Pali they were used with or without the case forms of nouns e.g, Sk. *tasya samīpe* or *tat-samīpe* 'near that.' Pali—*gotamasya santike, nibbāṇa-santike.* The same is the case in Ap. and NIA.[91] Due to the deterioration of the old declensional system in Ap. we find the wide use of post-positions in post-Ap. period.

The following are some of the post-positions found in Ap. literature.

*honta, hontau, honti.*

§101. This is a pres. part of√*ho*<Sk.√*bhū* 'to be' (cf. *Hc.* 8.3.180). It is used with Abl. as noted by *Hc.* 8.4.355. It appears as *huṁto* or *hū̃ta* in old Hindi. Old H. *hū̃t* is a weakening of Ap. *hoṁtu* or *huṁtu.* Mod. Beng. possesses *haïte* which is traceable to OIA **havanta.* Beames explains the rationale of this usage 'by supposing the idea to be that of having previously been at a place but not being there now, which involves the idea of having come away from it.'[92] Thus Ap. '*tahā̃ hontau āgado*' (*Hc.* 8.4.355) seems to have developed in Old H. *tahā̃ hontā āyo*, Nep. *tahā̃ bhə̃ndā ayo*, Beng. *othā haïte āil.*

We find the use of *hontau* even before the time of Hemacandra. e.g.,

*tāvasu puvva-jammi haū̃* hontao,
*Kosiu ṇāmeṁ nayari vasantao.* *BhK.* 88.8.

'*Having been* an ascetic in my former birth, I lived in the city of Kosiu.'

Here or elsewhere in *BhK.* 81.1, 294.5, 300.1, 351.7 etc., we do not find the Abl. sense developed, nor is it used with Abl. We do not meet with the use of this in other WAp. works (*e.g., Sdd., Pd.*) of the 10th cent. A.D. There is paucity of published WAp. works of the 11th cent. In the 12th cent. we do not find it in *Sc.*

*aha hontu (ki) na saccaviu*

'If it *was*, why was it not seen?' (*Sc.* 490.2). Here it is used as an ordinary pres. part. So is its Fem. *hunti* in *Sc.* 744.5. The absence of *-honta* in the Abl. sense in SEAp literature, and in WAp. works like *Sc.* even

90 Speyer, *Ved. u. Sansk. Syntax.* §§ 89, 91, 93 as quoted by Bloch, *FLM* § 197.

91 Bloch, *L'indo-aryen*, pp. 179-83, also see *FLM*. §§ 197-202.

92 Beames, *Comp. Gram.* II, 237.

of the 12th cent., leads one to believe that the use of *hontaü* was of a late WAp. origin, and was current in speech in Gujarat, Rajputana and other adjacent districts *c.* 1150 A.D. It is after that period that it travelled to Bengal and other Eastern provinces during Proto-NIA period. In old M. there is the use of the postpositions *hoüni, hauni, honi* in Abl. sense[93] *e.g. parvatā* hauni *daḷavaḍe*[94] (in 1273 A.D.) *pātāḷā* hõni *nimna*[95] (in 1290 A.D.) in both of which *hauni* and *hõni* means 'more than.' Father STEPHENS notes the use of *hounu* in Koṇk.[96] BLOCH does not connect M. *hõun* or *hū̃n* to Ap. *hontau.*[97]

### *ṭhiu*

§102. When this post-position is coupled with Loc. it yields the sense of Abl. *e.g.*

*hiaa-ṭṭhiu jai ṇīsarahi, jāṇau Muṁja sa rosu.*

'I shall consider that to be anger, if you go out from my heart.[98] (*Hc.* 8.4.439). PISCHEL takes it as 'in the heart reposed,' but ALSDORF takes it as an Abl.[99]

The use of √ *sthā* with Loc. in Abl. sense is due to the influence of MIA on Sansrit and not *vice versa.* The quotation from the *Hitopadeśa* given in ALSDORF's *Ap. Studien*[100] *viz., vivarābhyantare sthitvā* 'from the hole,' goes to prove the same as such hyper-sanskritisations are quite natural in a popular text like the *Hitopadeśa*, WAp. works of the 10th cent. A.D., do not show this Abl. sense of Loc. + √*sthā* or the postposition *ṭhia.* There is no such instance in *BhK.* Other works follow the OIA idiom. *e.g.*,

93 It is possible to trace the beginning of this usage in SAp. of 1100 A.D. There are constructions like the following in *KKc. tumhi homti hoï rajju, tumhi homti dhammakajju.* 'If you survive, the kingdom will survive. Righteous deeds are possible if you exist.'(*KKc.*1.13.4). As queen Padmāvatī is addressing her husband, can we not translate *homti* as 'from' thus : 'kingdom and religious deeds proceed *from* you' ?

94 *Śiśupālavadha,* 934 (V.L. BHAVE's Edition).

95 *Jñāneśvarī* 16.329 (RAJWADE's Ed.)

96 *Koṅkani Grammar* § 523 as quoted by S.M. KATRE, *Form. Koṅk* § 219.

97 BLOCH, *FLM* § 264 and § 195.

98 P. L. VAIDYA, Hemacandra's *Pk. Gram.* — Notes p. 69.

99 The original Translations are quoted below : PISCHEL : O Munja, wenn du fortgehst, *m Herzen ruhend,* dann weiss ich, (was) der Zoru (besagen will)—*Materialien.* ALSDORF : Gehst du (aber) *aus* meinem *Herzen heraus* dann weiss ich, o Munja, das ist Zoru. —*Ap. Studien,* pp. 22-6. *hiaa-ṭṭhiu* is a compound (Loc. tatpuruṣa). There is no need to take *hiaa-* as an independent word in Loc. case.

100 ALSDORF, *Ap. Studien,* p. 25.

*ahavā timiru ṇa ṭhāharai sūrahu* gayani thiena

'Or darkness does not stand by the sun's *being in the sky.*'

*aha dāvāṇalu kim karaï* paṇyia-gahira-ṭhiyāha. (*Sdd.* 132)

'Now what can a forest-conflagration do *to a person standing in deep water* (*Sdd.* 214).

These are the two instances of the use of *ṭhia* in *Sdd.* In *Pd.* we find:

*ṇillakkhaṇu itthībāhirau akulīṇau* mahu maṇi ṭhiyau.

The underlined words mean "... are staying in my mind" (*Pd.* 99)[101]

*kīlaï appu pareṇa sihu ṇimmala-jhāṇa-ṭhiya-haṁ.*

'The soul of *a person established in pure mediation* plays with another.' (*Pd.* 110).

*deha ṇa picchaï appaṇiya* jahiṁ *Siu santu* thiyāiṁ.

'He does not see his own body *wherein stays* that quiescent *Śiva*,' (*Pd.* 180).[102]

These are the only uses of *ṭhia* in WAp. of the 10th cent.[103]

Alsdorf quotes the Abl. use of Loc. from *Hv.* 88.21.2, 91.16.5, 91.18.5 89.10.2.[104] But there is no *ṭhiu*. Thus *tahĩ ṇiggau* 'went out from that' (*Hv.* 88.21.2), *tahĩ cuyāu* 'fell down from that' (*Hv.* 91.16.5), *tahĩ tahĩ ṇisaraï* 'goes out from that' (*Hv.* 91.18.5) and finally, *muhĕ ṇiggaya ṇau kaḍuayara vāya* 'No more bitter word passed out from the mouth' (*Hv.* 89. 10.2) show the fusion of the Loc. with Abl. in SAp. in 965 A.D., and not the use of postposition *ṭhiu*.

The following are the uses of *ṭhia*- and √ *ṭhā* - in EAp. :

*patta-caüṭṭhaa* caü-muṇāla ṭhia mahā-suhabāsĕ

'The four petals are situated under the four stems in the repose of great bliss.' (*DKK.* 5.)

*beṇṇi rahia tasu niccala* ṭhāi.

'(The breath) being devoid of both (movements) *rests* motionless' (*DKK.* 13).

---

101 H. L. Jain, translates them in Hindi as '*mere man me vasā hai*' - *Pd.* p. 31.

102 H. L. Jain translates it : '*jahā̃ santa śiva sthita hai*' (*Pd.* p. 55).

103 The only use of *ṭhiya* is in *BhK.* 79,7 where it means 'stood, stayed' (See *BhK*, glossar, p. 153).

104 Alsdorf, *Ap. Studien*, pp. 25-6.

Whatever be the date of *DKK*. √*sthā* is not used in an Abl. sense anywhere in *DKK*. The same is the case with *DKs*.

*jaï guru-buttabo hiahi païsaï*

*nihia* hattha-ṭṭhia *bia u dīsaï*.

*hattha-ṭṭhia*='placed or kept on hand.' (*DKs*. 20).

*kamala-kulisi* bebi majjha ṭhiu *jo so suraa- bilāsa*.

*bebi..ṭhiu* : 'Placed or staying in the midst of both.' (*DKs*. 96). In *DKs*. 105 we have :

gharahi ma thakku. 'Do not stay at home'. (*DKs*. 105).

saalu nirantara bhoi ṭhia *kahĩ bhaba kahĩ nibbāṇa*.

'Where is the worldly existence and where the Final Beautitude, i knowledge (*bohi*) be everywhere or all-pervading without any vacuum?.' (*DKS*. 105).

*ṇau ghare ṇau baṇe bohi ṭhiu*, 'Knowledge is neither in the house nor in the forest' (*DKs*. 106).

*caüjaha* bhubaṇẽ ṭhiaü *nirantara*. 'It *is* in the 14 worlds everywhere.' (*DKs*. 91). The use of √*ṭhā* in *DKs*. 40, 45 is in the ordinary sense of standing.

The main object of investigating every use of √*sthā*- in WSEAp. of the 10th cent., is to find out whether the use of *ṭhiu*- in the Abl. sense was current in 1000 A.D. The facts show that it was *not* so in WEAp., nor in SAp. even in ALDORF's illustrations.

The use of the post-positions derived from √*sthā*[105] is found in Guj. Beng. Or. Koṅk etc. This indicates its use in Ap. It might be a popular usage in the 12th cent. A.D., but Ap. literature upto 1100 A.D. shows little trace of it.

### *keraa, kera.*

§103. *keraa, kera* Fem. *kerī*(<OIA *kārya*) is used in the sense of 'an order' (e.g., *Mp*. 16.6.9) and 'related to' as in *Hc*. 8.1.246. It is in the latter sense that it was used as a Gen. post-position. Its use in Pkts. is noted by PICHEL[106] but its use as a Gen. post-position is a peculiarity of Ap.

---

105 When a post-position is traceable to MIA √*thakka* or √*ṭhakka* (e.g. Koṅk. *thākā* or *ṭhāka*) it is better to trace its derivation from IE **sthak-na-ti*<**st(se)aqe-*<**st(se)a-* 'to stand' - See GRAY *JAOS*. 60, p. 364.

106 *Grammatik*, § 176, § 434.

Historically it is not found in EAp. 700 A.D. (*DKk.*) nor in 1000 A.D., (*DKs.*) except *tāhara*<**tāha-ara*=*tasya-kārya* 'related to him, his' (*DKs.* 92) but in which -(*a*)*ra* is a Gen. suffix rather than a post-position. cf. Beng. -*er*, Oriyā -*ār* today.

This post-position was definitely used in WAp. in the 10th cent. A.D., *e.g.*, *kammahaṁ keraü* 'pertaining to karmas' (*Pd.* 36—the only example in *Pd.*) In *BhK.* it appears as *keraü* thrice (*BhK.* 75.7, 125.10, 189.5), and as *kerī* (Fem.) thrice (*BhK.* 99.3, 187.5, 290.8) and is used with Gen. e.g., *tau kerau* 'For you' (*BhK.* 75.7 125.10), *Sarūvahe kerau* 'pertaining to or belonging to S.' (*BhK.* 189.5).

Though there is no example of this in *Sdd.* the instances are enough to prove the prevalence of this usage in 1000 A.D. But it is older still. In 600 A.D., (?) it appears four times in *PPr. viz.*, *kerā* (*PPr.* 1.73, 2.69), *keraï* (*PPr.* 1.29), and *keraü* (*PPr.* 2.29). It was popular later in 1200 A.D. For example in *Hc.* we find *jahe keraü* (*Hc.* 8.4.359), *tumhahaṁ keraüṁ* (*Hc.* 8.4.373), *jasu keraeṁ* (*Hc.* 8.4.422.20). All this amply proves the popularity of this in WAp. from 600-1200 A.D. Its use in pronominal compounds in which it is reduced to a suffix both in WAp. and NIA of that region, shows that it has been a stable characteristic of the speech of that region during the last 1400 years.

It was used in SAp. in 1000 A.D., e.g., *rāyaho kerī* 'pertaining to the king' (*JC.* 1.9.2), *Rāvaṇa-Rāmahu keraü* 'relating to Rāvaṇa and Rāma' (*Mp.* 69.2.11) and also in *Hv.* 85.7.10, 81.2.7, 88.10.7, But it seems to have disappeared in proto-NIA period as we do not find a trace of it in old Marathi of the 13th cent. A.D. Thus we can trace the use of *kera-* as follows :

WAp. 600—1200 A.D.>NIA (both as a post-position and suffix.)

SAp. 1000 A.D.>Lost in NIA.

EAp. 1000 A.D. -as-*ara.*>NIA (as a suffix.)

*taṇa.*

§104. *taṇa* 'pertaining to' is used as one of the *nipātas*, and is construed with the Instr. e.g., *kehiṁ taṇeṇa*, *tehiṁ taṇeṇa* (*Hc.* 8.4.425). It is optionally and to a greater extent used with Gen. e.g., *vaḍḍattaṇaho taṇeṇa* (*Hc.* 8.4.425) and *taṇaüṁ* (*Hc.* 8.4.361), *taṇā* (*Hc.* 8.4.378, 380, 417, 422.)

*taṇa* is used as early as 600 A.D. in *PPr.* [107] e.g., *mahuṁ taṇai* =*madīyena* (*PPr.* 2.186). In 1000 A.D., it was used with Gen. *tasu*

107 A. N. Upadhye, Intro. to PPr. p. 51.

*taṇaïm* 'pertaining to him' (*Sdd.* 205) is the only example in *Sdd.* In *Pd.* 88 *siddhattaṇa-hu taṇeṇa* 'for the sake of siddha-hood,' and in *Pd.* 214 *gharu ḍajjhaï indiyataṇau* 'the house *belonging to the organs of senses,*' we have two uses out of which one is a clear Gen. while the other is a compound. In *BhK.* it is widely used, and *taṇaya* 'pertaining to' is used nine times in Masc. and Neut. direct sing., four times in Fem., once in Gen. and thrice in Loc. (17 times in all, for which see *BhK. Glossar,* p. 154). In *BhK.* 46.7 *taho taṇayaho nāmaho* 'of his name' is a double Gen. In *BhK.* 8.4.

*gaya diṭṭhi tāsu tahĕⁿtaṇaï dehi.*

'His gaze (sight) was attracted to her person.' *taṇaï* though a Loc. sg. is used with Gen. *But there is no Instr. as we find it in Hc.* 8.4.425. In *Sc.* (1200 A.D.) *taṇa* is used only twice *viz.*, *antara-rogaha- taṇai* 'pertaining to inner disease' (*Sc.* 775.6) and *rakkhasa-taṇaũ valu* 'The army of the demons' (*Sc.* 590.4). One is a Gen. post-position while the other is a compound. Its uses in *Hc.* are quoted above. It is not found in EAp.

From this data it appears that *taṇa* is rather a Gen. post-position than an Instr. one in WAp. Chronologically its use us as an Instr. post-position is in WAp. first, as in *PPr.* 2.186. It is seen in SAp. e.g., *sukaihiṁ taṇāiṁ* 'pertaining to good poets' (*Mp.* 1.12.8). Its popularity as an Instr. post-position in WAp. is a later development (of the 12th cent. A.D.) although it is used throughout our period (600-1200 A.D.) in that region.

## NUMERALS

§105. WSEAp. *ēka, ekka, ĕkka,* WAp. *ikka, iga, iya* (both Masc. and Fem.), WSAp. *ekkalla,* WAp. *ekalla* (*-alla* pleonastic)—all these show the predominance of *ekka* as the common MIA base all over India, although classicisms e.g., *eka, iga* and *eya* are met with. The gemination of *-k-* in WAp. *ekkekka, ikkikka* (<*ekaika*), *ĕkkĕkkama* (<**ekaikama*), SAp. *ekkamekka* (*ekaika*) cf. M. *ekmek*, and other combinations e.g., *aṇṇekka* (*anyaika*), WAp. *ekkaï* (*ekākinī*) show the same. The NIA forms for 'one' are the descendants of Ap. *ekka.* cf. M. Guj. H. Nep. *ek.* The doubling of *-k-* in *ekka* was probably due to the necessity of MIA speakers to distinguish between the cognates of OIA *etad-* and *eka-*.

This is the only numeral which shows the distinction of genders. It is declined as other *-a* stems with *-u* or zero as the term. of the direct sing. and -*hiṁ*, -*hĩ*, -*hi* as Loc. sgs.[108] The use of *eka* as indeterminative is as old as the *Atharva Veda*, [109] and is not a speciality of Ap.

§106. SEAp. *be*, WSAp., *ve*, *doṇṇi*, SAp. *biṇṇi*, EAp. *beṇṇi*, *biṇṇa* (<OIA *dva*-) show that even in Ap. period there was a confusion about the treatment of *dv*- (see §64) due to the interborrowing in WSAp. EAp. consistently uses *b*-<*dv*- treatment. The -*o* and -*u*- elements in the declension are due to -*au* e.g., WSAp. *doṇṇi*, *duṇṇi*, *dohiṁ*, *dohĩ*, WAp. *dohi*, SAp. *duṇham*, *dūṇa* (*dviguṇa*). cf. M. *duṇẽ*, *H. dūṇā*, *duhaḍi* (*dvighaṭi*). With the exception of EAp. the early isoglosses regarding the treatment of *dv*- seem to have been blurred and mixed up (cf. §63) already in Pkts.

As to its declension, we find SEAp. *biṇṇi*, EAp. *biṇṇa*, WSAp. *doṇṇi*' *duṇṇi* on the analogy of OIA *trīṇi*, SAp. *ve*, SEAp. *be* <OIA *dve* in the direct case. The Ins. and Loc. take -*hiṁ*, -*hĩ*, -*hi* e.g., WSAp. *dohiṁ*, *dohĩ*, *dohi*, SAp. *bihiṁ*. Gen. is SAp. *duṇhaṁ*, WAp. *doṇha*. In compositions OIA *dva*- become *bā*- in Ap. [110] (See §113, §115 below.)

§107. SWAp. *tiṇṇi*, EAp. *tiṇṇa*, SAp. *tiṁ* are used for OIA *trīṇi*. cf. Pā. *tīni*, Pkt. *tiṇṇi* M. H. *tīn*, Beng. Nep. *tin*, Punj. *tinn*. In Ap. compounds OIA *tri* becomes *ti*-, *tai*-, *te*. e.g., *tiviha* (*trividha*), *tiga* (*trika*), EAp. *teloa*, WAp. *taïloya* (*trailokya*), SAp. *taïya* (*trika*).

The direct case has SWAp. *tiṇṇi*, EAp. *tiṇṇa*, SAp. *tiṁ* irrespective of gender. The Instr. Loc. takes -*him* and -*hi* as usual *e.g.*, SAp. *tihiṁ*, WAp. *tihi*, *tihimi*. Gen. ends in -*ha* e.g., *tīha*.[111]

§108. Four is WSEAp. *caü* (*catur*), WSAp. *cayāri* (**catāri*<*cattāri* <OIA *catvāri*). This is pronounced in NIA (M. H. Guj. Panj. Nep.) as *cār* with palatal *c*-. In Ap. compounds it became *caü*-. e. g., EAp. *caüṭṭhaa* (*catvṣṭaya*), WAp. *cauvviha*, SAp. *cauviha* (*caturvidha*), *caurāsī* (*caturaśīti*).[112] -*ā*- in *cāuddisi* (*catvrdikṣu*) in *Sn*. 18.442 is rather puzzling but the text is uncritical.[113]

§109. WSAp. *paṁca* (*pañcan*) presents no difficulty. cf. Pā. Pkt. *pañca*, M. H. Guj. Beng. Nep. *pāc*, Panj. *pañj*, Sdh. *pañjā*. The direct

---

108 For the treatment of *eka* in Pkts. see PISCHEL, *Gram.* § 435.

109 BLOCH, *L'indo-aryen*, p. 187.

110 For the Pkt. forms of *dvi* see PISCHEL, *Grammatik*, §§ 436-7. For NIA forms see *FLM* § 214.

111 For the Pkt. forms of 3 see PISCHEL, *Grammatik* § 438 and for NIA ones, BLOCH, *FLM* § 215.

112 Cf. M. *cauryāṁśī*. For the nasal in the M. form see *FLM*. § 223.

113 For the Pkts. forms of 4 see PISCHEL, *Gram.* § 439, and for NIA ones BLOCH, *FLM.* § 216.

case takes no termination while the Ins. Loc. takes *-hĩ* and Dat. Gen. Abl. has *-hā̃* and *-ha* as desinences. In compounds *paṁca-* remains unchanged or is transformed to *paṇṇa-* or *paṇa-*.[114]. Thus we have WAp. *paṁca-guru* (°*gurūn*), SAp. *paṇu-vīsa*, *paṁcuttaravīsa* (*pañcottara-viṁśati*), WAp. *paṇṇaraha* (*pañca-daśa*)[115]. cf. H. *pandrah*, M. *paṇdhrā*, Sdh. *pandrahā* etc.

§110. Six is in WSAp. *cha*, *chaha* (**ṣaṣa*)[116]. We have its descendants all over NIA *e.g.*, Guj. H. *cha*, *chcha*, Sdh. *cha*, *chaha*, M. *sahā*, Singh. *sa*, *saya*, Beng. *chaya*. The Ap. compounds of *cha-* are directly derived from OIA via Pkts. Thus WSAp. *chaddaṁsaṇa*, *chaddarisaṇa* (*ṣaḍ-darśana*), *chaṇṇ*(*-nn-*)*avaï* (*ṣaṇṇavati*), SAp. *chaṇṇaudima* (*ṣaṇṇavati-tama*), *chappaya* (*ṣaṭpada*). *sol*(*-ḷ-*)*asa*(*-ha*)<*ṣoḍaṣa* is common to other Pk. dialects.[117]

§111. *satta* (*saptan*), *aṭṭha* (*aṣṭan*), *ṇava* (*navan*) are quite regular. Their NIA derivatives are equally simple. Thus Ap. *satta*>M. Guj. H. Beng. *sāt*, Oriyā- *sāta*, Panj. *satta* ; Ap. *aṭṭha*>M. Guj. H. Oriyā *āṭh*(*a*), Beng. *āṭa*, Panj. *aṭṭh*(*a*) and Ap. *ṇava* >M. Guj. H. Nep. *naü*, Panj. *naũ*.

Their compounds e.g., *sattaṭṭha* (*saptāṣṭa*), *cauraṭṭha* (*caturaṣṭa*) are quite easy.

In the direct case they generally take no term.. In Ins. Loc. they have *-ehiṁ*, *-ihiṁ* or *-ahĩ*, *-ihĩ*. The Gen. takes *-hā̃*, *-ha*. Thus *aṭṭha* (sometimes *aṭṭhaïṁ*), *aṭṭha-hiṁ*, °*hĩ sattihĩ* are some of the declined forms.[118] The gender sense was blurred in Ap. Hence we find such usages e.g., *aṭṭhaïṁ mūlaguṇā* (*mulaguṇāḥ*) : Masc. qualified by Neut. form of the Numeral.

§112. Literary Ap. contains two forms viz., *dasa* and *daha* for OIA *daśan* (cf. Pā. *dasa* only). *daha* is found even in EAp. (*DKs*. 45) and it is the only form in that region as appears from the Tibetan version of *DKs*. 30 which suggests '*daha-dihahi*' as the original reading. The Eastern Pkts. conserved the sibilants in *daśan*.[119] In NIA the distribution of the forms *daṣa* and *daha* (*e.g.*, Guj. H. *das*, M. Panj. *dahā*, Sdh. *ḍaha*), and the state of affairs described in *FLM* §220 have no distinct regional basis in Ap. literature as *dasa* and *daha* are freely mixed in Ap.

114 For its explanation see PISCHEL, *Grammatik*, § 273, especially B. KUHN's opinion (*KZ*. 33, 478) quoted therein.

115 For the Pkt. forms see PISCHEL, *Gram*. § 440, and for NIA. BLOCH, *FLM*. § 217.

116 Ibid. § 441, but *-ha* on the analogy of *daha*. See BLOCH, *FLM*. § 218, for more explanation.

117 See PISCHEL, *Gram*. § 441, BLOCH, *FLM*. § 218 for Pkt. and NIA. For the problem of MIA and NIA *cha* : *ṣaṣ* see *ODB* § 517.

118 For the Pkt. background of these see PISCHEL, *Gram*. § 442 and for NIA *FLM* §219.

119 PISCHEL, *Gram*., § 262.

As in Pkts. *daśan* as a second member of the compound in numerals from 11 to 18 (except 14 and 16) corresponds to *-raha* in Ap. Thus we find :

11 = WSAp. *eyāraha* (*ékādaśa*) cf. Pk. *ekkārasa*, *eggāraha*, *eāraha*. NIA.—M. *akrā*, Guj. *agyār*, H. *egāraha*, Nep. *eghāra*.

12 = *bāraha*, *bārasa* (*dvādaśa*) cf. Aśok. Inscr. *duvād*(*-ḍ*)*-asa*, Pk. *duvālasa*, *bārasa* ; NIA.—M. *bārā*, Nep. and Guj. *bār*, H. *bārah*.

13 = WSAp. *teraha* (*trayodaśa*) cf. Pā. *teḷasa*, *telasa*, Pk. *terasa*, *teraha*. NIA. M. *terā*, H. *terah*. Nep. *tera*, Guj. *ter*.

15 = WSAp. *paṇṇaraha*, SAp. *paṇṇāraha* in Hv. <*pañcadaśa*. cf. Pā. *pañcadasa*, *pannarasa*, *paṇṇarasa*, Pkt. *paṇṇarasa*. NIA.—M. *pandhrā*, Guj. *pandar*, Oriya-*pandara*, Panj. *pandrā̃*, Sdh. *pandrāhā*. Nep. *pandra*. *daha-paṁca* in *Pk. Pingala* is a poetic expression.

18 = WAp. *aṭṭhārasa*, SAp. *aṭṭhāraha* (*aṣṭādaśa*). cf. Pā. Pk. *aṭṭhārasa*. NIA. —M. *athrā*, Guj. *arāḍ*(*h*), *aḍhār*, H. *atthārah*, Nep. *aṭhāraha*.

The MIA background and NIA developments of the Ap. numerals are juxtaposed to evaluate the exact contribution of Ap. to Proto-NIA.[120]

14 = *coddaha*, *caüddaha*, and *cāuddaha* (in *Pk.piṅgala*) <*caturdaśa*. cf. Pā. *catuddasa*, *cuddasa*, Pk. *caüddasa*, *coddasa*, *coddaha*. NIA. M. *caudā* or *cavdā*, H. *caüdah*, Guj. *caud*, Nep. *cauda*.

16 = *sol*(*-ḷ-*)*asa*, *sol*(*-ḷ-*)*aha* (*ṣoḍaṣa*). cf. Pa. *soḷasa* Pk. *soḷasa*, *soḷah*^a^ *soḷa*. NIA. · M. *soḷā*, Guj. *soḷ*. Oriya—*soḷı*, Sgh. *soḷasa*, H· *solah* Nep. *sora*.

These two forms in Ap. are, of course, regularly traceable to OIA.

§113. The numerals in the ten's places are as follows :

10 : Already discussed above §112.

20 : WSAp. *vīsa*<**viṁśat*=*viṁśati*, changed on the analogy of *triṁśat*. cf. Pā. *vīsa*(*ti*), Pk. *vīsa*(*i*), NIA. : M. *vīs*, Guj. *vīś*, Sdh. *vīha*, Panj. *vīh*, H. *bīs*, Nep. Beng. *bis*.

30 : WSAp. *tīsa*<*triṁśat*. cf. Pā. *tiṁsa* (Fem.). Pkt. *tīsa*, *tīsaī*, NIA.: M. H. *tīs*, Sgh. *tisa*, *tiha*, Panj. *tīh*. The original OIA *tr-* is preserved in Dardic forms.[121]

---

120 Pischel (*Gram.* § 443) and Bloch (*FLM* § 221) give different explanations for the modification of *-d-*> *-r-* in Pkts. The latter appears more satisfactory.

121 Turner, *Nepali Dictionary*, 286.

The phonological changes in the above two are perfectly normal.

40 : SAp. *cālīsa*, WAp. *cālisa*, *tālisa* ; as a second member of the compound *-ālisa*, *-yāla*<OIA *catvāriṁśat*. cf. Pā. *cattālīsa*, *cattārīsa*, Pkt. *cattālīsa*, *cāyālīsa* (<**cātālīsa*<*cattālīsa*). NIA.—M. Guj. *cāḷīs*, Sdh. *cālīh*, Panj. *cālī*, H. *cālīs*, Beng. *callīs*, Sgh. *sataḷiho*, *sāḷis*.[122] SAp. recognises only *-cālīsa* forms and not *-tāli-sa* ones *e.g*, *chāyālīsa* 'Forty six.'[123]

50 : WSAp. *paṇṇāsa* <*pañcāśat*. cf. Pā. *paññāsa*, *paṇṇāsa*, Pkt. *paṇṇāsa*. NIA.: M. *pannās*, Guj. H. Nep. *pacās*. The change *-ñc-*>*-ṇṇ* was already in vogue in pre-Ap. NIA.[124]

60 : WSAp. *saṭṭhi*<*ṣaṣṭi* cf. Pā. Pk. *saṭṭhi* (Fem.) NIA: M. Guj. H. *sāṭh*, Sdh. *sāṭh*, *sāṭhi* Panj. *saṭṭh*, Nep. *sāṭhi*. A regular phonological change in MIA.

70 : WAp. *sattari*, *sattara*<OIA *saptati*. cf. Pā. *sattati*, Pk. *sattari*. NIA : M. H. Panj. Beng. *sattari*, Sdh. *satar* Oriya-*satori*, Nep. *sattari*. The *-ra-* element is of Pkt. period.[125]

80 : *asiti*, *asii*, *-asī*<OIA *aśīti* cf. Pk. *asii*. NIA. M. *aīsī*.[126] Guj. *ẽśi*, Nep. *assi*, *asi*. Ap. *-asī*<Pk. *-asii*<Sk. *aśīti* is evident.

90 : *ṇavadi*, *ṇavaī*, *ṇaudi* and SAp. *-nauya*<OIA *navati*. cf. Pā. *navati*, Pk. *ṇaüi* NIA. M. *navvad*, Guj. *nevũ*, Sdh. *nave*, H. Panj. *navve*, Nep. *nabbe*.

§114: The different forms of the numerals from 1-8 are combined with the forms in the ten's places to form different numbers. We meet with the common forms in Pkts. and Ap., and with some slight modifications they are current in NIA. A few numerals from Ap. literature are given below:

21 : SAp. *ekka-vīsa* (*eka-viṁśat*), cf. M. Guj. *ekvīs*, H. *ekāis*, Nep. *ekkāis*.

22 : WSAp. *bāīsa* (*dvā-viṁśat*) cf. Pā. *dvāvīsati*.

25 : *paṁcuttaravīsa* (*pañcottara-viṁśat*), *paṇuvīsaṁ*, SAp. *paṁcavīsa* (*pañca-viṁśat*), cf. Pā. *pañcavīsa*, *paṇṇavīsati*, *paṇṇuvīsa-*, Pk. *paṇuvīsa*, NIA. M. *pañcvīs*, H. Guj. *pacīs*. Nep. *pacis*.

---

122 For the change of *-ṭ-*>*-ḷ-* in MIA see BLOCH *FLM* § 223. The optional *-tāḷis* forms, though given by MOLESWORTH and followed by BLOCH, are not current in standard Marathi. Nor are they so in spoken Poona Marathi.

123 See also ALSDORF, Intro. to *Hv*. § 53.

124 PISCHEL, *Gram*. §§ 81, 148, 445, BLOCH, *La langue marathe* § 223.

125 Vide PISCHEL, *Gram*. § 446 but better still BLOCH, *FLM* § 221-3.

126 M. *aśśi* though given by TURNER *Nep. Dictionary* 29 is not current in M.

28 : SAp. *aṭṭhāvīsa* (*aṣṭāviṁśat*), cf. Pā. *aṭṭhavīsati*, Pkt. *aṭṭhāvīsaṁ*. NIA. M. *aṭṭhāvīs*, Guj. *aṭhāvīs*, H. *aṭhāīs*, Nep. *aṭhāis*.

33 : WAp. *tettiya*, *tīyatiṁsa* (*trāyastriṁśat*), SAp. *tettīsa* (*trayastriṁśat*), cf. Pā. *tettiṁsa*, Pk. *tettīsa*, NIA. M. *tettīs* (coll. *tehatīs*), Guj. *tetris*, H. *tetīs*, Nep. *tettis*.

34 : *cautīsa* (*catustriṁśat*), cf. Pk. *cottīsaṁ*, NIA. M. *cautīs* Guj. *cotrīs*, H. *caũtīs*, Nep. *caũtis*.

38 : *aṭṭhatīsa* (*aṣṭatriṁśat*.)

46 : SAp. *chāyālīsa*<Pk. *cha*(*ha*)-*cālīsa*<*ṣaṭ-catvāriṁśat*. cf. Pk. *chāyālīsa*. NIA. M. *secāḷīs*, Guj. *chētāḷīs*,, H. *chiyālīs*, Nep. *chāyāḷis*.

48 : WAp. *aṭṭhayāla* (*aṣṭa-catvāriṁśat*). cf. Pā. *aṭṭha-cattārīsa*, Pk. *aṭṭhacattālīsa*, °*cattāla*. M. *atthecāḷ* (not *aṭṭhetāḷ* as TURNER thinks in *Nep. Dictionary*), Guj. *aḍtālis*.

49 : SAp. *ekkūṇaī paṇṇāsa*<*ekonapañcāśat*. cf. M. *ekkuṇapannāsa*, but Guj. *ogaṇpacās*.

55 : SAp. *paṇa-paṇṇāsa* (*pañca-pañcāśat*). cf. Pā. *pañcapaññasa*, Pk. *paṇavaṇṇa*, Deśi *paṁcāvaṇṇā*. NIA. M. *paṁcāvan*, Guj. *pācāvan*, Oriya. *pacāwana*, H. *pacpan*, Nep. *pacpan*, *pacpanna*.

56 : SAp. *chappaṇṇa* (*ṣaṭpañcāśat*). cf. Pk. *chappaṇṇaṁ*, *chavaṇṇaṁ*. NIA M. *chappan*(*n*), Guj. H. Nep. *chappan*.

66 : WAp. *chāvaṭṭhi* (*ṣaṭṣasti*) cf. Pk. *chācaṭṭhiṁ*. NIA. M. *sāsaṭ*, *sāsaṣṭ*, Guj. *chāsaṭh*, H. *chiyāsaṭh*, Sdh. *chāsaṭhi*, Beng. *chesaṭṭi*, Nep. *chayasaṭṭhi*.

75 : *paṁca-sattara*, °*sattari* (*pañca-saptati*). cf. Pk. *pañcahattari*, *paṇṇattari*. NIA. M. *pācyāhattar*, *pacyāttar*, Guj. *pācoter*, Oriya, *pañcattari*, Nep. *pacahattar*.

84 : WSAp. *caurāsī* (*caturaśīti*). cf. Pā. *cullāsīti*, Pk. *caurāsīi*, NIA. M. *cauryāsī* (see 80 in §113 and the footnotes), Guj. *corāsī*, H. *caurāsī*, Nep. *caurāsi*.

96 : WAp. *channavaī*, *channaudi* (*ṣaṇṇavati*), cf. Pk. *chaṇaüi*, NIA : M. *śāṇṇav*, Guj. *chaṇṇū*, Nep. *chayānabbe*.

99 : SAp. *ṇavaṇauyaī* (*varisaī*)<*nava-navati-*. cf. Pk. *ṇavaṇaüi* (Fem.), NIA: M. *navyā* (-*vvyā*-) *ṇṇava*, H. *ninyānabe*.

There has been so much interborrowing in numerals that a regional classification or isoglossal treatment is impossible. Ap. has contributed but little to these numerals except a few phonetic changes here and there.

§115. For 100 and its numeral compounds we find WAp. *saa*, SAp. *saya* (*śata*), cf. M. *śe*, *ekkottara-saya* (*ekottara-śata*), *duttara-saya* (*dvyuttara-śata*), WAp. *aṭṭhuttara-saya* (*aṣṭottara-śata*), *caüsaa* (*catuḥ-śata*). For 1000 we find *sahassa*, *sahāsa* (*sahasra*). cf. Koṅk. *sõsrõ*. WSAp. *lakkha* (*lakṣa*), cf. M. Guj. H. Beng. Nep. *lākh*, Sgh. *lakhu*, Panj. *lakkh*, Oriya *lākha*. A crore in WSEAp. *koḍi* (*koṭi*).

Most of these formations belong to Pre-Ap. MIA period.

### FRACTIONALS

§116. Ap. follows Pkts. in fractionals as well. Thus ½ is *addha aḍḍha* (*ardha*), *saddha* (*sārdha*). Other fractionals associate the word *-ardha* to the next number to indicate a number less than that *e.g.*, *diyaḍḍha* (*dvyardha*), cf. M. *dīḍ*, Guj. *doḍh*, H. Panj. *deḍha*, Beng. *deḍa*, 3½ is *āüṭṭha*<MIA *addha-uṭṭha*<OIA. *ardha-* turtha*. cf. M. *auṭ*, Guj. *ŭṭhu*, *ūṭh*.

### ORDINALS

§117. The following are the ordinals in Ap.:

1st : *paḍhama* (*prathama*) by cerebralisation (see§§45,46) WSAp. *pahila*, *pahilaa*, *pahilla*, *pahilliya* (**pratha -ila*, *-ilaka*, *-illa*, *-illika*) *pahilāraa*, Fem. *pahilārī*, (**prathila tara-ka*)[127].

2nd: SWAp. *bīa*, *bīya* (*vīya* according to ALSDORF), *bīyaa*, WAp. *duiya*, *duijja* (*dvitīya*). There is no suffix like *-sara* in Ap. though it is found in NIA all over India. It might be in spoken Ap. upto 1200 A.D.

3rd: SAp. *taïya*, *taïyaa*, WAp. *tijjau* (*tṛtīya*) *-ijja* is a WAp. suffix for 2nd and 3rd.

4th: WSAp. *cauṭṭha*, SAp. *cauṭṭha*, *cotthaa* (*caturtha*). cf. M. *cauthā*, Guj. *cotho*., H. Panj. Nep. *cauthā*.

From 5th onwards (except 6th) the suffix *-ma* which is sometimes changed to *-va* in SAp., is added to the cardinal. Thus we get for 5th WSAp. *paṁcama* (°*va*), 7th WSAp. *sattama* (°*va*), 8th *aṭṭhama*, 9th *ṇavama* etc. As a matter of fact these are all Pkt. forms.

---

127 For the discussion of NIA forms for 1st see BLOCH, *FLM*. § 226.

6th: WSAp. *chaṭṭhaya*, SAp. *chaṭṭha* (*ṣaṣṭha*), Fem. *chaṭṭhī* (*ṣaṣṭhī*) is older than Ap. All these, being adjectives, have different forms for Masc. and Fem. genders, the latter generally taking *-ī* (or *-mī*) suffix.

If the *puṣpikās* in *Mp.* be of Puṣpadanta's composition we have a list of ordinals from 1-102 Though it is a lexicographer's work to enlist them all, ordinals from 81-102 are given below, as such higher ordinals are seldom met with in Ap. literature.

81st : *ekkāsītima* (*ekāśīti-tama*).

82nd : *duvāsīma* (*dvyaśīti-tama*).

83rd : *teyāsītima* (**traya-aśīti-tama*).

84th : *caürāsīma* (*caturaśīti-tama*).

85th : *paṁcāsīma* (*pañcāśīti-*). *-y-* in M. *paṃcyāṃśī*, is to show the palatal pronunciation of *-c-*.

86th : *chāsītima* (*ṣaḍ-aśīti*>*cha-* or *chaha-asii*).

87th : *sattāsītima* (*saptāśīti-*).

88th : *aṭṭhāsitima* (*aṣṭāsīti-*).

89th : *ekkūṇa-ṇavadima* (*ekona-navati-*).

90th : *ṇavadima* (*navati-*).

91st : *ekka-ṇavadima* (*eka-navati-*).

92nd : *duṇaüdima* (*dvā-navati-*).

93rd : *ti-ṇavadima* (*tri-navati-*).

94th : *caü-ṇaudima* (*catur-navati-*).

95th : *paṁca-ṇavadima* (*pañca-navati-*).

96th : *chaṇṇaüdima* (*ṣaṇṇavati-*).

97th : *sattaṇaüdima* (*satpa-navati-*).

98th : *aṭṭha ṇaüdima* (*aṣṭa-navati-*).

99th : *ṇavaṇavadima* (*nava-navati-*).

100th : *sayamo* (*śata-*).

101st : *ekottarasayama* (*ekottara-śata-*)

102nd : *duttara-sayama* (*dvyuttara-śatā-*)

## PRONOUNS

§118. Pronouns form an interesting category of words in IA as they show much phonetic disintegration such as we find it in the different forms of pronouns in NIA. Morphologically they belong to the same class as nouns and the pre-Ap. tendencies of normalisation, phonetic decay, etc. are evident in Ap. The variety of pronominal forms provides us with a sure basis for the multiplicity of forms in NIA.

## PRSONAL PRONOUNS

§119. Out of the different kinds of pronouns, personal pronouns of the 1st and 2nd person present a rich variety of forms. A reference to the relevant sections of Pk. grammars gives us the following tables of declension. (Only the number of the *sūtra* is quoted to conserve space).

## FIRST PERSON PRONOUN

§119A. Pkt. grammarians supply us with the following declension of the 1st person Pronoun :

*Singular*

Nom. : *haüṁ* (*Hc*. 375, *Tr. Ld*. 4.45, *Sh*. 53). *hamuṁ* (*Ki*. 40) *hamu* (*Rt*. 23, *Mk*. 48).

Acc. : *maïṁ* (*Hc*. 337, *Tr. Ld*. 4.46, *Sh*. 55, *Mk*. 51, *Rt*. 23) *maï* (*Pu*. 66, *Ki*. 43), *maṁ* (*Rt*. 9), *mo* (*Mk*. 78).

Instr. & Loc.: *maïṁ* (The same as Acc.), *aïṁ* ? (*Ki*. 43).

Abl. Gen.: *mahu* (*Hc*. 379, *Tr. Ld*. 4.47, *Sh*. 57), *mahuṁ* (*Pu*. 67, *Ki*. 45, *Mk*. 53),
*majjhu* (*Hc*. 379, *Sh*. 57, *Pu*. 67, *Rt*. 23).
*majjha* (*Tr. Ld*. 4.47, *Ki*. 45, *Rt*. 23, *Mk*. 53).
*maha* (*Pu*. 67, *Rt*. 23, *Mk*. 53).

*Plural*

Nom. Acc.: *amhe* (*Hc*. 376, *Sh*. 54, *Ki*. 41, *Mk*. 50), *amhaïṁ* (*Hc*. 376, *Tr. Ld*. 4.48, *Sh*. 54, *Rt*. 23, *Mk*. 49).
*amhehiṁ* ? (*Tr. Ld*. 4.48) *Mk*. 78 gives *mo* as a form. cf. Acc. plur.

Instr. : *amhehiṁ* (*Hc*. 378, *Sh*. 56, *Ki*. 44, *Mk*. 52),
*amhe, amha-hiṁ* (*Rt*. 23, *Mk*. 52), *amhaïṁ*,
*amhahaṁ* (*Mk*. 52), *amhehi* (*Tr. Ld*. 4.49, *Rt*. 23).

Abl. and Gen. : *amhahaṁ* (*Hc*. 380, *Tr. Ld*. 4.44).
*amhaha*, *amhahiṁ* (*Mk*. 55 ). *amha* (*Ki*. 47, *Rt*. 23).
*Mk*. adds the Pk. forms of Abl. and Gen. plur to these. *Rt*. 23 gives *ṇo* as an additional form of Gen. plur.

Loc. : *amhāsu* (*Hc*. 381, *Tr. Ld*. 4.50, *Sh*. 59, *Ki*. 49, *Mk*. 54) *amhasu* (*Mk*. 54).

The following are the declensional forms of this personal pronoun in Pkts. :

*Singular*

Nom. : *ahaṁ*, *ahaaṁ*, JM. *ahayaṁ*, *haṁ* (*amhi*, *ammi*, *mmi ahammi*) ; Mg. *hage*, *hagge*, (*hake*, *ahake*).

Acc. : *maṁ mamaṁ*, *mahaaṁ*, *me* (*mi*, *mimaṁ*, *ammi*,*amhaṁ*, *amha*, *mamha*, *ahaṁ*, *hammi*, *ṇe*, *ṇaṁ*.)

Instr. : *mae*, *maï* (*mamae*, *mamāï*, *maāi*), *me* (*mi*, *mamaṁ*, *ṇe*).

Abl. : (*matto*, *mamatto*, *mahatto*, *majjhatto*, *maïtto*) *mamāo* (*mamāu mamāhi*), *mamāhiṃto*. Pais. (*mamāto*, *mamātu*).

Gen. : *mama*, *maha*, *majjha*, *mamaṁ*, *mahaṁ*, *majjhaṁ*, *me mi*. (*maï amha*, *amhaṁ*).

Loc. : (*mae*), *maï*, (*me*, *mi*, *mamāï*), *mamammi* (*mahammi*, *majjhammi*, *ahamammi*).

*Plural*

Nom. : *amhe* (*amha*, *amho*, *mo*, *bhe*), *Ḍh*. *vaaṁ*, Amg. JM. also *vayam*, Mg. also (*hage*), Pais. *vayam*, *ampha*, *amhe*.

Acc. *amhe*, *amha* (*amho*), *ṇo*, *ṇe*.

Instr. : *amhehiṁ* (*amhāhiṁ*, *amhe*, *amha*), *ṇe*.

Abl. : (*amhatto amhāhiṁto*, °*suṁto*, *amhesuṁto*, *mamatto*, *mamāhiṁto* °*suṁto*, *mamesuṁto*). JM. *amhe-hiṁto*.

Gen. : *amhāṇaṁ*,° *ṇa*, *amha*, *amhaṁ*, *mha*, (*amhāhṇ*), *amhe*, (*amho*, *mamāṇaṁ*, °*ṇa*, *mahāṇaṁ*, °*ṇa*, *majjhāṇaṁ*, a, *majjha*, *ṇe*), *no*, *ṇe*.

Loc. : *amhesu*, *amhāsu* (*amhasu*, *mamesu*, *mamasu*, *mahesu*, *mahasu*, *majjhesu*, *majjhasu*.)

A close comparison of the forms in literary Ap. (§119A) and those in grammarians' Ap. shows that the following forms from grammatical treatises are not attested to in Ap. literature.

Nom. sg. *hamuṁ*. Ins.-Loc. *aiṁ* (?).

Nom. Plur. *amhehiṁ*, Acc. Plur. *mo*, *amhehiṁ*,

Loc. Plur. *amhe*, *amhahaṁ*, Gen. Plur. *amhahiṁ ṇo*.

Differences due to *anusvāra* (or its absence) are not noted as they may be scribal errors.

A reference to Com. Table §119A. and to PISCHEL *Gram* §415 quoted above is enough to prove that the following forms are the relics of Pkts. in Ap. literature :

*Singular*: Nom. *ahayaṁ*, *haṁ*, Acc. *maṁ*, *mamaṁ*, Instr. *maē*, *maĩ* (?) *me*;

Dat. Gen. Abl. *mama*, *me*, *maha*, *mahaṁ*, *majjha*, *majjhaṁ*.

*Plural* : Nom. *amhe*, Instr. Loc. *amhehi* Dat. Gen. Abl. *amha* (?) *amhāṇa*, *amhāṇam*.

The greatest number of Prakritisms are found in WAp. and the least in EAp.

The bases of 1st p. pronoun are *aha-*, *ma-* in Sing. and *amha-*(*asma-*) in Plur. Out of these *aha-* is found in Nom. sg. and the latter for the remaining cases in sg. number. Out of the declined forms in Literary Ap. Nom. sg. *haũ* or *haüṁ* is a stable form found in texts from 500-1200 A.D. (e.g. *Vk. PPr.* to *Kp.*) and in all regions. It is derived from OIA *aha-ka* (changed to *hage* in Mg.) and is attested to as *ahaya* in WSAp. The Ap. developments of OIA *ahaka* are the basis of Panj. and Beng. *haũ*, Guj. *hāu*, *hũ*, Koṇk. *hā̃v* etc. The Acc. Instr. Loc. sg. *maĩ* shows a merging of the cases. Is the nasal (-*ĩ*) due to the influence of Loc. sg -*hĩ* (-*smin*) ? It is a normal -*ĩ* term. of the Ins. sg. of Masc. -*a* stems. (see §81). WSEAp. *maĩ* (with *ya*- śruti viz. *mayĩ* in EAp.) is the only stable form giving rise to H. *maĩ*, M. *mī* in NIA. The other alternate forms of the Ins. sg. are *maï* (unnasalised *maĩ* or OIA *mayi*), *mae* and *me* (Prākritisms from OIA *mayā*) and *maeṇa* (*ma*+Ins. sg. *eṇa* of nouns.) Dat. Gen. Abl. sg. *majjhu* (cf. Pk. *majjha*, *majjhaṁ*) is traceable to OIA *mahyam*, -*u* in -*jjhu* being a characteristic of the Ap. period. In the same way *mahu* may be traced to Pkt. *maha* <OIA *mahyaṁ*,[128] and its older form is *mahuṁ* in *PPr*. (See § 119A). This -*hu* is common to all regions in 1000 A.D. -*ho* is found in *KKc*. (SAp. 1100 A.D.), and is a normal term. of Gen. sg. of Masc. -*a* stems (See. §83).

128 PISCHEL, *Grammatik*, § 418, P. 294.

The base of the plural form is *amha-* (*asma-*). It takes the plural neut. term. *-aĩ* in the direct case which appears to have been extended to Loc. Instr., although it must be admitted that *-aĩ* is a regular Loc. Instr., sg. term. of *-a* stems (See §81) which might have been extended to this. For analogically Dat. Gen. Abl. : *ma-ha* : *amha-ha* : Loc. Instr. *ma-ĩ* : *amha-ĩ* is not improbable. If *amhaïṁ*, in *JC.* 4.4.7, *amhaiṁ mucchaiṁ mucchiya mayacchi*, be a part of Loc. Absolute construction there is no difficulty. But its normal *chāyā* is *āvayoḥ mūrchayā* 'by our swooning' and as such it is a Gen. plur. form, though *-iṁ* in Gen. plur. is rather difficult for explanation unless we accept some Gen. plur. form in *-hiṁ* (cf. *amhahiṁ* in *MK.* 55 quoted above) as its predecessor. The rest of the terms. e.g., *-ahiṁ* of Instr. pl. *-hā̃*, *-ha* of Dat. Gen. Abl. plur. have been already discussed (See. §§85, 86, 83). The only point worth noting is the confusion of numbers in admitting *-ha* of Gen. sg. to this plur. The original WAp. form ends in *-hā̃* in 1000 A.D., and it was later denasalized to *-ha*; but both were simultaneous in SAp. This confusion of numbers is, however, older than 1000 A.D., as we find it in other cases as well.

The Comp. chrono-regional Table of *asmad-* (§119A) will show that there is much stability in these forms although there is a fusion of cases and a confusion of numbers. As will be seen later in §120, this declension has affected that of the 2nd person pronoun.

119A. 1st Person Pronoun—Singular Number

| A.D. | WAp. | SAp. | EAp. |
|---|---|---|---|
| 500 | *haũ* .. | .. | .. |
| 600-1000 | *haũ* | .. | .. |
| 700-1200 | .. | .. | .. *haũ* |
| 1000 | *haüṁ*, *haũ* | *haüṁ haü*, *ahayaṁ* (*Jc.* 2.3.4) *haṁ* (*Jc.* 2.3.6). | |
| 1100 | .. | *haüṁ*. | |
| 1200 | *haüṁ*, *haũ*, *ahayaṁ* (*Sc.* 648.1) | | .. |

Accusative Singular

| A.D. | WAp. | SAp. | EAp. |
|---|---|---|---|
| 500 ? | *maĩ* | | |
| 600-1000 | *maĩ*, *maĩ* | .. | .. |
| 700-1200 | .. | .. | .. |
| 1000 | *maĩ* | *maïṁ* | .. |
| 1100 | *maṁ* | *maïṁ* | .. |
| 1200 | *maĩ*, *maṁ* (*Sn.* 77-176). *mamaṁ* (*Sc.* 672.7). | | |

INSTRU. LOC. SING.

| | | | |
|---|---|---|---|
| 500 ? | *maī* | .. | .. |
| 600-1000 | (1) *maĩ*<br>(2) *maï* | .. | .. |
| 700-1200 | .. | .. | (1) *maĩ*<br>(2) *mayĩ*. |

| A.D. | WAp. | SAp. |
|---|---|---|
| 1000 | (1) *maïṁ, maē* (*BhK*. 69-10) | (1) *maïṁ, maĩ maï, mae* (*Jc*. 2-1-15.) |
| 1100 | .. | (1) *maïṁ*<br>(2) *maeṇa* (*KKc*. 1.10-6). |
| 1200 | *maïṁ, maï, maĩ*<br>*maē* (*Kp. J*. 65.1*), *me* (*Kp*. S. 100.1*) | |

DAT. GEN. ABL. SING.

| | | | |
|---|---|---|---|
| 500? | *majjhu* | .. | .. |
| 600-1000 | *mahũ, mahu* | .. | .. |
| 700-1200 | .. | .. | *mahu*. |
| 1000 | *mahu, majjhu* | *mahu, majjhu, mahaṁ* (*Mp*. 1-10-3), *majjhaṁ* (*MP*. 1-10-12). | |
| 1100 | *majjhu, mahu*<br>*me* (*Mt*. 5) *mama* (*Mt*. 20) | *maha, mahe* (*KKc*. 2.4.10).<br>*mahu* (*KKc*. 1.2.10). | |
| 1200 | *maha, majjha* (*Sc. Kp*.)<br>*mahu, majjhu* (*Hc. Kp*.) | | |

1ST PERSON PRONOUN—PLURAL NUMBER.

DIRECT PLURAL

| A.D. | WAp. | SAp. | EAp. |
|---|---|---|---|
| 500 | .. | .. | .. |
| 600-1000 | .. | .. | .. |
| 700-1200 | .. | .. | .. |
| 1000 | *amhaĩ, amhiṁ* (*BhK*. 28.6) | *amhaĩ* | |
| 1100 | .. | *amhaĩ* | .. |
| 1200 | *amhe* (*Kc., Kp*.),<br>*amhi* (*Sc., Kp*. ), | *amhaĩ* | .. |

### Instr. Loc. Plural.

| | | | |
|---|---|---|---|
| 500 | .. | .. | .. |
| 600-1000 | .. | .. | .. |
| 700-1200- | | .. | .. |
| 1000 | *amhaĩ*<br>*amha* (*BhK*. 111.4).<br>*amha-hiṁ* (*Pd*. 138). | *amhaĩ*,<br>*amhahĩ*.<br>*amhehĩ* (*Hv*. Intro. § 46.). | |
| 1100 | .. | .. | .. |
| 1200 | *amhehĩ*,<br>*amhihĩ* (*Kp*. S. 66.3). | | |

### Dat. Gen. Abl. Plural.

| | | | |
|---|---|---|---|
| 500 | .. | .. | .. |
| 600-1000? | .. | .. | .. |
| 700 | .. | .. | .. |
| 1000 | *amha-hã amha* (*Bh.K*. 143 *Pd*. 138.)<br>*amhāṇa* (*Pkt.*) *BhK*. 69.11. | *amha-ha*, *amhaĩ* (*Jc*. 4.4.7)<br>*amha-hã* (Intro. to Hv. § 46.)<br>*amhāṇa* (*Jc*. 1.15.12) Pktsm. | |
| 1100 | *amhāṇaṁ* (*Mt*. 4) | *amhahaṁ*, *amhaho*. | |
| 1200 | *amha-haṁ*, *amha-hã*,<br>*amha-ha*, *amha*,<br>*amhāṇa* (Pktsm.) | | |

## §119B. First Person Pronoun

*Base* : -(*a*)*ha* -*ka*.

### Nom. Singular.

| Cent. A.D. | WAp. | SAp. | EAp. |
|---|---|---|---|
| 500 | -*ũ* | .. | .. |
| 600-1000 | -*ũ* | .. | .. |
| 700-1200 | .. | .. | -*ũ* |
| 1000 | -*uṁ*, -*ũ* | -*uṁ*, -*ũ*, -(*a*)*ṁ* | .. |
| 1100 | .. | -*uṁ* .. | .. |
| 1200 | -*uṁ*, -*ũ*<br>-(*a*)*ṁ* (*Sc*. 648.1) | .. | .. |

Acc. Singular. *Base* : *ma-*

| | | | |
|---|---|---|---|
| 500 ? | *-ĩ* | .. | .. |
| 600-1000 | *-ĩ -i* | .. | .. |
| 700-1200 | .. | .. | .. |
| 1000 | *-ĩ* | *-iṁ* | .. |
| 1100 | *-ṁ* | *-iṁ* | .. |
| 1200 | *-ĩ, -ṁ* (*Sc.* 672.7 *Sn.* 77-176) | .. | .. |

Instr. and Loc. Singular.

| | | | |
|---|---|---|---|
| 500 ? | *-ĩ* | .. | .. |
| 600-1000 | *-ĩ, -i* | .. | .. |
| 700-1200 | .. | .. | .. |
| 1000 | *-iṁ* , *-e* (*Pkt.*) | *-iṁ; ĩ, -i, -e* | .. |
| 1100 | .. | *-iṁ, -eṇa* (*KKc.* 1.10.6) | .. |
| 1200 | *-iṁ, -ī -i, -ē* | .. | .. |

Dat. Gen. Abl. Singular

| Cent. A.D. | WAp. | SAp. | EAp. |
|---|---|---|---|
| 500 | *-jjhu* | .. | .. |
| 600-1000 | (1) *-hu̐* (i.e., *-hũ*) (2) *-hu* | .. | .. |
| 700-1200 | .. | .. | *-hu* |
| 1000 | *-hu, -jjhu* | *-hu, -jjhu, -jjhaṁ -haṁ* | .. |
| 1100 | *-hu, -jjhu* | *-ha, -ho, -hu* | .. |
| 1200 | *-ha, -jjha* (*Sc. KP.*) *-hu, -jjhu* (*Hc. Kp.*) | .. | .. |

Nom. Acct. Plural. *Base* : *amha-*

| | | | |
|---|---|---|---|
| 500 ? | .. | .. | .. |
| 600-1000 | . | .. | .. |
| 700-1200 | .. | | .. |
| 1000 | -(*a*), *-ĩ, -iṁ* | *-ĩ* | .. |
| 1100 | .. | .. | .. |
| 1200 | zero, -(*a*) *ĩ -i -e* | . . | .. |

INSTR. LOC. PLURAL.

| | | | |
|---|---|---|---|
| 500 | .. | .. | .. |
| 600-1000 | .. | .. | .. |
| 700-1200 | .. | .. | .. |
| 1000 | -(*a*) *ĩ*, -zero, (*Bh.K.*)<br>-*hiṁ* (*Pd.* 138) | -(*a*) *ĩ*<br>-(*a*) *hĩ*, -(*e*) *hĩ* | .. |
| 1100 | .. | .. | .. |
| 1200 | -*ehĩ* (*Hc. Kc.*)<br>-*ihĩ* (*Kp.*) | .. | .. |

| Cent. A.D. | WAp. | SAp. | EAp. |
|---|---|---|---|
| 500 | .. | .. | .. |
| 600-1000 | .. | .. | .. |
| 700-1200 | .. | .. | .. |
| 1000 | -*haṁ*, zero | -*ha*, -*ĩ* (*Jc.* 4.4.7)<br>-*hã* | .. |
| 1100 | -(*ā*)*ṇaṁ* Pktism. | -*haṁ*, -*ho* | .. |
| 1200 | -*haṁ*, -*hã*, -*ha*<br>zero, -(*ā*)*ṇa* Pktism. | .. | .. |

SECOND PERSON PRONOUN.

§120. The following are the Ap. forms of 2nd person pronoun according to Pk. grammarians :—

*Singular.*

Nom. *tuhuṁ* (*Hc.* 368, *Tr. Ld.* 4.37, *Sh.* 46). *tuhaṁ* (*Pu.* 17.64, *Ki.* 40. *Rt.* 22, *Mk.* 41).

Acc. : *paiṁ* (*Hc.* 370, *Rt.* 22).
*taiṁ* (*Hc.* 370, *Tr. Ld.* 4.40, *Sh.* 48, *Ki.* 43, *Mk.* 44).
*tomaṁ* ? (*Rt.* 31), *to* (*Mk.* 78).
*eiṁ* (*Tr. Ld.* 4.40, *Sh.* 48).

Ins. Loc., *païṁ*: *taïṁ* Loc. has *eiṁ* also (The same as Acc.)
Dat. Gen. Abl: *tau* (*Hc.* 372, *Sh.* 50, *Tr. Ld.* 4.41).
*tujjha* (*Hc.* 372, *Tr. Ld.* 4.41, *Ki.* 46, *Mk.* 49).
*tudhra* (*Hc.* 372, *Sh.* 50, *Tr. Ld.* 4.41), *tumbha* (*Rt.* 22).
*tuha* (*Ki.* 45, *Rt.* 22, *Mk.* 46, *Ld.* 4.41).
*timha* *Mk.* 46, *Rt.* 22), *tubbha* (*ki.* 45, *Mk.* 46).
*tuhuṁ* (*Ki.* 45), *tujjhu* (*Sh.* 50), *tao* (*Ld.* 4.41).
*tumhe* (*Rt.* 22).

*Plural.*

Nom. Acc. *tumhe* (*Hc.* 369, *Tr. Ld.* 4.38, *Sh.* 47, *Ki.* 41, *Rt.* 22, *Mk.* 43).
*tumhaïṁ* (*Hc*, 369, *Tr. Ld.* 4.38, *Sh.* 47, *Mk.* 42).
*tumhāïṁ* (*Pu.* 65), *tumbhaiṁ*, (*Rt.* 22).

Instr. : *tumhehiṁ* (*Hc.* 371, *Sh.* 49, *Pu.* 66, *Ki.* 44.)
*tumhahiṁ* (*Rt.* 22), *tumhāhiṁ* (*Mk.* 45).

Dat. Abl. Gen. *tumhahaṁ* (*Hc.* 373, *Tr. Ld.* 4.43, *Sh.* 51. *Ki.* 44.)
*tumha* (*Ki.* 47), *tumhahim*, *°ha* (*Mk.* 55).

Loc: *tumhāsu* (*Hc.* 374, *Sh.* 52, *Tr. Ld.* 4.42, *Ki.* 49, *Mk.* 47).
*tumhasu* (*Mk.* 47).

The MIA background of these forms will be clear from the following declension in Pkts. [129]

*Singular.*

Nom : *tumaṁ*, *tuṁ*, *taṁ* (*tuha*, *tuvaṁ*), Ḍh. *tuhaṁ*.

Acc. : *tumaṁ* (*tuṁ*, *taṁ*), *te* (*tuha*, *tuvaṁ*, *tume*, *tue*) ; Ś. Mg. also *de* ; Ḍh. *tuham*.

Instr. : *tae*, *taï*, *tue*, *tui*, (*tumaṁ*), *tumae* (*tumaï*), *tumāi*, *tume*, *te*, *de*, (*di*, *bhe*).

Abl : *tatto*, *tumāhi*, *tumāhiṁto*, *tumāo*, (*tumāu*, *tumā*, *tumatto*, *taïtto*, *tuitto*), *tuvatto*, (*tuhatto*, *tvbbbhatto*, *tumhatto* *tujjhatto*). Pais. (*tumāto*, *tumātu*).

Gen. : *tava*, *tujjha*, *tuha*, *tuhaṁ*, *tubbha*, *tubbhaṁ*, *tumha*, *tumhaṁ* *te*, *de*, (*taï*), *tu*, (*tuva*, *tuma*), *tumaṁ*, *tumma* (*tumo* *tume*, *tumāi* *etc.*, Ś. *tuha*, *de*. Mg. *tava*, *tuha*, *de*.

Loc. *tai*, *tumammi*, *tume*, *tuvi*, *tui*, (*tue*, *tae*, *tumae*, *tumai* etc.) AMg. *tumaṁsi*, Ś. *taï*, *tui*.

*Plural.*

Nom: *tvmhe*, *tubbhe* (*tubbha*, *tumha*, *tujjhe* etc.) *AMg.* *tumhe*, *tubbhe* ; Ś. Mg. (?) *tumhe*.

Acc. : The same as Nom. AMg. *bhe*.

Instr. : *tumhehiṁ*, *tubbhehiṁ* (*-ehiṁ* added to *tujjha*, *tuyha-*, *tumma-*, *umha-* etc.)

129 Pischel, *Grammatik*, § 420.

Abl. : (*-atto* added to *tumha-*, *tubbha-*, *tujjha-*, *tuyha-* etc.)

Gen. : *tumhāṇaṁ*, °*ṇa* (*-āṇaṃ*, *-āṇa* applied to *tubbha-*, *tujjha-*, *tuha-*, *tuva-*, *tuma-*),

Loc. : (*-esu* affixed to *tumha-*, *tubbha,- tujjha-*, *tuha*, - *tuva-*, *tuma-*, *tumhăsu*, *tusu*.)

A comparison of the paradigms of 2nd p. pronoun in the Ap. sections of Pk. grammars and in Ap. literature shows that many forms in the Ap. of the Pk. grammarians are *not* represented in Ap. literature. e.g., Acc. sg. *tomaṁ*, *to*, *eiṁ* ; Gen. sg. *tumbha*, *timha*, *tubbha* and the *tumbha-* and *tubbha-* plurals. Perhaps as PISCHEL[130] and BLOCH[131] think, they may be grammarians' creations or analogical formations in spoken Ap. which the Pk. grammarians knew personally or through tradition.

Out of the forms found in Ap. literature, the following are found in Pkts. :

Nom. sg. *tumaṁ*, Ins. sg. *taï*, Gen. sg. *tujjha*, *tuha*, *tuhaṁ* ;

Nom. Plur. *tumhe*, Ins. Plur. *tumhe-hiṁ*, Gen. Plur. *tumha*.

The bases of 2nd p. pronoun are *tu-* (sometimes changed to *ta-*) and *pa-* in the sing., and these are clear developments of OIA *tva-* (cf. §62). In Nom. sg. *-h-* (as in *tu-h-uṁ*,*-tu-h-ũ*, *tu-h-aṁ*, *tu-h-u*) presents some difficulty as Ved. *t*(*u*)*vam*, Sk. *tvam*, Pā. Pk. *tuvaṁ*, Pk. *tumaṁ* contain no *-h*. It is probably on the analogy OIA *asma-* : *aha-* : : **tuṣma* : *tuha-*. The Ap. developments of these are obviously *amha* : *haũ* : : *tumha* : *tuhũ*. cf. Ḍh. *tuhaṁ*. *tuhũ* became mixed up with unnasalised *tū-* derived from MIA *to*<OIA *tava*, and it is found in Pashai and Tirahi in the direct [132]case. *tumaṁ* is a Prākritism, and Kanakāmara is the only author who uses *paiṁ* in all cases. (See *KKc*. 3-10-6 Nom. sg. 3.20.4 for Acc. sg., 1.10-9 for Instr. sg. and 3.11-9 for Dat. sg).

Acc. Instr. Loc. sgs. *paiṁ* and *taïṁ* show that *-iṁ* or *-ĩ* was the common term. applied to *pa-* and *ta-*< OIA *tva-* (cf. §62.)

Gen. sg. *tu-jjha*, °*jjhu*, °*jjha-ha*, °*jjhuṁ* (cf. Pk. *-jjha*) are traceable to Pā. *tuhyam* on the analogy of OIA *mahyam*. It appears that *tu-* and *tujjha-* became the oblique bases, and we find the following pair of series:

*tu* : *tu-ha*, *tu-haṁ*, *tu-hu* : : *tujjha* : *tujjha-ha*, *tujjhu tujjhuṁ* (*Sn*.)

*tua* is found in uncritical editions like *DŚ*.

130 PISCHEL, *Grammatik* § 416.
131 BLOCH, *La langue marathe* § 207.
132 BLOCH, *L'indo-aryen* p. 191.

NIA accepts *tujjhu-* and *to-* (<*tava*) as the oblique bases. SAp. *tau* and EAp. *to* are directly derived from OIA *tava*. SAp. *tūsa* is unsupported by Pkt. grammarians though it is clearly traceable to OIA **tvasya* (cf. Niya Pk. *tūsa*), while *tudhra* though sanctioned by Pkt. grammarians like *Hc. Tr. Ld.* and *Sh.*, and though illustrated by Hemacandra in *Kc.*, is very rarely met with in Ap. literature. In *tu-ha* and *tujjha-ha*, *-ha* is the normal Ap. Gen. sg. term. *tua* (*DS*. 4.5.3) and *taha* (*JC* 1.7.13) are probably scribal errors for *tau* and *tuha* respectively.

The 2nd p. Plur. forms are based on *tumha-* (cf. Pā. Pk. *tumha* <OIA **tuṣma-*), and the desinences Direct *-ĩ*, Loc. Instr. *-ehĩ*, *-ihĩ*, Gen. *-hã*, *-ha* and zero are the same as those of the 1st p. pronoun and masc. stems in *-a*. Aśokan *tup(p)ha-* seems to be at the basis of *tubbha-* and *tumbha-* forms in grammarians' Ap. The assumption of the existence of such forms in spoken Ap. is based firstly on their close similarity with *tumha-* in literary Ap., and secondly on their conservance in NIA. [133]. Forms in NIA e.g., M. *tumhĩ*, Abl. *tumhā̃*, Guj. *tame*, *taṁ*, Braj. *tuṁ*, *tumhaũ*, Beng. *tumi*, *tomī*, H. *tuṁ*, are simply a continuation of Ap. *tumha-*. Can we not regard the **tuhva-* forms in NIA, as another development of *tumhau* ?

The comparative table of terms. in literary Ap. (§ 120 A) shows that in spite of the variety of terms. noted above, literary Ap. discloses much stability throughout the Ap. period. A comparison of the paradigms of the 1st and 2nd p. pronouns in literary Ap. indicates that they developed on similar lines in Ap. and that it is the 1st person pronoun that influenced the latter. As a matter of fact, it was practically one set of terms. which was applied to *ma-* : *amha-* in the 1st person and *tu-* and *ta-* : *tumha-* in the 2nd person. This set of terms. is practically the same as that of Masc. *-a* stems with a few relics of old Pkt. and OIA ones.

### §120A. SECOND PERSON PRONOUN

| A.D. | WAp. | SAp. | EAp. |
|---|---|---|---|
| | NOM. SG. | | |
| 500 | | .. | .. |
| 600-1000 | *tuhu* ⊙ | .. | .. |
| 700-1200 | .. | .. | *tuhu* |

133 *Ibid.*, p. 192.

| | | | |
|---|---|---|---|
| 1000 | *tuhuṁ*, *tum*? (*BhK*. 262.3) *paĩ* (Acc. to JAIN in *Pd*. 179). | *tuhuṁ*. *tumam* (*Nc*. 2.3.19) | |
| 1100 | .. | *tuhũ* | .. |
| 1200 | *tuhũ*, °*huṁ*. | | |

ACC. INS. LOC. SINGULAR.

| | | | |
|---|---|---|---|
| 500 ? | *paĩ* | | |
| 600-1000 | .. | .. | .. |
| 700-1200 | .. | .. | .. |
| 1000 | *paĩ*<br>Ins. *timaĩ* (*BhK*. 144.9) | *paiṁ* | .. |
| 1100 | Ins. *paĩ* | *paiṁ* | .. |
| 1200 | *paĩ*<br>Ins. *taĩ* | ..<br>.. | ..<br>.. |

DAT. GEN. ABL. SINGULAR

| | | | |
|---|---|---|---|
| 500 ? | *tujjhu*, *tujjha-ha* | .. | .. |
| 600-1000 | *tuha*, *tujjha* | .. | .. |
| 700-1200 | .. | .. | *to* (*DKK*. 29) |
| 1000 | *tujjhu*, *tau* (*BhK*. 19.8), *tuddhu* (*BhK*. 125.8) *tvhiṁ* (*Pd*. 219). *paĩ* (*Sdd*. 112.) | *tuha*, *tujjhu*, *tujjha*, *tūsa* (*Jc*. 1.7.11), *taha* (*Jc*. 1.7.13). | |
| A.D. | WAp. | SAp. | EAp. |
| 1100 | *tujjhu*, *tua* (*DS*. 4.5.2) *tuhaṁ* (*Mt*. 5) | *tujjha*, *tuha*, *tau* (*KKc*. 2.5.9). | .. |
| 1200 | *tujjhuṁ*, *tuhu*, *tuha*, *tujjha*. | | |

SECOND PERSON PRONOUN—PLURAL

| | | | |
|---|---|---|---|
| 500 | .. | .. | .. |
| 600-1000 | .. | .. | .. |
| 700-1200 | .. | .. | .. |
| 1000 | *tumhaĩ*, *tumhi*,<br>Acc. *tumha* (*BhK*. 99.4) | *tumhaĩ*. | |
| 1100 | .. | *tumhaiṁ*, *tumhi*. | |

| | | | |
|---|---|---|---|
| 1200 | *tumhi*, *tumhaiṁ*, *tumhe*, *tubbhē* (*Sc.* 565.1). *tubbhi* (*Sc.* 486.3). | | |

INST. PLURAL.

| | | | |
|---|---|---|---|
| 500 | .. | .. | .. |
| 600-1000 | .. | .. | .. |
| 700-1200 | .. | .. | .. |
| 1000 | *tumhi* (*BhK.* 113.4), *tumhaĩ* (*Bh.K.* 101.7). | *tumhehiṁ*. | |
| 1200 | do. | do. | |
| 1200 | *tumhēhĩ*. | | |

DAT. GEN. ABL. PLURAL.

| A.D. | WAp. | SAp. | EAp. |
|---|---|---|---|
| 500 | .. | .. | .. |
| 600-1000 | .. | .. | .. |
| 700-1200 | .. | .. | .. |
| 1000 | *tumhahã*, *tumha*, *tumhāṇa* (Pkt.) | *tumhaha*, *tumhahã* | |
| 1100 | .. | *tumhahaṁ* | .. |
| 1200 | *tumha*, *tumhaha*, *tumhahã* | .. | .. |

LOCATIVE PLURAL.

| | | | |
|---|---|---|---|
| 500 ? | .. | .. | .. |
| 600-1000 | .. | .. | .. |
| 700-1200 | .. | .. | .. |
| 1000 | .. | .. | .. |
| 1100 | .. | .. | .. |
| 1200 | *tumhāsu* (*Hc.* 4.374) | .. | .. |

§120B. SECOND PERSON PRONOUN

NOM. SINGULAR :

*Base* : *tu-*

| A.D. | WAp. | SAp. | EAp. |
|---|---|---|---|
| 500 ? | .. | .. | .. |
| 600 | *-huṁ* | .. | .. |

| | | | |
|---|---|---|---|
| 700-1200 | .. | .. | *hu* |
| 1000 | *-huṁ, -ṁ* | *-huṁ* <br> *-maṁ* (Pktsm.) | .. |
| 1100 | .. | *-hũ* | .. |
| 1200 | *-huṁ* | .. | .. |

ACC. & INS. SINGUALR. Base *pa-*

| | | | |
|---|---|---|---|
| 500 ? | *-ĩ* | .. | .. |
| 600-1000 | .. | .. | .. |
| 700-1200 | .. | .. | .. |
| 1000 | *-ĩ* | *-iṁ* | .. |
| 1100 | *-ĩ* | *-iṁ* | .. |
| 1200 | *-ĩ* <br> (*-ta-*) *ĩ* | .. | .. |

DAT. GEN. ABL. SINGULAR. Base : *tu-*

| | | | |
|---|---|---|---|
| 500 ? | *-jjhu, jjhha-ha* | .. | .. |
| 600- 100 | *-haö -jjha* | .. | .. |
| 700-1200 | .. | .. | *-o* ?(*DKK.* 29) |
| 1000 | *-jjhu, -ddhu* (*BhK.* 125.8) <br> *-hiṁ* (*Pd.* 219) | *-ha-, -jjhu, -jjha* <br> *-sa*( ? ) *-ha.* | .. <br> .. |
| 1100 | *-jjhu, -haṁ* | *-jjha, -ha* | .. |
| 1200 | *-jjha -jjhuṁ* <br> *-hu, -ha.* | .. | .. |

SECOND PERSON PRONOUN PLURAL NUMBER.

DIRECT PLURAL : Forms in *Vk.*, *PPr.*, *Ys.*, *DKK*, *Dks.* were not found. Base: *tumha-*

| A.D. | WAp. | SAp. | .. |
|---|---|---|---|
| 1000 | *-iṁ. -ĩ, -i* <br> zero | *-ĩ* | .. |

| | | | |
|---|---|---|---|
| 1100 | .. | *-iṁ, -i* | .. |
| 1200 | *-iṁ, -i, -e* | .. | .. |

INSTR. PLURAL.

| | | | |
|---|---|---|---|
| 1000 | *-ĩ- -i* | *-ehiṁ* | .. |
| 1100 | .. | *-ehiṁ* | .. |
| 1200 | *-ehĩ* | .. | .. |

DAT. GEN. ABL. PLURAL.

| | | | |
|---|---|---|---|
| 1000 | *-hā̃*, -zero | *-ha, -hā̃* | .. |
| 1100 | .. | *-haṁ* | .. |
| 1200 | *-ha, -haṁ*, -zero | .. | .. |

## THE ADJECTIVAL PRONOUNS

§121. The next group of Pronouns consists of the 3rd person, Remote Demonstrative and Correlative Pronoun *-ta* (<OIA *tad*), the Proximate Demonstratives *ea-*, *eya-* (<OIA *etad*), and *-āya-*, *āya- āa-* (=OIA *idam* which incorporates **a-* forms in its declension), the Relative *ja-* (OIA *yad-*) ; the Interrogative *ka-* (<OIA **ka-*), *kavaṇa* (cf. Pā. *kopana, kiṁpana* which is a development of MIA **ka-pana*<Sk. *kiṁ punaḥ*?) and the Reflexive *appa-* (**ātpman*<**āpIman*=*ātman*.[134] These are designated 'adjectival' from the functional point of view. As in Pkts., in Ap. also they show a continuous process of simplification of themes and paradigms. Thus we do not find OIA *adas-* (with the exception of a few forms noted by Pk. grammarians e.g., *Hc.* 8.4.364), the Pkt. stem *ima-* for OIA *idaṁ* (Masc. and Fem.) and *atta* (OIA *ātman* in Ap. literature. The rare forms of *adas- viz.*, Nom. Acc. Plur. *oi* is traceable to II. **ave*<*ava*.[135]

Generally these pronouns adopt the inflections of the nouns associated with and qualified by them. As such the pronominal declension also shows a confusion of gender and number and a fusion of cases. It is hence, perhaps, that we do not get any detailed exposition of the declension of these pronouns in Pk. grammars. It is not improbable that Ap. literature which does not possess many pronominal forms —so much so that many cases of some pronouns, especially of Fem. gender and plural number are not met with or are very scarce in some Ap. texts—formed the limitation of their authors.

---

134 S. M. KATRE, *Form. of Konk.* § 254 Footnote 1.
135 PISCHEL, *Grammatik* § 432 and BLOCH, *L'indo-aryen* p. 149.
For their relics in NIA, see *L'indo-aryen*, p. 197.

## The Third Person, Remote Demonstrative and Correlative Pronoun *ta-*

§122. Out of the above-mentioned adjectival pronouns (in §121), the 3rd person, Remote Demonstrative and Correlative Pronoun *ta-* (*tad*), the Relative Pron. *ja-* (*yad*) and the Interrogative *ka-* (**ka-* though usually written as *kim*), are declined exactly alike. Unlike the pronouns of the 1st and 2nd Person, these have different forms for different genders. *ta-*, *ja-* and *ka-* are the Masc. and Neut. bases for *tad-*, *yad-*, and *kim-* respectively. As noted by PISCHEL[136] their feminine bases end in *-ā* and *-ī*. A comparison of the terms. of these (both Masc. and Fem.) with those of the Masc. and Fem. nouns shows that they share the same set of desinences as is found in the case of nouns of the same region and century. Even Pkts. show a similar tendency[137].

§123. As Pk. grammarians are generally silent regarding the details of the declension of these pronouns in the *sūtras*, we have to deduce the forms from the illustrations. The following are the forms of 3rd p. pronoun in *Hc.* 8.4.329-448.

(i) *ta-* (MASC. AND NEUT.)

| | *Singular* | *Plural* |
|---|---|---|
| Direct : | Masc. *so*, *su* | *te*, *ti*. |
| (Acc. | *-taṁ*, a Pktsm.) | |
| Neut. | *taṁ*, *traṁ* *Hc.* 360.) | Neut. *tāiṁ*, *teṁ* |
| Instr. | *teṇa*, *teṁ*. | *tehiṁ* |
| Abl. | *tā* (*Hc.* 370.1), *to* (PISCHEL, *Gram* §425) *tahāṁ* (*Hc.* 355). | |
| Dat. : Gen.: | *tasu*, *tāsu*, *tassu*, *taho*. | *tahaṁ*, *tāhaṁ*, *tāṇa*. |
| Loc. : | *tahiṁ*, *tadru* (*Ki.* 5.50). | *tahiṁ* (*Hc.* 422.18). |

136 PISCHEL, *Grammatik* § 424.
137 *Ibid.*, §§ 425-8.

FEMININE

Nom. sg. *sā* ; Acc. sg. *taṁ* ; Instr. sg. *tāe*, Abl. Gen. sg. *tahe, tāsu*.

The *sa*- forms both here and in Pkts. are Sanskritisms and may be omitted here.[138]

(ii) The following is the declension of 3rd p. pronoun in Pkts.[139].

MASC. AND NEUT.

*Singular.*

Nom. Acc.: Masc. *so*, Amg. *se*, Mg. *śe*,
Neut. *taṁ* (all dialects).

Instr. : *teṇa* (all dialects), *teṇaṁ* (AMg.), *tiṇā* (M. *Hc.* 3.69).

Abl.: *tā* (M. JM. JŚ. Ś. Mg. Ḍh, Ā) ; *tāo* (Amg. JM.); *tatto, tao; tado* (Ś. Mg.); *to, tamhā* (Amg. JŚ.) *to* (M. AMg. JM. Mg.); *taohiṁto* (AMg.)

Gen.: *tassa* (M. AMg. JM. JŚ. Ś. Ḍh.); *tasa* (PG), *tāha* (Mg.) *tāsa* (M.)
Loc. *tammi* (M. JM. ) ; *taṁsi, tammi, taṁmi* (AMg.) *tassiṁ* (Ś.)

*Plural*

Nom.: *te* (Masc.) ; Neut. *tāiṁ* (All dialects), *tāṇi* (AMg. JM.)

Acc.: *te* (also JŚ).

Ins.: *tehiṁ*.

Abl. *tebbho* (AMg.) ; *tehiṁto* (AMg. JM.) (*tehiṁ* (JM.)

Gen.: *tāṇaṁ, tāṇa* (M.) ; *tesiṁ* (also JM.). *tesi* (AMg.)

Loc. *tesu* (also Ś.) ; *tesuṁ* (Ś).

(iii) FEMININE

*Singular*

Instr.: *tīe, tīa* (M.) ; *tīe, tāe* (AMg. JM.) *tāe* (Ś. Mg.)

Gen.: *tissā, tīe, tīa* (M.) ; also *tīā, tīi* (*Hc.* 3.64).
*tīse, tāe, tīe* (AMg.) JM). ; *tāe*(Ś. Mg.,) ; *tīe* (Pais),

---

138 *Ibid.*, § 423.
139 *Ibid.*, § 425.

Loc.: *tīe, tīa, tāhiṁ, tāe* (M.) ; *tīse,* (AMg.), *tāhe* (M. AMg. JM.)

*Plural*

Instr.: *tāhiṁ,* (M. AMg. JM.); *tehi, tāhi* (Ś.)

Gen.: *tāṇaṁ* (Ś. JS.) ; *tāsiṁ* (AMg. JS.) ; *tāsi* (AMg.)

Loc. : *tāsu.* (JM. Ś.).

### (iv) Singular Number

The Nom. and Acc. sings. in literary Ap. show the same tendencies as in noun declension *viz.*, the process of the formation of the Direct case, and the use of *-u* on a wider scale. The conservative forces *e.g.*, the use of *sa-* for Nom. (as well as for the Acc.) are there, and Pk. *so* remained a popular form in Ap. literature upto 1200 A.D.[140] The use of *ta-* even in Nom. sg. appears first in Neut. gender in WAp. (500 A.D. ?) but that is extended to Masc. in WSAp. from 1000 A.D., although *ta-*forms e.g., *te* (*DKs.* 107), *tā* (*DKs.* 7, 8) appear to be limited to EAp. in the 10th cent. A.D., Morphologically there is nothing new either in the Direct case or in the Indirect ones. We may note only the peculiar forms in this as well as in other cases.

Neut. Nom. sing. *tā* <OIA *tad* first appears in *VK.* i.e., WAp. of 500 A.D., (*Mt.* 24), and again in EAp. in the 10th cent. A.D. (only twice viz., *DKs.* 7, 8). In both these regions the forms were not very popular. One need not suspect any borrowal from WAp. to EAp. here. Masc. and Neut. Direct sing. in *-a* and *e-* is a special characteristic feature of EAp. (For the same in Noun-Declension see §80). *ta*<*tad* (Mt. 20) is an exceptional example in WAp. (1100 A.D.) Neut. direct sing. *taü*<**tako*<*ta-ka-ḥ* is an extended form of *ta-* in *Pd.* 11. Masc. Acc. sg. *tā*<*taṁ* in *Sc.* 603.8 is an illustration of *-ṁ*>nasalisation of the surrounding vowel, although this is the only example in the case of *ta-*.

Ins. sg. *-ẽ, -ẽṁ-, ẽṇa, iṇā* need no discussion (For their history see §81). *tiṇi*<*tena* in *Kp.* (only 1+2 forms[141]) is probably *teṇa-i* <**tena-cit* (?), but we have no *-iṇi* term. in Noun-declension. In the same text we find Masc. and Neut. Ins. sg. of *yad-* as *jiṇi* (*Kp.* S. 52.4 also *Jdc.* 8.3) though there is no form like **kiṇi.* (For *jīṇi* see later §126). Taking into account the correlation between *ja-* and *ta-*, it is natural that these

140 For the use of *sa-* in NIA, see Bloch, *L.'indo-aryen*, p. 196.

141 Alsdorf, Intro. to *Kp.* § 28(a).

forms should be limited to these two pronouns. -*i* in *iṇi* is, however difficult to explain.

Though the general set of terms for Dat. Gen. Abl. is the same for Nouns and Pronouns, a detailed comparison discloses the difference. Thus in *PPr.* and *Ys.*, *ta-* takes -*ā̆su* and -*hu*, while the Nouns (-*a* stems have -*haŭ* (see §§83A and 83). In EAp. -*su* and even -*hĩ* (*DKK.* 24) are applied to *ta-*, while the nouns (-*a* stems) take -*ha*, -*ho* and -*hŏ*. In WAp (1000 A.D.) -*ha*, -*haṁ*, and zero are not the terms. of *ta-* though nouns ending in -*a* require them. Normally *tā̆su* and *tahŏ*, °*hu* appear to be the stable forms of this case in WSAp. *tahĩ*=*tasya* (*DKK.* 24) is an extension of the Loc. to the Gen., as the converse example of Loc. sg. *tasu* (*DKK.* 22) shows, how the fusion of Loc. and Gen. began as early as 700 A.D. in EAp.[142] (cf. *kahĩ* in *DKK.* 24). -*āhara* in *tāhara* (*DKs.* 92) is a possessive, suffix although SHAHIDULLA[143] equates it with OIA *tasya*[144].

*tehaiṁ* (*Pd.* 103) is regarded as the Loc. sg. of *ta-* by H. L. JAIN[145]. It is a Loc. sg. but it is of Ap. *teha-*<*taïsa*<*tādṛśa*. cf. *jeha keha*, *eha* from OIA *yādṛśa*, **kādṛśa* (=*kīdṛśa*), **ādṛśa* (=*īdṛśa*[146]. The meaning of that line supports this view. The line in question runs thus :

*tahiṁ tehaïṁ vaḍha avasarahiṁ vitalā sumaraï deu* 'Oh dullard! Rare are those who remember God *in that kind of* period' (*Pd.* 103). H. L. JAIN's Hindi rendering takes it simply as '*us avasar par*'.[147] In *Hc.* 8.4.357 also we have *tahiṁ tehaï bhaḍa-nivahe* 'in that type of host of warriors[148]. *temaï* in *Pd.* 91 is an adverb though it is explained as *tasmin* in *Pd.* glossary, p. 85. *tasu* (*DKK.* 22) is regarded as the extension of the Gen. to Loc., as Gen. is the most accommodative case even in OIA, and we have the fusion of Gen. and Loc. sgs. in Fem. nouns in Pkts. The alternate theory that this -*su* is a plur. term. applied to Loc. sg. is not tenable, as we have no other instance of Loc. -*su* sing. or plur. even in the Noun declension in EAp. WSAp. *tammi* is a clear Prakritism.

PLURAL

(v) The Direct case requires no remark as Nom. *te* is a stable form from OIA to NIA. Ap. extended *te* to the Acc. The weakening of *te*>

142 The fusion of Loc. and Gen. sings. is found in the declensions of Fem. nouns in Pkts. See PISCHEL, *Gram.* §§ 374,385.
143 *Les Chants Mystiques*, p. 210.
144 For the descendants of these Dat. Gen. Abl. forms in NIA see BLOCH, *L'indo-aryen*, p. 196.
145 Glossary to *Pd.*, p. 84.
146 PISCHEL, *Grammatik* § 262.
147 *Pāhuḍadohā*, p. 31.
148 P. L. VAIDYA takes *tehai* as *tādṛśe* (Ed. of *Hc.* p. 43) though the translation 'in the midst of host' is general.

*ti* in 1200 A.D., is quite clear. An NIA type of internal *sandhi* is observed in *tiṁ* =*tān* (*BhK*. 295.2). The original seems to be the neut. form *ta-*+ *ãiṁ*>*tõ-iṁ*>*teṁ* which is also found in *BhK*. 108.6 and later in *Hc*. 8.4.339[149]. The use of Neut. terms. for Masc. direct plur. is quite common in 1000 A.D., (see §84). This type of internal *sandhi* began in WAp. of the 10th cent. A.D. So far as this case is concerned, contemporary SAp. seems to be rather conservative, as we do not find such forms in the works of Puṣpadanta.

The Instr. Loc. is quite easy of explanation as Ins. plur. *-ehiṁ*, *-ehĩ*, *-ehi* (the only desinence in EAp. of 1000 A.D.)<Ved. *-ebhiḥ*, and Loc. plur. *-hiṁ*, *-hi*<Loc. sg. *-smin* have been already discussed ( §85.)

*-ãhaṁ*, *-ãhã* of the Dat. Gen. Abl. have been discussed in noun declension (§86). SAp. favours *-āhaṁ*, *-āhã*, while the mixture *-ahaṁ* (*-ahã*) and *-āhaṁ* (*-āhã*) is found in WAp. from *PPr*. down *Sc*., *Sn*., *Kp*. (600-1200 A.D.), if we take a synthetic view of the desinences upto 1200 A.D., *tāhi* in *Jdu*. 24.2 is difficult to explain but it is an uncritically edited text. The rest are Prakritisms.

### FEMININE GENDER

#### (vi) Singular Number

In the direct sing. *sā* belongs to the pre-Ap. period (both OIA and MIA), the speciality of Ap. being its extension to the Acc. *sẽ* (*DKs*. 49) is not an Ardhamāgadhīsm as the identity of forms may lead one to believe, but it is rather the confusion of genders (use of Masc. for the Fem.) which is amply illustrated in Nominal and Pronominal declension in EAp. (For noun declension see §§88, 94, 97; for pronominal declension see later.)

In Instr. also we find the Masc. Instr. sing. *-eṁ*, *-ẽ*, *-iṁ* *-ĩ* applied to Fem. *tā-* and *tī-*. *Jc*. 3.10.12 uses *teṇa* for Fem. Instr. sg. *tayā*.

---

149 The line containing *tiṁ* runs as follows:
*puṇaravi tiṁ paesa parisakkai*. 'Again he crosses those regions.' (*BhK*. 295.2) In Intro. to *BhK*. p. *38 Jacobi explains *tiṁ* as *ta-iṁ* with the loss of *-a-*. In spite of careful search for the forms, we did not come across a single instance of *phaliṁ* ∠ *phalāiṁ* or *jiṁ jāi*. Hence *tiṁ* should be regarded as a weakening of *teṁ*. In *BhK*. 1 8.6 we have.

*payaphaṃseṁ parimaliya vasundhara*
*taṁ ji viṇou jeu teṁ vāsara.*

Here as *teṁ* qualifies *vāsara* days' (Neut. direct plu.) *teṁ* or *te* should be regarded as the contraction of *tāī*. Later on in *Hc*. 8,4,339 we find

*teṃ avaḍa-yaḍi vasanti.*

They (grass) grow on the slope of a ditch.' *teṃ*<*taiṃ* is obvious, *tahiṁ avasari ta teṇa ji jaṁpiu.*

'So it was spoken *by her* at that time.'

The desinences *-hĩ* and *-hi* for Instr. sg. in 1200 A.D., shows how the Loc. and Instr. became identified by the 12th cent. even in WAp. *tĩi* in WAp. (1200 A.D.) is a weakening of *tīe*. *tā* in *MP*. 1.6.15 is somewhat inexplicable. Is it a contraction of Pk. **tāa* on the analogy of *tīa*?[150] The application of *-hiṁ*, *-hĩ* to Fem. *ta* shows a confusion of genders.

Dat. Gen. Abl. terms *-(ă)ha*, *-(ă)he*, *-(ă)hẽ*, (*-(ă)hi* are discussed in Noun-declension. (see §§83, 91). *taho* in *Bhk*. 160.8 is the use of the Masc. for the Fem. The rest are Prakritisms, and there is little remarkable from a chrono-regional point of view.

PLURAL

(vii) The direct case of Fem. *tā-* was formed in OIA. Instr. Loc. *-hiṁ*, *-hĩ* are already discussed (see §93.2, 85). For the discussion of Dat. Gen. Abl. *-(ă)hã* see §93.3, 87. In *tāhiṁ* (*KKc*. 6.15.8) *-hiṁ* is probably the same as Instr. Loc. *-hiṁ* and serves as a proof of the absorption of Instr. Loc. in Dat. Gen. Abl. in SAp. of 11th Cent. A.D.

### 123A. (iv) THE DEMONSTRATIVE AND 3RD PERSONAL PRONOUN MASC. AND NEUT. DIRECT SING.

| A.D. | WAp. | SAp. | EAp. |
|---|---|---|---|
| 500 ? | Masc. *so*<br>*taṁ* (Acc. Pkt.)<br>Neut. *tu*, *tā taṁ*. | .. | .. |
| 600-1000 | Masc. *so* (Nom. Acc.)<br>Neut. *so*. | .. | .. |
| 700-1200 | .. | .. | Masc. *sa*, *so*.<br>Acc. : *taṁ* (*DKs*. 43)<br>Neut. *se* (*Dks*. 90,106)<br>*sa* (*DKs*. 67.<br>*te* (*DKs*. 107)<br>*tã* (*DKs*. 7.8). |

150 PISCHEL, *Grammatik*, § 425.

| A.D. | WAp. | SAp. |
|---|---|---|
| 1000 | Masc. *so*, *sō*, *su* *to* (*Pd.* 76) Acc. *taṁ*, *so* (*BhK.* 1.11. Pd. 46-160. Neut. *taṁ*, *taü* (Pd. 11). Neut. *taṁ*, *taü* (Pd. 11). | Masc. : Nom. *sō*, *so*, *to* (*Nc.* 1.17.16). Acc. *sō*, *taṁ* |
| 1100 | Masc. *su* (*DS.* 4.-32). *so* (*Mt.* 20) Neut. *ta*, *taṁ*. | Masc. *so*, Acc. *taṁ*. Neut. *taṁ* |

| A.D. | WAp. | |
|---|---|---|
| 1200 | Masc. *sō*, *so*, *su*. Neut. *taṁ su*. | Acc. *sō*, *su*, *taṁ*, *tā* *traṁ*, and *druṁ* in Pk. grammars are merely substitue *for tad*. |

INSTRUMENTAL SINGULAR

| A.D. | WAp. | SAp. | EAp. |
|---|---|---|---|
| 500 ? | .. | .. | .. |
| 600-1000 | *tiṁ*, *te* ᵕ̇ (i.e. *tē*) *tēṇa*, *te* (*PPr.* 2.26) | .. .. | .. .. |
| 700-1200 | .. | .. | .. *tē*, *teṇa*. *tena* (*DKK.* 17). |
| 1000 | *teṁ*, *tiṁ*, *teṇa* | *teṁ*, *tiṁ* (*Jc.* 3.25.5) *tēṇa*, *tiṇā* (*Jc.* 1.18.9) Pkt. Sm. | .. |
| 1100 | .. | *teṁ*, *teṇa* | .. |
| 1200 | *tēṇa*, *teṇa*, *tiṇa* *tiṇi* (*Kp.*) | .. | .. |

DAT. GEN. ABL. SINGULAR

| | | | |
|---|---|---|---|
| 500 | Abl. *tā* (*Mt.* 24) | .. | .. |
| 600-1000 | *tasu*, *tāsu* | .. | .. |
| 700- | *tahu* ᵕ̇ (-°*hŭ*) .. | .. | *tasu* |

| A.D. | WAp. | SAp. | EAp. |
|---|---|---|---|
| 1200 | | | *tahĩ* (*DKK*.24)<br>*tāhara* (*DKs*.92) |
| 1000 | *tasu*, *tāsu*, *tassa* (Pkt.)<br>*tasa* (*Pd*. 89) *tāsai* (*BhK*. 102.3)<br>*taho*, *tahu*, *tahi* (*Pd*. 174)<br>Abl. *tamhā* (*Sdd*. 101) AMg. | *tahŏ*, *tahu*, *tāsu* | |
| 1100 | *tahu* | *taho*, *tāsu*,<br>Abl. *tamhā*, Amgism. | |
| 1200 | *tasu*, *tāsu*, *tassu*(*Sc.Hc.*),<br>*tassa* (Pkt.), *taho*, *tahu*. | | |

LOCATIVE SINGULAR

| A.D. | WAp. | SAp. | EAp. |
|---|---|---|---|
| 500 ? | *tahĩ* .. | .. | .. |
| 600-1000 | *tahĩ* | .. | .. |
| 700-1200 | .. | .. | *tahĩ*<br>*tasu* (*DKK*.22) |
| 1000 | *tahiṁ*, *tahĩ*<br>*tahaiṁ* (*Pd*. 103), *temai* (*Pd*. 91)<br>*tammi* (Pkt.) | *tahĩ* | .. |
| 1100 | *tahiṁ* | *tahiṁ*,<br>*tammi* (Pktism.) | |
| 1200 | *tahiṁ*, *tahĩ*,<br>*tammi* (Pkt.) | | |

## §123A. (v). THE DEMONSTRATIVE AND 3RD PERSON PRONOUN *ta* PLURAL NUMBER

DIRECT PLURAL

| A.D. | WAp. | SAp. | EAp. |
|---|---|---|---|
| 500 ? | .. | .. | .. |
| 600-1000 | Masc. : *te* (Nom. Acc.)<br>Neut. : *te* (PPr. 1.61)<br>*tāi* | | |

| | | | |
|---|---|---|---|
| 700-1200 | .. | .. | .. |
| 1000 | Masc. : *te*<br>*tiṁ* (*BhK*. 295.2),<br>*tẽ* (*BhK*. 108.6)<br>Neut. : *tāiṁ taĩ*. | Masc. : *te*<br>Neut. : *tāĩ* , *tāiṁ*. | .. |
| 1100 | .. | Masc. : *te*<br>Neut. : *tāiṁ*. | .. |
| 1200 | Masc. : *tẽ*, *te*,<br>*ti* (*Jdc. Sc.*)<br>Neut. : *tāĩ*<br>*teṁ* (*Hc*. 4.339). | | |

INSTRUMENTAL PLURAL

| | | | |
|---|---|---|---|
| 500 ? | .. | .. | .. |
| 600-1000 | .. | .. | .. |
| 100-1200 | | .. | *tehi* (*DKs*. 58). |
| 1000 | *tẽhĩ*, *tehiṁ* | *tehiṁ*, *tehĩ* | .. |
| 1100 | .. | *tehiṁ* | .. |
| 1200 | *tẽhĩ tehĩ*, *tehiṁ*. | .. | |

DAT. GEN. ABL. PLURAL

| A.D. | WAp. | SAp. | EAp. |
|---|---|---|---|
| 500 ? | .. | .. | .. |
| 600-1000 | *taha*, ◡ *tāha* ◡ | .. | .. |
| 700-1200 | .. | .. | .. |
| 1000 | *tāhaṁ*, *tāhā*<br>*tahaṁ*, *tahã*<br>Pkt. *tāṇaṁ* | *tāhaṁ*, *tāhā*.<br>*tāha*<br>Pkt. *tāṇaṁ*. | |
| 1100 | .. | *tāhaṁ*, | .. |
| 1200 | *tahaṁ*, *tahã*<br>*tāhaṁ*, *tāhã*<br>*tāhi* (*Jdu*. 24.2).<br>Pkt. *tāna*, *tesĩ*, *tesiṁ*. | | |

LOC. PLURAL

| | | | |
|---|---|---|---|
| 500? | .. | .. | .. |
| 600-1000 | .. | .. | .. |
| 700-1200 | .. | .. | .. |
| 1000 | .. | .. | .. |

| | | | |
|---|---|---|---|
| 1100 | .. | .. | .. |
| 1200 | *tahiṁ* (*Hc.*), *tihi* (*Sc.* 517.2) | .. | .. |

### §123A. (vi) The Demonstrative & 3rd P. Pronoun. Fem Gender Singular Number

#### The Direct Case

| A.D. | WAp. | SAp. | EAp. |
|---|---|---|---|
| 500 ? | *sā* | .. | .. |
| 600-1000 | *sā* ? (Acc. *PPr.* 2.46*1) | .. | .. |
| 700-1200 | .. | .. | *sĕ* (*DKs.* 49) |
| 1000 | *sā*<br>Pkt. *taṁ* (Acc. *BhK.* 13.6) | *sā*<br>Pkt. *taṁ*. | .. |
| 1100 | .. | *sā* | .. |
| 1200 | *sā, sa*<br>Pkt. *taṁ* (Acc.). | | .. |

#### Instumental Singular

| A.D. | WAp. | SAp. | EAp. |
|---|---|---|---|
| 500 ? | .. | .. | .. |
| 600-1000 | .. | .. | .. |
| 700-1200 | .. | .. | .. |
| 1000 | *tāe, taĩ,*<br>*tāeṁ* (*BhK.* 2.5) | *tāe, tīe,*<br>*tā* (*MP.* 1.6.15), *taṇa* (*Jc.* 3.10.12)<br>*tāe tāeṁ.*<br>*tāīṁ* (*KKc.* 6.10.2)<br>*tīeṁ* (*KKc.* 1.8.2). | .. |
| 1200 | *tāe, tīi,*<br>*tahĩ, tahi* | | .. |

#### Dat. Gen. Abl. Singular.

| A.D. | WAp. | SAp. | EAp. |
|---|---|---|---|
| 500 ? | *tāha* | | .. |
| 600-1000 | .. | .. | .. |
| 700-1200 | .. | .. | .. |
| 1000 | *tāhĕ, tahĕ* | *tahi, tahe.* | .. |

| | | | |
|---|---|---|---|
| | *taho* (*BhK*. 160.8) | *tāhĕ* | |
| 1100 | *tĭe*, (*Mt*. 16) | *tahĕ*, *tāhĕ*<br>*tāhu* (*KK* . 7.8.1) | .. |
| 1200 | *tahe tahi*<br>*tĭe*, *tasu* | .. | .. |

Loc. Singular

| | | | |
|---|---|---|---|
| 500 ? | .. | .. | .. |
| 600-1000 | *tahiṁ* (*PPr*. 2.46*1) | .. | .. |
| 700-1200 | .. | .. | .. |
| 1000 | *tahĩ*, *tahi* (*BhK*. 73.3) | *tāsu* | .. |
| 1100 | .. | *tahiṁ* | .. |
| 1200 | *tahĩ* (*Sc*. 538.6) | .. | .. |

## §123A. (vii) Fem. *ta-* Plural Number

*The Direct Case*

| A.D. | WAp. | SAp. | EAp. |
|---|---|---|---|
| 500 ? | .. | .. | .. |
| 600-1000 | .. | .. | .. |
| 700-1200 | .. | .. | .. |
| 1000 | *tāu*<br>*tāo* (Pktsm.) | *tāu* | .. |
| 1100 | .. | *tāu* | .. |
| 1200 | *tāu* | .. | .. |

Instrumental & Locative

| | | | |
|---|---|---|---|
| 500 | .. | .. | .. |
| 600-1000 | .. | .. | .. |
| 700-1200 | .. | .. | .. |
| 1000 | .. | .. | .. |
| 1100 | .. | *tāhiṁ* | .. |
| 1200 | *tīhĩ* | .. | .. |

DAT. GEN. ABL.

| | | | |
|---|---|---|---|
| 500 ? | .. | .. | .. |
| 600-1200 | .. | .. | .. |
| 700-1200 | .. | .. | .. |
| 1000 | .. | .. | .. |
| 1100 | .. | *tāhiṁ* | .. |
| 1200 | *tahã tāhã* *tāsĩ* | .. | .. |

## THE PROXIMATE DEMONSTRATIVE PRONOUN *etad*

§124. In Ap., OIA *etad* assumes two forms viz., *ĕa*- and *ĕya*- and sometimes *āa*- (=OIA *idaṁ*) forms are confused with these. Although there is such a confusion of *ĕa*- and *āa*- forms, they are separately tabulated in the chrono-regional comp. tables (§§ 124A, 125A).

Hemacandra gives the following paradigm of OIA *etad* in Ap.:

*Singular*

Nom. Acc. Masc. *esa, eho, ehā* (445), Neut. Masc. *ehu*. Fem. *eha, eu*.

*Plural*

Nom. Acc. Masc. *ei*; Neut. *ehaüṁ*.

Though the anthology of Ap. verses in *Hc*. does not give more than these forms, Ap. literature is comparatively richer in these than *Hc*. Its variety is, however, less than that of Personal Pronouns.

The following is the pre-Ap. MIA background (*i.e.*, declension in Pkts.) of this pronoun[151].

*Singular*

Nom. : Masc. *eso* (M. JM. JŚ. Ś. Ā.D.), *ese* (AMg.) *esu* (*Ḍh*).

Fem. *esa, esā*.

Neut. *esa, eaṁ* (M.) ; *eyaṁ* (AMg. JM.), *edaṁ* (Ś. Mg. Ā.D.)

Acc. : (all genders) *eaṁ* (M.), *eyaṁ* (AMg. JM.), *edam* (Ś. Mg.)

Ins. : *eeṇa* (M.), *eeṇaṁ* (AMg.), *eiṇā* (JM.), *edeṇa* (Ś. Mg.)

Fem. : *eyāe, eïe*, (JM.) The latter for Abl. Gen.. Loc. sing. *edāe* (Ś. Mg.) also for Gen. and Loc.

151 PISCHEL, *Grammatik*, § 426.

Abl. *ĕtto, edādo, °dādu, °dāhi* (Vararuci) ; *ettāhe, eāo, eāu, eāhi, °hiṁto, eā* (*Hc.*) ; *ettha* (*Ki.*)

Gen. : *eassa* (M. AMg. JM.) ; *edassa* (Ś.) ; *edāha* (Mg.)

Loc. : *eassiṁ eammi* (M.) ; *ēyammi, eyammi* (AMg. JM.) *eyaṁsi* (AMg.) *edassiṁ* (Ś.)

*Plural*

Nom.: Masc. *ee* (M. AMg. JM.) ; *ede* (JŚ. Ś.)

Neut. *ede* (Mg.), *eāi* (M.) ; *eyāiṁ* (AMg. JM.) ; *eyāṇi* (AMg. JM.)

Fem. *eāo* (M.), *eyāo* (AMg. JM.); *edāo* (Ś.), *eyā* (JM.)

Acc. : Masc. *ee* (AMg. JM.)

Ins. : *eehiṁ, eehi* (M. JM.) ; *edehiṁ* (Ś. Mg.)

Fem. *eyāhiṁ* (AMg. JM.)

Gen. : *eāṇa* (M.), *etesi* (PG.), *eesiṁ, eesi* (AMg. JM.), *eyāṇam* (JM.), *edāṇaṁ* (Ś).

Fem. *eāṇa* (M.) *eīṇaṁ, eāṇaṁ* (*Hc.* 3.32.), *eyāsiṁ* (AMg. JM.) *eyāṇaṁ* (JM.)

Loc. : *eesu, eesuṁ* (M. AMg. JM.), *edesuṁ, edeśu* (Ś.)

SINGULAR

(i) In Pkts . *esa-* is the base of Nom. sg. (cf. OIA *eṣa-*) Ap. *eha-* (<OIA *eṣa-*) and *eha-a* (<*eṣaka*) are the result of the tendency to *h*-pronounciation of the sibilants in OIA. (See §§54.vii). The desinence *-u* of the direct sing. and the weakening of initial *e-* to *-i* are the developments in Ap. The extension of the Masc. term. *-o* to Neut. direct sg. e.g., *eho* (*DKK.* 27), *eso* (*DKK.* 29) shows a confusion of genders, and is a characteristic of EAp. in 700 A.D. *e* in *emaï kahiye* 'when this has been told by me' (*DKs.* 62) is a plui. form used in sing. In WAp. (1200 A.D.) we find two unusual forms viz., *ehā* (*Hc.* 4.445) and *eyaṁ Sc.* and *Kp.* J. 44.1*). The former is traceable to OIA **eṣa-ka*>*eha-a*>*ehā*, and the latter is a Neut. direct sg. found in AMg. JM.[152] *eha* is derived from *īdṛśa* or better **ādṛśa*>*aïsa* >*aïsa*>*esa* in *PPr.* 2.157, *BhK.* 21.2, *Hv.* 84.1.13, 82.8.7, *JC.* 3.9.14, *Hc.* 8.4.402.

After 900 A.D., there is a tendency to use *-ea* as the base in direct sing. in WAp. In *BhK.* we find *ĕu, īu* used frequently along with

152 *Ibid.*, § 426.

*eho, ehu.* SAp. remained immune from that tendency for some time, but the frequent use of *ēu* as Neut. direct sg. in *Hv.* shows that the base *ea-* was to some extent successful in driving out *eha-* from this gender. Though Alsdorf gives *ēu* (14) with no optional form in Neut. direct sg.,[153] we find *ehau* =*etad* in the works of Puṣpadanta elsewhere, and later in *KKc.* The conservance of this *-ha* element in SAp. is responsible for the Marathi declension of the proximate demonstrative *ha-* :
Sing : *hā, hī, hẽ,* Oblique Masc. Sing. *hyā-*[154].
Plur. : *he hya, hī̃* oblique Masc. Plur. *hyā̃-*

The frequency of *eha-* and *ea-* (*ia-*) forms shows that in *Kp.* (1194 A.D.) *e*(*i*)*a-* forms are restricted to Neut. (contrast *Sc.* of the same century)[155] According to Alsdorf we have [156].

Masc. Nom. Sg.: *iha* (3+1), *ihu* (3+1), *ēhu* (3), *esa.*

Neut. direct Sg.: *iu* (2+2), *ēu* (10), *ihu* (1+1), *ēhu* (3) *ehu*[157].

Ins. sg. has very few forms peculiar to Ap. as *eṇa eeṇa* etc. appear already in Pkts. As in OIA, the *eha-*<*eṣa-* forms are not used in oblique cases. In SAp. (1000 A.D.) *ēeṁ* is obviously *ea*+*eṁ*, *-eṁ* being the usual terms. of this case. In *DKs.* 4, *e* is traceable to *ē*<**eē.* The line runs thus :

*sīsau bāhiya* e *jaḍa-bhārẽ*

'The head is bound by this mass of hair' *i.e.*, these sages grow a burdensome mass of hair on their heads (*DKs.* 4). But the Dat. Gen. Abl. form *ehu* (*DKK.*8) shows that the base in EAp. was *e-* and not *ea-*;*-hŏ* of the noun declension and *-hu* here represent the same sound. Few as the forms are of this case, we find *-ho* of the 10th cent. giving place to *-ha* in the 12th cent. A.D., in WAp.—a tendency already observed in Noun declension (See §§83, 83A). Loc. sg. *ihi* in *Sc.* 707.9 is *ehiṁ*>*ihī* *-hi* being OIA *-smin.*

### Plural

(ii) The direct plur. has *ea-* and *eya-* as the alternate bases, but the Pkt. form *ēē* wielded considerable influence in the works of Puṣpadanta. The corresponding forms in WAp. (1000 A.D.) are *eya, ēya, iya. ē* in

153 Alsdorf, Intro. to *Hv.* § 48b.
154 There is no nasal on the Oblique Sing. *hyā-* in Marathi although Bloch gives it in *L'indo-aryen,* p. 198.
155 Jacobi, Intro. to *Sc.* p. 15 (Grammatik).
156 Intro. to *Kp.* § 28(b), p. 60.
157 For its NIA descendants, see *L'indo-aryen,* pp. 197-8.

*Mp.* 2.8.3 is an abbreviation of *ēē* (which is common in SAp. of the 10th cent.), but *e* in *Sdd.* 18 may be derived from *ea-* with zero term. *ē= etāni* is a Neut. direct plur. (cf. Neut. direct plurs. *e.g.*, *ghara*, *vattha*, *saya* in Noun-declension §84A). But 1100 A.D. WAp. ignored *eya-* forms, adopted *ēī*<*ēē*. *ehaüṁ* <**eṣa-kaṁ* in *Hc.* 8.4.362 is the use of the sing. for the plur[158].

The remaining cases have no peculiar forms needing special explanation. In Ins. Plur. *eya-hiṁ -hiṁ* is the usual term. The same is the case with gen. plur. *eya-hã*. *āyahaṁ* in *Mp.* 2.10.19 is originally the Gen. plur. of *idaṁ* used in the place of *etad.*

FEMININE GENDER.

(iii) The direct sg. of Fem. *etad* corroborates the findings in the case of Masc. Neut. and *eha-* forms the speciality of SAp. all through. Ins. sg. forms are the same as in Pkts. The Dat. Gen. Abl. terms. *-he* and *-hi* are the same as in the declension of Fem. *-a* stems. (See §91). The few forms of the plural—both Direct and Oblique—are quite clear. *eyahũ* in SAp. (1000 A.D.) is the extension of Masc. *-huṁ* (cf. *soṇiya-huṁ* in *JC.* 3.34.13. This desinence is very popular with Masc. *-i*, *-u* stem. See §96, also §99). WAp. *eya-hã* (*Sc.* 484.3) has the regular term. of Masc. and Fem. Dat. Gen. Plur. (See §§ 86, 91.)

The following comparative table of frequency will be interesting

| *Hv.* (SAp. 965 A.D.) | *Kp.* (WAp. 1194 A.D.) |
|---|---|
| *Singular* | |
| Nom. Acc. : | Nom. Acc.: |
| Masc. *ēhu*(13), *ehu* (10), *ehaü* (2) | Masc. *iha* (3+1), *ihu* (3+1) *ēhu* (3), *esa.* |
| Neut. *ēu.* | Neut. *iu* (2+2), *ēu* (10), *ihu* (1+1), *ēhu* (3), *ehu.* |
| Fem. *ēha* (8), *ēhī* (2) | Fem. *eha* (1) |
| Ins. | Ins. |
| *ēeṁ* (4), *eeṇa* (1) | *eeṇa.* |
| Fem. *ēyae* | |
| Dat. Gen. | Dat. Gen. |
| Masc. *ēyahõ* (15) | *eyaha* (3+1), *eyassa.* |
| Fem. *eyahẽ* (4) | |

158 Here P. L. VAIDYA's *chāyā* and translation of *Hc.* (Notes p. 45) is followed. But *ehaüṁ*... *cintantāhã* can be taken as *etat*... *cintamānānām.*

159 ALSDORF : Intro. to *Hv.* § 48 (b) ; Intro. to *Kp.* § 28(b) p. 60.

| | *Plural* |
|---|---|
| Nom. Acc. | Nom. Acc. |
| Masc. *ĕĕ*(2), *ĕ* (3) | |
| Neut. *ĕyaĭ* (3) | Neut. *ĕyāĭ* (2), *eyaĭ*. |
| Fem. *eyau* (6) | |
| Dat. Gen. | |
| Masc. Neut. *ĕyahā̃* | Masc. *āyahā̃* |
| Fem. *eyahū* | Fem. *eahi* (7) in *Kaḍavakas* S. 78-86. |

The forms underlined show chrono-regional difference.[160]

§124A. (i) THE PROXIMATE DEMONSTRATIVE PRONOUN

(a) *etad ea-, eya-*

MASC. AND NEUT. (SINGULAR NUMBER)

*The Direct Case.*

| A.D. | WAp. | SAp. | EAp. |
|---|---|---|---|
| 500? | Neut. *ehu* | .. | .. |
| 600-1000 | Masc. *ĕhu, ihū* | .. | .. |
| | Neut. *ehaüṁ, ehu.* | | |
| 700-1200 | .. | .. | Masc. *ehu, esa.* Neut. *ehu, eho* (*DKK.* 27.) *eso* (*DKK.* 29) *e*(*DKs.* 62.) |
| 1000 | Masc. *ĕhu, ehaü eho* (*BhK.*) *ēu eu, iu.* Neut. *ihu, ĕhu, ēhaü* (*Pd.* 79), *eha, ēu, iü* (*BhK.*) | Masc. *ĕhu, ehu, ĕhaü.* Neut. *ĕu, ehaü.* | |

160 For further development of *etad* in NIA see *L'indo-aryen*, pp. 197-ff.

| | | |
|---|---|---|
| 1100 | Masc. *ehu* | Masc. *ehu* |
| | Neut. *ehu* ? (*Mt.* 15) | Neut. *ehaü*, *eha*, *ehaṁ*, *ihu*. |
| 1200 | | WAp. |
| | Masc. *ehõ*, *ĕhu*, *ēu*, *iha*, *ihu*, *esa*, *eso* (?), *ehā* (*Hc.* 4.445). | |
| | Neut. *ĕhu*, *ihu*, *ēu*, *iu*, *ĕyaṁ* (*Sc. KP.* J.44.1*). | |

INSTRUMENTAL SING.

| A.D. | WAp. | SAp. | EAp. |
|---|---|---|---|
| 500 ? | .. | .. | .. |
| 600-100 | .. | .. | .. |
| 700-1200 | .. | .. | *eṇa* (*DKK.* 29)<br>*e* (*DKs.* 4) |
| 1000 | *eṇa* | *ĕeṁ*,<br>*ĕeṇa*. | .. |
| 1100 | .. | .. | .. |
| 1200 | *ĕēṇa*,<br>*ĕiṇa* (*Sc.* 733.6) | .. | .. |

DAT. GEN. ABL. SING.

| A.D. | WAp. | SAp. | EAp. |
|---|---|---|---|
| 500 | .. | .. | .. |
| 600-1000 | .. | .. | .. |
| 700-1200 | .. | *ehu* ? (*DKK.* 8). | |
| 1000 | *ĕyaho* | *ĕyahõ*<br>*eyahū* ? (*MP.* 2.16.7) | .. |
| 1100 | .. | *eyaho* | .. |
| 1200 | *ĕyaha*<br>*eyassa*<br>*eyassu*. | .. | .. |

LOCATIVE SING.

| A.D. | WAp. | SAp. | EAp. |
|---|---|---|---|
| 500 ? | .. | .. | .. |
| 600-1000 | .. | .. | .. |
| 700-1200 | .. | .. | .. |

| | | | |
|---|---|---|---|
| 1000 | .. | .. | .. |
| 1100- | .. | .. | .. |
| 1200 | *ihi* (*Sc.* 707.9) | .. | .. |

## § 124A. (ii) The Proximate Demonstrative Pronoun

*ea- eya-*

### Plural Number

*The Direct Case*

| A.D | WAp. | SAp. | EAp. |
|---|---|---|---|
| 500? | .. | .. | .. |
| 600-1000 | Masc. *e*<br>Neut. *e*, *eyaĩ̐* | .. | .. |
| 700-1200 | .. | .. | .. |
| 1000 | Masc. *ēya*, *iya*<br>Neut. *e* (*Sdd.* 18) | Masc. *ēē*, *ē* (*MP.* 2.8.3)<br>Neut. *ēyāĩ*, °*iṁ*. | ..<br>.. |
| 1100 | .. | .. | .. |
| 1200 | Masc. *ēi*<br>Neut. *ēyaĩ*, *eyāĩṁ*, *eyāĩ* *eyāṇi* *ēi* (*Sc.* 752.6). *ehaüṁ* (*Hc.* 362.) | .. | .. |

### Instrumental Plural

| | | | |
|---|---|---|---|
| 500 ? | .. | .. | .. |
| 600-1000 | *eyahĩ̐* | .. | .. |
| 700-1200 | .. | .. | .. |
| 1000 | *eyahĩ* | *eyahiṁ* | .. |
| 1100 | .. | *eyahiṁ*, *eehiṁ* (*KKc.* 7.8.5) | .. |
| 1200 | *ēēhiṁ*, °*hĩ* | .. | .. |

DAT. GEN. ABL. PLURAL

| A.D. | WAp. | SAp. | EAp. |
|---|---|---|---|
| 500 ? | .. | .. | .. |
| 600-1000 | *eyahaṁ* | .. | .. |
| 700-1200 | .. | .. | .. |
| 1000 | *ēyahā̃*<br>*ēyāṇa* (*Pktism.*) | *ēyahaṁ* ? (*Mp.* 2.10.19). | |
| 1100 | .. | .. | .. |
| 1200 | *ēyahā̃* (*Sc.* 484.3 ?)<br>*eyāṇa* (*Pktism.*) | .. | .. |

No separate pure Ap. Loc. plur. forms were traced.

## § 124A. (iii) THE PROXIMATE DEMONSTRATIVE PRONOUN *etad-*

FEMININE GENDER—SINGULAR NUMBER.

*The Direct Case*

| A.D. | WAp. | SAp. | EAp. |
|---|---|---|---|
| 500? | .. | .. | .. |
| 600-1000 | *ehu* (*PPr.* 2.28) | .. | .. |
| 700-1200 | .. | .. | .. |
| 1000 | *ēha, ehī, iha*<br>*ēya* (*iya*), *eyāiṁ* ? (*Pd.* 203). | *ēha, ēhī* | .. |
| 1100 | .. | *eha* | .. |
| 1200 | *ēha, iha* (*Sc.*)<br>*ēsa, ēya.* | .. | .. |

INSTRUMENTAL SING.

| | | | |
|---|---|---|---|
| 500 ? | .. | .. | .. |
| 600-1000 | .. | .. | .. |
| 700-1200 | .. | .. | .. |
| 1000 | .. | *ēyae* | .. |
| 1100 | .. | .. | .. |
| 1200 | *ēie* (*Sc.* 669.3) | .. | .. |

DAT. GEN. ABL. SING.

| | | | |
|---|---|---|---|
| 500 | .. | .. | .. |
| 600-1000 | .. | .. | .. |
| 700-1200 | .. | .. | |
| 1000 | *ēyahe, eyahi.* | *ēyahĕ* | |
| 1100 | .. | .. | |
| 1200 | *ēie* (*Sc.* 492.7)<br>*ēahi* (*Kp.* S, 79.2) | .. | |

No. Loc. forms were found.

PLURAL NUMBER

THE DIRECT CASE—(As no plural forms previous to 1000 A.D. were traced, the first 3 groups are omitted here to conserve space).

| A.D. | WAp. | SAp. | EAp. |
|---|---|---|---|
| 1000 | *eyao, iyao,* | *ēyaü* | .. |
| 1100 | .. | .. | .. |
| 1200 | *ēyāu* (*Sc.* 659·1) | .. | .. |

INSTR. LOC. PLURAL.

| | | | |
|---|---|---|---|
| 600-1000 | *ehiṁ̐* | .. | .. |
| 1000 | *ehiṁ* | .. | .. |
| 1100 | .. | .. | .. |
| 1200 | .. | .. | .. |

DAT. GEN. ABL. PLURAL.

| | | | |
|---|---|---|---|
| 1000 | .. | *ēyahŭ* | .. |
| 1100 | .. | .. | .. |
| 1200 | *eya-hā* (*Sc.* 484.3) | .. | .. |

(2) *idam.*

§125. The next Proximate Demonstrative Pronoun *idaṁ* has *aya-*, *ima-*, *ana-*, *ena-* and *a-* as the bases in OIA. In Pkts. *ima-*, *ana-* and *ena-* became more popular.[161] In Ap. *āya-* and *āa-*<OIA *ā-* or *aya-* plus the stem-widening *-ka*, are the main bases.

(*i*) The following is the paradigm of *idam* in Pkts.[161]

*Singular*

Nom. : Masc. *ayaṁ* (AMg. JM.) *aaṁ* (Ś.Ḍh.), *imo* (M.) *ime* (AMg.

Neut. *ayaṁ* (AMg.), *imaṁ* (Mg.), *idaṁ* (M. AMg. Ś.) *iṇam* (M.)

Fem. *imā*, *imiā*, *iaṁ* (Ś), *ayaṁ* (Pa. AMg.)

Acc. : Masc. Fem. Neut. *imaṁ* ; Masc. *iṇaṁ* (AMg.).

Masc. *eṇaṁ* (M. Ś. Mg.).

Ins. : Masc. *-eṇa* (M.), *aṇeṇa*, °*ṇam* (AMg.), *imeṇa* (M. JM. AMg.), *imiṇā* (JM. Ś. Mg.), *imeṇaṁ* (AMg.).

Fem. *imie*, *imīa* (M.), *imāe* (Ś.)

Abl. : Masc. *ā*, *imāo* (JM. AMg.), *imādo* (Ś. Mg.)

Gen. : Masc. *assa* (M. JM.), *imassa*, *imaśśa* (Mg.).

Fem. *imīe*, *imīa* (M. JM. Ś.), *imīse* (AMg.), *imāe* (JM.)

Loc. : Masc. *assiṁ* (M. AMg.), *ayaṁsi* (AMg.) *imammi* (M. AMg.), *imaṁsi* (AMg.), *imassiṁ* (Ś.), *imaśśiṁ* (Mg.).

Fem. *imīse* (AMg.), *imāi* (JM.)

*Plural*

Nom. : Masc. *ime*, Neut.; *imāiṁ* (Ś.), *imāṇi* (AMg. JM.)

Fem. *imāo*, *imā*, *imīu* (M.)

Instr. : Masc. *ehi*, *ehiṁ* (AMg. Ḍh.), *imehi* (M.), *imehiṁ* (M.), *imehiṁ* (AMg. Ś.)

161 PISCHEL, *Grammatik*, §§ 429-31.

Fem. *ā-hi, imāhiṁ* (AMg.)

Gen. : Masc. *esiṁ* (M.), *imāṇa* (M.), *imesiṁ* (AMg.)

Fem. *imāṇaṁ* (M.Ś.), *imiṇam* (M.), *imāsiṁ* (AMg.)

Loc. : Masc. *esu* (JM.), *imesu* (M Ś.) *imesuṁ* (Ś.)

*Ṇa* declension of OIA-*idaṁ* is given by PISCHEL in *Grammatik* § 431.

(*ii*) The terms. of this pronoun are the same as those of corresponding nouns of Masc. Fem. Neut. stems. ending in *-a*. In the declension of this pronoun there appears to be a mixture of *e-* and *eya-* bases which are more correctly traced to OIA *etad*. Thus *e* in *DKs*. 4 is the use of the stem *e* (<*etad*> *ēa*) itself in the direct case rather than *āa*+*e*>**ā*+*e*>*e*, *-e* being the EAp. desinence of Nom. sg. (For other *-a* and *-e* ending forms of *-a* declension in EAp. see §§80, 81A). The alternative explanation is rather far fetched. We have other examples of *ea-*, *eya-* for OIA *idaṁ*. In SAp. (1000 A.D.) Masc. Gen. sg. *eya-hũ* (*Mp*. 2.16.7) implies *eya-* (<*etad*) as the base for *idaṁ*. *-hũ* must be regarded as the extension of the plur. to sing. as the usual term. is *-ho* (See comp. Table §125A). *isu* in *Jdu*. 51.3 (WAp. 1200 A.D.) implies *i-*<*e-*<*ea-* as the base. Similarly Loc. sing. *eyaĩ* in SAp. (1000 A.D.). These illustrations are enough to show how freely *etad* and *idam* forms got mixed up in Ap., as the context implies *idaṁ* forms and not *etad* ones in the cases mentioned above.

Ins. Sg. *ẽ* in *Vk*. (500 A.D. WAp.) is a *sandhi* of **ā-ẽ-*<*āa -ẽ*. Thus the rest of the forms of Masc. and Neut. gender, and sing. no., take the normal desinences of *-a* stems.

Masc. and Neut. direct plur. presents one remarkable form in SAp. (1000 A.D.) viz., *āyahiṁ—etāni* (*Jc*. 1.17.15-6) as will be apparent from the line

*kahiṁ āyahiṁ bālaiṁ ṇiru somālaiṁ hā khala vihi haya-suyaṇa-suha.*

*bālaiṁ* and *somālaiṁ* show that *āyahiṁ* is probably a scribal error for *āyaiṁ*. It will be rather a far-fetched relation to connect it with the words . . *kiṁ ṇa bhutta vasuha* (*Jc*. 1.17.16) as they have a separate subject-*eyahiṁ*- immediately preceding the word *kiṁ* and *eyahiṁ kiṁ ṇa bhutta vasuha* "why have not these enjoyed the earth ? " is a complete sentence. The remaining forms take the desinences of Masc. *-a* stems and are quite regular.

*Feminine Gender*

(*iii*) There are very few Fem. forms of this pronoun. Most of them accept the terms of Fem. *-a* stems. There are two forms viz.

*āya-hĩ* (*BhK*. 114.7) and *āya-hi* (*BhK*. 114.9) which JACOBI seems to take as sings. (at least the question marks used by him before these forms in *BhK*. *Glossar*, p. 129, show that he does so). But the context is quite clear and they *are* of the plural no. From his Intr. to *BhK*. pp. *35-*38, it seems that JACOBI also did not come across a single Fem. form with Instr. sg. *-hi*, *-hiṁ*. Instr. sing. *āṇae=anayā* (*Hv*. 91-8-5, 91-11-9) shows that the base *āṇa-* is probably a contamination of Pkt. Fem. bases. *ā-* plus *aṇa-*. *-e* is of course the normal term. of Fem. Ins. sg. of *-a* stems. *eya-i* in SAp. (1000 A.D.) is another illustration of the use of *eya* (<*etad-*) for OIA *idam*.

Plural forms are also quite regular. Gen. plur. *āya-hā̃* in WAp. of the 10th cent. (in which the normal form *āya-hĩ* is also found) shows the extension of the Masc. terms. to Fem. stems.[162]

### 125A. (*ii*) THE PROXIMATE DEMONSTRATIVE PRONOUN

*b*) *idam-* Ap. *āya-*, *āa-*, and *ima-*.

MASC. AND NEUT. SING. NUMBER.

THE DIRECT CASE

| A.D. | WAp. | SAp. | EAp. |
|---|---|---|---|
| 500 ? | .. | .. | .. |
| 600- | Masc. *ihu* (*PPr*. 2.142) | .. | .. |
| 1000 | | | |
| | Neut. *iü*. | | |
| 700- | | | |
| 1200 | .. | .. | Neut. *e* (*DKs*. 4) |
| 1000 | Masc. *āyaü* | Masc. *āya*. | .. |
| | *āü* (*BhK*. 274.10). | | |
| | Neut. *āyaü*, *āü*. | | |
| | Pkt. *imaṁ* (*BhK*. 205.24). | | |
| 1100 | .. | .. | *ima*, *emu*, *imuṁ*, *e*(*Pu*). |
| 1200 | Masc. *imo* | .. | .. |
| | Neut. *imu* | .. | .. |

162 For the relation of the Ap. demonstratives with NIA ones see BLOCH, *L'indo-aryen* pp. 196-9.

INSTRUMENTAL SINGULAR

| | | | |
|---|---|---|---|
| 500 ? | *ē ẽ*<br>*eṇae* | .. | .. |
| 600-1000 | .. | .. | .. |
| 700-1200 | .. | .. | .. |
| 1000 | *āeṁ*<br>*eṇa, eṇaṁ* (*BhK*. 56.8)<br>*iṇi* (*Sdd*. 205.) | *ēṇa* | .. |
| 1100 | .. | *eṁ, eṇeṁ* (=*eṇa* +*eṁ*)<br>double Instr. (*KKc*. 10.4.7) | |
| 1200 | *āeṇa, imiṇa* (*Kp*. J. 104.1) | | |

DAT. GEN. ABL. SINGULAR.

| A.D. | WAp. | SAp. | EAp |
|---|---|---|---|
| 500 ? | .. | .. | .. |
| 600-1000 | .. | .. | .. |
| 700-1200 | .. | .. | *ehu* (*DKK*.8) |
| 1000 | *āyaho* | (2) *eyahũ* (*Mp*. 2.16.7)<br>(1) *āyaho* (*Hv*. 81.16.4) | |
| 1100 | .. | *eho* (*KKc*. 10.17.10)x | .. |
| 1200 | *āyaho*<br>*imassu, imasu* (*Sc*.)<br>*isu* (*Jdu*. 51.3)<br>*imassa* (*Kp*. S.40.3) | | |

LOCATIVE SING.

| | | | |
|---|---|---|---|
| 500 ? | .. | .. | .. |
| 600-1000 | .. | .. | .. |
| 700-1200 | .. | .. | .. |
| 1000 | .. | *eyaï* | |
| 1100 | .. | .. | .. |
| 1200 | *āyahiṁ*<br>*imammi* (*Sc*. 628.7) | .. | .. |

PLURAL NUMBER.

THE DIRECT CASE

| | | | |
|---|---|---|---|
| 1000 | Masc.<br>Neut. *āyaiṁ* | Neut. *āyahiṁ* (*Jc*. 1.17.15) | |
| 1100 | | .. | .. |

| | | | |
|---|---|---|---|
| 1200 | Masc.: *ime* (*Kp. A.* 8.3) | .. | .. |
| | Neut. *āyaïṁ*, *āyaï* | .. | .. |

Loc. Instr. Plu. : No forms were traced even after careful search.

DAT. GEN. ABL. PLURAL.

| A.D. | WAp. | SAp. | EAp. |
|---|---|---|---|
| 1000 | *āyahaṁ* | *āyahaṁ* | .. |
| 1100 | .. | .. | .. |
| 1200 | *imāṇa* (*Kp.J.* 40.2) | .. | .. |

## 125A. (*iii*) THE PROXIMATE DEMONSTRATIVE PRONOUN *idam*

### FEMININE GENDER.

Very few pure Ap. declensional forms of Fem. *idam* are met with in Ap. literature. Most of them appear from the 10th cent. A.D.

SINGULAR NUMBER.

| A.D. | WAp. | SAp. | EAp. |
|---|---|---|---|

INSTRUMENTAL SING. (No forms of the direct case and Loc. sing. were seen. In *PPr.* 2.182 Acc. Sg. *ihu* is an example of confusion of genders.)

| | | | |
|---|---|---|---|
| 1000 | *āyae* | *eyai* (?), *āṇae* (*Hv.* 91.8.5) | |
| 1100 | .. | .. | .. |
| 1200 | .. | .. | .. |

DAT. GEN. ABL. SING.

| | | | |
|---|---|---|---|
| 1000 | *āyahĕ* *ĕyaho* | *āyaho* (*Hv.* 81.16.4) | .. |
| 1100 | .. | .. | .. |
| 1200 | .. | .. | .. |

PLURAL NUMBER.

THE DIRECT CASE

| | | | |
|---|---|---|---|
| 1000 | .. | .. | .. |
| 1100 | .. | .. | .. |

| | | | |
|---|---|---|---|
| 1200 | *imāu* (*Sc.* 596.8, *Kp.* A. 14-.3) | .. | .. |

LOC. INSTR. PLURAL

| | | | |
|---|---|---|---|
| 1000 | *āyahī̃*, *āyahi*, *ẽhī̃* | | |
| 1100 | .. | .. | .. |
| 1200 | .. | .. | .. |

DAT. GEN. ABL. PLURAL.

| A.D. | WAp. | SAp. | EAp. |
|---|---|---|---|
| 1000 | *āyahā*<br>*āyahī̃*. | .. | .. |

None in the remaining periods were found.

§125 B & 125 D. PROXIMATE DEMONSTRATIVE PRONOUNS.

MASC. & NEUT. (SING. NO.)

| A.D. | WAp. | SAp. | EAp. |
|---|---|---|---|
| 500 ? | Neut. *-u* | | |
| 600-1000 | Masc. *-u*,<br>*-aü*<br>Neut. *-u*<br>*-(a)üṁ* | | |
| 700-1200 | .. | ..<br><br><br><br>..<br><br>.. | Masc. *-u*<br>zero<br>Neut. *-u*<br>*-o*<br>zero<br>*-e*(*DKs.* 4) |
| 1000 | Masc. *-u*, *-aü*<br>*-o*<br>Neut. *-u*, *-aü*<br>zero. | Masc. *-u* *-aü*<br>Neut. *-u*, *-aü* | .. |
| 1100 | Masc. *-u*<br>Neut. *-u* | Masc. *-u*<br>Neut. *-u* , *-aü*.<br>zero<br>*-ṁ* | In Pu. zero<br>*u*<br>*-uṁ*<br>*-e* |

| | | | |
|---|---|---|---|
| 1200 | Masc. Nom. -ŏ<br>-u<br>-zero<br>-ā (*Hc.* 445) | .. | .. |
| | Neut. Nom. and Acc.<br>-u<br>-ṁ (*Sc. Kp.*)<br>*etad-, idam* | | |

INSTRUMENTAL SG.

| A.D. | WAp. | WAp. | EAp. |
|---|---|---|---|
| 500 | -*ẽ*<br>-*e* | .. | .. |
| 600-1000 | .. | .. | .. |
| 700-1200 | .. | .. | -(*e*)*ṇa*<br>-zero. |
| 1000 | -(*e*)*eṇa*<br>-*eṁ*<br>-(*e*)*ṇam*<br>-*i* (*Sdd.* 205) | -*eṁ*<br>-*eṇa* | |
| 1100 | .. | -*eṁ* | .. |
| 1200 | -*eṇa*<br>-*iṇa*<br>-*iṇā* | .. | .. |
| | DAT. GEN. ABLATIVE SG. | | |
| 500 | .. | .. | .. |
| 600-1000 | .. | .. | .. |
| 700-1200 | .. | .. | -*hu* |
| 1000 | -*ho* | -*hŏ*<br>-*hû*?(*Mp.* 2.16.7) | .. |
| 1100 | .. | -*ho* | .. |
| 1200 | -*ha*, -*ho*<br>-*ssu*, -*su*<br>-*ssa* | .. | .. |

### Loc. Sing.

No forms upto 1000 A.D. were traced.

| | | | |
|---|---|---|---|
| 1000 | .. | *-i* | .. |
| 1100 | .. | .. | .. |
| 1200 | *-hi*<br>*-hiṁ*<br>*-mmi* (Pkt.) | .. | .. |

### Nom. & Acc. Plural.

| | | | |
|---|---|---|---|
| 500 | .. | .. | .. |
| 600-1000 | Masc. zero<br>Neut. zero<br>*-ai̐* | .. | .. |
| 100-1200 | .. | .. | .. |
| 1000 | Masc. zero<br>Neut. Nom Acc.<br>(1) zero<br>(2) *-iṁ* | Masc. zero<br>*-e* (Skt. ism.)<br>Neut. *-āĩ*<br>*-āĩṁ*<br>*-hiṁ* (*Jc.* 1.17.15) | |
| 1100 | .. | .. | .. |
| 1200 | Neut. *-aĩ, aĩṁ*<br>*-āim, āĩ*<br>*āṇi*<br>*-i* (*Sc.* 752.6)<br>*-auṁ* (*Hc.* 362.)<br>Masc. *-i*, ? | | |

### Instrumental Plural.

| A.D. | WAp. | SAp. | EAp. |
|---|---|---|---|
| 500 | .. | .. | .. |
| 600-1000 | *hi-̐* | .. | .. |
| 700-1200 | .. | .. | .. |
| 1000 | *-hĩ* | *-hiṁ* | .. |
| 1100 | .. | *-hiṁ* | .. |
| 1200 | *ehĩ*<br>*-°hiṁ* | .. | .. |

*Dat. Gen. Abl.*

| | | | |
|---|---|---|---|
| 500 | .. | .. | .. |
| 600-1000 | *-haṁ* | .. | .. |
| 700-1200 | .. | .. | .. |
| 1000 | *-hā̃*<br>*-āṇa* (Pkt.) | *-haṁ* | .. |
| 1100 | .. | .. | .. |
| 1200 | *-hā̃*<br>*-āṇa* (*Kp* J. 40.2)<br>Pkt. | .. | .. |

No separate pure Ap. forms for Loc. plural were traced.

## 125 E. The Proximate Demonstrative Pronoun

### *Feminine Gender*

Nom. and Acc. Sg.

| A.D. | WAp. | SAp. | EAp. |
|---|---|---|---|
| 500 | .. | .. | .. |
| 600-1000 | *-u* (*PPr.* 2.28)<br>(2.182) | | |
| 700-1200 | .. | .. | .. |
| 1000 | zero<br>-(*ā*)*iṁ* (*Pd.* 203) | zero<br>.. | ..<br>.. |
| 1100 | .. | zero | .. |
| 1200 | zero | .. | .. |

Instrumental Sg.

No forms till 1000 A.D. were found.

| | | | |
|---|---|---|---|
| 1000 | *-e* | *-e*<br>*-i* | .. |
| 1100 | .. | .. | .. |
| 1200 | *-e* | .. | .. |

### Dat. Gen. Abl. Sg.

No forms upto 1000 A.D. are attested to in Ap. lit.

| | | | |
|---|---|---|---|
| 1000 | *-he*<br>*-hi*<br>*-ho* | *-ha*<br>*-ho* (*Hv.* 81.16.4) | .. |
| 1100 | .. | .. | .. |
| 1200 | *ēhi*<br>*-e* ? (*Sc.* 492.7) | .. | .. |

No Loc. forms were traced.

### Plural Number

### The Direct Case

| A.D. | WAp. | SAp. | EAp. |
|---|---|---|---|
| 500 | Forms upto 1000 A.D. are not traced. | | |
| 1000 | -(*a*)*o* | -(*a*)*ü* | .. |
| 1100 | .. | .. | .. |
| 1200 | -(*ā*)*u* | .. | .. |
| *Instr. Loc. Plural.* | | | |
| 500 | .. | .. | .. |
| 600-1000 | *-hi̐*, *-hiṁ* | .. | .. |
| 700-1200 | .. | .. | .. |
| 1000 | *-hiṁ*, *-hĩ*<br>*-hi* | .. | .. |
| 1100 | .. | .. | .. |
| 1200 | .. | .. | .. |

*Dat Gen. Abl. Plural.*

No forms upto 1000 A.D. were found.

| | | | |
|---|---|---|---|
| 1000 | *-hā̃*, *-hĩ* | *-hū̃* | .. |
| 1100 | .. | .. | .. |
| 1200 | *-hā̃* (*Sc.* (*Sc.* 484.3) | .. | .. |

32

## The Relative Pronoun. *ja-*

§126. The OIA pronoun *ya-* is conserved intact throughout IA as a relative pronoun, and forms the basis of pronominal adjectives, relative adverbs, correlatives, interrogatives and indefinite pronouns, as well. Ap. *jo, jaïsa, jettula, jāva* (and *tāva*), *jaṁ* (and *taṁ*), *jahā̃, jamhā jahĩ* etc., illustrate the use of this theme in different parts of speech and have their descendants in NIA. To limit ourselves to M. and H. we have[163] M. H. *jo*, H. *jaisā*, M. *jasā*, H. *jitnā*, M. *jitkā*, H. *jab*, M. *jāv*. etc.

The following Pkt. forms supply us the MIA. background of this pronoun in Ap.[164]

*Singular*

Nom. Masc. - *jo*, Fem. -*jā* Neut. *jaṁ*.

Acc. Masc. *jaṁ*. Neut. *jaṁ*.

Ins. *jeṇa jiṇā*.

Abl. *jẵo, jado, jato jamhā, jā*.

Gen. *jassa, yaśśa, yāha* (Mg.)

Fem. *jīa, jīe, jissā, jīā, jīi, jīse, jāe* (Ś.)

Loc. *jaṁsi, jaṁsī* (AMg.), *jahiṁ*.

Fem. *jāe* , *jīe, jāhiṁ*.

*Plural*

Nom. Masc. *je*, Neut. *jāiṁ* (AMg.)

Abl. *jehiṁto* (AMg.)

Gen. *jōṇa* (M. JM.) *jāṇaṁ* ( J.M.Ś. ), *jesiṁ, jesi* (AMg.)

Fem. *jāsiṁ* (AMg.)

### Masculine and Neuter in Ap.

(*i*) The declension of *ja-* is similar to that of its correlative and 3rd per. Pron. *ta-*. The direct sing. takes -*u* and -*o* (and occasionally -*ṁ* in Prakritic forms) as usual. There is no -*e* term. in EAp. direct sing. In Ins. sg. -*ẽ* (-*eṁ*) and -*eṇa* are common to WSEAp., but in *Hv.* (SAp.

---

163 For other NIA forms see Bloch, *L'indo-aryen*, pp. 200-201.

164 Pischel, *Grammatik*, § 427.

1000 A.D.) their proportion is 6 : 17 as opposed to that in Noun- declension of *-a* stems where it is 580 : 355.[165] In *Kp.* (WAp. 1194 A.D.), *-eṁ* is absent, the proportion of these forms being *jēṇa* (1+2), *jiṇa* (1+1), *jiṇi* (*jiṁ* E. 35).[166] In noun declension also *-eṇa* is the prevailing term.[167] It seems that the conservation of *-e(i)ṇa* is due to the strong influence of Pkts. and that appears to be considerable on the declension of *ja-* and *ta-* in Hv.[168] *jiṁ* is a weakened form of *jeṁ* and its presence in *PPr.* shows the antiquity of *-eṁ*. *jiṁ* is found in SAp. (*e.g.*, *JC.* 4.1.4) but it is not so common. *jẽ* (*jeĕ* or *jeṁ*), *jiṁ* and *jeṇa* are the stable forms in WSAp. *jiṇa* in *Jdc.* 7.1 *Sc.* 588.4, *Kp.* J. 9.4 (all in WAp. of 1200 A.D.) is a weakened form of *jeṇa*. So also *jiṇi* in *Kp.* S. 52.4, *Jdc.* 8.3 (For corresponding *tiṇi* forms, though in different context and its history see §123). In EAp. *jo* appears to have been used for OIA *yena*. Thus in

*jŏ natthu niccala kiaü maṇa*

*so dhammakkhara—pāsa*

*pabaṇaho bajjhaï ......* (*DKK.* 23).

*jo....kiaü*= *yena kṛtam.* But that is a Nom. sg. form used probably to correspond to its correlative *so..bajjhaï* in the next line.[169] In '*jahĩ mana mānasa kimpi na kijjaï.* (*DKK.* 20), *jahĩ* stands for *yena.*[170] It is probably due to the fusion of Instr. and Loc. (See §81) and *-a-hĩ* *-a-smin* is obvious. There are practically no *-ha* forms of Dat. Gen. Abl. except. *jāha* (*Pd.* 14). In EAp. *jẽ* (*DKK.* 30) is really Ins. sg. though it is used in the Gen. sense. Thus *jĕ bujjhia abirala sahaja-khaṇa*=*yena buddhā aviralāḥ sahaja-kṣaṇāḥ.* Gen. sg. *-ā -su* is the only uniform term. throughout this period in WSEAp. The Loc. sing. *-a-hiṁ* or *-a-hĩ*< OIA *-a-smin* is already familiar (See §82).

Plural forms are quite regular.

FEMININE GENDER

(*ii*) The declension of Fem. *jă* follows the normal noun-declension of Fem. *-ă* stems. Only irregular forms are noted here.

---

165 ALSDORF, Intro. to *Hv.* § 49 and 41. Also § 81 of the present dissertation.

166 ALSDORF, Intro. to *Kp.* § 29 p. 60.

167 *Ibid.*, § 21, p. 57.

168 See Intro. to *Hv.* § 48(a) and § 49. In acc. sg. *so* (3) : *taṃ* (8) and Fem. *sā* (1) : *taṃ* (2) point to the same conclusion.

169 SHAHIDULLA translates these lines as follows : "Le souffle du maitre qui a rendn l'esprit immobile aux côtés de la lettre de l'Idéal, est entrave". —*Les Chants Mystiques*, p. 87.

170 *Ibid.*, *Vocabulaire*, p. 101.

Instr. sg. *jā-ẽ* in *BhK.* 209-10 is the application of a Masc. term. to the Fem. base *jā-*: In Dat. Gen. Abl. we find Masc. *jăsu* was used for Fem. gender attesting to the tendency of using Masc. forms for Fem. in Pronominal declension between 1000-1200 A.D. The use of *-hi* both for Gen. and Loc. shows the influence of compound Gen. Loc. case of Pkts. on Ap.

Fem. plural forms are quite regular like the declension of Fem. *-ă* stems.

It is noteworthy that *dhruṁ* which is sanctioned by Pkt. grammarians is conspicuous by its absence in Ap. literature except in *Hc.* 8.4.360 and *Kc.* where Hemacandra specially illustrates it. The use of *dhruṁ* (*Hc.* 8.4.360), *jruṁ* (=*yad*) in *Kī* 5.49, *yadru* (=*yasmin*) in *Kī.* 5.50 is not found in Ap. literature except in the cases noted by PISCHEL.[171]

126A (*i*). THE RELATIVE PRONOUN *ja-* (*yad*).

MASC. AND NEUT. SING.

THE DIRECT SING.

| A.D. | WAp. | SAp. | EAp. |
|---|---|---|---|
| 500 ? | Neut. *ju, jaṁ.* | .. | .. |
| 600-1000 | Masc. *ju, jo, jaṁ* (Acc.)<br>Neut. *jaṁ.* | .. | .. |
| 700-1200 | .. | .. | Masc. *jo.* |
| 1000 | Masc. *jo* | Masc. *jo* | .. |
| | Neut. *ju, jaṁ.* | Neut. *jaṁ.* | .. |
| 1200 | Masc. *ju, jo*<br>*jaṁ* (Acc.) | | |
| | Neut. *ju, jaṁ.* | *dhruṁ* and *jruṁ* in Pk. grammars is linguistically unconnected with *ja-* | |

INSTRUMENTAL SINGULAR.

| | | | |
|---|---|---|---|
| 500 ? | .. | .. | .. |
| 600-1000 | *je*ऺ (i.e., *jẽ*)<br>*jiṁ, jeṇa* | .. | .. |

171 PISCHEL, *Gram.* § 427. For the development of *ja-* in NIA, see *L'indo-aryen* pp. 200-201.

| | | | |
|---|---|---|---|
| 700-1200 | .. | .. | *jẽ, jeṇa*<br>*jo* (*DKK.* 23)<br>*jahĩ* (*DKK.*20) |
| 1000 | *jeṁ, jiṁ,* | *jẽṁ, jiṁ* (*Jc.* 4.1.4) | .. |
| | *jeṇa* | *jeṇa.* | |
| 1100 | *jeṇa* | *jeṁ* | .. |
| 1200 | *jeṁ, jiṁ* (*Kp. E.* 35) | | |
| | *jẽṇa, jiṇa* (*Jdc.*, *Sc. KP.*) | .. | .. |
| | *jiṇi* (*KP.* , *Jdc.*) | | |

Dat. Gen. Abl. Singular

| A.D. | WAp. | SAp. | EAp. |
|---|---|---|---|
| 500 ? | .. | .. | .. |
| 600-1000 | *jasu, jāsu* | .. | .. |
| 700-1200 | .. | .. | *jāsu*<br>*jẽ* (*DKK.*30) |
| 1000 | *jasu, jāsu* | *jāsu* | .. |
| | *jāha* (*Pd.* 14) | *jasu* | .. |
| | *jassa* (Pkt.) | | |
| 1100 | .. | *jāsu, jasu* | .. |
| 1200 | *jasu, jāsu* | .. | .. |
| | *jassa* (Pkt.) | .. | .. |
| | *jamhā* (*Kp. J.* 48.2*) | | |
| | Ablative. | | |

Loc. Singular.

| | | | |
|---|---|---|---|
| 500 ? | .. | .. | .. |
| 600-1000 | .. | .. | .. |
| 700-1200 | .. | .. | *jahĩ* (*DKK.*24) |
| 1000 | *jahiṁ, jahĩ* | *jahiṁ, jahĩ* | .. |
| | *jammi* (Pkt.) | | |

| | | | |
|---|---|---|---|
| 1100 | Pkt. *jammi* (*Mt.* 20) | *jahiṁ jāhiṁ* | .. |
| 1200 | *jahiṁ, jahĩ* | .. | .. |

PLURAL NUMBER

THE DIRECT PLURAL

| | | | |
|---|---|---|---|
| 500 ? | .. | .. | .. |
| 600-1000 | Masc. *jĕ* | .. | .. |
| | Neut. *jāi̐* | .. | .. |

| A.D. | WAp. | SAp. | EAp. |
|---|---|---|---|
| 700-1200 | .. | .. | .. |
| 1000 | Masc. *je, ji* (*Pd.* 86) | Masc. *jĕ* | .. |
| | Neut. *jāĩ* | | |
| 1200 | Masc. *jē̆ ji* (*Kp.* A. 13.1) | .. | .. |
| | Neut. *ji* (*Kp.* J. 54.1) | | |

INSTR. LOC. PLURAL.

| | | | |
|---|---|---|---|
| 500 ? | .. | .. | .. |
| 600-1000 | *jehiṁ* | .. | .. |
| 700-1200 | .. | .. | *jehi* |
| 1000 | *jehiṁ, jehĩ* | *jehĩ* | .. |
| 1100 | .. | .. | .. |
| 1200 | *jehiṁ, jehĩ* | .. | .. |

DAT. GEN. ABL. PLURAL.

| | | | |
|---|---|---|---|
| 500 | .. | .. | .. |
| 600-1000 | *jahã, jāhã* | .. | .. |
| 700-1200 | .. | .. | .. |
| 1000 | *jāha,* | *jāhaṁ* | |
| | *jāhaṁ, jāhiṁ.* | *jahuṁ* (*Jc.* 2.12.19). | |

| | | | |
|---|---|---|---|
| 1100 | .. | .. | .. |
| 1200 | *jahã* (*Kp.* J. 28.5) | .. | .. |
| | *jāhaṁ.* | .. | .. |

## §126A (*ii*). The Relative Pronoun *ja-* Feminine Gender

### Singular Number

### Direct Sing.

| A.D. | WAp. | SAp. | EAp. |
|---|---|---|---|
| 500 ? | *jā* | .. | .. |
| 600-1000 | *jā* (*PPr.* 2.46*1) | .. | .. |
| 700-1200 | .. | .. | .. |
| 1000 | *jā* | *jā* | .. |
| 1100 | .. .. | *jā* | .. |
| 1200 | *jā* | .. | .. |
| | **Instrumental Sing.** | | |
| 500 | .. | .. | .. |
| 600-1000 | .. | .. | .. |
| 700-1200 | .. | .. | .. |
| 1000 | *jāĕ* (*BhK.* 209.10) | *jāe, jāi* | .. |
| 1100 | .. | .. | .. |
| 1200 | .. | .. | .. |
| | **Dat. Abl. Gen. Sing.** | | |
| 1000 | *jāhi* | *jāhe, jāhi* | .. |
| 1200 | *jasu, jāsu* | | |
| | *jahe* (*Hc.* 4.359), *jīe* (*Sc.* 484.4) | .. | .. |

Loc. Sing.

No forms till 1000 A.D. were traced.

| | | | |
|---|---|---|---|
| 1000 | *jāhi* (*BhK.*149.5) | .. | .. |
| 1100 | .. | *jahiṁ* (*KKc.* 6.16.7) | .. |
| 1200 | .. | .. | .. |

PLURAL NUMBER

THE DIRECT CASE

| A.D. | WAp. | SAp. | EAp. |
|---|---|---|---|
| 500 ? | .. | .. | .. |
| 600-1000 | .. | .. | .. |
| 700-1200 | .. | .. | .. |
| 1000 | *jāo* | *jāü* | |
| 1100 | .. | *jāü* | |
| 1200 | *jāü* | .. | .. |

*Instr. Loc. Plural. Dat. Gen. Abl. Plural.*

No forms were traced.

INTERROGATIVE PRONOUN

§127. The interrogative Pronoun *kiṁ* assumes three bases in Ap. viz., *ka- ki-* and *kavaṇa-*.[172] These form the basis of the three types of Interrogatives in NIA. Thus we find ;

(*i*) *ka-* type : *e.g.*, Shina, Nep. *ko* ; Kashmiri *ku- su*; Braj. *kaü, ko.*

(*ii*) *ki-* type : *e.g.*, Maith. *kī*, Beng. Oriyā *ki*, H. *kyā.* Punj. *ki*, Singh. *kimda.*

(*iii*) *kavaṇa-* type : Raj. Punj. *kauṇ* ; H. Awadhi *kaun* Guj. M. *koṇ* ; Nep. *kun* ; Beng. *kon.*

172 The base *kavaṇa-* is variously derived. PISCHEL quotes some similar OIA forms e.g., *kavapatha, kavāgni, kavoṣṇa* (*Gram.* §§ 428,246), and postulates **ku-* in OIA. HOERNLE connects it with *kevaḍū* (*Gauḍian Grammar*, p. 219) K. P. KULKARNI with OIA *kaḥ* + *cana* (*Marathī Bhāṣā Ulgamā va Vikīsa*, p. 348), S. G. TULPULE with Pkt. Abl. sing. *kiṇo* (*Yādava Kālīna Marāṭhī Bhāṣā*, p. 208). K. P. KULKARNI and TULPULE fail to explain the labial element *-va-* in that base. For its derivation, see next page.

Out of these three bases *ka-* and *ki-* and are found in OIA and MIA[173] *kavaṇa-* is better traced to Pali **ka-pana* underlying the forms. *ko-pana kiṁ-pana* (<OIA *kiṁ punaḥ* ?)[174]

(*i*) The following is the Paradigm of this pronoun, implied in *Hc.*[175] and other Pk. grammarians

SINGULAR

Nom.: Masc. *kavaṇu, ko.* Fem. *kavaṇa, kă.*

Neut.: *kim, kăiṁ, ki* ? (*Hc.* 340).

Instr.: *kavaṇeṇa.*

Abl.: *kau, kahāṁ.*

Dat. Gen.: Masc.: *kavaṇa-hẽ, kassu, kāsu.*

Fem.: *kahe.*

PLURAL

Nom.: *ke.* Neut. *kāiṁ, kāĩ.*

(*ii*) In Pkts. we have *ka-* and *ki-* bases. The following forms are noted by PISCHEL[176]

(*i*) *ka-*

SINGULAR

Abl.: *kăo, kado, katto, kamhā; kahiṁto* (AMg.)

Gen.: *kassa, kāsa* ; *kāha* (Mg. also Fem.)

Loc. *kammi* (M.) ; *kaṁsi, kamhi* (AMg.) ; *kassiṁ* (Ś.) ; *kahiṁ, kattha, kahi, kaha* (*Hc.* 8.2.161).

Fem.: *kāe, kāhiṁ; kāhe* (AMg.).

PLURAL

Nom.: *kā* (Fem. Ś.)

Gen·: *kāṇaṁ* , *kāṇa* (M.); *kesiṁ* (AMg. JM.)

(*ii*) *ki-*

---

173 For MIA see PISCHEL, *Grammatik*, § 428.

174 The relations between Pali and Ap. are not properly appreciated by scholars (except a few like Helmer SMITH, Jules BLOCH). Hence the different postulates noted in Footnote No. 172 above.

175 *Hc.* 8.4.329—448.

176 For MIA see PISCHEL, *Grammatik*, § 428.

SINGULAR

Nom.: Ac,: Neut. *kiṁ* (all dialects) ; *kitti* (Ś.)

Ins.: *kiṇā* (M. also AMg.)

Abl.: *kiṇo*, *kīsa*. cf. Pā *kissa*.

Gen.: Fem. *kissā*, *kīse*, *kīā̆*, *kīi*, *kīe*.

DECLENSION IN AP. MASC. AND NEUT.

(iii) The direct sing. has three bases *ka*- *ki* -and *kavaṇa*-. Out of these *ki*- is found in Neut. as in OIA. *kavaṇa*- is not seen in EAp. It first appeared in *PPr.* (WAp. 600 A.D.) and is continuously found in WAp. upto the end of our period (1200 A.D.). In the works of Puṣpadanta (SAp. 1000 A.D.) there are some *kavaṇa* forms in the direct case e.g., *kavaṇu* (*Hv.* 88.2.10), *kavaṇa* (*Hv.* 87.16.5) but they are not found in other cases, though later on it attained popularity, as there is only *kavaṇa*- as the base of this pronoun in Marāṭhī from the oldest period.

*ku* (*ka*+*u*) appears first in 600 A.D., in WAp. In SAp. of the 10th cent. *ko* is the main form, and *ku* is seen only occasionally while it is not used in EAp. at all. Even the Neut. *kāiṁ* which, according to *Hc.* 8.4.367 is a substitute for *kiṁ* is nothing but the extension of the Neut. direct plur. *ka*+*āiṁ* to the sing. *kāĩ* and *kaĩ* are the two alternative forms in WSAp. direct sing. though *kiṁ* or *ki*- forms alone are found in EAp. *ki*- forms are still very popular in Maithili, Bengali, Oriya and other Eastern NIA languages. As seen above and elsewhere (see §84 for Noun - declension of -*a* stems) -*aĩ* and -*āĩ* are desinences of Neut. direct Plur. Thus *kāĩṁ* and *kāĩ* are originally Neut. direct plur. forms used for the sing., and this use is found as early as 500 A.D. WAp. in the direct case. They were naturally used for the plur. also (see Comp. Table §127A). As *ki*- is the only base in the EAp., *kaï* (<*kaĩ*) noted in *Pu.* 17.25 and *Ki* 5.13 is due to the influence of the WAp. literature and western grammarians. The particles *i* (<*cit.*), *vi*, *bi* (<*api*) etc., used to express indefiniteness, need not be considered here. *kiṇṇa* in *BhK*. 148.6 (also in *Pd.* 19) is a sandhi of *kiṁ*+*ṇa*. *kau* in *BhK*. 118.5 is due to the extension of the base *ka*-.

The use of *ki* (<*kiṁ*) without any term. appears first in *PPr.* 1.98 (WAp. 600 A.D.) and is continuous upto 1000 A.D., as is clear from the use of *ki* in *Pd.*, *Sdd.* But EAp. is the only region where it was very popular, as it recurs 21 times in *DKs.* (1000 A.D.), though *kiṁ* (2) and *kiṁpi* (2) show the remnants of OIA and MIA influence in that period. There is one unusual form needing explanation in EAp. viz., *kuccha*

(*DKK*. 10) -*ch*- this reminds us of Pali *koci, kiṁci*, Aśokan Inscr. *kecha, kiṁchi*, a survival of OIA *kaścit*. In Eastern NIA, we get Beng. *kichu*, Oriya *kichi*. Is H. *kuch* a borrowal from the East ? Acc. sg. *ko* in WAp. of the 6th cent. A.D., shows the formation of the direct case as early as 600 A.D.

The variety of forms in the direct case shows :

(1) that the direct case was formed in WAp. from 600 A.D.

(2) that *ki*- was a very popular base in EAp., wherein *kavaṇa*- was absent, and that *kavaṇa*- came to be used first in WAp. (600 A.D.) and later in SAp. (1000 A.D.) in which region it became very popular in the NIA period.

(3) that the plur. forms *kā̃ĩ* came to be used for the sing. from the beginning of this period.

(4) that forms in Aśokan Inscriptions are found in Ap. of those regions.

(5) that these forms of the direct case satisfactorily explain the NIA forms of the corresponding regions.

Ins. sg. *kavaṇeṁ, kavaṇeṇa* are limited to WAp. only, thus corroborating the above finding regarding its original venue. The terms. -*eṇa*, -*ẽ* are quite common. *kiṇa* (*Sc*. 604.3) is a weakening of *keṇa* possibly due to the following *api* (*vi*).

The terms. of the Dat. Gen. Abl. are the same as those of -*a*- stems. (Compare §83A). Only the forms in EAp. deserve attention. In Noun-declension -*a* stems has -*ha*, -*hŏ*, -*ho* terms. But *kāhiu* (*kasmin*) is a Loc. form used in this sense. So *kāhĩ* in *DKK*. 30. *kāsu* <MIA *kassa* being obvious, -*su* need not be discussed though it is not seen in -*a* stems (Masc.). The influence of OIA and MIA declensions have left their traces on Ap. *kassa* is a Prakritism. Loc. sg. forms in -*hiṁ*, -*hĩ* and -*hi* (in EAp.) are regular.

Plural forms of *ka*- follow the normal declension of -*a* stems.

## Feminine Gender

(*iv*) Fem. direct sing. contains no *ki*- forms. The use of *kă* and *kavaṇa* directly without any term. is as usual *ka-u* (*Sdd*. 68) and *kāyau* < *kā-ka-u* (a usual extension of stem in *Sdd*. 189) show the use of Masc. terms. with Fem. stems—an example of confusion of genders. The remaining forms, being few and regular, may not be discussed.

§127A. (*iii*) INTERROGATIVE PRONOUN *kim*

(A) *ka*- (B) *kavaṇa*.

DIRECT SING.

| A.D. | WAp. | SAp. | EAp. |
|---|---|---|---|
| 500 ? | Masc. *ko*, *ko͝*<br>Neut. *kiṁ*, *kaĩ ko*. | .. | .. |
| 600-1000 | Masc. *ko*, *ku*<br>*kavuṇa* or *kavaṇu* (*PPr*. 2.171)<br>Neut. *kāĩ* (*PPr*. 1.27) ? *ki* (*PPr*. 1.98)<br>Neut. *ki*, *ko*. | .. | .. |
| 700-1200 | .. | Masc. *ko*, *koi* (*DKs*. 18), *kobi* (*DKs*. 10).<br>Neut. *kiṁ*, *kimpi* (*DKK*. 12). *ki* (*DKs*. 21). 21 times. *kiccha* (*DK*. 10). | |
| 1000 | Masc. *ko*, *ko vi*<br>*ku vi*, *ku i* (*BhK*.)<br>*kaṁ* (Acc. Pktism.)<br>Neut. *kiṁ kiṇṇa* (*BhK*. *kaĩ*(*vi*). (*Pd*.)<br>*kāĩṁ kima* (*Pd*. 42)<br>*kau* (*BhK*. 118.5), *ki* (*Pd*. Sdd.)<br>(B) *kavaṇu*, *kavaṇa* (*Sdd*.) | Masc. *ko*, (*ku*(*vi*)<br>Neut. *kiṁ*.<br>*kāi* (*mi*), *kāĩ*) | |
| 1100 | Neut. *kiṁ* (*pi*)<br>*kavaṇu* (*Mt*. 16) | Masc.: *ko*, *ku*<br>Neut. *kavaṇu*, *kāiṁ*. | Neut. *kaĩ* (*Pu*. 17.25). |

| A.D. | WAp. | SAp. | EAp. |
|---|---|---|---|
| 1200 | Masc. *kō, ko(vi) ku,* (B) *kavaṇu.* Neut. *kiṁ, kĩ kaĩ, kaĩ, kāiṁ* (B) *kavaṇu.* | | |
| | **INSTRUMENTAL SING.** | | |
| 500 ? | .. | .. | .. |
| 600-1000 | .. | .. | .. |
| 700-1200 | .. | .. | *keṇa* |
| 1000 | *keṇa, kavaṇeṁ* | *keṇa* | .. |
| 1100 | .. | *keṇa, keṁ* | .. |
| 1200 | *kēṇa kiṇa* (*Sc.*) *kavaṇeṇa* (*Sc.* 530.7) | | |
| | **DAT. GEN. ABL. SING.** | | |
| 500 ? | *kaĩ* (Abl. -*Mt.* 25) | | .. |
| 600-1000 | .. | .. | .. |
| 700-1200 | .. | .. | *kāhĩ* (*DKK.*29) *kāsu* (*DKs.* 60.75) Pkt. *kassa* (*DKs.* 96) |
| 1000 | *kaho, kahu kasu, kāsu* | *kaho, kahŏ kassa, kāsu* | .. |
| 1100 | *kāsu* (*Sc.* 33-624) a quotation. | *kāsu* Abl. *kīsa* (*KKc.* 10-1-3) | *kāsa* (*Pu.* 17. 25) |
| 1200 | *kasu, kassu, kāsu kassa* | .. | .. |

Loc. Sing.

| A. D. | WAp. | SAp. | EAp. |
|---|---|---|---|
| 500 ? | .. | .. | .. |
| 600-1000 | .. | .. | .. |
| 700-1200 | .. | .. | *kāhi* (*DKK*. 30) *kahi* (*DKs*. 93) 4 times. |
| 1000 | *kahiṁ*, *kahĩ* | *kahĩ* | .. |
| | *kahi* | *kahi* (*mi*) | |
| 1100 | *kahiṁ* | *kahiṁ* | .. |
| 1200 | *kahĩ*, *kavaṇahiṁ* (*Hc*. 425.) | .. | .. |

Plural Number

Direct Case

| A. D. | WAp. | SAp. | EAp. |
|---|---|---|---|
| 500 ? | .. | .. | .. |
| 600-1000 | Masc. *ke*, *ki* | .. | .. |
| 700-1200 | .. | .. | .. |
| 1000 | Masc. *kē*, *ki* (*vi*) | *kē*, *ki* (*vi*) | .. |
| 1100 | .. | Masc. *ke* | .. |
| 1200 | Masc. *kē*, *ki* (*vi*) | .. | .. |
| | Neut. *kaĩ* | | |

Instrumental-Locative Plural

| A. D. | WAp. | SAp. | EAp. |
|---|---|---|---|
| 500 ? | .. | .. | .. |
| 600-1000 | .. | .. | .. |
| 700-1200 | .. | .. | .. |
| 1000 | .. | *kēhi*(*mi*) | .. |
| 1100 | .. | *kehiṁ* | .. |
| 1200 | .. | .. | .. |

## § 127A (*iv*) Interrogative Pronoun *ka-* (fem.)

### Direct Case Sing.

| A. D. | WAp. | SAp. | EAp. |
|---|---|---|---|
| 1000 | *kā, ka* | *kā, ka* | .. |
| | *kaü* (*Sdd.* 68), *kāyau* (*Sdd.*189) | | |
| | (B) *kavaṇa* | (B) *kavaṇa* (*Hv.* 87.16.5) | |
| 1100 | .. | *ka, kā(i)*. | .. |
| 1200 | *kā, ka* | .. | .. |

### Instrumental Sing.

| | | | |
|---|---|---|---|
| 500 ? | .. | .. | .. |
| 600-1000 | | .. | .. |
| 700-1200 | .. | .. | .. |
| 1000 | .. | *kāe* | .. |
| 1000 | .. | *kāiṁ* | .. |
| 1200 | .. | .. | .. |

### Dat. Gen. Abl. Sing.

| | | | |
|---|---|---|---|
| 500 ? | .. | .. | .. |
| 600-1000 | .. | .. | .. |
| 700-1200 | .. | .. | .. |
| 1000 | *ka-hi* | *kā-hĕ* | .. |
| | | *kā-hi* | |
| 1100 | .. | .. | .. |
| 1200 | *ka-he* | .. | .. |
| | *kī-i* (*Kp.* E. 25) | | |

DIRECT PLURAL

| A. D. | WAp. | SAp. | EAp. |
|---|---|---|---|
| No forms upto 1000 A. D. were traced. | | | |
| 1100 | .. | .. | .. |
| 1200 | *kāu* | .. | .. |

§ 127B. PRONOUNS MASCULINE AND NEUTER

*ta-* (*tad*), *ja-* (*yad*), *ka-* (*kim*)

NOM. ACC. SINGULAR

| A. D. | WAp. | SAp. | EAp. |
|---|---|---|---|
| 500 | Masc. Nom.: *-o*, *-ŏ*, *-u* | .. | .. |
| | Acc.: *-ṁ*. | | |
| | Neut. Nom. Acc. (1) *-u* | | |
| | (2) *-ā* | | |
| | (3) *-ṁ*. | | |
| | (4) [*ka*]- (*a*) *ĩ* | | |
| | (5) *-o*. | | |
| 600-1000 | Masc. Nom. : *-o*, *-ŏ*. | | |
| | *-u*, zero-. | | |
| | Acc. : *-ŏ* | | |
| | *-ṁ* | | |
| | Neut. Nom. & Acc. : | | |
| | (1) (*ka*)-*āiṁ* (*PPr.* 1.27) ? *kavaṇa* substituted for *kiṁ*. | | |
| | (2) (*ka*)-*i* (*PPr.* 1.98). | | |
| | (3, 4) *-ṁ*, *-o*. | | |

| A. D. | WAp. | SAp. | EAp. |
|---|---|---|---|
| 700-1200 | .. | .. | Masc. Nom.: -zero |
| | | | *-o*. |
| | | | Acc.: *-ṁ*. |
| | | | Neut. Nom. & Acc.: *-e* |
| | | | -zero |
| | | | *-ā* (*DKs*. 7.8) (viz. *tā*) |
| | | | [*ka-*] *-iṁ* |
| | | | *-i* (*DKs*. 21.) |
| 1000 | Masc. Nom.: *-o*, *-ō* | Masc. Nom.: *-ō*, *-o* | .. |
| | *-u* | [*-ka*]*-u*(*vi*) | |
| | Acc.: *-ō* | Acc.: *-ō* | |
| | *-ṁ* | *-ṁ* | |
| | Neut. Nom. & Acc.: | Neut. Nom. & Acc.: | |
| | (1) *ṁ* | *-ṁ* | |
| | (2, 3) -(*a*)*u*, *-u* | [*ka-*] *āi* (*mi*) | |
| | (4, 5, 6) zero, *-iṁ*, *-ima* | *-āĩ* (*ṁ*) | |
| | (7, 8) (*ka*) *-āĩ*, *-i* (*Pd*., *Sdd.*) | *-āĩ* (*vi*) | |
| 1100 | Masc.: *-u* | Masc.: Nom.: *-o* | |
| | *-o* | | |
| | Acc. *-ṁ* | Acc. *-ṁ* | |
| | Neut. Nom. & Acc. : | Neut. Nom. Acc. : | Neut. Nom. & Acc.: |
| | -nil | *-ṁ* | |
| | *-ṁ*, [*ka*] *-iṁ* (*pi*) | *-o* | *-ĩ* (*Pu*. 17.25) |
| | (*kavaṇa*) *-u* (*Mt*. 16) | *-u* | (*Ki*. 5.13). |
| | | *-āiṁ*. | |

| A.D. | WAp. | SAp. | EAp. |
|---|---|---|---|
| 1200 | Masc. Nom.: -*ō*, -*o* | also [*kavaṇa*] -*u* (*SN.*, *Hc.*) | |
| | -*u* | | |
| | Acc.: -*ṁ* | | |
| | -*ō*, -*oi* | | |
| | -*u* | | |
| | Neut. Nom. & Acc.: -*ṁ*. | | |
| | (*ka*)-*iṁ* -*ĩ*, -*ā̆im* | | |
| | -*āĩ* -*u*. | | |

INSTRUMENTAL SINGULAR

| A.D. | WAp. | SAp. | EAp. |
|---|---|---|---|
| 500 | .. | .. | .. |
| 600-1000 | -*iṁ* | .. | .. |
| | -*ē̐* or -*ẽ* | | |
| | -*eṇa* | | |
| 700-1200 | .. | .. | -*ẽ* |
| | | | -*eṇa*, -*eṇa* |
| | | | [*ja*] -*o* (*DKK.* 23) |
| | | | ,, -*hĩ* ,, 20 |
| 1000 | -*iṁ* | -*ēṇa* | .. |
| | -*eṁ* | -*eṁ* | |
| | -*eṇa* | -*iṁ* | |
| | | -*iṇa* | |
| 1100 | -*eṇa* | -*eṁ* | |
| | | -*eṇa* | |
| 1200 | -*ēṇa* | .. | .. |
| | -*eṇa* | | |
| | -*iṇa* | | |
| | -*iṇi* (*Kp.*, *Jdc.*) | | |
| | [*Ja*] -*eṁ* | | |
| | [*Ja*] -*iṁ* | | |

| A.D. | WAp. | SAp. | EAp. |
| --- | --- | --- | --- |
| | **DATIVE-GENITIVE-ABLATIVE SINGULAR** | | |
| 500 | Abl.: *-ā* | .. | .. |
| | [*ka*] *-aĩ* (Mt. 25) | | |
| 600-1000 | Gen.: -(*a*) *su* | .. | .. |
| | -(*ā*) *su* | | |
| | -(*a*) *hũ* | | |
| 700-1200 | .. | .. | Gen.: (*ā̆*)-*su* |
| | | | (*ā̆*)-*hĩ* |
| | | | -*āhara* (*ta*-*DKs*. 92) |
| | | | [*ja*] -*ẽ* (*DKK*. 30) |
| | | | [*ka*] -*ssa* (*DKs*. 96) |
| 1000 | Abl.: *mhā* (*Sdd*. 101) (Pkt.) | Abl.: -*hŏ* | .. |
| | Gen.: -*ho* | Gen.: -*hŏ*, -*ho* | |
| | -*hu* | -*hu* | |
| | -(*ā̆*)*su* | -(*ā̆*) *su* | |
| | -(*ā*) *ha* | (*ka*) -*ssa*. | |
| | -*sa* | | |
| | -*hi* | | |
| | -(*ā*) *saï* | | |
| | -*ssa* | | |
| 1100 | | Abl.: -*mhā* | |
| | | -(*ĭ*) *sa* (*RKc*. 10.1.3) | |
| | Gen.: -*hu* | Gen.: -(*ā̆*)*su* | -(*ā*)*sa* (*Pu*. 17.75) |
| | -(*ā*)*su* | -*ho* | |
| 1200 | -(*a*) *su* | | |
| | -(*ā*) *su* | | |
| | | Abl. [*ja*-] -*mhā* (*Kp*. J. 48.2*) | |
| | -*hu* | | |
| | -*ho* | | |
| | -*ssu* | | |
| | -*ssa* | | |

| A.D. | WAp. | SAp. | EAp. |
|---|---|---|---|
| | **LOCATIVE SINGULAR** | | |
| 500 | *-hĩ* | .. | .. |
| 600-1000 | *-hi̐* | .. | .. |
| 700-1200 | .. | .. | *-hĩ*<br>*-(ā̆) hi*<br>*-su*<br>(*ta* - *DKK*. 22) |
| 1000 | *-hiṁ*, *-hĩ*<br>(*ka*) *-hi*<br>*-ehaiṁ* (*Pd*. 103. *ta-*)<br>*emaï*<br>*-mmi*. | *-hĩ*<br>*-hiṁ*<br>(*ka*) *-hi* (*mi*) | .. |
| 1100 | *-hiṁ*<br>*-mmi* (Pkt.) | (*ā̆*)*-him*<br>*-mmi* (Pkt.) | .. |
| 1200 | *-hiṁ*<br>*-hĩ*<br>*-mmi* | .. | .. |
| | **NOM. ACC. PLURAL (MASC. NEUT.)** | | |
| 500 | .. | .. | .. |
| 600-1000 | Masc. Nom.: *-ē*<br>*-i*<br>Acc.<br>Neut. Nom. & Acc.<br>*-e*<br>*-āi̐* | .. | .. |
| 700-1200 | .. | .. | .. |

| A.D. | WAp. | SAp. | EAp. |
|---|---|---|---|
| 1000 | Masc. Nom.: *-e*<br>*-i*(Pd. 86)<br>Acc.: *-e*<br>*-iṁ*<br>*-ĕṁ* (*Bh.K.* 108.6)<br>[*ka*]-*vi*<br>Neut. Nom & Acc.:<br>*-(ā̆)iṁ*<br>*-(ā̆)ĭ* | Masc. Nom. Acc.: *-e*, *-ĕ*<br>[*ka*] *-i* (*vi*)<br>Neut. Nom. Acc.:<br>*-(ā̆)ĭ*, *-(ā̆)iṁ*<br>*-(ā̆)u* ? | |
| 1100 | .. | Masc.: *-e*<br>Neut.: *-(ā̆)iṁ* | .. |
| 1200 | Masc. Nom. & Acc.:<br>*-ĕ*<br>*-e*<br>*-i* (Acc. also)<br>*-i* (*vi*)<br>Neut. Nom. & Acc.:<br>*-(ā̆) ĭ*<br>*-eṁ* (*Hc.* 339)<br>(*ja-*) *-i* (*Kp.* J. 54.1) | .. | .. |

INSTRUMENTAL AND LOCATIVE PLURAL

| | | | |
|---|---|---|---|
| 500 | .. | .. | .. |
| 600-1000 | *-ehiṁ* | .. | .. |
| 700-1200 | .. | .. | *-ehi* |

| A.D. | WAp. | SAp. | EAp. |
|---|---|---|---|
| 1000 | -ēhĩ | -ehiṁ | .. |
| | -ēhiṁ | -ehĩ | |
| | | (ka) -ehi (mi) | |
| 1100 | .. | -ehiṁ | .. |
| 1200 | -ēhĩ | .. | .. |
| | -ehĩ | | |
| | -ehiṁ | | |
| | Loc.: -hiṁ | | |
| | -ihi (Sc. 517.2) | | |

DATIVE-GENITIVE -ABLATIVE PLURAL

| | | | |
|---|---|---|---|
| 500 | .. | .. | .. |
| 600-1000 | Gen.: -(a)haũ | | |
| | -(ā)haũ | | |
| 700-1200 | .. | .. | .. |
| 1000 | -(ā)haṁ | -(ā) hã, -(ā)haṁ | .. |
| | -(ā)hã | -(ā) ha (Nc. 1.14.9) | |
| | -(a)haṁ | -(a)huṁ (Jc. 2.12.19) | |
| | -(a)hã | -(ā)ṇaṁ (Pkt.) | |
| | -(ā)ha | | |
| | -(ā)ṇaṁ | | |
| | -(ā)hiṁ (Pd.) | | |
| 1100 | .. | -(ā)haṁ | .. |
| 1200 | -(a)haṁ, -(a)hã | .. | .. |
| | -(ā)haṁ, -(ā)hã | | |
| | -(ā)hi (Jdu. 2.42.) | | |
| | -(ā)ṇa, -(ē) si (Sc.) | | |

## § 127 C. Feminine Gender.

*tă-* / *-tī-* } <*tad-* ; *jă-* / *jī-* } <*yad-* ; *kă-* <*kim.*

### Nom. Acc. Singular: (*sā* for *tad*)

| A. D. | WAp. | SAp. | EAp. |
|---|---|---|---|
| 500 | -(*ă*) zero | .. | .. |
| 600-1000 | zero | .. | .. |
| 700-1200 | .. | | -*e*(*DKs.* 49) |
| 1000 | Nom. :-(*ā*) zero | Nom.: -(*ă*) zero | |
| | -(*a*) zero | (in *kavaṇa* also) | |
| | (*a*)*ü*, -*u*- (*Sdd.* 180) | Acc.: -(*ā*) zero | |
| | Acc.: -(*ā*)zero | -(*a*) *ṁ*. | |
| | -(*a*)*ṁ* (*BhK.* 13.6) | | |
| | *kavaṇa* - (*a*) zero | | |
| 1100 | Nom. : ˘ | -zero | |
| 1200 | Nom. :-(*ā*) zero | | |
| | Acc. (*ă*) zero | | |
| | -(*a*)*ṁ* (*Sn.* 30-231) | | |
| | Pkt. | | |

### Fem. Instr. Sing.

No forms up to 1000 A.D. were traced.

| | | |
|---|---|---|
| 1000 | -(*ā*)*e* | -(*ā*)*e* |
| | -(*ă*)*ĩ* | -(*ī*)*e* |
| | -(*ā*)*eṁ* (*BhK.* 2.5) | -(*ā*) zero |
| | -(*ā*)*ẽ* (*BhK.* 209.10) | -*eṇa* |
| | | -(*ā*)*ĩ* |

| A.D. | WAp. | SAp. | EAp. |
|---|---|---|---|
| 1100 | .. | -(ā)e | |
| | | -(ā)eṁ | |
| | | -(ī)eṁ (*KKc.* 1.8.2) | |
| | | -(ā)iṁ. | |
| 1200 | -(ī) | | |
| | -(a)hĩ | | |
| | -(a)hi | | |
| | -(ā)e | | |

DAT. GEN.-ABL.-SINGULAR

| A.D. | WAp. | SAp. | EAp. |
|---|---|---|---|
| 500 | -(ā)ha | .. | .. |
| 600-1000 | .. | .. | .. |
| 700-1200 | .. | .. | .. |
| 1000 | -(ā)hĕ | -(ā̆)hi | |
| | -(a)hĕ | -(ā̆)hĕ | |
| | -(a)ho (*BhK.* 160.8) | | |
| | -(ā̆)hi (*BhK*) | | |
| 1100 | -(ī)a | -(a)hĕ | |
| | | -(ā)hĕ | |
| | | -(ā)hu (*KKc.* 7.8.1) | |
| 1200 | -(a)he | | |
| | -(a)hi | | |
| | -(ā̆)su | | |
| | -(ī̆)e | | |
| | -(ī)i vi (*KpE.* 25) | | |
| 500 | .. | .. | .. |
| 600-1000 | -(a)hi̐ (*PPr.* 2.46*1) | .. | .. |
| 700-1200 | .. | .. | .. |
| 1000 | -(a)hĩ | | |
| | -(ā)hi (*BhK.* 73.3.) | -(ā)su (*Jc.* 3.1.20) | .. |
| 1100 | .. | -(a)hiṁ | .. |

| A.D. | WAp. | SAp. | EAp. |
|---|---|---|---|
| 1200 | -(*a*)*hī* | .. | .. |

FEMININE *yad*, *tad*, *kim* (Plural.)

NOM. AND ACC. PLURAL.

No forms upto 1000 A.D. were traced.

| | | | |
|---|---|---|---|
| 1000 | Nom.: -(*ā*)*u*<br>-(*ā*)*o* | -(*ā*)*u* | .. |
| | Acc.: -(*ā*)*u* | -(*ā*)*u* | |
| 1100 | .. | -(*ā*)*u* | .. |
| 1200 | Nom. Acc.: -(*ā*)*u* | .. | .. |

INSTR. & LOC. PLURAL.

Forms upto 1000 A.D. were not traced.

| | | | |
|---|---|---|---|
| 1100 | .. | -(*ā*)*hiṁ* | |
| 1200 | Ins.: -(*ī*)*hī* (*Kp.*) | .. | .. |

FEM. DAT. GEN. ABL. PLURAL

No forms upto 1000 A.D. are recorded in Ap. texts

| | | | |
|---|---|---|---|
| 1100 | .. | -(*ā*)*hiṁ* | |
| 1200 | -(*a*)*hā̃*<br>-(*ā*)*hā̃*<br>-(*ā*)*sī* | | |

INDEFINITE PRONOUNS

§ 128. Many Indefinite Pronouns are formed by adding -*i* (<*cit* or *api*), *vi*, *bi* (<*api*), *mi* to *ka*-. They are generally added after declining the pronoun regularly. The final vowel of the declined form, if long, is many times shortened before them. A few examples of the use of *ka*- as an indefinite pronoun are given below :

Direct. sg. Masc. WSEAp. *kā̃ī*, WSAp. *kovi*, *kuvi*; EAp. *kobi*.

Neut. WEAp. *kiṁpi*, WAp. *kiṁci*, *kā̃ī mi*,

EAp. *kuccha*.

Fem. WSAp. *kăvi*, WAp. *kāyau*.

Instr. sg. Masc., Neut.: *keṇa vi*.

Dat. Gen. Abl. sg. Masc.: *kāsu vi*, *kaho vi*, *kahu vi*.

Fem.: *kāhivi*.

Loc. sg. Masc., Neut.: *kahẽ mi*, *kahiṁ vi*.

Direct Plur. *ke vi*, *ki vi*.

Out of these *ko* (*ci*) or *ko* (*vi*) resulted into H. Panj. Raj. *koi*, Oriya *kei*, Shina *ko* etc. In NIA we have similar formations of *ka-* e.g., M. *koṇhī*, *koṇī*, H. *kōū*, Bihari *keu*, Beng. *keho*, *keu*; Neut. M. *kāhī*, Guj. *kāī*, Marwari *kĩ* .[176]

REFLEXIVE PRONOUN

§ 129. Out of the two Pkt. developments of OIA *ātman* (*viz*., *appa-* and *-atta-*), Ap. conserves only *appa-* which is a predecessor of a number of NIA forms such as H. Panj. *āp* or *āpe*, Beng. *āpā*, *apṇī*, Guj. *āpṇo*, M. *āpaṇ* etc. This *appa-* seems to be derived from spoken OIA **ātpman* for *ātman*.[177] The stem-widening of OIA *ātman* +*a*+*ka*>Ap. *appăṇa-* has also been very popular in Ap. and remained so in NIA.[178] Thus *appa-* and *appaṇa-* are the two bases of reflexives *ātman-* (?) in Ap. The latter, though a later development, is found in Pkts. PISCHEL traces both these forms to OIA **ātmānaḥ*.[179]

The following forms of this pronoun are recorded by *Hc.*:

*Singular.*

Nom. Acc. *appa-u*, *°ũ* (*Hc.* 422.3 PISCHEL), *appaṇā*, *appaṇu*.

Instr.: *appaṇeṁ*.

Dat. Gen. Abl.: *appa-ho*.

(There are no plural forms of *appa-* in Ap.)

The following Pkt. declension of *appa-* base of OIA *ātman*, shows that *appa-* forms in Ap. are a natural development out of Pkts. In PISCHEL's *Grammatik* § 401, it is a part of Noun declension and has both sing. and plural numbers, and two bases *appa-* and *atta-*.

176 BLOCH, *L'indo-aryen*, p. 202.
177 S. M. KATRE, *Form. Koṅk.* § 254 Footnote 1. *ABORI*, 20.2.155 (1940).
178 See BLOCH, *L'indo-aryen*, *p*. 203-4.
179 PISCHEL, *Grammatik*, § 401, p. 281.

*appa-* (OIA *ātman*)

*Singular*

Nom.: *appā* (M. AMg. JM. JŚ.), *appo appāṇo* (M. JM.)

Acc.: *appāṇaṁ* (M. AMg. JM. JŚ. Ḍh.), *appaṁ* (AMg.) *appaṇaaṁ* (M.)

Ins. : *appaṇa* (M. AMg. JM. Ś.), *appeṇa*, °*ṇaṁ* (AMg.) *appāṇeṇaṁ* (AMg.), *appaṇena* (M.).

Abl.: *appappaṇo* (JM.), *appā-o*, °*u*, °*hi*, °*hinto*, *appā*.

Gen.: *appaṇo* (M. AMg. JM. JŚ. D.A.) *appāṇassa* (JM.) *appāṇaassa* (M.)

Loc.: *appe*, *appāṇe* (M.)

*Plural*

Nom.: *appāṇo*, *appā* (M.), *appāṇā* (AMg.)

Instr.: *appehi*.

Abl.: *appāsuṁto*.

Gen.: *appāṇaṁ*.

Loc.: *appesu*.

In Ap. literature there is nothing peculiar in the declension of this pronoun except the use of *appuṇu* in the oblique in WAp. It is used in the direct case and the Instr. in SAp. of the 10th and 11th centuries. Can we not trace *-u-* in Ap. *appuṇu* to OIA **ātpuman-* rather than to **ātpman-*? the last *-u* is a regular Ap. term.

*appāṇa* forms e.g., Nom. *appāṇa* (WEAp. 1000 A.D.) *appāṇu* (WAp. (WAp. 1200 A.D.) Gen. *appāṇa* (*Sdd.* 25. *i.e.*, WAp. 1000 A.D.) are traced to OIA **ātmānaḥ* by Pischel. Without denying the linguistic possibility of OIA **ātmanaḥ* (=*ātmā*) developing into Ap. *appaṇa-*, it may be suggested that OIA **ātpmanaka* may be the original form as such stem-widening is a common tendency in Ap. The remaining *appāṇa-* forms are explained by Pischel,[180] the gen. sg. *appaṇa* (*Sdd.* 84) and *appāṇa* (*Sdd.* 25) are directly traceable to OIA **ātpmānaḥ*=*ātmanaḥ*. The *appa-* forms follow the declension of Masc. *-a* stems.[181]

*uppahiṁ*=*ātmanā*[182] in *Sdd.* 84 is inexplicable. The line is question runs as follows :

*uppahiṁ corahaṁ appiyayü khoju ṇa pattaü keṇa* (*Sdd.* 84). H. L. Jain, the editor, translates this in Hindi as follows : '*upat kar corã ko diye hue*

180 Pischel, *Grammatik*, § 401.
181 Compare § 130A and § 81A—and § 84A.
182 Glossary to *Sdd.*, p. 75.

*dhan kā khoj kis-ne pāyā hai?*'[183] In *uppahiṁ*, *-hiṁ* may be construed as the Loc. or Instr. sing. But *uppa-* = *appa-* is a riddle, unless we take *u-* as a scribal error for *a-*.

Lastly a reference may be made to ALSDORF's equation *appaṇ*$^{a}$ =*ātmīya*.[184] He quotes the following verse to support his view :

*rakkhejjahu, taruṇaho : appaṇā bāla hẽ jāā visama thaṇa.*

*phondenti je hiaḍaũ appaṇaũ tāhā parāī kavaṇa ghaṇa* (*Hc.* 8.4.350-.2) Phonologically the equation is doubtful.

## §129A. THE REFLEXIVE PRONOUN *appa-*(*ātman*) MASC. SING.

### THE DIRECT CASE.

| A.D. | WAp. | SAp. | EAp. |
|---|---|---|---|
| 500 ? | .. | .. | .. |
| 600-1000 | *appā*<br>*paramappu* (*PPr.* 1.14) | .. | .. |
| 700-1200 | .. | .. | *appa, appā*<br>*appāṇa* (*DKs.*29). |
| 1000 | *appā, appa*<br>*appu, appaü*<br>*appāṇa*<br>Acc. *appaṇaü*<br>*appaṁ* (*BhK.* 102.1). | 2. *appaüṁ*<br>1. { *appuṇu*,<br>*appaṇu*. | |
| 1100 | *appā*<br>*appu, appaüṁ*<br>(*Sn.* 270-190 A quotation). | *appuṇu*<br>*appāṇau* (*KKc.* 9.4.4) | |
| 1200 | *appa, appu, appa-u,*<br>*appa-ū* (*Sc.*), *appaṇu*,<br>*appāṇu, appaṇā*. | | |

### INSTRUMENTAL

| A.D. | WAp. | SAp. | EAp. |
|---|---|---|---|
| 500 ? | .. | .. | .. |
| 600-1000 | *appẽ*<br>*appiṁ* (*PPr.* 1.76)<br>*appu* ? (*PPr.* 1.30) | | |

183 *Sdd.*, p. 27.
184 ALSDORF, *Ap. Studien*, pp. 68-9.

| | | | |
|---|---|---|---|
| 700-1200 | .. | .. | *appa-hi* (*DKs.* 62). |
| 1000 | *appā-e* | *appaeṇa* | .. |
| | *appuṇu* (*Pd.* 83) | *appuṇu*. | |
| 1100 | .. | .. | .. |
| 1200 | *appaṇeṁ* | .. | .. |

DAT. GEN. ABL.

| | | | |
|---|---|---|---|
| 600-1000 | *appaha.ŭ* | .. | .. |
| | *appā* ? (*PPr.* 1.30) | | |
| 700-1200 | .. | .. | .. |
| 1000 | *appa-hu* | .. | .. |
| | *appaṇa*, *appāṇa* | .. | .. |
| 1100 | *appaṇu* | .. | .. |
| 1200 | *appaha* | .. | .. |
| | *appa-ho* | .. | .. |

LOCATIVE

| | | | |
|---|---|---|---|
| 500 ? | .. | .. | .. |
| 600-1000 | *appaĕ* | .. | .. |
| 700-1200 | .. | .. | .. |
| 1000 | *appi* | .. | .. |
| 1100 | .. | .. | .. |
| 1200 | .. | .. | .. |

## §129B. THE REFLEXIVE PRONOUN *-appa*

### MASC. SING. NUMBER

### THE DIRECT CASE

| A.D. | WAp. | SAp. | FAp. |
|---|---|---|---|
| 500 ? | .. | .. | .. |
| 600-1000 | zero | .. | .. |
| | *-u* | | |

| A.D. | WAp. | SAp. | EAp. |
|---|---|---|---|
| 700-1200 | .. | .. | (ă) zero |
| 1000 | (ă) zero | *-u* | .. |
| | *-u* | *-uṁ* | |
| | *-aü* | | |
| | *-ṁ* (Acc.) | | |
| 1100 | zero | *-u* | .. |
| | *-u* | | |
| | *-auṁ* (*Sn.* 20-190) | | |
| 1200 | *-u*, *-aü* | .. | .. |
| | zero | | |
| | *-aũ* (Acc.) | | |
| | **INSTRUMENTAL** | | |
| 500 ? | .. | .. | .. |
| 600-1000ȯ | *-e.* (*-ẽ*) | .. | .. |
| | *-iṁ* (*PPr.* 1.76) | | |
| 700-1200 | zero ? (*PPr.* 1.30) | | *-hi* |
| 1000 | *-*(*ā*)*e* | *-eṇa* | .. |
| | *-u* ? (*Pd.* 83) | *-u* ? | .. |
| 1100 | .. | .. | .. |
| 1200 | *-eṁ* | .. | .. |
| | **DAT. GEN. ABL.** | | |
| 500 | .. | .. | .. |
| 600-1000 | *-ha*ȯ | | |
| | zero ? (*PPr.* 1.30) | | |
| 700-1200 | .. | .. | .. |
| 1000 | *-hu* | .. | .. |
| | zero | | |
| 1100 | *-u* ? | .. | .. |
| 1200 | *-ha* | | |
| | *-ho* | | |

LOCATIVE

| A.D. | WAp. | SAp. | EAp. |
|---|---|---|---|
| 500 ? | .. | .. | .. |
| 600-1000 | -*e* | .. | .. |
| 700-1200 | .. | .. | .. |
| 1000 | -*i* | .. | .. |
| 1100 | .. | .. | .. |
| 1200 | .. | .. | .. |

## MISCELLANEOUS PRONOUNS

§130. Out of the remaining pronouns *anya*, *sarva* and *itara* are more important. The number of their forms is too small and too unimportant to require chrono-regional analysis. They are not, therefore, tabulated in Comp. Tables. Their Pkt. forms are recorded by PISCHEL in *Grammatik* §§ 433-4.

(a) *anya*-

The following forms are found in Ap. literature :

Nom. Acc. Sg.: WSEAp. *aṇṇa*, *aṇṇu*; WEAp. *anna*, WAp. *aṇu*.

Gen. sing. : *aṇṇaha*.

Instr. Plur. *aṇṇoṇṇa-hĩ*, *annonnihĩ*, *aṇṇahĩ*. (The first two are traceable to OIA (*anyonya*-).

Prakritisms need not be noted. The terms. are also the normal ones of the -*a* stems.

(b) *sarva*-

The form *sāha*<*śāśvat*,[185] is not popular though it is sanctioned as a substitute for *sarva* by *Hc*. 8.4.366. The following are some of the declined forms in Ap. literature :

Nom. Acc. sg.: *savva*, *savu* (cf. H. *sab*), *sahu*, *sāhu*, *savvui* (<*sarva cit* in *BhK*. 12.12.7 GUNE's Ed.)

185 PISCHEL, *Grammatik*, §§ 64, 262, 434.

Abl. sg.: *savva-ho, savvattau* (<*sarvata-kaḥ* used adverbially in *BhK*. 12.12.7 GUNE's Ed.)

Gen. sg.: *savva-ho*.

Abl. Gen. Plur.: *savva-haṁ*.

Morphologically this corresponds to the declension of *-a* stems.

(c) *itara*.

This is declined like other normal *-a* stems. To mention a few forms :

Nom. Acc. sg.: Masc. Neut. *iyaru* ; Fem. *iyara*.

Gen. sg.: *iyara-hu, iyara-ssu-*

Nom. Acc. Plur. *iyare* (cf. OIA Masc. Plur. *sarve* etc)

Gen. Plur. *iyaresi* (Prākritism).

As there is nothing remarkable regarding the declension of thesel we can pass on to Pronominal Adjectives.

PRONOMIMAL ADJECTIVES.

§131. Personal, demonstrative, relative, interrogative and other pronouns have contributed different types of adjectives to Ap. literature. Though the formative suffixes are noted in a separate chapter later on (Ch. IV. *Nominal Stem-Formation in Apabhraṁśa.*), a few adjectival suffixes are noted in passing here.

1—4 *-ăra, -āraa*, Fem. *-erī* :

Possessive adjectives which form an important class of pronomina, adjectives, take these suffixes. They are traceable to MIA**kāra* **-kārī* <*kārya* which are usually used with Gen. form. (Compare the use of the post-positions *kera, keraa*<OIA *kārya.*<See §103). We have the following possessive adjectives from the above suffixes :

1st Person : Sing. —*mahāra, mahāraü*.

Fem. *mahārī* (<*maha- *kārī*) ; *hamāra,° rī* (by Metathesis of the above) ; *mera* (<**ma-kera*), *merī* (<**ma-kerī*).

Plural : *amhāraya, amhārā, amhārī* (<*asma-kāra-ka °kārī*).

2nd Person: sing. —*tuhāra, tuhāraa, tuhāraü* (*tuha- *kāra*) *terau*,

Fem. *terī* (<*tva*>*ta kera, °kerī*).

3rd Person: EAp. *tāhara* (<**tāha-kara* ? )

*maha-* and *tuha-* are the Gen. sings. and the use of *kera* with Gen. is a common Ap. idiom. (See §103). Proto-Marathi seems to have lost it at some period between 1150-1250 A.D., though it is found in SAp. of the 10th and the 11th centuries. Other branches of NIA have preserved these forms.

5-6 *-isa, -risa.*

*-isa* and *-risa* ( OIA *-dṛśa*) are added to Pronominal themes to form adjectives in Ap. e.g., *jaïsa* (*yādṛśa*), *taïsa* (*tādṛśa*), *kaïsa* (**kā-dṛśa*) *aïsa* (**a-dṛśa*), *kerisa* (*kīdṛśa*), *hārīsa* (*asmādṛśa*), *tumharisa* (**tuṣmā-dṛśa*), *annāïsa* (*anyādṛśa*), *avarāïsa* (* *aparādṛśa*). NIA forms *e.g.,* M. *jasā, tasā, kasā, asā,* H. *kaisā, aisā* etc., are traceable to these Ap. forms.

7. *-eha*

The *-sa* element in the above (5-6) suffixes is changed to *-ha* in Ap. e.g., *kehaü, kehaya,* Fem. *kehī* (<*kīdṛśa kaïsa*). So also *eha* <Ap. *aïsa, jeha*<Ap. *jaisa, teha* <Ap. *taïsa* etc.[186]

Adjectives showing extent are of two types : (1) *kiyat* type and (*ii*) -**vṛddha* type. The following are the suffixes of the first type :

8-10. -(*e-, i-*)*ttiya*, -(*e-, -i-*)*ttila*, -(*e-i-*)*ttula*. e.g., *kettiya, kittiu* (*kiyat*) cf. Pali. *kittaka, ettiya* (*iyat*) cf. Pali *ettaka*; *ettiu* (*etāvat*), *jettiya, tetti-ya* etc. Sometimes these take pleonastic *-la* giving us *ettila, jettila, tettila, kettila* and *jettula, tettula, kettula* and others.

(*ii*) Adjectives of the second type take the following suffixes :

11-12. *-vaḍḍha, -vaḍu.* e.g., *jevaḍu, tevaḍu, kevaḍḍha, evaḍḍha* etc.

PISCHEL traces these *evaḍu* and *evaḍḍa* forms to **ayavaddra*.[187] Thus **kiyadvṛddha*>**ke-vṛddha*>*kevaḍḍha, kevaḍu* is the history of these forms. The same is the case with other *-vaḍha* and *-vaḍu* adjectival forms.

Both these types are conserved in NIA *e.g.,* H. *itnā*, M. *itkā* (<*īyat*) ; H. *kitnā*, M. *kitī* (<*kiyat*). So also with *evaḍhā, kevaḍhā, tevaḍhā* and other Marathi forms.[188] Marathi retained the older suffix *-vaḍḍha* while Guj. prefers the later *-vaḍu* development.

186 PISCHEL, *Grammatik*, § 262.
187 PISCHEL, *Grammatik*, § 434.
188 For more NIA forms and the connection of **vṛddha*, see BLOCH, *L'indo-aryen*, p. 203.

## CHAPTER III

# CONJUGATION IN APABHRAMŚA

§ 132. The verbal system in Ap. is chiefly based on the phonological and morphological simplification of this system in OIA and Pkts. As in declension, the verbal system in IA shows a continuous process of simplification and modification, and conjugation in Ap. forms the medial stage between Pkts. and old NIA.[1] There are relics of some OIA archaisms out of which some are unrepresented in classical Sk. These have percolated to Ap. either through Pkt. speech or through the influence of AMg. which is rich in such forms.[2] Most of the Ap. writers being Jains, the influence of AMg. on Ap. is understandable.

As shown by Jules Bloch in 'La Phrase nominale en Sanskrit',[3] and *L'indo-aryen*, the substitution of the nominal phrase for verb-system is the normal rule in epic Sk., MIA and NIA. Ap. is, of course, no exception to it. The gradual change in the verbal system of IA reached such a stage in Ap. as made it (the verbal-system in Ap.) appear to be based on :

(1) the verbal group depending on the Present Indicative of OIA (and to a certain extent the Future and the Imperative in pre-Ap. IA), and

(2) a group of nominal forms based on the verbal system noted above.

We find a similar state in Conjugation in NIA.[5]

### *Themes*

§ 133. As in Pkts. verbal themes in Ap. repose on the following systems in OIA :

(*i*) The Present System—the basis of the Present and Future Indicative, the Present Imperative, the Present Participle and the Infinitive.

(*ii*) The Past Passive Participles.

Ap. roots are either transitive or intransitive, the former being many times active in sense. Again Ap. roots may be either primitive (simple) or causative in form.

---

1 For the development of the verbal system in pre-Ap. IA. see Bloch, *L'indo-aryen*, pp. 207-36. Bloch's treatment of Pk. verbal system (p. 235-6) is very brief.

2 See Pischel, *Grammatik*, §§515-8.

3 *MSL.* XIV. 31 ff.

4 *L.indo-aryen*, pp. 251-86.

5 See Bloch, *L'indo-aryen*, p. 238.

The sources of verbal bases in Ap. are (*i*) Present Active bases, (*ii*) Present Passive bases, (*iii*) Past Passive Participles, and (*iv*) Onomatopoetic.[6] The following are some of the examples.

(i) *Present Active bases:*

(1) OIA verbal bases of the present with the *-a* suffix in Ap., though originally they belonged to different classes ( *gaṇas* ) in OIA e.g., *pāvaï* (**prāpati=prāpnoti*), *ruvaï*, *ruaï* (**rudati=roditi*), *karaï* (**karati= karoti*), *bīhaï* (*bibheti*), *ukkhiṇaï* (*utkṣiṇati* but *ut-khanati* according to some editors e.g., Jacobi see *BhK. Glossar*, p. 132), *haṇaï* (**hanati=hanti*).

Under these, we may include roots of the 10th class and denominatives, where the Ap. forms do not inherit the augment *-aya-*, but the original roots.

e.g., *āyaṇṇaï* (*ā-karṇa-*), *cinta-hiṁ* (*cinta-*), [illegible]*tāḍ-*), *vāvāraï* (*vyāpāra-*) SAp. *tandijjaï* (*tandrā-*), EAp. *bakkhāṇaï* (*vyākhyana*). Relics of *-aya-* are sometimes found in forms like *abbhatthemi* (*abhi-* √*arthay*).

(2) Stem forms of OIA which are to be reconstructed, e.g., *dekkhaï* (**dṛkṣ-*), *muṇaï* (<*man-* cf. *muni* 'a sage').

(3) Themes with a nasal which generally signifies some conjunct consonant in the original form. e.g., *jampaï* (*jalp-*), *gunthaï* (*grathnāti* <*gṛth* ?), *jiṁghai* (*jighra=ghrā*), *vindhaï* (*vidhya-*).

(ii) *Present Passive bases* :

Themes with the suffix *-ya*, under which category we can include OIA passive verbs. e.g., *uppajjaï* (*-ut-pad-ya*), *ghippaï* (**ghṛp-ya-=kṣip-*) *callaï* (*cal-ya*), *thippaï* (*stip-ya-*), *phiṭṭaï* (*sphiṭ-ya-*), *bujjhaï* (*budh-ya-*) but *bojjhu*<*budhyasva* (*DKs.* 53) is active, *lippaï* (*iip-ya-*).

(*iii*) *Past Passive Participles:*

PP. participles in OIA supply a great many verbal bases in Ap. *e.g.*, EAp. *mukkeï*, WSAp. *mukkaï* (**mukna=mukta*) EAp. *païṭṭhaï* (*praviṣṭa-*) WSAp. *saṁṭhaḍaï* (*saṁstṛta-*), *lagga-ï* (*lagna-*, *lag-ya* is also possible).

(iv) *Onomatopoeic* :

In Ap. narrative works, there are many onomatopoeic verbs e.g., *gulagulaï* "trumpets" (like an elephant), *salasalaï* "rustles," *pupphuvaï* "hisses," *lalalalanti* cf. M. *laḷalaḷaṇẽ*, *kilikilanti* "exult with joy" (? *Hv.*

6 Grierson's classification of verbal bases in MIA is from a different standpoint. See 'The Prākrit Dhātvādeśas according to the Western and Eastern School of Prakrit Grammarians.' *JASB.*, 1924.

84.5.9). The number of such onomatopoeic expressions and reduplicatives is very large in Ap.

Enlargement of bases by the addition of *-ra*, *-ḍa*, *-alla*, *-illa*, *-ulla* etc. are discussed in Ch. IV § 158.

*Causatives*

§134. Causative formations in Ap. take the augment *-ava* in WSAp. and *-aba* in EAp., (cf. OIA *-paya*, Pali. *-paya*, *-pe*, Inscriptional Pkt. *-apa*).

e.g., WSAp. *dāvaï* (*dā-*), *ṭhāvaï* (*ṭhā-*=*sthā-*), *viṇṇavaï* (*vi-jñā-*), *cintavai* (*cint-*), SAp. *jemāvaï* (√*jima* "to eat, to take one's meals"), *bollāvaï* (*bollaï* '(to speak'), *tosāvaï* (*tuṣ-*), EAp. *paribhābaï* (*pari-bhū-*), *dahābia* (*dah-*).

(1) Sometimes t[illegible] is a *vṛddhi* of the radical vowel (chiefly of *-a-*, and *guṇa* of radical *-i-*, *-u-*) of the primitive root, and the morpheme *-aya-* is added to it.

e.g., *jhaṁkhāaï* (√*jhaṁkha* "to get angry" vide *Hc.* 8.4.140), here *-a* being followed by the nasal, is not lengthened. SAp. *ṇāsaï* (*naś-*), *rāvaï* (*ram-* but usually equated with √*rañj-*), *bhesāvaï* (*bhī-*). cf. OIA *bhīṣayati*, *lehāviya* (*likh-*). cf. *likhapita* in Inscr. Pkts., *mellāviya* (*milla*=*muc-*), WAp. *khāviya* (*khād-*).

(2) Sometimes *-āva-* is simply added to the primitive root *e.g.*

SAp. *ṇaccāvaï* (*nṛtya*=*nṛt-*), *bollāvaï* (*bolla-*) *lhikkāvaï* (*lhikka* 'to conceal'), WAp. *caḍāviya* (√**cṛt* 'to ascend' or IE **qelde*[7]), *khaṇāviya* (*khan-*), *viyasāvaï* (*vi-kas-*).

(3) Some primitive and causal forms are identical. e.g., *ṇāsaï* (*naśyati*, *nāśayati*). *pāvaï* (**prāpati* : *prāpayati*), *dalaï* (*dalati* : *dalayati*), *khavaï* (*kṣamati* : *kṣāmayati*.√*kṣap-* also), *gamaï* (**gamati* : *gamayati*), *ṇamaï* (*namati*: *namayati*).

(4) There are some cases of double causatives: *e.g.*, *kārāviya* (*kar-*), *khāvāviya* (*khād-*), *devāviya* (*dā-*), *mārāviya* (*mar-*), *hārāvei* (*har-*).

(5) Some causative affixes of NIA type *e.g.*, *-āḍ*, *-āṛ*, *-āl*, were observed in Ap. *e.g.*, *bhamāḍaï* (*bhram-*) cf. Guj. *bhamāḍvū̃*, *paisāraï* (*pra-viś*) cf. Guj. *pesārvū̃*, H. *paisāra* 'access, admission.' *vaïsāraï* (*upa-viś-*) cf. Guj. *besāḍvū̃* *vaddhāraï* (*vṛddha*<*vṛdh-*) cf. Guj. *vadhāro*, *dekkhālaï* (**dṛkṣ-*) cf. *H. dikhlānā*

---

7 L. H. Gray, 'Fifteen Prākrit Indo-European Etymologies,' *JAOS.* 60, pp. 360-9.

(6) Ap. literature, being classical, contains a number of Sanskritisms. e.g., *appaï* (*arpayati*), *jaṇaï* (*janayati*), *āvaṭṭaï* (*āvartayati*), *darisaï*, *daṁsaï* (*darśayati*), *pāḍhaï* (*pāṭhayati*), *māraï* (*mārayati*).

§135. The study of these causal formations shows the following types of regularising process corresponding to those in NIA.

(1) The *guṇating* of the radical vowel,[8] *vṛddhi* of radical -*a*- e.g., √*mar*- *maraï* : *māraï* ; √*paṭh*- *paḍhaï*: *pāḍhaï*, √*ḍhala*-*ḍhalaï* : *ḍhālaï*; √*jiṁ*- *jimaï*: *jemāvaï* √*dyut*-*jovaï*: *joavaï* (?); √*tuṣ*- *tusaï*: *tōsāvaï*: √*chuha*-*chuhaï*: *ch*(*s*-)*ohaï*; √*truṭ*- *vittuḍaï*: *toḍaï*.

(2) Corresponding to the 2nd type e.g., H. *paknā*: *pakānā*, *sukhnā*: *sukhānā*:[9] we have :

√**nṛtya*- *ṇaccaï* : *naccāvaï*; *bolla*- *bollaï* : *bollāvaï*

√*lhikka*-*lhikkaï* : *lhikkāvaï*; *vi*-√*kas*- *viyasaï* : *viyasāvaï*.

(3) The suffixes -*āṛ*, -*aḍ*, -*āl* of the NIA type are noted above in 135. (5).

PRESENT INDICATIVE

§136. The following are the desinences of the Present Indicative according to Pk. grammarians :

SINGULAR

1st Person :

-*mi* (*Hc*. 4.385, *Ld*. 4.51).
-*āmi* (*Rt*. 26).
-*uṁ* (*Hc*. 4.385).
-*u* (*Ld*. 4.54).

2nd Person :

-*hi*, -*si*, (*Hc*. 4.383 so also *Tr*. *Ld*., *Rt*. 26,27).

3rd Person :

-*i*
-*di* (*Pu*. 72, *Hc*. 4.393 ex., *Rt*. 26, 27).
-*edi* (*Rt*. 26, 27).
-*e* -do-

---

8 BLOCH, *L'indo-aryen*, pp. 241-3.
9 *Ibid*., pp. 243-5.

PLURAL

1st Person :

*-mu* (*Hc.* 4.386, *Ld.* 4.55).

*-huṁ* (*Hc.* 4.386, *Tr. Ld.*, 4.55, *Pu.* 72, *Mk.* 58, *Rt.* 26).

*-mo* (*Ld.* 4.55).

*-ma* -do-

2nd Person :

*-hu* (*Hc.* 4.384, *Tr. Ld.* 4.53, *Rt.* 27).

*-ha* (*Hc.* 4.384, *Ld.* 4.53).

*-iddhā* (*Ld.* 4.53).

3rd Person :

*-hiṁ* (*Hc.* 4.382, *Tr. Ld.* 4.51, *Rt.* 27).

*-nti* (*Hc.* 4.382, *Ld.* 4.51).

*-nte* (*Ld.* 4.51).

*-ire* -do-

The pre-Ap. MIA background will be clear from the following Pali and Pkt., terms.

PALI

| | *Sing.* | *Plur.* |
|---|---|---|
| 1st Person | *-āmi* (<OIA *-āmi*) | *-āma* (<OIA *-āmaḥ*, *-āmo*) |
| 2nd Person | *-asi* (<OIA *-asi*) | *-atha* (<OIA *-atha*). |
| 3rd Person | *-ati* (<OIA *-ati*) | *-anti* (<OIA *-anti*). |

LITERARY PRAKRITS[10]

| | | |
|---|---|---|
| 1st Person | *-ami*, *-e* | *-āmo*. |
| 2nd Person | *-asi*, *-ase* | *-aha*, JŚ. Mg. Dh. *-adha*. P. CP. *-atha*. |
| 3rd Person | *-aï*, *-ae* | *anti*. |
| JŚ. Ś. Mg. Ḍh. | *-adi*, *-ade* | *-ante* |
| P. CP. | *-ati*. | |

Out of the two chief alternative terms. (viz. *-ami* and *-aũ*), *-aũ* (i.e., *-ü*ᴗ *-ũ*, *u*) is a *bona fide* Ap. desinence. *-ami*, *emi*, *-imi* (the latter ones

10 PISCHEL, *Grammatik*, §§453-7.

are comparatively rare), are the same as or altered forms of OIA *-ami*. *-aṽi* in *Hv*. (and it is limited to that work) is nothing but *-ami* with the change of intervocalic *-m->-ṽ-*. (vide *Hc*. 8.4.397, also 59). Even in *Hv*. it is rare as is seen from ALSDORF's calculation of terms. of Pres. Ind. 1 P. sing.[11] *-aũ* is an important desinence, as it is conserved in old NIA.[12] It is not traceable to Pk. *-amu<*-aṽu>-aũ*, but it is the influence of 1 P. Nom. sg. pronominal ending *-aũ*. We have such instances in MIA *e.g.*, Pali 1 sing. Optative *vatteyyāham *vatteyaṁ aham*, and Aśokan *vaṭṭe'ham*.[13]

Although we have both of these terms. for 1st per. sing., a calculation of morphological frequency shows that *aũ* became more popular than *-ami* during the centuries between *Vk*. (500 A.D.?) and *Kp*. (1194 A.D.) in WAp. In *Vk*. *-aũ* forms are absent, while in *Kp*. the proportion of *-aũ -emi* and *-imi* is 11 : 4—that is all types of *-mi* endings are only one-third of *-aũ* ones.[14] In SAp. of 100 A.D., (if *Hv*. be the representative text) the proportion of *-ami*: *-aṽi*: *-aü* is 86 7:1.[15] Probably Puṣpadanta was a purist and wished to emulate Sk. and Pkt. epics, hence *-aũ* may be an exceptional form. But if that be the real spoken stage (and SAp. is much conservative) *-ami* seems to be very popular in Mahārāṣṭra in 965 A.D. Are we to connect 1 P. sg. *-ẽ*, *ĩ-* in Old M. (*e.g.*, in the *Jnāneśvarī*) to this? The intermediate stage *-aṽi* is represented in *Hv*., and it is more popular than *-aũ*. Thus *-ami* may be taken as the characteristic term. of SAp., while in WAp. *-ami* gave place to *-aũ* during the 700 years between *Vk*. and *Kp*. We find both in EAp.

*2nd P. Sing.*

Out of the two chief terms. *-asi* (*-esi*, *-isi*) and *-ahi* (*-ehi -hi*), *-ahi* is the real Ap. development. Jules BLOCH[16] and L. H. GRAY[17] trace it to Imp. 2p. **-dhi*. In earlier WAp. texts *-ahi* endings were in overwhelming majority, and the term. remained popular throughout the Ap. period (*at least in speech*) as there is no *-sa* element in Pres. 2p sg. of the NIA languages of that region. e.g., Guj. *cāle* (√*cala*) Jaipuri *calai*, Awadhi *calai*, Braj. *calai*, H. *cale*. Due to the strong

---

11 ALSDORF, Intro. to Hv. §55.

12 BLOCH, *L'indo-aryen*, pp. 248-9 ; also R. HOERNLE, *Comparative Grammar of Guadian Languages*, London, 1880, p. 335.

13 Louis H. GRAY sees some II. influence in the 1st P. pronoun in MIA and here (*BSOS* VIII-ii-iii, p. 567). He points out that PISCHEL's comparison of *-aã* with OIA *-aki* forms e.g., *yāmaki=yāmi* (*Grammatik* § 454) is improbable. cf. L. RENOU—*Grammaire Sanscrite* Paris, 1930, p. 247 quoted by GRAY in *BSOS* VIII, ii-iii above.

14 ALSDORF's calculation of forms (as is given in Intro. to *Kp*. § 35a) is followed here.

15 ALSDORF, Intro. to *Hv*. § 55.

16 *L'indo-aryen*, p. 247 implicitly.

17 *BSOS* VIII ii-iii, 567.

influence of Sk. and Pkt., WAp. texts show a growth of *-asi* forms. The following table of frequencies will make this point clear.

| | | |
|---|---|---|
| BhK. | (1000 A.D.) | *-ahi* (47) : *-asi* (2) |
| Sc. | (1158 A.D.) | *-asi.* |
| Kp. | (1194 A.D.) | *-ahi* (7) : *-asi* (13). |

(*Kp.* has *-asi* (7), *-ēsi* (5), *-ahi* (4+1), *-ēhi* (2), W. *desi*[18]

In SAp. in the 10th cent. A.D., the proportion between *-asi* and *-ahi* is 2 : 25,[19] but due to the revival of Brahmanism and Sk. during 1100-1300 A.D., in Mahārāṣṭra, *-s-* element predominated again, and we find *-asi* and *-isi* 2p. sgs. in Old Marathi. *-asu* in forms e.g., *bhuṁjejjasu* (*bhuj-*), *ṇi-vasijjasu* (*ni-√vas-*) in *Jc.*, is clearly traceable to OIA *-sva* of Imp. 2p. sg.

In EAp. *-asi* is the only desinence and *-sa* is seen in Pres. 2p. sg. of Beng. Maith. and other modern representatives of EAp. cf. Pres. 2 sg. Beng. *calis* 'thou walkest,' Maith. *dekhasi* 'thou seest'.

### *3rd P. Sing.*

The 3rd p. sing. is common throughout the Ap. period of all regions, and is an undisputed predecessor of most of NIA terms. of Pres. 3 p. sg. A few forms in EAp. deserve notice. SHAHIDULLA supposes that *paḍihāa* (*DKs.* 87), *bhāya* (*DKK.* 19), *mara* (*DKs.* 93). are the special forms in the *Dohākoṣas* taking *-aa* and *-a* desinences, though they were probably pronounced as *-aï* or *-i.*[20] The following is the context of these forms :

(1) *siddho so puṇa takkhaṇe ṇaü jarā-maraṇa-ha-* bhāya.

'The very moment he is a Perfect Soul, he has no fear from old age and death' (*DKK.* 19). Here *bhāya* is not *bibheti* as SHAHIDULLA takes it[21] but rather* *bhāta=bhīta* PP. of √ *bhī-*. cf. *bhāyayati, bhāpayati bhī.-*

(2) *ṇia pāsa baiṭṭhi citte bhatthī joinimahu* paḍihāa (*Dks.* 87.)

Here *paḍihāa-=prati-*bhāta*, and not a verb *pratibhāti* as SHAHIDULLA takes it.[22]

---

18 ALSDORF, Intro. to *Kp.* § 35(a).
19 ALSDORF, Intro. to *Hv.* § 55.
20 SHAHIDULLA, Intro. to *Les Chants Mystiques*, p. 43.
21 *Vocabulaire, Les Chants Mystiques*, p. 105.
22 *Less Chants Mystiques*, p. 43, 212. On p. 179 SHAHIDULLA translates the verse as follows : 'Assise près de son époux, corrompue dans l'esprit—ainsi m'apparaît une femme ascete.'

(3) *jima tisia tisittaṇe dhābai*

mara *sose nabhajjalv kahĩ pābaï.*

'Just as the thirsty one runs out of thirst and *dies* with a dry throat.... (*DKs.* 93). Here *mara* appears to stand for *marai* (**maratï=mriyate*),[23] the contraction *-aï*>*-a* being *metri causa.* These special desinences of EAp. viz., *-aa* and *-a* are otherwise difficult to explain. Forms in *-i* and *-aī* in EAp. are passive ones.

In WAp. the special forms in *-di* (e.g., *bruvadi* in *Hc. Kc.*) and *-a-* (e.g., *cintae* in *Kp.* J. 34.1*) are Prakritisms, the former a Śaurasenism,

*Plural*

Out of the Plur. number, the 2nd p. has *-ahã*, *-aha* and *-ahu* endings. Bloch[24] and Gray[25] trace it to Pres. 2 plur. **-thas* (on the analogy of 1 Plur. *-mas*) rather than the ordinary *-(a)tha* giving *-aha* in Pkt. That there is some contamination or confusion between the desinences of the Pres. Ind. and the Imp. in 2nd pers., is clear from the fact that *-ahu* and *-aha* are used for Imp. 2 plur. *-ahu* of SAp. which appears as frequently as *-aha,*[26] can thus be satisfactorily explained. Desinences of 2 plur. in NIA *e.g.*, M. *-ā*, *-ā̃*, Sdh. *-o*, Lahndi*-o*, Cameali *-ā*, Guj. Mar. (Jaipuri) *-o*, Awadhi, *-u* (i.e., *-au*), H. *-o*, Braj. *-u*—all are traceable to these Ap. terms. It is the *-h-* in these which accounts for the otherwise inexplicable *-h* in 1st and 3rd p. plur. *ahũ* and *-ahĩ*.

*1st Plural*

The 1st Plur. term. *-ahũ* has been a bone of contention among linguists for a long time. Hoernle supposes that the form-*ahũ* probably contains a euphonic *-h-* for *-aũ*<Pk. *-amu*, perhaps to distinguish it from the 1st p. sing. *-aũ* ... and to assimilate it to the 3rd p. plur. *-ahĩ*.[27] Cowell gives optional 1st p. plur. terms. *-amho*, *-amha* (e.g., *hasamho*, *hasamha*<√*has-*).[28] These, if correct, would account for the *-h-* in Ap. *-ahũ*. Cowell, however, admits that he knows no authority for them. Pischel admits the obscurity of the origin of this 1st p. plur. *-hũ* though he suggests the similarity between this and Abl. plur. *-hũ*.[29] Bloch traces in it the influence of *-hu* of the 2nd plur.

---

23 cf. *Less Chants Mystiques*, p. 43, p. 216.
24 Bloch, *L'indo-aryen*, p. 247, though indirectly.
25 L. H. Gray, *BSOS*, VIII, ii-iii, p. 567.
26 See Alsdorf, Intro. to *Hv.* § 55.
27 R. Hoernle, *Comp. Gram.* § 497.
28 Cowell, [*Prākṛta Prakāśa* XXIX. Also Lassen, *Institutiones* 335.
29 Pischel, *Grammatik*, § 455.

pers. and of Pk. *-amho*.[30] According to Louis H. Gray Ap. *vaṭṭahũ* is from OIA **vartatham*<*vartatha*~Ap. *vaṭṭaũ*.[31]

In Ap. Morphology vowel+*-sm-*+vowel resulted into vowel+*-h-*+nasalized vowel e.g., *tasmāt*>*tahā̃*, *tasmin*>*tahĩ*. We can thus trace *-ahũ* to OIA *asmaka*, the Nom. plur. of 1st pers. Pronoun. In Pali also we have *vatteyā̆mhe*<*vattey amheā̆*. The nasal in *-ahũ* is due to the influence of 1st p. sg. *-aũ*. It may not be impossible that the *-h-* element in 2nd p. plur. had some influence in having a *-h-* in 1st p. plur. also. This *-ahũ* is the source of 1st p. plur. in NIA. *e.g.*, M. *-o*, *-ū̃*, Sdh. *-ū̃*, Nep. *-(a) ũ*, Maith. Beng. *-õ*. to mention a few important NIA languages.

*3rd Plural*

Out of the two terms. of 3rd p. plur. *-anti* is a continuation of pre-Ap. IA, and *-ahĩ* is the real Ap. development. It can never be traced to *-anti*, but is an analogical formation atter the 1st Pers.:

1st p. sg. *-aũ* : Plur *-ahũ*.
3rd p. sg. *-aï* : ,, *-ahĩ*.

*-h-* in both might be due to *-h-* in 2nd p. plur.

In WAp. *-anti* was the only term. in *Vk.*, but that term. was dying out fast and giving place to *-ahĩ* which appears first in *PPr.* The following is the frequency of *-antĩ* and *-ahĩ* from 1000 A.D., in WAp. (The calculation is adopted from the relevant sections of Introductions to these works.)

| | *-anti* | : | *-ahĩ* |
|---|---|---|---|
| *BhK.* (1000 A.D.) | 65 | : | 10 |
| *Sc.* (1158 A.D.) | 10 | : | 30 |
| *Kp.* (1194 A.D.) | 5 | : | 33 |

This fact is borne out by the 3rd p. plur. terms. of NIA of that region e.g., Guj., Mar., H., Braj. In SAp. *-ahĩ* is rare, and 3rd p. plur. of M. and Koṅk. is evolved out of *-anti*. The same is the case with EAp. and NIA languages of the East e.g., Maith., Beng.[32]

The special terms. of the 'Eastern' Pkt. grammarians viz., 1 p. pl. *-mha* (*Mk.*.58,50), and 3 p. sg. *-di*, *-edi*, *-e* (*Rt.* 26, 27) are not represented in EAp.

30 Bloch, *L'indo-aryen*, p. 247.
31 Gray, *BSOS.* VIII, ii-iii pp. 563-77.
32 See Bloch, *L'indo-aryen*, p. 246.

## 136A. Present Indicative.

*1st Person Sing.*

| A.D. | WAp. | SAp. | EAp. |
|---|---|---|---|
| 500 ? | *pāvami*<br>*abbhatthemi*<br>*pucchimi* | .. | .. |
| 600- | *bhaṇami, akkhami* | .. | .. |
| 1000 | *vandauṁ, kijjaüṁ* | | |
| 700- | .. | .. | *acchaũ, jāṇaũ* |
| 1200 | | | *jāṇami* (*DKs.* 92) |
| 1000 | (1) *karaüṁ*, °*ũ*, *jovaüṁ*<br>*caḍāvaüṁ*<br>(2) *akkhami, karami,*<br>*sikkhavami,*<br>*ukkhiṇami, acchami,*<br>*samāsami.* | (1) *kahaüṁ karaüṁ*<br>*lehuṁ* (*Hv.* 84.15.6)<br>(2) *ghallami, acchami*<br>*ṇihālami, pheḍami,*<br>*dakkhālami*<br>*samāsami, lemi* | .. |
| 1100 | *savaü*<br>*pekkhami, bīhemi* | *chaṇḍauṁ*<br>*sarami, heremi,*<br>*karami.* | |
| 1200 | *laggaüṁ, pariyāṇauṁ, kaḍḍhaüṁ, haraüm, karaüṁ, giṇhaüṁ,*<br>*bandhijjaũ* (*Kp. J.* 63.2) (2) *karimi, ṭhāimi,*<br>(3, 4) *salahemi, muṇāmi.* | | |

*2nd Person Sing.*

| A.D. | WAp. | SAp. | EAp. |
|---|---|---|---|
| 500 ? | .. | .. | .. |
| 600-1000 | *mĕllahi, hohi*<br>*muṇahi, pāvahi* | | |
| 700-1200 | .. | .. | *bujjha-si*<br>*pābasi.* |

| A.D. | WAp. | SAp. | EAp. |
|---|---|---|---|
| 1000 | *ḍarahi, ullūriyahi,*<br>*acchahi,*<br>*karahi,*<br>*ṇehi*<br>*paḍīsi* (*Pd.* 91) | *ghallahi, nivasahi,*<br>*ghattahi,*<br>*bhuṁjejjasu, ṇivasijjasu.* | |
| 1100 | .. | *jampahi, acchahi* | .. |
| 1200 | *karahi, bubbuyahi,*<br>*pecchahi, muṇahi.*<br>*hārāvehi, saccavēhi.*<br>*karasi, hārasi, pattijjasi* ;<br>*muṇesi.* | | |

3rd *Person Sing.*

| A.D. | WAp. | SAp. | EAp. |
|---|---|---|---|
| 500 ? | *ottharai, mellaï, parisakkaï*<br>*varisei.* | .. | .. |
| 600-1000 | *phāsaï, dekhaï, muṇaï,*<br>*vilāï*<br>*havei, galei, muṇei.* | .. | .. |
| 700-1200 | .. | | (1) *bhamijjaï, kijjaï, muṇaï, pucchaï, chaḍḍaï, takkaï, dekkhaï, dei.*<br>(2) *muṇiaï.*<br>(3) *bhāya* (*DKK.* 19) *paḍihāa* (*DKs.* 87), *mara* (*DKs.* 93). |
| 1000 | (1) *ṭhāharaï, buḍḍaï, caḍhaï, bujjhaï, ṇavaï vaḍavaḍaï, phiṭṭai, choḍaï, karaï, khampaï*<br>(2) *karei, mailei, bhamei.* | *ghoṭṭaï, thakkai, ḍollaï jokkhaï, dāvaï, viṇṇavaï, dubbhaï, cakkhaï.* | .. |
| 1100 | (1) *jampaï, muṇaï, gheppaï, hoi, dijjaï.*<br>(2) *raṇetti* (*DS.* 4.5.1) | (1) *pabhaṇaï, acchaï, sambhavai kīraï*<br>(2) *pujji* (*KKc.* 10.4.5) | |

| A.D. | WAp. |
|---|---|
| 1200 | (1) *āyaṇṇaï, akkandaï, jāṇaï, bihiyai, suyaï, jhalahalaï, lahalahaï muṇaï, ṭhāi, karaï.* |
| | (2) *pecchēi, cintei, karei, cintae* (*Kp.* J. 34.1*) |
| | Special forms : *bruvaï, vuñaï, prassadi, gṛṇhaï* (*Kc.* & *Hc.*) |

*1st Person Plural*

| A.D. | WAp. | SAp. | EAp. |
|---|---|---|---|
| | No forms upto 1000 A.D., were traced. | | |
| 1000 | (1) *khamāvahã, ghallahã, jāṇahã, jāhã.* (2) *jāhū, muṇahū.* | *avayarahuṁ gacchāmo* (Pkt.) | .. |
| 1100 | .. | *karahuṁ, ṇavahuṁ. dekkhahuṁ jāhuṁ* (?) | .. |
| 1200 | (1) *akkhahuṁ, muṇahuṁ karahū, jāyahū* (2) *viṇṇavimō* | .. | .. |

*2nd Person Plural*

| A.D. | WAp. | SAp. | EAp. |
|---|---|---|---|
| | No forms upto 1000 A.D., were found. | | |
| 1000 | (1) *acchahu, saṁcallahu, karahu, cintijjahu* (2) *ghallah* (?) | *karaha, paḍivajjaha* | .. |
| 1100 | *icchahu* | .. | .. |
| 1200 | *acchahu, icchahu acchaha, icchaha.* | .. | .. |

*3rd Person Plural*

| A.D. | WAp. | SAp. | EAp. |
|---|---|---|---|
| 500 ? | *kīlanti* | .. | .. |
| 600-1000 | (1) *acchah , vacchah· ,* | .. | .. |
| 1000 | *maṇṇahiṁ, bujjhahiṁ.* | | .. |
| 700-1200 | (2) *bhaṇanti, mucanti* | | .. |

| A.D. | WAp. | SAp. |
|---|---|---|
| 1000 | (1) *karahiṁ, laggahiṁ, pūrahim, lahahiṁ, kaṭṭahī.* | (1) *melavahiṁ, harahiṁ, hiṇḍahiṁ.* |
| | (2) *uppajjaïṁ.* (Sdd. 22) *ḍasanti* | (2) *hūlanti, moḍantī, rahanti, ghoṭṭanti, loṭṭanti.* |
| | (3) *vaccanti, ṭhanti, dharanti, karanti,* | |
| 1100 | *acchanti, ghippanti.* | (1) *phalahiṁ, jāhiṁ, saṁcallahiṁ.* |
| | | (2) *haraïṁ, āvahiṁ.* |

| A.D. | WAp. |
|---|---|
| 1200 | (1) *āvahī, karahī, vaccahī, lahahī, khillahī, ṇi-suṇahī, dharahiṁ, cintahiṁ, daṁsahiṁ, pasaṁsahiṁ.* |
| | (2) *payampahi* (*Jdc.* 11.1), *bhaṇijjahi* (*Jdc.* 5.4). |
| | (3) *talanti, karanti, hunti, inti* (*Sn.* 15.296). |

## §136B. Present Indicative.

*1st Person Sing.*

| A.D. | WAp. | SAp. | EAp. |
|---|---|---|---|
| 500? | *-ami, -emi, -imi* | .. | .. |
| 600-1000 | *-ami* <br> *-aü̆.* | .. | .. |
| 700-1200 | .. | .. | (1) *-aũ* <br> (2) *-ami.* |
| 1000 | (1) *-aüṁ* <br> (2) *-ami* | (1) *-aüṁ, -uṁ* (*Hv.* 84.15.6) <br> (2) *-ami, -emi* (rare). | |
| 1100 | (1) *-aũ* <br> (2) *-ami, -emi* (rare) | (1) *-aüṁ* <br> (2) *-ami -emi* (*KKc.* 10.23.6) (rare). | |
| 1200 | *-aüṁ, -aũ* <br> *-ām̆i, -em - mi* (comparatively rare). | .. | .. |

| A.D. | WAp. | SAp. | EAp. |
|---|---|---|---|
| | *2nd Person Sing.* | | |
| 500 ? | .. | .. | .. |
| 600-1000 | *-ahi, -hi* | .. | .. |
| 700-1200 | .. | .. | *-asi.* |
| 1000 | *-ahi, -ehi* (not frequent)<br>*-isi* rare) | *-ahi*<br>*-asu* (*Jc.*) | ..<br>.. |
| 1100 | .. | *-ahi* | .. |
| 1200 | *-ahi*<br>*-ehi*<br>*-asi*<br>*-esi* (rare). | .. | .. |
| | *3rd Person Sing.* | | |
| 500 ? | *-aï*<br>*-eï* (rare, | .. | .. |
| 600-1000 | *-aï, -āi* (rare)<br>*-eï* (chiefly in *Cd.*) | .. | .. |
| 700-1200 | .. | .. | *-aï, -ī* (*DKs.*<br>*-iaï* (Pass.)<br>*-aa, -a* |
| 1000 | *-aï*<br>*-eï* (rare) | *-aï*<br>.. | ..<br>.. |
| 1100 | *-aï -ï* (rare<br>*etti* (*Ds.* 4.5.1) | *-aï*<br>*-ï* (rare)<br>(*KKc.* 10.4.5) | .. |
| 1200 | *-aï, -ï*<br>*-ei* (rare)<br>*-ae* (*Kp.* J. 34.1*)<br>*-di* (*Hc.* 4.393) | .. | .. |
| | *1st Person Plural* | | |
| | No forms upto 1000 A.D., were traced. | | |
| 1000 | (1) *-ahã*<br>(2) *-ahũ* | *-ahuṁ*<br>*-amo* (Pkt.) | |

| A.D. | WAp. | SAp. | EAp. |
|---|---|---|---|
| 1100 | .. | *-ahuṁ* | |
| 1200 | *-ahuṁ, -ahũ*<br>*-imō* (Pkt.) | .. | .. |

*2nd Person Plural*

No forms upto 1000 A.D. were found.

| A.D. | WAp. | SAp. | EAp. |
|---|---|---|---|
| 1000 | *-ahu*<br>*-ahã* | *-aha* | .. |
| 1100 | *-ahu* | .. | .. |
| 1200 | *-ahu*<br>*-aha.* | .. | .. |

*3rd Person Plural*

| A.D. | WAp. | SAp. | EAp. |
|---|---|---|---|
| 500 ? | *-anti* | .. | .. |
| 600-1000 | *-ahiṁ*<br>*-anti* | .. | .. |
| 700-1200 | .. | .. | .. |
| 1000 | *-ahiṁ, -ahĩ*<br>*-aiṁ,*<br>*-anti* | *-ahiṁ*<br>*-anti* | ..<br>.. |
| 1100 | *-anti* | *-ahiṁ*<br>*-aïṁ* | .. |
| 1200 | *-ahiṁ, -ahĩ*<br>*-ahĩ* (*Jdc.*)<br>*-anti, -nti.* | .. | .. |

§ 137. Even in OIA, Pres. Ind. was used in the sense of the past and the immediate Future.[33] In Ap. also it stood for the same, and was widely used for the Historical Present and for the immediate future. As this is in no way a special characteristic of Ap. it is not illustrated.

33 Bloch, *MSL.* XIV, pp. 35-6, 67 and *FLM.* §238 where he refers to Speyer, *Vedische u. Sanskrit Syntax* §§172-3.

## IMPERATIVE

§138. The following are the special terms. of the Imperative in Ap. according to Pk. grammarians. 1 p. plur. *-huṁ* (*K* 66); 2 p. sg. *-i,-u, -e, -h* (*Hc.* 4.387, *K* 64); 3p. sg. *-ū* (*K.* 65). The remaining are the same as in Pkt. In Pkts. we get the following set of terms. for this mood.[34]

*Singular*

1st p. (*-ămu*)

2nd p. zero (or *-a*), *-(a-, e-)su, -ehi,* Amg. also *-āhi.*

3rd p. *aü* Ś. Mg. Ḍh. *-adu.*

*Plural*

1st p. Amg. JM. *-āmo*; Mah. Ś. Mg. Ḍh. also JM. *-(a-, e-)mha*

2nd p. *-aha*; Ś. Mg. (Ḍh.) *-adha, -edha*; CP. *-atha.*

3rd p. *-antu.*

The Comp. Tables of the desinences of the Imp. ( §138A) show that there is a richer variety of terms. in Ap. literature than in Pk. grammars. Thus we have 11 terms. of 2. p. sg. in SAp. (1000 A.D.), 9 in WAp. (1200 A.D.), 7, but a different set of terms. in EAp. Secondly certain desinences recorded by Pk. grammarians *viz.*, 1 p. plur. *-huṁ*, 3 p. plur. *-ahĩ* (as recorded in Pischel's Gram. §467, but which is originally a term. of the Present Ind.) are either untraced or exceptional in Ap. literature. Thirdly out of this variety of morphemes only 6 are common to all regions. They are as follows :

2 p. sg. : zero (*i.e.*, *-a*), *-aha, -ahu*;

3 p. sg. : *-(a)u*, 3 p. plur. : *-(a)ntu.*

2 p. plur. : *-(a)hu*;

As expected there are no forms of 1 p. sing. and plur. *nehu* (*nayāma*) in *Sn.* 17-570 is the only exception. *-mu* in *bhañjimu* (*Sc.* 337.9), *geṇhimu* (*Sc.* 400.8) are Prakritisms.

In 2 p. sg. we have a gradual growth in the number of terms. In *Vk.* (500 A.D. ?) we have only one term. viz., *-ahi.* zero (*i.e.*, *-a*) as in *pasiya=prāsīda* is Sanskritic. This *-ahi* is traceable to OIA 'athematic' term. *-dhi* (e.g., *kṛdhi, juhudhi*) and has been extended to Pres. Ind. in Ap. (See §136). In the 10th Cent. A.D., *-ahi* srpead all over

34 Pischel. *Grammatik*. §467.

India and was the most popular term. in SAp. as is seen from ALSDORF's calculation of term. in *Hv.* [35] as given below :

*-ahi* (71), *-u* (22), *-i* (32).

It was widely used in *BhK. Sdd. Pd.* in WAp., but it (*-ahi*) is not much popular in EAp.

In 600 A.D., *-i*, *-hu*, and *-u* came to be used in WAp. (in *PPr.* and *Ys.*). Is this *-i* due to OIA passive base+zero or the loss of *-h-* in *-(a)hi* mentioned above? Thus *sevi* in *PPr.* is probably derived from OIA **sevya* if not from Ap. *sevahi.* We have *-ehi* in Pk. and *-āhi* in AMg. in pre-Ap. MIA. (See the Pk. terms. quoted above from PISCHEL's *Gram.* §467). *-hu* is obviously traceable to OIA **-thu*<OIA *-tha*~*-u* that is a contamination of Sk. 2 p. plur. *-tha* of Pres. Ind. and 3p. sg. *-u* of Imp. in Pkt. This *-u* of 3 p. sg. has affected the terms. of 2 p. sg. and plur. e.g., *-asu,* and *-esu* in Pkt., and 2 p. plur. *-ahu* and *esu* in Ap. L.H. GRAY regards this explanation of *-asu* and *-esu* more plausible[36] than the theory of regarding it as a transfer from the middle voice for OIA *-sva* and Pali *-ssu.*[37] According to PISCHEL OIA *-sva* becomes *-su.*[38] In Ap. *-u* is a characteristic ending which is added not only to terms. but to indeclinables also. Can we not apply the same reasoning to the *-u* ending terms. of Imperative 2 p. sing., instead of accepting the somewhat far-fetched process explained in GRAY's paper mentioned above.

Imp. 2 p. sg. *-u* is probably the extension of Imp. 3 p. sg. *-u* (<OIA *-tu*) to 2 p. sing. Such a direct application of terms. to the root (in suppression of the final vowel) is not unusual in Ap. e.g., Imp. 3. p. sg. *āu* 'let it come,' *aṇuhavu* (*anubhavatu*) in *Sdd.* and other texts. GRAYS in the paper mentioned above in *BSOS* VIII ii-iii, differs, and regard, Ap. *vaṭṭu* as derived from OIA **vartas*<*(a)vartas.*

In the 10th cent. A.D., a new term. viz., *-aha* appears, or is extended to Imp. 2 p. in Ap., though the forms are but few. It originated from Pres. Ind. 2 p. plur. *-(a)tha* in OIA. The confusion of numbers in Ap., and the use of the Pres. Ind. for Imp. (which is of the Pres. Tense even in OIA) are already exemplified elsewhere. *-aha* is normally unusual in contemporary SAp., although forms like *pasāheha*=*praśrāvaya* (*Jc.* 1.18.10) attest to its existence in Puṣpadanta.

Due to the paucity of published WAp. material of the 11th cent. A.D., we cannot trace all the desinences of the 10th cent. in it. In

---

35 Intro. to *Hv.* §56.
36 See *BSOS,* VIII ii-iii, 570.
37 BLOCH, *L'indo-aryen,* p. 249.
38 PISCHEL, *Grammatik,* §467.

1200 A.D., the influence of Pkt. appears very strong as the Pkt. desinences *-asu* and *-esu* (see PISCHEL *Gram.* §467) predominate. The following frequency of terms. in *Kp.* will clarify the point.[39]

Imp. 2 p. sg. : *-asu* (7), *-esu* (7), *-ahi* (2+2), *-ihi* (1), *-ĕhi* (3), *-i* (4+4), *-ā* (4), *-u* (1 in *Kp.* E. 29a)

In his remarks on these terms., ALSDORF observes that the form with *-u* ending is unusual in Somaprabha's Ap., and occurs once in a strophe in the history of Nala.[40] The fact is that *-u* was never popular in WAp. even in 1000 A.D., In SAp. of the 10th cent. (in *Hv.*), it stands for 3 p. sg. It is much more popular in EAp. where it stands next to *-aho* and *-ahu* in frequency, as will be seen from the following desinences arranged in a descending order of popularity: Imp. 2 p. sg. : *-aha, -ahu, -u, -ahi.* zero and *-ssa* are rare in EAp.

Due to the paucity of EAp. literature and unsettled chronology of some texts, it is very difficult to determine the mutual loans in WSEAp. What one finds is the popularity of certain sets of desinences in certain regions. Thus *-ahi -i* and *-u* are popular in SAp. (1000 A.D.) *-aha, -ahu* and *-u* are so in EAp.

In WAp. there is a continuous growth in the variety of terms., and these terms. have different frequencies in different centuries and works. Thus *-ahi* is very popular in 500 A.D., *-ahu, -ahi, -i* in 1000 A.D., and *-asu, -esu* in 1200 A.D.

### *3 P. Sing.*

*-u* or *-au* of 3 p. sing. is clearly traced to OIA *-tu*>Pk. *-u*. *-ahu* in WAp. (1000 A.D.) as in *accha-hu, kara-hu* is probably the extension of 2 p. sing. term. to 3 p. sing. In SAp. (1000 A.D.) we have two special terms. *-aï* and *-aïṁ*. *laïjjaï* in *Nc.* 3.7.8 is the use of the Pres. Ind. 3 p. sg. for Imp. *-aïṁ* in *vandijjaïṁ* (*Jc.* 3.31.8) is probably a scribal error for *-aï* as *-ṁ*. is inexplicable. The use of *ijja* shows the Optative influence.

### *2 P. Plural.*

1 p. plural forms are very rare and are already discussed above. The desinences of 2 p. plur. fall in three regional groups :

(1) WAp. : *-ahu, -ahŭ -aha* (1100 and 1200 A.D.)

(2) SAp. : *-ahaṁ, -aha, -ahu* (rarely).

(3) EAp. : *-aha, -ijja-ha, -ahu* (only in *DKs.*)

---

39 ALSDORF, Intro. to *Kp.* §35 (b).
40 *Ibid.*, p. 62.

As explained above *-ahu* is derived from **athu*<OIA 2 p. plur. -*(a)tha* of Pres. Ind. 13 p. sing. Imp. *-u* (<OIA-*tu*). It is the only term. in *Vk*. (500 A.D.) It persisted down to 1200 A.D., but it was superseded by *-aha* which began to appear in 1100 A.D. *-aha-* is the only term. in *Sc*. Its frequency in *Kp*. is as follows.[41]

*-aha* (2+1), *-ēha* (2), *-ahu* (1+1), *-ehu*. Suffice it to show that *-ahu* which is the only and original term. in WAp. grew less popular in the same region in the 12th cent. A.D., We can roughly indicate its history in our period thus :

i) 2 p.plur. *-ahu* { WAp. (500-1200 A.D.)
{ SAp. (slightly in 1000 A.D.)
EAp. (In Dks. in 1000 A.D.)

ii) The history of *-aha* in Ap. may be sketched as follows : Historically and linguistically it is the term. of Pres. Ind. 2 p. plur. in OIA., and has been applied to the Imp. in Ap. SAp. (1000 A.D.) uses it but rarely as in *Hv*. 87.5.16, the regular term. being *-ahaṁ*. It is popular in EAp. of the 10th cent. and WAp. of 1000-1200 A.D.

The nasal element in *-ahũ* is due to the plur. nature of the term. Thus, in Ap. Imp. 3 p. plur. is *-antu* and *-ahũ*, Pres. Ind. 1 p. plur. is *-ahũ*, 3 p. plur. is *-ahĩ*. This association of nasalisation with the plur. has descended to NIA (e.g. Marathi), though sometimes it is etymologically doubtful. *-ahũ* is thus an analogical formation from Ap. *-ahu*<OIA **-thu*. Although ALSDORF records *-ahu* as the most popular term. in *Hv*.[42] *-ahaṁ* and *-aha* are much more so in the works of Puṣpadanta. The relation between *-aha* : *-ahaṁ* is the same as that between 2 p. plur. *-ahu*: *-ahuṁ*, the nasal in the latter is analogically due to its plur. *-aha* <OIA -*(a)tha* developed in 2 p. plur *-ā* in M.

In EAp. we find *-aha*, *-ijjaha* and *-ahu* (only in *DKs*.). *-ijjaha* is nothing but the optative *-ijja*+*-aha* discussed above. *-ahu* is absent in *DKK*. and in *DKs*. It might be a loan from WAp. where it was well-established from 500 A.D.

### *3 p. plural.*

In 3 p. plur. *-antu* <Pk. OIA *-antu* is quite clear. *-ahuṁ*, *-ahũ* and *ahu* are discussed above, and this extension of 2 p. plur. found a favourable ground in Ap.

Pres. Ind. has 1 p. sg. -*(a)ũ* : Plur. -*(a)hũ*.
3 p. sg. -*(a)ĩ* : Plur. -*(a)hĩ*,

41 *Ibd*., 35 (b),
42 Intro. to *Hv*. 56.

so in Imp. we find 3 p. sg. -(*a*)*u* : plur. (*a*)*hũ*. There are many terms common to Pres. Ind. and Imp. (which is of the Present Tense from OIA. period) e.g., 2 p. sg. -*ahi*, -*hi*, -*asu*, 2 p. plur. -*ahu*, -*ahũ*, -*aha* (in corresponding centuries and in the same texts). The importance of 2 p. in Imp. made such extension more probable.

The relations between NIA 3 p. sing. -e.g., M. -*o*, Oriya -*u* Beng. -*uk*-, and Ap. -*aü*, between 3 p. plur. M. -*ot*, Oriya -*antu*, *untu*, Beng. -*un* and Ap. -*antu*, and also between Raj. Braj. 2 p. sg. -*a*, -*i* (in M. also),[43] -*ẽ*, -*ĩ* and Ap. -*ahi*, *ehi*, are already established.[44] The continuation of Imp. from MIA to NIA is well described by Bloch[45] and Ap. forms the essential connecting link between the two.

## § 138A. Imperative Mood.

*2nd p. sing.*

| A.D. | WAp. |
|---|---|
| 500 ? | (1) *akkhahi, uttārahi, ṇisammahi.* |
| | (2) *pasiya* (Sktism.) |
| 600-1000 | (1) *jāṇi, jōi, sēvi, kari.* |
| | (2) *jāṇu, laggu, viyāṇu.* |
| | (3) *cāha-hu, kahahu.* |
| | (4) Some forms of Pres. Ind. 2nd Person sg. e.g., *muṇahi, mellahi* are used in this sense. |

| A.D. | EAp. |
|---|---|
| 700- | (1) *ṇiahu, muṇahu, bhamahu, suṇahu, khāhu.* |
| 1200 | (2) *lagagha, jagaḍaha, mellaha, dekkhaha, muṇaha.* |
| | (3) *acchahi* (°*hu*), *karahi, puccha-hi.* |
| | (4) *karu, thakku, chāḍḍu, bujjhu, pekkhu.* |
| | (5-7) *cintassa* (*DKs.* 77), *puccha, cinta.* |

43 *e.g.*, ghei ghei *mājhe vāce goda nāma Vithobācē—Tukārāma.*

44 Bloch, *L'indo-aryen*, p. 249.

45 *La langue marathe* 239; *L'indo-aryen*, pp. 233 and 49.

| A.D. | WAp. | SAp. |
| --- | --- | --- |
| 1000 | (1) *bujjhahu, karahu, jāṇahu lehu, suṇahu, chaṇḍahu, cāhahu, uccallahu, galathallahu.* | (1) *suyarahi, ṇiyacchahi, ahiṇāṇahi, avaherahi, caḍavahi, paṭṭhavahi,* |
| | (2) *karahi, acchahi, millahi--harahi, dekkhahi, hohi, jhāvahi, gaṇijjahi, jampijjahi,* | *chaṇḍahi, sambharahi, khāhi.* (2-3) *tāḍahu, jāhu, āṇehu, pūrehu.* (4) *āu, haṇu, caḍu, uṭṭhuṭṭhu.* |
| | (3) *muṇehi, bhaṇehi, karahi, dehi.* | (5) *lai, melli, kari, hari, pecchi.* |
| | (4) *kari, chaṇḍi, bolli, bandhi, parihari, maṇṇi.* | (6) *mue, magge, kare.* (7) *jaya, jīva, pattiya* (Skt.) |
| | (5) *karu, viyaṇu, dikkhu, ūsaru.* | (8) *jāṇasu, kahasu, haṇasu, gacchasu, bīhasu.* |
| | (6) *pekkhaha* (*Sdd.*) | (9) *karejjasu, pujjejjasu.* (10, 11) *āyaṇṇahiṁ* (*Nc.* 1.3.1) *pasāheha* (*Jc.* 1.18.10); *ṇisuṇahuṁ* (*Jc.* 3.11.14) (Probably Infinitive). |
| 1100 | *lehi laī, dhari, geṇha.* | (1) *rovahi, jāhi, khavahi, saṁthavahi.* (2) *marehu, uttarehu, ṇavahu.* (3) *jaya* (Skt. sm.) |

| 1200 | WAp. |
| --- | --- |
| | *āgacchasu, giṇhasu, muṇasu, cintasu, bandhasu.* |
| | *ajjesu, pucchēsu, cintesu.* |
| | *karahi, dehi; muṇehi, lehi,* |
| | *sumari, kari, bhaṇi, rakkhi, kahi.* |
| | *vaccu, haru, acchu, laggu.* |
| | *peccha, vāha.* |
| | *āgaccha-ha* (*Sc.*) |
| | *kare* (*hc.*) |

*3rd Person Sing.*

| A.D. | WAp. | SAp. | EAp. |
|---|---|---|---|
| | No forms upto 1000 A.D. were found. | | |
| 1000 | (1) *aṇuhavu, āu, hou, acchaü bujjhaü, acchaü.* (2) *acchahu, karahu,* | (1) *uaḍḍaü, bhukkaü, ḍajjhaü, ṇivaḍaü, gamaü, huvaü, piṇijjau, pāvevvaü.* (2) *laïjjaï,* (*Nc.* 3.7.8) *vandijjaiṁ,* (*Jc.* 3.31.8) ? (3) *ho* (*Jc.* 2.1.17) | |
| 1100 | .. | *aṇusaraü, āruhau, leu, saṁpaḍaü.* | |
| 1200 | *ruṭṭhaü, māraü, hou, acchaü, kijjau, nisuṇaü. pecchijjaü.* | | |

*1st Person Plural.*

| | | | |
|---|---|---|---|
| 1200 | *ṇehu* (*Sn.* 17.570). *bhaṁjimu* (*Sc.* 337.9), *geṇhimu* (*Sc.* 400.8) Pktisms. | | |

*2nd Person Plural*

| | | | |
|---|---|---|---|
| 500 | *peccha-hu* | .. | |
| 600-1000 | *muṇahu, chaṇḍahu* (*Ys.*) | .. | .. |

| A.D. | SAp. | EAp. |
|---|---|---|
| 700-1200 | (1) *māṇaha, cintaha, karaha, pucchaha, dekkhaha; pattijjaha.* (2) *chaḍahu, khamahu, pellahu, dekkhahu, karahu, jāṇahu* (All in *DKs.*) | |

| A.D. | WAp. | SAp. |
|---|---|---|
| 1000 | (1) *rakkhejjahu, acchahu, akkhahu, karahu, dekkhahu.* (2) *ṇisuṇahũ.* | (1) *kuṇahaṁ, thuṇahaṁ, ṇavahaṁ, ṭhavahaṁ.* (2) *mellaha, saṁharaha.* (3) *āroḍahu, jāhu, pekkhahu.* |

| A.D. | WAp. | SAp. |
| --- | --- | --- |
| 1100 | *kahahu*<br>*cintaha* (*Sn.* 168-115 A quotation) | *aṇuhuṁjahu.*<br>*avalovahu.* |

| A.D. | WAp. |
| --- | --- |
| 1200 | (1) *muccahu, sārahu, ṇijojahu, jeyahu, karahu.*<br>(2) *acchaha, picchaha, avahīlaha, aṇuṭṭhaha, kuṇaha, āruhaha, cayaha, thuṇaha, vandijjaha,* (*Sc.* 173.7), *samejjaha* (*Sc.* 178.2); *avaharaha* (*Sc.* 599.3). |

*3rd Person Plural*

| A.D. | WAp. | SAp. |
| --- | --- | --- |
| | No forms upto 1000 A.D., were traced. | |
| 1000 | *dintu* (*Sād.*), *karantu*<br>*acchantu, karantu, jantu.* | *pasiyantu, dentu, hontu* (Intro. to *Hv.* § 56.) |
| 1100 | .. | (1) *avaharantu, saṁṭhāvantu, ghaḍantu.*<br>(2) *Saṁpajja-hauṁ.* |
| 1200 | (1) *pīḍantu*<br>(2) *vivva-hu* (*Sn.* 16-286) | |

## § 138B. Imperative Mood

*1st Person Singular*

No forms of Imperative 1st Person sing. were traced.

*2nd Person Singular*

| A.D. | WAp. | SAp. | EAp. |
| --- | --- | --- | --- |
| 500 ? | *-hi*<br>-zero (Sktism.) | .. | .. |
| 600-1000 | *-i*<br>*-u*<br>*-hu* | .. | .. |

(Sometimes *-hi* of the Pres. Ind. 2 p. sg.)

| A.D. | WAp. | SAp. | EAp. |
|---|---|---|---|
| 700-1200 | .. | .. | *-ahu*<br>*aha-*<br>*-ahi*<br>*-u*<br>*-ssa*<br>zero. |
| 1000 | *-ahu*<br>*-ahi, -ehi*<br>*-i*<br>*-u*<br>*-ha* | *-ahi*<br>*-ahu, -ehu.*<br>*-u*<br>*-i*<br>*-e*<br>*-a*<br>*-asu, -ejjasu*<br>*-ahiṁ*<br>*-eha* | .. |
| 1100 | *-ehi*<br>*-i*<br>zero (i.e., *-a*) | *-ahi, -hi*<br>*-(e)hu*<br>zero (i.e., *-a*) | |
| 1200 | *-asu, -esu*<br>*-ahi, -ehi*<br>*-i*<br>*-u*<br>zero (i.e., *-a*)<br>*-aha*<br>*-e* (rare). | .. | .. |

*3rd Person Singular*

No forms upto 1000 A.D., were traced.

| A.D. | WAp. | SAp. | EAp. |
|---|---|---|---|
| 1000 | *-aü, -u*<br>*-ahu* | *-aü, -u*<br>(*-ijja*) *-u*,<br>(*-evva*)*-v*,<br>(*-ijja*)*-i*<br>zero | .. |
| 1100 | .. | *-u* | .. |
| 1200 | *-aü, -u*<br>-(*-ijja*)*-u*. | .. | .. |

*1st Person Plural*

Only one form with *-ehu* in *Sn*, 17-570 (in 1200 A.D.) was found

*2nd Person Plural*

| A.D. | WAp. | SAp. | EAp. |
|---|---|---|---|
| 500 ? | *-ahu* | .. | .. |
| 600-1000 | *-ahu* (*Ys.*) | .. | .. |
| 700-1200 | .. | .. | *-aha*, *-ijjaha*<br>*-ahu* (All in *DKs.*) |
| 1000 | (1) *-ahu* | *-ahaṁ* | .. |
| | (2) *-ahũ* | *-aha*<br>*-ahu* (*Hv.* 86.9.3) | |
| 1100 | *-ahu*<br>*-aha* | *-ahu* | .. |
| 1200 | *-ahu*<br>*-aha*, (*-ijja*)*-ha*<br>*-eha* (*Sc.* 599.3) | | |

*3rd Person Plural*

Forms upto 1000 A.D., were not traced.

| A.D. | WAp. | SAp. | EAp. |
|---|---|---|---|
| 1000 | (*a*)*ntu* | -(*a*)*ntu* | .. |
| 1100 | .. | -(*a*)*ntu*<br>*-ahuṁ.* | .. |
| 1200 | (*a*)*ntu*<br>*ahu* (*Sn.* 16 286.) | .. | .. |

FUTURE

§ 139. In Ap. there are two sets of terms. of the Future—the *-sa* type, and the *-ha* type. In Pkts. also we meet with these two types.[46] The following are the desinences in Ap. literature :

46 Pischel, *Gram.*, § 520. For the discussion of different verbs, see §§ 521-34.

(i) THE *-sa* FUTURE.

*Singular.*

1 p. WSAp. *-esami, -sami*; WAp. *-isu, -esu, -su.*

2 p. WSAp. *-esahi*, WAp. *-sahi, -īsi, -issasi* (Sanskritism).

3 p. WSAp. ; *-esaï, -saï* WAp. *-isaï, -issaï* ( do. )

SAp. *-esahi.*

*Plural*

1 p. WSAp. *-esahũ*, WAp. *-issahũ*, *-isahũ*, SAp. *-sahiṁ.*

3 p. WSAp. *-sahiṁ*, WAp. *-esahiṁ*, *-issahĩ.*

(ii) THE *-ha* FUTURE.

*Singular*

1 p. WSAp. *-ī̆himi* , WAp. *-hissu* (*ha-issu*), WAp. *-hu.*

2 p. WSAp. *-ī̆hisi, -hi* ; WAp. *-ihahi, -hisi*, SAp. *-ehi.*

3 p. WAp. *-ihaï -ehaï, -ihihaï, -hii, -hī*, SAp. *-haï.*

*Plural.*

3 p. SAp *-ihinti, -hinti, -ihahĩ, -hahiṁ.*

These two sets of terms. disclose that the terms. of the Pres. Ind. are added to the augments *-sa* and *-ha*, both of which are traceable to OIA *-sya* of the 2nd Future. TURNER has shown that this *-ha* Future is 'a special treatment of *-ssa-*>*-s-* in a terminational element' seen also in Mg. Gen. sg. *puttāha*, Ap. *puttaha*, °*hŏ*. This *-ssa-*<OIA *-sya* is obvious.[47] As noted by JACOBI[48] *-ha* future is Prakritic, and *-esa, -issa, -isa* etc., are the augments derived from OIA *-sya.*

In SAp. *-sa* Future appears to be popular as 51 : 11 is the proportion of the two types in *Hv.*[49], and M. preserves only the *-sa* future (though a few *-ha* future forms are occasionally found in SAp.) WAp. discloses a confused state to which we can trace the different sets of Future desinences in NIA of that region e.g., the *-sa* future in Guj., the *-ha* future of Marwari, Braj., Bundeli, and the mixed state in Bhilli on the borders of Gujarat.[50] Although the confusion is witnessed in Ap. literature the bifurcations of these Futures are a post—Ap. development.

Future forms are rarely used in EAp. In *DKs.* 38, *basiau*<**basihau* <**vasiṣyatha*=*vatsyatha* is the only form.

47 TURNER, *JRAS* 1927, pp. 232-5 ; *BSOS* V (1930), 50, VI (1932), 531.
48 Intro. to *Sc.* I Grammatik § 24, p. 17.
49 ALSDORF, Intro. to *Hv.* § 58 (a) and (b).
50 BLOCH, *FLM.* § 241 ; also *L'indo-aryen*, p. 250.

## § 139A. Future

| A.D. | WAp. | SAp. | EAP. |
|---|---|---|---|
| | *1st Person Singular.* | | |
| 500 ? | *sahīhimi* | .. | .. |
| 600-1000 | .. | .. | .. |
| 700-1200 | .. | .. | .. |
| 1000 | *hosami* | *pariṇesami*<br>*kīlihimi, picchihimi* | .. |
| 1100 | .. | *hosomi, pālesami.* | .. |
| 1200 | *pāvisu, dalisu, jāïsu, kerisu,*<br>*desu, pekkhesu* (*Sc.*)<br>*hohissu* (*Sn.* 306-169).<br>*ṇamaṁsa-hu* (*Sn.* 238-271) | .. | .. |
| | *2nd Person Singular* | | |
| 500 ? | *jāṇihisi, karīhisi.* | .. | .. |
| 600-1000 | *karīsi, gamīsi, lahīsi*<br>*sahīsi.* | .. | .. |
| 700-1200 | .. | .. | .. |
| 1000 | (1) *pāvahi, jāhi,*<br>(2) *tarihahi* (*Sdd.* 67)<br>(3) *hosahi*<br>(4) *lahesahi.* | (1) *pekkhesahi*<br>(2) *bhamihīsı.*<br>(3) *paḍi-vajjahi, vivajjahi* (*Jc.*) | .. |
| 1100 | .. | (1) *lahesahi, karesahı pālesahi*<br>(2) *lahehi* (*KKc.* 2.8.10) | .. |
| 1200 | *ciṭṭhihisï, laṅghihısï.*<br>*hohısi, kāhisi* (<*kar*) *Kp.* S. 84.2) | | |
| | *3rd Person Singular* | | |
| 500 | .. | .. | .. |
| 600-1000 | *karesaï, lahesaï, hosaï* | .. | .. |

| A.D. | WAp. | SAp. | EAp. |
|---|---|---|---|
| 700-1200 | .. | .. | .. |
| 1000 | (1) *karesaï acchesaï, kahesaï lahesaï*<br>(2) *hosaï, esaï*<br>(3) *paḍisaï.* | (1) *mellesaï, luṇesaï, bajjhesaï, bhuṁjesaï.*<br>(2) *hosaï, pahosaï,*<br>(3) *āvesahi* (*Hv.*) | |
| 1100 | .. | *pāvesaï, āvesaï, lahesaï-hosaï,*<br>*hohaï,* (*KKc.* 1.16.15). | .. |
| 1200 | (1) *jiṇihaï, harihaï, karihaï, marihaï.*<br>(2) *laṅghihihaï* (*Kp.* E. 28).<br>(3) *hohii; pāḍijjihii* (*Sc.*)<br>(4 & 5) *hohī* (*Sn.*), *hohi, jāhī*<br>(6) *bhavissaï*<br>(7) *karisaï, hoisaï,*<br>(8) *hosaï.* | | |

*1st Person Plural*

Forms upto 1000 A.D., were not found.

| A.D. | WAp. | SAp. | EAp. |
|---|---|---|---|
| 1000 | .. | *hosahiṁ* (*Jc.* 2.22.5)<br>*laesahũ* (*Hv.* 85.20.5) | .. |
| 1100 | .. | .. | .. |
| 1200 | *purisahũ, sevissahũ*<br>*karisahũ, thakisahũ*<br>*jīvesahũ.* | .. | .. |

*2nd Person Plural*

None were traced.

*3rd Person Plural*

No forms upto 1000 A.D., were found.

| A.D. | WAp. | SAp. | EAp. |
|---|---|---|---|
| 1000 | *bhajesahiṁ*<br>*hosahī* | *karihinti*<br>*khāhinti.* | .. |
| 1100 | .. | *hosahiṁ, cadesahiṁ*<br>*hohahiṁ.* | .. |
| 1200 | *paḍissahī, jaṇissahī* | .. | .. |

## § 139B. Future.

| A.D. | WAp. | SAp. | EAp. |
|---|---|---|---|
| | *1st Person Singular.* | | |
| 500 | *-īhimi* | .. | .. |
| 600-1000 | .. | .. | .. |
| 700-1200 | .. | .. | .. |
| 1000 | *-sami* (*BhK.*) | *-esami*<br>*-ihimi* | .. |
| 1100 | .. | *-sami*<br>*-esami* | .. |
| 1200 | (1) *-isu*<br>(2) *-esu*, *-su* (*Sc.*)<br>(3) *-hissu* (*Sn.* 306-169)<br>(4) *-hu* (*Sn.* 238-271). | .. | .. |
| | *2nd Person Singular* | | |
| 500 ? | *-ĭhisi* | .. | .. |
| 600-1000 | *-īsi* | .. | .. |
| 700-1200 | .. | .. | .. |
| 1000 | (1) *-hi*<br>(2) *-ihahi*<br>(3) *-sahi*<br>(4) *-esahi.* | *-esahi*<br>*-ihīsi*<br>*-hi* (*Jc.*) | ..<br>.. |
| 1100 | .. | *-esahi*<br>*-ehi* (*KKc.* 2.8.10) | .. |
| 1200 | *-ihisi*<br>*-hisi.* | .. | .. |
| | *3rd Person Singular* | | |
| 500 ? | .. | .. | .. |
| 600-1000 | *-esaï*<br>*-saï* | ..<br>.. | ..<br>.. |
| 700-1200 | .. | .. | .. |

| A.D. | WAp. | SAp. | EAp. |
|---|---|---|---|
| 1000 | (1) *-esaï* | *-esaï* | .. |
| | (2) *-saï* | *-saï* | |
| | (3) *-isaï* | *-ēsahi* (*Hv.*) | |
| 1100 | .. | *-esaï* | .. |
| | | *-saï* | |
| | | *-haï* | .. |
| 1200 | (1) *-ihaï* | .. | |
| | (2) *-ihihaï* (*Kp.* E. 28) | | |
| | (3) *hii* | | |
| | (4) *-hī* (*Sn.* 15-141) | | |
| | (5) *-hi* (*Kp. Sc.*) | | |
| | (6) *-issaï* (*Sc.*) | | |
| | (7) *-isaï* (*Sc.*) | | |
| | (8) *-saï* | | |

*1st Person Plural*

Forms upto the 10th cent. A.D., were not traced.

| A.D. | WAp. | SAp. | EAp. |
|---|---|---|---|
| 1000 | (*esa*)*-hã* | *-sahiṁ* (*Jc.* 2.22.5) | |
| | (Intr. to *BhK.* § 36 p. *41) | *-esahũ* (*Hv.* 85.20.5) | |
| 1100 | .. | .. | .. |
| 1200 | (1) *-issahũ* | .. | .. |
| | (2) *-isahũ* | | |
| | (3) *-ēsahũ* | | |

*2nd Person Plural*

No forms of the 2nd Plural were found.

*3rd Person Plural*

No forms upto 1000 A.D. were found

| A.D. | WAp. | SAp. | EAp. |
|---|---|---|---|
| 1000 | *-esahiṁ* | *-ihinti* | .. |
| | *-sahī* | *-hinti* | |
| 1100 | .. | *-sahiṁ, -esahiṁ* | .. |
| | | *-hahiṁ.* | |
| 1200 | *-issahĩ* | .. | .. |

### THE PAST

§ 140. In Ap. the past tense was expressed by the pp. of the verb with the auxiliary √*as* or √*bhū* 'to be' expressed or implied (generally the latter), e.g., *Hv.* 81.10.9, 82.8.6 etc. The *-la* suffix of the Past does not yet appear to have gained literary status,[51] though it became an augment of the Past in many NIA languages. Sanskritisms of this tense in Ap. are exceptional. A few forms of the Past are given below : *ahēsi*=*abhūt* (*Sc.* 447.8), *ṇisuṇiuṁ*=*nyaśruṇvaṁ* (*Mp.* 2.4.12); *sahu*=*asahe*. For a few more forms of √*as* see §144.

### THE OPTATIVE

§ 141. As in Pkts. *-ijja* characterises the Optative in Ap. It is also the augment of the Passive in Ap., and it is sometimes difficult to distinguish between the two. The Optative *-ijja* is a successor of *-eyya* of the Primary Pkts., while the Passive *-ijja* is traceable to *-iya* or *-iy(y)a* of Literary Pkts. Optative forms without the augment *-ijja* e.g., 2 p. sg. *vaṭṭe* and Sanskritisms e.g. *soceya* (*śocayet*) are exceptional. *-ijja* forms are common to WSAp, and none were traced in EAp.

The following are some of the instances of the Optative in Ap. :
2 p. sg. : WAp *acchijjahi*, *acchijjahu* (*accha-* 'to be')

SAp. *bhuṁjejjasu* (*bhuj-*), *ṇivasijjasu* (*ni-vas-*) *jiṇejjasu* (*ji-*).
3 p. sg. : SAp. *viraijjaï* (*vi-rac-*), *saṁtosijjaï* (*saṁ-tuṣ-*), *vandijjaï* (*vand-*).

In *Kp.* we have *-ijja* for all persons : e.g., 2 p. sg. *dejja* (*dā-*), 3 p. sg. *caïjja* (*tyaj-*), *bhamijja* (*bhram*). SAp. *soceya* (*śuc-*) in *Nc.* 9.20.12 is a pure Sanskritism. *-iavva* forms are from OIA suffix of Pot. Part *-tavya*.

The Optative in Ap. is a continuation of pre-Ap. IA with due allowance to phonological changes.[52] The Optative in Ap. stands for the OIA Potential Mood (e.g. see *Nc.* 3.2.14, 3.3.10), and the Imperative, and as such shows possibility, necessity, compulsion, etc.

### DENOMINATIVES

§ 142. As in OIA, denominatives are used throughout the Ap. period and in all regions. To take a few examples :

WAp. *jh(j-)agaḍaï*, < *jhakaṭa* 'a quarrel,' *hakkāraï* <*hakāra* 'calling out,' *bubbuyahi* < *budbuda* "a bubble,"

---

51 In his Intro. to *Ap. kāvya-trayī*, L. B. GANDHI quotes 2 *-la* forms of the pest from the language of the Marathas in the 8th cent. A.D. The forms are *diṇṇale* (*dā-*), *gahille* (*grah-*) and are note l by Udyotana in *Kuvalayanālā* (1778 A.D.).
52 See BLOCH, *L'indo-aryen*, pp. 233-34 and PISCHEL, *Gram.* §§ 459-66.

EAp. *bakkhāṇaī bakkhāṇijja-i-*....................

SAp. *vakkhāṇaï* <*vyākhāna* 'a lecture,' *raṇḍami raṇḍā*, 'a widow, a term of abuse to women,' *duguṁcchavi* < *duguṁchā* = *jugupsā* 'disgust, abhorrence,' *sandāṇai*<*sandāna* 'a bond' cf. *Hc.* 8.4.67, *ahiṇāṇaï abhijñāna* 'recognition'

The conjugation of the denominatives is like that of other verbs in Ap.

## Duplicate Verbs

§ 143. The duplication of the verbal base to express intensity, frequency or repetition is quite common in OIA. In Ap. we find such forms, and sometimes they have become a part of the NIA verbal bases e.g., *vaḍavaḍaï* (*vad-*) 'to talk idly, to prattle' cf. M. *baḍbaḍṇẽ*; *ḍhaṇḍholanta* (=*bhramat*) cf. M. *dhāṇḍolṇẽ*, H. *dhandhornā*, *jhalahalaï* (√*jval-*) 'to shine' cf. M. *jhaḷajhaḷṇẽ* or *jhaḷāḷṇẽ*, H. *jhaljhalānā*; *dedehī* (*dā-*), *jajjāhi* (√*yā-*), *gammagammaï* (*gaṁgamyate*<√*gam-*) *gahagahaī* (*gāhate*). These bases are different from onomatopoeic reduplicatives e.g., WAp. *ghavaghavanta* (?) 'glittering,' EAp. *khusakhusahi* 'whispers', SAp. *salasalaï* 'rustles,' *gumagumanta* 'trumpeting of elephants.'

There is nothing peculiar regarding the conjugation of these verbs.

## Defective Verbs

§ 144. The verb √*as* 'to be' is defective in Ap. We find WSAp. *mhi* (*asmi*), WSEAp. *atthi* (*asti*) both Pres. and Past 3 p. sg., and *atthu* (*astu*) Imp. 3 p. sg. Forms of √*as* 'to be' noted by Pischel (in *Grammatik* §498) are occasionally met with in Ap., but they, being Prakritisms, are not mentioned here. √*ho* is related to √*bhū* and not to √*as-*. WSAp. *āsī* (*āsīt*) is the only Ap. past of √*as-* (e.g., *Hv.* 92.18.13), but is used in the 1st and 2nd p. as well.

## Negatives

§ 145. In Ap. negation is expressed by the use of OIA particles *na* and *mā*. With the exception of *Hc.* 8.4.418 and the illustrative verses (and those in *Kc.* also), OIA *mā* (Ap. *maṁ*) seems less in vogue, and the use of OIA *na*+√*as-* was more popular. Its regularisation was complete in NIA but Ap. forms *e.g.*, *ṇahiṁ*, *ṇāhĭ* or *ṇāhi*, *natthi*—all are traceable to OIA *nāsti*. These are found in WSEAp. regions, and are the predecessors of negatives in NIA.

## NOMINAL FORMS OF VERBS

§ 146. The Present, the Past Passive and the Future Participles, Infinitives and Absolutives are the important nominal forms of verbs in Ap. Out of these the last two are indeclinables. They are treated below in the above-mentioned order.

### PRESENT PARTICIPLES

§ 147. Apart from Sanskritisms and Prakritisms, Ap. takes *-anta* Fem. *-antī̆*), and *-māṇa* (Fem. *-māṇā*, *-māṇī*) with or without the stem-widening *-au* or *-ao* as the terms. of the Present Participles. *-anta* and *-māṇa* are found in Pkts. also. [53] We cannot follow ALSDORF in accepting *-ira* as the suffix of the Pres. Part. even in *Kp.*[54] *-ira* shows habit (*tācchīlye* ) which may sometimes be interpreted like the Pres. Part. e.g., *ṇiyacchira* (*ṇiyaccha-* 'to see'), *cāvira* (*carvat*) 'biting', *pathippira* (*pra-* √*stip-*) 'dripping down' in SAp. in the 10th cent. The 9 forms in *Kp.* e.g., *bhamira* (*bhram-*), *kampira* (*kamp-*), *hasira* (*has-*), *vĕvira* (*vep-*) etc. can be explained as habit-showing ones. EAp. does not possess *-ira* and- *māṇa*. It shows *-anta*, *-ante*, *-anto*, *-āte* which are nothing but different forms of *-anta*. *-anta* and *-māṇa* are found in WSAp. (irrespective of its original *pada* in OIA). These are uninterrupted developments of OIA and have been handed down to NIA.[55] Out of these *-anta* is very popular as it is found in WSEAp. and in NIA of all regions.[56]

Ap. being a 'classical' literature, is under the influence of Sanskrit and Prakrits, and archaisms e.g., *enta* (*ā-*√*i-*), *janta* (*yā-*), *denta* (*dā-*), *ṭhanta* (*sthā-*) are frequently met with. The details regarding the use of the Pres. Part. in IA[57] show that Ap. occupies a very important place in the formation of NIA tenses and syntax—a common ground where MIA shades off into different NIA usages.

### § 147A. PRESENT PARTICIPLES :

| A.D. | WAp. | | EAp. |
|---|---|---|---|
| 500 ? | *bhamanta*, *jantī* | .. | .. |
| 600-1000 | *jaṇantu*, *vasantu*, *muṇantu* | | |
| | *sahantu*; *lahanto*. | | |

53 PISCHEL, *Grammatik* §§ 560-63.

54 Intro. to *Kp.* § 35, p. 62. ALSDORF is, however, cautious in his statement : 'Dem. p. pr. *gleichwertig* ist das adj. auf. -ira, von dem in unsern Texten folgende 9 Bildungen vorkommen.' The underlining is ours.

55 BLOCH, *L'indo-aryen*, pp. 259-61.

56 BLOCH, *FLM*. § 255 and *L'indo-aryen*, p. 259.

57 *L'indo-aryen*, pp. 261-9.

| | | |
|---|---|---|
| 700-1200 | .. | *kahanta, pharanta, jāṇanta, janta,*<br>*abanta* ; *ramanto.*<br>*khāyante, cāhāte, milante.* |

| A.D. | WAp. | SAp. |
|---|---|---|
| 1000 | *joyanta, ḍhaṇḍholanta, rillanta.*<br>*khantu, jhāyantu* ;<br>*uttārantī, āucchantī, cavantī.* | *ohaṭṭanta, dhagadhaganta, magganta, vaccanta, kuṇanta, jiyanta honta, hunta, havanta hontau* (*Jc.* 3.37.17).<br>*vijjijamāṇa.*<br>*cāvira* (*Hv.* 85.11.14).<br>*pathippira* (*Jc.* 3.9.1) ? |
| 1100 | *denta, bhaṇanta*<br>*jantaü*; *āḍhantao* | *khanta, vihasantĭ*<br>*bhaggamāṇu.* |

| 1200 | WAp. |
|---|---|

*bahiranta, rasanta, ḍhalanta, āgacchanta, vilasanta, gaḍayaḍanta, buḍḍantaü, alahantau, paribhamantu, ṇiharantu, hammantu, haṇantaüṁ bhavantā* (√*bhram-*).
*āgamira, hallira, bhamira, parisakkira.*

## § 147B. Present Participles.

(The case terminations and Feminine suffixes are excluded.)

| A.D. | WAp. | SAp. | EAp. |
|---|---|---|---|
| 500 ? | *-anta, -nta* | .. | .. |
| 600-1000 | *-anta* | .. | .. |
| 700-1200 | .. | .. | *-anta,*<br>*-nta*<br>*-āta.* |
| 1000 | *-anta*<br>*-nta* | *-anta, -nta*<br>*-māṇa* } rarely.<br>*ira* ? } | |

| A.D. | WAp. | SAp. | EAp. |
|---|---|---|---|
| 1100 | *-anta, -nta* | *-anta, -nta*<br>*-māṇa* (rare). | .. |
| 1200 | *-anta, -nt*<br>*-ira*<br>(*-māṇa* Prakritic & rare). | .. | .. |

PAST PASSIVE PARTICIPLES

§ 148. A reference to Comp. Tables (§148A) will show that *-ia, -iu, -iya, -iyau, -iaa, -iau* are the suffixes of pp. participles in WSEAp. All these are traceable to OIA *-i-ta* which has been progressively normalised in Pāli and Pkt., and is found in the NIA of the midland today (and with *-la* in other provinces).[58] This *-ita* with or without the stem-widening pleonastic *-ka* is applied to :

(i) the Prakritic forms of Sanskrit roots. and (ii) the *deśī* roots.

Thus for example (i) Ap. *viṇṇaviya, bisariaü* are not directly derived from OIA *vi-√jñā, vi-√smṛ:-.* but from the Prākrit roots *√viṇṇava* and *√bisara* with the suffixes *-iya, -iaü* <OIA *-ita*, while (ii) *chaḍḍia* <*√chaḍḍa-*, *phullia*<*√phulla kokkiya*<*√kokka-* etc., are the examples of the latter. *-ita* is the chief suffix of pp. in all regions throughout the Ap. period.

In addition to these *-ita* forms we have the following types of pp. participles in Ap. :

1) Phonological descendants of OIA pp. forms both *seṭ* and *aniṭ* e.g.

WSAp. *kaa, kaya, kiya, kaïya* (*kṛta*), *catta* (*tyakta*),

SAp. *hua, hūvau, hūva* (*bhūta*).

EAp. *kahia, kahiya* (*kathita*).

2) Direct combination of the root (even *desī* ones) and the pp. suffixes. Such formations are found in NIA today.[59]

(i) In the case of Sk. roots : *diṇṇa* (**didna*), *ruṇṇa* (**rud-na*), *mukka* (**muk-na*), *naṭṭa* (**nṛtta*) etc. These are represented as *datta, rudita, mukta, nartita* in classical Sk.

(ii) In the case of deśī roots : *ghitta*<*√ghiva* or *√ghippa*, *abbhiṭṭa*<*√abbhiḍa*, also *abbhiḍia*, *vicchitta* <*vi-√chiva-* cf. *Hc.* 4.257-8, *chiddha*<*√chuha=kṣip-*, *ḍhukka*<*√ḍhauka* etc. These are *aniṭ* type of formations in *deśī* roots.

58 BLOCH, *FLM.* § 256 and *Ibid.*, pp. 269-70.
59 BLOCH, *L'indo-aryen*, pp. 269-70.

3) Phonological descendants of reconstructed OIA pp. participles See 2 (i) above. The geminated forms e.g., *latta* <**lap-ta*, *hitta*<*hṛta* are MIA modifications of colloquial OIA forms.

PP. forms in -*a* e.g., *phāraa*<*sphārita* (*DKs.* 109), *paruṭṭhāba*< *paristhāpita* (*DKs.* 50) are the speciality of EAp. -*ĭ* endings as in *aṇi*< *ānīta* (*Pd.* 99), *muṇḍī*<*muṇḍita* (*DKs.* 5), *khettī*<*kṣetrita* (*Sdd.* 55), *buḍḍī* <**buḍḍiya* 'sub-merged, lost' (*Jdu.* 62.2) are due to the loss of final -*a* in -*ia* or -*iya*<OIA -*ita*. -*uya* endings e.g., *caṭṭuya* 'purified,' *cāluya* 'sifted' are on the analogy of -*iya* suffix.

Ap. literature including EAp. (where the old Bengali chants ascribed to Kāṇha and Saraha give us a number of -*la* forms e.g., *rundhelā*, *āilā gelā*), does not attest to the -*la* past tense which is common in 'Outer', NIA languages. Was it current in spoken Ap. as attested in the forms *diṇṇale* (*dā*-), *gahille* (*grah*) in the 8th cent. A.D., in Udyotana's *Kuvalayamālā*? [60] The use of pp. and their influence on NIA are already traced by BLOCH.[61]

## § 148A. PAST PASSIVE PARTICIPLES

| A.D. | WAp. | SAp. | EAp. |
|---|---|---|---|
| 500 ? | (1) *pasaria*, *khuhia*, *jhakārie* (*Mt.* 31) | | .. |
| | (2) *kaa*, *diṇṇa*, *ṇaa*. | .. | .. |
| 600-1000 | (1) *viṇṇaviu*, *payāsia*, *pariṭṭhiyau*. (2) *tatta*, *vibhiṇṇau*, *pattu*, *ṇibhaṁtu*. | .. | .. |
| 700-1200 | .. | .. | (1) *muṇia*, *saṁjai*, *bisariaü*, *kahia*, *kahiya*, *tuḍia*, *tuṭṭiaa*, *birahia*, *sohiya*. (2) *muṇḍī* (*DKs.*5) *phāraa* (*DKs.*109), *pariṭṭhāba* (*DKs.* 50). |

60 L. B. GANDHI, *Intro. to Ap. Kāvyatrayī*.
61 BLOCH, *L'indo-aryen*, pp. 271-80.

| A.D. | WAp. | SAp. |
|---|---|---|
| 1000 | *chaḍḍia, phullia, vaviyau,* | (1) *gaṁjolliya, halliya,* |
| | *bhāiya, vasiya, purāiu, uṭṭiya,* | *kokkiya, kokkāviya,* |
| | *kappariya, ukkhambhiya,* | *ḍeviya, ohāmiya, ghuliyaü,* |
| | *allaviya, kisiya, kaiya.* | *acchoḍiu, caṭṭuya* (*Jc.*) |
| | (2) *catta, ṭṭhiya, rīṇa,* | *galatthi*(*cchi*)*ya,* |
| | *visaṭṭa, āṇī* (*Pd.* 99), *ālatta,* | *mokkaliya, uddāliya,* |
| | *ummilla, uvalagga, vihāya,* | *khuḍia, uḍḍāviya,* |
| | *kilīṇa, kaya, kiya.* | |

| A.D. | WAp. | SAp. |
|---|---|---|
| 1000 | | *baïṭṭha, hittiya, palhatthiya* |
| | | (*palhatthau.*) |
| | | (2) *abbhiṭṭa, vicchitta,* |
| | | *ghitta, ḍhukka, bhulla,* |
| | | *jhīṇau, hūvau, ruṇṇa, ṇaṭṭa,* |
| | | *hitta, latta, aṭṭa.* |
| 1100 | (1) *vahelia, calliu,* | (1) *turia, parajjiya,* |
| | *uṇṇāmia, ullasia, pīḍia,* | *uccāiu, piṇia, bolliu,* |
| | *vivillia.* | *uddāṇiya, chuddhiyā.* |
| | (2) *kantao, visaṭṭha.* | (2) *hūva, hu*(*KKc.* 1.2.7), *kīya.* |
| 1200 | (1) *ubbhaviu, dhariya, kaḍayaḍiya,* | |
| | *āvariya, jhampio, taliu,* | |
| | *jhalakkiyau.* | |
| | (2) *buḍḍī, appaḍihaya, āyaḍḍa,* | |
| | *palhattha, raḍḍa, chūḍha,* | |
| | *viḍhatta, ḍakka, bhugga.* | |
| | *palitta* | |

## § 148B. Past Passive Participles

(Case-terminations and Feminine suffixes are deleted).

Forms phonologically derived from Sk. *aniṭ* formations and analogical forms from *deśi* roots are not noted here.

| A.D. | WAp. | SAp. | EAp. |
|---|---|---|---|
| 500 | *-ia* | .. | .. |
| 600-1000 | *-ia, -iu, -iyaü* | .. | .. |
| 700-1200 | .. | .. | *-ia, -iya, -iaa, -iau. -a* |
| 1000 | *-ia, -iya* | *-iya* ; *-ia, -iu -uya.* -gemination. | .. |
| 1100 | *-ia, -iu* | *-ia, -iya -iu.* | |
| 1200 | *-iya, -iyau, -iu.* | | |

## Future and Obligatory Participles

§ 149. The following are the suffixes of these participles according to Pk. grammarians :

*-ievvaüṁ, -evvaüṁ, -evā* (*Hc.* 8.4.438),

*-evvaï, eppaï, -evva* (*Tr. Ld.* 3.3.17) ;

*-iavva, -ievvaüṁ* (for Neut. only *Pu.* 17.38),

*-ivvaṁ ?* (*Ki* 5.22)—the last four according to the Eastern School of Pk. grammarians.

In SAp. *-evva(ya)*, *-evaya*, Masc. Plur. *-evā* and Fem. *-evī* and Prākritisms ending in *-avvaũ* (*-tavyaka*), *-aṇijja* (*-anīya*) are found. WAp. favours *-avvu* especially in the latter half of the 12th cent. A.D., whence we have Guj. Infinitive in *-vũ*. In EAp. *-iba*<OIA *-tavya* is the most common term. upto 10th cent. i.e. in *DKS.* In *DKn* (circa 1300 A.D.) we find *-aï, -auï* and *-ao.*

Out of these OIA and Pali *-eyya* (e.g. Ved. *stuṣeyya*, *śapatheyya*, Pa, *pūjaneyya*<√*pūj-*), and Sk. *-tavya* developed into SAp. *-avva(va)*, *-evaya*. *-evā*. Most probbably *-tavya* developed into the Prakritisms in *-avvaũ* WAp. *-avvu* and EAp. *-ıba*. Prakritisms with *-anta* and *-māṇa* added to the *-ssa* augment of the Future are sometimes found.

### § 149A. Obligatory and Potential Passive Participles

| A.D. | WAp. | SAp. | EAp |
|---|---|---|---|
| 500 ? | *avicalliu* | .. | .. |
| 600-1000 | .. | .. | .. |
| 700-1200 | .. | .. | *sugoppa* (*DKs*. 95) *bādhā* (*DKs*. 90), *bande* (*DKs*. 10) |
| 1000 | *dekkhevaa* (*Sdd*. 39) In *BhK*. gerunds, e.g. *carivvau*, *khaṇḍivvau*. | *joevvau*, *dharevvau*, *jāṇevvī*, *mārevvau*, *vaṁcevvaa*, *jāevaa*. | |
| 1100 | .. | .. | .. |
| 1200 | *karievvaüṁ*; *karevvaüṁ*. *sarevau*, *karevā*. Pktism. e.g., *duggijjha*, *duggejjhaüṁ*. | .. | .. |

### § 149B. Obligatory and Potential Passive Participles

| A.D. | WAp. | SAp. | EAp. |
|---|---|---|---|

No Sanskritisms and Prakritisms are noticed here. Few pure Ap. developments upto 1000 A.D., were found.

| | | | |
|---|---|---|---|
| 1000 | *-evaa* *-ivvaü* | *-evvaü* *-evvaa* *-evva* *-evaa*. | |
| 1100 | .. | .. | .. |
| 1200 | *-evvaüṁ* *-evaü*, *-evā*. | .. | |

## Infinitive

§ 150. The Western and Southern Pk. grammarians—the 'Western School'—admit the following Infinitive suffixes : *-evaṁ, aṇa, aṇahaṁ, -aṇahiṁ*, and *-eppi, -eppiṇu -evi -eviṇu* (*Hc.* 4.491, *Tr.* 3.3.29, followed by *Sh.* and *Ld.*) The Eastern Pk. grammarians do the same, but *Pu.* 17.36 is a defective *sūtra.* '(*tumo*) + *edaṇahuṁ ṇaṁ ṇahiṁ* + *eppi eppiṇu -evayaḥ*' is the text in Nitti-Dolci's edition. According to her interpretation *-evaṁ* (?), *-nahuṁ, -ṇam, -nahiṁ, -eppi, -eppiṇu* and *-evi* are the Infinitive suffixes.[62] It appears that *Pu.* took into account the final *a* of the roots, and implied *-aṇaṁ, aṇahuṁ, -aṇahiṁ* in the suffixes *-ṇaṁ, ṇahuṁ* and *ṇahiṁ. Ki* 5.55 also prescribes *-evi, eppi, eppiṇu, -aṇaṁ, aüṁ*, and *-evvauṁ.*

The following are the Infinitive suffixes in Pkts.[63] *-iuṁ, -euṁ, (ve)uṁ, -uṁ*<OIA *-tum.* Absolutives terms. *-ṭṭu, -ittu, -ttā* are used for Infinitives. In Amg. *-ttae, -ettae, -ittae*, cf. Ved. *-tave* e.g., *vastave*<√*vas.*

Ap. literature shows the *-aṇa* group (*i.e., -aṇa, -aṇu, -aṇahaṁ, -aṇahiṁ*) as the most important one in WAp. This *-aṇa* is the Nom. sg. of the OIA action-noun corresponding to Sk. stem in *-aṇaṁ* (e.g., *karaṇaṁ* <√*kar-*). *-aṇu* has the usual *-u* which is added to many other terms. and indeclinables in this period. *-aṇahiṁ* < OIA - **aṇasmin* i.e., the Loc. sg. of *-aṇa.* Pischel regards *-aṇaham* as the Gen. plur. of *-aṇa.*[64] It appears first in WAp. literature, and it has persisted down to NIA as *-na* of the Infinitives e.g., Raj. *-no, -nu, H. -nā*, Braj. *-naü*, Sdh. *-nu*, Panj. *-ṇā, -nā.* M. has *-ṇẽ* < *-*anakaṁ* as SAp. preserves only *-aṇahaṁ.* In EAp. *-aṇa* is absent in *DKK.* and a rarity in *Dks.* It is probably a loan from the WAp. in *DKs.*, as Beng. has no *-na* Infinitive.

Another characteristic of WAp. is the use of Absolutive terms. for the Inf. Although it is sanctioned by Eastern Pk. grammarians, it is totally absent in EAp. Even in WAp. it became established roughly after 1000 A.D., and got recognition in the works of the 'Western School' of Pk. grammarians. It was very widely used in 12th cent. A.D.

In Pd. 105 we have *-la* in the Infinitive sense. The line runs thus :

*ve paha* java lā *darisiyaïṁ jahiṁ bhāvaï tahiṁ laggu.*

---

62 We do not know why Dr. Dinesh Chandra Sircar accepts *-eda* (*A Grammar of the Pkt. Language*, Calcutta (1943), p. 116), where Nitti Dolci, the original editor, is inclined to *-evaṁ* as the original reading. *-eda* is absent in other Pk. grammars and Ap. Literature.

63 Pischel, *Grammatik*, §§ 573-78.

64 Pischel, *Grammatik* § 579. In this connection it may be pointed out that Louis H. Gray traces this to OIA **-anatham* which is a combination of the term. *-no* of nouns of action and II formative *-tha*<*-tho* which is also used as *nomina actions* e.g., Sk. *gāthā*, Av. *gāθā* (*BSOS* VIII. ii-iii). This Plur. Inf. form may be regarded as exceptional as Inf. forms in Plur. are not known in the whole field of IE. (For details, see Gray's paper in *BSOS* VIII ii-iii mentioned above).

'These two ways *for going* (*java lā*) are shown. You may follow what you like.' H. L. JAIN, the editor, translates it in Hindi : '*Ye do path* jāne ke liye *batlā diye gaye haĩ*.[65] *-la* is traceable to -**laa*<-**laga*<√*lag-*. Like *attham* (*artham*) it is a post-position.

In SAp. *-huṁ* is the most popular suffix of the Infinitive, and is probably the origin of M. *-ū̃* e.g., M. *karū̃* <*kara-ūṁ* <*kara-huṁ*. In the 10th cent. in WAp. *-huṁ* and *-hu* are less common. So also in the works of Joïndu. Another special feature of SAp. of the 11th cent. A.D., is the use of obligatory *-evvaïṁ*, *-evaeṁ*<OIA -**tavyakaṁ* for Infinitive. Though these are not seen in WEAp. literature (forms in *-evaṁ* in WAp. are exceptional) it seems to have spread to those regions in the proto-NIA period. e.g., Guj. *-vũ*, Raj. *-bo*, Braj. *-ibaũ*, Beng. *-ibüă*. In M. it (i.e., *-vā -vī -vẽ*) is preserved in its original (obligatory) connotation.

In EAp. *-aï* is the special term. of the Infinitive. In EAp. Absolutives take *-i* suffix e.g., *gai*=*gatvā* (*DKs.* 82), *baisī* <*upaviśya* (*DKs.* 4), *mili*<**milya*=*militvā* (*DKK.* 27). In Ap. we have many other Absolutive terms. for the Infinitive. e.g., *-eppi*, *-eppiṇu*, *-evi*, *-eviṇu*. This *-i* or *-aï* of the Inf. is similarly an extension of Absolutive, and as such may be traced to OIA *-ya* (*-lyab*). Thus in EAp. *bhaṇaï*<**bhaṇya*=*bhaṇitum* (*DKs.* 60), *bhamaï* (**bhramya*) in *Dis.* 50. The few *-i* Infinitives in WAp. e.g. *vāhi*<**vāhya*=*voḍhuṁ*, *muṇi*<**mun-ya*=*mantuṁ* (both from *Jdu.*, 1200 WAp.) may be similarly explained. Here we cannot rule out the linguistic possibility of *-tavaī*>-**avaï* -**aaï*>*-aï*, and *-āya*> -**āi*>*-aï* for both *-tavaï*, and *-āya* are infinitive in sense. But the use of the Absolutive for Infinitive is a normal usage in WAp. in the 10th cent. A.D. Its existence in contemporary EAp. follows the same lines, although SAp. does not attest to such forms.

Sanskritisms and Prakritisms need not be discussed.[66]

## § 150 A. INFINITIVE

| V.D. | WAp. | SAp. | EAp. |
|---|---|---|---|
| 500 ? | - | - | - |
| 600- | *sahaṇa*, *saṁṭṭhavaṇa* | - | - |
| 100 | *sahaṇu*. | | |
| | *muṇahu* | | |
| | *leṇahẽ* (*PPr*.2.89) | | |
| 700- | - | - | *kahaṇa* (*DKS.* 54). |
| 1200 | - | - | *bhaṇaï* (*DKs*.60), *bhamaï* (*DKs.* 50) |

65 H. L. JAIN, *Pahuḍa-doha*, p. 33.

66 For the use of Infinitives in NIA see BLOCH, *L'indo-aryen*, p. 283-4.

| A.D. | WAp. | SAp. |
|---|---|---|
| 1000 | *dhavalaṇahaṁ*, *karaṇahaṁ*<br>*toḍahuṁ* (*Sdd.*)<br>*kahivi*, *karivi*.<br>*java lā* (*Pd.*105). | *karaṇahaṁ* (*Jc.*)<br>*vaṇṇahuṁ*, *sikkhahum*,<br>*khāhuṁ*.<br>*nāsahuṁ*, *dharahuṁ mārahũ*. |
| 1100 | - | *jiṇaṇahaṁ*<br>*vahevvaïṁ*, *tarevvaïṁ*<br>*devaṁ*.<br>*pekkaha-huṁ*. |

| A.D. | WAp. | |
|---|---|---|
| 1200 | (1) *karaṇa*, *bhuṁjana* | (2) *dharaṇu* (E *Jdu.*) |
| | (3) *sevaṇahaṁ* (*Kc.*) | (4) *muṁcaṇahiṁ* |
| | (5) *karevi* | (6) *kareviṇu*. |
| | (7) *kareppi* | (8) *kareppiṇu* |
| | (9) *caevaṁ* | (10) *hariu* (*Kp.*S.86.6) |
| | (11) *dharivi*, *jampivi*, *jiṇavi* | (12) *vāhi*, *muṇi*. |
| | (13) *niyatteüṁ* | |

## § 150 B. Infinitive

| A.D. | WAP. | SAp. | EAp. |
|---|---|---|---|
| 500 ? | - | - | - |
| 600 | -*aṇa*, -*aṇu* | - | - |
| 1000 | -*hu*<br>-(*e*) *ṇaha*ö *PPr.*2.87) | | |
| 700-1200 | - | - | -*aṇa*.<br>-*aï* |
| 1000 | -*aṇahaṁ*<br>-*huṁ*<br>-*ivi*<br>-*lā* (*Pd.*105). | -*aṇahaṁ*<br>-*huṁ* (most popular)<br>-*hũ*. | |
| 1100 | - | -*aṇahaṁ*<br>-*evvaiṁ*, -*evaeṁ*<br>-*huṁ* | - |

1200 *-aṇa, -aṇu*
*-aṇahaṁ -aṇahiṁ*
*-evi, eviṇu*
*-eppi, eppiṇu*
*-evaṁ*
*-iu.*
*-ivi,-avi.*
*-i.*
*-euṁ.*

## Absolutives

§ 151. The following are the desinences of the Absolutive according to Pk. grammarians. According to the Eastern Pk. grammarians, we have :

i) *-epi, -epiṇu, -evi, -eviṇu, -i, -ia* (*Pu.* 17.32-5) *Ki.* 5.53.-4, 58-9).

ii) *-ppi, -ppiṇu* in the case of √*brū*, *kr̥*, √*gam* and √*bhū* (?)

iii) *-eppi, -eppiṇu* (*Ki.* 5.53).

Out of these *-i, -eppi, -eppiṇu, -evi, -eviṇu* are recognized by *Hc.* 8.4.439 -42 and *-i, -eppi, -eppiṇu* by *Tr.* 3.3.18, 19. *Hc.* admits *-ppi, -ppiṇu* for √*brū* and √*gam* (*Hc.* 8.4.391 and 442 and exs.), but *Tr.* 3.3.21 restricts their use to √*gam* only. *Tr.* reconizes *-epi, -epiṇu* (3.3.19).

The terms. which are noticed only in the 'Western 'School' are as follows :

(iv) *-ttu, -tta, -ccā, -ṭṭu, -ṭṭuṁ, -tuṇa, -(i)o, -ppi* (if *Cd.* II.19 be an authentic *sūtra* as claimed by Gune—Intro. to *Bhk.*)

(v) *-iu, -ivi, -avi* (*Hc.* 8.4.439).

Out of these *-iu* is sanctioned by *Tr.* 3.3.18. *-eavi* is the only suffix peculiar to *Tr.* 3.3.18.

In Pkts. we find the following terms. of the Absolutives.[67]

*-ia(yă), -āe, -āyāe, -ttā, -tā, -ttāṇaṁ, -tuāṇaṁ, -°ṇa, -tūṇa, -ūṇaṁ, -dūṇa* (JŚ), *-ūṇa, -ccā -ccāṇam -ccāṇa.*

In Ap. literature, we find EAp. is characterised by *-ĭ* and *-iă*. Not that *-i* is absent in WSAp. (*Hc.* 8.4.339 and *Tr.* 3.3.18 also prescribe it), but its frequency is negligible when compared with that in EAp. According to Pischel *-ĭ, -iă* (and its WSAp. cognates *-iu, -iya* (*-ya*

67 Pischel, *Grammatik*, §§581-93.

<pleonastic *-ka*) developed out of OIA suffix *-ya* (*lyab*).[68] This *-ya* seems to be the origin of Ap. *-ia, -iya, -iu, -ĭ.*[69] *-ia* (*-iyă*) although found in Pkts,[70] was not much popular then, but it appears first in WAp. (1000 A.D.). There are only five examples in *BhK.*, but in *Kp.* (1194 A.D.) the frequency of alternate terms. is[71] : *-ivi* (56+4), *-ēvi* (9+2), *-eviṇu* (4), *-avi* (4), *-i* (3), *-iu* (1). In SAp. of the 10th cent. (*Hv.* ) we find[72] : *-ĕvi* (430), *-ēvi* (59), *-eppiṇu, gampi* (7), *gampiṇu* (2), *hoevi* (9), *hoeppiṇu* (3) and *hovi* (2) *i.e.*, there is no *-i* in *Hv.*, though we have a few ones e.g., *ṇava+-yāri* (Jc. 1.27.10) in other works of Puṣpadanta. The desinence persists in the bardic texts in Raj., in Guj., Old Hindi, Maith. and in some of the speeches in the Hindukush.[73]

It is, however, interesting that most of the desinences noted by 'Eastern' Pk. grammarians are not found in EAp.

Vedic Absolutive suffixes *-tvī, -tvīnaṁ* are regarded as the origin of Ap. *-eppi, -epi, -eppiṇu, -epiṇu, -evi, -eviṇu, -ivi, -avi, -ppi, -pi, -vi* and *-piṇu.*[74] In WAp. *VK.* uses *-eviṇu* only, while the works of Joïndu show only *-va* forms viz., *-evi, -vi, -eviṇu, -avi.* It is only once in *PPr.* 2.47 that we have an *-eppiṇu* form (viz *mueppiṇu=muktvā*). Though this term. appears more frequently from the 10th cent. A.D., it was not very productive in WSAp. *-tti* found in WAp. *visitti*<**viśitvī*<√*viś* 'to enter' is rare.

There are two clear currents in the Absolutive terms., one traceable to OIA *-tva-*, and the other to *-ya.* Out of these the former is absent in. EAp., while the latter (*i.e. -ya* forms) appears in WSAp. from 1000 A.D. Vedic Absolutive suffixes -**tvānam* became *-ttūṇa(ṁ), -tūṇa(ṁ), -dūṇa(ṁ), -ūṇa(ṁ)* in Pkts., the relics of which are scattered in Ap. literature. Such Prakritisms are more frequently met with in the works of Puṣpadanta rather than in *KKc.* EAp. is free from them.

Apart from the linguistic consideration put forth by BLOCH[75] the very fact that *-tūṇa* or *-(i)uṇa* has become practically obsolete in

68 *Ibid.*, § 594.

69 Louis H. GRAY differs. He suggests that this is a survival of a Loc. Infinitive in *-i*, of the same type as the Vedic infinitive *neṣaṇi* (only 8 examples. See MACDONELL, *Vedic Grammar*, p. 412) and Gatha Av. *fraxanī.* For the suffix *-ī* we find parallel in Vedic *vedī, vedi*, and some in II. and IE (GRAY, *BSOS*, VIII ii-iii, p. 575). Ap. and II or IE are chrono-regionally unconnected. GRAY's observations on MIA Morphology in *BSOS* VII ii-iii try to emphasize the relations of Pk. and Ap. with those of II and IE. Sometimes in a farfetched manner.

70 PISCHEL, *Grammatik*, § 589.

71 ALSDORF, Intro. to *Kp.* § 39, p. 63.

72 ALSDORF, Intro. to *Hv.* § 60.

73 BLOCH, *L'indo-aryen*, p. 285.

74 PISCHEL, *Grammatik*, § 588.

75 BLOCH, *La Langue Marathe*, § 264.

SAp. literature after being so much used in Pkts., is enough to show that we cannot connect M. *-ūna* with them. As suggested by KATRE, a contamination of OIA *-tvāna* and *-tvīna* giving *-*tūṇṇa*u, *-*tuaṇṇaï*, -*-tuaṇṇu* or *-*tuaṇṇi* in spoken Ap. should be regarded as the common source of Koṅk. and M. *ur*-forms *-*aunu*, *-*(v) auni*.[76] The difficulty of dentalization of cerebral *-ṇ* can be overcome by supposing two currents of pronunciation (*viz*., *-n* and *-ṇ-*) as we find them in coll. M. to-day.

As noted above Guj. Sdh. Singh. *-ī*, Panj. and H. *-i*(>*o*) and *-e*, Beng. *-iyā* (<*-ĭă* in EAp. with *-ya śruti*) are traceable to OIA *-ya* >WSEAp. *-ĭ*, *-iă*.[77]

## § 151A. ABSOLUTIVE

| A.D. | WAp. | SAp. | EAp. |
|---|---|---|---|
| 500? | *rundheviṇu* | .. | .. |
| 600-1000 | (1) *dhārĕvi, dĕvi, ṇavevi* | .. | .. |
| | (2) *mĕllivi, paṇavivi* | .. | .. |
| | (3) *mueviṇu, laheviṇu, kareviṇu* | .. | .. |
| | (4) *pariharavi, hoyavi.* | | |
| | (5) *mueppiṇu* (Only in *PPr*. 2.47) | | |
| 700-1200 | .. | | (1) *muṇi, chaḍḍi, mili, laï.* (2) *muṇia, hoia, upaṭṭia, paluṭia* ; *cintiā* (*matri*) *causa* (3) *baïsī, jālī, nibesī, bandhī, uḍḍī.* |

| A.D. | WAp. | SAp. |
|---|---|---|
| 1000 | (1) *cavevi, uḍḍevi, ubbhevi, khuḍĕvi.* (2) *phuṭṭivi, bujjhivi,* | (1) *phāḍevi, ṇiĕvi, thappevi, kapparevi, ubbhevi, laggevi, ṭhāevi,* |

76 S. M. KATRE, *Form. of Koṅk* § 291.
77 For the usage of Absolutive in Ap. and NIA, see BLOCH, *L'indo-aryen*, p. 285-86.

| A.D. | WA. | SAp. |
|---|---|---|
| | *bhuṁjāivi, laggivi, millivi,*<br>*phusivi, valivi, ghullivi,*<br>*apphālivi, ancivi,*<br>(3) *caḍeviṇu, paḍeviṇu,*<br>*āṇeviṇu, leviṇu.* | *pekkhevi, pallaṭṭevi.*<br>(2) *māṇivi, cappivi, osarivi,*<br>*veḍhivi, pallaṭṭivi,*<br>*laggivi, upphālivi,*<br>*kaḍḍhivi, samoḍivi.* |
| 1000 | (4) *ṇamakāreppiṇu, ghalleppiṇu.*<br>(5) *lahi, pilli, kari, utthalli*<br>(6) *iṁchiya, joiya.*<br>(7) *gampi.* | (3) *leviṇu, luṇeviṇu,*<br>*chaṇḍeviṇu* (not found in *Hv.*)<br>(4) *toḍeppiṇu, pelleppiṇu,*<br>*āṇeppiṇu, laeppiṇu,*<br>*haveppiṇu, hoeppiṇu,*<br>*huṇeppiṇu.*<br>(5) *jhaḍavi, jhampavi, hovi*<br>(6) *leppi, gampi*<br>(7) *ṭhaviūṇa, hakkiūṇa,*<br>*mantiūṇa.*<br>(8) *bhaṇiūṇaṁ, soūṇaṁ*<br>(9) *dāuṁ, kāuṁ, ṇieuṁ.*<br>(10) *pamottūṇa.*<br>(11) *ṇavayāri* (The same as (6) ?<br>(*Jc.* 1.27.10). |
| 1100 | (1) *suṇivi*<br>(2) *paḍicchavi*<br>(3) *vāli, visitti.*<br>(4) *ṇisuṇiu.* | (1) *caḍevi, ṇevi, pāvevi, ullalevi.*<br>(2) *dharivi, kalivi,*<br>*pekkhivi, karivi,*<br>*kokkāivi.*<br>(3) *vāhi.*<br>(4) *vāiuṇa, gāiuṇa,*<br>*sajjiuṇa, suṇiuṇa*<br>(5) *kareviṇu, moheviṇu.* |

| A.D. | WAp. |
|---|---|
| 1200 | (1-2)(*āṇevivi, ahiyāsivi, bhuṁjivi, karivi, karevi* (*Kc.* 77) *ṇamivi gacchivi, muṇivi, pecchivi, pecchevi* (*Kp. S.* 104.1)<br>*hakkārevi* (*Kp. S.* 49.7), *phedivi, ghuṇṭivi, ṇirumbhivi, a-lahivi.*<br>(3) *karavi, taravi, karāvi.*<br>(4) *kireviṇu, ṇisuṇeviṇu, kareviṇu.* |

(5) *bhaṇi, lahi, suṇi, ṇihoḍi, lahi, gacchi.*

(6) *ḍahiu* (*Sn.* 270-190), *āgantu* (*Sc.* 506.7), *kariu* (*Kc.* 76)

(7) *kareppi, gameppi.*

(8) *kareppiṇu, gameppiṇu.*

(9-10) *gamppi, gamppiṇu* (*Kc.* 80).

## § 151B. Absolutive.

| A.D. | WAp. | SAp. | EAp. |
|---|---|---|---|
| 500 ? | *-eviṇu* | .. | .. |
| 600-1000 | *-evi*<br>*-ivi*<br>*-ēviṇu*<br>*-avi, -vi*<br>*-eppiṇu* (only once *PPr.* 2.47.) | .. | .. |
| 700-1200 | .. | .. | *-i*<br>*-ia, -iā*<br>*-ī.* |
| 1000 | *-evi*<br>*-ivi*<br>*-eviṇu*<br>*-eppiṇu*<br>*-i*<br>*-iya*<br>*-pi* (*BhK.* 14.7) | *-evi, -ĕvi*<br>*-ivi*<br>*-eviṇu*<br>*-eppiṇu*<br>*-avi, -vi*<br>*-i* (?) e.g., *Jc.* 1.27.10)<br>*-p(p) i*<br>*-iūṇa, -iūṇaṁ*<br>*-ūṇaṁ*<br>*-uṁ*<br>*-euṁ*<br>*-ūṇa.* | |
| 1100 | *-ivi*<br>*-(a)vi*<br>*-i* | *-evi*<br>*-ivi*<br>*-i* | |

| A.D. | WAp. | SAp. | EAp. |
|---|---|---|---|
| 1100 | *-iu* | *-iuṇa*, *-īuṇa* *-eviṇu*. | |
| 1200. | *-ivi*, *-evi*. *-avi* *-eviṇu* *-i* *-iu* (*Sn*. 270-190, *Kc*. 76.) *-u* *-eppi*, *-eppiṇu*. *-ppi*, *-ppiṇu* (*Kc*. 80). | .. | .. |

## ADVERBS.

§ 152. Adverbs in Ap. are based on (i) nouns (ii) pronouns, and (iii) older adverbs and adverbial expressions :

(i) Adverbs based on nouns :

e.g., SAp. *taru* (*tvarā*) 'quickly,' *ṇicchaü* (*niścaya*) 'certainly, WAp. *accattham* (*atyartham*).

(ii) Adverbs based on pronouns :

OIA *kim* : WSE *kahiṁ*, *kahĩ*, WAp. *kahi* (=*kutra*) *kaü* (*kutaḥ*),

OIA *yad* : *jahiṁ*, *jahĩ* (=*yatra*), *jāma*, *jāmu*, *jā̆va* (*yāvat*), *jāmaï*, *jāvaï*, *jaïyaha* (*yadā*).

OIA *tad* : WAp. *to*, *tu* (*tataḥ*), WAp. *tavve*, EAp. *tabbe* (*tadvā*), *tahiṁ*, *tahĩ* (*tadā*), *tā*, *tāma*, *tāmu*, *tā̃va*, *tāvaĩ*, *tāvaï* (*tāvat*).

(iii) Adverbs based on older adverbs and adverbial expressions : SAp. *ajju*, WEAp. *ajja*, WAp. *aju* (*adya*); WAp. *itthu*, *itthi*, *ittha* (*itthā̆*=*atra*), WSAp. *ihu*, WAp. *ihā̆* (*iha*) ; SAp. *dhruva*, *dhruu* (*dhruvaṁ*) ; WSAp. *bāhiri*, WAp. *bahiraü*, *bāhiṁ*, SAp. *bāhira*, *bāhuḍi*, EAp. *bahi bahi* (*bahiḥ*) ; *aïreṇa*, *airiṇa* (*acireṇa*), *aggaï* (*agre*), WAp. *aha*, *heṭṭhā̆* (*adhastāt*).

§ 153. Adverbs in Ap. may be classified as (A) Adverbs of Time, (B) Adverbs of Place, (C) Adverbs of Manner, and (D) Miscellaneous Adverbs.

The following are the lists of some important adverbs. These are by no means exhaustive as this is not a lexical work.[78]

### (A) Adverbs of Time

1) WSAp. *ajju*, WEAp. *ajja*, W. *aju* (*adya*).

2) WAp. *aireṇa*, *airiṇa* (*acireṇa*), also SAp. *ciru* (*ciram*)

3) SAp. *ettahĕ* (*itas*=*atrāntare*) cf. *Hc*. 4.420.

4) SAp. *evahiṁ*=*adhunā*.

5) WSAp. *kayā*, *kaiyā̆*, WAp. *kaïyahā̃ mi* in *BhK*. 93.7), *kaiaha* in *Hc*. 8.4.422.1, EAp. *kabbe* (*kadvā*) in *DKs*. 62. —All used for OIA *kadā*.

6) WSAp. *jaïya*, WAp. *jaïya-haṁ*, °*huṁ*, EAp. *jai*, *jabbe* (*yadvā*)=*yadā*.

7) WSAp. *jāma*, *jā̃va*, EAp. *jāba*, WAp. *jāmu*, SAp. *jāhu*. (*yāvat*), but WAp. *jāmaï*, *jā̃vai* (*yadā*) in *PPr*. 2.41, 174, *jittiu* (*yāvan-mātra*).

8) WSAp. *tā*, *tāma*, *tāu*, *tau*, WAp. *tāmu*, *tāva* or *tā̃va* ; SAp. *tāva*, WAp. *tāvaï*, EAp. *tāba* (*tāvat*).

9) WAp. *tāmaï*, *tāvaï* in *PPr*. 2.41.174, *tavve*, EAp. *tabbe* (*tadvā*), SAp. *taïya*, °*hā̃*, °*hu*, *tā*, *to* (*tadā*), WSAp. *to*, WAp. *tu* (*tataḥ*).

10) EAp. *paccha*, SAp. *pacchae* (*paścāt*) cf. *Hc*. 8.4.120.

11) WAp. *saï* (*sadā*).

12) *sajjo* (*sadyaḥ*).

### (B) Adverbs of Place

1) SAp. *ihu* (*Jc*. 3.37.17), *ihā* (*Pd*. 162)<*iha*.

2) WSAp. *itthu*, *etthu*, *itthi* (*Sdd*. 71. v.l.)<**ittha*=*atra*. *etthau* (*Jc*. 1.25.1), *eu* (*Nc*. 1.15.15), *ettahe* (*Kc*. 75)—all used in the sense of 'here.'

3) *uppari* (*upari*) 'over.' In *sandhis* the last vowel of the first word is suppressed *e.g.*, *majj'-uppari*=*majjha* + *uppari* 'above me' (*Hv*. 88.19.13), *Kalas' upari*=*kalasa*+*upari* 'on the pitcher' (*Hv*. 85.9.16).

---

78 In these lists WAp. or SAp. does not mean that that form is exclusively limited to the region unless it is specially state to be so.

4) WAp. *kau*=*kutaḥ*, also *kahanti-hu* in *Kc.* 61 and *Hc.* 8.4.416. The latter form is not popular in Ap. literature.

5) WSAp. *kattha*, *ketthu*, *katthaï* (*kutra cit*) in *Jc.* 2.6.6. *kitthu* (*PPr.* 2.47)=*kutra.* In *BhK.* 57.11 *kahĩ*=*kutra*, Loc. sg. of *ka-* used adverbially. EAp. *kui*=*kutra* (*DKs.* 64).

6) *kayā* (*kadā*), WAp. *kaïyā vi*=*kadā'pi* (*Kp.* J. 46.1)

7) *jattha*, *jetthu*, *jitthu*, *jettahe* (*Hv.* 83.16.4), *jettahiṁ* (*Jc.* 3.12.6), *jattu*, (*Kc.* 52, *Hc.* 8.4.404), *jahiṁ* (*yasmin*)=*yatra.*

8) *tattha*, *tetthu*, *titthu*, *tettahe* (*Nc.* 5.2.2.), *tettahiṁ* (*Jc.* 3.12.6), *tettahi* (*Kc.* 75, *Hc.* 8.4.436), *tattu* (*Kc.* 52, *Hc.* 8.4.404), *tahiṁ*=*tatra.*

9) WSAp. *bāhiri*, WSEAp. *bāhira*, *bāhirau* (*Sdd.* 57), *bāhera* (*DKK* 2), *bāhiṁ* (*Kp.* S. 44.8)<*bahiḥ.* In *KKc.*) *bāhuḍi*=*bahiṣ* governs the Abl. or Gen. e.g., *bāhudi gau so ṇiyapuraho.* 'He went out of his own town.' (*KKc.* 1.12.10).

10) *savvattau*=*sarvataḥ* (*BhK.* 12.12.7 GUNE's edition), cf. *Pai. savatto sarvataḥ*

## (C) ADVERBS OF MANNER

1) WSAp. *avaropparu avarupparu* (*parasparam*) 'mutual.'

2) *aha*<*yathā* from *jaha.*

3) WAp. *ittiyaiṁ*, *ittiya* (*iyat*).

4) WSAp. *emu*, *eũ*, *iũ* *ema*, *eṁva*, *emaï*, *emvahiṁ*, *evahiṁ*, *evi* (*evaṁ*) ; *ēvahim*, *emahiṁ*=*idānīm*, *emēva* (*eva-meva*).

5) EAp. *eta* (*DKs.* 39, 63), WAp. *ettaḍaïṁ*, *ettula* (*etāvat*).

6) *ettiya*, *evaḍḍa*, *evaḍa*, *ēvaḍu*, *evaḍḍaa* (*iyat*).

7) WSAp. *kaha* (also *kahāmi*, *kaha-va* in WAp. *BhK.* 44.2, 42.7), *kiha*, *kema*, *keṽa* or *keṽva*, *keva* (*Jc.*), *kima*, WAp. *kimi*, *kiṁva* or *kiṽa*, *kiva*, *kīvaï*, *kēmaï*, SAp. *kiuṁ* (*KKc.* 1.10.2), also *kāhaü* (*Jc.* 2.28)=*katham.*

8) *kettiu*, *kittiu*, *kettiya* (*kiyat*) : also *kettula.* cf. *Hc.* 8.4.435 and *Kc.* 75.

9) *kūra*=*īṣat* (*Hv.* 85.19.9) cf. *Hc.* 8.2.29.

10) WSAp. *chuḍu*, *chuḍu chuḍu*=*kṣipram.*

11) WSAp. *jema, jima, jiṁva, jiṽa, jeṽa, jiva, jiha jehaü*, (*Jc*. 2.28.) =*yathā*. Also *jahā̃* (*Kc*. 26) cf. *Hc*. 8.4.355.

12) *jittiu*=*yāvanmātra* (*PPr*. 2.38).

13) WSAp. *jhatti*, SAp. *jhaḍatti*=*jhaṭiti*.

14) *ḍhāvu*=*śīghraṁ* (*Kc*. 35).

15) WSAp. *ṇirāriu*=*nitarām* (*Pd*. 120), *atiśayena* (*MP*. 13.7.13), *anivāritaṁ* (*MP*. 2.18.8), but *ṇirutta* (*Pd*. 121), *niruttau* (*Nc*. 2.13.11), *ṇiruttaüṁ*<*nirukta-kaṁ*=*nitarāṁ* (*KKc*. 1.2.4, 7.1.4), *ṇiru* (*Mp*. 1.1.9), (*Sn*. 25.2.2) cf. *Dn*. 4.30).

16) WSEAp. *ṇāhĩ*, *ṇāhi* (*nāsti*).

17) SAp. *taru*<**tvaram*=*śīghram* (*Mp*. 25.19.13).

18) WSAp. *taha, tiha, tema*, WAp. *tahā̃, tima, temu, timu tĕ͝va, tĕũa, tiṽa* (cf. *Hc*. 8.4.397, 401) *tiṁva*=*tathā*.

19) *tĕttaḍau, tittiḍaü*=*tāvan mātra* (*PPr*. 1.105).

20) WAp. *ḍaḍavaḍa*, SAp. *ḍavatti* (*MP*. 29.6.3), *daḍatti* (*MP*. 9.13.2) =*śīghraṁ*.

21) *dive dive*=*divā* (*Hc*. 8.4.419).

22) *puṇu* (*punaḥ*), WAp. *puṇo* (*Kp*. J. 41.2*).

23) *phuḍu* (*sphuṭam*).

24) *laï* 'much' (*Jc*. 3.10.4).

25) *saṇiuṁ*=*śanaiḥ*.

## (D) Miscellaneous Adverbs

1) WAp. *accattham* (*atyartham*).

2) WSAp. *avasa, avaseṁ*, WAp. *avasaya, avasu, avasi, avassu* (*avayśam*).

3) EAp. *ālĕ* (*alaṁ*).

4) WAp. *i* (*api*), EAp. *i*=*hi*.

5) WSAp. *ia, iya*, WAp. *iu* (*iti*).

6) WAp. *kau, kahantihu* (*kutaḥ*) as in *Hc*. 8.4.416.

7) WSAp. *kira*, WAp. *kiri* (*kira*=*kila*).

8) WAp. *ghaṇauṁ*=*prabhūtaṁ*.

9) SAp. *ciya*, *cciya*, EAp. *ceba* (*caiva*).

10) WAp. *jaṇi*, *jaṇu*=*iva*.

11) WSAp. *ji*, WAp.-*jja*, -*jji*.

12) WSAp. *ṇaṁ*, *ṇau*, *ṇāi*, *ṇāĩ*, *ṇāvaï*=*iva* cf. Ved. *na*, and *Hc*. 8.4.444.

13) WSAp. *ṇaṁ* (*nanu*).

14) WAp. *ṇahi*, *nahĩ*, SAp. *ṇeya*, WAp. *ṇea* (*naiva*=*na*), SWEAp. *ṇa*, WEAp. *ṇaï*, EAp. *ṇaü*, WAp. *ṇavi* (*nāpi*=*na*) all showing negation.

15) WAp. *ṇavari*, *ṇavaru*, *ṇavara* (*na para*=*kevalaṁ*).
Also used as conjunction in the sense of 'thereupon' (*Hv*. 82.15.4), 'however, yet' (*Hv*. 86.8.1)

16) SAp. *ṇicchaü* (*niścayam*), also *ṇikkhuttauṁ*.

17) WSAp. *ṇiru*, *ṇirāriu*, SAp. *ṇiruttaü* (*niruktaṁ*=***nitarām***).

18) WAp. *prāu*, *prāïva*, *prāïṁva*, *paggiṁva*=*prāyaḥ* (*Hc*. 8.4.414, *Kc*. 59).

19) *pi* (*api*) also changed as *vi*, EAp. *bi*, WSAp. *mi* as in *tuhũ mi*, *haũ mi*; also *va* in *Nc*. 6.10.12 '*ṇa peraï* kaha va *maṇu*.'

20) WSAp. *piva*, *viva*, *va*, EAp. *bia*, WAp. *viu*, -*vvava* (*iva*).

21) WSEAp. *puṇu*, WAp. *puṇo*, EAp. *puṇa* (*punaḥ*).

22) SAp. *phuḍu* (*sphutaṁ*).

23) WSAp. *ma*, WAp. *maṁ*, *maṇa*, *maṇāüṁ* (*Hc*. 4.418)=***mā***.

24) WAp. *maṇu*, *miva*=*iva* (*Cd*.)

25) WSAp. *vāra vāra* (*vāraṁvāraṁ*). WAp. *valivali*< (**vālyavālya*<√*val*-) is used in the sense of '*vāraṁvāraṁ*' in *PPr*. 2.137.

26) WSAp. *viṇu*, EAp. *biṇu* (*vinā*).

27) WSAp. *saïṁ*, *saĩ*, SAp. *sae*, EAp. *saï* (*svayena*=*svayaṁ*).

28) WSAp. *sahuṁ*, *sahu*, WAp. *sahu* (*PPr*. 2.109)<*saha*.

29) WSAp. *hu*<*kkhu*<**khlu*, an abbreviation of ***khalu***.

30) EAp. *hu*=*hi* (*DDK*. 21).

It is only EAp. which shows a different set, or rather a different phonological development in these adverbs. Most of the adverbs (with some exceptions) are common to WSAp. regions.

### Conjunctions

§154. In Ap. we have the same conjunctions as in Pkts., though some of them are slightly modified in form, a few unusual in Pkts. : e.g., *ahava*, *ahavaï* (*athavā*), WAp. *anu*, *annaha* (*anyathā*), WSAp. *chuḍu*=*yadi*, but adverbially *yadā* as in *BhK*. 121.10, WSAp. *jaï*-(*yadi*) with the corresponding *tā*, *to*, *toi*, *taha* etc., *je*<*jaï* (*yadi*) in Mt. 9, *ṇavari* 'thereupon' as in *Hv*. 82.15.4, 'however, yet' (*Hv*. 85.5.7,86.8.1). In *Hv*. 81.5.7 *ṇaṁ*..*to* are used to mean 'If not—so.' *va* is used for *vā*, but in *sn*. 355 27 '*ajja* ki *kalli* ' *ki*=*vā*.

This list is only suggestive.

### Interjections

§155. The following are some of the Interjections found in Ap. literature. Some of them are *tss*., while most of them are found in Pkt., and we cannot hence regard them as peculiar to Ap.

1) *ammie*=*aho*. To address a particular person cf. *amba*, *ambike* in OIA.

2) *ari*, *ariri*, *arari*, *are*<OIA *re re*, *are*.

3) *avvō*, *avvo avvo* 'oh mother!' (*Hv*. 89.10.12, 85.10.25) cf. *Dn*. 1.5 *avvā*=*ambā* 'mother.' It is found in Dravidian.

4) *ahaha* 'Alas' (*Sc*. 585.1) *ts*.

5) *aho*, *ahu*, *aho'hu*, *uhu* (*Hv*. 89.15.10)<*aho*.

6) *chī chī*, *thū thū* ; to express disgust.

7) *haüṁ haüṁ*=*hā hā* 'Alas,' as in
*haüṁ haüṁ lahivi sudhammihiṁ juttau*.
*chāyā* : *hā hā labdhvā sudharmaiḥ yuktaṁ*. -*Sn*. 308.169.

8) *hahā*, *hāhā*<*hā*, *dhiratthu*=*dhig astu* ('Fie' (*Kp*. A. 2.4, 8. 46.8).

9) *hali*, *hali hali*<*hale* 'oh', in addressing a friend (*Jc*. 2.7.2).

In *Kc*. 39 we have *ra*=*re* e.g., *āhara*=*ehi re*, *jāha ra*=*yāhi re*. In *Kc*. 68 and in *Hc*. 8.4.423 *huhuru*, *ghugghiu* are onomatopoeic expressions.

The above list is by no means exhaustive.

## *CHAPTER IV.*

# NOMINAL STEM-FORMATION IN APABHRAMŚA

§156. Ap. suffixes are divided as (I) Primary and (II) Secondary. Most of them are derivable from IA sources, although in a few cases Dravidian influence is suspected.

### I. Primary Suffixes

§157. The following is the list of important Primary Suffixes in Ap. :

1) *-a* <OIA *-ka* : 'agent, doer'. e.g., WAp. *khavaṇaa* (*kṣapaṇaka*), SAp. *bappīhaya* (*bāṣpa-īha-ka*), EAp. *biṇua* (*vijñuka*).

2) *-aṇa* <OIA *-ana* with or without pleonastic *-ka*: applied to verbs to make Abstract Substantives. Some forms are clear developments of OIA Abstract nouns. e.g., WAp. *ukkovaṇa* (*utkopana*), *payaḍiṇa* (*prakaṭana*), *-iṇa*<*-anna* by Umlaut; *avikkhaṇa* (*avekṣaṇa*) ; SAp. *khaṁcaṇa* (*karṣaṇa*), *paülaṇa* (*prajvalana*), WEAp. *ṭhāṇa* (*sthāna*) or MIA √*ṭha*+*aṇa*.

MIA roots take this Primary Affix as in the following examples : WAp. *jampaṇaya* ( √*jampa*<√*jalp-*), *caḍḍaṇa* (√*caḍḍa-*=√*mṛd-*) cf. *Hc.* 8.4.126, SAp. *khuṇṭaṇa* (√*khuṇṭa*=√*truṭ-*), *khamcaṇa* ( √*khaṁca*= √*kṛṣ-*), *ghaṭṭaṇa* (√*ghaṭṭa* usually connected with √*ghṛṣ-*).

3-4, *-ia*, *-iya*<OIA *-in*+pleonastic *-ka*; also from OIA *-ika* : 'action, agent.' e.g., SAp. *ullūriya* (*ullūra-iya*) 'a baker.'

5) *-ira* To show habit (*tācchīlye*). This is regarded by Alsdorf as an equivalent suffix of Pres. Part [1]. It must be admitted that OIA Pres. Part. forms can be cogently used in some of these examples (See §147). It is however a Primary Suffix showing habit. e.g., SAp. *kīllirī* (√*krīḍ-*)=*krīḍana-śīlā*, *himsira* ( √*himsa-* 'to neigh')=*heṣaṇaśīla*, *cāvira* (√*carv-*)=*carvaṇa-śīla*, *gasiru* ( √*gras-*)=*grasana-śīla*. Similarly WAp. *cuṁvira* (√*cumb-*), *kandira* ( √*krand-*) *hallira* (√*halla-* 'to move'), *hasira* ( √*has-*). EAp. has no forms with this suffix.

---

1 Alsdorf, Intro. to *Kp.* 35, p. 62, (See also § 148 Footnote 54).

6) *-illa*<OIA *-ra* or *-la* (?) : 'Agent, doer.' e.g., SAp. *kaṇailla* (√*kaṇa-*<*kvaṇ-*) 'a parrot.'

7) *-evva*<OIA *-tavya*: added to verbs to form Adjs. This is a suffix of Pot. Pass. Part. e.g., *vaṁcevva* (√*vañc-*), *jāṇevvī* (√*jāṇa-*) etc. For more see §149. Additional Suffixes are also discussed there.

8) *-ga*<OIA *-ka* : 'agent, doer.' e.g., WAp. *khamaga*=*kṣamaka* <√=*kṣam-*, *khavaga*=*kṣapaka*<√ *kṣap-*, *jāṇaga*(√*jāṇa-*) =*jñāyaka*.

9) *-tāra* OIA *-tṛ* : 'Agent, doer' e.g., *ahittāra* (*abhivak-tṛ*), *kattāra* (*kar-tṛ*).

As most of the OIA suffixes became so much identified with the original root, the sense of OIA root+suffix (e.g., *dhar-ma*) was lost quite early in pre-Ap. MIA. There is hence no propriety in analysing Ap. *carisu* (*cariṣṇu*), *jalahi* (*jaladhi*), or *kisi* (*kṛṣi*) into *cara-isu* (*-iṣṇu*), *jala-ha-i* (*-i* technically known as *ki* in Sk. grammar) or *kisa-* *-i* (*-i* known as *ik* in Sk. grammar).

## II. Secondary Suffixes

§158. The following is the list of important secondary suffixes. The powers of each suffix are indicated one after another :

1) *-a*<OIA *-ka* : pleonstic e.g., WAp. *bāḍhaa* (*vṛddhaka*), *santāviya-a* (*santāpitaka*), *ahāṇaa* (*ābhāṇaka*); SAp. *Joheya-a* (*Yaudheya-ka*), *bhaḍāra* (*bhaṭṭaraka*); EAp. *tuṭṭia-a* (*truṭitaka*), *bisariaa* (*vismṛtaka*), *paḍhia-a* (*paṭhita-ka*), *arabinda-a* (*aravindaka*).

2) *-a*<OIA *-ā* : Feminine gender. Sometimes used where normally OIA is seen. e.g., WSAp. *-gattia* (*-gātrikā*= *gātrī*), *taruṇa* (*taruṇī*).

3) *-aya*<OIA *-aka* : Pleonastic e.g., WAp. *accheraya* (*āścarya-ka*) SAp., *tṛya*, *tiya* (*strī-ka*), *Nīsiriya* (*Niḥśrīka*).

4) *-ara*<OIA *-kara* : added to substantives for forming Adjectives. e.g., SAp. *royara* (*ruci-kara*) in *Mp*. 17.12.7.

5-6) *-āra*, *-gāra-* : 'Agent, doer,' e.g., *soṇṇāra* (*suvarṇa-kāra*), *sūṇāra* (*sūnā* 'murder'+*kāra*) ; SAp. *jaṇeri* (**janaya-kārī*) and not *janayitrī* with which it is equated (See *Nc*. glossary. *ahagāra* (*agha-kāra*). For *-k->-g-* see *Hc*. 8.4.396.

7) *-āla*<OIA *-āla, -āra* : affixed to substantives to form Adjs. in the sense of 'possessing, full of.' It is very popular in SAp. and Marathi e.g., *khīrāla* (*kṣīra-*); *dāḍhāla* (*daṁṣṭrā-*) *haḍḍāla* (*haḍḍa-* 'a bone'), *guṇāla* (*guṇa-*), *sohāla* (*śobhā*); WAp. *payāla* (*prajvāla*) in *Pd.* 69, 84).

8) *-ālu* (*ya*) <OIA *-ālu, -āru* : Added to Substantives to make Adjs. chiefly in WSAp. e.g., *saddhāluya* (*śraddhā-*), *dayālu-a* (*dayā-*), *tiṭṭhālu-ya* (**tṛṣ-ṭā* 'thirst'), WAp. *giddhālu* *gṛddha-*). In these forms *-ya* and *-a* are derived from OIA peonastic *-ka*.

9) *-ī*<OIA *-ī*: For the Fem. gender, but many times used for OIA *-ā* suffix. These are traceable to OIA colloquial forms, though these are not recognised by the School of Pāṇini.

e.g., WAp. *païṭhi* (**praviṣṭī*—°*ṣṭā*), *-vadaṇī* (**-vadanī*=*vadana*), *-saṁkuḍī* (*-saṁkaṭā*), SAp. *kaṁpilli* (*kāmpilyā*) 'N. of a town,' *vayaṁsī* (**vayasyī*=*vayasyā*).

10) *-i*(*ya*)<OIA *-in* with pleonastic *-ka* : 'possessing, or having,' used to form Adjs. from Nouns. The Adjs. in *-in* were already formed in OIA e.g., *yoga*+*in*>*yogin* 'possessing or having yoga.' *yogin*>*joi* is a Pkt. form. Ap. adds pleonastic *-ya*<*-ka*, and the suffix appears as *-iya* in Ap. Really speaking it should be classed as *-ya* <*-ka* below. e.g., SEAp. *joiya* (*yogin-ka*), *vaïriya* (*vairin-ka*), WAp. *dehiya* (*dehin-ka*), *ahigāriya* (*adhikārin-ka*). SAp. *aṇṇāṇiya* (*ajñanin-ka*), *bandiya* (*bandin-ka*).

11) *-iya*< OIA *-kīya* (?): 'possessing, belonging to': To form Adjs. from Adjs. e.g. WAp. *parāiya* (*parakīya*), SAp. *mahaiya* (*mahat-*).

12) *-itta*< OIA *-i-tra* or *-i- tṛ* : 'having, possessing'. Applied to Nouns to make Adjs. It is rare and is found in WAp. e.g. *chadāitta* (*chanda—itra*=*chanda-vat*).

13) *-ima*< OIA *-ima*: Affixed to Adjs. to form Abstract nouns. e.g. WAp. *bhallima* (**bhad-la-ima*). SAp. *dhuttima* (*dhūrta-ima*): *kārima* (**kār-ima*=*kartrima*).

14) *-ira*:< To show habit (*tācchīlye*). This is regarded by ALSDORF as an equivalent suffix of Pres. Part. (See §147 Footnote) It must be admitted that OIA Pres. Part. forms can

be cogently used in some of these examlpes (see §147). It is, however, a Primary Suffix showing habit. e.g.SAp. *kīlirī* (√*krīḍ-*)=*krīḍana-śīla*, *hi iṁ sira* (√*hiṁsa-* 'to neigh')=*heṣaṇa-śīla*, *cāvira* (√*carv-*)=*carvaṇaśīla*, *gasiru* (√*gras-*)=*grasanaśīla*. Similarly WAp. *cuṁvira* (√*cumb-*), *kandira* (√*krand*), *hallira*(√*halla-* 'to move') *hasira* (√*has-*). EAp. has no forms with this suffix.

15) *-ira*< OIA *-ira*: 'possessing, having'. It is used with substantives to form Adjs. SAp. *surosira* (*suroṣa*), *ānandira* (*ānanda-ira*). This is closely allied with the Primary Suffix *-ira* noted above (See §157). It is applied to Adjs. to form Adjs. e.g. WAp. *gaggira* (*gadgada-*), SAp. *lambira* (*lamba*).

16) *-ila*< OIA *-la* pleonastic: e.g. WAp. *samīla* (*sama-*), SAp. *aṭṭhiliya* (*asthi-la-ika* ?). This suffix is another form of *-illa*.

17) *-illa*< Allied with OIA *-ila*? 'Pertaining to, possessing having'. e.g. WAp. *chailla* (*chāyā-*) of. *Hc*. 8.4.412 and PISCHEL, *Grammatik*, §595, WSAp. *kaḍilla* (*kaṭi-*) 'a dhoti' in *BhK*. 167.2 and *Hv*. 86.10.6, but'a thread round the waist' in *Mp*. 4.4.5., *sohilla* (*śobhā-*), SAp. *jhuṇilla*, (*dhvani-*), *ṇēhilla* (*sneha-*), *saṁkaḍilla* (*saṅkaṭa-*), *uvarilla* (**upara-*) cf. *Hc*.8.2.163. Generally it is adjectival. Pleonastically we have: WAp. *kuḍilliya* (*kuṭi-*), SAp. *samilla* (*sama-*).

18-20) *-ulla*, *-ullaya*, *-ullī* (Fem.)<OIA *-ṭa*: All these are pleonastic. Sometimes there are combinations of such *svārthe* suffixes like<OIA *-ka*, *-la*, *-ṭa* etc. cf. *Hc*. 8.4.430 The following are some of the examples. WSAp. *hia-ulla* (*hṛdaya*), WAp. *kuḍullī* (*kuṭī-*), *vilalulla* (*vilola-*), *kaṇṇulla-ḍa* (*karṇa-*), SAp. *morulla-a* (*mayūra-*), *bahiṇulla* (*bhaginī-*), *ciḍaulla* (*caṭaka-*?) probably cognate with *ceṭaka*<√**cṛt-* or*√*cṛ-* as KATRE[2] and S. K. CHATTERJI[3] take it, *maḍahulla* (*maḍa ha* 'small') see *Dn*. 6.117.

21) *-evva*<OIA *-tavya*: added to verbs to form Adjs. Pot. Pass. Participles e.g. *vaṁcevva* (*vañc-*), *jāṇevvī* (*jñā-*) etc. For more see §149. Additional suffixes are also discussed there.

---

2 S. M. KATRE, 'Prakrit, *uccidima* and *uccuḍai*, in *Festschrift Prof. P. V. Kane*, p. 258-9.
3 S. K. CHATTERJI, *New Ind. Ant.* 2, 421-7.

22) *-kka*<OIA pleonastic *-ka* geminated : e.g. *guruki* (*guru-*). In *BhK*. 126.7 it is an adj. of *āsaṁka* 'doubt'. It need not be connected with M. *guraknē* as JACABI does in *BhK* p. 146.

23) *-ḍa, -ḍī* (Fem.)<OIA *-ṭa* pleonastically. Its use and combinations with other pleonastic suffixes are sanctioned by Pk. grammarians of all schools.[4]

It is very popular in WAp. and especially so in *Sdd.* and NIA of that region. e.g.WAp *rukkha-ḍa* (**rukṣa-*)' a tree', *bhiṭṭa-ḍī* (*bhiṭṭa-*) 'a visit', *vaṭṭaḍiyā* (*vartman-*), *goraḍī* (**gauraṭī*) *vakkhāṇa-ḍa* (*vyākhyāna-*). SAp. *maṁchuḍu* (*maṅkṣu*). OIA *-kṣ-*>*-ch-* is found in SAp. and Marathi.[5] *ukkuruḍa* (*utkara-*); EAp. *khara-ḍa* (*khara-*). It is however rare in SEAp.

It is applied to Adverbs to form Adjs. e.g. *ettaḍaya* (*iyat-*), *tettaḍau*, *tittaḍau*=*tāvan-mātra*: EAp. *evaḍu* (*etāvat*). These forms are found in all regions.

24) *-ḍḍa*<OIA *-*dra* : WSAp. *tevaḍḍa* (**tayavadra*=*tāvat*), *evaḍḍa* (**ayavadra*=*iyat*).

25) *-ṇī*<OIA *-nī* : Fem. e.g. *sāhu-ṇī* (*sādhu-*), *thambha-ṇī* SAp. *candāṇī* (*candra-*) on the analogy of (*stambānī Indrāṇī*, *hāliṇī* (*hala-* 'a plough') 'a peasant woman', WSEAp. *joiṇī* (*yoginī*).

26) *-tta*<OIA *-tva* : added to Substantives to form Abstract Substantives e.g.WAp. *mantitta* (*mantrin*+*tva*), *maṇuyatta* (*manujatva*). EAp. *sallatta* (*śalya-*). These are Prakritisms.[6]

27) *-ttaṇa*<OIA *-tvana* : applied to substantives to make Abstract Nouns. e.g. WSAp. *maṇuya-ttaṇa* (*manuja*), *siddhantaṇa* (*siddha-*), *devattaṇa* (*deva*). SAp. *rora-ttaṇa* (*rora-*'poverty -stricken'), *carittaṇa-* (*cārin-*).

Both the above-mentioned suffixes are used with Adjs. to form Abstract Nouns. e.g. WAp. *bahutta* (*bahu-*), *cavala-ttaṇa* (*capala-*), *bhalla-ttaṇu* (**bhad-la*=*bhad-ra*); SAp. *pharusattaṇa* (*paruṣa-*), *thaḍḍha-ttaṇa* (*stabdha-*); EAp. *tisi-ttaṇa* (*tṛṣita-*).

28) *-ttiya*<OIA **-tika*<*-tā*+*ika* : added to Adverbs to form Adjs. e.g. WSAp. *ettiya* (**ayat-tika*)=*iyat*. PISCHEL traces this from

---

4 *e.g.*, *Pu.* 17.18-19 *Hc.* 8.4.429-32, *Tr. Ld.* 3.3.29-32 *Rt.* 3.2.6-7, *Mk.* 17.5.-7. Artificial combinations in *Sh.* 22. 4,29,33,34 are not found in actual literature.

5 BLOCH, *FLM.* § 104; TURNER *BSOS* VIII ii-iii, p. 797. For Ap. see Ch. I. § 61.

6 PISCHEL, *Grammatik*, § 597.

to OIA **ayattya*+**ayattiya*[7]. *kettiu*, *kittiu* (**kayat-tika*) though equated with **kayattya*, **kayattiya* by PISCHEL. The same is the case with *jettia*, *tettia* and others.

29) *-ttula*<OIA **-tula*<*-tā*+*ula*: This is affixed to make Adjs. from Adverbs. e.g. *ettula* (*etāvat*), *kettula* (*kiyat-*). *jettula* (*yāvat-*), *tittula* (*tāvat-*).

30) *-du*: pleonastic. This is found only in the works of 'Eastern', Pk. grammarians.[8] e.g. *rukkha-du* (**ruksa-*) 'a tree'. *taruṇi-du* (*taruṇi-*), *bhūmidu* (*bhūmi-*), *vaṇa-du* (*vana-*) Neither EAp. nor WSAp. attests to it.

31-32) *-ppa*, *-ppaṇa*<OIA *-tva*, *-tvana*, a labial development (See §62.2.3). Another development viz. *-tta*, and *-ttana* is noted above. These are added to Adjs. to make Abstract Substantives. e.g. *vaḍḍappaṇa*: *vaḍḍattaṇa*, *bhallappaṇa*: *bhallattaṇa*.

33) *-maī̆* < OIA *-matī* : As in Pk. the last member of Fem. proper Nouns. e.g. *Sirimai* (*Śrīmatī*), *Dhaṇamai* (*Dhanamatī*), *Kaṇaya-mai* (*kanaka-matī*).

34) *-ya*<OIA *-ka* : It is found as *-a*, *-ya*, *-a-ya*, *-i-ya*, *-u-ya*. It is directly applied to words or is used in combination with other pleonastic affixes in their different forms. As most of these are separately treated, the examples are not repeated here. *-ya* being common to Pkt., words, e.g. *Nīsiriya* (*Niḥśrīka*), *tiya* (*strīka*), need not be regarded as purely Ap.

35) *-va*<OIA *-vat*, *-mat* : Out of these Adjective-forming suffixes. *-va*<OIA *-vat* is an ordinary Pkt. development. We may presume OIA **-vat* >*-va* in the spoken stage, though classical Sk. uses *-mat* for them. e.g. *Haṇuva* <**Hanu-vat*=°*mat*. *-va* ending Ap. words e.g. *candakava* (*candraka-vat*) can be found in other Pkt. dialects.

36) *-vaṇḍa*<OIA *-*vṛnda* : It is added to substantives to make nouns. e.g. *balivaṇḍa* 'might, force' as in balivaṇḍae *dharantaho suravaihiṁ*. 'In spite of the mighty efforts of the king of gods to hold it up'. (*No.* 8.3.2). Is there some Dravidian influence on this rare suffix ?

---

7 *Ibid.*, § 153.

8 See *Pu.* 17.20, *Mk.* 17.7.

37) *-vanta*<OIA *-vanta-*=*vat* : 'possessing, having'. This adjectival suffix is too common in Pkts. to need any elaboration here.

38) *-vāla*<OIA *-vat* : 'possessing'. e.g. *dhandha*=*vāla -lajjāvat* (*Pd.*122) for *dhayadhandhā ṇara-lajjā*. *Dn.* 5.57. Can we trace modern *-wala* in proper nouns to this ?

39) *-vi(ya)*<OIA *-vin*+*-ka*: 'possessing'. This is not peculiar to Ap. as forms in *-viya* (e.g. SAp. *māyāviya*) are the normal Pk. development of *-vin-ka*.

40) *-ra*(?)<OIA *-ru*: Pleonastic e.g. *kappara* (√*kḷp-*). Is Deśi *maḍap-phara* 'pride', a contamination of *mada*+*darpa*+*ra* ?

41) *-riṇa*<OIA ? : Another rare suffix of Abstract nouns in SAp. e.g. *tila-riṇa* (*taila-tva*) 'oily'.

42) *-risa*<OIA-*dṛśa* applied to Adverbs to make Adjs. e.g., *erisa* (*īdṛśa*), *kerisa* (*kīdṛśa*) and the like.[9]

43-44) *-la*, *-lī* (Fem.)<OIA *-ṭa*. pleonastic. It is different from *-āla*, *-ālu*, *-illa*, *-ulla* which are traceable to OIA *-ra* or *-la*. It was much productive in Ap. of all regions. e.g. WSAp. *poṭṭa-lī* (*poṭṭa* 'stomach'), *andhalaya* (*andha-*), EAp. *naggala* (*nagna-*). *-alla* as in SAp. *navalla* (*nava-*), WAp. *mahalla* (*mahat-*) *Dn.* 6.143 may be included under this.

45) *-(e)ha-u* <MIA *-isa* OIA *-dṛśa* : applied to Adverbs for forming Adjs. e.g. *jehau* (*yādṛśa*), *tehau* (*tādṛśa*), *kehau* (*kīdṛśa*), etc.[10]

This list of secondary suffixes is not exhaustive, but it may be claimed to be fairly representative of this stage of IA though some of these suffixes are common to other MIA dialects.

§159. The following table of Ap. suffixes gives their classification according to their powers :

1) Suffixes added to substantives to form substantives : *-tta*, *-ttaṇa*, *-ppa*, *-ppaṇa*, *-maī*, *-riṇa* (?), *-vaṇḍa*.

2) Suffixes applied to Adjs. for forming Abstract Substantives: *-ima*, *-tta*, *-ttaṇa*, *-ppa*, *-ppaṇa*.

---

9 For the change of OIA *-dṛ-*> MIA *-ri-*, See PISCHEL, *Grammatik*, § 245.

10 PISCHEL, *Grammatik*, § 262.

3) Suffixes added to Substantives for forming Adjs.: *-ara*, *-āla*, *-ālu(ya)*' *-i(ya)*, *-itta*, *-illa*, *-ira* *-va*, *-vanta*, *-vi(ya)*.

4) Suffixes added to Adjs. to form Adjs.: *-iya*, *-i(e-)ra*.

5) Suffixes for forming Adjs. from Verbs: *-ira*, *-evva*, *-rima* (?).

6) Suffixes added to Adverbs to form Adjs. *-(a)ḍa*, *-(a)ḍḍa*, *-ttia* (*-ya*), *-ttula*, *-risa*, *-ha(u)*.

7) Pleonastic suffixes: *-a*, *-ya*, *-aya*, *-āla*, *-ālu*, *-iya*, *-illa*, *-uya*, *-ulla*_ *-kka* (rare), *-ḍă* *-ḍĭ* (fem.), *du* (only in Eastern Pk. Gram› mars), *-ra* (rarely), *-la*, *-lī* (fem.), and different combinations of the pleonastic suffixes, *-ka*, *-ḍa*, *-la*.

8) Fem. suffixes: *-ă*, *ĭ*, *-ṇī*.

Many of these are common to literary Pkts.

## AN INDEX VERBORUM OF Ap. WORDS OCCURRING IN 'A HISTORICAL GRAMMAR OF APABHRAṀŚA.'

This Index Verborum covers all the Ap. vocables occurring in the body of the thesis, and includes the morphological illustrations as well. As we have prepared a separate Index Verborum of Ap. words cited in Pk. grammars and commentaries on them, and in PISCHEL's *Grammatik*, and as this is not a lexicon of Ap. words, only those vocables (from different Ap. texts and Pk. grammars) which have been used in preparing the present work, are incorporated in this Index. It is thus quite natural that some Ap. works, which have not been mentioned herein, may contain that form or vocable. The abbreviations used herein have been already tabulated at the beginning. The remaining ones, being common to other standard works on Indian linguistics, can be easily understood. A single arabic figure indicates the verse number as in the cases of those coming after *DKK.*, *Dks. Mt.*, *Pd.*, *Sdd.*, etc. Three consecutive arabic figures (with dots to separate them) indicate the *sandhi*, *kaḍavaka* and line number ; for example figures after *MP. NC. JC. KKC.* etc. In every case we have followed the critical text and numbering of the editor. In *Hc.* all references are to Ch. VIII.4 unless mentioned otherwise. Though we have given etymological equations and cognates from OIA, MIA and NIA, this does not claim to be a comparative etymological Index Ap. vocables.

*aïra-* (*acira-*) Adverbially *-iṇa Sc.* 586.5, *-eṇa Sc.* 508.9.

*aïratti* (**ati -raktī*) Ins. sg. *-e Hc.* 438.

*aïsa* (**a-dṛśa=īdṛśa*) *DKK.* 24, *DKS* 10, 78, *Sh.* 22.61. 'here' *DKK* 20.

(SHAHIDULLA - *Les Chants Mystiques* p. 99).

Masc. Nom. sg. *-ē DKS.* 77, *-u Kc.* 52, *Ld. Tr.* 3. 3. 10, *-o Hc.* 403.

*aüho* (*ayudhaḥ*) *Mt.* 11.

*akayattha* (*akṛtārthaḥ*) *Kc.* 46.

*akkaṭa* (*akṛta*) *=āscarya* 'wonder' *DKS.* 78.

*akkanda-i* (*=ākrāmati*) *Sc.* 529.8, Abs. *-iuṇa, Sc.* 531.4 (cognate with Sk. *ākrānta* ?)

*akhaï* (*akṣati*) *=akṣaya Pd.* 169.

*akhaīṇi* (*akṣayinī*)

Loc. sg. zero *Pd.* 42 ('*akṣayinī ..par*' H. L. JAIN *Pd.* p.15).

*akkha* (*akṣa*) 'game at dice' *Kp*. 27.6.

*akkha-i-*(*ā-khyā-ti*) *BhK*. 25.5, Pres. Ind. *-mi BhK*. 95.6, *Sdd*. 1, *Ys*. 2. *-hi Mt*. 29. *-hā BhK*. 180.6. *-huṁ Kc*. 42. Imp. *-hi BhK*. 145.3. *-hu BhK*. 99. 6. pp. *-iya BhK*. 106.9 *MP*. 2.6.2.

*akkhara* (*akṣara*) *BhK*. 18.2, *DKK*. 23, *DKS*. 60, *KKC*. 1.7.7. Ins. Pl. *-hiṁ Sdd*.1

*akkharaḍa* (*akṣara-ṭa*) (pleonastic) *Pd*. 86.

*akkhāḍaya* (*akṣapāṭa*), *akṣavāṭa* (Sk.lex.) 'arena, place of combat' *Hv*. 86.6.13. (Pa. *akkhavāṭa*, M. *akhāḍā*, Punj. *akhāṛā*, Kāshmiri *-akahār*. For more discussion S. M. Katre, *Prākrit Languages*, p. 76).

*akkhi* (*akṣi*.) Loc. sg. *-hiṁ Hc*. 357, Acc. pl. zero *DKs* 2, 5. (M. H. Guz. *ākh*, M. *ākh*, Sdh. *akha*, Punj. *akkh*. Beng. Or. *khi*)

*akkhiya-mettī* (=*ākhyāta-mātreṇa*) *Mp*. 2.6.2

*akkheva* (*ākṣepa*) Ins. Sg. *-iṇa Sn*. 335-127.

*akkhoha* (*akṣobha*, *akṣobhya*) Ins. Pl. *-ehī DKK*. 3.

*agāa*(=*agamya*) *Nc*. 2. 3. 12.

*agga* (*agra*) Adv. *aggai*=*agre Sc*. 504.5.

*aggi* (*agni*) Acc. Sg. zero *DKS*. 2, Ins. Sg. *-eṁ*, *-ṁ*, *-ṇa*. *Hc*. 344. Loc. Sg. *-hiṁ Sdd*. 39. °*ya-ē*=*agninā PPr*. 1. 1. (Pa. Pk. *aggi* M.H. Guz. *āg*, Maith. *āgi*, Punj. *agga*).

*aṁga* (*ts*.) Ins. Sg. *-eṁ*. *Mt*. 32, cf. *Hc*. 396.4.

*aṁguli* (*ts*.) Nom. Pl. *-u BhK*. 167.8, *Hc*. 333. (M. *aṁgaḷī*, *aṁgulī*, Guz. *aṁguḷī* (°*lī*), *āṁgḷī*, H. *aṁgulī*, *uṁglī*, Sdh. *aṁguri*. Punj. *uṁgulī*).

*acokkha-u-*(*a-cokṣa-ka*) 'dirty' *Jc*. 3. 36. 17. (M. H. *cokh*, Guz. *cokkhũ*, Punj. *cokkhā*).

*accattham* Adv. *atyartham Kp*. S. 103.1*

*Accuya Acyuta* 'N. of a heaven in Jain mythology.'

*Hv*. 81. 11. 12; 92. 18. 13. also 90.6.9, 92.15.6.

√*accha*=√*as* 'to be,' 'to stand' cf. *Hc*. 215, but rather *ā-kṣi* '*nivāsa-gatyoḥ*., Pres. Ind. *-mi Bhk*. 82. 6, *Jc*. 3.21.6, *-ũ DKK*. 18. *-esi Pd*. 91. *-hi BhK*. 25. 7, *KKC*. 1. 15. 7. *-hu BhK*. 226.10.

-*i* BhK. 36. 2, KKC. 1. 11. 5, Pd. 58, 136. -(*a*)*nti* BhK.
24. 9. -*hĩ* PPr. 1. 5. Imp. 2p. sg. -*hi* BhK. 38. 2, DKS. 56.
-*hu* BhK. 28. 9. DKS. 59. -*u* BhK. 4. 1, Pd. 215, Sc. 516.7,
Sdd. 30. 2pl. -*ha* Jdu. 1. 3. -(*a*)*ntũ* BhK. 215.8, Fut. -*isu*
Sc. 142.8. -*esaï* Pd. 182. Pres. Part. -*anta* Pd. 122.

(Sk. *ākṣeti*, Pa. *acchati* 'abides, stays.' M. *asṇē* Nep.
\**chunu*, Guz. *chũ*, Mar. *chũ*, Maith. Beng. *āchi*, Or. *achi*.
For more discussion TURNER, BSOS 8. 2-3. 795-812).

*acchi* (*akṣi*) BhK. 250. 9, PPr. 1. 121, Sc. 584. 5. Loc. Sg. -*hĩ* Mt. 7.

*accheraya* (*āścaryaka*) BhK. 65. 1, Kp. K 3.2.

*acchoḍiu* (*ākṣoḍita*) =*āsphoṭita* in Jc. 3. 10. 8 Kp. J. 72.1. cf. *ācchoṭa*. 'das
Schlagen mit dem Schwanz' PWB as quoted by ALSDORF
in Kp. Glossar.

*ajoa* (*ayoga*) Ins. Sg. -*eṁ* BhK. 87. 6.

*aju* < *ajju*  (*adya*) Sc. 614.3.

*ajja* (*adya*) BhK. 10.7, Sc. 706.1, Sn. 355-27.

*ajju* (*adya*) BhK. 178.10, Jc. 4. 5. 12, Sc. 489.7 (Sk. *adya*, Pa. Pk. *ajja*, M.
H. Guz. *āj*, Beng. Or. *āji*, Sdh. *āju*, Punj. *ajj*).

*ajja* (*arjay*) Imp. 2p. Sg. -*esu* Kp. A. 6. 4.

*aṁca*( *arcay*) PP. -*iya* BhK. 114.13, JC. 2. 4. 1, Abs. -*ivi* BhK. 47. 1.

*aṁcāiṇi*(=*arcitā*) JC. 1. 9. 13.

*aṭṭa* (*ārta*) JC. 3. 21. 6.

*aṭṭha* (*aṣṭa*) BhK. 96. 4, Kp. J. 82.4, S. 31.2,\* 34.2\*, Sc. 470.5. Nom.
Acc. zero Sc. 602.3, 600.9. Neut. -*iṁ* Sdd. 26. Ins. -*hĩ*
Sc. 604.6, Gen. -*h* Sc. 601. 8. (Sk. *aṣṭā*: Pa. Pk. *aṭṭha*,
M. H. Guz. *āṭh*, Beng. *āṭ*, Punj *aṭṭh*).

*aṭṭhatīsa* (*aṣṭa-triṁśat*) Mp. 2. 5. 4. (Pa. *aṭṭha-tiṁsam* M. H. *aḍtīs*, Guz.
*aḍtrīs*).

*aṭṭhama* (*aṣṭama*) KKc. 10. 16. 4, Sdd. 15.

*aṭṭhami* fem. (*aṣṭamī*) Loc. Pl. -*hiṁ* Sdd. 13.

*aṭṭhayāla*=*aṣṭa-catvāriṁśat* BhK. 316. 1.
(Pa. *aṭṭhacattārīsa*, Pk. *aṭṭhacattālīsa*, *aṭṭhacattāla* > \**aṭṭhā-*
*catāla* leading to the Ap. vocable. M. *aṭṭhecāḷ*, *aṭṭhetaḷ*,
Guz. *aḍtālīs*, etc. TURNER 9[a]).

*aṭṭhuttara-saya* (*aṣṭottara-śata*) *Kp.* S. 31.2.

*aḍavaḍa* (*aṭapaṭa*) (Onomatopoeic) *Pd.* 6, 145.

*aḍavi* (*aṭavī*) Loc. Sg. *-hiṁ KKc.* 7. 1. 10.

*aṇaṇṇa* (*ananya*) *Kp.* A. 6, 3.

*aṇaṇṇāïsa* (*ananyādṛśa*) *Kc.* 58.

*aṇavarāïsa* (**anaparādṛśa=ananyādṛśa*) *Kc.* 58.

*aṇahijja* (f.) (*anabhijñā.*) Loc. Sg. *-e Mt.* 20.

*aṇāï* (*anādi*) Ins. Pl. *-hi Jc.* 1. 2. 26.

*aṇu*(*=anyat*) *PPr.* 2. 44.*=anyathā Hc.* 415, *Kc.* 60, *Ld.* 3. 3. 51, *Sh.* 22. 21. *Tr.* 3. 3. 51.

*aṇuṭṭha* (*anu √sthā.*) Imp. 2 pl. *-ha Sn.* 30-231.

*aṇuṇenti* f.](*anu-nayantī*) Loc. Sg. *-hī Mt.* 3.

*aṇupehā* (*anuprekṣā*) Acc. Pl. zero *Pd.* 211.

*aṇumaï* (*anumati*) Acc. Sg. zero *Sdd.* 16.

*aṇumagga* (*anumārga*) Ins. Sg. *-eṁ̆ BhK.* 46.11.

*aṇu-valla*(*=anu-pālaya-?*) (Jacobi *BhK.* p. 124). *-hi BhK.* 160.2.

*aṇu-sara-*(*anu √sṛ* (*sar-*)Pres. 3p. Pl. *-hiṁ Sdd.* 117. Imp. 3p. Sg. *-u KKc.* 9.7.4.

*aṇu-hara-* (*anu-√hṛ*) (*har-*) PPr. *-māṇaũ BhK.* 132. 5.

*aṇu-hava-* (*anu- √bhū-*) Imp. 3p. Sg. *-u BhK.* 145.10, 3p. Pl. *-ntu BhK.* 188.13.

*aṇu-huṁja-* (*anu- √bhuj-*) (*bhuñj-*). Imp. 2p. Pl. *-hu KKc.* 3.10.10.

*aṇṇa* (*anna*) *anya*, *anyat DKK.* 16, *DKs.* 40,104 *Hc.* 372, *PPr.* 2.45. *Sc.* 617-1. Masc. Nom. Sg. *-u Sc.* 490.8. Gen. Sg. *-ha Sc.* 735.3. Loc. Sg. *-hiṁ Hc.* 357.2, 383.3, 422.9, Neut. Direct Pl. *-iṁ Hc.* 427.1. Ins. Pl. *-ihī Sc.* 769.3. Fem. Gen. Sg. *-hi*, *-hĕ Hc.* 425.1

*aṇṇa*(*nn*)*aha* *anyathā Hc.* 415, *Kc.*, 60., *Sc.* 504.8.

*aṇṇ*(*nn*)*āïsa* *anyādṛśa Hc.* 413, *Tr. Ld.* 3.3.55, *Sh.* 66.

*aṇṇ'ekka* *anyaika Hv.* 82.13.9. Fem. Ins. Sg. *-i Jc.* 2,34,3,

| | |
|---|---|
| *aṇṇ'ettahĕ* | *anyatra Hv*. 81.11.1 |
| *aṇṇoṇṇa* | *anyonya*. Ins. Pl. -*hĩ Mt*. 13. |
| *atta* | *ārta Sc*. 692.7. |
| *atthamiya* | *astamita* Masc. Loc. Sg., -*iṁ Sdd*. 37. |
| *atthavaṇa* | *astamana* (*atthamaṇa* in *Hc*. 444.2). Loc. Sg. -*i PPr*. 2.132. |
| *atthi* | (Sktism) *asti BhK*. 84.5, *DKs*. 7. *Jc*. 1.3.4. *Kp*. J. 2.1, 46.1. *MP*. 1.17.1 (Sometimes Historical Present.) |
| *atthu* | (Sktism) *astu Kp*. A. 2.4, J. 51.5. |
| *adaa* | *advaya DKs*. 100. |
| *adaṁsaṇa* | *adarśana* Ins. Sg. -*i Jdc*. 9.4. |
| *addaṁsaṇa* | *adarśana* 'invisibility' *Hv*.82.4.3. 'invisible' *Hv*. 82.4.6. |
| *addaïya-vāya* | *advaita-vāda Hv*. 83.5.10. |
| *addiya* | *ārdrita BhK*. 40.5 |
| *anta-ḍa*, °-*ḍaa*, °-*ḍaaā*, °-*ḍiā*, °-*ḍī*=*antra* | *Sh*.. 28-34 but |
| *antra-ḍī* | =*antra* in *Hc*. 445.3. |
| *antara* (*ts*.) | Ins. and Loc. Sg. -*ẽ Mt*. 17,33. Loc. -*i Hc*. 434. |
| *antima-tigu* | °-*trikam Sn*. 15-286. |
| *Andhakaviṭṭhi* | °*vṛṣṇi Hv*. 83.11.14. |
| *andhāra* | *andhakāra DKs*. 99. Ins. Sg. -*iṁ Sdd*.6, Loc. Sg. -*ẽ DKK*. 22. -*i Hc*. 349.1. |
| *appa-i* | *arpayati* Abs. -*ivi KKc*. 2.6.5. |
| *appa* | *ātman Kp*. J. 4.9. Nom. Sg. zero *DKs*. 62, 107, *Pd*. 44. -*u BhK*. 243.4, 257.3, *Sc*. 489.4. Acc. Sg. -*u BhK*. 70.3, *Hc*. 422.3 *Mt*. 1. *Pd*. 129. *Sc*. 669.4. -*ũ Sc*. 515.8, -*ṁ BhK*. 102.1. -*uṁ Jc*. 3.7.2. *Sn*. 270-190. Ins. Sg. -*ĕ*,ŏ -*eṁ*, -*ĕ Pd*. 178. *PPr*. 1.56, 99. -*eṇa Jc*. 3.7.2. -*iṁ PPr*. 1.76. -*hi DKs*. 62. Dat. Gen. Sg. -*ho Hc*. 336. -*hu Sdd*. 104, -*ha Sc*. 589.9. -*haŏ PPr*. 2.155. Loc. Sg. -*e Pd*. 204, *PPr*. 1.102. -*i Pd*. 83, 10. -*hiṁ Pd*. 78. -*hi DKs*. 62. -*haṁ pd*. 133. |
| *appaḍihaya* | *apratihata Sc*. 470.2. |

| | |
|---|---|
| *appaṇa* | =*ātman* Direct Sg. -*u DKs.* 67, *Hc.* 337, 422, *Jc.* 2.10.15. Ins. Sg. -*eṁ Hc.* 416. *appaṇā* (Sktism) *Pd.* 119. Gen. Sg. zero *DKs.* 85, *Sdd.* 84. *appaṇu DKs.* 81, *Mt.* 13 (M. Guz. *āpaṇ*, Nep. *āphnu*). |
| *appattha* | *apathya* Ins. Sg. -*eṁ Sdd.* 41. |
| *appā* | *ātmā PPr.* 1.51. Direct Sg. zero *DKs.* 62, *Mt.* 13, *Pd.* 8.3. *PPr.*195, Ins. Sg. -*e*, *Pd.* 75. Gen. Sg. zero *PPr.* 1.30. |
| *appāṇa* | =*ātman.* Direct Sg. zero *DKs.* 98, *Pd.* 33. -*u Hc.* 396, *KKc.* 9.44. *Kp.* S. 12.2. *Pd.* 7, 139. *Sc.* 613.7. Gen. Sg. zero *DKs.* 108, *Pd.* 25. |
| *appia* | *apriya* Loc. Sg. -*e Hc.* 365.1. |
| *appuṇu* | =*ātmanā Jc.* 1.5.17. *Pd.* 83.<br>=*ātmanaḥ KKc.* 4.3.4. |
| *apphāla-i* | *āsphālayati* Abs. -*vi BhK.* 146.3. |
| *abadhūi* | *avadhūtī* Nom. Sg. zero *DKK.* 4. |
| *abejja* | *avidyā DKs.* 53. |
| *abhakkha* | °*kṣ-ya BhK.* 320.3. |
| *abhaṇiya* | °*ṇya* 'unbecoming, unseemly.' *Hv.* 91.2.5. |
| *abhha* | *abhra Sc.* 757.5 Direct Pl. -*ā Hc.* 445. |
| *abbhattha-* | *abhi-√arthay-* Pres. 1p. Sg. -*emi Mt.* 24. |
| *abbhiṭṭa* | =*abhigata Mp.* 32.6.13.<br>Prob. pp. of √*abbhiḍa* cf. Pk. *bhiṭṭana Hc.* 383.3 (*M. bheṭṇē* 'to meet each other,' 'to embrace.' Traceable to Sk. *abhi-* √*aṭ* -*abhyaṭati* ?) |
| *abbhukkhaṇu* | *abhyākhyānaṁ Sn.* 271-190. |
| *amaṇṭha* | **amṛṣṭa*=*amanojña, amarṣaṇa Hv.* 91.15.4. |
| *amaṇā* | *āgmana* °*gamana* ' coming and passing' *DKs.* 70. |
| *amaya* | *amṛta Sc.* 465.2. |
| *amayamaï* | *Amṛta-matī Jc.* 3.41.6. |
| *Amayavaï* | *Amṛtavatī Hv.* 91.7.8. |
| *amara* (*ts.*) | Nom. pl. zero *MP.* 87.16.12. |
| *Amarāurī* f. | *Amara-purī KKc.* 3.22.5. |

*amavāsa* — *amāvāsyā Hv.* 82.9.5.
(*Pk. amāvāsa* Guz. *amās,* M. *āvas amūs, amośā.* H. *amās,* Sdh *umāsu*

*amia* — *amṛta DKs.* 58, *KKc.* 2.15.6, *Sdd.*168.
Direct Sg. *-u Sdd.* 2.

*Amiyaveya Amita-vega KKc.* 5.4.2.

*amū* — *=adas.*
Direct Sg. zero *Tr. Ld.* 3.4.32 Ins. Sg. *-eṁ, -ṇa. Tr. Ld.* 3.4.35. Direct Pl. *-iṁ Tr. Ld.* 3.4.32.

*ammā* — *ambā* 'mother' *Hv.* 85.7.4.
Dat. Sg. *-hiṁ Jc.* 3.11.6. Voc. Sg. *ammi Hc.* 395. *ammīe Hc.* 396. Hence the Interjection *ammie=aho Pd.* 51. It is probably to this vocable that *ammāhīraa* 'lullaby' in *MP.* 4.4.13. is traceable.

*ambhāra* — **asma-kāra. Pu.* 17.30 (vide *amhāra-* below).

*ambhu* — *aśman Ld.* 3.3.2.

*-aṁvala* — or *-aṽala,°-kamala*
Direct Pl. *-ī Kc.* 47. cf. *Hc.* 4.397.

*amha* — *asma*
Direct: *-iṁ, BhK.* 28.6, *Tr. Ld.* 3.4.48,
*Sh.* 22.54. *-ī BhK.* 29.2, *Hc.* 376.
*-i Jdu.* 51.3. *Kp.* J. 4.6. *Sc.* 643.6.
*-e* (i.e. *amhe*) *Hc.* 376, *Kp.* E. 4. *Sh.* 22.54.
*-eiṁ Tr. Ld.* 3.4.48.
Instr. *-ī BhK.* 44.6. *Jc.* 4.4.2.
*-ihī Kp.*S. 66.3.
*-ehiṁ, °hī Hc.*378, *Sh.* 22.56.
*-ehi Tr. Ld.* 3.4.49
-zero *BhK.*111.4 *-hiṁ Pd.* 138.
Dat. Gen. zero *BhK.* 14.3, *Jc.* 3.2.12, *Kp.*J. 46.1,
*Pd.* 138, *Sc.* 561.2.
*-iṁ Jc.* 4.4.7.
*-hã, -haṁ, BhK.* 28.3, 41.7, *Hc.* 380,
*KKc.* 1.14.12, *Tr. Ld,* 3.4.44.
*Sc.* 601.1, *Sh.* 22.58
*-ha Kp.* J. 51.6. *Mp.* 1.4.6, *Sc.* 486.4.
*-ho KKc.* 3.12.10.
*-(ā)ṇa(ṁ) -Pkt.ism. BhK.* 69.11, *Jc.* 1.15.12,
*Kp.*J. 48.2*, *Mt:* 4, *Sn.* 17-570.

Loc. -(ā)su Hc. 381. Tr. Ld. 3.4.50, Sh. 22.59. (Sk. asme Instr. asmābhiḥ, Pa. Direct amhe, Instr. amhehiṁ, Pk. Direct amhe, Instr. amhehī. Gen. amha, amhāṇaṁ. Loc. amhāsu. In NIA: M. āmhī, Guz. ame, Bg. āmi 'I', Or. āmbhi.

amhāra — *asma-kāra (kārya) =asmadīya. -u Tr. Ld. 3.3.23. -uṁ Kc. 74. cf. Hc. 434. -ā Hv. 91.3.2, Sh. 22.65.

ayaṇḍi — -akāṇḍe Sc. 651.3.

ayāṇuya — =ajña (>*a-jānuka) Nom. Pl. zero Jdc.4.4

arabinda — -aravinda Nom. Sg. -ĕ DKK.6.

aravinda-rāya — °-rājan Gen. Sg. -ho BhK. 234.1.

arari — are re Sc. 582.6.

Arahanta — Arhat BhK. 1.9. Ins. Sg. -iṁ Sdd. 4. Gen. Sg. -ho Jc. 1.1.1.

ari(ri) — are(re) Pd. 92, Sc. 586.4, 591.6.

ari (ts.) — Gen. Sg. -hu MP. 85.4.15, Ins. Pl. -hī Sc. 447.4.

arisaya — arśa-ka Sc. 768.3.

ariha, — arhat Hv. 85.4.13.

arihanta — (Pkt.) arhat BhK. 329.7.

Aruha — Arhat BhK. 321.4, Hv. 82,6.5. Nom. Sg. -u MP. 1.6.16. °datta Arhadatta Hv. 82.13.11. °dāsa Arhaddāsa Hv. 81.3.8.

Aruhanta — Arhat MP. 1.1.10.

arere (ts.) — MK. 17.8

Alayāuri — Alakāpurī Loc.Sg. -hi MP. 90.2.17.

alahantau — a-labha-māna Sc. 516.2.

a-lahivi — alabdhvā (abs. in -ivi) Kp. S. 92.8.

allaviya — alāpita BhK. 223.15.

ali (ts.) — Nom. Pl. -a DKK.2.

*ava-gaṇṇa* -　*ava* -√*gaṇ*
Imp. 2 Sg. *-i Sdd.* 20.

*avattha*　*-avasthā*
Fem. Loc. Sg. *-hiṁ Pd.* 170.

*avayara*　*-ava* √*-tar*
Pres. 1 Pl. *-huṁ*. No. 6.5.9, but the Tippaṇa explains it as '*upakurmaḥ*'. Is it connected with *apa*√*kar* in the sense of *upa* √*kar*? PP. *-ia Nc.* 2.8.9.

*avara*　*apara*
Masc. Neut. Loc. Sg. *-i Jdc.* 6.3. Fem. Ins. Pl. (*ā*) *-hiṁ MP.* 87.13.3.

*avarupparu*　*parasparaṁ BhK.* 5.5, *Hc.* 4.409, *KC.* 55. *Kp.*S. 16.6,*Sn.* 30-231.

*avaro-pparu*　*parasparam Hv.* 82.7.5, *JC.* 1.15.15.

*avarovaru*　*parasparam Ld.* 3.3.54.

*ava-lova*　*ava-loka-ya.*
Imp. 2 Pl. *-hu KKc.* 5.15.5. Is Sg. used for Pl. here?

*avasa*　*avaśyam Hc.* 4.427, *Hv.* 92.3.10, *Kc.* 71.
Also *avasi Sn.* 21.287, *avasiṁ Jc* 1.7.15.
*avasu BhK.* 121.7, *avassu Sc.* 529.9.
*avaseṁ BhK.* 39.8, *Hv.* 85.2.12, *Kc.* 71, *MP.* 15.22.10.
*avasaiṁ Sdd.* 99. *avasaya Jdc.* 31.4.

*ava-hara*　*apa-*√*har*
Imp. 2 Pl. *-eha Sc.* 599.3.
Imp. 3 Pl. *-antu KKc.* 9.16.6.

*ava-hīla*　*ava-*√*dhīr-aya.*
Imp. 2 Pl. *-ha Sc,* 648.3.
(cf. M. *avahelaṇe*).

*ava-hēra-i*　*ava-dhīrayati.*
Pres. 2 Sg. *-hi Hv.* 92.12.4. PP. *-ia Nc.* 3.9.10.
The Tippaṇa explains it as '*vicāritam*' (cf. M *avherṇe*).

*avaheri*　Noun from the above. *Hv.* 91.13.2. (cf M. *avhēr*, H. *aver*).

*avāsa*　*avasyaṁ Ld.* 3.3.27, also *avāseṁ.*

*avāha*　*abādhā*
Fem. Ins. Sg. *-e Sc.* 452.1.

*avikkhaṇa* *avekṣaṇa BhK.* 278.3.

*avicallu* *avicālyaḥ Mt.* 30.

*avvo* Interjection 'Oh Mother' *Hv.* 89.10.12.
(cf. Dn. 1.5. *avvā*
'Mother', Dravidian -*avva* 'Mother' cf. Koṅk. *āvay*).

*asaï* *asatī*
Fem. Ins. Pl. -*hiṁ Hc.* 4.396.

*asaddha-māṇa* *aśraddadhāna Sc.* 772.7

*asavaṇṇa* *asāmānya Sc.* 667.2.

*asavāra* *aśvavāra* 'a rider' *Hv.* 88.7.14.
Prob. old Pers. loan cf. Pers. *aswār*, H. *asavā*, M. *swār*).

*asii* *aśīti Sc.* 527.1.
(cf. Pk. *asīi*, M. *aiś aiśi* G. *ēśī*, Nep. *assi*,
Bloch and Turner regard *aśśī* a. the M. form).

*asilaya* *asi-latā*
Acc. Sg. zero *KKc.* 2.3.10.

*asuṇṇa* *aśūnya DKK.* 10.

*aṁsu*, °*ya*, °*va*, *aśru-ka BhK.* 27.5,110.9,66.11.
(cf. Pa. *assu*, Pk. *aṁsu* M. *ā̆su*, G. *ā̆sū*, H. Nep. *ā̆sū*

*aha* *atha Sdd.* 200, *Sn.* 78-332. In the former it may be taken as *yathā*.

*ahakkamiṇa* *yathākrameṇa Sc.* 782.6.

*ahaṇisu* *aharniśaṁ Hv.* 82.12.5.

*aharattu* *ahorātram Nc.* 4.5.4.

*ahava* *athavā BhK.* 279.6, *Hc.* 4.419, *Kc.* 64. *Sc.* 469.6, *Sdd.* 6.

*ahavaï* *athavā BhK.* 38.<, *Hc.* 4.419, Ld. 3.3.47.

*ahaha* (*ts.*) *Sc.* 585.1.

*ahāṇaa* *ābhāṇaka Sdd.* 24. (cf. M.H. *ahāṇā*, 'saying').

*ahikaṁkhira* *abhikāṅkṣin Sc* 554.7.

*ahigāra* *adhikāra Kp.* S. 51.4.

√*ahiṇāṇa* Denom. from *abhijñāna*. Imp. 2 Sg. -*hi Hv.* 82.15.9.

*ahiyāsa-ī* *adhyāsaya-ti Sc. 778.4.
PPr. -anta Sc. 769.8, Abs. -ivi Sc. 781.2.

*ahuṭṭha-haṁ* =adhastāt Pd. 94.

*ahēsi* =abhūt Sc. 447.8.

*aho(hu)(ts.)* BhK. 39.7, aho'hu=aho ho BhK. 289.8.

*aho-gaĩṇaṁ* adho-gaāganam Jc. 2.2.3.

*ā*

*āa* See āya=idam below.
Neut. direct Sg. -u Sh. 22.41. cf. Hc. 4.365. direct Pl. -iṁ Sh. 22.42.

*ā-akkha* =ā√khyā. Imp. 2 Sg. -hi Mt. 24. Pp. -iu Mt 24.

*āïddha* āviddha=gṛhīta.
Neut. direct Sg. -u MP. 1.12.13.

*āïria, °ya* acārya Nc. 6.10.5, Sdd. 12.
Ins. Pl. -ehiṁ MP. 1.14.11.

*āü* āyus Hv. 81.13.7.Ys. 49.

*āüccha-i* āpṛccha-ti PPr. fem. -antī BhK. 25.8.

*āgaccha-* (ts.) Pres. 3 P. Sg. -i Sc. 531.6, Imp. 2 p. Sg. -su Sc. 515.2. -ha Sc. 740.2, PPr, -anta Sc. 644.8. -ira Sc. 595.8.

*āgama-* (ts.) DKK.2. Loc. Sg. -ā DKS. 81.

*āgara* ākara Sc. 444.6.

*-āḍova* āṭopa Sc. 582.7.

*āḍha* āḍhya BhK. 86.7.

*āḍhantao* =ādadhat Mt. 22.

*āṇa* ājñā Ins. Sg. -iṁ KKc. 1. 5. 6. (Pa. aññā, āṇā f. 'order.' Pk. āṇā, aṇṇā, M.G. āṇ. -'oath' Sgh. aṇa 'order' Sdh. āṇa 'submission.')

*āṇī (°ṇa)* ā-√nī-
Imp. 2 Sg. -ehu Jc. 1.8.4. PP. āṇī=ānītā Pd. 99.
Abs. -eppiṇu Nc. 1.15.15, -eviṇu BhK. 188.5.
-ivi Sc. 729.8, Ger. -ivvau BhK. 29.10.
(M. āṇaṇē, G. āṇvũ, H. ānanā, Sdh. āṇaṇũ).

*āmilla* = √*muñc*.
Imp. 2 P. Sg. *-hu BhK.* 176.3.

*āya* *āgata*
Masc. direct Sg. *-u KKc.* 1.11.7, *Hv.* 81.14.5.
*Hv.* 83.22.14, Direct Plur. zero, *Hv.* 81.17.2, Neut.-ī
*Hv.* 90.15.8 *-ā Hv.* 81.11.6. Fem. *-u Hv.* 84.2.9.

*āva* =*idam*
Masc. Sing. Direct *-u BhK.* 292.6, 132.3.
Neut *-u Bhk.* 274.10.
Ins. *-eṁ Bhk.* 39.8. *eṇa Bhk.* 6.4.58.6. *-eṇa Hc.* 4.365.
Dat. Gen. *-ho BhK.* 45.5. *Hc.* 4.365, *Hv.* 81.16.4.
*Kc.* 29. *-haṁ Nc.* 2.10.6, Loc. *-hiṁ Hc.* 4.383.
Neut Direct Plur. *-iṁ*, *-ī Hc.* 4.365, *Kc.* 29,
*-hiṁ Jc.* 1.17.15.
Gen. *-haṁ Mp.* 2.10.19.
Fem. Sing. Ins. *-e BhK.* 147.4., *-hī BhK.* 114.7 (?).
*-hi BhK.* 114.9(?), Gen. *-he BhK.* 146.6. *-ho BhK.* 171.10.
Plur. Ins. *-hī*, *-hi. BhK.* 114.7, 114.9 regarded as doubtful by Jacobi (see *BhK. Glossar*), *-ehī BhK.* 117.9
Gen. *-hā BhK.* 51.4, *-hī BhK.* 248.5.

*āya* *āpad* Loc. Sg. *-iṁ Pd.* 6.

*āyaḍḍa-* PP. of √*āyaḍḍa*=*vyāpriyate Hc.* 4.81, *Sc.* 662.2.

*āyaṇṇa* *ā-karṇay*
Pres. 3 Sg. *-i Sc.* 553.2, Imp. 2. Sg. *-hiṁ Nc.* 1.3.1.
PP. *-iya Sc.* 639.7.

*āyamba* *ātāmra KKc.* 3.11.4.

*āyariyaï* *ācāryaḥ Jdc.* 11.4.

*āra* *ākāra DKs.* 57.

*ārāva* *ārāma Hv.* 81.3.7.

*āruha* *ā*-√*ruh*
Pres. 3 Sg. *-i Sc.*536.2, Imp. 2 Sg. *-ha Sc.* 645.2.
3 P. Sg. *-u KKc.* 9.7.5. Abs. *-eviṇu Sc.* 530.3.

*ālatta* **ālapta*=*ālapita BhK.* 203.7.

*āle* *alaṁ DKs.* 35, 51.

*āva* √*āp* but many times equated with *ā*-√*i* or *ā* √*gam*.- or *ā*√*yā*. Pres. 3 Sg. -*i* *Hv*. 81.9.9. -*ei* *Hv*. 82.16.8, 3P. Plur. -*hiṁ*, *hī* *KKc*. 2.13.6 *Sc*. 457.5.
Imp. 2 Sg. -*ahi* *Hv*. 89.15.15, -*ehi* *Hv*. 84.11.14.
-*u* *Hv*. 85.9.9 3P. Sg. -*u* *Sdd*. 58. Fut. 2 Sg. -*esahi* *Hv*. 92.6.9, 3 Sg. -*esaï* *KKc*. 2.5.5.
PPr. -*antu* *Hv*. 90.4.14. Abs. -*eppinu* *Hv*. 81.4.11, -*evi* *Hv*. 82.10.6 -*ĕvi* *Hv*. 82.6.10.

*āvaï* *āpad* *Sc*. 681.8.

*āvariya* *āvṛta* *Sc*. 650.3.

*āsā̆* *āśā* *DKK*. 25, Nom. Sg. zero *Ys*. 49.

*āsi* Sktism for *āsīt* *Hv*. 92.18.1. *JC*. 2.8.5, *JdC* 5.1 *Kp*. J. 91.1, S. 5, 1. Used in 1 P. Sg. in *BhK*. 327.5, and in 2P. Sg. *BhK*. 28.4.

*āhasantae* **ābhāṣantake*=*ābhāṣamāṇe* *Mt*. 20.

*āhuṭṭha* *ardha* - **tŭrtha* 'Three and half' *MP*. 11.25.2.
(cf. Pk. *addhuṭṭha*, M. *auṭ*, *aūṭ* G. *ŭṭhu* *ūṭh*).

**i**

-*i* *cit*, *api*, *Mt*. 21.

*iü* =*iti* *Pd*. 52.

*iu* *etat* *Kp*. S. 47.2 *idam* *PPr*. 2.155.

*ika* *eka* *Sdd*. 161.

*ikka* *ekā* *Sdd*. 43. Mas. Neut. Gen. Sg. -*hu* *Sdd*. 111.

*i(e)kkasi* *ekaśaḥ* *Hc*. 4.428, *Kc*. 71.

*iga* *eka*
Masc. direct Sg. -*u* *Sc*. 666.7, Fem. direct Sg. zero *Sc*. 609.5.
(cf. Pk. *ekka*, M.G.H. Nep. *ek*).

*icchă* *icchā* Fem. Ins. Sg. -*ē* *DKs*. 81.

*iccha* √*iṣ*>*icch*-
Pres. 2P. Plu. -*ha* *Hc*. 4.384, -*hu* *Hc*. 4.384, *Mt*. 20. -*ira* showing habit. *hv*. 85.6.8. PPr.
Fem. -*antiyā*. Ins. Sg. -*ē* *KKc*. 1.16.2.

*icchu* *ikṣu* *Sc*. 586.2.

*iṁcha* √*icch* Abs. -*iya* *Sdd*. 63.

*iṇi* =*anena* or *enena* *Sdd*. 205.

*ittiya* *strī-kā* *BhK*. 50.8.

*ittiya* =*iyattika* Direct Plur. (Neut). -*iṁ* *Sdd*. 107. (Pk. *ettaa*, *ettia*, M. *itkā*, *itukā*, Panj. H. *itnā*, Guj. *eṭlo*, Sdh. *etiro*, Sinh. *eta-kin*).

*itthi*, *itthu* =*atra* *Jdc*. 36.1., *PPr*.1.101, 2.211. *Sdd*. 71, 172, 189.

*itthi-* *strī* *Sn*. 19-286.

*inti* =*yanti* *Sn*. 15-296.

*indi*, *īdi*, *indiya*=*indriya* -*DKS*. 69, 91. *Sdd*. 140.

*ima* =*idam* *Pu*. 17,59, *Tr*. *Ld*. 3.4.36.
Masc. Neut. direct Sg. -*u*. *Hc*. 361. *Kc*. 28, *Ld*. 3.4.36, *MK*. 17.36, *Sh*. 22.41, *Tr*. 3.4.36.
-*o* *Sc*. 647.5, *Tr*. *Ld*. 3.4.36.
-*uṁ* *Pu*. 17.57. Ins. Sg. -*eṁ* *Tr*. *Ld*. 3.4.2, -*eṇa*. *MK*. 17.36. Gen. Sg. -*ssa* *Kp*. S. 40.3, *MK*. 17.36. -*ssu* *Sc*. 751.2 -*su* *Sc*. 653.5, Loc. Sg. -*hiṁ*. *Tr*. *Ld*. 3.4.2., -*mmi* *Sc*. 628.7. Acc. *Pl*. *imē* *Kp*. A. 8.3. Fem. Nom. Pl. -*āu* *Sc*. 596.8.

*imerisa* =*etādṛśa* *Sc*. 751.3.

*iya* **ika<eka* *Sc*. 747.9.

*iya* *iti* *Jc*. 1.6.16.

*iyara* *itara*
Masc. Nom. Sg. -*o* *Sc*. 721.2, -*u* *Sc*. 574.1.
Gen. Sg. -*assu*, *Sc*, 676.1, -*hu* *MP*. 2.16.5. Masc. Nom. Pl. -*ē* (Skt. sm. ?) *Sc*. 461.4, Gen. Pl. -*esi*, *Sc*. 586.9. Fem. Nom. Sg. zero *Sc*. 485.6.

*iha* =*etad*.
Masc. Nom. Sg. -*u* *Kp*. S. 66.8, *Sc*. 548.9 -zero *Kp*. J. 11.3. Acc. Sg. -*u* *Kp*. S. 39.8, *PPr*. 2.142. Neut. direct Sg. -*u* *KKc*. 5.1.1., *Kp*., J. 63, *Sc*. 707.5, *Sdd*. 88. Loc. Sg. -*i* *Sc*. 707.9. Fem. Nom. Sg. zero *Sc*. 573.9. Acc. Sg. -*u* *PPr*. 2.182.

*ihu* *iha* *BhK*. 3.1., *Jc*. 3.37.17.

*ī*

*īria* <*āïria*=*ācārya*
Ins. Pl. -*ehiṁ* *MP*. 1.14.11.

*īst* *īṣat* *BhK*. 33.3, *Sc*. 485.3.
*īsıṁ* (*pi*) *īṣat* *Sc*. 675.9.

*īsisi* *īṣat* *Hv*. 82.7.10.

*u*

*uatti* *utpatti*. Nom. Sg. zero *DKK*. 8.

*uesa* *upadeśa* Nom. Sg. -*ē* *DKK* 24.

*ukkhala* **utkhala*=*udūkhala* *Hv*. 85.12.3.
(cf. M. Guj. *ukhal*, H. *ūkhalī*, *ūkhal*, Sdh. *ukhirī* *Dn*. *ukkhalīpiṭharam*. 1.88.

*ukkhambhiya* **ut-skambhita* *BhK*. 203.1 but *uttabhita* according to Jacobi *BhK*. P. 132.

*ukkhiṇa* *ut-*√*khan* or *ut-*√*kṣiṇ*
Pres. 1 Sg. -*mi* *BhK*. 246.7, Imp. 2 Sg. -*hu* *BhK*. 229.9.
Abs. -*ivi* *BhK*. 228.6.

*uggaya* *udgata* Neut. Nom. Pl. -zero *KKc*. 1.3.6.

*uccalla* **ut-calya*- 'to shake about, to swing.'
Imp. 2 Sg. -*hu* *BhK*. 54.10.

*uccāiu* also *uccāyiya* <*ud-cāyita*, caus. PP. of√*ci* *BhK*. 234.5, *KKc*. 2.1.7.

*ucchalia* =*utkṣipta* *Nc*. 2.9.7.
(cf. M. *ucchalana* 'coming up suddenly'=*usḷī*).

*ucchu* *ikṣu* *BhK*. 5.10, *Hv*. 90.10.1.
(cf. Pk. *ucchu*, *ikkhu*, M. Guj. *ūs*, H. *ūkh*, *īkh*, Beng. *āku*, Or. *ākhu*).

*Ujjanta*, *Ujjayanta* *Urjayanta* *Hv*. 89.17.13, 92.7.8.

*vjjavaṇa* *udyamana* *BhK*. 97.3.

*ujjāḍiya* =*uccāṭita* *BhK*. 163.3.
(cf. M. *ujāḍ* 'razed, desolate').

*Ūjjēṇi* *Ujjayinī* *Hv*. 89.9.7.
Loc. Sg. -*hiṁ*. *Hc*. 4.442.1. *Jc*. 2.30.10.

*Ujjenta* *Ūrjayanta* *Hv*. 92.21.2.

| | |
|---|---|
| *ujjoa* | *udyota.* Acc. Sg. zero *DKs.* 99. |
| *Ujjha* | *Ayodhyā Hv.* 90.11.4. |
| *ujjhā-* | *upādhyāya- BhK.* 17.14. |
| *uṭṭhiyā̆* | *utsthitā.* Ins. Sg. *-āe KKc.* 18.7. |
| *uṭṭhuṭṭhu* | *=uttiṣṭho-ttiṣṭha Jc.* 4.4.9. |
| *uḍu* | (*ts.*) Nom. Sg. zero PPr. 1.38. |
| *uḍḍa-* | *ut-√ḍī*<br>Abs. *-ī DKs.* 72. *-evi BhK.* 61.3. |
| *uḍḍāvanti* | Fem. Pres. Part. of the Caus. of √*uḍḍa* Ins. Sg. -(*a*)*e Hc.* 352. |
| *uḍḍāviya* | Caus. PP. of √*uḍḍa MP.* 2.13.2, *Nc.* 3.9.14. |
| *uṇa* | *punaḥ MK.* 17.10. |
| *uṇṇāmia* | *unnāmita Mt.* 15. |
| *utuṁga* | *utuṅga DKK.* 25. |
| *uttara* | *ut-* √*tar* Imp. 2P. Sg. *-ehu KKc.* 1.13.3. |
| *Uttarakuru* | (*ts.*) Loc. Sg. *-hi MP.* 90.15.20. |
| *Uttarāsāḍha* | °*ṣāḍhā*<br>Loc. Sg. *-i. MP.* 87.13.7. |
| *uttāra-* | *uttāraya* Imp. 2 Sg. *-hi Mt.* 33.<br>Fem. Pres. Part. *-antī Sdd.*86. |
| *uttiya* | *ukta* Neut. Nom. Pl. *-ā Ys.* 35. |
| *utthalla* | *=ucchal -Hc.* 4.174.<br>Pres. 3 Sg. *-i BhK.* 108.5. Abs. *-i BhK.* 230-6.<br>PP. *-iya BhK.* 111.6. |
| *uddālia* | *=āchinna Nc.*6.11.8 cf *Hc.* 4.124.<br>(Traceable to OIA *utdal*? In Old M.√*udāḷnẽ* connotes a cognate semantic significance, e.g. in the *Jñāneśvarī* 15.498 we have '*jaisī khaḷāḷīciyā udakā sarasī udāḷe candrikā.* |
| *-uddehiya* | *udrehikā* 'cankering worm, insect.'<br>See *PPr.* P. 277. Hindi Translation of verse 2.133.<br>Fem. Ins Sg. *-e PPr.* 2.133. |
| *uddhara* | *uddhura BhK.* 35.7. |

*upalāṇa -hiṁ* — *utpalāni* (?) or *utpalyānay-* (?) *Pd.* 42. In his notes on this verse H. L. JAIN the editor, prefers the latter. *Pd.* P. 109-10.

*upāṭṭia* — *utpātya* 'plucked out' *DKś.* 6.

*uppahiṁ* — *ātmanā* See *Pd.* 84 translation and glossary P. 75.

*upajja* — *utpad-ya*
Pres. 3 Pl. *-iṁ Sdd.* 22. (Pa. *uppajjati*) (Pk. *uppajjai*, M. *upajṇẽ*, G. *upajvũ*, Sdh. *upajaṇu*, H.*upajnā* 'to grow big.')

*uppaṇṇa* — *-utpanna*, Neut. Nom. Sg. *-u KKc.* 1.11.2.

*uppari* — *upari Hv.* 83.3.12.

*upparẽ* — *upareṇa Mt.* 15 (H. *upar*, M. *uppar*).

*uppariyaṇa* — *uparitana Hv.* 85.2.6. (cf. M. *upparṇẽ*).

*upiya* — *upeta* Masc. Nom. Sg. *-o BhK.* 343.2.

*upphāla* — *ut-pāṭay* or *utphal* (?)
Abs. *-ivi Jc.* 1.6.5. (Sk. *utphāla* 'jump'. M. *uphāḷnẽ*. See BLOCH- *FLM* vocabulary).

*ubbhaṁ* — *ūrdhvam BhK.* 171.12.
(Pa. *ubbhaṁ*, Pk. *ubbha*, M. *ubhā*, G. *ubhũ*, G. *ubhũ*, Sdh. *ubho* Nep. *ūbho*).

*ubbha* — *ūrdhvī-kṛ* Abs. *-evi BhK.* 119.10.

*ubbhavia* — **udbhavita-* =*udbhūta Jdc.* 8.1.

*ummaṇa* — *un-manas.* Loc. Sg. *-i Pd.* 104.

*ummattia* — *unmattikā* Ins. Pl. *-hī Mt.* 14.

*ummilla* — *unmīlita BhK.* 73.2 (M. *umaḷṇẽ*, Guj. *umalvũ*).

*ummūla* — *un-mūlaya-* Abs. *-ivi Pd.* 21.

*ura* — *uras* Loc. Sg. *-i Mt.* 17.

*ullala* — *ut-lā* 'catch hold of.' Abs. *-evi KKc.* 1.13.7.

*ullasiā* — *ullasita Mt.* 16.

*ullūriya* — *ut+lū+ra* (pleonastic). Equated with *truṭ* in *Hc.* 4.116. Here PP. is used as the root Pres. 2 Sg. *-hi Pd.* 112.

*ulukhaṇa* — *ulūkhala* or *udūkhala Hv.* 85.12.1.

*ulla* — *ud-la*=*ārdra* Masc. Neut. Loc. Sg. *-e Mt.* 17.

*ullova* *ulloca Hv*. 87.14.3

*ulhāviya* =*ārdrita Sdd*. 39. (cf. *ulla* above).

*uvarilla* *upara* (-*illa* pleonastic) *uparitana Hv*. 82.12.8.

*uvavāsa* *upavāsa* Loc. Ins. Pl. -*hiṁ Sdd*. 109.

*uvalagga* *upalagna BhK*. 105.10.

*uvahi* *udadhi BhK*. 78.12.

*uvvali* =*udvartana* (?) Pd. 98.

*Uvvaśī* *ūrvaśī Sc*. 451.3. Gen. Sg. -*e Sc*. 491.1.

*uvvasa* *udvasa* Masc. Nom. Sg. -*u PPr*. 1.44.

*uvvasia* *udvasita Sc*. 671. 5.

*uvvāra* **udvāra* (*ṇa*) 'Protection, lifting up.' *MP*. 16,21.11.

*uvvigga* *udvigna Sc*. 692.8.

*uvveya* *udvega Sc*. 758.3.

*uvvellia* *udvellita Mt*. 32.

*uvvellira* *udvella*+*ira Mt*. 33.

*uvvēva* *udvega* Nom. Sg. -*u BhK*. 147.4, Loc. Sg. -*i BhK*. 159.3
-*ira* '*tācchilya*' *Jc*. P. 109 glossary.

*ussisā* Skt.ism. *ucchīrṣāt Mt*. 3.

*uhu* Interjection *aho* 'oh' *Hv*. 89.15.10.

*ū*

*ūala* *utpala DKs*. 66.

*ūāra* *upakāra DKs*. 109.

*ūsava* *utsava Kp*. S. 9.1.

*ūsara* *ut*-√*sar* Imp. 2 Sg. -*u BhK*. 23.7.

*ūsāra* **utsāra BhK*. 223.11.

√*e* *ā*-√*i* Fut. 3 P. Sg. -*sai BhK*. 37.3.
*e* =*idam DKs*. 4.62.

*ea eya* *etad* (sometimes used or *idam*). Direct Sg. Masc. *ēu*, *eu BhK*. 93.8, 44.1. *BhK*. 81.1, *Sc*. 511.1. Neut. *ēu*, *eu*, *BhK*. 21.2, 21.7, 58.8, *Hc*. 4.4.38. *Jc*. 3.24.8, *Kp*. J. 9,5., *Pd*. 39, *Sdd*.

92, *eum̃ Sn.* 14-441. Masc. *esa DKs.* 92. *eso KP.J.* 50.1* *Sc.* 485.2 Neut. *eso DKK.* 29. Masc. *ehu BhK.* 15.5, *DKK.* 15,16. *Jc.* 1.25.15. *KKc.* 5.3.7., *Kp.* J. 50, 9. *Mt.* 15.22. *PPr.* 1.60, *Pu.* 17.61, *Sc.* 484.4, 486.9, *Sdd.* 24, *Sn.* 17-570. Neut. *ehu BhK.* 36.2, *DKK.*8, 26. *Dks.* 33, 67.28. *Hc.* 4.362, *KC.* 28, *KP.* J. 14.4, *KP.S.* 68, *Ld.* 3.4.32, *MK* 17.39. *Sc.* 465.7, 456.8. *Sh.* 22.43. Masc. *ehaü Jc.* 2.31.11. *Pd.* 26. *PPr.* 1.100. Neut *ehaü. Jc.* 3.9. 14, 3.25.5, *KKc.* 1.11.3, *Nc.* 1.15.15, *Pd.* 79, *ehaüm̃ PPr.* 1.80 Masc. *eho DKK* 27. *Hc.* 4.391, *Kc.* 28 *Ld.* 3.43.3. *MK* 17.39, *Pu.* 17.61, *Sh.* 22.43. Neut. *eho DKK.* 27. Neut. *eyam̃ Sc.* 464.1. Masc. *eha MK.* 17.38. *Pu* 17.60. Neut. *eha KKc.* 1.11.3 *MK.* 17.38. *Ld.* 3.4.33. *eham̃ KKc.* 6.4.6. Ins. Sg. *aṇa DKK* 29. *Jc.* 25.14. *eeṇa Kp.* J. 58.3. *eina Sc.* 733.6. *ẽ, em̃ KKc.* 10.4.3., *Mt.*25. *eṇem̃ KKc.* 10.4.7. *ẽṇae Mt.* 31. *edeṇa Ld.* 3.4.34. Dat. gen. Abl. Sg. *eya-ho BhK.* 79.6, *Jc.* 2.32.2. *KKc.* 6.15.6. *edem̃ Ld.*3.4.34. *eyaha Kp.* J. S. *Sc.* 758.1. *ehu DKK* 8. *eho KKc.* 10.17.10. *eyahū MP.* 2.16.7. *eyassa Kp.* S. 35.4 *ẽyassu Sc.* 575.7. Loc. Sg.

Plural Direct Masc. *e MP.* 2.8.3., *PPr.* 2.136, *Sdd.* 18. Neut *e PPr.* 2.24. *Pu* 17.62, *Ys.*11 *ẽya BhK.* 253.9, 25.6.3. *ei Hc.* 4.330, *Kc.* 29. *Ld.* 3.4.34, *Sc.* 752.6. *Sh.* 22.44. Neut *Sc.* 554.3. *ee* Neut *eyaim̃ eyaĩ Kp.* J. 25.4 *PPr.* 226. *eyāĩm, oĩ Kp.* S. 36.4. *Kp.* J. 40.1.* *Pd.* 144, *Sn.* 32-231. *eyāṇi Kp.* J. 42.2.*

*eim̃ Ld.* 3.4.32, *edāim̃ Ld.* 3.4.32. *ehaum̃ Hc.* 4.362. Ins. *BhK.* 44.13, *Jc.* 1.17.16, *KKc.* 2.8.2. *PPr.* 2.88. *eehim̃ KKc.* 7.5.8. *Kp.* J. 39.2*

*edahim̃ Ld.* 3.4.34. Gen. *eyahã BhK.* 152.7. *Kp. J.* 29.6. *PPr.* 2. 52. *Sc.* 484.3 (?).

*ẽyāṇa Kp.* J. 42.1* Fem. Direct Sing. *ẽha BhK.* 26.4. 135.6, 4.9., *KKc.* 1.6.5., 1.15.5., *Kp.* J. 23.2., *MK.* 17.38. *Nc.* 1.15.4. *Sc.* 605.5, 625.6, 574.7, *Sdd.* 179, *Sh.* 22.43. *ehā Hc.* 4.445 ?, *ehĩ Nc.* 1.15.4. *Pd.* 95. *ehu DKK.* 8. *PPr.* 21.28 *eho Ld.* 3.4.30. *eya BhK.* 278.5. Fem. Acc. Sg. *eyāĩm̃ Pd.* 203. Ins. Sg. *eie Sc.* 669.3, *edāṇa Ld.* 3.4.30. Gen. Sg.*eyahe °hi BhK.* 99.5. *KP.S.* 79.2., *eie Sc.* 492.7. Direct Plur. *eyao BhK.* 267.10, *ẽyāu Sc.* 659.1. *ei Ld.* 3.4. Gen. Plur. *eyahā Sc.* 484.3.

| | |
|---|---|
| *esa* | **adṛśa=īdṛśa.* |
| *eiṁ* | Loc. Ins. and Acc. Sg. of *yuṣmad Ld.* 3.4.40. |
| *eu* | *ettha Nc.* 1.15.15. |
| *eũ, euṁ* | *evaṁ BhK.* 275.8, *Hv.* 92.13.5, *PPr.* 2.73. |
| *ekka* | *eka DKs.* 19.43, *Kp.*J. 5.6, *Mt.*15 Fem. *Mt.* 12. Masc. Nom. Sg. zero *DKs.* 40, *-u DKK.* 1, *Kp.*E. 29 b. Loc. Sg. *hiṁ KKc.* 1.6.1. *hi Jc.* 2.31.9 (M. Guj. H. Nep. *ek*). |
| *ekkaï* | *ekākinī BhK.* 304.9. |
| *ekkamekka* | *ekaika BhK.* 41.1 cf. *Hc.* 8.3.1., *Hv.* 83.23.5, 88.8.2. |
| *ekkalla* | *eka* (+*alla* Pleonastic) cf. *Hc.* 2.165. Masc. Nom. Sg. *-u Kp.* A. 5.1, *-o BhK.* 38.7. Fem. *-ī. Hv.* 85.4.13. |
| *ekkekka* | *ekaika BhK.* 182.5, *Kp.* J. 25.2. |
| *ekkĕkkama* | **ekaikama Mt.* 27. |
| *egasi* | *ekaśaḥ Ld.* 3.3.28. |
| *eta* | *etāvat DKs.* 39,63. |
| *ettaḍa* (*-ya*) | *=iyat, etāvat* Masc. Nom. Sg. *-u BhK.* 153.7, Nom. Pl. *-im Sdd.* 53. |
| *ettahe* | *itas, atra- Hc.* 4.420, *Hv.* 82.5.9. *Kc.* 75, *Ld.* 3.3.48. |
| *ettia, °ya* | *iyat BhK.* 58.4. *Kp.* J. 64.6, cf. *Hc.* 2.157. Neut. direct Sg. *-u Jc* 2.12.20. |
| *ettula* | *etāvat, iyat Hc.* 4.408, *Kc.* 75, *Ld.* 3.3.12, *Sh.* 62. |
| *etthau* | *=atra Hv.* 81.17.9, *Jc.* 1.11.7, *ittha KKc.* 1.7. 3, *Ld.* 3.3.15. *Mt.* 24. |
| *etthu* | *=atra Jc.* 1.25.1. |
| *enta* | **āyānta* Pres. Part of *ā-√yā.* Loc. Sg. Masc. and Neut. *-i. Mt.* 18. |
| *ema* | *evam BhK.* 11.6, *Hc.* 4.418, *Hv.* 83.12.11, *Jc.* 1.7.11, *Ld.* 3.3.36, *Pd.* 4. |
| *emaï* | *evam(eva) Jc.* 3.26.5, *Ld.* 3.3.39. |
| *emahĩ* | *=idānīm BhK.* 114.6. |

*emu* *evam* *Ld.* 3.3.36, *PPr.* 1.65, *Pu.* 17.58.

*ĕm ĕva* *evameva* *Hv.* 81.2.7.

*eṁva, eva̐* *evaṁ* *BhK.* 76.6. *Hc.* 4.418.

*eṁvaī* *evaṁ* *Kc.* 65.

*eṁvahī* *evam* *BhK.* 182.9, *Hc.* 4.420.

*eyāraha* *ekādaśan* *Sdd.* 9.
°*ma* *ekādaśama* *MP.* 2.12. *Sdd.* 16.
(Pa. *ekādasa*, Pk. *ekkārasa*, *eggāraha*, M. *akrā*.
Guj. *agyār*. H. *egāraha*, Nep. *eghāra*).

*eyārisa* *etādṛśa* *Jc.* p. 109.

*erisa* *īdṛśa* *Kp.* J. 6.5. *Sdd.* 175.

*evaḍa,* *iyat* *Sh.* 22.62. -*u* *Hc.* 4.407, *Jc.* 4.1.7. *Ld.* 3.3.12.

*ĕvaḍḍa* **ayavadra*=*iyat*, *etāvat* *BhK.* 321.1. *Sdd.* 179.
Direct Sg. -*u* *BhK.* 165.10, *Hc.* 4.408, Gen. Sg. -*ho*
*Jc.* 3.37.11. Sg. -*u*

*evahiṁ* °*hī*- =*idānīm*, *BhK.* 21.5. *HC.* 4.420, *Hv.* 81.6.9.=*evam* *Jc.*
3.41.5., *Sdd.* 154.
=*adhunā* *KKc.* 1.10.10.

*evvahī* =*idānīm* *BhK.* 4. 4. °*hi* *Ld.* 3.3.34.

*evi* *evam* *Jc.* 2.6.8.

*eha*, °*ya* =*īdṛśa*.
Masc. Neut. direct Sg. -*u* *BhK.* 21.2, 24.3.
*Hv.* 84.1.13, *Sh.* 22.60, cf. *Hc.* 4.402.
Neut -*ū* *Hv.* 82.8.7, Loc. Sg. -*i* *BhK.* 60.11.
Fem. Direct Sg. *ehī* *BhK.* 24.10 *Hv.* 83.23.8, *PPr.* 2.157.

*o*

*oi* =*amūn* (cf. II. **ave*, Pischel *Gram*. p. 307, Bloch-*L'indo-aryen*, p. 149) *Hc.* 4.364. *Kc.* 29., *Ld.* 3.4.35.

*oṇaviya* *ava-namita* *Hv.* 86.8.7 (M. *oṇavā*)

*otthara-i* **ava-starati* *Mt.* 32. PP. -*iya* *Hv.* 8.8.11.2. cf. *Dn.* 1.169.

*otthāḍiya* =*avastṛta* *BhK.* 298.3.

*osara-* *apa-√sar* Abs. -*ivi* *Nc.* 8.15.10, 4.-12-13.

√ohaṭṭa apa-hṛta (?) Mp. 2.8.5.
(M. ohaṭṇẽ, Noun. ohaṭī, Guj. ōṭ)

√ohāma =√tul- PP. -iya Hv. 83.15.6., Nc. 1.14.7,
=ava- or -o-√hamma as in ohāmiya
=avaghātita MP. 2.7.3. cf. 4.25.

k

ka Interrogative Pronoun.
Masc. direct Sg. kō, ko BhK. 6.1, 21.8, 177.7, DKK. 15, DKS. 10, 18, 69. Hc. 4.370, 384, 415, KKC. 9.9.1, KP. S. 73.1, Kp. J. 53.3 MK. 17.30, Mt. 21, 35. Pd. 40,27. PPr. 2.9, Sc. 530.7, Sdd. 6. ku BhK. 118.11, Jc. 2.26. Jdc. 2.4, KKc. 9.7.10, Kp. E. 15, Kp. J. 10.1, Pd. 159, PPr. , Sc. 542.8, 629.8. Neut. Direct Sg. kim, BhK. 2.3, 2.6. DKK. 16, 20, 28, DKS 95, 55, Hc. 4.418, KP.S. 48.7, 72.8, Mt. 18,25, PPr. 2.5. Sc. 606.2, kĩ Sc. 579.9. ki DKK 16, 28. DKS. 21,35, Hc. 4.340 (used adverbially) Pd. 70. PPr 2.185, Sdd. 6, kāī BhK. 19.6, Hc. 4.349, Kc. 30. Ld. p.275 (3.3.53), Mk. 17, 56, Pd. 22, PPr. 1.27 Sdd. 62,172. kaī Hc. 4.426 Ld. p. 275, Mt. 25, kaï Pu. 17.25, kaü BhK. 118.5. kiṇṇa BhK. 148.6, kuccha DKK 10. (kiṁ na) Pd. 19. kimpradi, °du, kimpru, kira Pu. 17.25.
Ins. Sg. keṇa BhK. 23.10, 44.1, DKS. 24, 80, KKc. 9.6.3, Pd. 139, Sc. 607.1, kiṇa Sc. 586.8. ki PPr. 1.98. keṁ KKc. 10-1-4.
Gen. Sg. kāsu BhK. 25.5, 140.4 DKs. 60,75, Hc. 4.358, Hv. 85.7.8. Kc. 31,71, KKc. 1.6.8, Ld. 3.4.29, Pd. 139, Sdd. 178, Sh. 22.37. Sn. 33-624. kasu Hc. Kc. 17, Ld. 3.4.29. Sc. 539.1. kassa DKs. 96. kāsa Sh. 22.37, kassu Hc. 4.442.7. Ld. 3.4.29. kisa (Abl.) KKc. 10.1.3, Ld. 22.8. kaho BhK. 26.1, 223.4, Ld. 3.4.29. kahu BhK. 94.8. 274.2, BhK. 120.3 (Abl.)
Loc. Sg. kahim °hĩ BhK. 10.7, 59.4, KKc. 1.11.5 (adverbially), Mt. 17, Sdd. 194, 215 (adverbial) kahi BhK. 327.5, DKS. 93, 84. kāhĩ (also Abl.) DKK. 29, 30.
Direct Plur No. Masc. ke BhK. 85.4, Hc. 4.376, 387. KKc. 9.17, Kp. J. 5.4, PPr 1.50, Sc. 642.8. ki(vi). BhK 163-10, PPr. 1.50, Sn. 16-570.

Neut. *kāī Sc.* 735.8.
Ins. Loc.Pl. *kehiṁ*. *KKc*. 9.1.8 and Intro. to *Hv*. page 167 article No. 51.
Fem. direct Sg. *kă BhK*. 10.9, *KKc*. 9.2.3, *Kp*. E. 26. *Sc*. 735.8, 736·1.
Ins. Sg. *kāiṁ KKc*. 7.9.10.
Gen. Sg. *kahi vi BhK*. 11.2, *kāhi MP*. 2.1-14.
*kahe Hc*. 4.359, *Kc*. 27. *Sh*. 22.39, *kīi* (*vi*) *Kp*. E. 25.
Direct Pl. *kāü Sc*. 596.8.
Ins. Pl *kāhiṁ Jc*. 2.26.

*kaa* — *kṛta Mt*. 32.

*kai* — *kavi* Nom. Sg. zero *Nc*. 3.4.17.

*kaïsu* — =*kīdṛśa Ld*. 3.3.10.

*kaïyahā mi* — *kadāpi BhK*. 93.7, *Hc*. 4.422.1.

*kaïyā* — *kadā Kp*. J. 46.1.

*kaü* — *kutaḥ BhK*. 10.7, *Hc*. 4.416, *Kc*. 61, *Ld*. 3.3.46. *Mt*. 4, Sdd. 68.

*kaüsiya* — *kauśīkā MP*. 84.1.2.

*kakkhaḍa* — *karkaśa*=*niṣṭhura MP*. 11.13.10 but=*pīna* in *BhK*. 176.1.

*kaṁgu* — fem. *kaṅgu* 'N. of a plant'
Gen. Sg. *-he Hc*. 4.367.

*kacca* — 'raw' *Sdd*. 13 (M. H. *kaccā*) Loc. Sg. in *-haṁ* as in *kaccōsaṇa-haṁ* ?

*kacca* — *kāca* 'glass' *PPr*. 2.78.
Masc. Ins. Sg. *-eṇa Sdd*. 2.

*kaccha* — *kakṣā Hv*. 87.11.1.
(M *kās, kā̃s* 'udders', H. Punj. Sdh. *kaccha*)

*kajja* — *kārya* Ins. Sg. *-e DKs*. 2.
(Pa. Pk. *kajja* M. Guj. Nep. *kāj*.)

*Kaṁcāïṇi* — *kātyāyanī Jc*. 3.8.14.

*kaṁculiya* — *kañculikā* Nom. Sg. zero *Pd*. 15.

*kaṁjia* — **kamjī* or °*jikā* 'gruel,' Ins. Sg. *-eṇa Jc*. 3.31.1.
(cf. M. *kāmjī*).

√*kaṭṭa* — √*kṛt->kart-* 'to cut.'
Imp. 2p. Sg. -*hī BhK* 231. -4, *PP*. -*iya BhK*. 207.16.
Abs. -*ivi BhK*. 129.3 (See *kattariya* below).

*kaṭṭha-ḍa* — *kaṣṭa*.
Masc. Nom. Pl. -*ā Sdd*. 114.

*kaḍakkha* — *kaṭākṣa Sn*. 24.212.
°*ccha*<*kaṭākṣā* (Fem.) *Mt*. 12.

*kaḍayaḍiya* — =*parāvartita* Onomatopoeic *Sn*. 76-176.

*kaḍilla* — *kaṭi-illa* or -*lla* (Possessive Term.)
=*kaṭi-sūtra MP*. 4.4 5. but='a dhoti' *kaṭi-vastra* in *BhK*. 167.2, *Hv*. 86.10.6. cf. *Dn*. 2.52.

√*kaḍha* — √*kvath- Jc*. 3.5.11.
(Pa. *kaṭhita*, M. *kaḍhṇẽ*, Guj. *kaḍhvũ*, Sdh. *kaṛhaṇu*)

√*kaḍhakaḍha* — Reduplication of √*kaḍha-*, Onomatopoic also.
Pres. Part. -*antu Hv*. 88.8.3.

√*kaḍḍha-* — IE **qal-dhe*>OIA **kardh*—
Pres. 1 Sg. -*uṁ Kc*. 41.
Masc. Pres. Part. Gen. Sg. -*anta-haṁ Sdd*. 99. Neut.
Abs. -*ivi Jc*. 3.12.12, *KKc*. 10.13.7.
(Pa. *kaḍḍhati*, Pk. *kaḍḍhaï*, M. *kāḍhṇẽ*. Guj. *kāḍhvũ*, Panj. *kaḍḍṇā*, H. *kāṛhnā*. Bloch connects it to OIA *kṛṣṭa FLM* §112 and the Index to Vocables. Louis. H. Gray, derives Pa. Pk. *kaḍḍha*< OIA **kardh-* <IE **qaldhe JAOS* 60.361-2. This gets over the difficulty of positing the unusual change -*ṭṭh-*>-*ḍḍh-*)

*kaṇa* — (*ts*.) Ins. Pl. -(*a*)*hiṁ Pd*. 84.

*kaṇṇa*(*ya*) — *kanyā*.
Acc. Sg. zero *KKc*. 2.12.9. Direct Pl. -*u Sc*. 659.2.
Gen. Plur. -*hā*. *Sc*. 660.6, -(*yā*)*hā Sc*. 708.3. -*āṇa* (Pkt.). *KKc*. 8.10.1

*kaṇṇ*(*nn*)*ullaḍa* — *karṇa*+(*ulla-ḍa* Pleonastic). *Kc*. 73.
(Pa. Pk. *kaṇṇa*, M. Guj. H. Nep. *kān*).

√*kaṇḍa-* — 'to thrash grain.' Imp. 2P. Sg. -*i Pd*. 13 (cf. M. *kāṇḍṇẽ*).

√*kattariya-* — *kartarikā*< √*kṛt*.
Imp. 2P. Sg. -*hi MP*. 2.7.10.
(Pa. Pk. *kattarī*, Deśi *kaṭṭari*. cf. M. *kāṭar*, *kātrī*, Guj.

kātar, Sdh. katarī, Panj. kattara, Beng. kātāri).

kattiya — kārtika Hv. 87.13.6.

kattī — =kartarī Sn. 78 176.

kadhida — kathita Kc. 46. cf. Hc. 4.396.

kanta — 1) kānta
Masc. Acc. Sg. -u Mt. 10, Gen. Sg. -ha Ds. 4.32. -ho Hc. 8.4.395.
2) kāntā Ins. Sg. -e BhK. 291.4.
3) krānta Masc. Nom. Sg. -o Mt. 22.

kantilla — kānti-mat. Mp. 1.2.4.

kattha — =kutra Kp. S. 95.3, katthai Jc. 2.6.6. kattha-vi=kutrāpi Jc. 3.23.8, Si. 19-442.

√kappara — 'to cut,' √kḷp. (-ara pleonastic in MIA.)
PP. -iya BhK. 243.11. Abs. -evi Hv. 88.12.10.
(Pa. kappeti 'trims,' kappei 'cuts,' M. kāpṇẽ, Guj. kāpvũ, Sdh. kapaṇu, Sgh. kapanu).

kappa-aru — kalpa-taru
Nom. Sg. zero Mt. 23

kabbe — *kadvā=kadā DKs. 62.

Kambhūru — kāśmīra Ld. 3.3.2.

kamala — (ts.) Sc. 454.5, Acc. Sg. -u Jdc. 1.2.
Abl. Sg. -ho Nc. 2.12.2.
=°lā Fem. Ins. sg. -ẽ BhK. 27.9.

kamala māla — (ts.) Acc. Sg. zero Sc. 488.2.

kamala-siri — °-śrī Fem. Gen. Sg. -he BhK. 17.4.

kamma — karman
Ins. Sg.-(a)ĩ PPr. 1.63,76. Nom. Pl. -e DKK 29.
Gen. Pl. -haṁ Pd. 24,36. -āṇa (Pkt.) KKc. 9.12.1.
(Pa. Pk. kamma, M. Guj. H. Nep. kām̐).

kammuya — kārmuka 'a bow.'
Gen. Pl. -āhaṁ MP. 2.9.18.

kaya — kṛta Sdd. 17, Loc. Sg. -iṁ Jdc. 34.1.

kaya-uṇṇa — kṛta-puṇya Masc. Nom. Sg. -ũ BhK. 70.4.

*kayā* *kadā* as in *kaya i=kadācit Kp*. S. 5.1, °*vi=api Kp*. J. 5.1.

*kara* (*ts*.) Masc. Ins. Pl. -*hiṁ Hc*. 8.4.349.

√*kara* √*kṛ*-
Pres. I Sg. -(*a*)*uṁ*, -(*a*)*ũ* *BhK*. 79.6, *Jc*. 2.1.6. *Kp*. J. 8.8, *Pd*. 139. *Sdd*. 88. (*a*)*mi* *BhK*. 21.5. *KKc*. 2.6.3, *Pd*. 174. -*imi Jdc*. 1.3, *Kp*.S. 72.8, 2 P. Sg. -*hi BhK*. 44.2. *Kc*. 40, *Kp*. J. 8.3, -*si Kc*. 40. 3 P. Sg. -*i Kp*. J. 15.3. *Mk*. 17.69, *Pd*. 7, 42. -*ei DKS*. 99, *Kp*. J. 21.3, *Pd*. 15, 16. 1 P. Pl. -*huṁ*, -*hũ*, *KKc*. 2.11.8, 5.9.5, *Kp*. J. 46.4. 2 P. Pl. -*ha Mp*. 91.3.3, *hu BhK*. 128.7 3 P. Pl. -*anti BhK*. 187.12. *Kp*. E.4, *Pd*. 80. -*hiṁ*, -*hĩ*, *BhK*. 339.5. *Kc*. 40, *Kp*. J. 7.2, *Pd* 217, *Sdd*. 55,75,117. Imp. 2. Sg. -*i BhK*. 29.9. *KP*. S. 59.3. *Nc*. 1.3.10, *Pd*. 2, 18. *PPr*. 1.26. *Sdd*. 22, -*u DKS*. 27, 59.
-*e Kc*. 42, *Nc*. 9.17.25. -*ejjasu Nc*. 5.13.9. -(*a*)*hi BhK*. 24.9. *DKS*. 77, *Kp*. S. 49.9. *Pd*. 13,92, *Sdd*. 4,60. -(*e*)*hi BhK*. 38.2 3. Sg -*u BhK*. 2.10. 2P. Pl. -(*a*)*hi*. *BhK*. 90.3, *DKS*. 51, *Kp*. J. 64.5, -*ha DKS*. 106. 3 P. Pl. -*antu ts*. *BhK*, 2.8. Fut. 1 Sg. -*isu Sc*. 690.7.

2 P. Sg. -*ĭhisi MK*. 17.59, *Mt*. 22, -*ĭsi PPr*. 2.125, -*hisi* (*kāhisi*), *Kp*. S. 84.2.
3P. Sg. -*isaï Kp*. S. 44.3, -*ihaï Kp*. E. 28, *Sc*. 765. 5, -*esaï*, *BhK*. 19. 5, *PPr*. 2.188.
1P. Plur. -*isahũ*, *Sc*. 318.7, 3 P. Plur. -*ihinti Nc*. 4.5.5.
Pres. Part. -*anta Kp*.S. 47.7, Masc. Nom. Sg. -*o BhK*. 20.7,

Fem. -*ĭ BhK*. 77.7, 213.11, -*antiya BhK*. 131.12, Abs. -*avi Kc*. 76, *Ld*. 3.3.18, *Sn*. 334-127. -*āvi* (caus. Abs. *Jdc*. 18.3. -*i Kp*. J. 46.8, *Ld*. 33.18, *Pd*. 102.
-*iu Kc*. 76, *Ld*. 3.3.18. -*ivi BhK*. 21.6, *Hc*. 4.4 39, *Kc*. 76, *Kp*. J. 9.1. *Sn*. 306-169. -*e Ld*. 3.3.18, -*epi*, -*epiṇu Ld*. 3.3.19, -*eppi*, -*eppiṇu BhK*. 47.7. *Hc*. 4.440, *Kc*. 77, *Ld*. 3.3.19, -*evi BhK*. 11.7, *Hc*. 4.440, *Kc*. 77. -*eviṇu BhK*. 27.8, *Hc*. 440, *Kc*. 77, *KKc*. 1.10.8, *Kp*. S. 53.1, PPr. 1.8. Inf. *aüṁ Ld*.3.4.25. -*aṇa Jdc*. 2.4, *Sn*. 15-286, -*aĭ BhK*. 328.5. ?
-*aṇahā BhK*. 337.5, *Jc*. 1.8.2.
-*eppi*, *eppiṇu Kc*. 79, -*evi Kc*. 79.
-*eviṇu Kc*. 78. Pot. Part. -*ivvaü Kc*. 76.
-*evvaü*, °*uṁ Kc*. 76, *KKc*. 2.13.2, -*evĕ Kc*. 76.

*karaḍi* *karaṭin* Ins. Pl. -*hi Sn*. 76-176.-*hiṁ*. *Sn*. 76-176.

*karaṇābhāsa* (*ts.*) Abl. *-hv Kc.* 17.

*karaṇḍa* (*ts.*) Gen. Sg. *-ho DKK.* 21.

*karaha* *karabha* Neut. Acc. Sg *-ā DKS* 45.

*kari* *karin* 'an elephant'.
Direct Sg. zero *KKc.* 8.18.8, Gen. Sg. *-ha DKS.* Nom. Pl. zero *Mp.* 87.9.3
Ins. Pl. *-hiṁ KKc.*8.18.8.

*kari-kara-samoru* (*ts*) Fem. Ins. Pl. *Jc.* 1.17.9.

*kariṇi* °*ṇī* 'a female elephant'.
Loc. Sg. *-hiṁ Sdd.* 123.

*karuṇă* °*ṇā* Acc. Sg. zero *DKS.* 16.
Ins. Sg. *-(a)iṁ KKc.* 2.4.10.

*kala* *kalā DKS.* 55.

*√kala* *√kalay* 'to know'
Abs. *-ivi KKc.* 1.11.6.

*kalāpa* (*ts.*) Loc. Sg. *-e Mt.* 3.

*kali* (*ts.*) Loc. Sg. *-hi Hc.* 4.341.

*kaloyahi* *Kalodadhi* Loc. sg. *-hi Sc.* 471.4.

*kavaṇa* **ka-pana=kim Sdd.* 40.
Masc. Neut. direct Sg. *-u BhK.* 38.6, *Hc.* 4.395.6, *Kc.* 30,*KKc.* 6.6.2, *Tr. Ld.* 3.3.53. (*Ld. p.* 275). PPr. 2.171, *Sn.* 78-332. '*kiyan*' according to the Sk. *chāyā*. *-o* (Masc.) *Ld.* 3.3.53. *-eṇa Hc.* 367, *Sc* 530.7 *-eṁ BhK.* 261.3, Fem. direct Sg. zero. *Hc.* 4.350,367, *BhK.* 38.6, 99.5. Gen.Sg. *-he Hc.* 4.425. (OM. *kavaṇa*, M.Guj. *koṇ*, H. *kaun*,Braj. *kawan*, Nep. *kun*, all traceable to Sk. * *ka-pana*>Pa. *kopana*, *kim-pana*.

*kav̄ala* *kamala* Neut. direct Sg. *-u Hc.* 4.397.

*kavaḍḍiya* *kapardikā*,
Ins. Sg. *-iī Kp.* S. 56.4. (Pk. *kavaḍḍa*, °*ḍḍiya*, M. *kavḍī* fem. Guj. *kavaḍō* (Masc.), H. *koḍī* Sdh, *koḍu*)

*kavvāḍiya* 'a porter'. *Kp.* E. 31 b.
(Guj. *kāvaḍiyo*, H. *kāvaḍiyā* 'porter').

*kasaṇa* *kṛṣṇa Mt.* 32.

47

*kasāya* — *kaṣāya* Loc. pl. *-hi* ǒ*PPr.* 1.123.

*kaṁsa* — (*ts.*) Gen. Sg. *-ho Jc.* 3.29.7.

√*kaha* — √*kath*-
Press. 1.Sg. *-uṁ Nc.* 1.5.4, *-evi* (°*vi*ǒ). *PPr.* 1.11, Imp. 2 Sg. *-su Hv. Grammatik* §56, *-i Jdc.* 43.4, 2 Pl. *-hu Mt.* 20, PPr. 1.10. Fut. 3 Sg. *-esaï BhK.* 118.8. PPr. *-anta DKK* 16. PP. *-ia DKK* 10.26, (Masc. direct Sg. *-ā Kc.* 14. *-iya DKS.* 27. Masc. Nom. Sg. *-e DKs.* 60. Neut. direct Sg. *-e DKs.* 60. Fem. Ins. sg. *-(ā)i Jc.* 1.1.6.)
Abs. *-ivi KKc.* 5.12.6. Inf. *ivi Sdd.* 201. *-aṇa DKs.* 54.

*kaha* — *kathā*
Loc. Sg. *-āe BhK.* colophones, *Jc.* 1.1.5. Ins.Loc. Pl. *-hĩ Sc.* 457.2. Loc. Pl. *-āsu* (Pkt.sm.) *Sc.* 470.7.

*kaha* — *katham BhK.* 2.5, *Jc.* 3.23.3.
°*va* (*kathamapi*) *BhK.* 42.7 also *kahāmi BhK.* 44.2 °*vi* (*api*) *Sn.* 306-169.

*kahi* — =*kutra*, *kva* (original Loc. Sg. of *ka*-)

*kahĩ*, *-hiṁ* — *kasmin*=*kutra BhK.* 57.11, *Jc.* 3.11.2.
*PPr.* 1.90, *Sdd.* 86. *kahĩ*. . . . *kahĩ*=*kva*. . . . *kva Kp.* J. 6.7.

*kahu* — *kutaḥ Ld.* 3.3.46.

*kāṇha* — *Kṛṣṇa* Direct Sg. zero *DKK* 15,22.

*kāyaü* — *kā'pi Sdd.* 99, 189. *kimapi Sdd.* 189.

*kāya* — (*ts.*) Nom. Pl. *-ā DKs.* 9. Ins. Sg. *-iṁ Sdd.* 108. Ins. Pl. *-hiṁ Sdd.* 14.

*kāya-bāk-mana* — =*kāya-vāṅmanāṁsi DKs.* 85.

*kāya-maṇi* — *kāca-maṇi*
Acc. Sg. zero *Sn.* 31.-231.

*kāyavva* — *kartavya* Acc. Pl. *-āĩ Sc.* 459.4.

*kāraṇa* — (*ts.*) Ins. Sg. *-iṁ Sdd.* 30.

*kārima* — **kār-ima*=*kṛtrima Hv.* 84.3.4. *PPr.* 2.123.128, 129.

*kārima* — *karman* Nom. Sg. *-u Pd.* 9.

*kāla* — (*ts*) 'Time' Masc. direct Sg. *-u PPr.* 1.85.
(In *Cd.* as noted be UPADHYE, Intro. to *PPr.* p. 65 footnote 7),Instr. Sg. *-ĩ Jc.* 2.25.14. 'black, dark' Masc. Nom.

Pl. *-ā Sdd.* 65. Neut. direct Pl. *-ā Sdd.* 29. (Pa. *kāḷo* 'black', *kālo*, Pkt. *kālaa.* M. *kāḷā*, Guj. *kāḷo*, Sgh. *kaḷu*, H. Panj. *kālā*, Nep. *kālo.* Bloch supposes these forms to be of Dravidian origin *BSOS* 5.1).

***kālattaya*** °*traya-* Gen. sg. *-haṁ Sdd.* 5.

***kālāgni*** (*ts.*) Nom. sg. zero *DKK.* 14.

***kāliṁga*** *Kaliṅga Hv.* 81.14.3.

***kia*** *kṛta DKK.* 4,25, *DKs.*107. Neut. direct Sg. *-u PPr.* 2.133, 147.

***kiuṁ*** *kathaṁ KKc.* 1.10.2.

***kiṁkara*** (*ts.*) Ins. Pl. *-ehiṁ Mp*, 81.19.5.

***√kijja-*** *-ijja* Pass. of *√kar-*, sometimes used actively.
Pres. 1 Sg. *-mi Mt.* 18, *-uṁ* (actively) *PPr.*2.139. 160. 3 Sg. *-i Kp.S.* 42.6. Imp. 3 Sg. *-u Sc.* 760.8.
Pres. Part. *-anta Kp.S.* 45.3

***kittaṇa*** *kīrtana* Acc. Sg. *-u KKc.* 1.5.3.

***kitti*** *kīrti KKc.* 2.3.6.
Fem. Ins. Sg. *eṁ KKc.* 1.5.2 Gen. Sg. *hi* )*Pr.* 2.92.
Neut. Loc. Sg. *hi* (as the 2nd member of the comp.) *Sc.* 443.1.

***kittiu*** *kiyat Sdd.* 183.

***kitthu*** =*kutra PPr.* 2.47

***kima*** =*katham BhK.* 23.3, *Hc.* 4.401, *Ld.* 3.3.8.

***kimpradi,*** °*du*=*kiṁ Pu.* 17.25.

***kimpru*** *kiṁ Pu.* 17.25.

***kiya*** *kṛta Sdd.* 155. also *kīya* in *KKc.* 1.2.7.
Neut. direct Pl. *-āiṁ PPr.* 1.27.

***kira*** *kila Jdc.* 9.1, *Kp.* J. 21.1, *Ld.* 3.3.41, *Mp.* 1.3.8.

***kiraṇa*** (*ts.*) Neut. Acc. Pl. *-aiṁ Sdd.* 29.

***kiraṇāvali*** (*ts.*) Ins. sg. *-e Sdd.* 191.

***kiri*** *kila Kp.* J. 82.4.

***kiriyā*** *kriyā* Nom. Sg. zero *Pd.* 19.

√*kilikila-* 'to exult, to shout with joy.'
Pres. 3 Pl. -(*a*)*nti* *Hv*. 84.5.9.
(cf H. *kilkilāna* 'to be fretful'? M. *kilkilṇē*).

*kiva* =*katham* *Jdu*. 7.2.

*kiva̐,kiṁva* =*katham* *BhK*. 180.8.

*kisiya* **kṛśita* *BhK*. 305.5.

*kiha* =*katham* *Jc*. 3.11.13, *Sn*. 78-176.

*kihĩ* =*kṛte* *Kp*. E. 20. cf. *Hc*. 4.425.

*kira* *kiṁ* *Pu*. 17.25.

√*kīla-* √*krīḍ*.
Pres. 3 Sg. -*i* *Mt*. 27. Fut. 1 Sg. -*ihimi* *Jc*. 3.15.11. Fem. Pres. Part. direct Sg. -*anti*+zero *Mt*. 26, Fem. habit showing -*irī* *Hv*. 86.10.5.

*kui* *kutra* *DKs*. 34.

*kukaï* *kukavi* Gen. Sg. -*hi* MP. 87.1.10.

*kuṁkuva* *kuṅkuma* *BhK*. 199.6.

*kucchi* *kukṣi* *KKc*. 7.2.4. of. M. *kūs*.

*kuṭṭiṇī* °*nī* Fem. Dat. Sg. -*he* *KKc*. 8.5.7.
(M. *kumtaṇ*, Guj. *kuṭṇī*, H. *kuṭnī*, Or. *kuṭuṇī*).

*kuḍī* *kuṭī* Nom. Sg. zero *Pd*. 52.

*kuḍilliya* *kuṭī-* *Kc*. 72 *Hc*. 4.429. Loc. Sg. -*i* *PPr*. 2.95, -*iṁ* *Sdd*. 112.
(M. *kuḍī*)

*kuḍuṁba* *kuṭumba* Gen. Sg. -*ha* *Sdd*. 48.

*kuṇḍa* (*ts*.) Nom. Sg. -*ha* *Sn*. 78.332.

*kuṇḍiya* *kuṇḍikā* Ins. Pl. -*hi̐* *PPr*. 2.89.

√*kuṇa* √*kṛ-* Imp. 2 Pl. -*haṁ* *Jc*. 4.8.5-15.
Pres. Part. -*anta* *Nc*. 9.17.17.

*kupatta* *kupātra* Dat.Gen. Pl. -*haṁ* *Sdd*. 86.

*kumbhi* *kumbhin* Gen. Sg. -*he* *KKc*. 1.16.7.

*kumarī* *kumārī* Ins. Sg. -*e* *Jc*. 1.18.16.

*kumma* *kūrma* Gen. Sg. -*ha* *Sn*. 76.-176.

*kumāra* (*ts.*) Masc. direct pl. -(*a*) *iṁ Jc*. 3.41.4.

*kula* (*ts.*) Loc. pl. -*ehiṁ Jc*. 1.27.18.

*kum̃vara, kuṁvara kumāra BhK*. 203.8.

*kusuma* (*ts.*) Ins. Pl. -*hiṁ Sdt*. 186.

*kusuma-ura* °*pura* Abl. Sg. -*ho KKc*. 1.6.1.

*kusumatta* °-*dattā* Ins. sg. -*iṁ KKc*. 1.6.10.

*kuhiya* *kṣubhita* 'diseased' *Jc*. 3.14.10.

*kūra* =*īṣat Hv*. 85.19.9. of. *Hc*. 2.129.

*kṛvāṇu* *kṛpāṇaḥ Mk*. 18.4.

*keumai* *ketumatī* Ins. Sg. -*eṁ KKc*. 6.12.1.

*kettiya* *kiyat BhK*. 113.1, *PPr*. 2.141. *Hc*. 2.157.

*kettula* °*lu* =*kiyat Hc*. 4.435, *Kc*. 75, *Ld*. 3.3.12, *Sh*. 22.62.

*ketthu* =*kutra BhK*. 208.3, *Hv*. 91.4.3. *KKc*. 2.1. 10. *Ld*. 3.3.15, *PPr*. 2.47, of. *Hc*. 4.405.

*kema* =*katham BhK*. 10.5, *Ld*. 3.3.8, *PPṛ*. 1.121, *Sdd*. 138 cf. *Hc*. 4.401. *kemaī* (*kathamapi*) *Jdu*. 72.4. 4.401. *kemaï* (*kathamapi*) *Jdu*. 72.4.

*kera* 'an order' *Mp*. 16.6.9.

*kera*, °*a*, °*ya* Gen. postposition showing relation.
*Hc*. 2.146, *Nc*. 1.3.14, *Pd*. 36.
Masc. Nom. Sg. *Hv*. 85.7.10. *Pd*. 36, *PPr*. 2.29.
Loc. Sg. -*e Hv*. 81.2.7. *keraï PPr*. 1.99. *kerā*
*Hv*. 88.10.1, *PPr*. 1.73.

*kēli* (*ts.*) Acc. Sg. zero *BhK*. 20.7, *DKK* 28.

*kevaḍa* °*ḍu* *kiyat Ld*. 3.3.12, *Sh*. 22.62.

*keṽa* =*kathaṁ Hv*. 83.3.11, 89.16.8-9. *Kp*.S. 46.8, cf. *Hc*. 4.401.

*kesa* *keśa* Acc. Pl. -*ẽ*, *DKs*. 6, Loc. Pl. -*hiṁ Hc*. 4.370.

*kesari* (*ts.*) Nom. Sg. zero *Hc*. 4.335.

*keha* °*u*, °*va* =*kīdṛśa Hv*. 83.8.2, 88.17.10, *Ld*. 3.3.9. °-*o Sh*. 22.60.

*ehiṁ* =*arthe* 'for the sake of' cf. *Hc*. 4.425. *Kc*. 70.

| | |
|---|---|
| *kokka* | =*āhve-* 'to call' (onomatopoeic).<br>PP. -*iya MP.* 5.17.15, *Nc.* 3.13.7. |
| *koḍi* | *koṭi* Gen. Sg. -*ha DKK* 1.<br>=*kutūhala Pd.* 117. cf. *kuḍḍa Hc.* 2.174. *koḍaa Hc.* 4.422. |
| *konti* | *Kuntī Mp.* 87.7.6. |
| *Kosambı* | *Kauśāmbī* Loc. Sg. -*hi MP.* 90.16.4. |
| *koha-gaṇa* | *krodha-gaṇa* Ins. Pl. -*ehi DKK*.18. |

*kh*

| | |
|---|---|
| *khaga-vai* | °*pati*. Dat. Gen. Sg. -*he KKc.* 6.16.9. |
| *khaṁcaṇa* | =*karṣaṇa Nc.* 5.4.12 (M. *khēcaṇē*). |
| *khaḍillaü* | =*khalvāṭam PPr.* 2.139 (Metathesis of Pkt. *khallīḍa*). |
| *khaḍḍa* | =*gartā* 'a pit' Loc. Sg. -*ha* (-*i* ?) *Jdu.* 14.3. |
| *khaṇa* | *kṣaṇa DKK.* 30, Direct Sg. -*u Hc.* 4.446,<br>Ins. Sg. -*eṇa Hc.* 4.371, -*eṁ Hc.* 4,419.<br>Loc. Sg. -*e* (Skt.ism ?) *DS.* 4.5.2, -*i DKs.* 93.<br>Ins. Loc. Pl. -*ehi DKK* 18. |
| *khaṇaddha* | =*kṣanārdha KKc.* 1.10.6. |
| *khaddha* | =*khādita* Ins. Sg. -*iṁ Sdd.* 36. |
| *khandhāra* | *skandhāvāra* Neut. direct Sg. -*u Sdd.* 51. |
| *khappara* | **skarparaka Mt.* 15. |
| *khabaṇa* | *kṣapaṇaka* Ins. Sg. -*ehi DKs.* 6.<br>Gen. Pl. -*āṇa* (Pkt.ism) *DKs.* 8. |
| √*khama* | √*kṣam* Imp. 2 Pl. -*hu DKs.* 75.<br>Caus. Pres. 1.Pl. -*āva- hā BhK.* 210.8. |
| *khamaga* | **kṣamaka*=*kṣapaṇaka Kp. S.*88.1 |
| *khayara* | *khadira Pd.* 149. |
| *khala* | (ts.) Acc. Pl. -*īiṁ Hc.* 4.334,<br>Gen. Pl. -(*ā*)*haṁ* 3.37.8. |
| √*khalakhala* | Onomatopoeic cf. M. *khaḷāḷṇē*<br>Pres. Part. -(*a*)*nta Hv.* 88.11.9. |
| √*khalahala* | The same as above.<br>Pres. Part. -*antu Jc.* 4.7.4. |

√*khava* √*kṣap-aya* Imp. 2 Sg. -*hi* *KKc.* 1.11.3.

*khavaṇaa* *Kṣapaṇaka* Masc. Nom. Sg. -*u* *PPr.* 1.82.

√*khā* √*khād*
Imp. 2 Sg. -*hi* *Jc.* 2.9.7 -*hu* *DKs.* 57.
Fut. 3 Pl. -*hiṁti* *Jc.* 2.29.5, Pres. Part. -*anta.*
*KKc.* 1.3.8, *Pd.* 63, -*antẽ* *DKs.* 26. *PP.* -*ya* *BhK.* 118.9.

*khāiṁ* an expletive *Hc.* 4.424.

*khāra* *kṣāra* *Pd.* 195, *Sdd.* 81.

*khāla* =*khalla* *Kp.* S. 95.9 (cf. Guj. *khāḷ* 'drain-gutter, urinal.')

*khitti* *kṣiti* *DKK.* 9.

*khitta* *kṣetra* *Sc.* 444.9.

*khittaa* *kṣiptaka* Masc. Nom. Sg. -*u* *Mt.* 15.

√*khilla* =*krīḍ* cf. *Hc.* 4.168, also 4.382.
Pres. 3 Pl. -*hĩ* *Kp.* J. 25.6 (M. *kheḷnẽ*, Guj., H.,
Panj. Beng.√*khel*-).

*khilliya* *kīlikā*, Masc. Nom. Sg. -(*a*)*iṁ* *Sdd.* 106.
(M. *khiḷā*, Guj. *khilo*, H. *khīlā* *kīla*)

*khīṇa* *kṣīṇa* *KKc.* 7.1.6.

*khīra* *kṣīra* Ins. Sg. -*iṁ* *Jc.* 2.3.1. (M. Guj.
Panj. H. *khīr*).

*khīrāla* *kṣīravat* *Hv.* 87.12.8.

*khīliya* *kīlita* *Hv.* 91.2.15 (Pa. Pk. *khīla*).

*khuḍiya* =*truṭita* *Hv.* 84.4.3, *Nc.* 7.14.13, cf. *Hc.* 4.116, (cf. Sk. *khuṇḍ*,
Pk. *khuṭṭa*-, M. *khuḍṇẽ*, Guj. H. *khuṇṭ*).

√*khunda* √*kṣud*- Abs. -*mi* *Jc.* 1.5.12.

√*khuppa*- =√*kṣip* Pres. 3 Sg. -*i* *MP.* 25.9.9.
PP. *khutta* *MP.* 31.23.6.

*khuruppa* *kṣurapra* ? *MP.* 11.1 9.
Ins. Sg. -*iṁ* *Jc.* 3.7.11 (M. *khurapẽ*)

*khuhia*, °*ya* *kṣubhita* *BhK.* 43.5, *Mt.* 31.

*kheu* *kṣemam* (acc. Sg.) *Hv.* 91.22.10. but *kheuṁ* 'an embrace' *MP.*
29.19.2.

*khetta* *kṣetra KKc.* 1.3.8.

*khettī* *kṣetritā Sdd.* 55 (M. *śetī* Sdh. *khetī*, H. Beng. Panj. *khet(a)*.)

√*khella-* √*krīḍ-* Abs. *-evi Hv.* 91.20.11, *-vi Nc.* 3.12.10.

*kheviya* *khedita BhK.* 260.9.

*khoï* =*kṣapayitvā Pd.* 194. (*kṣapay-*>*khavatya-*>*khoya*>*khoa*+Abs.*-i*)

*khoja* *kṣoda* ? =*anveṣaṇa Sdd.* 84. (*H. khoj-*).

*g*

*gaaṇa* *gagana Mt.* 33. Nom. Sg. *-u Mt.* 16.

*gaï* *gati* Nom. Sg. zero *Mt.* 25,33. Acc. Sg.=*Mt.* 24, Dat. Sg. *-he Mp.* 2.3.35.

*gaïya* *gatā Pd.* 52.

*gaṁga* *Gaṅgā* Loc. Sg. *-i Pd.* 137, *-hiṁ KKc.* 10.13.2.

*Gaṁgā-ṇaī-Sindhu-hu*=*Gaṅgā-nadī-Shindhu-bhiḥ KKc.* 1.3.3.

*-gagana* (*ts.*) Direct Pl. zero *DKK.* 9.

*gaggira* *gadgada BhK.* 81.10.

√*gaccha* see under √*gaṁa* below

*gaṁjolliya* =1) *romāñcita Hv.* 83.9.1, *MP.* 14.12.12.
2) *kṣubdha Jc.* 3.36.5.
(Sk. *gañjana* 'disregard, insult,' M. *gāṁajṇē* 'to trouble, to harass,'' Guj. *gāṁjvū̃*, H. *gāṁjnā* 'to move,' Beng. *gaṁja-* 'insult').

√*gaḍayaḍa* 'to thunder' (onomatopoeic) cf. *Sc.* 537.4. *Kp.* P. 7.1. (M. *gaḍgaḍṇē* 'to thunder'.)

*gaḍḍāyara-u* =*phalaka* or *gartaka Sdd.* 58.

√*gaṇa-* √*gaṇay-*
F. Pres. Part. *-anti BhK.* 147.9. Ins. Sg. for Gen. Sg. *-e Hc.* 4.333. PP. *-iu KKc.* 1.11.3.
(M. *gaṇaṇē*, Guj. *gaṇvū̃*, H. *ginnā*, Panj. *giṇaṇā*)

*-gatta* *-gātrā* Ins. Sg. *-e Bhk.* 293.3.

*-gattia* *gātrikā*. Nom. Pl. *-o BhK.* 10.15.
Ins. pl. *-hi Mt.* 14.

*gantha* *grantha* Abl. Sg. *-haü PPr.* 2.49.

*gabba* — *garva* Masc. Acc. Sg. zero *DKK*. 1.

√*gama* — √*gam* (*gaccha*- forms are included here) Imp. 2 Sg. (*gaccha*-) -*su Jc*. 2.3.5. Fut. 2 Sg. -*isi PPr*. 2.141. Pres. Part. -*anta Kp*. S. 94.4 PP. *gadu Ld*. 3.3.46, Abs. (*gacch*) -*ivi Kp*. S. 40.6 80, *Ld*. 3.3.31 *gamppiṇu Kc*. 80, *Ld*. 3.3.21. -*eppi*, -*eppiṇu Kc*. 80, *Ld*. 3.3.21.

*gama* — *gama*(*na*) Direct Sg. -*u KKc* 1.6.1.

*gammagammai* Freq. Pres. 3 Sg. of √*gam Pd*. 83.

*gaya* — =*gaja* Masc. Nom. Pl. zero 87.9.2.
=*gata* Neut. direct Pl. zero *Sdd*. 206.

*garuva* — **garukā*=*gurvī* Loc. Sg. -*i Pd*. 137.

*galacchiya* / *galatthiya* — *kadarthita Jc*. 4.2.22, *MP*. 31.27.9.
*kṣipta BhK*. 134.4, *JHc*. 4.143, *Hv*. 88.6.5.
Masc. Gen. Pl. -*haṁ Sn*. 25-212.

*galia* — *galita* Neut. Ins. Sg. -*eṁ Jc*. 2.3.1.

*gahaṇa* — °*na* Ins. Sg. -*e DKs*. 8.

*gahia* — =*gṛhītvā DKs*. 103.

*gahirajjhuṇī* *gabhīra-dhvani* 'deep-voiced.'
Ins. Sg. -*ṇa Sc*. 457.4.

*gahṇa* — **gṛbhṇa*=√*grah* (*gṛhṇāti*)
Pres. 3 Sg. -*i*, -*di Ld*. 3.4.62.

*gāi* — *gāvī* Fem. Acc. Sg. zero *Sdd*. 92.

*gā-iuṇa* — Abs. of *gā* < √*gai* 'to sing' *KKc*. 1.12.2-3.

*gāma* — *grāma DKs*. 69. Masc. Nom. Sg. -*u PPr*. 1.44. Nom. Pl. -*aī BhK*. 5.6.

*gāva* — *garva Mp*. 1.8.1.

-*gāhiṇi* — -*grāhiṇī* Fem. Ins. Pl. -*hī BhK*. 17.6.

√*giṇha*- — *gṛh-ṇa* Pres. Part. 1 Sg. -*sū Kp*. S. 49.9.
3 Sg. -*i Kp*.S. 73.9, *Sdd*. 162, 3. Pl. -*ahī*.
*Kp*. S. 53.2. Imp. 2 Sg. -*asu KP*.S. 49.8.

*giddhālu* — =*gṛddha-ālu* Neut. direct Sg. zero *Sn*. 16.570.

-*giddhī* — -*gṛddhi* 'craving for meal' *PPr*. 1.111.3*

*gira* — *gīr, girā Sdd.* 178. Ins. Plur. *hī Śc.* 455.1. Loc. Sg. *hī Sc.* 597.6.

*giri* — (*ts.*) Masc. Nom. Sg. zero MP. 87.2.2, -*girī DKs.* 102. Dat. Gen. Sg. -*hi Jc.* 2.12.5, Abl. Sg. -*he Hc.* 4.341. -*hĕ* Kc. 19. -*hi Kc.* 20. -*hiṁ Jdu.* 6.1 Abl. Pl. *hū Kc.* 19. Abl. Pl. °*singa-hu Hc.* 4.337.

*guḍare* — =*guḍero Mt.* 17.

*guṇa* — (*ts.*) Ins. Pl. -(*a*)*hiṁ Hc.* 4.335. -(*ĕ*)*hī*. *BhK.* 18.9. Loc. Sg. -*ĕhī BhK.* 21.3.

*guṇavvaya* — °*vrata* Neut. direct Pl. zero *Sdd.* 11.

*gutti* — *gupti* Fem. Gen Loc. Sg. -*hi BhK.* 293.4.

*guru* — (*ts,*) Masc. Nom. Sg. zero *Pd.* 1, *PPr.* 2.1. Acc. Sg. zero *BhK.* 299.1. Gen. Sg. -*ha DKs.* 97. -*hu Ys.* 41, -*huṁ Pd.* 81, Acc. Pl. zero *Sdd.* 1.

*guru-kkī* — =*gurvī PPr.* 1.32.

*guruva* — *guru* Gen. Sg. -*hi Pd.* 174.

*guhila* — =*gahvara Hv.* 82.8. 9.

√*gṛhṇa* — =*gṛh Pu.* 17.86. Pres. 3. Sg. -*di Sh.* 22.67.

*gĕṇha* — *gṛhāṇa*. Imp. 2 Sg. of √*gṛh*- *Mt.* 5. (cf. M. *gheṇĕ*, Sdh. *giṇhaṇu*).

*gĕruya* — *gairika Hv.* 85.2.7. (Pk. *geria, geruya:* M. H. Guj. Panj. *gerŭ* Beng. *gerī*).

*goṁcha, guṁcha*=*guccha MP.* 1.3.7, *Nc.* 1.6.12. cf. M. *ghŏs.*

*gotta* — *gotra* Gen. Sg. -*hu Sdd.* 46.

*goraḍī* — **gavra-ṭī*=*gaurī Mt.* 12.

*gori, gaurī.* — Gen. Sg. -*he Hc.* 4.395.

*goria* — *gaurī-kā* Gen. Sg. -*he Hc.* 4.414.

*Govai* — *Gomatī Hv.* 90.18.10.

*gosa* — 'dawn' *MP.* 1.16.9 (still coll. in Koṅkan.)

gh

*ghaïṁ* An expletive *Hc.* 4.424, *Kc.* 69 *Ld.* 3.3.58.

*ghaggharoli* *ghagghārā*, +*āvali*=*kiṅkiṇī-paṅktiḥ*
Fem. Ins. Pl -*hiṁ* *Jc.* 1.16.5 (cf. M. *ghāgaryā*)

√*ghaḍa* √*ghaṭ*- Imp. 3. Pl. -*antu* *KKc.* 9.16.8.
(*Pk.* *ghaḍaï*, M. Guj. H. Sdh. Panj. √*ghāḍ*(*a*)-)

*ghaṇaüṁ* =*prabhūtam* *Jdc.* 9.4.

*ghaṇṭa* *ghaṇṭā* Fem. Nom. Pl. zero *Sdd.* 199.

*ghaṇḍā* *ghaṇṭā* Acc. Sg. zero *DKs.* 4.
(cf. Sdh. *ghaṇḍo*, Panj. *ghaṇḍā*, Nep. *gh ṛo*)

√*ghatta* =√*kṣip*- *Hc.* 4.143.
Imp. 2 S.g -*hi* *Hv.* 82.17.10, PP. *iya* *BhK.* 9.2. Abs. -*evi* *Hv.* 92.10.4.

*ghara* IE **gʷhoro*. Wrongly but usually traced to Sk. *gṛha*.
Direct sg. -*u* *Pd.* 13.
Loc. Sg. -*e*, -*ĕ* *DKK* 13, 28, Dks. 80. -*ẽ* *DKs.* 82. -(*a*)*hi* *DKs.* 14,21. -(*a*)*hiṁ* *Hc.* 4.422.15.°
Direct Pl. zero *BhK.* 65.5.
(Pa. Pk. *ghara.* M. G. Nep. *ghar*).

*gharṇī* =*gṛhiṇī*.
Nom. Sg. zero *DKK* 24, 28. Acc. Sg. zero. *DKK.* 31, *Hc.* 4.370. Ins. Sg. -*eṁ* *KKc.* 1.6.9, 10-10.6, -*ehi* *DKs.* 86. Gen. Sg. -*hĕ* *BhK.* 19.4. Loc. Sg. -*hi* *Jc.* 2.1.2.

√*ghalla* =√*kṣip* *Hc.* 4.334.
Pres. 1 Sg. -*mi* *Hv.* 91.7.4. 2 P. Sg. -*hi* *Hv.* 88.21.6, -*i* *Hv.* 83.22.8. 1 Pl. -*hã* *BhK.* 10.7.6. Pres. Part. -*antu* *Hv.* 84.7.8.
PP. -*iya* *Hv.* 82.4.12. Abs. -*ivi* *BhK.* 177.11. -*eppiṇu* *Pd.* 171. -*eviṇu* *BhK.* 181.4.
(M. *ghālṇẽ*. Guj. *ghālvũ*).

*ghāra* =*gṛdhra* *PPr.* 1.111. *4

*ghiṇā* *ghṛṇā* *PPr.* 2.151.

*ghitta* PP. of √*ghiva* or √*ghippa* *Jc.* 3.16.9. Many times equated with *kṣipta*

√*ghippa* =√*kṣip-* Pres. 3 Sg. -*i* *Sn* 168-115. 3 Pl. -*anti* *Pd.* 151.

√*gniva* =*kṣip-* *MP*. 2.18.6, *Nc*. 3.3.1, 8.1.7.√

√*ghuṇṭa* 'to drink' Abs. -*ivi* *Kp*.S. 110.4.
(cf. *Dn*. 2.109c. *Hc*. 4.10. M. *ghoṭaṇẽ*, H. *ghumtnā* *ghõṭnā*, Sdh. *ghuṭakaṇu*, Or. *ghuṭanā*).

√*ghula* =√*ghūrṇ-* of. *Hc*. 4.117 but *gholayati* in Sk. lex. PP. -*iya-u* *Jc*. 3.14.5.
Abs. -*ivi* *BhK*. 269.9.
(M. *gholṇẽ*, Guj. *gholvũ* 'agitates' H. *gholnā*, Nep. *gholnu*).

√*ghe* =√*grah-* Pres. 3 Sg. -*i* *Ld*. 3.4.62.

√*gheppa* =√*grah*. Traceable to **ghṛpyate*=*gṛhyate* ?
Pres. 3. Sg. -*i* *Mt*. 20.
(cf. M. *ghepṇẽ*, *gheṇẽ*).

√*ghoṭṭa* 'to drink' cf. *Hc*. 4.10.
Pres. 3 Sg. -*i* *Hv*. 85.10.4, 3 Pl. -*anti* *Nc*. 5.5.5. (For cognates see √*ghuṇṭa* above).

*ghoṇasa* *gonasa* *Jc*. 1.9.6.

C

*caü-* *catur-* *DKK*.5. Direct Pl. zero *Sdd*. 121.

*caükka* *catuṣka* *Kp*. S. 17.7, *Nc*. 9.21.2.
(Pa. *catukkaṁ*, Pk. *caükka* n., M. *cauk* Guj. *cok* Masc., H. Panj. *cauk*, Nep. *cok*.)

*caüṭṭha* *catuṣṭaya* *DKK*. 5.

*caütīsā* *catustriṁśat* *MP*. 1.18.7 (M. *cautīs*)

*caü-disa-hiṁ* =*catur-dikṣu* *MP*. 87.4.6 (Ins. Loc. Pl. -*hiṁ*)

*caüppaha* *cautṣpatha* Loc. Sg. -*i* *Mt*. 12.

*caübbeü* *caturvedāḥ* *DKs*.1.

*caüraṁsa* *caturasra* *BhK*. 34.5.

*caürāsī* *caturaśītī* *Pd*. 23.
(Pk. *caürāsīi*, M. *cauryāśi* H. *caurāsī*, Guj. *corāsī*, Nep. *caurāsi*).

*caüriya* *camarī* *KKc*. 7.7.10.

*cakka-la* *cakra-* 'round, extensive' *BhK*. 12.2.
°*tta*= °*tva* *KKc*. 5.1.9.

***cakkā*** *cakra-(vāk)* Neut. Nom. Sg. zero *Mt.* 26.

***cakki*** *cakrin=cakravartin*
Ins. Pl. *-hiṁ Sdd.* 177.

***√cakkha*** 'to eat, to taste, to relish'.
Pres. 3 Sg. *-i Hv.* 85.10.6. *Jc.* 3.23.6.
(cf. Sk. *caṣ-* 'to eat' quoted by Bloch in FLM Gloss. Pk. *cakkhaï*, M. Guj. Sdh. H. Beng. *√cākh-*, Panj. *√cakkh-*)

***caṁga*** Sk. lex. *caṅga* 'handsome'. *BhK.* 28.3.
Neut. Nom. Sg. *-c DKs.* 39, Loc. Sg. *-i BhK.* 10.6. (OM. *cāng* 'good', Nep. *camgā*).

***caṁcū*** (*ts.*) Acc. and Ins. Sg. zero *Jc.* 1.12.8.
(M.H. *cõc*, Sdh. *cũji*, Deśi *cumculī*)

***caṭṭa*** 1) 'a disciple' *Hv.* 82.12.2, *MP.* 1.16.1.
2) 'a mat'? acc. to Upadhye *PPr.* 2.89.
(Traceable to *√*cṛt-* See S.M. Katre, 'Pk. uccidima in *Festschrift Prof. P.V. Kane*). PP. 258-59.

***caṭṭuya*** *=utpūta Jc.* 3.5.14. 'scoop, drainer'. *Hv.* 83.3.4 cf. *Dn.* 3.1 *caṭṭū dāruhastaḥ.* For cognates see Bloch, *FLM* Glossary. under *cāṭū.*

***√caḍa-*** 'to ascend, to climb' cf. *Hc.* 4.206. Fut. 3 Pl. *-esahim KKc.* 2.8.3, PP. *-iya Pd.* 173.
Abs. *-eviṇu Pd.* 111, *-evi KKc.* 1.10.9.

***√caḍāva*** Pres. 1 Sg. *-uṁ Pd.* 49, Imp. 2 Sg. *-hi*
*Nc.* 1.4.1, PP. *-iya Jc.* 3.26.6.

***√caḍha*** *=ā-ruh* Pres. 3 Sg. *-i Sdd.* 105.
(M. *caḍhṇē*, Guj. *caḍhvū*, *Sdh. caṛhaṇu* H. Panj. *caṛhṇa* < Pk. *caḍha, caḍa.* Louis Gray traces it to IE **qelde* < **qele-* 'be high lift high.' *JAOS* 60.362 ff. Its *-dhe-* extension gives modern M. Guj. H. forms).

***caduvvũghaka*** *=caturmukha Sh.* 22.3.

***candima*** 'Moonlight' Ins. Sg. *-e Hc.* 4.349.

***candru*** *candraḥ Mk.* 17.4.

***campa*** *campā* Loc. Sg. *-hiṁ KKc.* 10.9.12.

***√caya*** *√tyaj-* Imp. 2 Pl. *-aha Kp.* J. 100.1*,
Abs. *-ēvi Kp.* J. 59.1. *PP. catta Kp.* S. 2.2 *Sdd.* 15.

*cayārı* — *catvāri*>*cattāri*>**catari* *Sdd*. 11.
(M. *cāri*, *cyār*, Guj. H. Panj. Nep. *cār*)

*caraṇa* — (*ts*.) Acc. Sg. *-u* *KKc*. 1.1.2, Direct Pl. zero *KKc*. 1.1.12.

*calaṇa* — *caraṇa* Loc. Pl. *-haṁ* *Sdd*. 173.

*callıu* — *calıtam* *Mt*. 14.

√*cava* — 'to tell, to speak' cf. *Hc*. 4.2
Imp. 2 Sg. *-hi* *Hv*. 91.18.11. 'to abandon'
Abs. *-evi* *Pd*. 66 also *Hv*. 90.6.12.

*cāa* — *tyāga* Ins. Sg. *-eṇa* *Jc*. 1.5.1.

*cāüttha* — *caturtha* *Nc*. 9.20.3.
(M. *cauthā*, Guj. *cotho*, H. Nep. Panj. *cauthā*)

*cāuddisi* — =*caturdikṣu* *Sn*. 18.442.

*cāḍuyasaa* — *caṭu-ka-śata* Ins. Pl. *-ihıṁ*. *Sn*. 168-115

*cārittaṇa* — *cārın*+*tva* *Nc*. 3.3.12.

*cāvira* — √*carv*+*ıra* (*tācchīlye*) *Hv*. 85.11.14.
(Pk. *cavviya*, M. *cāvṇē*, Guj. *cāvvū*, H. *cabāıā*,
Panj. *cabbṇā*, Sdh. *cabaṇu*)

√*cāha* — 'to like, to expect.' Imp. 2 Sg. *-hu* *BhK*. 147.3,
*Ys*.26. (M. *cāhṇē*, H. *cāhnā*.)

*cia* — **cita*<*cıtta* *DKK* 3.

√*ciṭṭha* — *tiṣṭha-*
Fut. 2 Sg. *-ihisi* Sc. 513.2.

*ciḍaulla* — =*caṭaka* *MP*. 9.8.14 (Traceable to √**cr* or *√*cṛt*. See S. M. KATRE's paper in *Festschrıft Prof. P.V.Kane*, p.258-59.)

*ciṇha* — *cinha*. Ins. Sg. *-ē* *Mt*. 24.

*citta* — (*ts*) Ins. Sg. *-ē* *DKs*. 80, Gen. Sg. *-hā* *PPr*. 2.70.
Ins. Pl. *-chi* *DKs*. 101 (used as Sg.).
Gen. Pl. *-ahā* *Sc*. 452.3, Loc. Pl. *-ahī* *Sc*. 777.4.

*citta* — *caitra* 'N. of a month' Gen. Sg. *-ha* *Sn*. 18-468 used locatively.

√*cinta* — *cintay-* Pres. 3 Sg. *-i* *DKs*. 39. *Kp*. S. 74.1, *-ei* *Kp*.S. 51.2. 3 Pl.—(*a*)*hiṁ* *Sn*. 77-176, *-anti* *Kp*.S.89.2. Imp. 2 Sg. -zero *DKs*. 88, *-ssa* *DKs*.77, *-asu* *Kp*. A. 11. 4 2 Pl. *-ha* *DKs*. 46,

Sn. 168.115. PP. Neut. direct Sg. *-iu KKc.*1.11.1. Abs. *-iā DKs.* 76. *-ivi Kp.*J. 97.2.

*cinta* — *cinta* Acc. Pl. zero *Pd.* 66.

*cintācinta* — °*cinte* (i.e Fem. Acc. Pl. -zero) *DKs.*59.

*ciya, ceya* — *eva MP.*1.11.14 also *cciya Nc.* 6.15.1.
*ceya* (*caiva*) in *Nc.* 7.14.8.

*ciru* — *ciram Nc.* 3.13.13.

*cillaṇa* — *celanā* (*devī*) *Nc.* 1.7.9.

*cihura* — *cikura* 'hair' *Mp.* 2.7.1.

*cukkha, cokkha* — *cokṣa* 'pure' *Kp.* E 34, but in *Kp.* E 22 *cokkha* means 'licking'.

*cuṁcu* — *cañcū Nc.* 2.11.12.
(Pk. *caṁcū.* But the Ap. form gives the NIA forms with *-o-* e.g. M. *cōc, coc,* Guj. *cac*).

*cumbhala* — =*śekhara Hv.* 88.5.3, *Nc.* 4.10.7. (cf. *Dn* 3.16 M. *cumbal*).

*cei-hara* — *caitya-gṛha* Loc. Sg. *-i Jdc.* 12.1.

*ceṇa* — *cetanā BhK* 330.4.

*ceya* — *cetanā BhK.* 247.10.

*cellu* — 'a disciple' *DKs.* 10. cf. H. *celā* connected with √**cṛt* or √**cṛ Festschrift Prof. P.V.Kaṇe* P. 258-59).

*cotthī* — *caturthī* Nc. 9.20.4.

*coddaha* — *caturdaśa Mp.* 1.2.6.
(Pa. *catuddasa, cuddasa,* Pk. *coddasa, coddaha* M. *caudā, cavdā,* H. *caudah,* Guj. *cauda*).

*coraḍā* — *cora- Sdd.* 75.

*ch*

*cha* — *ṣaṣ Nc.* 1.12.15. Ins. Pl. *-hiṁ Kp.*S. 37.1*

*chaïlla* — 'Beautiful' (*chāyā-illa*) *Kp.*E. 11.

√*chaḍḍa-* — √*chard*=*tyaj* cf. *Hc.* 4.91.
Pres. 3 Sg. *-i DKs.* 34. Imp. 2 Sg. *-u DKs.* 57.
2 Pl. *-hu DKs.* 51. PP. *-iü Sdd.* 39.
Abs. *-i DKs.* 16.

*chaṇa* — *kṣaṇa- BhK.* 12.3, *KKc.* 5.19.5, *Sdd.* 199.

| | |
|---|---|
| √*chaṇḍa* | √*chard=muc*<br>Pres. 1 Sg. -*üṁ KKc.* 2.4.6.<br>Imp. 2 Sg. -*i Pd.* 13, *Sdd.* 67. -*hı Jc.* 3.21. 11.<br>2Pl. -*hu Pd.* 69, *Ys.* 21. Abs. -*ı Pd.* 109,<br>-*ivi Pd.* 16.205. -*evıṇu Jc.* 3.38.3, *Pd.* 151 PPr. 1.74. |
| *chaṇṇavaī* | *ṣaṇṇavatı Sn.* 30-231. |
| *chaddarısaṇa* | *ṣaḍdarśana* Gen. Pl. zero *Jdc.* 2.1. |
| *chadāïtta* | *chanda-vat BhK.* 35.5. |
| *chappaṇṇa* | *ṣaṭpañcāśat Mp.* 2.6,4.<br>(M. *chappann*, Guj. H. Nep. *chappan*) |
| *chaha* | *ṣaṭ Sdd.* 20.<br>(II **kṣaṭ* or **kṣvaṭ*, Pa. Pk. *cha*, M. *sahā* Guj. Sdh. H. Nep. *cha*). |
| *chāvaṭṭhi* | =*ṣaṭṣaṣṭi Kp.* J. 66.3. |
| *chāyā* | (*ts*) *Hc.* 4.370, Acc. Sg. zero *Sdd.* 103. |
| *chāra* | *kṣāra PPr.* 2.90, *Hc.* 4.365.3. |
| *chōha* | *chōyā* Fem. Loc. Sg. -*hī Mt.* 14. |
| *chāhı* | =*pratibimbaṁ* (Tippaṇa) *MP.* 2.16.16. |
| *chi chi* | Interjection to express contempt. *Cd.* |
| *chıtta* | *kṣetra BhK.* 5.3 (cf. M. *śet*). |
| *chuḍu* | =*yadı BhK.* 54.8 *Hc.* 385, 401.1, *Hv.* 81.10.13, *Nc.* 3.9.11, *Sdd.* 58.<br>=*kṣipram Jc.* 3.13.18.<br>=*yadā BhK.* 121.10. |
| *chuddhiyā* | =*kṣipta KKc.* 1.7.3. cf. *Hc.* 4.143. |
| *churia*(*ya*) | *kṣurikā KKc.* 3.13.7, *Sc.* 654.6. (*M. surī*, °*rā*, Guj. Sdh. H. *churī*) |
| *chuha* | *kṣudhā KKc.* 5.10.4, *Kp.* J. 2.4, *Sc.* 554.5. |
| *chūḍha* | *kṣipta Kp.* S. 84.3. cf. *Hc.* 4.143. |
| *chetta* | *kṣetra KKc.* 1.3.3. (M. *śet* In other NIA languages *kh*-) |
| *choha* | *kṣobha MP.* 17.1.6, 29.18.8. |

ija　*yad*　*j*

Masc. Nom. Sg. *jo Cd.* 2.27.11, *DKK.* 16, *DKs.* 19. *Hc.* 4.330.4, 332.1, *Jdc.* 2.1, *KKc.* 6.3.7, *Kp.* J 4.3 *Pd.* 1, *Sc.* 527.1, Direct Sg. *ju Ds.* 4.32, *Hc.* 4.345, *Jdc.* 3.3, *Pd.* 161, *Sc.* 485.8, *Sn.* 271-190. Neut. direct Sg. *ju Hc.* 345, 350.1, *Ld.* 3.4.31. *Mt.* 22. Sc. 623.4.

*jaṁ Kc.* 28, *Kp.* J. 1.1. *Ld.* 3.4.32 *Pd.* 2, *PPr.* 1.42, 57.

*druṁ Ld.* 3.4.31, *dhruṁ Hc.* 4 360, *Kc.* 27.

Ins. Sg. *jeṁ, jẽ DKK.* 21,31. *DKs.* 10. *Hc.* 4.350. *KKc.* 6.3.2.

*jiṁ, jĩ Jc.* 4.1.4. *Kp.* E. 35, *Pd.* 71, 98.

*jeṇa DKK.* 17,19. *DKs.* 44, *Hc.* 4.414. *Kp.* S. 63.6, *Mt.* 18, *Pd.* 57,82. *Sc.* 491.1, *Sdd.* 2.

*jiṇa Jdc.* 7.1. *Kp.* J. 9.4, *Sc.* 588.4, *jiṇi Jdc.* 8.3. *Kp.* S. 52.4.

*jo DKK* 23 (?)

Dat. Gen. Sg. *jasu BhK.* 2.7, 4.6, *Jdu.* 4.2. *KKc.* 1.5.2, *Kp.* J. 25.4, *MP.* 1.11.12. *Pd.* 24. *Sc.* 503.8, *Sdd.* 5.

*jāsu BhK.* 3.3, 9.10, *DKs.* 89, *Hc.* 4.358, *KKc.* 1.5.5. *MP.* 1.1.17, *Pd.* 59,76. *jassa* is Pktism.

*jāha Pd.* 14, Loc. Sg. *jahiṁ, jahĩ BhK.* 5. 2. *DKK* 20 (used instrumentively), *Hc.* 4.386 (adverbially) *Kc.* 26, *KKc.* 5.4.6, *Kp.* J. 74.4, *Sc.* 476.3.

*jammi Mt.* 20 (Pkt. sm). *jāhiṁ KKc.* 1.3.6.

Masc. Direct Pl. *je BhK.* 146.10, *Hc.* 4,333, *Jdc.* 4.3. *Kp.* J. 5.4, *MK.* 17.40, *Pd.* 4, *Pv.* 17.62. *Sc.* 610.6, *Sdd.* 20 *ji Kp.* A. 13.1. *Pd.* 86, Neut. in *Kp.* J. 54.1

Neut direct Pl. *jāĩ BhK.* 204.5, *Ld.* 3.4.32 (*jaïṁ* also), *PPr.* 2.56

Ins. Pl. *jehiṁ jehĩ BhK.* 147.6, *Hc.* 4.439, *Pd.* 92. *PPr.* 1.61. *jehi DKs.* 58.

Gen. Pl. *jāhaṁ Hc.* 4.353, *Pd.* 102, *jāha Pd.* 14. *jahã Kp.* J. 28.5, *jahuṁ Jc.* 2.12.19. *jāhiṁ Pd.* 156. 217.

Fem. direct Sg. *jā BhK.* 4.2. 214.7. (Acc.) *BhK.* 140.4. *Hc.* 4.395.6, *KKc.* 5.15.4, (Acc.) *KKc.* 5.1.12, *Kp.* S.16.2. *Pd.* 19, *PPr.* 2.46*. 1, *Sc.* 736.5. Ins. Sg. *jāẽ BhK.* 209.10 Gen. Sg. *jāhi BhK.* 168.4, *Jc.* 3.7.7. *jāhe KKc.* 5.16.5, *jasu Hc.* 4.368, *Kp.* S. 12.1.3. *jāsu Kp.* S. 13.4, *jahe Hc.* 4.359, *Ld.* 3.4.30.

*jīe Sc.* 484.4. Loc. Sg. *jāhi BhK.* 149.5.

*jahiṁ KKc.* 6.16.7. Direct Pl. *jāo BhK.* 10.3, *jāü Kp.* S. 98.1.

jaï　1) *yadi Kp.* J. 46.9, *Nc.* 8.13.3, *PPr.* 2.5, *Sdd.* 25.

2) *yatra Ld.* 3.3.14.

*jaïṁ* An expletive (*pāda-pūraṇe*) *Pu.* 17.27.

*jaïa* =*jāta DKK.* 7.

*jaïvaṁ,* °*hu*, °*hā*=*yada Jc.* 3.34.6. *BhK.* 121.4. °*huṁ Nc.* 3.15.7.

*jaïsu* *yādṛda Ld.* 3.3.10.

*jaüṇā* *yamunā Hv.* 85.19.1, *KKc.* 10.12.9.

*jaga* *jagat*
Nom. Sg. -*u DKK.*27, Acc. Sg. zero *DKs.* 80.
Gen. Pl. -*ha Jc.* 1.6.1.

√*jagaḍa* 'to fight, to overpower.' Traced to Sk. *jhakaṭa Hc.* 422.2.
Imp. 2 Sg. -*ha* DKs. 25. Pres. Part. -*anta Nc.* 3.15.12.
(cf. *Hc.* 4.170 ' to hasten,' *Dn.* 3.44. *M.* jhagḍā)

*jajjariā* *jarjaritā* Nom. Pl. -(*ā*)*u Hc.* 4.333.

*jajjāhi* Intensive of √*jā* (<*yā*) Imp. 2 Sg. *Nc.* 6.12.11.

*jaṇa* *jana* Gen. Sg. -*hu Sc.* 769.5.
*jāna* Ins. Pl. -*hi KKc.* 2.2.4.

√*jaṇa* *janay.*
Fut. 3 Pl. -*isahī Sc.* 25.9 (Intro. to *Sc.* P. 17. §24)
Pres. Part. -*antu PPr.* 1.35.

*jaṇaṇi* *jananī* (Fem.)
Ins. Sg. -*i MP.* 87.13.15, -*e BhK.* 302.11
Gen. Sg. -*he* *BhK.* 73.8, 291.6.

*jaṇi* =*iva Hc.* 4.444. *Ki* 5.6, 7. *Kc.* 81, *Kp.* S. 10.6,
*Ld.* 3.3.24. *Pu.* 17.26.

*jaṇu* =*iva Hc.* 4.401.3, 444, *Kc.* 81, *Ld.* 3.3.24.

*janēri* =*janayitrī Nc.* 5.8.15. Gen. Sg. -*hi BhK.* 73.6.

*jatta* *yatra* (>*jattha*) *DKs.* 74.

*jattha* *yatra Kp.* J. 46.5, -*u DKs.* 31.

*japa-homĕ* °-*homāḥ* (*i.e.* Nom. pl. in -*e*) *DKK.* 29.

*jamuṇa* *janman* (>*jamma*). Loc. Sg. -*ĕ Mt.* 4.
*Yamunā* Nom. Sg. zero *DKs.* 49.

√*jaṁpe-* √*jalp-*
Pres. 2 Sg. *-hi KKc.* 1.10.4, 3 Sg. *-i Mt.* 18.
Pres. Part. *-antu BhK.* 177.6
PP. *-iya BhK.* 40.6, Abs. *-ivi BhK.* 43.2 *-eviṇu BhK.*

*jamma* *janman* Loc. Sg. *-iṁ Jc.* 2.19.1.

*jaya* (*ts*) (Imp. 2 Sg. of √*ii-*) *Jc.* 1.2.1, *KKc.* 1.1.3.

*jaya-siri* °*śrī* Acc. Sg. zero *Mp.* 87.5.15.

*jayāsi* *jayaśrī BhK.* 7.5. (Acc. to Jacobi).

*jarā* (*ts.*) Ins. Sg. *-e BhK.* 301.4.

*jarā-maraṇa-ha* °*maraṇayoḥ* (Gen. Pl. in *-ha*) *DKK* 19.

*jala* (*ts.*) Sg. Nom. *-u DKs.* 76, Loc. *-hi DKs.* 76. *-hī DKs.* 34.

*jalūa* *jalūkā, jalaukā Kp.* S. 53.2.
(Pa. *jalūkā,* Pk. *jalūgā,* M. *jaḷū,* Guj. *jaḷo,* Sdh. *jaru,* Panj. *jalogī*).

*java lā* =*yātum Pd.* 105 (cf. M. *jāy-lā,* H. *jāne ke liye* ; *lā*<*lag*).

*javalā* =*samīpe* (Traced to *yamala-ka*) *PPr.* 2.127. cf. M. *javaḷ.*

*javāïya* *jāmātṛka Kp.* E. 6a (Guj. *jamāi* H. *āwāi* Nep. *juwǎi*)

*Javuṇa* *Yamunā* Gen. Sg. *-he Kc.* 15.

*iahiṁ* 1) *yatra Jc.* 1.3.5, *Sdd.* 54, 61. *Sn.* 271-190.
2) *yathā* (?) *Sdd.* 71.

*jram* *yad.* Pu. 17.55.

*jā* √*yā-* Pres. 3 Sg. *-ī KKc.* 1.12.9, 1 Pl. *-ha*
*Bhk.* 207.1, *-huṁ, hū BhK.* 210.8, *KKc.* 3.5.2 (?)
3 Pl. *-hiṁ KKc.* 2.2.4, *-anti Sdd.* 8.
Imp. 2 Sg. *-hi KKc.* 1.13.6.
*-huṃ. KKc.* 3.5.2.
3 Pl. *-antu BhK.* 26.9. Fut. 1 Sg. *-isu Sc.* 153.7.
3 Sg. *-hi Sc.* 569.1. Pres. Part. *-anta Pd.* 52. *-antaü M* 8, Fem. *-antī Mt.* 29, Pot. Part.
*-evaa Nc.* 7.4.10.

*jā* *yāvat* (>*iāva*) *Hv.* 85.3.6, *Kp.* S. 27.7.

*jāüṁ* *Ld.* 3.3.11. *Hc.* 4.406. *yāvat.*

√*jāṇa-* √*jñā-* Pres. 1 Sg. -*ũ DKs.* 92, -*mi* DKs. 92.
3 Sg. -*i DKs.* 60, 91. *Jdc.* 2.2
1 Pl. -(*a*)*hã BhK.* 26·3. Imp. 2 Sg. -*asu*
(Intro. to *Hv.* §56), -*i PPr.* 1.107, 2.38, -*u PPr.* 1.94.
-*hu Sdd.* 82. 2 Pl. -*hu DKs.* 39, 64.
Fut. 2 Sg. -*ihisi Mt.* 24. Pass. Pres. 3 Sg. -*ijjaï Nc.* 3.3.7.
-*ī DKs.* 65. Pres. Part. -*anta DKs.* 1, PP. -*aü*, *DKs.* 92.
-*ia DKs.* 53. *KKc.* 1.11.2.
-*ıā Mt.* 21.
Fem. Pot. Part. -*evvī Jc.* 4.6.4.
(Pa. *jānāti*, Pk. *jāṇei*, M. Guj.√*jāṇ-*, H. Nep.√*jān-*

*jāma* *yāvat Hc.* 4.406. *Hv.* 84.2.5, *Ld.* 3.3.11, *PPr.* 2.81.
-*ĩ*=*yadā* (?) *PPr.* 2.174, -*u PPr.* 2.194.
-*hıṁ Hc.* 4.406.3, *Ld.* 303.11.

*ālī* **jvālya* Abs. of√*jvālay DKs.* 4.

*iāya-hũ* =*jāyāmahe Sc.* 465.8.

*jjāva* *yāvat Hv.* 88.13.6.

*jāvã* *yāvat Hc.* 4.395.3. *Hv.* 89.13.12. -*i PPr.* 2.41.

*jāvāya* *jāmātṛ. MP.* 23.4.16.

*jjāhu* *yāvat* (or *yathā*) *Jc.* 3.19.9.
=*eva* (*cit*) *Hc.* 358.1, 396.3, *Jc.* 2.7.5.,
*KKc.* 2.7.1, *Ld.* 3.3.35, *PPr.* 1.96, *Sdd.* 26, *Sh* 39.
=an expletive *Jc.* 3.10.12.

*jiṁgha-ï* *jighrati DKK.* 6. (-*ī* Metri causa).

√*jiṇa* √*ji-* Fut. 3 Sg. -*ihaï Kp.* E. 33.
Inf. -*aṇahaṁ KKc.* 8.14.10.

*Jiṇa-ṇāha* *Jina-nātha.* Gen. Sg. -*ha* ὀ *Ys.* 30.

*Jiṇa muṇi* °-*muni* Acc. Sg. zero *Sdd.* 116.

*Jiṇa-vara* *Jina-vara* Gen. Sg. -*ho KKc.* 1.1.2.
Acc. Pl. zero *PPr.* 1.6.

*Jiṇa-vayaṇa* *jina-vayana.* Ins. Pl. -*ihiṁ* Sn. 307-169.

*Jitta-sattu* *Jita-śatru Hv.* 89.19.9.

*jittiu* =*yāvan-mātra PPr.* 2.38.

*jitthu* =*yatra Jdc.* 181.

| | |
|---|---|
| *jidha* | =*yathā Ki.* 5.12, *Ld.* 3.3.8. |
| *jiva* | =*yathā Gū.* 2.27.11, *DKK.* 2, *Ki* 5.12, *Ld.* 3.3.8' *Pu.* 17.23. *Sdd.* 2. 'like, as' *Pu.* 17.26. |
| *jiva* | =*yathā Jdc.* 2.2, *Jdu.* 4.3, *Sn.* 17-570. |
| *jiva* (*jiṁva*) | =*yathā Hc.* 4.330.3, 336. *Kp.* J. 9.8, *Sn*, 89-177. |
| *jiha* | =*yathā Hc.* 4.337, *Jc.* 1.4.15, *Kp.* J. 15.6, *Pd.* 18, *Sdd.* 3. |
| *jīva-* | √*jīv-* Fut. 1 Pl. -*esahū* (Intro. to *Sc.* p. 17 *Gram.* §24). *jiyania*-Pres. Part. of √*jīva- Jc.* 3.41.8. |
| *jīva* | (*ts.*) Nom. Sg. -*ā Ys.* 33, Gen. Sg. -*ha Sdd.* 115, -*hao PPr.* 2.86. -*hu Pd.* 42.<br>Voc. Sg Zero (*jiya*) *PPr.* 1.23, *Sdd.* 4, 21.<br>Gen. Pl. -*haṁ PPr.* 2.106, *Sdd.* 3. |
| *jīvājīva* | (*ts.*) Acc. Pl. zero *PPr.* 1.30, Gen. Pl. -*ha* ṁ *Ys.* 38. |
| *Jīvaṁjasa* | 'N. of Kaṁsa's wife'. Ins. Sg. -*ī Mp.* 87.1.15. |
| *jīha* | *jihvā Kp.* J. 73.3, *Sn.* 16-570.<br>Ins. Sg. -*i Jc.* 2.5.11. |
| *juala* | *yugala.* Ins. Pl. -*ehiṁ Mt.* 10. |
| *jujha* | *jujjha* (*yuddha*) *KKc.* 2.96. |
| *jutta* | = *alīka* Gen. Pl. -*ha Jdu.* 77.1. *cf.* H. *jhūṭ.* |
| *juṇṇaü* | **jūrṇam*= *jīrṇam Jc.* 3.38.3. |
| *jutti* | *yukti* Ins. Sg. -*e BhK.* 290.7. |
| *juttha* | *yūtha* 'collection' *DKs.* 73. |
| *jūya* | *yuga* Gen. Sg. -*hu Sdd.* 3. |
| *jẽ, jai* | <*yadi Mt.* 9. |
| *jettahe* | *yatra Hv.* 83.16.4. |
| *jettula* | =*yāvat, Kc.* 75, *Ld.* 3.3.12. *Sh.* 22.62. |
| *jetthu* | =*yatra. Jc.* 1.5.10, *Mt.* 20. |
| *jema* | *yathā Jc.* 1.3.1, *Ki* 5.12, *Sdd.* 60. |
| *jẽva* | *yathā Hv.* 86.7.8 *Kp.* J. 50.1 (cf. *Hc.* 4.401). |
| *jevaḍu* | *yāvat Ld.* 3.3.12, *Sh.* 22.62. |
| *jeha* | *yādṛśa Sh.* 22.60. *Ld.* 3.3.9. -*u PPr.* 1.26, -*ō Ld.* 3.3.9. |

√*joa* (*-ya*) √*dyut->dyotate*
Pres. 1 Sg. *-uṁ*. *Pd*. 139, 175. 3 Sg. *-i Pd*. 51, 180.
Imp. 2 Sg. *-i Pd*. 52, *PPr*. 2.34. 2 Pl. *-hu Sn*. 18-442.
Pres. Part. Fem. *-antī* Gen. Sg. *-he Hc*. 4.332.
PP. *-iu MP*. 2.4.8, Inf. *-iuṁ Pd*. 179. Abs. *-iya Pd*. 42.
Pot. Part. *-evvaü Nc*. 5.2.6. (cf. Guj. *jovũ*).

*joi* (*-ya*) *yogin* (*-ka*) Nom. Sg. zero *PPr*. 1.35, 2.171,
Ins. Sg. *-ẽ* ◌̇ *PPr*. 2.157, Gen. Sg. *-hi* ◌̇ *PPr*. 2.160.
*-hi* Pd. 192, Voc. Sg. zero *Dks*. 34, *Pd*. 53, *Ys*. 38.
Nom. Pl. *-ā Cd*. 2.27.11. Ins. Pl. *-ihiṁ, ihĩ*. *Pd*.9, *Ys*. 38,
39. Gen. Pl. *-hā PPr*. 1.35. *-hi* ◌̇
*PPr*. 2.166. Voc. Pl. *-hu Ys*. 50.
(*-g-* retained in NIA as in M. Guj. Nep. *jogi*).

*joiṇi-māi* *yogiṇī-māyām Dks*. 88. (Acc. Sg. zero).

*joṇi* *yonī* Loc. Sg. *-hiṁ Jc*. 2.30.10.
Loc. Pl. *-hiṁ MP*. 82.10.11, *Pd*. 8.

*joṇha* *jyotsnā* Ins. Sg. *-i MP*. 87.12.7.
Loc. Sg. *-hĩ Mt*. 14.

*jh*

*jhaḍatti* *jhaṭiti* 'immediately' *Hv*. 82.6.9.

*jhaḍavi* 'immediately.' *Jc*. 3.8.4.

*jhatti* *jhaṭiti Hv*. 84.2.15, *PPr*. 2.184 *Sn*. 236-270.

√*jhampa* 'to cover' PP. Masc. Nom. Sg. *-io Kp*. E. 8·4.
Abs. *-avi Jc*. 1.6.4. (cf. H. *jhā̃pnā*, M. *jhāpaḍ* 'cover')

*jhara* *kṣar-*(but, √*kṣi* acc. to *Hc*. 4.20) *Nc*. 2.2.5.

√*jhalakka* 'to burn' PP. *-iyaü Kp*. E. 3. (Traceable to √*jval-*

*jhalakka* *jhalakkā* (pWB **grosse Flamme*) *Hv*. 83.13.1.
(cf. M. Guj. *jhaḷak* 'splendour, lustre).'

*jhalajhala-i* Freq. of √*jval- Hv*. 84.5.6 cf. *jhala-halai Sn*. 217-186.
(M. *jhaḷāḷnẽ*, *jhaḷjhaḷṇẽ*, H. *jhaḷjhalānā*)

*jhāṇā* *dhyāna*. Ins. Sg. *-ẽ Dks*. 22, 24.

√*jhā-* (*ya*, *-va*)*-i* *dhyāyati*.
Imp. 2 Sg. *-hi Pd* 37, Pres. Part *-antau Pd*. 3.

√*jhijja-* √*kṣi+va* (Pass :)
Pres. Part. *-anta Hv*. 91.16.3.

*ihīṇa* *kṣīṇa* Masc. Nom. Sg. *-u Hv.* 81. 15. 7. *Jc.* 3.19.5.

*jhuṇilla* *dhvani-vat Hv.* 87.12.5 (*-illa* Poss. Suff.)

*jhendua* =*kanduka*. Masc. Nom. Sg. *-u Mp.* 1.16.10.

*ṭ*

*ṭikka* *ṭīkā* Fem. Ins. Sg. *-iṁ Sdd.* 193.

*ṭh*

√*ṭhā* √*sthā* Pres. 1 Sg. *-imi Kp.* S. 92.3.
3 Sg- *i DKK.* 13, *DKs.* 40, *Kp.* S. 73.6. *Sdd.* 197.
3 Pl. *-anti Sdd.* 54.
*ṭhāvaï Kp.* E. 11.
Opt. 3 Sg. *-ejja Kp.* J. 104.1*, Fut. 3 Sg. *-ēsaï Kp.* S 44.5, Pres. Part. *-antu Kp.* S. 40·9, PP. *-ia DKK.* 5 *DKs.* 20, *Kp.* S. 81.2 *Sdd.* 132. *-iaa DKs.* 91.

*ṭhāṇa* *sthāna DKs.* 54. Neut. Acc. Sg. *-a DKs.* 80.
Direct Pl. *-aiṁ Sdd.* 18.

*ṭhōba* *sthāman DKK.* 16.

*ṭhāhara-ï* =*tiṣṭhati Sdd.* 132. cf. H. *ṭhaharnā*.

*-ṭṭhiya* *sthita*. Direct Sg. *-u Pd.* 102.

*ḍ*

*ḍakkha* =*daṣṭa Kp.* S. 107.4 ct. *Hc.* 2.89.
(M. Guj. *daṁkh*, Sdh. *dãgu*, Panj. *daṁg*, *ḍaṁk*, H. *daṁk*).

*ḍajjha-ï* *dahyate Hc.* 4.365.3. *Nc.* 3.15.5.

*ḍamaṇo* *damanaḥ MK* 18.5.

√*ḍara* 1. 'to fear' Pres. 1 Sg. *-mi Jc.* 2·28·6.
(Sk. *darati* Pk. *ḍarai*, M. Guj. Sdh. Panj. H. Beng. √*ḍar-* 'to fear'.)
2. 'to fall', Pres. 2 Sg. *-hi Sdd.* 156.

√*ḍasa-* √*daṁś-*Pres. 3 Pl. *-anti Mt.* 10.

*ḍaha* *dahara* 'a child' *Jc.* P. 125.

√*ḍaha* √*dah-*
Abs. *-iu Sn.* 270-190. caus. PP. *-āba+iao DKs.* 2.

| | |
|---|---|
| *ḍāla* | =*śākhā* Fem. Gen. Sg. -*ha* *Sdd.* 61. Loc. Sg. -*haṁ* *Sdd.* 95. Acc. Pl. -*aiṁ* *Hc.* 445.4. (M. *ḍhāḷı*, *ḍāhli*, °*ḷā*, Guj. *ḍāḷ* Sdh. *ḍāru*, Panj. H. Beng. *ḍāl*). |
| *ḍuṁgara* | =*śaila* Masc. Loc. Pl. -*ihiṁ* *Hc.* 4.445.2. |
| *ḍoṁgara* | ' a mountain' Nom. Pl. zero *Hc.* 422.2. (M. *ḍongar* Guj. *ḍungarm* Sdh. *ḍomgaru*). |
| *ḍora* | *davaraka* 'a rope' Ins. Sg. -*eṁ* *Jc.* 3.8.11. (Pk. *davara*, *dora*, M. *dor*, *ḍor*, Nep. *ḍoro*. Guj. Beng. H. Panj. *dor*.) |
| *ḍollaï* | *dolayati* M P 4.18.2. (M. Guj. H. Sdh.√*ḍol*-, Sdh.√*ḍoṛ*-). |

*ḍh*

| | |
|---|---|
| *ḍhaṁkha* | ='dry,' *śuṣka* *Jc.* 1.13.3, *MP.* 29.13.5. |
| *ḍhaṁḍholanta*- | *bhramat* *Pd.* 152. cf. *Hc.* 4.161. (M. *ḍhānḍolṇẽ*, Sdh.√*ḍhunḍh*-) |
| *ḍhala* | =√*kṣar*- Pres. Part. -*anta* *Kc.* 24. *PP.* *iya*-*ũ* *Hv.* 90.4.6 (cf. M. *ḍhaḷṇẽ*, Guj. *ḍhalvũ*, H. *ḍhalṇā*). |
| *ḍhāvu* | =*śīghram* *Kc.* 35. |
| *ḍhilla* | *śithila* Masc. Nom. Sg. -*u* *Pd.* 43, *Sdd.* 129. (Pk. *siḍhila*, *ḍhilla* M. *ḍhilā*, H. *ḍhīlā*, Guj. *ḍhīlũ*, Sdh. *ḍhilo*, Panj. *ḍhillā*, Beng. Or. *ḍhil*). |
| *ḍhuraḍhullıa* | ='wandered.' Masc. Nom. Sg. -*o* *Pd.* 23. |
| √*ḍhekkara*- | 'to bellow' cf. *Hc.* 4.99. Pres. Part. Masc. Nom. Sg. -*aṁtu* *Hv.* 84.17.6. cf. M. *dhẽk* 'roar', also *dhẽkar*. Sdh. *dhikṇu*. |
| *ḍholla* | =*viṭa*. Masc. Nom. Sg. -*ā* *Hc.* 4.330.1.2. |

*ṇ*(*n*)

| | |
|---|---|
| *ṇa* | =*iva* *Pu.* 17.26. 2 *ṇa* *Sdd.* 199. (cf. Ved. *ıa* 'lıke') |
| *ṇaa* | *nata*. Ins. Sg. -*e* *Mt.* 31. |
| *ṇaï* | =1. *iva* *Ld.* 3.3.24., *Pu.* 17.26. 2. *nāpi* *Mt.* 34. |

*ṇaü* =1 *na Hv.* 81.2.1. 2 *iva Hc.* 4.444, *Jc.* 2.5.9. *Kc.* 81.

*ṇaṁ* =1. *iva Hc.* 4.444. *Hv.* 81.7.5. *KKc.* 1.3.11. Kc. 80. *Ld.* 3.3.24, *Jc.* 2.3.2. *MP.* 1.12.2.
2. *nanu Jc.* 1.18.9, *Sn.* 217-186.

*ṇakka* Deśi 'nose' Ins. Sg. -*iṁ Jc.* 3·22·3.
(M. Guj. H. Beng. *nāk.* Sdh. *nāku*, Panj. *nakk*).

*ṇaggala* *nagna-ṭa* Masc. direct Pl. zero *DKs.* 6.
(M. *nāgḍā* °*vā* Guj. *nāgũ* Sdh. *naṁgo*, Panj. H. *naṁgā*, Or. *naṁglā*).

*ṇa-carisu* =*na-cariṣṇu*
Masc. Nom. Sg. zero *Pd.* 58.

*ṇaccaï* *nṛtyati Sdd.* 162.

*ṇaṭṭa* *nṛtta Hv.* 81.1.11.

*nattha* *nātha.* Masc. Nom. Sg. -*u DKK.* 23.

*ṇatthi* *nāsti DKs.* 44.

√*ṇama-* √*nam-* Abs. -*ivi Jdc.* 1.1.

*ṇaṁakār-eppiṇu* *namaskṛtya Sdd.* 1.

*ṇayaṇāṇandiira*=*nayanānandakara*
Gen. Sg. -*āsu BhK.* 342.7.

*ṇara* *nara.* Masc. Nom. Pl. zero *Pd.* 5. Ins. Pl. -*ihĩ Sc.* 459.2.

*ṇaraya* *naraka* Loc. Sg. -*haṁ* (Scribal error for -*iṁ* ? ) *Pd.* 5.

*ṇara-rūa* *nara-rūpa.* Direct Sg. -*u KKc.* 1.10.8.

*ṇara-vaï* *narapati* Direct Sg. (and Voc.) zero *KKc.* 1.10.6.
Gen. Sg. -*ṇo Jc.* 1.19.1 (Pkt. ism.)

*Naravaï-viṭṭhi*= *Narapati-vṛṣṇi Hv.* 84.8.14.

*ṇaravara* *nara-*○ Dat. Gen. Sg. -(*ā*)*su KKc.* 1.10.5.

*ṇarinda* *narendra.* Gen. Sg. -*ho KKc.* 1.2.3.

*ṇaliṇi* *nalinī* Loc. Pl. -*ihiṁ Sdd.* 191.

√*ṇava-* √*nam* Pres. 3 Sg. -*i Pd.* 77. (with *pari- Pd.* 14).
1 Pl. -*huṁ KKc.* 4.1.9. Imp. 2 Sg. -*hu KKc.* 4.1.7.
2 Pl. -*haṁ Jc.* 4.8.13. Abs. -*evi PPr.* 1.7.

*ṇavakāra* *namaskāra Jdu.* 71.3.

| | |
|---|---|
| *ṇavama* | *navama Sdd.* 15. |
| *ṇavayāri* | =*namaskṛtya* (Abs. in -*i*) *Jc.* 1.27.10. |
| *ṇavara* | =1. *na paraṁ*=*kevalam Hc.* 4.401. *Jc.* 3.33.8.<br>2. 'there upon'. *Hv.* 82.15.4.<br>3. 'however, yet.' *Hv.* 85.5.7. |
| *ṇavari* | =1. *kevalaṁ Hc.* 4.377, 401.<br>2. 'afterwards.' *Pd.* 153. cf. *Hc.* 2.188. |
| *ṇavi* | *naiva PPr.* 1.31. |
| *navullaḍaa* | *nava*(-*ulla*-*ṭa*)<br>Masc. Acc. Pl. zero *Kc.* 73. |
| *ṇaha* | *nabhas* Neut. nom. Sg. -*u PPr.* 2.20.<br>Loc. Sg. -*hĩ Mt.* 19. -*ammi* (Pkt. ism.) *Jc.* 1.16.14. |
| *ṇahayala* | *nabha-tala* Abl. Sg. -*hu Sc.* 264.8. Intro. to *Sc.* Gram. §16. |
| *ṇaha-siri* | *nabha-śrī.* Fem. Gen. Sg. -*hi Jc.* 2.12.5. |
| *ṇāï* | =*iva Hc.* 4.444, *Hv.* 81.4.5. *Kc.* 81. *K̇p.* J. 6.4. *Ld.* 3.3.24 *Nc.*, 3.12.6, *Pu.* 17.26. |
| *ṇāïṁ*, *o*ĩ | =*iva Mp.* 1.12.4, *Pd.* 158. |
| *ṇāïkka* | *nāyaka* Ins. Sg. -*eṁ Sdd.* 51. |
| *ṇāïṇiya* | *nāgiṇikā Jc.* 2.10.6. |
| *ṇāü* | *nāman* (direct Sg. -*u*) *Mt.* 3, *PPr.* 1.19, 2.206. |
| -*ṇāü* | -*snāyu* 'muscle.'<br>Neut. Acc. Pl. zero *MP.* 100.5.3. |
| *ṇāṇi* | *jñānin.*<br>Masc. Ins. Sg. -*iṁ PPr.* 2.73.<br>Direct Pl. zero *PPr.* 2.19, Ins. Pl. -*hiṁ PPr.* 2.16.<br>Gen. Pl. -*haṁ PPr.* 1.122. -*hiṁ PPr*, 2.30. |
| *ṇāma* | *nāman* Ins. Sg. -*e DKs.* 109.<br>Gen. Sg. -*hu Mt.* 3. |
| *ṇāmāla* | *nāmavat* (-*āla* suff.) *Hv.* 81.8.4. |
| *ṇāri* | *nārī* Fem. direct Sg. zero *KKc.* 7.1.3.<br>Ins. Pl. -*hiṁ KKc.* 3.1.11. |
| *ṇāvaï* | =*iva. Hc.* 4.444, *Hv.* 81.14.5. *Kc.* 81, *Ld.* 3.3.24. *Mt.* 19, *Nc.* 1.7.6. *Pu.* 17.26. |

| | |
|---|---|
| *ṇāha* | *nātha*. Masc. Nom. Sg. *-v* *DKK*. 31, *DS*. 4.3.2. |
| *ṇāhala* | =*bhilla* Ins. Pl. *-hiṁ* *MP*. 82.10.6. |
| *ṇāhi* | *nāsti*, *na hi* *DKK*. 10, *DKs*. 67,90. *Ld*, 3.3.37. *Pd*. 94, *Sdd*. 13. °*hĭ* in *DKs*. 19. |
| *ṇāhiyă* | *nābhikā* 'the navel .' Fem. Gen. Sg. *-he* *KKc*. 1.16.6. |
| √*ṇia-* | Connected with Sk.√*nī* cf. *netra*, *nayana* =*dṛś-* in *Hc*. 4.181. Pres. 2. Sg. *-ehi* *Pd*. 186. Imp. 2. Sg. *-hu* *DKK*. 26. |
| *ṇikka* | *nīkā* (=*iḍā*) Fem. Gen. Sg. *-hĕ* *Kc*. 24. |
| *ṇikkhanta* | *niṣkrāntā*. Fem. direct Pl. *-u* *Hv*. 92.19.6. |
| *ṇigghiṇa* | *nirghṛṇa* *KKc*. 9.4.10. |
| *ṇiccala* | *niścala* *DKK*. 20, *DKs*. 68. Fem. Nom. Sg. zero *DKK*. 13. |
| *ṇiccu* | *nityam* *Jdc*. 6.4. *PPr*. 1.89. |
| *ṇicchaü* | *niścayaṁ* *Hv*. 84.7.13. |
| *ṇicchaï* | *niścayena* *Jdc*. 26.3, *Sn*. 18-286. °*iṁ*, °*ī*. *Kc*. 43. *KKc*. 1.10.10. |
| √*ṇi-joja-* | *ni-yōjaya* (<*yuj*). Imp. 2 Pl. *-hu* *Kc*. 20. |
| *ṇitaṁba* | *nitamba*. Gen. Pl. *-ha* *DKs*. 7. |
| *ṇitthara-* | *ni-star-* Pres. 3 Pl. *-hiṁ* *Kp*. P. 3.5, Abs. *-ivi* *Kp*. P. 7.5. |
| *ṇidda* | *nidrā*. Fem. Ins. Sg. *-e* *Hc*. 4.330, *Mt*. 16. (M. H. *nīdo*, Singh. *nidi*, *nidu*). |
| *ṇiddhā* | *nidrā* *Ld*. 3.3.43. |
| *ṇinda* | *nidrā* *Jc*. 3.20.9. cf. *H*. *nīṁd*. |
| √*ṇippīla-* | *niṣ*-√*pīḍ* Abs. *-ivi* *Kp*. *S*. 53.4. |
| *ṇibesī* | *ni-veśya*. (Abs. in *-ī*) *DKs*. 5. |
| *ṇibbāṇa* | *nirvāṇa*. Neut. nom. sg. *-o* *DKK*. 22. |
| *ṇibhantu* | *nir-bhrāntam* *PPr*. 1.120, 2.88. |

√ṇiya- 'to see' cf. *Hc*. 4.181. See √*ṇia*- above.
Pres. 3 Sg. -*i* *Hv*. 91.195.
Abs. -*ēvi* *Hv*. 85.5.11, 86.5.10.

*ṇiyaccha*- 'to see' cf. *Hv*. 4.181.
Imp. 2 Sg. -*hi* *Hv*. 87.9.10. Habit showing -*ira* *Hv*.86.5.9.

√*ṇiyatta*- *nir*-√*vart*. Inf. -*ēuṁ* *Kp*. J. 41.1*

*ṇiyama* *niyama*. Ins. Sg. -*ē̆* *PPr*. 2.62.

*ṇiyala* *nigaḍa* Neut. direct Pl. -*iṁ* *Sdd*. 211.

*ṇiya-satti* *nija-śakti*. Ins. Sg. zero *Sdd*. 121.

*ṇiyaṁsaṇa* *nivasana* *Nc*. 3.11.11.

*ṇirasa* *nirasa*. Loc. Sg. -*mi* *Jc*. 1.15.16.

*ṇirāriu* =1. *nitarām*. 'verily, indeed.' *Hv*. 83.8.6, *Nc*. 7.2.6, *Pd*. 120.
=2. *atiśayena* *MP*. 13.7.13.
=3. *anivāritaṁ* *MP*. 2.18.8.

*ṇirāsa* *nirāśa* = *nirasta*.
Masc. direct Pl. zero *DKK*. 23.

*ṇirikka* 'thief.' Connected with *nir-īkṣ*- ? *MP*. 29.17.3, *Nc*. 7.7.3.

*ṇiru* =*nitarāṁ* *Hv*. 81.4.2, *MP*. 1.1.19, 13.11.11, *Nc*. 1.1.8, *Sn*. 25-212 (*chāyā-niścitam*).

*ṇiruttaü* *niruktaṁ*=*niścitam*, *nitarām*.
*KKc*. 1.2.4, 7.1.4, *Nc*. 2.13.11, *Pd*. 121. cf. *Dn*. 4.30. (cf. M. *nirutē*)

√*ṇi-rumbha*- =*ni*-√*rudh*-
Abs. -*ivi* *KP*. S. 97.3.5.

*ṇiva* *nṛpa*. Masc. Nom. Pl. zero *KKc*. 4.1.4.

*ṇivaï* *nṛpati*. Loc. Sg. -*mmi* *Sc*. 479.4.

√*ṇivaḍa*- *ni*-√*pat*.
Imp. 3 Sg. -*u* *Jc*. 2.1.5.

√*ṇi-vasa* *ni*-√*vas*- Pres. 2 Sg. -*hi* *MP*. .1.3.10.

*ṇivitti* *nivṛtti*. Fem. Nom. Sg. zero *Sdd*. 10.
Gen. Pl. -*hi* *PPr*. 2.52.

| | |
|---|---|
| *ṇisa* | *niśā*. Fem. Loc. Sg. *-hi* *DKs*. 89. *-i* *Jdc*. 16.3. (Prob. Skt. ism.). |
| √*ṇisamma-* | *ni-*√*śāmaya*.<br>Imp. 2 Sg. *-hi* *Mt*. 24. |
| *ṇisāḍa* | =*niśācara* *MP*. 16.26.8. |
| *ṇisāsuṇha-ï* | =*niḥśvāsosṇayā* 'sighing out hotly.'<br>(Ins. Sg. in *-ï*) *MP*. 100.6.7. |
| *ṇisi* | *niśā* Fem. Loc. Sg. *-hi* *Jdc*. 18.2. *-hĩ* *Sc*. 452.3. |
| √*ṇi-suṇa* | . *ni-*√*śṛ-* (*ṇu*)<br>Imp. 2. Sg. *-i* *PPr*. 1 11, 2.2, *-huṁ* *Jc*. 3.11.14. (Pl.?) 3 Sg. *-u* *Sc*. 494.9, 2 Pl. *-hũ* *BhK*. 1.2. Prob. *Jc*. 3.11.14 above. Abs. *-eviṇu* *Jdc*. 15.4.<br>*-iu* *Mt*. 9, 10. |
| *nihasaṇa* | *nigharṣaṇa*=*nikaṣaṇa* *Hv*. 91.15.3. |
| √*ṇihāla-* | *ni-bhāl-* Pres. 1 Sg. *-mi* *Nc*. 4.12.7. cf. M. *nihāḷṇē* 'to look attentively.' |
| *-ṇihi* | *-nidhi* Masc. Nom. Sg. zero *MP*. 85.7.14. |
| *ṇihitta* | *nihita* (properly *nikṣipta*) *Hv*. 82.14.11, *Kp*. E. 3. cf. *Hc*. 2.99. |
| *ṇīra* | *nīra* Neut. Nom. Sg. zero *DKK*. 4. |
| *ṇīsa* | *anīśa* *Pd*. 27. |
| √*ṇīhara-* | *niḥ*√*sar-* Pres. Part. *-antu* *Kp*. J. 83.2. PP. *-iya* (Fem.) *Kp*. E. 32, Caus. Abs. *ṇīhārivi* *Kp*. *S*. 69.8. |
| *nṛ* | (*ts*) 'a man' *Hv*. 83.5.8 . 88.14.2<br>°*sīha*=*nṛ-siṁha* *Hv*. 86.6.12. |
| *nṛva* | *nṛpa*. *Hv*. 81.1.9.<br>°*-urasi* (Skt. ism.) *Kc*. 83. -°*jāla* *Hv*. 92.3.3. |
| √*ṇe* | √*nī* Imp. Pl. *-hu* *Sn*. 7-570. Abs. *-vi* *KKc*. 2.5.4 |
| *ṇea* | *naiva* (=*na*) *Kp*. *S*. 82.4. |
| *-ṇetta* | *-netrā*. Fem. Ins. Sg. *-ẽ* *BhK*. 293.3. |
| *ṇettha* | *nepathya* (=*ābharaṇa* in *Ṭippaṇa*). *Nc*. 9.18.12. |
| *ṇēya* | *naiva*=*na* *Hv*. 82.4.6. |
| *Ṇēriya* | *Nairṛta* *Hv*. 87.15.6. |

*ṇēsara* (*di-*)*neśvara* 'the Sun' *Hv.* 83.21.9, *Mp.* 1.1.1.

*ṇeha* *sneha.* Ins. Sg. *-e DKK.* 29.

*ṇehā* *na+iha* (*-ā* metri causa ?) *Pd.* 162.

*ṇēhilla* *snehala* (prop. *-illa* suff.) *Hv.* 81.10.13.

*ta* *tad-* Demonstrative and Correlative Pron. Masc. and Neut. Sing. Masc. Nom. *so. BhK.* 2.7. *KKc.* 1.5.10, *Ld.* 3.4.31, *Mk.* 78.6, *Mt.* 20. *Pd.* 16, 23. *Sc.* 491.6, *Sdd.* 27,28. *Sn.* 31.231. *sa DKK.* 16,19. *su BhK.* 291.5 *Ds.* 43.2, *Jdc.* 6.2. *Ld.* 3.4.31. *Pd.* 68, *Sc.* 471.2, *Sn.* 31.231. *to Nc.* 1.17.16. Acc. *so. BhK.* 1.11, *Pd.* 46,160. *Sc.* 513.5. *su Sc.* 514.3. *taṁ BhK.* 78.3. *DKs.* 43. *KKc.* 1.14.11.*Sc.* 464.2. *tā̃ Sc.* 603.8. Neut. direct *taṁ BhK.* 6.1., *Hc.* 4.350. *Kc.* 28, *KKc.* 1.8.9. *Pd.* 3,10. *Sc.* 502.1., *Sdd.* 4. *tā̃ Sc.* 623.5 *taü Pd.* 11. *te DKs.* 87. *sa DKs.* 67. *su se. DKs.* 90,106. 16.19. *PPr.* 1.30, 2.7.9. *Sc.* 648.8. *traṁ Kc.* 27. *truṁ Ld.* 3,4.32. *Sh.* 22.40. Ins. *teṇa BhK.* 4.1, *DKK.* 17, *DKs.* 100. *Hc.* 4.365. *KKc.* 1.6.1., *Pd.* 2. 10, *Sc.* 515.3, *tiṇa Jdc.* 2.2, *Sc.* 567.7, *tiṇā Jc.* 1.18.9. *teṁ*, *tẽ DKK* 30, 32. *KKc.* 1.6.9, 2.1.3. *tiṁ Jc.* 3.25.5, *te PPr.* 2.26. Dat. Gen. *tasu BhK.* 29.5, *DKK.* 13, *DKs.* 18.40. *Hc.* 4.338, *Jdc.* 2.4. *Sc.* 498.8, *Sdd.* 32,184, *Sn*, 217-186, 19-468. *tāsu BhK.* 5.2., *Hc.* 4.358, *Jdc.* 9.4., *Ld.* 3.4.31. *Pd.* 45,50, *Sdd.* 5, *tāsaï BhK*102.3, *Hc.* 4.419, *Sc.* 450.1., *taho BhK.* 4.7. *Hc.* 4.356, *Jc.* 1.5.20, *KKc.* 1.11.6. *tahu MP.* 1.11.10, *Mt.* 3, *Pd.* 71. *Sdd.* 187. *tahi Pd.* 174, *tāhara DKs.* 92, *tasa Pd.* 89, *tahī̃* (Loc. for Gen.) *DKK.* 24. *tamhā* (Pkt.) *KKc.* 1.2.11, *Sdd.* 101. Abl. *tā Mt.* 34. *to=tataḥ KKc.* 1.2.8. Loc. *tahiṁ*, °*hī̃ BhK.* 4.8, *DKK.* 12,14. *DKs.* 24. *Hc.* 4.357, *KKc.* 1.9.11 *Mt.* 34, *Pd.* 38,48. *Sc.* 501.2, 725.4. *Sn.* 107-178. *tammi* (Pkt.)*BhK.* 59.1. *KKc.* 1.4.4, *Sc.* 636.3. Loc. Ins. *tiṇi Jdu.* 8.1.2. *tasu DKK.* 22. *tehaï Pd.* 103. Masc. Pl. Nom. *te* (*ts.*) *BhK.* 147.6, *Hc.* 4.353. *Jdc.* 7.4, *KKc.* 1.10.6, *Pd.* 4. *Sc.* 702.5, 763.1. *ti Hc.* 4.344. *Jdc.* 4.3. *Sc.* 562.8. Acc. *te BhK.* 108, 6, *Hc.* 4.336, *PPr.* 1.2, 62 *ti Sc.* 775.9., *tiṁ BhK.* 295.2. *tẽ*(?) *BhK.* 108.6. Neut. direct *tāïṁ* °*ī̃ BhK.* 20.2, *KKc.* 1.9.4. *Ld.* 3.4.32, *PPr.* 2.16. *Sdd.* 59. *te PPr.* 1.61. *teṁ Hc.* 4.339. Ins. *tehiṁ*, °*hī̃ BhK.* 36.1. *Hc.* 4.370, *KKc.* 1.11.5. *Jc.* 1.14.11, *Sc.* 581.1. *tehi DKs.* 58. Dat. Gen. *tahaṁ*, °*hā̃ BhK.* 256.5, *Hc.* 422.3. *Pd.* 67,

*Sc.* 460,8, *Sdd.* 31, *Sn.* 30-231. *tāhaṁ*, °*hā* *BhK.* 2.9, *Gd.* 1.5., *Hc.* 4.350, *KKc.* 1.12.8, *Pd.* 47, 102, *Sdd.* 30. *tāha* *Nc.* 1.14.9. *tāṇaṁ* (Pkt.) *BhK.* 329.7, *Jc.* 3.37.2. *tāṇa* *Hc.* 333. Loc. *tihi* *Sc.* 517.2 *tahiṁ* *Hc.* 422.18. Fem. Sg. Nom. *sā* *BhK.* 12.1. *Hc.* 4.439. *KKc.* 5.2.9. *Sc.* 488.4. *sa* *Mt.* 24,25. *Sc.* 640.5. Acc. *sā* *BhK.* 77.8, *KKc.* 5.3.7, 5.7.5. *PPr.* 2.46*, *Sc.* 498.2 *sa* *Sc.* 498.1. *sc* *DKs.* 49. *taṁ* *Sn.* 30.231. Ins. *tāe* *BhK.* 106.7, *Hc.* 4.370, *KKc.* 1.8.5, 2.6.10. *tāīṁ*, °*ī* *BhK.* 11.9, *KKc.* 6.10.2. *tāeṁ*, °*ī* *BhK.* 2.5, *KKc.* 2.6.10, 6.11.1. *tīe* *Jc.* 2.1.4, *KKc.* 1.12.5. *tīeṁ* *KKc.* 1.8.2 *tahī* *Sc.* 6.22.2, *tahi* *Sc.* 637.2. *teṇa* *Jc.* 3.10.13. Ḍat. Gen. *tahe* *BhK.* 8.3. *Hc.* 4.380. *KKc.* 1.17.10, 6.8.9. *Ld.* 3.4.30, *Sh.* 22.39. *tāhe* *BhK.* 13.1, *KKc.* 2.6.8, 6.11.7, *taho* *BhK.* 160.8, *tahi* *Jc.* 2.6.8, *Sc.* 637.2. *taü* *Jc.* 2.284. *tasu* *Sc.* 497.8. *tāsu* 22.39. *tāha* *Mt.* 34, *tāhu* *KKc.* 7.8.1. *tīa* *Mt.* 16. *tīe* *Sc.* 500.1. Loc. *tahī* *BhK.* 147.3, *KKc.* 6.1.3, *PPr.* 2.46.*1. *Sc.* 538.6. *tāsu* *Jc.* 3.1.20. *tāhi*(?) *BhK.* 73.3. Fem. Plur. Direct *tāü* *BhK.* 10.3, 3.11.3. *Sc.* 602.3, 603.8. Ins. *tāhiṁ* *KKc.* 6.15.8. Gen. *tāsī* *Sc.* 599.6. *tahā* *Sc.* 708. *tāhā* *Sc.* 516.5. Loc. *tāsu* (Pkt.) 1.8.5. (Forms in the grammatical sections in the introductions of different works are not indicated here.)

*taï* =*tatra* *Ld.* 3.3.14.

*taïya* *tṛtīya* Neut. Nom. Sg. -*u* *Nc.* 1.5.8.
Masc. Ins. Sg. -*eṇa* *MP.* 2.11.

*taïya-haṁ* =*tadā* *Jc.* 3.7.4. °*hī̃* *Kp.* E. 24.

*taī-loya-haṁ* *trai-lokyasya* *Pd.* 68, *Ys.* 28.

*taïsu* *tādṛśa* *Ld.* 3.3.10. °*sau* *Hc.* 4.403, *Kc.* 51.
(M. *tasā*, H. *taisā*).

*taü-lagi* =*tāvat-lagnam* *KKc.* 8.2.10.

*takkhaṇa* *tat-kṣaṇa.* Loc. Sg. -*e* *DKK.* 19. -*ammi* Pkt. *KKc.* 1.10.2.

*taccu* *tatvam* *Pd.* 25, *PPr.* 1.79.

*taṇaa* 'belonging, to, pertaining to.' *MP* 1.3.2. *Nc.* 3.9.16, *Hc.* 4.361 ex.

*taṇu* *tanu* Fem. Acc. Sg. zero *BhK.* 25.4, *PPr.* 2.182.

*taṇu-vaṇa* *tṛṇa-vana* *KKc.* 2.4.7.

*taṇha* *tṛṣṇā* *Hv.* 82.7.8, *KKc.* 2.16.5, *Sc.* 570.8.

*tatta* 1) *tatva DKs.* 9. *Sc.* 565.7.
2) *tatra DKs.* 74, 76.
3) *tapta* Gen. Pl. *-āhã PPr.* 1.10.

*tatti* =*tatparatā Hv.* 81.11.6, *Nc.* 8.14.4. (cf. *Dn.* 5.20) Loc. Ins. Sg. *-iṁ Pd.* 121. Here '*tatta*' seems to be the original vocable.

*tatru* *tatra Pu.* 17.56. (Literally it is the Loc. Sg. of *tad-* in *Pu.*)

*tattha* *tatra DKs.* 38, *Sc.* 448.1.

*tappaṇa* *Tapana Hv.* 91.16.8.

*tama* *tamas* Ins. Sg. *-iṇa Sdd.* 2.

*tambira* *tāmra MP.* 1.16.9.

√*tara-* √*tar.* Fut. 2 Sg. *-ihahi Sdd.* 67.
Inf. *-evvaïṁ KKc.* 1.2.5, Abs. *-avi Sn.* 334-127.

*taralacchi* *taralākṣī* Gen. Pl. *-hũ Mt.* 17.

*taru* **tvaram* 'quickly' *MP.* 25.19.13.

*taru* (*ts.*) Acc. Sg. zero *Sdd.* 52. Abl. Sg. *-he Hc.* 4.341. *Kc.* 19, Loc. Sg. *-(a)mmi KKc.* 8.7.7. Gen. Abl. Pl. *-huṁ. Hc.* 4.340, 341, *Kc.* 19.

*taruara* °*vara.* Loc. Pl. *-haṁ Hc.* 4.422.9.

*tarugaṇa* (*ts.*) Nom. Pl. zero *Kc.* 21.

*taru-mūla* (*ts.*) Loc. Sg. *-i MP.* 100.6.3.

*taruṇa* (*ts.*) Voc. Pl. *-ho Hc.* 4.346.

*taruṇi* *taruṇī* Voc. Sg. zero *DKK.* 29, Nom. Pl. *-(ī)u Sc.* 445.4, 477.4. Voc. Pl. *-ho Hc.* 4.346.

*taruṇi-du* *taruṇī Mk.* 17.7.

√*tala-* **talay-* PP. *-iu*, 'friend' *Kp.* J. 72.3.
(M. *taḷṇẽ*, Guj. *taḷvũ*, H. *talnā*, Panj. *talṇā*).

*talāu* *taḍāgaḥ Sdd.* 170.

*taḷī* =*taḍit Mt.* 21.

*tava* *tapas.* Ins. Sg. *-eṇa PPr.* 1.42.

*tavve* *tad-vā Mt.* 22. (cf. Coll. M. *tavā* H. *taũ tõ*)

| | |
|---|---|
| *tasa* | *trasa* Nom. Sg. -*u* *DKK* 13. |
| *taha* | *tatra* *Sdd*. 61. |
| *taha* | *tathā* *KKc*. 1.2.1. |
| *tahiṁ*, °*hĩ* | *tatra* (*Lit*. *tasmin*) *Jc*. 1.3.16. *PPr*. 2.162. *Sdd*. 54,71. |
| *tā* | *tāvat* *DKs*. 69, *Jc*.1.8.9, *Kp*. S. 27.7, *PPr*. 1.108. *Sn*. 270-190. |
| *tāü* | *tāvat* *DKs*. 19, *KKc*. 1.6.1. |
| *tāüṁ* | *tāvat* *Ld*. 3.3.11. cf. *Hc*. 4.406. |
| *tāḍ-ijjaï* | *tāḍyate* *MP*. 2.5.10. |
| *tāba* | *tāvat* *DKs*. 85, 90. |
| *tāma* | *tāvat* *Hc*. 4.406. *Hv*. 84.2.5, 85.3.6, 88.23.13 *KKc*. 1.14.3.*Ld*. 3.3.11, *Nc*. 1.14.9, *PPr*. 2.81, *Pu*. 17.23. |
| *tāma-ï* | *tāvat* *PPr*. 2.41. °*iṁ̐* *PPr*. 2.174. °*hiṁ* *Ld*. 3.3.11, cf. *Hc*. 4.406. |
| *tĕya* | *tāta* Gen. Sg. -*ho* *KKc*. 2.8.12. |
| *tāyatiṁsa* | *trayastriṁśa* *Hv*. 89.13.7. |
| *tārisa* | *tādṛśa* *Sc*. 571.9. |
| √*tāla*- | √*tāḍay* Pres. 3 Pl. -(*a*)*nti* *Sn*. 16-570. |
| *tālā* | Neut. Nom. Sg. *tālakaṁ* 'lock' *DKK*. 22. |
| *tālū* | *tālu* Fem. Acc. Sg. zero *Pd*. 97. |
| *tāva* | *tāvat* *Hv*. 88.13.6. *Kp*. E. 21. °*iṁ* *Sdd*. 52. |
| *tāv̆a* | *tāvat* *Hv*. 83.19.3, *Mt*. 18. |
| *ti*- | *tri* Masc. Nom. *tia* *Mk*. 17.78. Neut. direct *tiṇṇi* *Mk*. 17.78. *Nc*, 1.8.2. Ins. *tihiṁ* *Nc*. 3.3.11, *KKc*, 3.8.2. Gen. *tīha* *Jc*. 1.6.1. Fem. Loc. Pl. *tihi* *Sdd*. 12, *tihiṁ* *Sdd*. 68. |
| *tiga* | *trika* *Kp*.S. 44.6. |
| *tijjaa* | *tṛtīya* Masc. Nom. Sg. -*u* *Sdd*. 12. cf. M. *tijā*, *tīj*. |
| *tiṭṭhā̃* | **tṛṣ-ṭā* 'thirst'. *Hv*. 81.1.11, *PPr*. 2.132. |
| *tiṭṭhāluya* | **tṛṣṭāluka* 'thirsty' *Hv*. 88.12.6. |
| *tiṭṭhi* | **tṛṣṭi* 'thirst' *Nc*. 9.14.1. |
| *tiṇa* | *tṛṇa* *Sc*. 497.5. Acc. Sg. -*u* *KKc*. 8.19.8. |

| | |
|---|---|
| *titti* | *tṛpti KKc.* 10.10.5. |
| *tittiḍaü* | *tāvan-mātraṁ PPr.* 1.105. |
| *tittula* | *tāvat Hc.* 4.435, *Kc.* 75. |
| *tittha* | *tīrtha.* Loc. Pl. *-hiṁ Ys.* 42. |
| *titthu* | *=tatra Jc.* 3.41.2, *PPr.* 1.111. 2.137. |
| *tima* | 1) *tathā Cd.* 2.27.11 *Ki.* 5.12, *Tr. Ld.* 3.3.8. *PPr.* 1,85,102. 2) *tāvat Pu.* 17.23. |
| *timira* | (*ts.*) *Hc.* 4.382. Gen. Sg. *-hu Sdd.* 183. |
| *tiya* | *strī-(kā) Hv.* 85.21.3 cf. H. *tiyā, tiy.* |
| *tiricchī* | *tiryakṣī Hc.* 4.420.3, *Mt.* 12. |
| *tilariṇa* | *=tailatva KKc.* 6.10.15, *Nc..* 1.18.6. |
| *tilla* | *taila.* Ins. Sg. *-eṁ Sdd.* 184. |
| *tiṽa* | *=tathā Hc.* 4.376.2, 395.1 *Kc.* 49, *Kp. J.* 24.2, *Mt.* 1. *Sn.* 89-177, 78-332. |
| *Tiveya* | *Trivedā* Gen. Sg. *-hĕ BhK* 290.9. |
| *tisa* | *tṛṣā* Gen. Sg. *-he Hc.* 4.395. |
| *tisi* | **tṛṣi* 'thirst' Ins. Sg. *-e DKs.* 58. |
| *tisia* | *tṛṣita DKs.* 58.93. |
| *tisittaṇa* | *tṛṣitatva DKs.* 93. |
| *tiha* | *=tathā Hv.* 87.5.8. *Kc.* 49, *Ld.* 3.3.8, *Sdd.* 3, *Tr., Ld.* 3.3.3. cf. *Hc.* 4.401. |
| *tihi-pavva-hi* | *=tithi-parvasu Jdc.* 33.4. |
| *tihuyaṇa* | *tribhuvana.* Gen. Sg. *-hu Sc.* 477.2, Loc. Sg. *-i PPr.* 1.4. |
| *tīsa* | *triṁśat Sn* 335-127. (Pa. *tiṁsa*, Pk. *tīsa.* M. Guj. H. Maith. *tīs*, Panī. *tīh*, Singh. *tisa, tiha* OIA *-r-* is conserved in Or. *trisa*, Sdh. *ṭrīha*, Guj. *trīs*). |
| *tu<tŏ* | *=tataḥ* (*chāyā* on *DS.* 4.5.2). |
| *tuṭṭiaa* | *=truṭita DKs.* 31. |
| *tuṭṭhi* | *tuṣṭi* Loc. Sg. *-hi MP.* 87.9.15. |
| *tuḍia* | *truṭita.* Masc. Nom. Pl. zero *DKK.*30 *-ā DKK.*5. |

*tumibiṇi* °*nī* Fem. Gen. Sg. -*he* *Hc*. 4.427.

*tumbhāra* =*tvadīya* *Pu* 17.30.

*tuṁha-* **tuṣma*-=*yuṣma*- 2nd Pl. base. Pl. Direct. *tumhaïṁ*, °*ī* *BhK*. 111.5, *Hc*. 4.369, *KKc*. 8.13.10, *Nc*. 2.6.11. *tumhaï* *Ld*, 3.4.47, *tumhe* *Ld*. 3.4.47. *tumhi* *BhK*. 115.9. *Jdu*. 1.2. *KKc*. 1.13.4, Sc. 645.1. Nom. *tubbhẽ* Sc. 565.1, *tubbhi* *Sc*. 486.3, Acc. *tumha* *BhK*. 99.4. Ins. *tumhehī* *Hc*. 4.371, *KKc*. 3.11.10. *Ld*. 3.4.39, *Sc*. 755.1. *tumhi* *BhK*. 113.4, *tumhaī* *BhK*. 101.7. Dat. Gen. *tumha* *BhK*. 44.6, *Sc*. 599.5, *Sn*. 25-22 *tumhahã*, °*haṁ* *BhK*. 26.11, *KKc*. 2.4.6. *Ld*. 3.4.43, *Sc*. 567.6. *tumhaha* *Sn*. 26-23. *tumhāṇa* (Pkt.) *BhK*. 69.10. Loc. *tumhāsu* *Hc*. 4.3.74. *Ld*. 3.4.42.

*tumhāra* **tuṣma-kārya* 'belonging or pertaining to you' *Sh*. 22.65, -*uṁ* *Kc*. 74.

*turanga* (*ts*.) Gen. Pl. -*ha* *DKs*. 8.

√*tura-* √*tvar* Pres. Part. -*anta* *KKc*. 2.15.3, *Sc*. 510.1. PP. -*ia* *KKc*. 2.10.7, *Sc*. 487.9.

*tusa* *tuṣa*. Acc. Pl. zero *Pd*. 13.

*tuhāra* **tuha-kārya*. cf. *Hc*. 4.434, *KKc*. 2.18.5. Masc. Nom. Sg. -*u* *Pd*. 56.

*tuhũ* 2 P. Pron. Sing. No. Nom. *tuhũ* *BhK*. 24.1. *Hc*. 330.2,3,368. *Jc*. 1.1.11, *KKc*. 1.10.3, 2.8.10, *Ld*. 3.4.47. *Mk*. 17.6, *MP*. 1.6.5, *Nc*. 1.4.1, *Pd*. 11.13.17, *PPr*. 1.29, *Sh*. 22.46. *tuhu* *DKs*. 77. *tuṁ* (?), *Bhk*. 262.3, *tumaṁ* *Nc*. 2.3.19. *paiṁ* *KKc*. 3.10.5. Acc. *païṁ* °*ī* *BhK*. 24.7, *KKc*. 3.20.4, *MP*. 1.5.13, *Mt*. 22,24,29, *Pd*. 106, *Sc*. 534.5, 707.6, *Sdd*. 112. Ins. *païṁ*, °*ī* *BhK*. 21.7, *Hc*. 4.370, *Jc*. 1.15.14, 2.29.5. *KKc*. 1.10.9, *MP*. 1.6.11, *Mt*. 11,25,29,33, *Pd*. 111, *Sdd*. 155, *Sc*. 489.4, 518.2. *tumaī* *BhK*. 144.9. *taīṁ* *BhK*. 252.11, *Ld*. 3.4.40, *eiṁ* *Ld*. 3.4.40. Dat. Gen. *tau* *BhK*. 19.8, *KKc*. 2.5.9. *Ld*. 3.4.41. *tao* *Ld*. 3.4.41. *tujjha* *Jc*. 1.7.12. *KKc*. 2.4.6. 3.11.5, *Ld*. 3.4.41, *PPr*. 2.182, *Sc*. 639.1, *tujjha-ha* *Mt*. 35. *tujjhu* *BhK*. 14.5. *MP*. 1.6.12. *Mt*.15, 24. *Pd*. 119, 208. *tujjhuṁ* *Sn*. 16-441, *tuddhu* *BhK*. 125.8. *tuha* *Hc*. 4.361, *Jc*. 1.7.5. *KKc*. 1.6.8, 1.10.6, 3.13.8, *Ld*. 3.4.41, *Sc*. 455.4. *tuhaṁ*. °*hã* *Mt*. 5, *PPr*. 2.171. *tuhiṁ* *Pd*. 219, *tuhu* *Sn*. 28-213. *tua* *DS*. 4.5.2. *tudhra* *Hc*. 4.372, *Ld*. 3.4.41. *taha* *Jc*. 1.7.13, *tūsa* *Hc*. 1.7.11, *to* *DKK*. 29. *païṁ* *KKc*. 3.11.9 (Dat.?) *tera* *Rt*. 3.2.5, *terau* *Jc*. 3.40.4, *KKc*. 3.21.5. Loc. *paī* *BhK*. 44.12, *Hc*. 4.370.

*tūra* — *tūrya* Ins. Pl. *-ehĩ Mt.* 23, Gen. *-haṁ Jc.* 2.12.8.

*tṛya* — *strī Hv.* 89.13.4, *MP.* 9.22.9.

*tetta-hi* — *=tatra Hc.* 4.436, *Kc.* 75. °*hiṁ Jc.* 3.12.6.
°*hẽ Hv.* 83.16.4.*Nc.* 5.2.2. °*hō=tatratas Hv.* 81.11.13.

*tettiya* — *trayastriṁśat MP.* 2.7.16.

*tettula* — *tāvat Hc.* 4.407, *Sh.* 22.62, °*lu Ld.* 3.3.12.

*tetthu* — *tatra Hv.* 81.15.12.cf. *Hc.* 4.404, *Jc.* 1.5.10.

*tema* — *tathā Ki.* 5.12, *Tr. Ld.* 3.3.8, *PPr.* 1.102.

*teraha* — *trayodaśa* Gen. Pl. *-haṁ MP.* 2.10.19. °*ma.* Ins. Sg. *-i MP.* 2.12.
(Pa. *teḷasa, telasa,* Pk. *terasa, teraha,* M. *tera,* Guj. *tera,* H. *terah,* Nep. *tera.*)

*tevada* — **tayavadra=tāvat Sh.* 22.62, *-u Hc.* 395, 407, *Tr. Ld.* 3.3.12.

*tevaḍḍa* — **tayavadra Hv.* 83.17.6, cf. *Hc.* 4.371. (M. *tevaḍhā*).

*tĕva* — *=tathā Hv.* 81.8.10, *KP.*J. 50.3, cf. *Hc.* 4.397, 401.
°*i=tathā Hc.* 4.401, *Kc.* 49.

*tĕha* — *=tādṛś* (>*taïsa*) *Ld.* 3.3.9. °*u Hc.* 4.402, *Kc.* 51, *PPr.* 2. 149 Loc. Sg. *-i Jc.* 1.11.9.

*tehiṁ* — *=arthe* (governs the Gen.) *Kc.* 71.

*to* — *=tataḥ, tadā Hc.* 4.417, *Kc.* 60, *KKc.* 1.2.8, *Ld.* 3.3.50, *Pd.* 51, *Sn.* 89-177. *tōi Kp.*E. 31b, *to vi Pd.* 36

√*toḍa-* — √*troṭay-*
Inf. *-huṁ Sdd.* 64. Abs. *-eppiṇu MP.* 1.3.2. *-eviṇu KKc.* 10.27.2.

*toṇḍa* — *tuṇḍa Hv.* 86.8.8 (OIA* *tauṇḍa-*, *M. toṇḍ,* G. Beng. *tõḍ*)

*tolā* — *tulā- KKc.* 2.2.2.

*tohāraṁ* — *=tvadīyam Rt.* 3.2.5.

*th*

√*thakka* — IE **staq-ne*, but usually equated with OIA√*sthā.*
cf. *Pu.* 17 17.77.
Pres. 3 Sg. *-i DKs.* 17, 61, *Hv.* 87.6.8, *MK.* 17.67. cf. *Hc.* 4.16, 307.3, 3 Pl. *-iṁ Sdd.* 53.
Imp. 2 Sg. *-u DKs.* 105, Fut. 1 Pl. *-isahū Sc.* 84.6 (Intro.

| | |
|---|---|
| | to *Sc.* p. 17, Gram. §24). PP. *thakka.* Neut. Nom. Sg.-*ā* *Pd.* 104. (M.H.Sdh.√*thak-*, Panj.√*thakk-*, Guj. Beng.√*thāk*). |
| *-thaḍi* | =*sthali* Fem. Loc. Sg. -*hiṁ* *Pd.* 151. cf. M. *thaḍ* |
| *thaḍḍhattaṇa* | (*stabdhatva*) |
| *thatti* | **sthapti* 'room, space'. Acc. Sg. zero *Hv.* 83.19.1 cf. *thitti* in *Hv.* 83.18.10. cf. *Dn.* 5.26 *thattiam viśrāmaḥ.* |
| √*thappa-* | *sthāpay-* Abs. -*ĕvi* *Hv.* 85.5.3. (M. Guj. H. Sdh. *thāp-*) |
| *-thali* | -*sthali* Fem. Loc. Sg. -*hiṁ* *Pd.* 112. |
| √*thava-* | 1. *stav->stu-* Fem. Pres. Part.-*antī* *Hv.* 91.12.21. 2. *sthāpay-* Abs. -*eppiṇu* *Hv.* 82.8.15. -*ivi* *Nc.* 7.10.1. |
| *thava* | *stabaka.* *MP.* 12.9.19. (Pk. *thavaa,* M. *thavā*). |
| √*thā-* | √*sthā-* Abs. -*evı* *Nc.* 6.1.6. |
| *hāvara* | *sthāvara.* Loc. Pl. -*hiṁ* *MP.* 82.10.11. |
| *thitti* | *sthiti* Fem. Gen. Sg. -*hĕ* *Hv.* 83,18.10. |
| *thira* | *sthira* Gen. Sg. -*hu* *Mt.* 18. |
| *thī* | *stri* *Kp.*A. 7.3. |
| √*thuṇa* | √*stu-* Pres. 3. Sg. -*i* *KP.* S. 31.2*, Imp. 2 Sg. -*aha* *Kp.* S. 111.1* |
| *theva* | =*stoka* *Kp.*J. 64.9. cf. *Hc.* 2.125. |
| *thoḍa* | *stoka-* Masc. Nom. Sg. -*u* *Sdd.* 23, Loc. Sg. -*ı* *Kp.*E. 2a. (Pa. *thoka,* Pk. *thoa.* -*ḍa* extension in M. *thoḍā* Guj. *thoḍū,* Panj. H. *thorā.* Sdh. *thoro*). |
| *thova* | *stoka* *Kp.* J. 38.2. Masc. direct Plur. -*ā* *Hc.* 376.1, Loc. Pl. -*ĕhĩ* *BhK.* 19.10. |
| *thovaḍaü* | *stokaṁ* *Sdd.* 90. |

*d*

| | |
|---|---|
| *daïa* | *dayita* Masc. Ins. Sg. -*eṁ* *Hc.* 4.333. |
| *-daïya* | *dayitā* Fem. Gen. Sg. -*ha* *Sc.* 455.1. |
| √*dakkhava-* | Caus. of√**dṛkṣ-* Imp. 2 Sg. -*hi* *Nc.* 1.16.2. Pres. part. -*anta* *Nc.* 1.1.6. Cf. *Hc.* 4.32. |

*dakkhāla-mi* =*darśayāmi Jc.* 3.33.10.

*daḍatti* Onomatopoeic 'suddenly' *MP.* 9.13.2.
cf. M. *dhāḍkan.*

*daḍavaḍa* =*śīghramṁ Cd.* 2.27. *Hc.* 4.330.2, -*u Hc.* 4.422.18.

*daṇḍadhara-hu* =*daṇḍa-dharāḥ* (Voc. Pl. in -*hu*) *Sn.* 19-442.

-*danta* (*ts.*) Ins. pl. -*hiṁ KKc.* 3.3.4.

*danti* °*tin* Gen. Sg. -*hi MP.* 87.2.9.

*dayo* *dayā* Nom. Sg. zero *Sdd.* 40. Acc. Sg. zero *Sdd.* 60.

*daramaliya* =*durmṛdiṭa KKc.* 8.19.4.

*dal-isu* *daliṣyāmi* (Fut. 1 Sg. -*isu*) *Sc.* 653.5.

*davakkaḍiya* *dāvāgni* -(*ḍa-ka*) 'a small fire' *Pd.* 102.

*davva* *dravya.* Neut. direct Pl. -*aï PPr.* 2.15, *Ys.* 35.

*dasa-disi-hiṁ* =*daśa-dikṣu* (Loc. Pl. -*hiṁ*) *KKc.* 8.8.3)

*dasa-vīsa-* =*daśa-viṁśat.* Ins. -*ha* (scribal error for *i* ?) *Jdu.* 55.2.

√*daṁśa-* *darśay-* Pres. 3 Pl. -*hiṁ Sn.* 48.249.
-*ira* (habit showing suff.) *Jc.* 1.3.10.

*daṁsaṇa* *darśana Hc.* 4.401. Direct Sg. -*u Cd.* 2.27.11.
Ins. Sg. -*i Jc.* 1.6.19.

*daṁsaṇa-bhūmi* *darśana-* Abl. Sg. -*hiṁ Sdd.* 57.

*daha* *daśan Kp.* E. 24, *MP.* 2.5.9.
(Pk. *dasa, daha.* -*s*- is preserved in Guj. H. Maith. Beng Or. Panj. *das*, and -*h*- in M. *dahā*, Sdh. *ḍā̃h*).

*daha-diha-hĩ* =*daśa-dikṣu* (Loc. Pl. in -*hĩ*) *DKs.* 45.

*dahama* *daśama.* Ins. Sg. -*eṁ MP.* 2.12. -*ī BhK.* 300.2.

*dahi* *dadhi.* Acc. Sg. -*u KKc.* 8.13.6. Ins. Sg. -*eṁ BhK.* 270.4.

*dāïjja* *dāyada Nc.* 4.8.9.

*dāïya* *dāyada Nc.* 3.14.13.

*dāḍha* *daṁṣṭrā.* Gen. Pl. -*ha Sn.* 217-186. (Pa. *dāṭhā*, Pk. M. Guj. *dāḍh*, Sdh. *ḍarhi*, Panj. *ḍārh*, Beng. *ḍāṛ*).

*dāḍhāla* *daṁṣṭrā*+*āla* (possessive suff.) *Jc.* 2.17.4.

*dāṇa* *dāna.* Ins. Sg. -*iṁ PPr.* 2.72.

*dāṇaccaṇa-vihi* *dānārcana-vidhi.* Acc. Pl. zero *Sdd.* 117.

*dāyāra* **dātāra*<*dātṛ* Masc. Nom. Sg. -*u* *Sn.* 237-191.

*dāva* 'to show.' Pres. 3. Sg. -*i* *Nc.* 10.4. cf. *Hc.* 4.32. Coll. M. *dāvṇē*

*dāvaṇa* *dāman* *Kp.* J. 94.4. Neut. direct Sg. *u* *Pd.* 42 (M. *dāvaṇ*, *dāvẽ*, Guj. *dāmṇi*, H. *dāman*, *dāvan*, Sdh. *ḍāvaṇu*, Panj. *deū*).

*dikkha* *dīkṣā* Fem. Acc. Sg. zero *BhK.* 290.6.

*dijja-i* *dīyatām* (*dā*+*ijja* optative) *Sn.* 355-27.

*diṭṭha* *dṛṣṭa* *DKK.* 3.11. *DKs.* 10, *PPr.* 2.132. Ins. Sg. -*ẽ* *PPr.* 1.27, Loc. Sg. -*i* *Hc.* 365.1, -(*a*) -(*a*)*mmi* *Mt.* 20 Fem. Nom. Sg. zero *Sdd.* 55.

*diṭṭhaa* *dṛṣṭa-ka* *DKs.* 50.

*diṭṭhi* *dṛṣṭi* *DKs.* 36. *Sdd.* 63, Direct Sg. zero. *Mt.* 24,25, 26. Ins. Sg. (Pl.?) -*hiṁ* *Sdd.* 63. Loc. Sg. -*i* *Jc.* 3.10.4. Loc. Sg. -*hiṁ.* *Jc.* 2.20.2

*diḍha* *dṛḍha* *DKK.* 22, *DKs.* 59.

*diṇṇa* **didna*=*datta* *Mt.* 32. Neut. Nom. Sg. -*ā* *DKs.* 85. Loc. Sg. -*i* *Jc.* 3.21.17.

*dintu* =*yacchantu* (Imp. 3 Pl. -*antu*) *Sdd.* 223.

*divasa* (*ts.*) Loc. Pl. -*ahi* *BhK.* 19.10.

*divaha-ḍa* *divasa-ṭa* (pleonastic). Masc. Nom. Pl.*ā* *Pd.* 17.

*dive* *divā* *Hc.* 4,419. *Ld.* 3.3.43.

*divva-cakkhu* *divya-cakṣu* Masc. Nom. Sg. zero. *KKc.* 7.1.4.

*divvaṁbara* *divyāmbara* Neut. direct Pl. zero *Sdd.* 203.

*divva-vāṇi* *divya-vāṇi* Acc. Sg. zero *KKc.* 2.5.1.

*disa* *disā* Fem. Acc. Sg. *Mt.* 32, Loc. Sg. -*iṁ* *BhK.* 75.4, -*i* (Skt. ism). *Sdd.* 56. Gen. Pl. *āham* *KKc.* 7.13.8.

*disi* **diśi*=*diś* Fem. Dat. Sg. -*heṁ* *KKc.* 2.2.10, Loc. Sg. -*hiṁ* *KKc.* 4. 2. 4, 7.12.5. Ins. Pl. -*hiṁ* *Hc.* 4.340.

| | |
|---|---|
| *dissa-i* | *dṛśyate DKs.* 83. |
| *diha* | *diśā* Fem. Loc. Pl. *-hiṁ Pd.* 175. |
| *dihi* | *dhṛti Hv.* 82, 18, 12. 92.20.9. |
| *dība* | *dīpa* Masc. Nom. Sg. *-ho DKK.* 22. Acc. Pl. *-ā DKs.* 4. |
| *dīvaa* | *dīpaka.* Masc. Ins. Pl. *-ehiṁ KKc.* 3. 3. 9. |
| *Dīvāyaṇa* | *Dvīpāyana Hv.* 92. 6. 1. |
| *dīviya* | *dīpikā* Fem. Ins. Pl. *-hĩ BhK.* 77.2. |
| *dīsaï* | *dṛśyate DKs.* 69, 81. *PPr.* 1.100, 120. |
| *du* | *tu* 'again' *MP.* 2.5.2. |
| *duāra* | *dvāra DKK.* 22. |
| *duijja* | *dvitīya Kp.* J. 33.2* |
| *duiya* | *dvitīya Kp.* J. 28.4. |
| *duguṇa* | *dvi-guṇa Sc.* 495.5. |
| *duguṇia* | *dvi-guṇita Kp.* P. 6.2.? *Sc.* 454.7. |
| *duggijjha* | *durgrāhya Kp.* S. 98.1. |
| *duggejjhauṁ* | *durgrāhyaṁ Sn.* 168-115. |
| *Dujaḍa* | *Dvijaṭa Kv.* 91.6.6. |
| *duddhaḷā* | *dugdha-ṭa-ka Mt.* 4. |
| *dubbha-ï* | *duhyate Jc.* 3.21.9. |
| *Dumaya* | *Drupada Hv.* 92.8.2. |
| *dummeha* | *durmedhas.* Masc. Nom. Pl. *-ā Pd.* 98. |
| *dureha* | *dvi-repha Kp.* S. 102.8. |
| *Duvaya* | *Drupada Hv.* 92.18.4. |
| *duṽa* | *druma Hv.* 82.5.7. |
| *duviha* | *dvividha BhK.* 60. 13. |
| *duvvayaṇa* | *durvacana.* Ins. Pl. *-ehĩ BhK.* 21.3 |
| *dusaṁga-susaṁga-ha*=°*susaṅgānām Jdc.* 10.3. (Gen. Pl. in *-ha* | |
| *dusaha* | *duḥsaha* Masc. Nom. Sg. *-ā Pd.* 102. |
| *duha* | *dvidhā Sc.* 545.8. |

*-duha* — *duḥkha* Neut. Nom. Pl. *-ī PPr.* 1.28

*duhaḍi* — *dvi-ghaṭi Jc.* 3.30.13.

*duhikkha* — *durbhikṣa Hv.* 87.1.2.

*duhiya* — *duhitā* (°*tṛ*) Fem. Gen. Pl. *-hā Sc.* 662.8.

*dūṇa* — *dviguṇa Nc.* 8.1.9. (cf. M. *duṇē*, H. *dūṇa*).

*dure* — (*ts.*) *DKK.* 27, *Hc.* 349.1.

√*de-* — =*dā*
Imp. 2 Sg. *-hi Pd.* 18 *Sn.* 17.570 3 Pl. *-ntu* Intro. to *Hv.* §56. *de-de-hi* (intensive '*bhṛśārthe.*') *Nc.* 6.12.11 Fut. 1 Sg. *-su Sc.* 635.9. Pres. Part. *-nta Mt.* 7, *-evaem. KKc.* 1.5.5., *evaṁ Ld.* 3.3.20.

√*dekkha-* — √**dṛkṣ- Pu.* 17.79. Pres. 2 Sg. *-hi Pd.* 197. 3 Sg. *-i DKs.* 64, *MK.* 17.64. *PPr.* 1.64, 1 Pl. *-huṁ KKc.* 3.4.7.
Imp. 2 Sg. zero (or *-a*) *MK.* 17.11, *-u Pd.* 190. *-ha DKs.* 85. 2 Pl. *-hu BhK.* 99.6, *DKs.* 57. Pres. Part. *-anta Pd.* 196. Pot. Part. *-evaa. Sdd.* 39. Caus. Pres. 3 Sg. *-āva-i MK.* 17.65.

*debī* — *devī* Fem. Nom. Sg. zero. *DKK.* 18.

*deva* — Voc. Sg. zero *KKc.* 1.1.3
Abstract noun. *-ttaṇa.* Loc. Sg. *-i Sn.* 34-199.

*devaya* — *devatā* Fem. Gen. Pl. *-hā Sc.* 466.1.

*devala* — *devālaya.* Loc. Pl. *-ihiṁ Ys.* 43.

*devī* — *devī* Fem. Gen. Sg. *-hi Jc.* 2.8.10. *Sc.* 474.1, Voc. Sg. zero *Sc.* 455.2, Ins. Pl. *-hiṁ MP.* 87.13.1 *Pd.* 3 (can we not take it as Gen. Pl.? The line runs as follows : *devi hīṁ koḍi ramantu.* ' With crores of goddesses.')

*desa* — *deśa* Loc. Sg. *-i Hc.* 4.425. *-hi DKs.* 86. *-hiṁ Hc.* 4.386.1. *dveṣa.* Masc. Nom. Sg. *-u PPr.* 2.49.

*desaḍa* — *deśa-* (*ṭa*). Masc. Loc. Sg. *-i Hc.* 4.419.3.

*desa-bhāsa* — *-deśa-bhāṣā* Fem. Nom. Pl. *-aī BhK.* 52.4.

*deha* — 1) (*ts.*) Ins. Sg. *-e DKK* 29. Gen. Sg. *-haṁ PPr.* 1.71. Loc. sg. *-hi DKK.* 3. Abl. Pl. *-haṁ Pd.* 40.
2) *dvaidha* Loc. *-e Hv.* 91.5.7.

*dehā-devali* — =*deha-devālaye* (Loc. Sg. in *-i*) *Pd.* 53.

*dehā-deha* (*ts.*) Loc. Pl. *-hi PPr.* 1.29.

*-dehi* *-dehī* Fem. Loc. Sg. *-hĩ Mt.* 7.

*dehiya* *dehi-ka* (*-dehin*) Gen. Pl. *-ha PPr.* 2.26.

*do* *dvau* Numeral *Sc.* 642.3, *Sdd.* 28. Direct Pl. *doṇṇi Jc.* 1.27.15, *KKc.* 2.18.3, *MK.* 17.78, *Sn.* 33-624. *dui Pd.* 17. *duṇṇi Kp.* J. 32.2,* Sdd. 222 (Neut.) *beṇṇi MK.* 17.78. Ins. Pl. *dohiṁ*, *°hĩ Jc.* 2.24.10, *Kp.S.* 37.1,* 16.7. *Pd.* 72, *PPr.* 2.71. Gen. Pl. *dohi Jc.* 2.3.3, *Sdd.* 25, *doṇha Mt.* 16. *duṇhaṁ Nc.* 5.10.1 *duha Sn.* 217-186. Loc. Pl. *dohi Jc.* 1.26.18, 19 *PPr.* 1.59.

*Dovaï* *Draupadī Sc.* 451.4.

*dovālasa* *dvādaśa KKc.* 10.16.6.

*dosa* *doṣa.* Masc. Ins. Sg. *-iṇa Sn.* 272-191. Acc. pl. *-ĩ BhK.* 3.4, Gen. Pl. *-haṁ Sdd.* 19. (used for Sing).

*dosa-guṇa* *doṣa-guṇa* Acc. Pl. *-ā DKs.* 76.

*dosa-ḍa* *doṣa* Masc. direct Pl. zero *Hc.* 4.379.1. *Kc.* 72.

*dohā* *dodhakaḥ DKs.* 94.

*dohāī-huya* *dvi-bhāgībhūta* Masc. Loc. Sg. *-ĕ Hv.* 88.1.16.

*dohāviya* *dvidhā-kṛta Jc.* 3.7.11.

*dh*

*dhagadhaga-nta* 'shining, glittering' *Hv.* 86.1.14. cf. M. H. *dhagdhag-*

*dhaṇa* *dhanyā.* Fem. Nom. Sg. zero *Hc.* 4.330.

*dhaṇa dhāra* *dhana-dhārā* 'shower of wealth.'

*Dhaṇamaī* *Dhanamatī KKc.* 10.10.8.

*dhaṇu* *dhanuḥ* Acc. Sg. zero *Bh.K* 295.2.

*dhaṇṇa* *dhanya.* Masc. Nom. Sg. *-ā DKs.* 71.

*dhandhă* *dhandhatā* (Sk. Com. on *DKs.* 34 *Les Chants Mystiques*, p. 189) Acc. Sg. zero *DKs.* 34.

*dhandha* =1 *vyavasāya* Loc. Sg. *-i Pd.* 91. cf. M. *dhandā*, H. *dhandhā* 2. *dhāṁdha* (?) Brahmadeva on *PPr.* 2.121. Sk. *dvandva*?

*dhandha-vāla* =*lajjāvat Pd.* 122 of *Dn.* 5.57 *dhaya-dhandhā ṇaralajjā.*

*dhamma* *dharma.*Gen. Sg. *-ho BhK.* 249.2 Loc. Sg. *-e DKs.* 29.

*dhamma-gaï* *dharma-gati* Acc. Sg. zero *DKK*. 16.

*dhammādhamma* *dharmādharma*. Masc. Acc. Pl. zero *DKs*. 3.

*dhamma-dheṇu* *dharma-dhenu* Fem. Nom. Sg. zero *Sdd*. 222.

*dhamma-maï* *dharma-matiḥ Sc*. 448.

*dhara-* *dhṛ->dhar-* Pres. 3. Pl. *-anti Pd*. 4.
Imp. 2 Sg. *-i Mt*. 5. *PP*. *-iya Sn*. 6-480.
Inf. *-aṇu Jdu*. 12.1, *-ivi Sn*. 155-296.
Abs. *-ivi KKc*. 1. 2.1. Pot. Part. *-evvaü Ṅc*. 2.8.4.

*dharaṇi* (*ts*) Fem. Dat. Gen. Sg. *-he MP*. 1.15.10.
Loc. Sg. *-hiṁ -hĩ Sc*. 446.1., *Sdd*. 90.

*dhavala-* *dhavalaya-* Inf. *-aṇahaṁ Sdd*. 194.

*Dhāḍaisaṇḍa* *Dhātakī-ṣaṇḍa* Loc. Sg. *-e Hv*. 90. 15. 13.

*dhāra-* *dhāraya-* (but used primitively) Abs. *-ēvi PPr* 2.25.

*dhijjaï* *=dhriyate* (*-ijja* Passive) *DS*. 4.5.2.

*dhiṭṭha* 1 *dhṛṣṭa KKc*. 3.19.2.
2. *adhiṣṭhita KKc*. 1.17.4

*dhīya* **dhītā* (<*duhitṛ*). Acc. Sg. zero *MP*. 87.1.11. cf. Pa. *dhītā*

*dhuttima* *=dhūrtatva Pd*. 80.

*dhruva* *dhruvaṁ Hv*. 81.8.9.

*dhruvu* *dhruvaṁ Hc*. 4.418, *Kc*. 62, *Ld*. 3.3.27, *MP*. 2.7.12.

*dhūa* *dhūma* Sdd. 39.
(cf. *dhūa* also TURNER *Nep. Dictionary* 331a under *dhuwā̃*)

*dhūma* *ts*. Ins. Sg. *-ē DKs*. 2.

*dhūya* *duhitā*. Fem. Dat. Gen. Sg. *-he KKc*. 7.7.9.
Acc. Pl. zero *Sc*. 600.9 Gen. Pl. *-hā Sc*. 660.8.

*p.*

*paa* *pada* Loc. Sg. *-i Hc*. 4.406.1, *Mt*. 12.

*Paāvaï* *Prajāpati* Masc. Loc. Sg. *-hiṁ Mt*. 19.

*paija* *pratijñā* Acc. Sg. zero *KKc*. 4.1.12. *ojja* in *BhK*. 145.6.
(N. H. Panj. *paij*, Sdh. *paij* Masc.)

*païṭṭha* *praviṣṭa* Neut. Nom. pl. zero *DKK*. 11.

*paümiṇi* *padminī* Fem.Loc. Sg. *-hiṁ Sdd.* 203.

*paülaṇa* *prajvalana MP.* 7.6.12. cf. M. *polṇẽ* and the cognates given by Bloch under it in *FLM*.

*paesa* *pradeśa*. Ins. Pl. *-hiṁ PPr.* 2.22.

*pakokkiu* *-āhūtaḥ* (Masc. Nom. Sg. *-u*) *Jc.* 3.34.7.

*pakkhara* *upaskara- =turaga-sannāha Kp.* S. 42-8 cf. *Dn.* 6.10 (M. Guj. Panj. H. *pākhar*, Sdh. *pākhiru* (with ref. to camels).)

*pagāma* *prakāmam Pd.* 112.

*paggima* *-prāyaḥ* Ld. 3.3.42.

*paggiṁva*,°ǚ *va =prāyaḥ Hc.* 414.4, *Kc.* 59.

*paṁka* (*ts.*) Loc. Sg. *-i Mt.* 19.

*paṁkaa* *paṅkaja* Loc. Sg. *-i Hc.* 357-3, Direct Pl. *-a Mc.* 19.

*paṁkkayaruha* *paṅkaja-ruha*. Gen. Pl. *-āhaṁ KKc.* 9.16.1.

*paṁkaya-siri* *paṅkaja-śrī*. Fem. Gen. Sg. *-hẽ BhK.* 17.2.

*paṁkhi* *pakṣin* Masc. Nom. Sg. zero *Sdd.* 87.

*paccala* *pratyala* (*ṁ*) *Kp.* J. 9.3. cf. *Dn.* 6.69.

*pacchaï* *paścāt Hc.* 362, 420, *Ld.* 3.3.49.

*pacchae* *paścāt Hv.* 83.12.11. cf. Guj. *pāche*

*pacchaliu* *-pratyuta Ld.* 3.3.38. *-cc* in *Hc.* 420.5.

*pacchittu* *prāyaścittam Jc.* 3.38.15, *Mp.* 1.6.12.

*pacchiṽa* *paścima Hv.* 81.6.13.

*paṁca* (*ts.*) *DKK*. 25. Plur. Nom. zero *DKK*. 7. *Kp.* J. 25.4, Acc. zero *Kp.* J. 7.1. Ins. *-ehĩ DKK.* 8, (*a*)*hĩ Hc.* 4.422.14. *Kp.* S 37.1* Gen. *-hã Hc.* 4.422.14. *Kp.* J. 29.6, (*a*) *ha Kp.* J. 64.2. (Pa. Pk. *pañca*, M. Guj. H. Beng. Nep. *pā̃c*. Or. *pāñca*, Panj. *pañj*, Sdh. *pañjā*).

*paṁca-guru* (*ts.*) Acc. pl. zero *Sdd.* 1.

*pamcame* (*ts.*) Masc. Nom. Sg. *-u Sdd.* 15, Ins. Sg. *-eṇa MP.* 2.11.
°*-gaï* °*gati*. Fem. Acc. Sg. zero *Ys.* 48.

*paṁcamī* (*ts.*) Fem. Gen. Sg. *-hi Sdd.* 185.

*paṁca-vīsa* *pañca-viṁśa MP.* 2.10.1 (see *paṁcuttaravīsa* below).

*paṁca-sattari* °*saptati MP.* 2.9.7.

*paṁcānana* *ts.* Ins. pl. *-ehĩ DKK.* 25. (Sing. No.?)

*paṁcāṇuvvaya* *pañcānuvrata.* Neut. direct Pl. zero *Sdd.* 11.

*Paṁcālī* *pāñcālī Hv.* 92.10.1.

*paṁcumbara* *pañcodumbara.* Gen. Pl. *-haṃ Sdd.* 10.

*paṁcuttaravīsa* *pañcottaraviṃśat MP.* 2.9.12. (Pa. *pañcavīsa,* M. *pañcvīs,* Guj. H. *pacīs,* Nep. *pacis*).

*paṁjali* *prāñjali* Masc. Ins. Sg. *-ṇā MP.* 87.14.10.

*paṭṭha* *pṛṣṭha* Loc. Sg. *-i MP.* 2.16.15.

√*paṭṭhava-* *pra-* √*sthāpay-* Imp. 2 Sg. *-hi Nc.* 4.14.1. (M. *pāṭhavṇẽ,* Sdh. *paṭhṇu,* Panj. *paṭhāṇā*).

√*paḍa-* √*pat-* (Pres. 2 Sg. *-īsi Pd.* 91, 3 Sg. *-i Hc.* 422.4. *-ei DKs.* 72. 3 Pl. *-(a)nti Hc.* 422.20, *-(a)hiṁ Hc.* 388. Fut. 3 Sg. *-isaï Pd.* 155, 3 Pl. *-issahī Sc.* 264.8 (See Intro. to *Sc.* p. 17). PP. *-ia Kp.* J. 95.3. *-iya Pd.* 7, 116. Abs. *-eviṇu Pd.* 21 (Pa. *patati,* Pk. *paḍaï,* M. Guj.√*paḍ,* H. *paṛnā* Nep. *parnu*).

*paḍi*] *prati DKs.* 104.

*paḍicchavi* **pratīcchatvī=pratīṣva Mt.* 14.

*paḍibakkha* *pratipakṣa.* Nom. Sg. *-ā DKs.* 76.

*paḍima* *pratimā.* Fem. Ins. Sg. *-iṁ Sdd.* 193, Nom. Pl. *-u Nc.* 1.12.6.

*paḍivajja-* *prati-pad-ya* Pres. 2 Sg. *-hi Jc.* 2.37.12. Pres. 2 Pl. *-ha MP.* 91.3.4.

*paḍivatti* *pratipatti* Fem. Acc. Pl. zero *Sc.* 461.1.

√*paḍha-* √*paṭh-* Pres. 3 Sg. *-i DKK* 12. Abs. *-ivi KKc.* 3.8.8. Pres. Part. Ins. Sg. *-anta-ehī DKs.* 53. Fem. Loc. Pl. *-antī -hī Sc.* 468.1.

*paḍhama* *prathama DKs.* 36. Masc. Nom. Sg. *-u Sdd.* 10. Loc. Sg. *-ẽ DKs.* 36.

*paṇaiṇi* *praṇayinī* Dat. Gen. *-hĕ BhK.* 23.1.

√*paṇava-* *pra-*√*nam* Abs. *-ivi PPr.* 1.8.

| | |
|---|---|
| *paṇuvīsa* | *pañca-viṁśat MP.* 2.10.1. |
| *paṁḍava* | *pāṇḍava Hv.* 91. 20. 8. Nom. Pl. zero *Jc.* 3.29.7. Gen. Pl. -(*a*)*hā Sc.* 451.4. |
| *paṁḍia-loa* | *paṇḍita-loka* Voc. Pl. -*hu DKs.* 95. |
| *paṁḍitta* | *paṇḍita.* Nom. Pl. -*ā DKK.* 2. |
| *paṇṇāsa* | *pañcāśat MP* 2.9.21, *Nc.* 5.11.7. (Pa. *paññāsa, paṇṇāsa,* Pk. *paṇṇāsa,* M. *pannās,* Guj. H. Nep. *pacās*). |
| *patta* | *prāpta.* Neut. direct Sg. -*u PPr.* 1.9. |
| *-patti* | *patnī* Fem. Ins. Sg. -*i MP.* 87.14.8. |
| *pattija-ha* | =*pratiyāta DKs.* 35. (Imp. 2 Pl. -*ha*). |
| *pattijja-si* | =*pratīṣe Kp.* J. 26.6. |
| *pattiya* | *prati-i* Imp. 2 Sg. -zero or -*a* (Intro. to *Hv.* §56). |
| *pattiya* | *patrikā.* Direct pl. -zero *Pd.* 158, 59. cf. M.H. *pattī.* |
| √*pa-thippa-* | *pra-*√*stip-ya.* -*ira* (showing habit, frequency, etc.) *Jc.* 3.9.1. |
| *padesa* | *pradeśa* Neut. direct Pl. zero *PPr.* 2.24. |
| *-panti* | *paṅkti* Fem. Acc. Sg. zero *Sdd.* 167. (In comp.s) Neut. Loc. Sg. -*hi Sc.* 443.2. |
| *paṁtha* | =*pathin* Loc. Sg. -*hĩ Mt.* 8. |
| *pabana* | *pavana* Masc. Nom. Sg. -*hŏ DKK.* 23. Gen. Sg. -*ho DKs.* 32. |
| *pa-bhaṇa-i* | *prabhaṇati* (Pres. 3 Sg. -i) *KKc.* 1.11.4. |
| *pamāa* | *pramāda* Loc. Sg. -*i* (used for Ins.) *Sn.* 308-169. |
| *pamāṇa* | *pramāṇa Sc.* 555.3. Acc. Sg. -*u PPr.* 1.51, Acc. Pl. -*i Jdc.* 2.1. |
| *payāgama* | *pataṅgama DKs.* 73. |
| *payaḍa* | *prakaṭa* Masc. direct (Acc.) Pl. -*ā Hc.* 338. |
| *payaḍiṇa* | *prakaṭana Kp.* S. 27.2. |
| *payaṁpa-* | *pra-*√*jalp- Hc.* 4.2. *Nc.* 5.9.9. Pres. 1 Sg. -*mi Jc.* 3.11.11. 3 Pl. -*hi Jdc.* 11.1. |
| *payāra* | *prakāra.* Ins. Pl. -*ehiṁ Hc.* 4.367. |

| | |
|---|---|
| *payāla* | *prajāla* (*-āla* suff.) *Pd.* 69.84. |
| *payāsiya* | *prakāśita* Masc. Nom. Pl. zero *PPr.* 1.6. |
| *para* | (*ts.*) 1 Gen. Sg. *-ssu Hc.* 4.338.<br>2. *paraṃ Lc.* 3.3.28. |
| *paraa* | =*paredyuḥ MP.* 32.26.8. Loc. Sg. *-i MP.* 16.20.12. |
| *parajjiya* | *parājita Hv.* 82.8.3, *KKc.* 2.3.1. *Nc.* 1.3.6. 1.14.10. |
| *paramattha* | *paramārtha.* Masc. Nom. Sg. zero. *DKK.* 31.<br>°*ya* (=*ka*) *-e DKs.* 63. |
| *parama-muṇi* | °*muni.* Masc. Nom. Sg. zero. *Ys.* 36. |
| *paramesara* | *parameśvara* Nom. Sg. *-u DKs.* 83. Gen. Sg. *-āsu BhK.*253.4. |
| *para-hara-* | *para-√har*<br>Imp. 2 Sg. *-i Sdd.* 52. |
| *para-huya* | *parabhṛta Sc.* 450.7. |
| *parāiya* | *parakīyā Pd.* 43. cf. H. *parāī.* |
| *parāhiṇa* | *parhīna MK.* 17.350. |
| *pariṁ* | *paraṁ PPr* 1.28 |
| *pariṭṭhāba* | *paristhāpita DKs.* 50 |
| *pariṭṭhiya* | *pratiṣṭhita Kp.* J. 26.3 cf. *Hc.* 1.38. Masc. Nom. Sg. *-u PPr.* 1.14. |
| *pari-ṇesami* | *pari-ṇeṣyāmi Nc,* 5.8.3 (Fut. 1 Sg. *-esami*) |
| *paripuṇṇa* | °*pūrṇa.* Masc. Nom. Sg. *-e DKK.* 8. |
| *pari-bhamantu* | °*bhraman Sc.* 516.3 (Pres. Part. *-anta-u*). |
| *pari-māna-ha* | =°*mānayata* (Imp. 2 Pl. *-ha DKK.* 9. |
| *pariyaṇa* | °*jana* Acc. Sg. *-u Pd.* 13. |
| *parivāḍi* | °*pāṭi* Fem. Nom. Sg. zero *Pd.* 17. |
| *pari-sakka-ï* | °*ṣvaṣkati Mt.* 30. *-ira Kp.* P. 8.3. |
| *pari-hara-* | °*-√har.* Imp. 2 Sg. *-i Sdd.* 20, *-hi Sdd.* 22. Abs.-(*a*)*vi PPr.* 2.4. |
| *√parīsa-* | *√spṛś-* Imp. 2 Pl. *-hu DKs.* 57. |
| *palāṇa* | *palāyana* Direct Sg. *-u Hv.* 83.13.4. |

| | |
|---|---|
| *palitta* | *pradīpta Kp.* S. 97.9 cf. *Hc.* 1.221. |
| *pallaṭṭa-* | =*paryastaṁ kṛ-* Abs. -*evi Jc.* 2.37.1, -*vi Nc.* 2.6.3. (M. *pālaṭṇẽ*, Guj. *pāl̆aṭvũ*, Sdh. *palaṭṇu* H. *palaṭnā*.) |
| *palhattha* | *paryasta Hv.* 83.10.4. cf. *Hc.* 4.258. *Kp.* S. 18.4, PP. -*iu Hv.* 85.15.5. -*u Jc.* 3.39.15. (M. *pǝlthā*. See *pallaṭṭa* above). |
| *pavasanta* | Pres. Part. of *pra-√vas-* Ins. Sg. -*eṇa Hc.* 4.333. |
| *pavāṇa* | *pramāṇa Sdd.* 27. |
| *pavva* | *parvan* Loc. Sg. -*i Jc.* 3.31.3. |
| *pasaria* | **prasarita Mt.* 23, 30. |
| *pasaṁsa-* | *pra-śaṁs-* (with -i *iya* of the pass.) Pres. 3 Pl. -*hiṁ Jdc*, 4.3, 6.4. |
| *pasāha* | =*pra-kathaya-* Imp. 2 Sg. -*ha Jc.* 1.18.10. |
| *pasāhiya* | *prasādhita* (PP. in -*iya*) *Jc.* 2.4.4. |
| *pasiya-* | *pra-sīd-* Imp. 2 Sg. zero *Mt.* 31 (Skt. ism.) also) 3 Pl. -(*a*)*ntu* (Intro. to *Hv.* §.56). |
| *pasuya* | *paśuka* Masc. Nom. Pl. zero *PPr.* 2.5. |
| *pasu-vāha-mi* | *paśu-vadhe* (Loc. Sg. in -*mi*) *Pd.* 127. |
| *pahaṭṭha* | *prahṛṣṭa* Masc. Nom. Sg. -*u Sc*, 692.3. |
| *pahāra* | *prahāra* Ins. Sg. -*eṁ Mt.* 29. |
| *pahāṇa* | *pradhāna* Loc. Sg. -*hiṁ KKc.* 1.3.1. |
| *pahirāviya* | *paridhāpita KKc.* 7.8.6. (M. *peherṇẽ*, H *pahrānā*). |
| *pahila* | **prathila*=*prathama Nc.* 1.5.8., *Pd.* 218. Neut. direct Sg. -*u Nc.* 1.5.8. Loc. Sg. -*e Hv.* 84.2.1. -*āro* (Comp. suff.) *Hv.* 82.1.7. *Jc.* 4.8.17, *Nc.* 1.6.1. Fem. -*ārī* (pleonastic) 4.6.4. |
| *pahilla* | **prathillaka*=*prathama Hv.* 82 *dhruvaka* (Pk. *pahilla-*, °*a*, M. *pahilā*, Guj. *pahelũ*, Nep. *pailo*). |
| *pahua* | *prabhṛti Jc.* 1.2.9a. |
| *pahu-kero* | ('pertaining to'=*kera*) -*prabhoḥ*. *DKK*, 21. |
| *pahūi* | *prabhṛti Hv.* 91.19.12. |

*paho-saï* — *prabhaviṣyati* (Fut. 3 Sg. *-saï*) *Hv.* 87.6.5.

*praā(yā)vadi* — *prajāpati Hc.* 4.404.

*prangaṇa* — *prāṅgaṇa Hv.* 83.4.3.

√*prassa* — 'to see' *Pu.* 17.79.

*pāa* — 1. *pāda* Direct Pl. *-ā DKs.* 19.
2. *pāpa* Direct Sg. *-v Pd.* 59.

*pāanta* — *pādānta* Loc. Sg. *-i Mt.* 3.

*pāikka* — *pādika=padāti Hv.* 83.20.3. cf. *Hc.* 2.138. cf. old M. *pāīk* 'a servant.'

*pāüsa* — *prāvṛṣ Sc.* 446.8. (Pa. *pāvusa*, Pk. *pāusa*, M. *pāūs*, Guj. *pāvas*, H. *pāwas*, *pāūs*)

*pāḍ-ijjihii* — =Pass Fut. 3 Sg. *pātaya-* (ending in *-ihii*) *Sc*, **661.8.**

*pāḍihera* — *prātihārya MP.* 1.18.9

*pāṇa* — *prāṇa* Masc. Acc. Pl. zero *Sn.* 217-186.

*pāṇī* — *pānīya DKs.* 66.
(Pa. *pānīyam*, Pk. *pāṇia*, M. Guj. *pāṇī* Panj. Sdh. *pāṇī* Masc. Or. H. *pānī*, Beng. Nep. *pāni*).

*pāṇia* — *pānīya* Loc. Ins. Sg. *-ehi DKK.* 32.

*pāba-si* — **prapa-si=prāpnoṣi DKs.* 62.

*pāya* — *pāda* Acc. pl. zero *KKc.* 4.11.6.

*pāyaḍa* — 1. *prakaṭa Hv.* 83.2.4. cf. *Hc.* 1.44.
Vb. Pres. 1 Pl. *-hũ Hv.* 84.2.11.

*pāya-poma* — *pāda-padma.* Dat. Gen. Pl. *-āṇa KKc.* 3.14.4.

*pāraddhi* — *pārardhikā* 'hunting' *Sdd.* 47 but *pāpardhi* according to H. L. Jain *KKc.* p. 218 glossary.
Loc. Sg. *-hiṁ KKc.* 7.444. (M. *pāradh*, Guj. *paradh*).

*pāla-* — *pālaya-*
Fut. 1 Sg. *-esami KKc.* 2.6.3. 2 Sg. *-esahi KKc.* 2.5.6. **2.6.2.**

√*pāva-* — √*prāp-* Pres. 1 Sg. *-mi Mt*, 34. 2 Sg. *-hi Ys.* 15. Fut. 1 Sg. *-isu Sn.* 306-169. 2 Sg. *-hi Sdd.* 208. 3 Sg. *-esai KKc.* 2.8.3. Pot. 3 Sg. *-evva-u. Jc.* 3.36.3. Abs. *-evī KKc.* 2.5.4.
(Pa. *pāpeti*, Pk. *pāvei*, *pāvaï*, M. *pāvṇẽ*, Nep. *pāunu*).

*pāsa* — *pārśva*. Loc. Sg. -*(a)hiṁ* *Nc*. 1.10.10 -*i* *KKc*. 2.8.7 -*e* *DKs*. 5 (M. *pās*, Guj. *pāsū*, Sdh. *pāsu*).

*pāsāa* — *prāsāda* Ins. Sg. -*eṁ* *Pd*. 81.

*pāhāṇa* — *pāṣāṇa* *Sdd*. 161.

*prāiṁa*, °*va*, — °*va*=*prāyaḥ* *Hc*. 414, *Kc*. 59, *Ld*. 3.3.42.

*prāü* — *prāyaḥ* *Hc*. 414, *Kc*. 59, *Ld*. 3.3.42.

*prāṇa* — (*ts*.) *Hv*. 84.7.9.

*pi* — *api* *Mt*. 18.

*pia* — 1. *priya* Mt. 8. Direct Sg. -*u* *Ld*. 3.3.5. Ins. Sg. -*eṁ* *Hc*. 410. 2. *priyā* *Mt*. 22, 29. Abl. Sg. -*hu* *Mt*. 13. °*ḍā* *Mk*. 17.5.

*pia-ama* — *priyatamā* *Mt*. 31.

*piu* — *pitṛ* *KKc*. 6.1.8, *Kp*. S. 46.6.9. Ins. Sg. -*ṇā*. *Kp*. S. 48.9. Gen. Sg. -*hi* *MP*. 87.1.2. -*hu* *Sc*. 564.5

√*pikkha*- — *prekṣ* Abs. -*avi* *Pd*. 33.

√*piccha*- — √*prekṣ*- Pres. 3 Sg. -*i* *Pd*. 180. *Sdd*. 167.
Imp. 2 Pl. -*ha* *Jdu*. 1.4.
Fut. 1 Sg. -*ihimi* *Jc*. 3.15.11.

*picchī* — *picchikā* *DKs*. 8.

*piḍa* — *pīḍā*. Fem. Loc. Sg. -*i* *Sdd*. 8.

*pidu*, °*do* — *pitā* *Ld*. 3.3.1.

*piya* — *priyā*. Ins. Loc. Sg. -*hã* *Sc*. 198.1.2 (Intro. p. 12)
°*sahi* °*sakhī* Ins. Pl. -*hĩ* *Sc*. 485.4.

*piyārau* — =*priyatama* *MP*. 2.21.7.

√*pilla*- — *prer*- Abs. -*i* *Pd*. 220.

*pilla* — 'young one.' Neut. direct Pl. -*āiṁ* *Jc*. 3.13.17.

*piva* — =*iva* *Cd*.

*pisuṇattaṇa* — *piśunatva* *Sdd*. 144.

*priu* — *priya* *Ld*. 3.3.35 *priya* In *Hv*. 81.3.12.

√*pīḍa* — √*pīḍ*- Imp. 3. Pl. -*antu* *Hc*. 385. *Sc*. 400.6 (Intro. to *Sc*. §22, p. 16).
PP. -*ia* *Mt*. 7.

√pīṇa- prī-ṇa- Opt. 3 Sg. -ijjau Jc. 3.8.14.
PP. -ia Neut. direct Sg. -u KKc. 1.5.2.

pukkāra =āhvāna śabda. Acc. Sg. zero KKc. 2.1.9. cf. M. **pukārā**
H. pukār.

√puccha- √pṛcch-
Pres. 1 Sg. -imi Mt. 29, 3. Sg. -i DKs. 64.
Imp. 2 Sg. -esu Kp. J. 28.1 -hi DKs. 31.
2 Pl. -ha DKs. 52. PP. -iu Mt. 35, PPr. 2.2.

pujja pūjā Acc. Sg. zero Pd. 49.

√pujja √pūj- Pres. 3 Sg. -i KKc. 10.4.5.
Imp. 2 Sg. -ejja-su (Hv. Intro. §56.)

puṭṭhi 1. pṛṣṭha Sc. 763.8.
2. puṣṭi Loc. Sg. -hi MP. 87.9.16.

puṇu punaḥ Jc. 1.3.1 Kp. J. 7.6. Kp. S. 94.7. Ld. 3.3.26, Mt. 14,16,
24, PPr. 2.211. Sdd. 5.17.

puṇo Sn. 78-332. punaḥ Kp. J. 41.2*

puṁḍucchu puṇḍra-ikṣu Nc. 1.6.11.

puṇṇāli =puṁścalī Fem. Gen. Sg. -hi Jc. 2.9.16.

putta putra. Voc. Sg. -ā Kc. 14. Ins. Pl. -ehim MP. 82.13.13.

puppha puṣpa. Neut. Nom. Pl. -aï MP. 87.15.13.

pupphavaī puṣpavatī Fem. Ins. Pl. -hiṁ Hc. 438.

pubba pūrva DKs. 84.

√pura √pūr- Imp. 2 Sg. -ehu Jc. 18.4.
Fut. 1 Pl. -issahũ Sc. 318.8. (Intro. to Sc. §24, p. 17).

purāiu purākṛta Pd. 77.

purisa =puruṣa Ins. Pl. -ihĩ Sc. 460.4.

puvva pūrva. Fem. Loc. Sg. -(ā)hiṁ KKc. 7.12.5.

Puvva-videha Pūrva-videha Loc. Sg. -i MP. 100.9.1.

puvvilla pūrva-illa (=mat 'possessing') MP. 1.2.4.

pusiu *spṛśita=spṛṣṭa Nc. 2.8.1.

puhaï (°vi) pṛthavī KKc. 3.9.4. Loc. Sg. -hi ȯPPr. 2.131.

pūya pūjā Acc. Sg. zero Sc. 466.2.

*pūra-hiṁ* — *pūrayanti Sdd.* 97 (Pres. 3 Pl. *-hiṁ*)

*pūhabi* — *pṛthavī DKK* 8.

*peiyā* — *peṭikā KKc.* 1.7.2.

*pekkha-* — *prekṣ-* Pres. 1 Sg. *-mı Mt.* 8, 3 Sg. *-ı DKs.* 19. Imp. 2. Sg. *-u DKs.* 45. *Mt.* 34. zero *PPr.* 1.71. *-ha Sdd.* 52. Pl. *-ha DKs.* 73. *-hu MP.* 91.3.5. Fut. 1 Sg. *-ıhımı Mt.* 22. *-esu Sc.* 635.7. 2 Sg. *-esahı Nc.* 2.4.4. Inf. *-huṁ KKc.* 4.3.2. Abs. *-ıvı -esahı Nc.* 2.4.4. Inf. *-huṁ KKc.* 4.3.2. Abs. *-ıvı KKc.* 2.3.9.

√*peccha-* — *prekṣ-* Pres. Sg. *-ahi Kp.*S. 79.2. 3 Sg. *-ēi Kp.* S. 32.1* Imp. 2 Sg. zero *Kp.* S. 63.1. *-i Jc.* 3.33.10. 2 Pl. *-hu Mt.* 30. Pass. Imp. 3 Sg. *-ijja-u* 68.9. Abs. *-ivi Kp.* J. 91.3. *-evi Kp.* S. 104.1

*peranta* — *paryanta Kp.* S. 59.2.

√*pella-* — *prer-* Pres. 3 Sg. *-i Jc.* 3.24.5. *Nc.* 3.17.14. Imp. 2 Pl. *-hu DKs.* 57. PP. *iya MP.* 2.13.22. Abs. *-ivi Nc.* 4.7.16. *-eppiṇu Nc.* 9.25.14. cf. *Hc.* 4.143.

*pesa* — *praveśa* Masc. Acc. Sg. *-u Pd.* 77, 193.

*poṭṭullaü* — =*poṭṭa-ullaa* (pleonastic) *Jc.* 2.28.7.

*potthā-picchiya* — =*pustaka-picchikā.* Ins. Pl. *-iṁ, -ī* ◌ *Ys* 47.

*popphalī* — *pūgī-phala MP.* 22.7.13.
cf. M. *po-phaḷ*, Guj *phophaḷ*

*Pomāvaī* — *Padmāvatī KKc.* 10.13.10.

*pomāvayā* — =*Padmāvatī* Fem. Ins. Sg. *-eṁ KKc.* 2.6.7.

*polaī* — *prajvalati DKs.* 82.

*ph.*

*phaṇi* — *phaṇin* Masc. Ins. Sg. *-ṇā MP.* 100. 4.15.

*pharanta* — Pres. Part. of √*sphur*? *DKK.* 16. (Pres. Part in *-anta*).

*pharusa* — *paruṣa Hv.* 89.17.10, *Nc.* 9.20.8. but *pharasa* in *BhK.* 244.7. cf. *Hc.* 1.232. °*ttaṇa* (*-tva*) *Nc.* 3.3.16.

*phala* — 1. (*ts.*) Neut. direct Pl. zero *Hc.* 335.
2. Vb. Pres. 3 Pl. *-hiṁ KKc.* 1.14.6.
(M. *phaḷ*, *-l* in Guj. Panj. H. Beng. Sdh.)

| | |
|---|---|
| *√phāḍa* | *sphāṭaya-* Abs. *-evi Hv.* 84.12.12. cf. M. *phāḍṇē.* |
| *phāraa* | *sphārita DKs.* 109. |
| *phāsa* | *sparśa.* Masc. Ins. Pl. *-hi PPr.* 2.112. |
| *phiṭṭa-i* | *=bhraṣyati, naśyati Ds.* 4.3.2.<br>(M. Guj. Sdh. *√phiṭ-*). |
| *phukka* | *phūtkā* 'hissing' *Kp.* P. 4.2. |
| *√phukka-* | *=sphāy-* Pass.Pres. 3 Pl. *-ijja-nti Pd.* 151. cf. M. *phuṁkṇē*<br>H. *phūṅknā.* |
| *√phuṭṭa-* | *sphuṭ-ya* Abs. *-ivi Sdd.* 100.<br>(M. *phuṭṇē,* Guj. *phuṭvũ,* Sdh. *phuṭaṇu,* Panj. *phuṭṇā,* H. *phuṭnā,* Nep. *phuṭnu*). |
| *phuḍu* | *sphuṭam Hv.* 81.11.7. |
| *√phura-* | *√sphur-* Pres. Part. *-anta Sc.* 528.5. |
| *phulla-tthāṇaya* | *=phulla-sthāna* Gen. Sg. *-hi Sdd.* 34. |
| *phullia* | *phullita=puṣpita. Sdd.* 35.<br>(Pa. Pk. *phulla,* M. Guj. *phūl,* Beng. Nep. *phul.* H. *phūl* Masc.). |
| *√phusa-* | *√spṛś=√mṛj.* Abs. *-ivi Pd.* 157. |
| *√pheḍa* | caus. of *√sphiṭ-* cf. *Hc.* 4.105.<br>Pres. 1 Sg. *-mi Jc.* 4.6.2. Abs. *-ivi Kp.*J. 10.1. (M. *pheḍṇē,* Guj. *pheḍvũ,* Beng. *phelite*). |

*b*

| | |
|---|---|
| *√baïsa-* | *up-viśa.* Abs. *-ī DKs.* 4. |
| *baïsaṇaa(-ya)* | *upaveśana-ka* Neut. direct Sg. *-u Jdc.* 21.3. |
| *bajja-ī* | *varjyate DKs.* 56. |
| *baḍha* | *=vatsa* or 'a fool' Voc. Sg. zero *DKK.* 11. *-e DKK.*8. |
| *Baṇārasi* | *Vārāṇasī DKs.* 49. (Fem. Nom. Sg. -zero). |
| *baddha* | (*ts.*) Ins. Sg. *-iṇa Sdd.* 60. |
| *bande* | *vandya DKs.* 10. |
| *√bandha-* | *√badh-*<br>Imp. 2 Sg. *-asu Kp.*J. 62.2*. *-i Sdd.* 208.<br>Abs. *-ivi Kp.*J. 26.7. *-ī DKs.* 5. |

| | |
|---|---|
| *bandha* | (*ts.*) Ins. Sg. *-e DKs.* 107. |
| *bandhu* | (*ts.*) Gen. Pl. *-hum*, *-haṁ Kc.* 18. |
| *batthu* | *vastu* Neut. Nom. Sg. zero *DKs.* 54. |
| *baṁbhaṇa* | *brāhmaṇa* Gen. Pl. *-haṁ Jc.* 3.40.18. |
| *baṁbhaṇa-cāra* | *=brahmacarya Nc.* 9.9.9. |
| *bara-ṇāla* | *vara-nāla* Acc. Pl. *-ẽ DKs.* 51. |
| *balāla* | *bala-āla(=vat) Hv.* 85.10.21. |
| *bali* | (*ts.*) Acc. Sg. zero *Hc.* 338. |
| *baliya* | °*ka.* Gen. Pl. *-haṁ Sdd.* 147. |
| *bali-vaṇḍa* | *bali-vṛnda* (*-vaṇḍa=vat*). *Nc.* 1.6.14, 8.3.2. |
| *baṁhaṇa* | *brāhmaṇa* Ins. Pl. *-ehĩ. DKs.* 1. |
| *baṁhiṇa* | *barhiṇa Mt.* 24 (Voc. Sg. -zero). |
| √*baha* | 1.√*badh* 'to bind'. Abs. *-eppiṇu Hv.* 92.19.3.<br>2.√*vah-* Pres. Part. *-anta.* Ins. Sg. *-eṇa DKK.* 17. |
| *bahiṇi* | *bhaginī KP.*S. 64.9. Loc. Sg. *-hi Sdd.* 42. (Gen. Sg. ?) Voc. *-e KKc.* 2.1.13. (M. *bahīṇ*, Guj. *behen*, Initial aspirate in Sk. conserved in others). |
| *bahiṇullī* | *bhaginī+ullī* (pleonastic) *Jc.* 1.15.4. |
| *bahiranta* | *=badhīrayantāḥ Sn.* 16-570 (Nom. Pl. -zero). |
| *bahu* | (*ts.*) Neut. Acc. Pl. zero *Jdc.* 7.3.<br>°*ya=bahuka*, Masc. Acc. Pl. zero Sdd. 85. |
| *bahutta* | *bahu* 'abundant' *Jdc.* 37.1. 46.4. |
| *bāca* | *vācā* Fem. Ins. Sg. *-ẽ DKs.* 35. |
| *-bādha* | *-bādhya.* Neut. Nom. Sg. *-ā DKs.* 90. |
| *bārasa* | *dvādśa Kp.*S. 55.1. cf. M. *bārasẽ* °*sa.* |
| *bāraha* | *dvādśa. Kp.*A. 1.3, *Pd.* 211, *Sdd.* 59.<br>°*ma MP.* 2.12.<br>(Pa. *dvādasa*, As. *duvāda(ḍa)sa*, Pk. *duvālasa bārasa.* M. *bārā* Guj. *bār*, H. *bārah*). |
| *Bārāvaïpura* | *Dvārāvatī-pura Hv.* 83.12.1 |

| | |
|---|---|
| *bāla* | *bālā*. *KKc*. 1.15.4. Gen. Sg. *-he Hc*. 350. 376.3. *Mk*. 17.14. Ins. Pl. *-hiṁ KKc*. 1.3.8. |
| *bāvīsa* | *dvāviṁśat*. *Jc*. p. 146. *Kp*.S. 97.1. *Sn*. 7-440. °*ma*=*dvāviṁśatitama Nc*. 6.5.11. (Pa. *dvāvīsa*(*ti*), Pk. *bāvīsa*, M. Guj. *bāvīs*, H. *bāīs*, Nep. *bāis*). |
| *bāsa* | *vāsa* Masc. Nom. Sg. *-e DKK*. 8. |
| *bāsia* | **vāsita DKs*. 78. |
| *bāhiṁ* | adv. *bahiḥ Kp*.S. 44.8. |
| *bāhira* | *bahiḥ DKs*. 64,82, *Nc*. 3.2.6, °*u Sdd*. 57. °*ri Kp*.K. 2.3, *Mp*. 16.3.3, *Pd*. 61. with *-ita* (term. of Loc. Sg.) *DKK*.2. (Pa. Pk. *bāhira*, M. Guj. *bāher*, H. *bāhīr*, Panj. H. *bāhar*, Beng. *bāhīr*). |
| *bāhuḍi* | *bahih KKc*. 1.12.10. |
| *bāhera* | *bahiḥ DKK*. 2 (See *bāhira* above). |
| *biappa* | *vikalpa* Nom. Sg. *-u DKs*. 92, Acc. Sg. zero *DKs*. 102. Nom. Pl. zero *DKK*. 30. |
| *biijjaya* | *dvitīya Kp*. S. 4.1. |
| *bikhaṇḍia* | *vikhaṇḍita*. Neut. Nom. Pl. zero *DKs*. 70. |
| *Biṭṭhu* | *Viṣṇu* Nom. Sg. zero *DKs*. 52. |
| *bidia* | *dvitīya Sdd*. 17. |
| *biphāria* | *visphārita*. Neut. Nom. Sg. *-ā DKK*. 17. |
| *biṁala-maï* | *vimala-mati* Masc. Nom. Sg. zero *DKs*. 71. |
| *biyaa* | *dvitīya*. Masc. Nom. Sg. *-u Sdd*. 11. |
| *birala* | *virala*. Masc. Nom. Sg. *-ā DKs*. 97. |
| *bisa*(*ya*) | *viṣaya* Masc. Ins. Pl. *-hi DKs*. 66 (Sing. according to SHAHIDULLA). |
| *bisaya* | *viṣaya* Masc. Nom. Pl. *-ā DKK*. 23. °*yā-satti*=°*ya-śakti* Fem. Loc. Sg. zero *DKs*. 73. |
| *bisaria* | *vismṛta*. Masc. Nom. Sg. *-ü DKs*. 92. |
| *bisarisa* | *visadṛśa*. *DKs*. 86, 88. |
| *bisuddha* | *viśuddha* Neut. Nom. Sg. *-o DKs* 36 |

*bīaya* — =*dvitīya Kp*.S. 70.8.

*bīyaa* — =*dvitīya* Neut. Nom. Sg. -*u Nc*. 1 5.8. *Sdd*. 11.

*bīra* — *vīra DKK*. 6.

*bīrahia* — *virahita DKs*. 104.

√*biha* — √*bhi*- Pres. 1 Sg. -*emi Mt*. 9. Imp. 2 Sg. -*su Jc*. 1.15.5. Pass. Pres. 3 Sg. -*iyaï Jdc*. 27.3.

√*bujjha*- — *budh-ya*- Pres. 2 Sg. -*si DKs*. 62. 3 Sg. -*i DKs*. 36, 65. *Pd*. 127. 3 Pl. -*hi PPr*. 2.212. Imp. 2 Sg. -*u DKs*. 53, 63. -*hu Pd*. 40. 3 Sg. -*u Pd*. 40. Pres. Part. -*anta Pd*. 125, PP. -*ia DKK*. 21, 30, -*iya Pd*. 22, 40. Abs. -*ivi Sdd*. 78. (M. Sdh. H, Beng. Or. √*bujh*- Guj. √*buj*-, Panj. √*bujjh*).

*buḍḍa* — =1 √*masj*- Pres. 3 Sg. -*i Sdd*. 161, PP. *buḍḍa*=*naṣṭa Jdu*. 62.2. cf. M. *buḍṇē*.
2. √*bruḍ*- Neut. Pres. Part. acc. Sg. -*anta*- *u Sn*. 236-270. (Cf. M. Guj. Sdh. Beng. √*buḍ*-, H. √*būḍ*-)

*buddhi* — (*ts*.) Fem. Acc. Sg. zero *DKK*. 9. Ins. Sg. -*e MK*. 17.26, Nc. 1.4.2.

√*bubbuya*- — 'to bleat, to cry', Pres. 2 Sg. -*hi Kp*.E. 26.

*būḍhaü* — *vṛddha-kaḥ KKc*. 9.5,4. *PPr*. 1.91. (H. *būḍhā*, M. *buḍḍhā*.)

*be* — *dve* (Always in Pl.) Masc. Direct *be Hc*. 4.379, *PPr*. 1.12.1 *beṇṇi Jc*. 2.22.5, *beṇṇa DKK* 5. Neut. direct *beṇṇi DKs*. 17. *biṇṇi Jc*. 4.4.3, *biṇṇa*- *DKs*.56. Ins. *behiṁ Hc*. 4.119, *bihiṁ Jc*. 4.3.11, 4.4.2, *MP*. 2.4.7. *Sdd*. 74.

*Bea* — *Veda DKK*. 2.
°*purāṇa*. Neut. direct Pl. zero *DKK*. 30.

*beaṇa* — *vedanā* Fem. Acc. Sg. -*u DKs*. 77.

*beṭṭā* — =*putraḥ Jdu*. 63.1. Fem. -*ī* (i.e. *beṭṭī*) *Jdu*. 63.1.

*beṇima* — *dvidhā DKs*. 51.

*bojjhu* — =*buddhyasva DKs*. 53.

*boḍḍia* — *boḍḍikā* 'a cowrie' Fem. Acc. Sg. zero *Hc*. 335.

*bori* — *badarī* Fem. Ins. Pl. -*hiṁ Sdd*. 110. (Pk. *bora*, *borī*. M. Guj. *bor*, H. *ber*, Sdh. *beru*, Beng. bair)

√*bola* 'to go' Pres. Part. Loc. Sg. *-anta-i Mt.* 18.

√*bolla-* 'to speak', Imp. 2 Sg. *-i Sdd.* 88.
(Pk. *bolla-*, M. Guj. Sdh. Panj. H. Beng.√*bol*).

*bohi* *bodhi, DKs.* 105. Fem. direct Sg. zero *DKK.* 29, *Pd.*8.

*bohi-cia* *bodhi-citta* Masc. Nom. Sg. zero *DKK.*3.

√*bro-di* =*bruvati Mt.* 18.10.

*bh*

*bhaabā* *bhagavān DKs.* 3. cf. AMg. *bhagavam.*

*bhaïya* =*bhaya* Ins. Sg. *-e Hv.* 81.14.5.

*bhauhā* =*bhṛkuṭi* Fem. Ins. Pl. *-hiṁ Jc.* 1.17.13.

*bhaũhā* =*bhrū MP.* 1.3.13. (Pa. *bhamuka*, Pk. *bhumaā*, *bhamuhā*, M. *bhavãī*, Guj. *bhavũ*, H. *bhaũ*, Panj. *bhaũh*, Beng. *bhomā*).

*bhagga* *bhagna.* Neut. direct Sg. *-ẽ Pd.* 104, Masc. direct Pl. *-iṁ Hc.* 386.

*bhagga-māṇa* =**bhagna-māna* 'running away.'
Masc. direct Sg. *-u KKc.* 1.13.1.
(Guj. H. Beng. Assam.√*bhāg-* 'to run away').

*bhaṁga* (*ts.*) Masc. Nom. Sg. *-e DKK.* 27.

*bhaṁgāla* *bhṛṅga-āla* (poss. suff.) *Jc.* 1.3.6.

√*bhaja-* √*bhañj-* Fut. 3 Pl. *-esahiṁ Pd.* 83.

*bhajja* *bhāryā.* Fem. Ins. Sg. *-ĕ DKs.* 21. (Pk. *bhajjā*, M. *bhājā*).

*bhaṭhṭhī* *bhraṣṭā DKs.* 87.

*bhaḍāra(ya)* *bhaṭṭāraka BhK.* 352.7, Voc. Sg. *-ā MP.* 2.4.3.

*bhaḍāriya* *bhaṭṭārikā*<*bhartārikā BhK.* 95.2. Fem. Voc. Sg. *-e KKc.* 1.11.10.

*bhaḍārī* *bhaṭṭārikā Jc.* 3.34.4.

√*bhaṇa-* √*bhaṇ-* Pres. 1 Sg. *-mi PPr.* 1.30, 1 Pl. *-huṁ MK.* 17.58, 3 Pl. *-anti. PPr.* 1.30. Imp. 2 Sg. *-i Sn.* 16-441. *-u Sdd.* 55. *ehi* Pd. 25. Pres. Part. Gen. Sg. *-anta-hŏ Mt.* 2. Inf. *-(a)ï DKs.* 60, Abs. *-i Sn.* 271-190.

*bhattāra* **bhartāra.* Acc. Sg. *-ha DKs.* 82.

*bhatti* — *bhakti* Fem. Acc. Sg. zero *DKs.* 59, Ins. Sg. -*e* *PPr.* 2.61 (also 1.6), -*ṇa* *Sc.* 489.1.

*bhanti* — *bhrānti* Fem. Nom. Sg. zero *Jc.* 3.26.2. Ins. Sg. -*a* *DKs.* 78. -*e* *BhK.* 76.1. *Jc.* 3.26.2. *PPr.* 2.177.

*bhappara* — *bhasman* *Jc.* 1.13.8.

*bhaba* — *bhava.* Acc. Sg. zero *DKK.* 22.

*bhaba-mudda* — *bhava-mudrā.* Fem. Ins. Sg. -*ẽ* *DKs.* 24.

√*bhama-* — √*bhram-*
Pres. 3 Sg. -*i* *DKs.* 50, 65, *Mt.* 15. -*ei* *Pd.* 16. Imp. 2 Sg. -*hu* *DKs.* 57. Fut. 2 Sg. -*ihĩsi* *Jc.* 3.32.6. Pres. Part. -*anta* *Mt.* 22, 24, 33. Gen. Pl. -*ahaṁ.* *KKc.* 9.8.1. -*ira* (to show habit) *Kp.* J. 2.7. Inf. -*aï* *DḲs.* 50.

*bhamara* — *bhramara.* Nom. Sg. -*ū* *DKs.* 73, -*u* *Hc.* 368.

*bharaha* — **bharatha*=*bhṛta*=*ācchādita* *Jc.* 1.3.3.

*Bharahesara* — **Bharatheśvara* *KKc.* 4.4.10.

*bhalla* — **bhad-la.* Neut. direct Sg. -*uṁ* *Jc.* 3.38.6. Loc. Sg. -*i* *Jc.* 1.24.2 Masc. Nom. Pl. -*ā* *Sdd.* 65.

*bhallattaṇa*, °*ppaṇa* — =**bhad-la-tva* (Abs. noun). Neut. direct Sg. -*u* *Kc.* 76.

*bhallima* — **bhad-la-ima* (=*tva* Abs. Noun). *Kp.* E. 17.

*bhallūa* — *bhallūka.* Ins. Pl. -*ehiṁ* *KKc.* 1.17.6.

*bhava* — (*ts.*) Loc. Pl. -*hiṁ* *Sdd.* 74.

*bhava-jalahi* — °*jaladhi.* Masc. Acc. Sg. zero *Sdd.* 85.

*bhava-nivvāṇa* — °*nirvāṇa.* Neut. Nom. Pl. -*ā* *DKs.* 43.

*bhava-sindhu* — (*ts.*) Masc. Nom. Sg. zero *Sdd.* 108.

*bhavaru* — *Bhramaraḥ* *Hc.* 4.397.

*bhaviya* — *bhavya*-*Jdc.* 8.2. *Sdd.* 33.

*bhaviya-sāra* — *bhavya*-Acc. Pl. zero *KKc.* 1.1.4.

*bhāi* — *bhrātṛ* Gen. Pl. -*hũ* *BhK.* 185.7.

*bhāiya* — 1. *bhrātṛka* *KKc.* 4.3.10.
2. *bhāvita* *Sdd.* 213.

| | |
|---|---|
| *hābābhābā* | *bhāvābhāva* Masc. Nom. Pl. zero *DKs.* 22.. Loc. Pl. -*ē* *DKs.* 61. |
| *bhāya* | *bhrātṛ* *KKc.* 3.5.2. Nom. Pl. zero *KKc.* 5.4.1. |
| *bhāyaṇi* | *bhājinī* Gen. Sg. -*hẽⁿ* *BhK.* 27.12. |
| -*bhārayā* | -*bhārakāḥ* *MP.* 87.9.1. |
| *Bhārahī* | **Bhārathī* *MP.* 1.10. |
| -*bhāriya* | *bhāryā.* Fem. Gen. Pl. -*hā* *Sc.* 462.1. |
| *bhāva-mi* | —*bhrāmyāmi* *Mt.* 34. |
| *bhāviṇi* | *bhāminī* *MP.* 2.1.2. |
| *bhikkha* | *bhikṣā* Fem. Acc. Sg. zero *Pd.* 186, *Ys.* 43. |
| *bhikkhu* | *bhikṣu.* Nom. Sg. zero *DKs.* 10. |
| *bhicca* | *bhṛtya* *PPr.* 1.89. |
| *bhiṇṇa* | *bhinna* Neut. Nom. Sg. -*ā* *DKs.* 85. |
| *bhitti* | (*ts.*) Gen. Sg. -*e* *BhK.* 76.1 Loc. Sg. -*hi* *BhK.* 74.7 cf. coll. M. *bhīt.* |
| *bhintara* | *abhyantara* *Pa.* 154 cf. M. *bhītarī* (°*r*). |
| *bhisa* | *bisa* *Nc.* 2.11.12. contrast *Hc.* 1.238. and *Vararuci* 2.38. *Sdd.* 34. |
| *bhīsiya* | *bṛsikā*=*ṛṣiṇāmāsanaṁ* Gloss. *Hv.* 83-18-4. |
| *bhītaru* | *abhyantaram* *Kc.* 15. (M. Guj. Beng. *bhitar*, Or. *bhitara*, H. *bhītar*). |
| *bhīsa* | *bhīṣma* *Hv.* 84.5.3. Neut. direct Pl. *āiṁ* *Jc.* 1.16.9. |
| √*bhukka* | 'to bark.' Imp. 3 Sg. -*u* *MP.* 1.8.7. cf. *Hc.* 4.186. (M. Guj. H. √*bhuk.*, Sdh. *bhaũkaṇu*) |
| *bhukkhā* | *bubhukṣā* *KKc.* 2.16.5. *Nc.* 1.11.10. (Pk. *bubhukkhā.* M. *bhūk*, H. Guj. *bhūkh*, Nep. *bhok*) |
| *bhugga* | *bhugna*=*bhukta* *Kp.* J. 69.3. |
| √*bhuṁja*- | *bhuñj*- Pres. Part. Gen. Pl. -*anta-hā* *Sc.* 452.2. Abs. -*ivi* *Sn.* 22-287. Caus. Abs. -*ivi* *Sdd.* 59. |
| *bhubaṇa* | *bhuvana* Loc. Sg. -*ẽ* *DKs.* 91. |
| √*bhumaya* | =√*bhram* Pres. 3 Pl. -*anti* *DKK.* 2. |

*bhulla* =*bhraṣṭa Nc*. 9.19.2. *Pd*. 17. cf. *Hc*. 4.177.
Neut. Nom. Sg. -*ẽ DKs*. 3. (Pk. *bhullaï*<**bhulyati* cf. *bhurāti*. M. *bhulaviṇẽ*, Guj. *bhulāvvũ*. H. *bhulānā* Nep. *bhulnu*, *bhulāunu*).

*bhullallio* =*bhrāntimān Mt*. 16.

*bhūta* (*ts*.) Neut. direct Pl. -*ā DKK* 7.

*bhūmi* (*ts*.) Direct Sg. zero *Jc*. 2.4.1. Loc. Sg. -*hi MP*. 2.21.5. -*hiṁ KKc*. 4.2.6.
Nom. Pl. -*u Jc*. 2.4.9.

*bhūva* *bhūta* Abl. Pl. -*hiṁ Pd*. 104.

*bhea* *bheda* Masc. Acc. Sg. -*u Pd*. 1.

*bho* Interjection (*ts*.) *Kp*. J. 64.4.

*bhoga* (*ts*.) Gen. Pl. -*haṁ* (used locatively). *Sdd*. 5.

*bhoṁa* *bhauma*. Neut. direct pl. -*aiṁ Jc*. 3.26.17.

*bhoya* *bhoga* Gen. Pl. -*haṁ*. *Sdd*. 221 (used locatively).

*bhoya-dhara* *bhoga-dharā* Fem. Gen. Sg. -*haṁ Sdd*. 190.

*bholaa* *bahulaka* 'a simpleton.' Masc. Nom. Sg. -*u Jdc*. 39.4. *MP*. 2.20.7. cf. M. *bhoḷa*.

*bholaviya* PP. from √*bholava* cf. Guj. *bhoḷavvũ*. 'to mislead, to deceive.' *Kp*. J. 85.2.

*m*

*ma* *mā Nc*. 2.4.4., *PPr*. 1.101. but *maṁ* in *PPr*. 2.107. 109 and *Ld*. 3-3.45.

*maacchi* *mṛgākṣī Mt*.

*Maaṇa* *Madana* Nom. Sg. -*i*, -*o MK*. 17.12.

*maaranda* *makaranda* Acc. Sg. -*ẽ DKK* 6.

*maïla* 1. **mradilla* 'dirty' *Jc*. 3.19.12,.Fem. Nom. Pl. -(*ā*)*u Jc*. 3.27.3.
2. 'to become dirty.' Pres. 3 Sg. -*ei Sdd*. 36 PP. -*iya Jc*. 4.2.19.

*magga* 1. *mārga* Loc. Pl. -*ehiṁ Hc*. 4.347.
2. √*mārgay*- Imp. 2 P. Sg. -*e* Intro to *Hv* § 56.
Pres. Part. -*anta*. *Nc*. 4.4.3. PP. -*iya Nc*. 3.16.13.

*magha* *makha* Nom. Sg. *-u* *MK*. 17.2.

*-majjha* *madhya* Loc. Sg *-ĕ* *DKK*. 11. *-mi* *Pd*. 23.

*majjhima* *madhyama* *Kp*. J. 10.1.

*maṁchu-ḍu* *maṅkṣu* *Hv*. 92. 13.3.

*manjari* °*rī* Fem. Loc. Sg. *-hiṁ* *Pd*. 152.

*maṁjūsa* °*ṣā* Fem. Loc. Sg. *-iṁ* *KKc*. 1.6.10.

*maṭṭī* *mṛttikā* Fem. Acc. Sg. zero *DKs*. 2.

*maḍahulla* =*laghu* (*-ulla* pleonastic) *Nc*. 3.4.12 cf. *Dn*. 6. 117 *lahummi maḍahaṁ*

*maṇa* *manas* Direct Sg. *-u* *KKc*. 1.5.8. Loc. Sg. *-e* *DKK* 15, *KKc*. 1.1.12. *-i* *KKc*. 1.2.1.

*maṇa-vaya-kāya* *manovākkāya*. Ins. Pl. *-hiṁ* *Sdd*. 60

*maṇāuṁ* *manāk* *Ld*. 3.3.47.

*maṇuyatta* *manujatva* *Kp*. S. 51 3

*maṇuyattaṇa* *manujatva*. Loc. Sg. *-i* *Sdd*. 3.

*maṇuva* *manuja* Masc. Gen. Pl. *-haṁ* *KKc*. 1.10.7.

*maṇoraha* *manoratha* Acc Pl zero *Sdd* 190

*maṇṭha* *mṛṣṭa* *Jc*. 3.1.13.

*maṇṇa-* *man-ya*. Pres. 3 Pl. *-ahiŭ* *Ys*. 56.

*-matta* (*ts*.) Masc. Gen. Pl. *-haṁ* *Hc*. 4.345.

*mattha* *masta* Ins. Sg. *-eṁ* *Mt*. 4.

*manta* *mantra*. Masc. Gen. Pl. *-āṇu* *KKc*. .1.1.5.

*mantaṇa* *mantraṇā* Fem. Ins. Sg. *-i* *MP*. 87.5.11.

*manti* *mantrin* Masc. direct Sg. zero *KKc*. 8.1.10. Gen. Sg. *-he* *KKc*. 8.1.11. Ins. Pl. *-hiṁ* *KKc*. 3.1.1. *MP*. 87.5.10.

*mantitta* *mantritva* *Kp*. S. 49.3.

*mandira* (*ts*.) Abl. Sg. *-āsu* *BhK*. 342.7.

*maya* *mṛga*. Nom. Pl. zero *PPr*. 1.112.

*mayaga* *mṛtaka* 'N. of a song.' *Kp*. S. 63.5.

*mayāsi* *amṛtāśī* 'a god' *MP*. 14.1.4.

√*mara-* √*mṛ-* Imp. 2 Sg. -*ehu* *KKc*. 1.13.3.
*maragaa* *marakata*. Nom. Sg. -*u* *PPr*. 2.78.

*maraṇa* (*ts*.) Gen. Sg. -(*ā*)*haṁ* *Sdd*. 156.

*marutthali* °*sthali* Loc. Sg. -*hī* *DKs*. 58.

*mahaevi* *mahādevī* Fem. Gen. Sg. -*e* *Jc*. 2.3.5.

*mahalla* *mahat* (-*alla* pleonastic) *Kp*. J. 4.3. cf. *Dn*. 6.143.

*mahāṇara* °*nara*. Gen. Sg. -*āsu* *BhK*. 345.2.

*mahābhūta* (*ts*.) Neut. direct Pl. -*ā* *DKK*. 7·

*mahāraa*(*ya*) -*madīya* (suff. -*kārya*.) *Jc*. 3.9.9. *Kp*. 45.9. *Nc*. 5.3.13. cf. *Hc*. 4.434. (H. *hamāra*, Marw. *mhārā* ?

*mahā-lacchi* °*lakṣmī* Fem. Loc. Sg. -*hī* *Mt*. 7.

*mahā-saī* °*satī* Fem. Ins. Sg. -*eṁ* *KKc*. 6.11.1.

*mahi* (*ts*.) Acc. Sg. zero *BhK*. 79.7. Gen. Sg. -*hi* *Sc*. 485.2. Loc. Sg. -*hi* *Hc*. 352. -*hī* *Sc*. 469.1. Loc. Pl. -*su* *Jc*. 1.1.7.

*mahila* °*lā* Fem. Gen. Sg. -*hi* *MP* 87.4.2. Gen. Pl. -*haṁ*. -*hā* *BhK*. 53.10, *Sn*. 108.115. -*āṇa* (Pkt.) *Pd* 157.

*mahu* (*ts*.) Direct Sg. zero *Mt*. 26. *Sdd*. 77. Acc. Sg. -*ṁ* *MP*. 100.4.10.

*mahūsava* *mahotsava* *Kp*. S. 9.1.

*mahalia* *mahelikā*=*mahilā* Fem. Gen. Sg. -*hu* *DS*. 4.32.1.

*mahovahi* *mahodadhi* *KKc*. 1.1.4.

*māi* *mātṛ* *DKs*. 86. Voc. Sg. zero *Jc*. 2.13.15. 4.4.9. also *māe* *Hv*. 89.12.14. (M. Guj. Marw. Sdh. H. *māī*. Beng. *mā*.)

*māuya* *mātṛka* *Hv*. 91.22.11.
(H. Panj. *māū*. Sdh. *māu*, Singh. *mav*. *mā*.)

*māucchiyā* *mātṛ-ṣvasṛkā*. Fem. Ins. Pl. -*hiṁ* *Jc*. 3.9.9.
(Pk. *māussiā*, *māucchā*. - M. *māvśī*, Guj. Panj. Beng. Sdh. *māsī* H. *mausī*. *māsī*.)

*māṇa* 1. *māna* Masc. Acc. Sg. zero *DKK*. 2.
2. Vb. √*mānay* Imp. 2 Pl. -*ha* *DKK*. 9. Abs. -*ivi* *MP*. 2.20.13.

| | |
|---|---|
| *māṇusa* | *mānuṣa*. Nom. Sg. *-u Kc*. 21. Gen. Sg. *-ha Sdd*. 54. |
| *māya* | *mātṛ KKc*. 3.9.1. Nom. Sg. zero *KP*. A. 3.1. Gen. Sg. *-haṁ Hc*. 399. |
| *māyaṇhiya* | *mṛga-tṛṣṇikā MP* 20.20.7. |
| *māyari* | *mātṛ* Acc. Sg. zero *MP*. 87.14.7. |
| √*māra-* | *māray-* Imp. 3 Sg. *-u Sn*. 308.169. Pot. Part. *-eva Jc*. 1.11.7., *Nc*. 3.15.4. cf. *Hc*. 4.438. |
| *mālaï* | *malatī* Fem. Gen. Sg. *-hı Sc*. 483.2. |
| *-māli* | *mōlın* Gen. Sg. *-hı KKc*. 1.14.4. |
| *māha* | *māgha* Loc. Sg. *-hĩ Mt*. 17. |
| *mi* | *=api Hv*. 81.4.5., *Pd*. 26.55. |
| *Mıkaṇḍa* | *Mṛkaṇḍā Hv*. 81.16.9. |
| *mıccha* | **mıthya* 'a heretic.' Ins. Pl. *-ehĩ DKs*. 3. |
| *mıcchatta* | *mıthyātva Sdd*. 136. |
| *mıcchattıya* | *mıthyātvika=°tvin Pd*. 20. |
| √*milla* | =√*muc*. Imp. 2 Sg. *-hī Sdd*. 133. Abs. *-i DKK*. 27. *-ivı Pd*. 29. |
| *mua-* | √*muc-* Imp. 2 Sg. *-e Hv*. (Intro § 56.) Abs. *-eppiṇu PPr*. 2.47. *-ēviṇu PPr*. 2.9. |
| *mua* | *mṛta KKc*. 3.21.3. |
| *muiya* | *mṛtā KKc*. 10.20.10. |
| *mukka* | *mukta*. Gen. Pl. *-(ā)haũ PPr*. 1.47. *-(ā)haṁ Sdd*. 18. |
| *mukkha* | *mokṣa Kp*. J. 85.2. |
| √*muca-* | √*muc-* Pres. 3 Sg. *-anti Ys*. 63. |
| *mucca-* | *muc-ya* Imp. 2 Pl. *-hu Jdu* 1.2. |
| *mucchā* | *mūrcchā*. Fem. Ins. Sg. *-iṁ KKc*. 6.15.4. |
| *muṭṭhi* | *muṣṭi* Loc. Sg. *-hi BhK*. 78.7. |
| √*muṇa-* | √*man-* but usually equated with *jñā-* cf. *Hc* 4.7. Pres 1 Sg. *-āmi Kp*. E. 27, 2 Sg. *-ahi Kp*. J. 6. 4. *-esi*. *Kp*. S. 96.9.3 Sg. *-i DKs*. 89, *Kp*. S. 44.3. *Mt*. 17, *PPr*. 1.64. 1 Pl. *-(a)hũ BhK*. 55.8. *Kp*. J. 46.8. Imp. 2 Sg. *-ha DKs*. |

34. -(*a*)*hi PPr* 1.15, *Ys*. 15. -(*ĕ*)*hi Kp*. S. 80.4. -*hu DKs*. 34. -(*a*)*su Kp*. A. 13. 2. 2Pl. -*hu Ys*. 21. Pres. Part. -*antu PPr*. 1.76, 2.35 PP. -*iya* -*ia DKs*. 80. *Kp*. S. 43.1.* Inf. -(*a*)*hu PPr*. 1.23. Abs. -*i DKs*. 41, -*ia DKs*. 80. -*ivi Kp*. S. 39.8 Pass. Pres. 3 Sg. -*īa-i DKs*. 73. Pres. Part. -*ijja-māṇu Kp*. J. 75.3.

*muṇāla* — *mṛṇāla DKK*. 5, *KKc*. 7.2.8.

*muṇi* — *muni* Masc. Sing. Nom. zero *Pd*. 60. Acc. zero. *KKc*. 7.1.4. Dat. Gen.-*hi* Sdd. 93. Plur. Ins. -*hiṁ MP*. 100.1.12 Gen -*haṁ Hc*. 414.3.

√*muṇḍa* — √*muṇḍ*- pp. -*ī* 5. Caus. Abs. -*āivi Pd*. 125.

*mutta* — *mūtra*. Gen. Sg. -*haṁ Pd*. 196.

*mutti* — *mukti* Fem. Nom. Sg. zero *DKs*. 7.

*mudda* — *mudrā* Fem. Nom. Sg. zero *PPr*. 1.22. Acc. Sg. -*ṁ Mt*. 5

*muddha* — *mugdhā* Ins. Sg. -*ı MP*. 87.12.11. Gen. Sg. -*he Hc*. 357.3. Voc. Sg. -*e Mt*. 5. -*i Hc*. 376.

*Mura-riu* — °*ripu* Masc. Gen. Sg. -*hũ* Sc. 451.1.

*murukkha* — *mūrkha Kp*. S. 57.2 cf. *Hc*. 2.112.

*muha* — *mukha* Nom. Sg. -*ū DS*. 4.52. Abl. Pl. -*hṽ Hc*. 22.204

*mūḍha* — (*ts*.) Nom. Sg. -*o Pd*. 85. (Pkt. sm.) Voc. Sg. -*ā Pd*. 13, Gen. Pl. -*haũ Ys*. 29.

*mūla-guṇa* — (*ts*.) Nom. Pl. zero *Ys*. 29.

*mṛga* — (*ts*.) *MP*. 2.14.4.
°*jūdhu* < °*yūthaṁ MK*. 17.4.

*Mṛgāyaṇa* — 'N. of a sage.' *Hv*. 82.8.10.

*meiṇı* — *medinī*. Fem. Acc. Sg. zero *KKc*. 2.8.3.

*memmāyanta* — 'bleating' (Pres. Part. in -*anta*) *Jc*. 3.11.5. Onomatopoeic.

√*melava*- — Caus. of √*mil*- Pres. 3 Pl. -*ahiṁ MP*. 2.6.11. (M. *milṇẽ*, H. *milnā*, Nep. *milnu*.)

√*mella*- — √*muc*- Pres. 3 Sg. -*i Hv*. 83.2.6. *Mt*. 34. Imp. 2 Sg. -*hi Hv*. 84.15.2. *PPr*. 1.12, -*i Hv*. 85.9.33. 3 Sg. -*u Hv*. 85.6.5.. 2Pl. -*ha DKs*. 47, *Hv*. 87.5.16. Fut. 3 Sg. -*esaï Hv*. 87.16.6.

Pres. Part. Fem. Gen. Sg. *-anti-he Hc.* 370. Abs. *-evi Hv.* 81.9.7. *-ivi PPr.* 1.92. *-eppiṇu Hv.* 88.12.5. Caus. PP. *-āviu. Hv.* 85.6.12. *-āviya* (direct Pl. zero) *Jc.* 1.11.5.

*mokaliya* =*mukta* Neut. direct Pl. *-iṁ Sdd.* 66.

*mokkala* =*-mukta* Neut. Nom. Pl. *-ā Sdd.* 128.

*mokkalliu* *-mukta MP.* 1.9.18.

*mokkha* *mokṣa Sdd.* 74. Nom. Sg. zero *Ys.* 29. Gen. Sg. *-ha Pd.* 62 *-haü Ys.* 33.

√*moḍe-* *moṭay-* Pres. 3 Pl. *-anti Nc.* 5.5.5. (Pk. *moḍei*, M. *moḍṇẽ*, Guj. *moḍvũ*, H. *moṛnā*, Nep. *moṛnu.*)

*mora* *mayūra*. Masc. Nom. Sg. *-u Mt.* 3. Voc. Sg. *-ā Mt.* 35. (M. Guj. Panj. H. *mor*. Sdh. *moru*.)

√*moha-* 'to deceive.' Abs. *-eviṇu KKc.* 1.3.8.

*moha-mahoyahi* °*mahodadhi*. Masc. Acc. Sg. zero *Sn.* 334-127.

*mhi* *asmi Kp.* S. 106.5.

*y*

*ycala-i* *calati* (Pres. 3 Sg. *-i*) *MK.* 18.2.
*yjala-i* *jvalati* (Pres. 3 Sg. *-i*) *MK.* 18.2.

*r*

*rai* *rati*. Fem. Direct Sg. zero *PPr.* 2.43, *Pd.* 13. *-ī* (elongation of final vowel) *Nc.* 6.5.8. Gen. Sg. *-hi Sc.* 491.1. -zero *BhK.* 21.4. (Is '*rai*' in that line ; *rai saṁgami avagaṇṇaī*, the 1st member of Gen. Tat. comp.?)

*Raïveya* *Ratívegā*. Fem. Gen. Sg. *-he KKc.* 7.14.1. *-heṁ KKc.* 7.7.5.

*rakkha* *rakṣā Sc.* 466.9.

√*rakkha-* √*rakṣ-*
Imp. 2 Sg. *-i Sn.* 77-176. *-hu Sdd.* 195. *-ejja-hu Hc.* 350.2, 2 Pl. *-ejja-hu BhK.* 226.7, Inf. *-huṁ KKc.* 5.18.2. Pass. Pres. 3 Sg. *-ijjai Sdd.* 98. (Pa *rakkhati*, Pk. *rakkhaï* M. *rākhṇẽ*, Guj. *rākhvũ*, H. *rākhnā*, Nep. *rākhnu.*)

*rakkhavāla* *rakṣāpāla KKc.* 1.15.3. cf. M. *rakhavāl-dār*, *rakhavalī*.

*rakkhasi* *rākṣasī KKc.* 2.11.1. Ins. Sg. *-ē BhK.* 22.3.

*raṁkholira* =*vilasana-śila* (Suff. *-ira*) *MP.* 3.2.1.

*raḍḍa* — PP. of √*raḍa*<√*raṭ* 'to cry.' *Kp.* S. 79.3. (Pa. *raṭati*, Pk. *raḍaï*, M. Guj. √*raḍ-*, Sdh. *raṛaṇu*)

√*raṇa-* — √*raṇ-* Pres. 3 Sg. *-etti* (?) *Ds.* 4.5.1.

*raṇa-gaya* — °*gata*. Loc. Pl. *-hiṁ Hc.* 370.

*raṇṇa* — *araṇya Nc.* 6.16.19. cf. *Hc.* 1.66. Ins. Sg. *-ẽ Mt.* 34. Loc. Sg. *-e Mt.* 24, 35. (Pa. *araññaṁ*, Pk. *araṇṇa*, M. Guj. *rān*, H. *rān* (Masc.), Singh. *riṇa*.)

*Radi* — *Rati* Ins. Sg. *-e Hc.* 446.

*rabi-śaśī* — =*ravi-śaśinau* (Nom. Pl. zero). *DKK.* 5.

*ramaṇi* — *ramaṇī* Ins. Pl. *-hiṁ Sn.* 77.176. °*yaā* Direct Pl. *-(ā)v KKc.* 3.2.1.

*ramanti-ya* — *ramantī* Fem. Nom. Pl. *-u KKc.* 3.9.10.

*raya* — *rajas*. Gen. Pl. *-haṁ Sdd.* 183.

*rayaṇa* — *ratna*. Direct Pl. *-āiṁ Hc.* 334.

*rayaṇattaya* — *ratnatraya*. Gen. Sg. *-hao PPr.* 2.95.

*rayaṇi* — 1. (*a*)*ratni* 'a hand.' *MP.* 2.7.5.
2. *rajanī* Fem. Loc. Sg. *-hi Jc.* 2.21.7. *MP.* 87.11.12. *-him*, *-hĩ BhK.* 21.4., *Jc.* 2.12.11 *Sc.* 445.1.

*rayaṇi-vahu* — *rajanī-vadhū* Gen. Sg. *-hi Jc.* 2.2.10.

*-rayā* — *-ratā*. Fem. Gen. Sg. *-hi MP.* 87.4.2.

*ravi-sasi* — °*śaśi* Masc. Ins. Pl. *-hiṁ Pd.* 219.

*rasa* — (*ts.*) Loc. Sg. *-ẽ DKK.* 19. Loc. Pl. *-(a)hiṁ Pd.* 132.

*rasanta* — Pres. Part. of √*ras-* (*-anta*) *Sn.* 217-186.

*rasaṇa* — *rasāyana DKs.* 53.

*raha* — 1. *ratha*. Nom. Pl. zero *MP.* 83.3.15.
2. √*rakṣ-* Pres. 2 Sg. *-hi Nc.* 6.1.5. 3 Pl. *-anti*. *Nc.* 1.5.9. *Sdd.* 138 PP. *-iya*+Masc. Nom. Sg. *-ĕ DKs.* 60 Pass. Pres. 3 Sg. *-ijja-i Nc.* 6.4.7. (M. Guj. Sdh. Panj. H. √*rah-* Beng. *rahite*).

*rahaṭṭa* — *araghaṭṭa MP.* 27.1.4. (M. *rahāṭ*, H. *rahaṭ*, Panj. *raṭṭa*)

*rāu* — *rājan MK.* 17.10. (Pa. *rājā* Pk. *rāyā* M. *rāo*, *rāy*, Guj. *rāy rāv*. Sdh. Panj. *rāu*, H. *rāo*.)

*rāṇaa(-ya)* =**ṛāñja-ka* 'a king.' *Hv*. 81.17.14. Nom. Sg. -*u* *Jc*. 4.2.10.

*rānī* *rājñī* *Hv*. 85.15.4. *Jc*. 2.31.7. -*i* before terms. and suff. e.g., °*ya* *Hv*. 82.5.5. (with -*he* of Gen. Sg. (Pa. *raṇṇī*, Pk. *raṇṇī* *rāṇiā* M. Guj. Sdh. Panj, H. *rāṇī*, Nep. Or. *rāṇi*.)

*Rāma* 1. (*ts*.) Gen. Sg. -*hu* *MP*. 69.2.3. Gen. Pl. -*hu* *MP*. 69.2.11. -*haṁ* *Hc*. 407.
2. *rāmā* 'a beautiful woman.' Loc. Sg. -*iṁ* *Pd*. 42

*Rāmaṇu* *Rāvaṇaḥ* śNom. Sg. -*u*) *Sdd*.63.

*rāya* 1. *rāga* Loc. Pl. -*hiṁ* *Pd*. 107.
2. *rājan* Gen. Sg. -*ho* *Jc*. 1.9.2. -*ha* (used for Acc.) *Sn*. 48-249. For cognates see *rāu* above.

*rāya-rosa* *rāga-roṣa* Acc. Pl. zero *Ys*. 48.

*rāyāṇī* **rājānī*- √*rājñī* *Hv*. 81.12.7. Nom. Pl. -zero *Jc*. 4.2.7.

*riu* 1. *ṛtu* *Sc*. 546.8.
2. *ripu* Gen. Pl. -*huṁ* *MP*. 87.5.18.

*riu-maddaṇa* *ripu-mardana*. Gen. Sg. -(*ā*)*su* *Jc*. 4.2.4.

*riṇa* *ṛṇa* *KKc*. 2.18.2. cf. M. *rīṇ* 'debt.'

*riṇiya* *ṛṇika* 'a debtor' *Kp*. J. 96.4.

*riddhi* *ṛddhi* *Kp*. J. 97. 1. *Sc*. 456.3. Ins. Sg. -(*i*) *e* *Sc*. 471.1. Gen. Sg. -*he* *KKc*. 1.15.1. Ins. Pl. -*hiṁ* *MP*. 100.10.1.

*riyā* **ṛcā*=*ṛc* Fem. Nom. Pl. -(*ā*)*u* *Jc*. 3.29.1.

*Risaha* *Ṛṣabha*. Ins. Sg. -*iṁ* *Jc*. 3.30.7.

*risiṁda* *ṛṣīndra* *KKc*. 6.1.9.

*rīṇa* **ṛ-ṇa* (PP. of √*ṛ*-). 'come, tired.' *Jc*. 3.19.5. *Pd*. 115.

*rukkha* **rukṣa* Masc. Nom. Sg. -*ho* *MK*. 17.11.
Acc. Sg. zero *KKc*. 1.13.7. Ins. Sg. -*eṁ* *PPr*. 2.133. Loc. Pl. -(*a*)*hiṁ* *MP*. 83.8.13. (Pa. Pk. *rukkha* H. M. Guj. *rūkh*, Panj. *rukkh*-, Nep. *rukh*.)

*rukkha-ḍa* **rukṣa-ṭa* (pleonastic). Nom. Pl. -*ā* *Sdd*. 190. °*ḍu*, °*ullu* (pleonastic) *Ld*. 3.3.29. °*du* *MK*. 17.7. In these -*u* is Nom. Sg. ending.

√*ruṭṭha* *ruṣṭa*< √*ruṣ*. Imp. 3 Sg. -*u* *Sn*. 308-169.

*uṇṇa* **rudna* cf. *Hc*. 1.209. Neut. Nom. Sg. -*ā* *Hv*. 83.7.7.

√*rundha-* *rundk-<rudh- Abs. *-eviṇu*

√*ruhacuha* Onomatopoeic for warbling of birds. Pres. 3 Pl. *-anti* *Hv.* 83.9.6.

*rūa* *rūpa* Ins. Sg. *-ĕ* *DKK.* 6.

*rūva* *rūpa* Loc. Pl. *-hiṁ* *Pd.* 101.

*rei* *rājate* *Sdd.* 174.

*roya* *roga* Acc. Pl. zero *PPr.* 1.70.

*royara* *rucikara* *MP.* 17.12.7.

*rora-ttaṇu* =*dāridrya* (*-ttaṇu* suff. of Abs. nouns.) Neut. direct Sg. in *-u.* *Jc.* 2.26.17.

√*rova-* =*rōd-< √*rud* 'to cry.' Imp. 2 Sg. *-hi* *KKc.* 2.1.13.

*rohiṇi* °*ṇī* 'A kind of fast.' Fem. Ins, Pl. *-hiṁ* *Sdd.* 188.

*l*

*laï* 'much' *Jc.* 3.10.14. cf. coll. M. *lai.*

*laüḍa* *lakuṭa.* Ins. Sg. *-i* *Jdu.* 19.4.

*laüḍi* *lakuṭa* *Hv.* 88.5.8.

*lakkaḍiya* *lakuṭa.* Gen. Sg. *-haṁ* *Sdd.* 148.

*lakkuḍa* *lakuṭa* *Hv.* 85.5.3. (Pa. *laguḷa*, M. *lākaḍ*, *lākūḍ*, Guj. *lākaḍi*, *lakaḍ*, Panj. *lakkaḍ*, H. *lakḍā*, Beng. *laguḍa*, *lagī* cf. *Dn.* *lakkuḍo lakuṭah.* The original word **lak*, **lag* is regarded as Austro-Asiatic.)

*lakkha-* 1.√*lakṣ-*. Pres. 3 Sg. *-i* *DKK.* 24, *DKs.* 19. PP. *-iya.* *DKs.* 28. Pass. Pres. 3 Sg. *-ijja-i* *Mt.* 25.
2. *lakṣa* 'a hundred thousand,' Ins. Pl. *-ehiṁ* *Hc.* 335.
(Pa. Pk. *lakkha*, M. Guj. H. Beng. Nep. *lākh*, Singh. *lakhu*, Panj. *lakkh*, Or. *lākha.*)

*lakkhaṇa* 1. *lakṣaṇa* *Sc.* 467.7. Ins. Pl. *-hiṁ* *PPr.* 1.25.
2. *Lakṣmaṇa* *Nc.* 3.14.5.
3. °*ṇā* *Hv.* 88.17.3.

*lakkhārasa* *lākṣā-* *KKc.* 3.2.4.

√*lagga* *lagna*< √*lag-* Pres. 1 Sg. *-uṁ* *Sn.* 236-270. 3 Sg. *-ı* *Kp.* J. 64-8. 3 Pl. *-hiṁ* *Sdd.* 75. Imp. 2 Sg. *-u* *Kp.* E. 29a. *PPr.* 2. 127. *PP. lagga* *DKs.* 16, *KKc.* 1.11.4. Abs. *-evi* *Nc.* 2.1.9. *-ivi* *Nc.*6.1.11. *Sdd.* 106. (NIA post-positions e.g., M. *lāgī*, Guj. *lāgu* Sdh. *lagi* are traceable to this.)

√*langha*  *laṅgh-* Fut. 2. Sg. *-ihihisi Kp.* S. 83.4. 3. Sg. *-ihihai Kp.* E. 28. Pass. Press. 3 Sg. *iyaï Kp.* E. 18.

*Lacchi*  *Lakṣmī BhK.* 32.3, *Hv.* 81.3.8, *KKc.* 6.2.1. *Kp.* S. 73.4. *Sc.* 606.9, Ins. Sg. *e BhK.* 28.1. *-i MP.* 1.12.6. Gen. Sg. *-he MP.* 1.12.2. *-hi Sdd.* 187.

*Lacchima*  *Lakṣmīḥ Sdd.* 191.

*lajja*  *lajjā.* Ins. Sg. *-ha Sn.* 168-115. (Pa. Pk. *lajjā* M. Guj. H. Beng. Nep. *lāj*, Or. *lāja*, Panj. *lajj*, Sdh. *laja*).

*lanjiya*  =*dāsī* Ins. Sg. *-i Jc.* 3.9.11.

*latta*  **lapta Nc.* 9.17.27.

*laya*  *latā.* Fem. Gen. Pl. *-hā Sc.* 484.1.

*lalaṇā-rasaṇā* (*ts.*) Nom. Pl. zero *DKK.* 5.

√*lalala-*  Intensive √*lal-*. Pres. 3 Pl. *-anti Hv.* 84.5.6. cf. M. *laḷalaḷṇe*

*lahalaha-i*  =*lālayate Sn.* 217.186.

√*laha-*  √*labh-* Pres. 3 Sg. *-i Hc.* 335. Pres. 3 Pl. *-hiṁ Pd.* 4. Fut. 2 Sg. *-esahi BhK.* 130.5. *KKc.* 2.4.2. *-ehi KKc.* 2.8.10. *-īsi PPr.* 2.141.
3 Sg. *-esaī BhK.* 74.3. *KKc.* 2.5.7. *PPr.* 2.47. Pres. Part. *-anta PPr.* 65.1*. Abs. *-i Jdc.* 3.4. Sdd. 220. *-ivi Sdd.* 221. *-eviṇu PPr.* 1.95. also *Cd.* 2.27.11.

*lahiri*  (*ts.*) Ins. pl. *-hiṁ KKc.* 8.12.9. (M. H. *lahar*, Guj. *leher*, *ler*, Panj. *lahir.*)

*lhasuṇa*  *laśūna Sdd.* 34. (cf. Pa. *lasuṇ(n)am*, Pk. *lasaṇa*, *lasuṇa*. M. *lasūṇ* H. *lahasun*, Panj. *lasaṇ*.)

√*lā-*  See under √*le-*

*lāla*  *lālā.* Fem. Ins. Sg. *-iṁ Sdd.* 146. cf. M. Guj. *lāḷ*.

*lirāra*  =*lalāṭa.* Loc. Sg. *-e DKs.* 85.

*livi*  *lipi* Fem. Nom. Pl. *-u Nc.* 3.1.1.

*lihia*  *likhita* Neut. direct Pl. *-ā Hc.* 335.

*līla*  *līlā.* Acc. Sg. zero *KKc.* 4.1.14. Ins. Sg. *-e BhK.* 27.3. *Sc.* 603.4. *-ē BhK.* 19.9. 76.10. *-ha Sn.* 334-127.

*līlāvaī*  *Līlāvatī* Ins. Pl. *-hiṁ Mt.* 19.

*līha*  *lekhā Pd.* 83.

*√luṇa-* *√lu* Pres. 1 Sg. *-evi Hv.* 82.10.3.
Fut. 3 Sg. *-ēsai Hv.* 92.2.27. PP. *lūya Hv.* 84.10.4. Abs. *-evi Hv.* 84.11.5. *-eviṇu Jc.* 3.11.6.

*√le-, √lā* *√lag-*. To avoid confusion the full form is quoted. Pres. 1 Sg. *lemi Hv.* 84.14.11. 3 Sg. *lēi. Hv.* 81.5.8. 1 Pl. *lehū Hv.* 84.15.6.

Imp. 2 Sg. *lehi Kp.* S. 56.3. *Mt.* 11, *Sdd.* 119. 3 Sg. *leu KKc.* 1.13.6. *-laïjjaï* (?) *Nc.* 3.7.8. Inf. *leṇahaṁ* Abs. *laï DKK.* 7. *PPr.* 2.87. Fut. 1 Pl. *laesahū. Hv.* 85.20.5. PP. *laiya Pd.* 91 *Sdd.* 119. *lēvi Hv.* 81.4.9. *leppiṇu Hv.* 82.7.13. *Nc.* 5.8.13. *laeppiṇu Nc.* 1.15.13. *leviṇu Nc.* 1.10.1).

*lekkha-hi* *lakṣaya* (Imp. 2 Sg. *-hi*) *MP.* 2.5.2.

*-lehi* *-lekhā.* Fem. Loc. Sg. *-hī Mt.* 7.

*loa* *loka* Nom. Sg. *-ha DKK.* 1. Voc. Pl. *-ho Kc.* 22, *Hc.* 346.

*loaṇa* *locana DKs.* 68. Ins. Pl. *-ehiṁ Hc.* 350.
°*vanta*=*locana-vat.* Neut. Nom. Sg. *-ũ. Mt.* 8.

*√loṭṭa-* *√luṭ-ya.* Pres. 3 Pl. *-anti Nc.* 5.5.5. PP. *loṭṭa Nc.* 7.7.6. (M. *loṭṇē.* Guj. Panj. H. Beng. *√loṭ*)

*loṇiu* *navanītaṁ* (Neut. direct Sg. *-u*) *Sdd.* 25.
(M. *loṇī.* H. *lonī, lunī,* Or. *lahuṇi,* Beng. *lanī*).

*loha* *lobha-* Ins. Sg. *-iṁ Pd.* 81.

*v*

*va* 1. *iva Kp.* J. 70.4, 71.3.4. S. 8.2. A. 12.3. *Nc.* 1.7.1.
2. *vā BhK.* 1.4.8 (Gūṇe).

*vaaṇa* *vadana.* Direct Sg. *-u Mt.* 7. Ins. Sg., *-ẽ Mt.* 24. Loc. Sg. *-mmi Mt.* 15. Ins Pl. *-ehĩ Mt.* 19.

*vaī* Inter. to express regret *Pu.* 17.28.

*vaïkaṇtha* *Vaikuṇṭha* 'N. of Viṣṇu' *Nc.* 7.12.7.

*vaïri* *vairin* Gen. Pl. *-huṁ Nc.* 1.4.4.

°*ya* „ Gen. Sg. *-ha Sn.* 34.199.

*vakka* *vyagra Jdu.* 43.2.

*vakkhāṇa-i* *vyākhyānayati* (Pres. 3. Sg. *-i*) *Nc.* 3.1.16, 9.5.11.

*vakkhāṇa-ḍa* *vyākhyāna-ṭa* (pleonastic).
Acc. Pl. *-ā Pd.* 84.

*vaggha* — *vyāghra Nc.* 6.8.9 (Pk. *vaggha*. M. Guj. *vāgh*. Panj. H. Beng. Nep. *bāgh*, Sdh. *vāghu*, Singh. *wag*).

√*vacca-* — **vṛtyate*=√*vraj*. Pres. 3s J. -*i Nc.* 1.10.9. 7.6.1. 3 Pl. -*anti Sdd.* 147. Pres. Part. -*anta Nc.* 7.1.10. (cf. Old M. *vacṇẽ* 'to go.' also *Hc.* 4.225. Aśok *vacca*. TURNER (429b) traces this to Sk. *vacyate* cf. *vañcayati*).

*vaccha* — *vṛkṣa PPr.* 2.133. Abl. Sg. -*he Hc.* 4.336.

*vaccha-yala* — **vakṣa-tala BhK.* 269.9.

*vacchi* — **vatsī*=*vatsā*. Gen. Sg. -*hi Sn.* 14.141. Voc. Sg. zero *Sn.* 16-441.

*vajjanta* — *vādyat* (Pres. Part. in -*anta*). Ins. Pl. -*ehĩ Mt.* 23. Fem. Loc. Plur. *ntī-hiṁ Jc.* 2.20.3.

√*vaṁca-* — 1. 'to go. Pres.. 3 Sg. -*i MK.* 17.70. 2 (*ts.*) 'to deceive'. Pot. Part. -*evaa. Nc.* 3.2.12.

*vaṭṭa* — *vartman*, *Hv.* 85.24.7. (Pk. *vaṭṭaṁ*, *vaṭṭā*. M. Guj. *vāṭ*, Singh. *vat*, *vaṭu*)).

*vaṭṭaḍiyā* — *vartman*- (pleonastic -*ṭikā*) Acc. Sg. zero *Pd.* 47.

*vaṭṭula* — *vartula Nc.* 3.4.8.

*vaḍa* — =*ukta*. 'prattling, talk'. Ins. Sg. -*iṇa Pd.* 145.

*vaḍavaḍa-i* — =*pralapati* (onomatopoeic ?) *Pd.* 6. cf. *Hc.* 4.148. and M. *baḍbaḍṇẽ*.

*vaḍḍa-ü* — *vartatām* (Imp. 3 Sg. -*u*) *MP.* 1.12.6.

*vaḍha* — =*mūrkha*, *vatsa*. 'a term of endearment in addressing' *Kc.* 67, *Pd.* 2,22. *PPr.* 2.19, 154. cf. *baḍha* above.

*vaḍḍha* — *vṛddha KKc.* 10.3.5.

*vaṇa* — *vana* Direct Sg. -*u MK.* 17.10. Loc. Sg. -*i Nc.* 2.9.4.5. *vaṇṇami*<*vaṇammi* in *KKc.* 1.14.9.

*vaṇa-kīla* — *vana-krīḍā* Fem. Acc. Sg. zero *BhK.* 295.3.

*vaṇa-rāi* — *vana-rāji* Fem. Loc. Sg. -*mmi Sc.* 479.3.

√*vaṇṇa* — √*varṇ*- Pass. Pres. 3 Sg. -*iya-ï Jdc.* 5.1.

*aṇāsaï* — *vanaspati MP.* 2.1.5.

*vattha* — *vastra*. Neut. Nom. Pl. zero *Sdd*. 203.

√*vanda-* — √*vand-* Pres. 1 Sg. -*uṁ* *PPr*. 1.4. Pass. Imp. or Pot. 3 Sg. -*ijja-ï* *Jc*. 3.31.8.

*vandi* — =*bandin* Ins. Sg. -*ṇa* *Sc*. 459.2. Loc. Sg. (Pl. ?) -*hiṁ* *Sc*. 459.5.

*vaya* — *vrata* *KKc*. 3.20.9. Direct Pl. zero *Sdd*. 206.

*vayaṇa* — *vacana*. Acc. Sg. -*u* *KKc*. 1.8.9. Loc. Pl. -*hiṁ* *Jc*. 2.42.1.

-*vayaṇiyā* — -*vadanikā*=*vadanā*. Fem. Ins. Sg. -*e* *Sc*. 669.2.

*vayaṁsī*, °*a*, °*ya* — **vayasyikā*=*vayasyā*. *Hv*. 90.6.8. Fem. Ins. Sg. -*e* *Nc*. 2.2.14. Gei Plur. -*hu* *Hc*. 351.

*vayaṁsulliya* — *vayasya-ullikā* (pleonastic) Fem. *Hv*. 90.8.10.

*varaïtta* — **varayitra* 'husband.' Masc. Nom. Sg. -*u* *Jc*. 4.2.15.

*varāḍiya* — *varāṭikā*. Fem. Ins. Sg. -*iṁ* *Sdd*. 209.

*vari* — =*varaṃ* *MP*. 1.3.12.

*varisa* — 1. *varṣa*. Loc. Sg. -*i* *MP*. 1.3.1 (M. *varīs*, H. *baras*, Panj. *varah*, Or. *barasa*).
2.√*varṣ-* Pres. 3 Sg. -*ei* *Mt*. 21.

√*vala-* — √*val-* Abs. -*ivi* Pd. 51. Caus. Abs. -*i* viz., *vāli*<**vālya* *Mt*. 8.

*valaa*(°*ya*) — *valaya*. Nom. Sg. zero *Ds*. 4.5.2. Direct Pl. -*ā* *Hc*. 352.

*valagga* — *avalagna* *Hv*. 81.4.5. '*āruḍha*' in Hc. 4.206.

*valli* — (*ts*.) Fem. Loc. Pl. -*hiṁ* *Mt*. 17.

√*vava* — √*vap-* Pres. 3 Sg. -*i* *DS*. 4.5.1. *PP*. -*iya-u* *Sdd*. 70.

√*vasa* — *vas-* Pres. Part. -*antu* PPr. 1.36. PP. -*iya* *Sdd*. 35.

*vasahi* — **vṛṣabhi* 'an ox' *Kp*. J. 71.4. ALSDORF records this as a contamination of *vṛṣabha* and '*vahati* an ox.'

√*vaha-* — √*vah-* Pres. Part. Fem. -*antia*. Ins. Pl. -*hī* *Mt*. 14. Inf. -*evvaïṁ* *KKc*. 1.5.5. Caus. *vāha*. Inf. -*i* *Jdu*. 75.2. Abs. -*i* *KKc*. 1.13.6.

-*vahu* — -*vadhū* Fem. Gen. Sg. -*hi* *Jc*. 2.2.10. -*hu* *Sc*. 444.1.

*vahuya* — *vadhūkā* Fem. Gen. Sg. -*huṁ* *MP*. 100.3.9.

*vahelia* — **avaheḍita*. *Mt*. 19.

*vāŭ* — *vāyu* *MK*. 17.9. Ins. Sg. -*eṇa* *MK*. 17.24.

*vāuḍa* — *vyāpṛta* *Nc*. 1.9.7.

| | |
|---|---|
| *Vāṇārasi* | *Varāṇasī* Fem. Loc. Sg. *-hıṁ Hc.* 442. |
| *vāya* | 1. *vācā* Fem. Ins. Sg. *-e MP.* 1.6.15.<br>2. *vāda* Masc. Nom. Pl. *-ī BhK.* 43.2. |
| *vāra* | *dvāra BhK.* 7.6. *Kp.* J. 2.9. S. 38.7. |
| *vāravāra* | *vāraṁ vāram Jc.* 2.25.18. *Sdd.* 156. |
| *vāvaṇa* | *vāmana Jc.* 3.2.9. |
| *vāvı* | *vāpī* Fem. Loc. Sg. *-hẽ Nc.* 2.8.3.<br>(M. H. *bāva-ḍī* Guj. *vāī, vāo* Sing. *vava*). |
| √*vāha* | 'to see' *Jdu.* 22.1, *PPr.* 2.142. (connected with *paśya*>*pāsa-*?) |
| *vāhi* | *vyādhi.* Fem. Acc. Sg. zero *Pd.* 210. |
| *vāhiyāli* | *vāhyāli* 'Training ground for elephants.' *Jc.* 1.4.3. |
| *Vrāsa* | *Vyāsa* Masc. Nom. Sg. *-u Ld.* 3.3.6. *MK.* 17.3. |
| *vrākrosu* | *vyākrośa. MK.* 17.3. |
| *vrāḍi* | *vyāḍi MK.* 17.3. |
| *vrāgaraṇu* | *vyākaraṇaṁ MK.* 17.3. |
| *vi* | *apı Mt.* 2, 4, 16. |
| *viaggha* | *vidagdha.* Ins. Sg. *-eṇa DS.* 4.6.2. |
| *viu* | *=iva Kp.* S. 110.4. |
| *Vıula-ıri* | *Vıpula-gırı.* Masc. Loc. Sg. *-hı MP.* 100.1.2. |
| *vıuvviṭṭhī* | *vyudviṣṭā*<*vi-ud-viṣ- Mt.* 19. |
| *viusa* | **viduṣa*=*vidvas Nc.* 3.4.2. (*Jc.* p. 160), *Sc.* 449.1.<br>°*ttaṇa*=*vidvatva Nc.* 3.5.11. |
| *vigutta* | *vigupta* Masc. Nom. Pl. *-āiṁ Hc.* 421. |
| *vicca* | **vṛtta* =*vartman Hc.* 421, *Kc.* 67, *Pd.* 188.<br>Loc. Sg. *-i Jc.* 2.26.10. *Ld.* 3.3.53. records *vıccha* for °*cca* |
| *vicintirī* | *vi-*√*cint*+*ira*(habit showing suff.)used as Pres. Part. *Sc.* 5301. |
| *vichitta* | PP. of *vi-*√*chiva* 'to touch' cf. *Hc.* 257. *Dn.* 3.27. Neut.<br>Nom. Sg. *-ũ Hv.* 83.16.13. |
| *vicchoya* | *vikṣobha*=*viraha KKc.* 10.1.4. |
| *vijja* | *vidyā.* Fem. Nom. Pl. *-u KKc.* 2.4.10. |
| *vijjappaha* | *vidyutprabha Nc.* 6.2.2. |

*vijjaya* *dvitīyaka BhK.* 354.6.

*vijjā-sāla* *vidyā-śālā.* Fem. Abl. Sg. *-ho BhK.* 18.10. °*-hariya vidyādharī KKc.* 1.15.10.

*vijjijjamāṇa* Pass. Pres. Part. of *vīj.* (*-ijja-māṇa*) *Nc.* 2.11.2.

*vijjula* *vidyullatā MP.* 2.14.8. cf. H. *bijlī.*

*vijjhaviya* *vidhyāpita Kp.* S. 75.4. cf. M. *vijhavṇẽ* but *vikṣāpita* acc. to ALSDORF.

*Viṁjha* *Vindhya.* Nom. Sg. *-u KKc.* 1.12.8, 2.2.11. Loc. Sg. *-i Jc.* 3.35.15.

*viṭṭala* *apavitra-la* Nom. Sg. *-u Hv.* 90.3.14. *Jc.* 3.18.4. (M. *viṭāl,* Guj. *vaṭāl,* Beng. *viṭāl,* Sd. *viṭāraṇu.* BLOCH connects M. *viṭaḷ,* to Sk. *viṣṭhā.* See *FLM* §§ 109, 150).

*Viṭṭhu* *Viṣṇu Hv.* 83.14.10, *KKc.* 7.7.3. *Nc.* 4.9.11. cf. M. *Viṭhu, Viṭhobā.*

*viḍavi* *viṭapi* Masc. Ins. Pl. *-hiṁ Sc.* 481.1.

*viḍhatta* PP. of√*viḍghava*√*arj- Kp.* A. 5.2. cf. *Hc.* 4.108.

*viṇāsa-ho* *vināśinah* (Gen. Sg. *-ho*) *KKc.* 1.1.1.

*viṇu* *viṇā DKs.* 107, *Hv.* 82.9.5, *Jdc.* 7.2. *Kc.* 71. (cf. *Hc.* 426), *Mt.* 13,34, *PPr.* 1.42, 2.59. *Sdd.* 6.18. *Sn.* 272-191. This is used with the Acc. and the Instr. cases.

*viṇṭala-u* =*veṣṭanakaḥ Jdc.* 23.2 cf. M. *vẽṭolẽ.*

√*viṇṇava-* *vi-*√*jñap-* Pres. 3 Sg. *-i Kp.*S. 35.3.1, *Nc.* 1.8.12. 1 Pl. *-imo Kp.*J. 45.1* Imp. 2 Pl. *aha Kp.*J. 45.2* PP. *-ia, Nc.* 1.16. 7, *PPr.* 1.8. (M. *vinavṇẽ,* Guj. *vinavavũ,* H. *binaunā*).

*vitti-ṇivitti* *vṛtti-nivṛtti.* Loc. Pl. *-hi PPr.* 2.52.

*viddāṇiya* *vidīrṇa KKc.* 1.10.3.

*vidisi-hiṁ* =*vidikṣu* (Fem. Loc. Pl. *-hiṁ*) *Sdd.* 66.

*vinda* *vṛnda.* Ins. Pl. *-hiṁ PPr.* 1.39 Gen. Pl. *-hā̃ PPr.* 1.110.

*viṁbhariya* **vismarita MP.* 1.13.3.

*viyakkhaṇu* *-vicakṣaṇaḥ PPr.*

*viyambhiya* *vijṛmbhita PPr.* 2.158.

*ai-yāṇu* *vi-jānīhi* (Imp. 2 Sg. *-u*) *PPr.* 1,53 *Sdd.* 19.

| | |
|---|---|
| *-vilaya* | =*vanitā*. Fem. Gen. Sg. *-hĕ BhK*. 17.8. |
| *vilalullu* | =*vilola*+*ulla-u* (pleonastic+nom. Sg. *-u*) *DS*. 4.5.2. |
| *vilāsiṇī* | *vilāsinī* Fem. Ins. Pl. *-hĭ BhK*. 17.7. |
| *viva* | =*iva*. *Hv*. 85.2.2. *Nc*. 3.8.3. cf. *Hc*. 2.182. |
| *vīvarera* | =*viparīta*+*ira* (showing habit) *Jc*. 3.29.13. *Pd*. 125, 129. |
| *viuva-hu* | =*vīyatāṁ Sn*. 16-286. |
| *visaa* | *viṣaya* Ins. Pl. *-ehiṁ Kc*. 22. |
| *visa-kaṇiya* | *viṣa-kaṇikā*. Fem. Ins. Sg. *-iṁ Sdd*. 207. |
| *visaya* | *viṣaya*. Gen. Pl. zero *Kc*. 22. *-ha* ̐ *Ys*. 50. |
| *visarisa* | *visadṛśa*. *Sc*. 584.1. |
| *visāṁvū* | =*viśrāmaḥ Kc*. 26. |
| *visitti* | **viśitī*< √*viś* Abso. Mt. 18. |
| *vihīṇa* | °*na*. Neut. Direct Pl. zero *PPr*. 2.23. |
| *vīhau* | =*vibhītaḥ Pd*. 74. |
| *vīhayv* | =*vīkṣitā* Fem. Ins. Sg. *-(ā)e KKc*. 1.13.2. |
| *vuṭṭhi* | *vṛṣṭi Kp*. S. 18.3. |
| *vutta* | *ukta Kc*. 67, *Ld*. 3.3.53.cf. *Hc*. 4.421. |
| *vuttanta* | *vṛttānta*. *Kp*.S. 39.8. |
| *vṛnda* | (*ts*.) *Hv*. 81.18.3. |
| *ve* | *dvi BhK*. 291.2, *Nc*. 9.20.11. *Pd*. 213. *Sdd*. 36.<br>Ins. Pl. *vihi Nc*. 3.5.5. |
| *veilla* | *vicakila Hv*. 84.1.2. |
| *Vegavaï* | *Vegavatī* Dat. Gen. Sg. *-he KKc*. 6.14.7. |
| *Veya* | *Veda*. Nom. Pl. *-iṁ Jc*. 3.29.12. Ins.Pl. *-hi*̐ *PPr*. 1.23. |
| *veyaṇa* | *vedanā* Fem. Acc. Sg. zero *Pd*. 74. |
| *vesa* | 1. *dveṣya* Masc. Nom. Sg. *-u MP*. 1.4.5.<br>2. *veśyā* Fem. Sg. *-hiṁ Sdd*. 44. |
| *vesi* | =*vetsi* (Skt.sm.) *Nc*. 6.13.8. |
| *voccheya* | =*vyuccheda Hv*. 90.1.7. |

*vonda* — *vṛnda Hv*. 90.13.12. Cf. *Hc*. 1.131.

*volīṇa* — =*vyatītā* Fem. Ins. Pl. -*hi MP*. 2.4.6. But the Tippaṇa takes it as Loc. Sg.

### *s*

*saa* — 1. *śata* Ins. Sg. -*eṇa Hc*. 332, Ins. Pl. -*hĩ Mt*. 13. Loc. Pl. -*ehiṁ Hc*. 345. (Pa. *sata*, Pk. *saa*(*ya*), M. Guj. *śẽ*, H. Panj. Nep. *sai*, Sdh. *saü*).
2. *svaka* Ins. Sg. -*e* ? =*svayaṁ Nc*. 9.21.5.

*saï* — 1. *satī* Fem. Dat. Sg. -*hi MP*. 87.12.12.
2. *sadā*. *Sn*. 26.213.

*saĩ*, °*iṁ* — *svayena* =*svayaṁ Jc*. 2.12.16; *Mt*. 11, *Nc*. 3.4.17

*saücca* — *śauca*. Direct Sg. -*u Sdd*. 7. Ins. Sg. -*ẽ*. *Nc*. 1.4.4.

*saüṇi* — *śakuni* Masc. Gen. Pl. *ihaṁ Hc*. 340.

*saũ* — 1 *samaṁ Kp*. S. 7.2.
2. *sva* (Alsdorf) *Kp*.E. 10b.

*saṁkaḍilla* — *saṅkaṭa*+*illa* (=possessing, full of). *Jc*. 1.3.2.

*saṁkala* — *śṛṅkhalā Kp*.A. 1.2. cf. *Hc*. 1.189.

*saṁkhala* — *śṛṅkhalā Hv*. 88.11.9 (Pa. Pk. *saṅkhalā*. Pk. *siṅkhalā*, M. *sãkhaḷ*, *sā̃kaḷ*, *sākaḷ*. Guj. *sā̃kaḷ*, H. *sākal*, Or. *saṅkoḷi*, Nep. *saṅlo*).

*saṁkheva* — *saṁkṣepa*. Ins. Sg. -*eṁ Sdd*. 1.

*Saṁkhohaṇikā* — *Saṁkṣobhaṇikā* (N. of a *vidyā*) *Nc*. 6.6.11.

*saṁgahia* — *saṁgṛhīta KKc*. 5.10.1.

*sanga* — (*ts*.) Gen. Sg. -*ho BhK*. 205.2.

*saccava* — 'to see' cf. *Hc*. 4.181. Imp. 2 Sg. -*ēhi Kp*. S. 80.3.

*saccha* — *sākṣāt BhK*. 252.7.

*sajjaṇa* — °*na*. Gen. Pl. -(*ā*)*haṁ KKc*. 1.5.7.

*sajjo* — *sadyaḥ* (adv.) *Jc*. 3.11.1

*sa-jhuṭṭha* — =*sa-juṣṭa*-'false' *Nc*. 6.13.15. cf. H.M. *jhūṭ*(*h*).

√*saṁ-calla-* — *saṁ*-√*cal-ya*- Pres. 3 Pl. -*hiṁ KKc*. 1.3.7.

| | |
|---|---|
| √*saṁjaia* | *sañjāta DKK.*7. |
| *saṁjha* | *sandhyā Kp.*S. 40.4. Loc. Sg. (*ā*)*i Jc.* 2.9.4. Loc. Pl. zero *Sdd.* 68, -*i Sdd.* 12 (M. Beng. H. Nep. *sā̃jh*, Guj. Nep. *sā̃j*). |
| *saḍḍha* | *sārdha MP.* 2.5.4. |
| *saṇiuṁ* | *śanaiḥ. Jc.* 3.12.8. |
| *saṇṇāha* | *sannāha.* Ins. Sg. -*eṁ Sdd.* 60. |
| √*saṇthava* | 1. *saṁ-stav-* Inf. -*aṇa PPr.* 2.137. 2. *saṁ-sthāpay* Imp. 2 Sg. -*hi KKc.* 1.11.10. |
| *satta* | *sapta Kp.* J. 31.2,* Plur. Direct zero *Kp.*S. 4.4, *Pd.* 220. Instr. -*ehiṁ Kp.*S. 37.1*. Loc. -*ihĩ Kp*, 74.3. (Pa. Pk. *satta*, M. Guj. H. Beng. *sāt*, Or. *sāta*, Panj. *satt*). |
| *sattama* | *saptama Kp.*J. 58.9, *Sdd.*15. |
| *sattāva-i* | =*santāpayati Pd.* 64. |
| -*satti* | *śakti* Fem. Ins. Sg. -*e BhK.* 18.3, *Sdd.* 9. |
| *sattu* | *śatru* Masc. Acc. Sg. zero *PPr.* 2.45. |
| *Sattuhaṇa* | *Śatrughna Hv.* 89.19.91. |
| *sattha* | =*śastra.* Ins. Pl. -*ihiṁ Hc.* 358, *Sn.* 24-212. |
| *sadda* | *śabda.* Ins. Sg. -*eṇa DKs.* 94. |
| *santāvia-o* | **santāpitakaḥ*=°*pitaḥ Mt.* 28. |
| *saṁthavantu* | *saṁstavantu* (Imp. 3 Pl. -*antu*) *KKc.* 9.18.3. |
| *sandhukkī* | *sandhukṣita Pd.* 87, cf. *Hc.* 4.152. |
| *sappa* | *sarpa.* Ins. Sg. -*iṁ Pd.* 15, Nom. Pl. zero *Sdd.* 65. |
| *śabara* | (*ts.*) Ins. Sg. -*e DKK.* 25. |
| *sama* | *ts.* Masc. Acc. Pl. zero *DKs.* 76. |
| *Samaï* | *Samati.* Masc. Gen. Sg. -*hi MP.* 90.16.4. |
| *samara* | *śabara Jc.* 3.29.13. *Nc.* 5.13.6. |
| *sama-sīla* | °*sīlā.* Fem. Ins. Pl. -*hiṁ KKc.* 3.6.1. |
| *samāṇu* | *samānaṁ*=*samaṁ Ld.* 3.3.40. |
| √*samāsa-* | 'to speak', Pres. 1 Sg. -*mi Hv.* 90.15.9. PP. -*iu BhK.* 171.6. |

| | |
|---|---|
| *samāhi* | *samādhi* Fem. (?) Ins. Sg. *-e Sdd.* 224.<br>Loc. Gen. Sg. *-hi Sdd.* 193. |
| *samidi* | *samiti Nc.* 1.12.3. (Śaurasenism). |
| *samiddha* | *samṛddha Kp.* J. 82.2 |
| *samubbaha-i* | *samudvahati DKK* 1 (Pres. 3 Sg. *-i*). |
| *samuhū̃* | *sammukhaṁ Hv.* 88.11.11. cf. *saũhū̃. Hv.* 86.2.4. and *samuha Mt.* 12. |
| √*samoḍa* | *sam-moṭay-*<br>Abs. *-ivi Jc.* 3.12.12. cf. M. *moḍṇẽ.* |
| √*saṁpajja-* | *sampad-ya-* Imp. 3 Pl. *-huṁ KKc.* 9.16.3. |
| *saṁpaḍa-u* | *sam-patatu* (Imp. 3 Sg. in *-u*) *KKc.* 9.16.4. |
| *saṁpaya* | *sampad-* Gen. Pl. *-hã BhK.* 252.12 |
| *saṁprāiya-ū̃* | *samprāptaḥ* (Masc. Nom. Sg. *-ū̃*) *Hv.* 87.7.2. |
| *saṁbea-i* | **saṁ-vedati*=*saṁvetti DKK* 16. |
| *sambhara-* | 1. *saṁ-*√*smar-* Imp. 2 Sg. *-hi Jc.* 3.40.17.<br>Imp. 2 Pl. *-ha Hv.* 92.21.14. PP. *-iya Jdc.* 11.4<br>2. *saṁsmṛta Jc.* 4.5.5. |
| *saya* | *śata.* Neut. direct Pl. zero *BhK.* 39.9 *-ĩ Sdd.* 222. |
| *sayattha* | *svārtha.* Ins. Pl. *-hĩ Kp.* J. 46.6. |
| *sayaṇijja* | *śayanīya* Abl. Sg. *-ha Sc.* 459.3. |
| *sayala* | *sakala.* Neut. Gen. Pl. *-haũ PPr.* 2.198.<br>Fem. Acc. Sg. zero *MP.* 100.1.1. Acc. Pl. *-iṁ Pd.* 66. |
| √*sara* | √1. *smar-* Pres. 1. Sg. *-mi KKc.* 1.1.2.<br>Abs. *-ivi Nc.* 7.6.7. Pot. Part. *-evaa-u Jdu.* 66.4.<br>2. *saras* 'a lake'. Ins. Pl. *-ehiṁ Hc.* 423.<br>3. *smara Hv.* 81.1.1. *Nc.* 1.17.15. |
| *saraṇī* | (*ts.*) Fem. Nom. Pl. *-u Sc.* 445.4. |
| *sara-vara* | *saro-vara* Loc. Sg. *-i Sdd.* 186. Loc. Pl. *-haṁ Sdd.* 18. |
| *Saraha* | 'N. of the author of *DKs.*' Masc. Nom. Sg. zero *DKs.* .80, Ins. Sg. *-ẽ DKs.* 41. |
| *Sarāsaī* | *Sarasvatī MP.* 1.2.8. Acc. Sg. zero *KKc.* 1.2.1. |
| *sarī* | *sarit* Fem. Ins. Pl. *-hiṁ Hc.* 422.11. |

| | |
|---|---|
| *saria* | *sarit* Fem. Nom. Sg. zero *Mt.* 25. |
| *saricchu* | *sadṛkṣaḥ* (Masc. Nom. Sg. -*u*) *Mt.* 9. |
| *sari-ṇāu* | *sadṛśa-nāmā* (Masc. Nom. Sg. -*u*) *Mt.* 3. |
| *sarisa* | *sadṛśa DKs.* 78,86. *Kp.*S. 75.5. °*a DKs.* 50. |
| *sarisava* | *sarṣapa Kp.*S. 106.4. |
| *sarīra* | *śa*- Sing. Loc. -*hi DKs.* 91. Gen. Pl. -*haṁ Nc.* 1.12.10. |
| *sarīso* | *sadṛśaḥ* (Masc. Nom. Sg. *o*) *DKs.* 78. |
| *saro-sira* | *saroṣa-ira* Masc. Nom. Sg. -*u Sn.* 273-191. |
| √*salaha*- | √*ślāgh*- Pres. 1 Sg. -*emi Kp.*S. 35.8.<br>Pres. Part. Fem. Ins. Sg. -*anti-e Hv.* 92.17.8. |
| *sallai* | *sallakī* Sing. Loc. -*hiṁ Hc.* 422, Direct pl. -*u Hc.* 387.1. |
| -*saloṇa* | -*salavaṇa* 'beautiful'. Masc. Nom. Sg. -*u Hv.* 87.2.9. cf. *Hc.* 4.420.5, 444.4. but '*sadṛśa*' in *Hv.* 92.9.7. |
| √*sava*- | √*śap*- Pres. 1 Sg. -*ũ Mt.* 4. |
| *savva* | *sarva* Masc. Nom. Sg. *savvu Kc.* 30. *sahu Pd.* 89, *sahu Kc.*30. also in Neut. *Jdu.* 17.3. *sāha Ld.* 3.3.51. *sāho*, °*hu Sh.* 22.21.<br>Gen. *sāha-haṁ. Sh.* 22.22. Gen. Sg. -*ho Kc.*17,31. -*ssu Kc.* 17. Masc. Nom. Pl. *savvi Jdu.* 24.4. Acc. in *Kp.* A. 8.3. *savvaĩ Jdc.* 11.4. Neut. Direct Pl. -*aiṁ Pd.* 27. *Ys.* 31. -*āī Sc.* 459.3. but *sahi* in *Jdc.* 43.3. Gen. Pl. -*haṁ Sdd.* 42. |
| *savvettahe* | =*sarvatra Ld.* 3.3.13. |
| *saṁsāra* | (*ts.*) Acc. Sg. -*u Pd.* 16. Gen. Sg. -*haṁ Sdd.* 192. also in *KKc.* 9.8.9. Loc. Sg. -*i PPr.* 1.9. |
| *sasi-rāhu* | *śaśi*- Masc. Nom. Pl. zero *Hc.* 382. |
| *sa-siri* | *sa-śrī-(ka)* Masc. Loc. Sg. -*hi MP.* 100.1.2. |
| √*saha*- | √*sah*- Fut. 1 Sg. -*ihimi Mt.* 22 Pres. Part. -*anta. PPr.* .2.36. Inf -*aṇa* (°*ṇu*) *PPr.* 2.120. In *Jc.* 2.33.9. *sahu* is Impf. 1 Sg. |
| *sahaja* | *ts.* Ins. Sg. -*ẽ DKK* 19. |
| *sahayarī* | *sahacarī* Fem. Ins. Pl. -*hiṁ KKc.* 3.6.7. |
| *sahā̃* | *sabhā* Fem.Loc. Sg. -*e BhK.* 2.3. |
| *sahāa* | *svabhāva.* Masc. Nom. Sg. -*u PPr.* 2.197. |

*sahāba* *svabhāva* Nom. Sg. *-e* *DKs*. 85, Ins. *-ẽ* Sg. *DKs*. 79.

*sahāsa* *sahasra* *Hv*. 82.11.4, *MP*. 1.11.14.

*sahi* *sakhī* Fem. Voc. Sg. zero *DKs*. 45, *Jdc*. 8.4. Gen. Pl. *-huṁ*, *-haṁ* *Kc*. 18.

*sahiya* **sakhi-ka*=*sakhī* Fem. Ins. Pl. *-hiṁ* *KKc*, 6.15.3.

*sahuṁ*, °*hũ* *saha* *Hv*. 81.10.2, *Jdc*. 32.1. *Kp*.S. 53.4. *Kp*. J. 87.4, *Lá*. 3.3.44, *PPr*. 2.109. cf. *Hc*. 4.419.

*sāiṇi* *śākinī* Fem. Nom. Pl. *-u* *Jc*. 1.16.11.

*sākhaṇḍa* *śākhāraṇḍa* (=*drohī*) Masc. Nom. Sg. *-u* *Sdd*. 61.

*sāmaggi* *sāmagri* Masc. Nom. Pl. *-ẽ* *DKK*. 7.

*sāmala* *śyāmala* *Mt*. 14, 21, *Sc*. 580.3. Masc. Nom. Sg. *-u* *PPr*. 1.80. Neut. direct Sg. *-i* *Ds*. 4.5.2.

*sāmi* *svāmin*. Masc. Gen. Sg. *-hi* *Jc*. 2.26.9, *MP*. 100.7.8 Abl. Pl. *-huṁ* *Hc*. 341.

*sāmi-sālā* *svāmi-sāra*=*svāmin* *KKc*. 1.7.4. 1.11.5. *Kp*.J. 10.3. *Nc*. 1.15.5.

*sāya* *svāda*. Abl. Sg. *-hu* *Sdd*. 35.

*sāyatta* *sapatnī* *Nc*. 3.9.9. cf. M. *savat*, H. *saut*.

*sāyara* *sāgara*. Gen. Sg. *-ho* *Hc*. 395.

*sāyara-gaya* *sāyara-gata* Loc. Sg. *-hiṁ* *Sdd*. 3.

*sāvaya* *śrāvaka*. Gen. Pl. -(*ă*)*haṁ* *KKc*. 9.16.2. *Sdd*. 31.

*sāsu* *sasyam* *Sdd*. 83. (Neut. Nom. Sg. *-u*).

*sāhāraa* *sahakāra* 'a mango tree' *Nc*. 3.6.13.

*-sāhi* *śākhin* Masc. Ins. Pl. *-hiṁ* *Sc*. 476.1.

*sāhu* *sādhu* Masc. Direct Pl. zero (elongation of *-u*) *PPr*. 2.10. Gen. Pl. *-huṁ* *Sn*. 17-286.

*Sia* *Śiva* Masc. Nom. Sg. *-u* *KKc*. 4.3.1.

*śiāla* *śṛgāla* *DKs*. 7.

√*sikkha-* √*śikṣ-* Imp. 2 Sg. *-i* *Pd*. 84 PP. *-ia* *Mt*. 25, Pot. Part. *-iyavya* *Pd*. 98. Inf. *-huṁ* *Nc*. 5.8.2. Caus. Pres. 1 Sg. -(*a*) *va-mi* *Pd*.106. (Pa. *sikkhati*, Pk. *sikhaï*, M. *śikṇe*, Guj. H. √*sikh-*, Panj. *sikkṇā*).

*sikkha-vaya* — *śikṣā-vrata*. Direct Pl. *-iṁ* *Sdd.* 11.

*siddha* — (*ts.*) Nom. Sg. zero *DKK.* 19.

*siddha-ttaṇa* — *siddha-tva* Gen. Sg. *-hu* *Pd.* 88.

*siddhi* — (*ts.*) Fem. Direct Sg. zero (elongation of *-i*) *Mt.* 19.
Gen. Sg. *-hi* *PPr.* 2.48. *-hiṁ̐* *PPr.* 2.69.
Loc. Sg. *-hi* *PPr.* 1.26. (It is plural in sense though Sg. in the *chāyā*.) Ins. Pl. *-hiṁ* *MP.* 100.10.1.

*siddhi-suha* — °*sukha*. Acc. Sg. zero *Ys.* 30.

*-sindhu* — (*ts.*) Ins. Pl. *-hu* *KKc.* 1.3.3.

*Sippa* — *śi*(*kṣi*)*prā* *Jc.* 3.1.2.

*sippi* — **śilpi* 'Mother of pearl.' Fem. Loc. Sg. *-hiṁ* *Sdd.* 91.

*simira* — *śibira* *Nc.* 5.1.1.

*siya-* — *śri-ka* *Nc.* 9.4.3. in comps. *e.g.*, *Nc.* 5.11.12.

*siri* — *śrī* *Hv.* 81.3.12. *Nc.* 1.1.11. *Sc.* 451.1. Gen. Sg. *-hĩ* (?) *Sc.* 484.1.

*sila* — *śilā* *Hc.* 337. Loc. Sg. *-ẽ* *PPr.* 1.123. *-i* *Ys.* 44.

*Siva* — *Śiva* Neut. Acc. Sg. zero *Pd.* 55.

*Śiva-devi* — *Siva-devī* Fem. Ins. Sg. *-i* *MP.* 87.11.13.
Loc. Sg. *-hi* *MP.* 87.10.8.

*Siva-paha* — *Siva-patha*. Loc. Sg. *-e* *KKc.* 1.1.4.

*Siva-mai* — *Śiva-mati* Fem. Acc. Sg. ̐ *PPr.* 2.56.

*Siva-satti* — *Śiva-śakti* Gen. Pl. *-hiṁ* *Pd.* 127.

*siviṇa* — *svapna*. Neut. direct Pl. *-aĩ* *Jc.* 461.1.

*śihara* — *śikhara* *DKK.* 25.

*sihiṇa* — *stana* *MP.* 2.16.2.

*sīya* — *sītā* Fem. Gen. Sg. *-ha* *Sc.* 491.2.

*sīyalatta* — *śītalatva* *KKc.* 3.10.8.

*sīsakka* — *śīrṣaska* 'helmet' Neut. Nom. Pl. *-ĩ* *MP.* 88.5.7.

*Sīhaura* — *Siṁhapura* *Nc.* 7.4.7.

*suaṇa* — *sujana* Masc. Gen. Sg. *-ssu* *Hc.* 338. Acc. Pl. *-aĩ* *BhK.* 35.5.

*-suā* *sutā*. Fem. Gen. Sg.-*heṁ* *KKc*. 7.7.5.

*suī-ṇaṁ* *śrutīnām* (Pkt. sm.) *Pd*. 98 (Gen. Pl. in -*ṇaṁ*)

*sukaī* *sukavi*. Masc. Nom. Pl. zero. *Jdc*. 6.3.
Ins. Pl. -*hiṁ* *Jdc*. 4.2. *MP*. 1.12.8.

*ukasaṇiya* **sukṛṣṇita* *Hv*. 83.13.11.

*ukka* *śuṣka* Gen. Sg. -*ha* *Sdd*. 52. cf. *M*. *sukā*.

*ukkila* *śukla* Nom. Sg. -*u* *Nc*. 1.14.2.

*sukhiya* *sukhita* 'happy' Masc. Nom. Sg. -*u* *Sdd*. 2.

*suggai-maggu* =*sugati-mārgaḥ* *Sn*. 273-191.

*sugha* *sukha* Ins. Sg. -*ĕ* *Kc*. 56.

*succhanda* *succhandas* Ins. Sg. -*iṇa* *Jdc*. 3. 3.

√*suṇa-* 1.√*sr-ṇu* Pres. 3 Sg. -*i* *DKK* 12. *DKs*. 75. Imp. 2 Sg. -*hu* *DKs*. 57, *Sdd*. 42. Abs. -*i* *Jdc*. 8.3, -*ivi* *Mt*. 16. -*īuṇa* *KKc*. 8.4.1. -*ūṇaṁ* *Jc*. 1.12.15.

*suṇa* *śvan* *DKs*. 7. (Pa. *sunakha*, *Pk*. *suṇaa*, M. poetic *suṇĕ*, H. *sūnā*.)

*suṇaha* *śvan-* Masc. Ins. Pl. -*hi* *Jc*. 1.5.16.

*suṇṇa* *sūṇya* Nom. Sg. -*ĕ* *DKK* 8.

*sunnāsunna* Loc. Sg. -(*a*)*hi* *DKs*. 77. *śūnyāśūnya* (Nom. Pl. zero) *DKK*. 11. Gen. Pl. zero *DKK*. 13.

*suttā* *suptā*. Fem. Ins. Sg. -*e* *MP*. 87.11.12.

*Sudatta* (*ts*.) Masc. Nom. Sg. -*u* *Jc*. 3.34.15.

*suddhi* *śuddhi* Fem. Ins. Sg. -*e* *Sdd*. 56.

*sundēra* *saundarya*. *Hv*. 90.8.12. cf. *Hc*. 1.57.

*su-pottha-i* *su-pustaka* (Loc. Sg. -*i*) *Sn*. 16.286.

*sumaī* *sumati* Gen. Sg. -*hu* *MP*. 90.16.4.

*sumiṭṭhāhāra* *sumiṣṭāhāra* zero Acc. Sg. *Pd*. 18.

*suya-ï* **svapati*=*svapiti* *Sn*. 272-191.

*suyaṇa* *sujana* Voc. Pl. -*hu* *Sc*. Intro. P. 12. -16.

*suya-paṁcami* *śruta-pañcamī* Fem. Gen. Sg. -*hi* *Sdd*. 185.

√*suyara-* — *sumar-< *smṛ-* Pres. 3 Sg. *-i Hv.* 81.16.5. PP. *-iu Hv.* 83.15.11. Abs. *-eppiṇu Hv.* 90.4.9.

*sura-giri* — (*ts.*) Loc. Sg. *-hiṁ Sdd.* 196.

*sura-guru* — (*ts.*) Gen. Sg. *-hu Jdc.* 4.4.

*sura-vara* — (*ts.*) Masc. Nom. Pl. zero *MP.* 87.14.6.

*surāsura* — (*ts.*) Masc. Direct Pl. zero *DKK* 8.

*suva-paṁcamī* — *śruta-*° Fem. Gen. Sg. *-hĕ BhK.* 1.2.

*suvisuddha-maï* — *su-viśuddha-mati* Nom. Sg. zero *Sdd.* 10.

*suvihāṇa* — *su-vibhāna* 'dawn' Loc. Sg. *-iŏ Nc.* 2.7.7.

*susamāhi* — *susamādhi* Acc. Sg. zero *Ys.* 40.

*suha* — 1. *sukha* Neut. Direct Sg. zero *Pd.* 5. *-u Pd.* 3, *PPr.* 2.199. Nom. Pl. *-ā Pd.* 17.
2. *śvā* 'a dog' *Jc.* 2.35.10.

*suhi* — *suhṛd Nc.* 2.7.10.

*suhuma* — *sūkṣma.* Gen. Pl. *-haṁ MP.* 2.7.10.

*suhelli* — *sukha-keli Nc.* 1.13.2. but '*sukha*' in *Dn.* 7.36.

*sūri* — (*ts.*) Gen. Sg. *-hi Jdc.* 1.4. *Sdd.* 7.

*sṛya* — *śrī Hv.* 82.1.9, 92.7.6.

*seṇṇa* — *sainya* Neut. direct Pl. *-iṁ KKc.* 4.1. *ghattā* cf. *M. śeṇvī* 'N of a caste.'

*seṁbali* — *śālmali KKc.* 8.7.7.

*seṁbha* — *śleṣmā MP.* 20.14.10. (cf. M. *śĕmbūḍ*, *śemb*, H. *sembhā*, Singh. *sem(a)* Pk. *simbha*, *sembha*).

*sĕraya* — *svaira-ka Hv.* 85.1.14.

√*seva-* — √*sev-* Fut. 1 Pl. *-issahũ* Intro. to *Sc.* p. 17, § 24.

*sesāsi-hiṁ* — *śeṣāśīrbhiḥ* (Ins. Pl. *-hiṁ*) *MP.* 87.17.1.

*soceya* — *śocayet* (Skt.ism) *Nc.* 9.20.12.

*sojjha*, °*u* — *śuddhi DKs.* 53, 80.

*soṇaiya* — *śaunika.* Gen. Pl. *-huṁ Jc.* 3.34.13.

*ṇiyā* — *ṇī* Fem. Gen. Pl. *-hiṁ KKc.* 1.16.5.

*soṇṇāra* *suvarṇakāra MP*. 31.7.2. cf. M. Guj. H. *sonār*.

*solaha-ma* *ṣoḍaśama*. *Nc*. 4.5.1. (Pa. *solasa*, Pk. *solaha*, *soḷā*, M. *solā* hence M. *soḷāvā* Guj. *soḷ*, Or. *soḷa* H. *solaha*).

*soha* *śobhā* Acc. Sg. zero *Sn*. 273-191.

*soha-choṇı* *śobhā-kṣoṇı-ḥ* *Mp*. 1.2.7.

*sohi* *śuddhi Sn*. 32-231.

*sohiya* *śodhita DKs*. 40,41.

*sohilla* *śobhā-illa* ( =*yukta* 'possessing,' 'having' ) *MP*. 2.17.9. cf. *BhK*. 68.4.

*h*

*haa* *haya* Acc. Pl. -*ĕ* *Nc*. 6.13.11.

*haũ* 1st P. Pron. Sing. Nom. *haũ*, °*uṁ BhK*. 21.5. 24.5, *DKK* 1, *DKs*. 70. *Hc*. 375, *Jc*. 1.6.9. *Jdc*. 45.2. *Kc*. 37, *KKc*. 2.5.8. *Kp*. *J* 8.4. 63.2. *Ld*. 3.4.45., *Mt*. 29, *Pd*. 26,31. *PPr*. 1.3, 80. *Sc*. 465.9, *Sh*. 22.53, *Sn*. 306-169. 18-468. *ahayaṁ Jc*. 2.3.4., *Sc*. 648.1. *haṁ Jc*. 2.3.6. *huṁ Jc*. 2.28.4. Acc. *maĩ BhK*. 57.9, 82.7., *Hc*. 377. *Jc*. 2.35.4, *Kc*. 38, *KKc*. 1.16.16, *Kp*. J. 10.2. *Ld*. 3.4.46. *Sc*. 612.9, *Sh*. 22.55, *maṁ Mt*. 11, 24, *Sn*. 77-176. *mamaṁ Sc*. 672.7. Ins. *maĩ BhK*. 21.2., 22.4, *DKK* 26, *DKs*. 50, 95. *Hc*. *Kc*. *Ld*. *Sh*. the same as the Acc. *Jdc*. 45.4, *KKc*. 1.2.7, *Kp*. J. 10.2. *Pd*. 208, *PPr*. 1.9, 2.211, *Sc*. 485.5. *maï Jdc*. 46.1, *PPr*. 2.212, *mae BhK*. 69.10, *Jc*. 2.1.15, *Kp*. J. 65.1* *maeṇa KKc*. 1.10.6. *me Kp*. S. 100.1* Gen. *maha KKc*. 1.10.7, *Kp*. J. 9.2, *Sc*. 465.6. *Sn*. 217-186. 14-441. *mahaṁ MP*. 1.10.3, *mahu BhK*. 27.12, 37.5. *DKs*. 9,95. *Hc*. 379, *Kc*. 39, *KKc*. 1.2.10, *Kp*. S. 45.7, *Ld*. 3.4.47, *Pd*. 99,186, *PPr*. 1.1.22, *Sh*. 22.57. *mahũ PPr*. 2.186. *maho KKc*. 1.6.9, 2.4.10, 4.5.10. *majjha Kp*. J. 6.3, *Ld*. 3.4.47, *Sc*. 482.3, *Sn*. 11-441. *majjhaṁ MP*. 1.10.12. *majjhu BhK*. 38.3, 41.8. *Hc*. 379, *Kc*. 39, *KKc*. 3.11.7, *Mt*. 13.24, *Pd*. 119, *Sh*. 22.57. Forms in -*era* e.g. *meraum*, *Jc*. 3.21.11 are not a part of this declension. Loc. *maĩ* °*iṁ Hc*. 377, *Kc*. 38, *Kp*. S. 74.2, *Ld*. 3.4.46, *Sc*. 620.5, *Sh*. 22.55.

*hauṁ haüṁ* *hā hā Sn*. 308-169.

√*hakkāra* 'to call near' cf. M. *hakārṇẽ*. Abs. -*evi Kp*. S. 49,7 cf. also √*hakka* 'to drive' as in *hakkiūṇa Nc*. 6.13.11. (M. Guj. H. Beng. *hā̃k-*, Panj.√*hakk-*)

| | |
|---|---|
| *hamkāra* | *ahankāra* Nom. Sg. *-o DKK* 4. |
| *haḍḍāla* | *=asthi-yukta* (*-āla* suff.) Neut. direct. pl. *-aim Jc.* 3.4.9. (Sk. lex. *haḍḍa*, Pa. Pk. *haḍḍa*, M. Guj. *hāḍ*, H. Nep. *hāḍ*). |
| √*haṇa* | √*han-* Imp. 2 Sg. *-u Nc.* 4.7.12, *-su Nc.* 3.3.14. Pres. Part. *-anta Kc.* 25, Inf. *-hum KKc.* 2.3.10. Pot. Part. *-evvaa. Nc.* 4.89. The pass base √*hamma-* is found in *Kp.* S. 46.5 and elsewhere cf. M. *hanaṇẽ*. |
| *hattha* | *hasta* Ins. Pl. *-ihim Hc.* 358, *Sc.* 487. 2. (Pa. Pk. *hattha*, Guj. H. *hāth*, M. Nep. *hāt*, Panj. *hatth*). |
| √*hara* | √*hṛ-* Pres. 1 Sg. *-emi KKc.* 10.23.6, *-aũ Kp.* E. 30b, 3 Pl. *-anti Jdc.* 7.1. *-him Jc.* 2.26.17. *-im KKc.* 10.29.15. Imp. 2 Sg. *-i Jc.* 1.9.14. Fut. 3 Sg. *-ihai Kp.* E. 28 PP. *-iya Kp.* S. 14.1 Inf. *-iu Kp.* S. 86.6 Caus. Pres. 2 Sg. *hārasi Kp.* S. 96. 9. *hārā-vehi Kp.* S. 56.4. |
| *Hari* | (*ts.*) Nom. Sg. zero *MP.* 85.1.4, Acc. Sg. *-m*(*ts*)*Jc.* 3.3.10. Gen. Sg. *-hi MP.* 87.59. *Sh.* 22.26, *-he Sh.* 22.26, Loc. Sg. *-hi Jc.* 1.25.27. *Sh.* 22.26, *-he Sh.* 22.26. |
| *hariṇa* | (*ts.*) Neut. direct Pl. *-(a)im KKc.* 1.5.6. |
| *harisa* | *harṣa* Ins. Sg. *-im KKc.* 1.14.11. |
| *Hari-Hara-Bamhu* | *=°Brahmāṇaḥ PPr.* 2.8. |
| *hali* | (*ts.*) Ins. Sg. *-ṇā MP.* 87.6.4. *hale* (at the time of addressing) *Jc.* 2.7.2. |
| *halola* | *hillola Pd.* 220. cf. H. *hilor*. |
| √*halla-* | *=*√*kamp-* Pres. 3 Sg. *-i MP.* 14.5.12. PP. *-iya MP.* 1.12.5, *-ira* (*tācchīlye*) *Kp.* K. 3.5. cf. *Dn. halliam calitam* (M. *hālṇẽ*, Guj. *hālvũ*, H. *hālnā*, Sdh. *halnũ*, Panj. *hallaṇā*). |
| √*hava-* | *bhav-* Pres. 3 Sg. *-i Sdd.* 87. Abso. *-eppiṇu Nc.* 9.13.3. |
| *hamsa* | (*ts.*) Nom. Sg. *-u Kc.* 16. |
| *hamsiṇi* | *=*hamsinī=hamsī* Ins. Sg. *-em KKc.* 6.13.10. |
| *hãhā* | *=hā* 'fie' *Kp.* A. 2.4., *Kp.*S. 46.8. |
| *hara* | (*ts.*) Masc. Acc. Pl. *-(a)ĩ BhK.* 17.11. |
| *hia* | *hṛd-*, *hṛdaya DKs.* 26, 75, Ins. Sg. *-em Mt.* 24, Loc. Sg. *-i Mt.* 12. |

| | |
|---|---|
| hia-ḍa | hṛdaya (-ḍa pleonastic) Masc. Nom. Sg. -ā *Mk.* 17.5, Loc. Sg. -i *Pd.* 5. |
| hitta | hṛta *Hv.* 89.17.4, Neut. direct Sg. -vĭ *Hv.* 81.16.3. |
| hiya | hṛd-(ya) *Nc.* 7.6.19, *Sn.* 19-468. Loc. Sg. -e *DKs.* 41, -iṁ *KKc.* 1.14.12. -i *Pd.* 2. -ulla (pleonastic) *Nc.* 3.6.6. |
| hiyaya | hṛdaya *Kp.* J. 84.4. *Nc.* 1.17.13. |
| hiyavaa | (°ya)=hṛdaya *Hv.* 82.3.6. *Nc.* 2.6.1. (cf. Pais. hitapakā). Loc. Sg. -i *Jc.* 3.38.9. |
| hiyavaḍa | hṛdaya Loc. Sg. -e *PPr.* 1.12.1. |
| Ḥiri | Hrī *Hv.* 87.13.1. |
| hiṁsa | hīṁsā. Ins. Sg. -e *Jc.* 3.29.9. |
| hiṁsira | hiṁsa-ira (tācchīlye) 'neighing' cf. H. hiṁsnā *Nc.* 3.14.1. |
| hu | 1. *khlu=khalu *Ds.* 4.3.2. *Mt.* 13,16,25. 2. bhūta *KKc.* 1.2.7. |
| √hŭla- | =√-kṣip- cf. *Hc.* 4.143. also H. hūlnā Pres. 3 Sg. -i *Hv.* 88.8.11.3 Pl. -(a)nti *Hv.* 84.6.4. |
| huhuru | Onomatopoeic *Kc.* 68. |
| √hŭ- | bhū- Pres. 3 Pl. -nti *Jdc.* 29.4. Imp. or Benedictive 3 Sg. -jja-u *Sdd.* 224. |
| heu | hetu Masc. Acc. Sg. zero *Pd.* 24, *PPr.* 1.40, *Sc.* 499.2. |
| √ho- | bho<bhū Pres. 2 Sg. -hi *PPr.* 2.14. 3 Sg. -i *KKc.*1.13.4. *Kp.* J 46.9. *Mt.* 2, 8, 9, *Sdd.* 6. -ī *Ds.* 4.5.2. 3 Pl. hunti *Kp.* J 6. 8, *Jdc.* 29.4. Imp. 2 Sg. -zero *Jc.* 2.1.17, -hi *Kp.* A. 12.4. *Nc.* 1.3.10. *Pd.* 43, 3 Sg. -u *Kp.* S. 62.5, *Sdd.* 2. kuvau in *Jc.* 1.6.28. 3 Pl. -ntu (Intro. to *Hv.* §56). Fut. 1 Sg. -sami. *BhK.* 302.6, *KKc.* 5.18.7.-hissu *Sn.* 306-169. 2 Sg. -sahi *BhK.* 100.4. -hisi *Kp.* S. 55.4. 3 Sg. -saï *BhK* 28.10, *Jc.* 1.7.15. *KKc.* 2.5.6, *Kp.* E. 12, 28. *Nc.* 2.6.4. *Sc.* 50.3, 262.4 (Intro. to *Sc.* §24). -isaï *Kp.* E. 3, -haï *KKc.* 1.16. 15. -hi *Kp.* S. 3.4. -hī *Sn.* 15-141. -hii *Sc.* 455.4 -hihidi *MK.* 17.59. 1 Pl. -sahiṁ *Jc.* 2.22.5. 3 Pl. -sahiṁ °hĭ *BhK.* 42.9 *KKc.* 2.5.7. -hahiṁ *KKc.* 2.4.10. Pres. Part. -nta, -ntau *Jc.* 3.37.17. 2.25.12, *Kp.* S. 36, *Nc.* 3.15.5, 13. havanta *Nc.* 3.3.10. hontau as Fut. Part. *Ld.* 3.3. 22. PP. hua(ya) *Kp.* S. 92.9,*Kp.*J.60.2,*Sn.* 308-169. hūva *KKc.* 1.7.8.hu *KKc.* 1.2.7. hūi Fem. *KKc.* 5.11.3. Abs. -eppiṇu *Jc.* 1.8.1. -evi *KKc.* 2.3.5. -eviṇu *KKc.* 3.10.10.-vi *KKc.* 5.11.3. -avi *PPr.* 2.27. |